Lecture Notes in Computer Science 14405

The series Lecture Notes in Computer Science (LNCS), including its subseries Lecture Notes in Artificial Intelligence (LNAI) and Lecture Notes in Bioinformatics (LNBI), has established itself as a medium for the publication of new developments in computer science and information technology research, teaching, and education.

LNCS enjoys close cooperation with the computer science R & D community, the series counts many renowned academics among its volume editors and paper authors, and collaborates with prestigious societies. Its mission is to serve this international community by providing an invaluable service, mainly focused on the publication of conference and workshop proceedings and postproceedings. LNCS commenced publication in 1973.

Chung-Kil Hur
Editor

Programming Languages and Systems

21st Asian Symposium, APLAS 2023
Taipei, Taiwan, November 26–29, 2023
Proceedings

Springer

Editor
Chung-Kil Hur
Seoul National University
Seoul, Korea (Republic of)

ISSN 0302-9743 ISSN 1611-3349 (electronic)
Lecture Notes in Computer Science
ISBN 978-981-99-8310-0 ISBN 978-981-99-8311-7 (eBook)
https://doi.org/10.1007/978-981-99-8311-7

This Springer imprint is published by the registered company Springer Nature Singapore Pte Ltd.
The registered company address is: 152 Beach Road, #21-01/04 Gateway East, Singapore 189721, Singapore

Preface

This volume contains the papers presented at the 21st Asian Symposium on Programming Languages and Systems (APLAS 2023), held in Taipei, Taiwan during November 26–29, 2023. APLAS aims to stimulate programming language research by providing a forum for the presentation of the latest results and the exchange of ideas in programming languages and systems. APLAS is based in Asia but is an international forum that serves the worldwide programming languages community.

APLAS 2023 solicited contributions in the form of regular research papers. Among others, solicited topics included the following: semantics, logics, and foundational theory; design of languages, type systems, and foundational calculi; domain-specific languages; compilers, interpreters, and abstract machines; program derivation, synthesis, and transformation; program analysis, verification, and model-checking; logic, constraint, probabilistic, and quantum programming; software security; concurrency and parallelism; tools and environments for programming and implementation; and applications of SAT/SMT to programming and implementation.

This year we employed a lightweight double-blind reviewing process with an author response period. Each paper received at least three reviews before the author response period, which was followed by a 12-day period of Program Committee (PC) discussion. We received 36 submissions, out of which 4 submissions were desk-rejected due to formatting issues. After a rigorous assessment, the PC accepted 15 papers. Additionally, after reviewing the final versions of papers, the PC discussed and selected the following paper as the best paper, deserving of this extra recognition.

- A Fresh Look at Commutativity: Free Algebraic Structures via Fresh Lists. Clemens Kupke, Fredrik Nordvall Forsberg, Sean Watters.

We were also honored to include three invited talks by distinguished researchers:

- Hakjoo Oh (Korea University, South Korea) on "Data-Driven Static Analysis"
- Bow-Yaw Wang (Academia Sinica, Taiwan) on "Certified Automatic Verification of Industrial Cryptographic Primitive Programs"
- Yong Kiam Tan (Institute for Infocomm Research, A*STAR, Singapore) on "Covering the Last Mile in Trustworthy Automated Reasoning with CakeML"

The success of this program owes a debt of gratitude to the dedicated individuals whose efforts were instrumental. I extend my sincere thanks to the Program Committee, sub-reviewers, and external expert reviewers for their diligent work in selecting robust papers and providing constructive feedback in their reviews.

Special appreciation goes to Shin-Cheng Mu (Academia Sinica, Taiwan), who, as the General Chair of APLAS 2023, carefully managed all conference details. Ryosuke Sato (University of Tokyo, Japan), in his role as the Publicity Chair, was consistently responsive and invaluable. I also wish to express my deep gratitude to the APLAS Steering Committee for their leadership. Finally, I would like to acknowledge the organizers of the associated events that contributed to the success of APLAS 2023: the Poster Session and Student Research Competition, led by Hsiang-Shang 'Josh' Ko (Academia Sinica, Taiwan), and the APLAS Workshop on New Ideas and Emerging Results, held by Atsushi Igarashi (Kyoto University, Japan).

October 2023 Chung-Kil Hur

Organization

General Chair

Shin-Cheng Mu	Academia Sinica, Taiwan

Publicity Chair

Ryosuke Sato	University of Tokyo, Japan

Program Chair

Chung-Kil Hur	Seoul National University, South Korea

Program Committee

Soham Chakraborty	TU Delft, The Netherlands
Yu-Fang Chen	Academia Sinica, Taiwan
Ronghui Gu	Columbia University, USA
Ichiro Hasuo	National Institute of Informatics, Japan
Ralf Jung	ETH Zurich, Switzerland
Ohad Kammar	University of Edinburgh, UK
Jeehoon Kang	KAIST, South Korea
Jieung Kim	Inha University, South Korea
Robbert Krebbers	Radboud University Nijmegen, The Netherlands
Ori Lahav	Tel Aviv University, Israel
Doug Lea	State University of New York at Oswego, USA
Woosuk Lee	Hanyang University, South Korea
Hongjin Liang	Nanjing University, China
Nuno P. Lopes	University of Lisbon, Portugal
Chandrakana Nandi	Certora, USA
Liam O'Connor	University of Edinburgh, UK
Bruno C. d. S. Oliveira	University of Hong Kong, China
Jihyeok Park	Korea University, South Korea
Clément Pit-Claudel	EPFL, Switzerland
Matthieu Sozeau	Inria, France

Kohei Suenaga	Kyoto University, Japan
Tarmo Uustalu	Reykjavik University, Iceland
John Wickerson	Imperial College London, UK
Danfeng Zhang	Penn State University, USA

SRC and Posters Chair

Hsiang-Shang 'Josh' Ko	Academia Sinica, Taiwan

Workshop on New Ideas and Emerging Results Organizer

Atsushi Igarashi	Kyoto University, Japan

Additional Reviewers

Philipp Joram
Xupeng Li
Dylan McDermott
Matthew Might
Yaozhu Sun
Jinhao Tan
Runzhou Tao
Jianan Yao

Contents

Types

Compilation Semantics for a Programming Language with Versions 3
Yudai Tanabe, Luthfan Anshar Lubis, Tomoyuki Aotani, and Hidehiko Masuhara

What Types Are Needed for Typing Dynamic Objects? A Python-Based Empirical Study 24
Ke Sun, Sheng Chen, Meng Wang, and Dan Hao

Types and Semantics for Extensible Data Types 46
Cas van der Rest and Casper Bach Poulsen

Functional Languages

A Diamond Machine for Strong Evaluation 69
Beniamino Accattoli and Pablo Barenbaum

Proofs as Terms, Terms as Graphs 91
Jui-Hsuan Wu

Typed Non-determinism in Functional and Concurrent Calculi 112
Bas van den Heuvel, Joseph W. N. Paulus, Daniele Nantes-Sobrinho, and Jorge A. Pérez

Interactive Theorem Proving

A Fresh Look at Commutativity: Free Algebraic Structures via Fresh Lists 135
Clemens Kupke, Fredrik Nordvall Forsberg, and Sean Watters

Oracle Computability and Turing Reducibility in the Calculus of Inductive Constructions 155
Yannick Forster, Dominik Kirst, and Niklas Mück

Experimenting with an Intrinsically-Typed Probabilistic Programming Language in Coq 182
Ayumu Saito and Reynald Affeldt

Verification

Towards a Framework for Developing Verified Assemblers for the ELF Format ... 205
Jinhua Wu, Yuting Wang, Meng Sun, Xiangzhe Xu, and Yichen Song

Transport via Partial Galois Connections and Equivalences ... 225
Kevin Kappelmann

Argument Reduction of Constrained Horn Clauses Using Equality Constraints ... 246
Ryo Ikeda, Ryosuke Sato, and Naoki Kobayashi

Static Analysis and Testing

Incorrectness Proofs for Object-Oriented Programs via Subclass Reflection ... 269
Wenhua Li, Quang Loc Le, Yahui Song, and Wei-Ngan Chin

m-CFA Exhibits Perfect Stack Precision ... 290
Kimball Germane

TorchProbe: Fuzzing Dynamic Deep Learning Compilers ... 310
Qidong Su, Chuqin Geng, Gennady Pekhimenko, and Xujie Si

Author Index ... 333

Types

Compilation Semantics for a Programming Language with Versions

Yudai Tanabe[1(✉)], Luthfan Anshar Lubis[2], Tomoyuki Aotani[3], and Hidehiko Masuhara[2]

[1] Kyoto University, Kyoto, Japan
yudaitnb@fos.kuis.kyoto-u.ac.jp
[2] Tokyo Institute of Technology, Tokyo, Japan
luthfanlubis@prg.is.titech.ac.jp, masuhara@acm.org
[3] Sanyo-Onoda City University, Yamaguchi, Japan
aotani@rs.socu.ac.jp

Abstract. *Programming with versions* is a paradigm that allows a program to use multiple versions of a module so that the programmer can selectively use functions from both older and newer versions of a single module. Previous work formalized λ_{VL}, a core calculus for programming with versions, but it has not been integrated into practical programming languages. In this paper, we propose VL, a Haskell-subset surface language for λ_{VL} along with its compilation method. We formally describe the core part of the VL compiler, which translates from the surface language to the core language by leveraging Girard's translation, soundly infers the consistent version of expressions along with their types, and generates a multi-version interface by bundling specific-version interfaces. We conduct a case study to show how VL supports practical software evolution scenarios and discuss the method's scalability.

Keywords: Type system · Type inference · Version control system

1 Introduction

Updating dependent software packages is one of the major issues in software development. Even though a newer version of a package brings improvements, it also brings the risk of breaking changes, which can make the entire software defective.

We argue that this issue originates from the principle of most programming languages that only allow the use of one version of a package at a time. Due to this principle, developers are faced with the decision to either update to a new, improved version of a package that requires many changes or to remain with an older version. The problem gets worse when a package is indirectly used. This dilemma often results in delays in adopting upgrades, leading to stagnation in software development and maintenance [2,16].

Programming with versions [15,28,29,31] is a recent proposal that allows programming languages to support multiple versions of programming elements

C.-K. Hur (Ed.): APLAS 2023, LNCS 14405, pp. 3–23, 2023.
https://doi.org/10.1007/978-981-99-8311-7_1

at a time so that the developer can flexibly cope with incompatible changes. λ_{VL} is the core calculus in which a *versioned value* encapsulates multiple versions of a value (including a function value). The λ_{VL} type system checks the consistency of each term so that a value produced in a version is always passed to functions in the same version. The calculus and the type system design are based on coeffect calculus [3,20].

While λ_{VL} offers the essential language constructs to support multiple versions in a program, the language is far from practical. For example, with multiple versions of a module, each version of the function must be manually represented inside a versioned value (i.e., a record-like expression). λ_{VL} is as simple as lambda calculus, yet it has a verbose syntax due to the coeffect calculus. In short, there are aspects of versioning in λ_{VL} that a surface language compiler can automate.

We propose the functional language VL as a surface language for λ_{VL} along with its compilation method. In VL, a function name imported from an external module represents a multi-version term, where each occurrence of the function name can reference a different version of the function. The VL compiler translates a program into an intermediate language VLMini, a version-label-free variant of λ_{VL}, determines the version for each name occurrence based on a type and version inference algorithm, and translates it back into a version-specialized Haskell program. VL also offers the constructs to explicitly control versions of expressions, which are useful to keep using an older version for some reason.

This paper presents the following techniques in VL: (a) *an application of Girard's translation* for translating VL into VLMini, (b) *the bundling* for making a top-level function act as a versioned value, and (c) *a type and version inference algorithm* for identifying the version of each expression with respect to the λ_{VL} type system. Finally, we prove the soundness of the inference system and implement a VL compiler. Code generation converts a VL program into a version-specialized Haskell program using the solution obtained from z3 [18].

Paper Organization. Section 2 introduces incompatibility issues and fundamental concepts in programming with versions with λ_{VL} and VL. Section 3 introduces bundling and Girard's transformation. Section 4 presents an algorithmic version inference for VL. Section 5 features an implementation of VL, and Sect. 6 introduces a case study that simulates an incompatible update made in a Haskell library. Finally, Sect. 7 discusses further language development and concludes the paper by presenting related work and a conclusion.

2 Overview

2.1 Motivating Example

First, we will explain a small example to clarify incompatibility issues. Consider a scenario where an incompatible change is made to a dependent package. Figure 1 shows the package dependencies in a file explorer **`App`** based on a hash-based file search. This function is developed using the system library **`Dir`** and the cryptography library **`Hash`**. For simplicity, we equate packages and modules here

```
module App where
import Dir
import Hash
main () =
  let s = getArg ()
      digest = mkHash s in
  if exists digest
    then print "Found"
    else error "Not found"
```

```
module Dir where
import Hash
-- version 1.0.0
exists hash =
  let fs = getFiles () in
  foldLeft
    (\(acc, f) ->
      acc || match f hash)
    false fs
```

version 2.0.0 version 1.0.0

```
module Hash where
-- version 2.0.0
mkHash s = {- SHA-3 hash -}
match s hash =
    mkHash s == hash
```

```
module Hash where
-- version 1.0.0
mkHash s = {- MD5 hash -}
match s hash =
    mkHash s == hash
```

The `exists` provided from **`Dir`** (which depends on version 1 of **`Hash`**) expects an MD5 hash as an argument. However, after the dependency update of **App** on **`Hash`**, the value assigned to `digest` is a SHA-3 hash.

Fig. 1. Minimal module configuration before and after the dependency update causing an error due to inconsistency expected to the dependent package.

(each package consists of a single module), and we only focus on the version of **`Hash`**. The pseudocode is written in a Haskell-like language.

Before its update, **App** depends on version 1.0.0 of **`Hash`** (denoted by ⇢). The **App**'s `main` function implements file search by a string from standard input using `mkHash` and `exists`. The function `mkHash` is in version 1.0.0 of **`Hash`**, and it generates a hash value using the MD5 algorithm from a given string. **`Hash`** also provides a function `match` that determines if the argument string and hash value match under `mkHash`. The function `exists` is in version 1.0.0 of **`Dir`**, which is also dependent on version 1.0.0 of **`Hash`**, and it determines if a file with a name corresponding to a given hash exists.

Due to security issues, the developer of **App** updated **`Hash`** to version 2.0.0 (denoted by ⟶). In version 2.0.0 of **`Hash`**, SHA-3 is adopted as the new hash algorithm. Since **`Dir`** continues to use version 1.0.0 of **`Hash`**, **App** needs two different versions of **`Hash`**. Various circumstances can lead to this situation: **`Dir`** may have already discontinued maintenance, or functions in **`Dir`**, other than `exists`, might still require the features provided by version 1.0.0 of **`Hash`**.

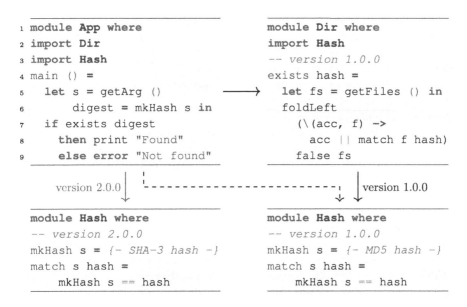

Although the update does not modify **App**, it causes errors within **App**. Even if a file with an input filename exists, the program returns `Not Found` error contrary to the expected behavior. The cause of the unexpected output lies in the differences between the two versions required for `main`. In line 6 of **App**, an SHA-3 hash value is generated by `mkHash` and assigned to `digest`. Since `exists` evaluates hash equivalence using MD5, `exists digest` compares hashes generated by different algorithms, evaluating to `false`.

This example highlights the importance of version compatibility when dealing with functions provided by external packages. Using different versions of **Hash** in separate program parts is fine, but comparing results may be semantically incorrect. Even more subtle changes than those shown in Fig. 1 can lead to significant errors, especially when introducing side effects or algorithm modifications that break the application's implicit assumptions. Manually managing version compatibility for all external functions is unfeasible.

In practical programming languages, dependency analysis is performed before the build process to prevent such errors, and package configurations requiring multiple versions of the same package are rejected. However, this approach tends towards conservative error reporting. In cases where a core package, which many other libraries depend on, receives an incompatible change, no matter how minuscule, it requires coordinated updates of diverse packages across the entire package ecosystem [2,29,32].

2.2 λ_{VL}

λ_{VL} [28,29] is a core calculus designed to follow the principles: (1) enabling simultaneous usage of multiple versions of a package, (2) ensuring version consistency within a program. λ_{VL} works by encapsulating relevant terms across multiple versions into a record-like term, tagged with a label indicating the specific module version. Record-like terms accessible to any of its several versions are referred to as *versioned values*, and the associated labels are called *version labels*.

Version Labels. Figure 2 shows the syntax of λ_{VL}. Given modules and their versions, the corresponding set of version labels characterizes the variation of programs of a versioned value. In λ_{VL}, version labels are implicitly generated for all external module-version combinations, in which M_i is unique, with the universal set of these labels denoted by $\mathcal{L}$. Specifically, in the example illustared in Fig. 1, $\mathcal{L} = \{l_1, l_2\}$ and $l_1 = \{$**Hash** $= 1.0.0$, **Dir** $= 1.0.0\}, l_2 = \{$**Hash** $=$ $2.0.0$, **Dir** $= 1.0.0\}$. The size of $\mathcal{L}$ is proportional to V^M where M is the number of modules and V is the maximum number of versions.

Syntax of λ_{VL}. λ_{VL} extends $\ell\mathcal{R}$PCF [3] and GrMini [20] with additional terms that facilitate introducing and eliminating versioned values. Versioned values can be introduced through versioned records $\{\overline{l_i = t_i}\}$ and promotions $[t]$. A versioned record encapsulates related definitions $t_1, \ldots, t_n$ across multiple versions

λ_{VL} **syntax**

$$t ::= n \mid x \mid t_1\, t_2 \mid \lambda x.t \mid \textbf{let}\ [x] = t_1\ \textbf{in}\ t_2 \mid u.l \mid \langle \overline{l_i = t_i} \mid l_k \rangle \mid u \qquad \text{(terms)}$$

$$u ::= [t] \mid \{\overline{l_i = t_i}\} \quad \text{(versioned values)} \qquad r ::= \bot \mid \{\overline{l_i}\} \quad \text{(resources)}$$

$$A, B ::= \mathsf{Int} \mid A \to B \mid \Box_r A \quad \text{(types)} \qquad \mathcal{L} \ni l ::= \{\overline{M_i = V_i}\} \quad \text{(version labels)}$$

M_i and V_i are metavariables over module names and versions of M_i, respectively.

Fig. 2. The syntax of λ_{VL}.

and their version labels $l_1, \ldots, l_n$. For instance, the two versions of `mkHash` in Fig. 1 can be bundled as the following version record.

$$mkHash \quad := \quad \begin{array}{l}\{l_1 = \lambda s.\texttt{\{- make MD5 hash -\}},\\ \;\; l_2 = \lambda s.\texttt{\{- make SHA-3 hash -\}}\}\end{array}$$

In λ_{VL}, programs are constructed via function application of versioned values. A function application of `mkHash` to the string `s` can be written as follows.

$$app \quad := \quad \begin{array}{l}\textbf{let}\ [mkHash'] = mkHash\ \textbf{in}\\ \textbf{let}\ [s] = [\text{“}\texttt{compiler.vl}\text{”}]\ \textbf{in}\ [mkHash'\ s]\end{array}$$

This program (*app* hereafter) makes a hash for the string “`compiler.vl`" and is available for both l_1 and l_2. The contextual let-binding $\textbf{let}\ [x] = t_1\ \textbf{in}\ t_2$ provides the elimination of version values by binding a versioned value for t_1 to x, thus making it accessible in t_2. Promotion $[x]$ offers an alternative way to introduce versioned values, making any term t act as a versioned value.

The evaluation of terms t_i stored in a versioned value $\{\overline{l_i = t_i}\}$ and $[t]$ is postponed until a specific version label is later specified. To proceed with a postponed evaluation of a versioned value, we use extraction $u.l_k$. Extraction specifies one versioned label l_k for the versioned value u and recursively extracts the inner term t_k corresponding to l_k from $\{l_i = t_i\}$, and t from $[t]$ as follows.

$$\begin{array}{lcl} app\#l_1 & := & \begin{array}{l}\textbf{let}\ [mkHash'] = mkHash\ \textbf{in}\\ \textbf{let}\ [s] = [\text{“}\texttt{compiler.vl}\text{”}]\ \textbf{in}\ [mkHash'\ s].l_1\end{array}\\ & \longrightarrow^* & (\lambda s.\texttt{\{- make MD5 hash -\}})\ \text{“}\texttt{compiler.vl}\text{”}\\ & \longrightarrow & \texttt{4dcb6ebe3c6520d1f57c906541cf3823}\end{array}$$

Consequently, $app\#l_1$ evaluates into an MD5 hash corresponding to l_1.

Type of Versioned Values. The type of a versioned value is expressed as $\Box_r A$, assigning a set of version labels r, called *version resources*, to a type A. Intuitively, the type of a versioned value represents the versions available to that versioned value. For example, *mkHash* and *app* are typed as follows.

$$mkHash : \Box_{\{l_1, l_2\}}\,(\mathsf{String} \to \mathsf{String}) \qquad app : \Box_{\{l_1, l_2\}}\,(\mathsf{String} \to \mathsf{String})$$

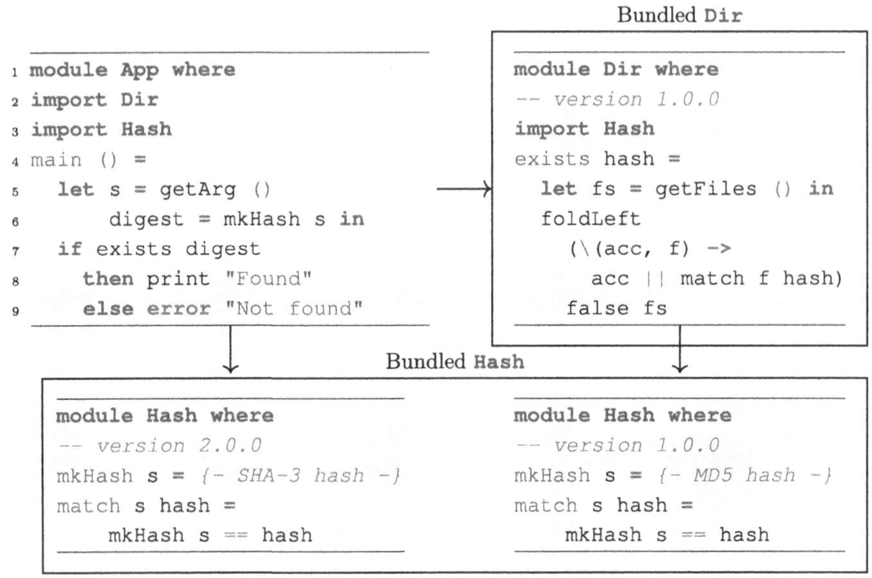

The versions of each external module are bundled. Programs using a bundled module can refer to the definitions of all versions of the bundled module.

Fig. 3. The programs in Fig. 1 in VL.

The types have $\{l_1, l_2\}$ as their version resource, illustrating that the versioned values have definitions of l_1 and l_2. For function application, the type system computes the intersection of the version resource of subterms. Since the promoted term is considered to be available in all versions, the version resource of the entire function application indicates $\{l_1, l_2\} = \{l_1, l_2\} \cap \mathcal{L}$.

For extractions, the type system verifies if the version resource contains the specified version as follows.

$$app\#l_1 : \mathsf{String} \to \mathsf{String} \quad app\#l_3 : (rejected)$$

Assuming $\mathcal{L} = \{l_1, l_2, l_3\}$, $app\#l_3$ is rejected by type checking because the version resource of *app* does not contain l_3. Conversely, $app\#l_1$ is well-typed, but note that the resultant type lost its version resource. It is attributed to the design principle that it could be used in other versions upon extraction.

The λ_{VL} type system incorporates the notion of version consistency in addition to the standard notions of preservation and progress. Proofs of these theorems can be found in Appendix C [30].

2.3 Programming with Versions in VL

Our contributions enjoy the benefits of programming with versions on a λ-calculus-based functional language VL. To achieve this, we develop a compilation method between lambda calculus and VLMini, a version-label free variant

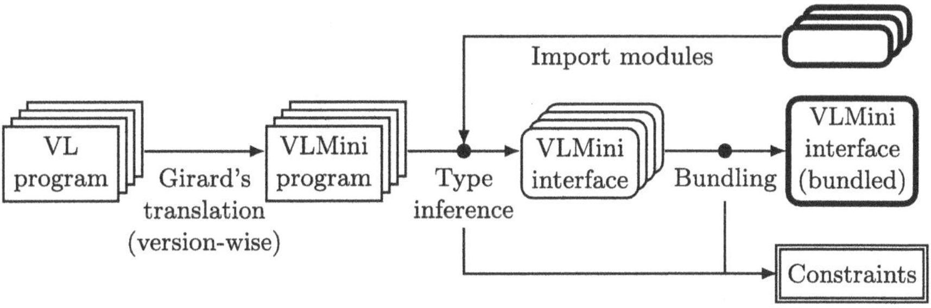

Fig. 4. The translation phases for a single module with multiple versions.

of λ_{VL}, and a version inference algorithm to infer the appropriate version of expressions.

In VL, (1) all versions are available for every module, and (2) the version of each expression is determined by expression-level dependency analysis. This approach differs from existing languages that determine one version for each dependent package. Figure 3 shows how the programs in Fig. 1 are interpreted in VL. The VL compiler bundles the interfaces of multiple versions and generates a cross-version interface to make external functions available in multiple versions. The VL type system enforces version consistency in `main` and selects a newer version if multiple versions are available. Thus it gives the version label {**Hash** = 2.0.0, **Dir** = 1.0.0} to dependent expressions of `main`. As a result, since **Hash** version referenced from **Dir** is no longer limited to 1.0.0, `exists digest` is evaluated using SHA-3 under the context of **Hash** version 2.0.0.

Furthermore, VL provides *version control terms* to convey the programmer's intentions of versions to the compiler. For example, to enforce the evaluation in Fig. 3 to MD5, a programmer can rewrite line 7 of **App** as follows.

```
7  if ver [Hash=1.0.0] of (exists digest)
```

The program dictates that `exists digest` is evaluated within the context of the **Hash** version 1.0.0. Consequently, both `mkHash` and `match`, which depend on `exists digest`, are chosen to align with version 1.0.0 of **Hash**. Moreover, VL provides **`unversion`** `t`. It eliminates the dependencies associated with term `t`, facilitating its collaboration with other versions under the programmer's responsibility, all while maintaining version consistency within its subterm. Thus, VL not only ensures version consistency but also offers the flexibility to control the version of a particular part of the program.

3 Compilation

The entire translation consists of three parts: (1) *Girard's translation*, (2) an *algorithmic type inference*, and (3) *bundling*. Figure 4 shows the translation process of a single module. First, through Girard's translation, each version of the VL program undergoes a version-wise translation into the VLMini program. Second, the type inference synthesizes types and constraints for top-level symbols. Variables imported from external modules reference the bundled interface generated in the subsequent step. Finally, to make the external variables act as multi-version expressions, bundling consolidates each version's interface into one VLMini interface. These translations are carried out in order from downstream of the dependency tree. By resolving all constraints up to the main module, the appropriate version for every external variable is determined.

It is essential to note that the translations focus on generating constraints for dispatching external variables into version-specific code. While implementing versioned records in λ_{VL} presents challenges, such as handling many version labels and their code clones, our method is a constraint-based approach in VLMini that enables static inference of version labels without their explicit declaration.

In the context of coeffect languages, constraint generation in VL can be seen as the automatic generation of type declarations paired with resource constraints. Granule [20] can handle various resources as coeffects, but it requires type declarations to indicate resource constraints. VL restricts its resources solely to the version label set. This specialization enables the automatic collection of version information from external sources outside the codebase.

3.1 An Intermediate Language, VLMini

Syntax of VLMini. Figure 5 shows the syntax of VLMini. VLMini encompasses all the terms in λ_{VL} except for versioned records $\{l_i = t_i\}$, intermediate term $\langle \overline{l_i = t_i} \mid l_k \rangle$, and extractions $t.l_k$. As a result, its terms are analogous to those in $\ell\mathcal{R}$PCF [3] and GrMini [20]. However, VLMini is specialized to treat version resources as coeffects. We also introduce data constructors by introduction $C\, t_1, ..., t_n$ and elimination **case** t **of** $\overline{p_i \mapsto t_i}$ for lists and pairs, and version control terms **unversion** t and **version** $\{\overline{M_i = V_i}\}$ **of** t. Here, contextual-let in λ_{VL} is a syntax sugar of lambda abstraction applied to a promoted pattern.

$$\textbf{let } [x] = t_1 \textbf{ in } t_2 \triangleq (\lambda[x].t_2)\, t_1$$

Types, version labels, and version resources are almost the same as λ_{VL}. Type constructors are also added to the type in response to the VLMini term having a data constructor. The remaining difference from λ_{VL} is type variables α. Since VLMini is a monomorphic language, type variables act as unification variables; type variables are introduced during the type inference and are expected to be either concrete types or a set of version labels as a result of constraint resolution. To distinguish those two kinds of type variables, we introduce kinds κ. The kind Labels is given to type variables that can take a set of labels $\{\overline{l_i}\}$ and is used to distinguish them from those of kind Type during algorithmic type inference.

Constraints. The lower part of Fig. 5 shows constraints generated through bundling and type inference. Dependency constraints comprise *variable dependencies* and *label dependencies* in addition to propositional formulae. Variable

VLMini syntax (w/o data constructors and version control terms)

$$t ::= n \mid x \mid t_1\, t_2 \mid \lambda p.t \mid [t] \quad \text{(terms)} \qquad \Gamma ::= \emptyset \mid \Gamma, x : A \mid \Gamma, x : [A]_r \quad \text{(contexts)}$$
$$p ::= x \mid [x] \quad \text{(patterns)} \qquad \Sigma ::= \emptyset \mid \Sigma, \alpha : \kappa \quad \text{(type variable kinds)}$$
$$A, B ::= \mathsf{Int} \mid \alpha \mid A \to B \mid \Box_r A \quad \text{(types)} \qquad R ::= - \mid r \quad \text{(resource contexts)}$$
$$\kappa ::= \mathsf{Type} \mid \mathsf{Labels} \quad \text{(kinds)}$$

Extended with data constructors

$$t ::= \dots \mid C\,\overline{t_i} \mid \textbf{case}\ t\ \textbf{of}\ \overline{p_i \mapsto t_i} \quad \text{(terms)} \qquad A, B ::= \dots \mid K\,\overline{A_i} \quad \text{(types)}$$
$$p ::= \dots \mid C\,\overline{p_i} \quad \text{(patterns)} \qquad K ::= (,) \mid [,] \quad \text{(type constructors)}$$
$$C ::= (,) \mid [,] \quad \text{(constructors)}$$

Extended with version control terms

$$t ::= \dots \mid \textbf{version}\ \{\overline{M_i = V_i}\}\ \textbf{of}\ t \mid \textbf{unversion}\ t \quad \text{(terms)}$$

VLMini constraints

$$\mathcal{C} ::= \underbrace{\top \mid \mathcal{C}_1 \wedge \mathcal{C}_2 \mid \mathcal{C}_1 \vee \mathcal{C}_2}_{\text{propositional formulae}} \mid \underbrace{\alpha \preceq \alpha'}_{\text{variable dependencies}} \mid \underbrace{\alpha \preceq \mathcal{D}}_{\text{label dependencies}} \quad \text{(dependency constraints)}$$
$$\mathcal{D} ::= \langle\langle \overline{M_i = V_i} \rangle\rangle \quad \text{(dependent labels)}$$
$$\Theta ::= \top \mid \Theta_1 \wedge \Theta_2 \mid \{A \sim B\} \quad \text{(type constraints)}$$

Fig. 5. The syntax of VLMini.

dependencies $\alpha \sqsubseteq \alpha'$ require that if a version label for α' expects a specific version for a module, then α also expects the same version. Similarly, label dependencies $\alpha \preceq \langle\langle \overline{M_i = V_i} \rangle\rangle$ require that a version label expected for α must be V_i for M_i. For example, assuming that versions 1.0.0 and 2.0.0 exist for both modules **A** and **B**, the minimal upper bound set of version labels satisfying $\alpha \preceq \langle\langle \mathbf{A} \mapsto 1.0.0 \rangle\rangle$ is $\alpha = \{\{\mathbf{A} = 1.0.0, \mathbf{B} = 1.0.0\}, \{\mathbf{A} = 1.0.0, \mathbf{B} = 2.0.0\}\}$. If the constraint resolution is successful, α will be specialized with either of two labels. Θ is a set of type equations resolved by the type unification.

3.2 Girard's Translation for VLMini

We extend Girard's translation between VL (lambda calculus) to VLMini following Orchard's approach [20].

$$[\![n]\!] \equiv n \qquad [\![x]\!] \equiv x \qquad [\![\lambda x.t]\!] \equiv \lambda[x].[\![t]\!] \qquad [\![t\ s]\!] \equiv [\![t]\!]\ [[\![s]\!]]$$

The translation replaces lambda abstractions and function applications of VL by lambda abstraction with promoted pattern and promotion of VLMini, respectively. From the aspect of types, this translation replaces all occurrences of $A \to B$ with $\Box_r A \to B$ with a version resource r. This translation inserts a syntactic annotation $[*]$ at each location where a version resource needs to be addressed. Subsequent type inference will compute the resource at the specified location and produce constraints to ensure version consistency at that point.

The original Girard's translation [11] is well-known as a translation between the simply-typed λ-calculus and an intuitionistic linear calculus. The approach involves replacing every intuitionistic arrow $A \to B$ with $!A \multimap B$, and subsequently unboxing via let-in abstraction and promoting during application [20].

3.3 Bundling

Bundling produces an interface encompassing types and versions from every module version, allowing top-level symbols to act as multi-version expressions. During this process, bundling reviews interfaces from across module versions, identifies symbols with the same names and types after removing $\square_r$ using Girard's transformation, and treats them as multiple versions of a singular symbol (also discussed in Sect. 7). In a constraint-based approach, bundling integrates label dependencies derived from module versions, ensuring they align with the version information in the typing rule for versioned records of λ_{VL}.

For example, assuming that the *id* that takes an Int value as an argument is available in version 1.0.0 and 2.0.0 of $\mathbf{M}$ as follows:

$$id : \square_{\alpha_1}(\square_{\alpha_2}\mathsf{Int} \to \mathsf{Int}) \mid \mathcal{C}_1 \qquad \text{(version 1.0.0)}$$

$$id : \square_{\beta_1}(\square_{\beta_2}\mathsf{Int} \to \mathsf{Int}) \mid \mathcal{C}_2 \qquad \text{(version 2.0.0)}$$

where α_1 and α_2 are version resource variables given from type inference. They capture the version resources of *id* and its argument value in version 1.0.0. $\mathcal{C}_1$ is the constraints that resource variables of version 1.0.0 will satisfy. Likewise for β_1, β_2, and $\mathcal{C}_2$. Since the types of *id* in both versions become $\mathsf{Int} \to \mathsf{Int}$ via Girard's translation, they can be bundled as follows:

$$\begin{aligned} id : \square_{\gamma_1}(\square_{\gamma_2}\mathsf{Int} \to \mathsf{Int}) \mid \mathcal{C}_1 \land \mathcal{C}_2 \land \Big(&(\gamma_1 \preceq \langle\!\langle \mathbf{M} = 1.0.0 \rangle\!\rangle \land \gamma_1 \preceq \alpha_1 \land \gamma_2 \preceq \alpha_2) \\ &\lor (\gamma_1 \preceq \langle\!\langle \mathbf{M} = 2.0.0 \rangle\!\rangle \land \gamma_1 \preceq \beta_1 \land \gamma_2 \preceq \beta_2) \Big) \end{aligned}$$

where γ_1 and γ_2 are introduced by this conversion for the bundled *id* interface, with label and variable dependencies that they will satisfy. γ_1 captures the version resource of the bundled *id*. The generated label dependencies $\gamma_1 \preceq \langle\!\langle \mathbf{M} = 1.0.0 \rangle\!\rangle$ and $\gamma_1 \preceq \langle\!\langle \mathbf{M} = 2.0.0 \rangle\!\rangle$ indicate that *id* is available in either version 1.0.0 or 2.0.0 of $\mathbf{M}$. These label dependencies are exclusively[1] generated during bundling. The other new variable dependencies indicate that the *id* bundled interface depends on one of the two version interfaces. The dependency is made apparent by pairing the new resource variables with their respective version resource variable for each version. These constraints are retained globally, and the type definition of the bundled interface is used for type-checking modules importing *id*.

[1] In the type checking rules for **version** l **of** t, type inference exceptionally generates label dependencies. Please see Appendix B.4 [30].

VLMini pattern type synthesis $\boxed{\Sigma, R \vdash p : A \rhd \Gamma; \Sigma'; \Theta; \mathcal{C}}$

$$\frac{}{\Sigma; - \vdash x : A \rhd x : A; \Sigma; \top; \top}\ (\text{pVar}) \qquad \frac{}{\Sigma; r \vdash x : A \rhd x : [A]_r; \Sigma; \top; \top}\ ([\text{pVar}])$$

$$\frac{\Sigma, \alpha : \mathsf{Labels}, \beta : \mathsf{Type}; \alpha \vdash x : \beta \rhd \Delta; \Sigma'; \Theta; \mathcal{C}}{\Sigma; - \vdash [x] : A \rhd \Delta; \Sigma'; \Theta \wedge \{A \sim \Box_\alpha \beta\}; \mathcal{C}}\ (\text{p}\Box)$$

VLMini type synthesis (excerpt) $\boxed{\Sigma; \Gamma \vdash t \Rightarrow A; \Sigma'; \Theta; \mathcal{C}}$

$$\frac{x : A \in \Gamma}{\Sigma; \Gamma \vdash x \Rightarrow A; \Sigma; x : A; \top; \top}\ (\Rightarrow_{\text{LIN}}) \qquad \frac{x : [A]_r \in \Gamma}{\Sigma; \Gamma \vdash x \Rightarrow A; \Sigma; x : [A]_1; \top; \top}\ (\Rightarrow_{\text{GR}})$$

$$\frac{\Sigma_1, \alpha : \mathsf{Type}; - \vdash p : \alpha \rhd \Gamma'; \Sigma_2; \Theta_1 \quad \Sigma_2; \Gamma, \Gamma' \vdash t \Rightarrow B; \Sigma_3; \Delta; \Theta_2; \mathcal{C}}{\Sigma_1; \Gamma \vdash \lambda p.t \Rightarrow \alpha \to B; \Sigma_3; \Delta \backslash \Gamma'; \Theta_1 \wedge \Theta_2; \mathcal{C}}\ (\Rightarrow_{\text{ABS}})$$

$$\frac{\begin{array}{c}\Sigma_1 \vdash [\Gamma \cap \mathsf{FV}(t)]_{\mathsf{Labels}} \rhd \Gamma' \quad \Sigma_1; \Gamma' \vdash t \Rightarrow A; \Sigma_2; \Delta; \Theta; \mathcal{C}_1 \\ \Sigma_3 = \Sigma_2, \alpha : \mathsf{Labels} \quad \Sigma_3 \vdash \alpha \sqsubseteq_c \Gamma' \rhd \mathcal{C}_2\end{array}}{\Sigma_1; \Gamma \vdash [t] \Rightarrow \Box_\alpha A; \Sigma_3; \alpha \cdot \Delta; \Theta; \mathcal{C}_1 \wedge \mathcal{C}_2}\ (\Rightarrow_{\text{PR}})$$

VLMini constraints generation $\boxed{\Sigma \vdash \alpha \sqsubseteq_c \Gamma \rhd \mathcal{C}}$

$$\frac{}{\Sigma \vdash \alpha \sqsubseteq_c \emptyset \rhd \top}\ (\emptyset) \qquad \frac{\Sigma \vdash \alpha \sqsubseteq_c \Gamma \rhd \mathcal{C}}{\Sigma \vdash \alpha \sqsubseteq_c (x : [A]_r, \Gamma) \rhd (\alpha \preceq r \wedge \mathcal{C})}\ (\alpha)$$

Fig. 6. VLMini algorithmic typing.

4 Algorithmic Type Inference

We develop the algorithmic type inference for VLMini derived from the declarative type system of λ_{VL} [28,29]. The type inference consists of two judgments: *type synthesis* and *pattern type synthesis*. The judgment forms are similar to Gr [20], which is similarly based on coeffect calculus. While Gr provides type-checking rules in a bidirectional approach [8,9] to describe resource constraint annotations and performs unifications inside the type inference, VLMini only provides synthesis rules and unification performs after the type inference. In addition, Gr supports user-defined data types and multiple computational resources, while VLMini supports only built-in data structures and specializes in version resources. The inference system is developed to be sound for declarative typing in λ_{VL}, with the proof detailed in Appendix D [30]. Type synthesis takes type variable kinds Σ, a typing context Γ of term variables, and a term t as inputs. Type variable kinds Σ are added to account for distinct unification variables for types and version resources. The synthesis produces as outputs a type A, type variable kinds Σ', type constraints Θ, and dependency constraints $\mathcal{C}$. The type variable kinds Σ and Σ' always satisfy $\Sigma \subseteq \Sigma'$ due to the additional type variables added in this phase.

Pattern type synthesis takes a pattern p, type variable kinds Σ, and resource environment R as inputs. It synthesizes outputs, including typing context Γ, type variable kinds Σ', and type and dependency constraints Θ and $\mathcal{C}$. Pattern type synthesis appears in the inference rules for λ-abstractions and case expressions. It generates a typing context from the input pattern p for typing λ-bodies and branch expressions in case statements. When checking a nested promoted pattern, the resource context R captures version resources inside a pattern.

4.1 Pattern Type Synthesis

Pattern type synthesis conveys the version resources captured by promoted patterns to the output typing context. The rules are classified into two categories, whether or not it has resources in the input resource context R. The base rules are pVar, p$\Box$, while the other rules are resource-aware versions of the corresponding rules. The resource-aware rules assume they are triggered within the promoted pattern and collect version resource r in the resource context.

The rules for variables pVar and [pVar] differ in whether the variable pattern occurs within a promoted pattern. pVar has no resources in the resource context because the original pattern is not inside a promoted pattern. Therefore, this pattern produces typing context $x : A$. [pVar] is for a variable pattern within the promoted pattern, and a resource r is recorded in the resource context. The rule assigns the collected resource r to the type A and outputs it as a versioned assumption $x : [A]_r$.

The rules for promoted patterns p$\Box$ propagate version resources to the subpattern synthesis. The input type A is expected to be a versioned type, so the rule generates the fresh type variables α and β, then performs the subpattern synthesis considering A as $\Box_\alpha \beta$. Here, the resource α captured by the promoted pattern is recorded in the resource context. Finally, the rule unifies A and $\Box_\alpha \beta$ and produces the type constraints Θ' for type refinement.

4.2 Type Synthesis

The algorithmic typing rules for VLMini, derived from declarative typing rules for λ_{VL}, are listed in Fig. 6. We explain a few important rules in excerpts.

The rule $\Rightarrow_{\mathrm{ABS}}$ generates a type variable α, along with the binding pattern p of the λ-abstraction generating the typing context Γ'. Then the rule synthesizes a type B for the λ-body under Γ', and the resulting type of the λ-abstraction is $\alpha \rightarrow B$ with the tentatively generated α. With the syntax sugar, the type rules of the contextual-let are integrated into $\Rightarrow_{\mathrm{ABS}}$. Instead, λ-abstraction does not just bind a single variable but is generalized to pattern matching, which leverages pattern typing, as extended by promoted patterns and data constructors.

The rule $\Rightarrow_{\mathrm{PR}}$ is the only rule that introduces constraints in the entire type inference algorithm. This rule intuitively infers consistent version resources for the typing context Γ. Since we implicitly allow for weakening, we generate a constraint from Γ' that contains only the free variables in t, produced by *context grading* denoted as $[\Gamma]_{\mathsf{Labels}}$. Context grading converts all assumptions in the input environment into versioned assumptions by assigning the empty set for the assumption with no version resource.

Finally, the rule generates constraints from Γ' and a fresh type variable α by constraints generation defined in the lower part of Fig. 6. The rules assert that the input type variable α is a subset of all the resources of the versioned assumptions in the input environment Γ. The following judgment is the simplest example triggered by the type synthesis of $[f\,x]$.

$$r : \mathsf{Labels}, s : \mathsf{Labels} \vdash \alpha \sqsubseteq_c f : [\mathsf{Int} \to \mathsf{Int}]_r, x : [\mathsf{Int}]_s \rhd \alpha \preceq r \wedge \alpha \preceq s$$

The inputs are type variable α and the type environment $(f : [\mathsf{Int} \to \mathsf{Int}]_r, x : [\mathsf{Int}]_s)$. In this case, the rules generate variable dependencies for r and s, each resource of the assumptions, and return a constraint combined with $\wedge$.

4.3 Extensions

Version Control Terms. The rule for **version** l **of** t uses the same trick as $(\Rightarrow_{\mathrm{PR}})$, and generates label dependencies from the input environment Γ to $\langle\langle l \rangle\rangle$. Since **version** l **of** t only instructs the type inference system, the resulting type is the same as t. **unversion** t removes the version resource from the type of t, which is assumed to be a versioned value. We extend Girard's translation so that t is always a versioned value. Since a new resource variable is given to the term by the promotion outside of **unversion**, the inference system guarantees the version consistency inside and outside the boundary of **unversion**. The list of the rules is provided in Appendix B.4 [30].

Data Structures. To support data structures, Hughes et al. suggest that coeffectful data types are required to consider the interaction between the resources inside and outside the constructor [13]. They introduce the derivation algorithm for *push* and *pull* for an arbitrary type constructor K to address this.

```
push : ∀{a b: Type, r: Labels}. (a,b)[r] -> (a[r],b[r])
push [(x, y)] = ([x], [y])
pull : ∀{a b: Type, m n: Labels}. (a[n],b[m]) -> (a,b)[n⊓m]
pull ([x], [y]) = [(x, y)]
```

Following their approach, we developed inference rules for pairs and lists. When a data structure value p is applied to a function f, the function application $f\,p$ is implicitly interpreted as $f\,(pull\,p)$. As a dual, a pattern match for a data structure value **case** p **of** $\overline{p_i \mapsto t_i}$ is interpreted as **case** $(push\,p)$ **of** $\overline{p_i \mapsto t_i}$. Appendix B.5 [30] provides the complete set of extended rules.

5 Implementation

We implement the VL compiler[2] on GHC (v9.2.4) with haskell-src-exts[3] as its parser with an extension of versioned control terms, and z3 [18] as its constraint

[2] https://github.com/yudaitnb/vl.
[3] https://hackage.haskell.org/package/haskell-src-exts.

Table 1. Availability of functions in hmatrix before and after tha update.

version	`join`	`vjoin`	`udot`, `sortVector`, `roundVector`
< 0.15	available	undefined	undefined
≥ 0.16	deleted	available	available

solver. The VL compiler performs the code generation by compiling VLMini programs back into λ-calculus via Girard's translation and then translating them into Haskell ASTs using the version in the result version labels.

Ad-hoc Version Polymorphism via Duplication. The VL compiler replicates external variables to assign individual versions to homonymous external variables. Duplication is performed before type checking of individual versions and renames every external variable along with the type and constraint environments generated from the import declarations. Such ad hoc conversions are necessary because VLMini is monomorphic, and the type inference of VLMini generates constraints by referring only to the variable's name in the type environment. Therefore, assigning different versions to homonymous variables requires manual renaming in the preliminary step of the type inference. A further discussion on version polymorphism can be found in Sect. 7.

Constraints Solving with z3. We use sbv[4] as the binding of z3. The sbv library internally converts constraints into SMT-LIB2 scripts [1] and supplies it to z3. Dependency constraints are represented as vectors of symbolic integers, where the length of the vector equals the number of external modules, and the elements are unique integers signifying each module's version number. Constraint resolution identifies the expected vectors for symbolic variables, corresponding to the label on which external identifiers in VL should depend. If more than one label satisfies the constraints, the default action is to select a newer one.

6 Case Study and Evaluation

6.1 Case Study

We demonstrate that VL programming achieves the two benefits of programming with versions. The case study simulated the incompatibility of hmatrix,[5] a popular Haskell library for numeric linear algebra and matrix computations, in the VL module **`Matrix`**. This simulation involved updating the applications **`Main`** depending on **`Matrix`** to reflect incompatible changes.

Table 1 shows the changes introduced in version 0.16 of hmatrix. Before version 0.15, hmatrix provided a `join` function for concatenating multiple vectors.

[4] https://hackage.haskell.org/package/sbv-9.0.

[5] https://github.com/haskell-numerics/hmatrix/blob/master/packages/base/CHANGELOG.

```
module Main where
import Matrix
import List
main = let
  vec = [2, 1]
  sorted = sortVector vec
  m22 = join -- [[1,2],[2,1]]
          (singleton sorted)
          (singleton vec)
  in determinant m22
-- error: version inconsistent
```

```
module Main where
import Matrix
import List
main = let
  vec = [2, 1]
  sorted = unversion
             (sortVector vec)
  m22 = join -- [[1,2],[2,1]]
          (singleton sorted)
          (singleton vec)
  in determinant m22 -- ->* -3
```

Fig. 7. Snippets of `Main` before (left) and after (right) rewriting.

The update from version 0.15 to 0.16 replaced `join` with `vjoin`. Moreover, several new functions were introduced. We implement two versions of **`Matrix`** to simulate backward incompatible changes in VL. Also, due to the absence of user-defined types in VL, we represent `Vector a` and `Matrix a` as `List Int` and `List (List Int)` respectively, using **`List`**, a partial port of `Data.List` from the Haskell standard library.

We implement **`Main`** working with two conflicting versions of **`Matrix`**. The left side of Fig. 7 shows a snippet of **`Main`** in the process of updating **`Matrix`** from version 0.15.0 to 0.16.0. `main` uses functions from both versions of **`Matrix`** together: `join` and `sortVector` are available only in version 0.15.0 and 0.16.0 respectively, hence **`Main`** has conflicting dependencies on both versions of **`Matrix`**. Therefore, it will be impossible to successfully build this program in existing languages unless the developer gives up using either `join` or `sortVector`.

- **Detecting Inconsistent Version**: VL can accept **`Main`** in two stages. First, the compiler flags a version inconsistency error. It is unclear which **`Matrix`** version the `main` function depends on as `join` requires version 0.15.0 while `sortVector` requires version 0.16.0. The error prevents using such incompatible version combinations, which are not allowed in a single expression.
- **Simultaneous Use of Multiple Versions**: In this case, using `join` and `sortVector` simultaneously is acceptable, as their return values are vectors and matrices. Therefore, we apply **`unversion`** `t` for t to collaborate with other versions. The right side of Fig. 7 shows a rewritten snippet of **`Main`**, where `sortVector vec` is replaced by **`unversion`** (sortVector vec). Assuming we avoid using programs that depend on a specific version elsewhere in the program, we can successfully compile and execute `main`.

6.2 Scalability of Constraint Resolution

We conducted experiments on the constraint resolution time of the VL compiler. In the experiment, we duplicated a VL module, renaming it to #mod

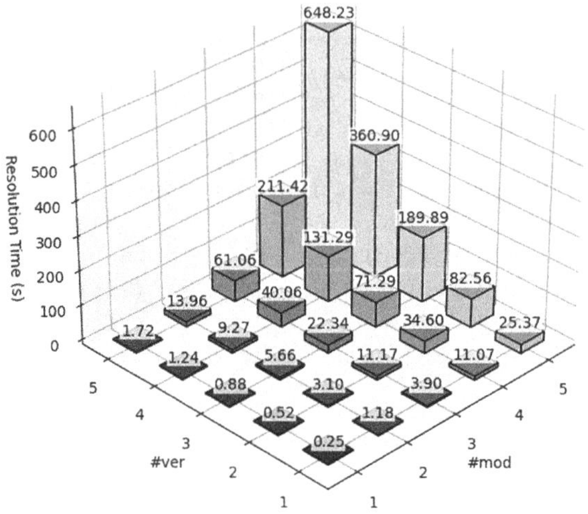

Fig. 8. Constraint resolution time for the duplicated **`List`** by `#mod` × `#ver`.

like **`List_i`**, and imported each module sequentially. Every module had the same number of versions, denoted as `#ver`. Each module version was implemented identically to **`List`**, with top-level symbols distinguished by the module name, such as `concat_List_i`. The experiments were performed ten times on a Ryzen 9 7950X running Ubuntu 22.04, with `#mod` and `#ver` ranging from 1 to 5.

Figure 8 shows the average constraint resolution time. The data suggests that the resolution time increases polynomially (at least square) for both `#mod` and `#ver`. Several issues in the current implementation contribute to this inefficiency: First, we employ sbv as a z3 interface, generating numerous redundant variables in the SMT-Lib2 script. For instance, in a code comprising 2600 LOC (with `#mod` = 5 and `#ver` = 5), the VL compiler produces 6090 version resource variables and the sbv library creates SMT-Lib2 scripts with approximately 210,000 intermediate symbolic variables. Second, z3 solves versions for all AST nodes, whereas the compiler's main focus should be on external variables and the subterms of **`unversion`**. Third, the current VL nests the constraint network, combined with $\vee$, `#mod` times at each bundling. This approach results in an overly complex constraint network for standard programs. Hence, to accelerate constraint solving, we can develop a more efficient constraint compiler for SMT-Lib2 scripts, implement preprocess to reduce constraints, and employ a greedy constraint resolution for each module.

7 Related Work, Future Work, and Conclusion

Managing Dependency Hell. Mainstream techniques for addressing dependency hell stand in stark contrast to our approach, which seeks to manage dependencies at a finer granularity. *Container* [17] encapsulates each application with all its dependencies in an isolated environment, a container, facilitating multiple library versions to coexist on one physical machine. However, it does not handle internal dependencies within the container. *Monorepository* [10,21] versions logically distinct libraries within a single repository, allowing updates across multiple libraries with one commit. It eases testing and bug finding but can lower the system modularity.

Toward a Language Considering Compatibility. The next step in this research is to embed compatibility tracking within the language system. The current VL considers different version labels incompatible unless a programmer uses **`unversion`**. Since many updates maintain backward compatibility and change only minor parts of the previous version, the existing type system is overly restrictive.

To illustrate, consider Fig. 3 again with more version history. The module **`Hash`** uses the MD5 algorithm for `mkHash` and `match` in the 1.x.x series. However, it adopts the SHA-3 algorithm in version 2.0.0, leaving other functions the same. The hash by `mkHash` version 1.0.1 (an MD5 hash) aligns with any MD5 hash from the 1.x.x series. Therefore, we know that comparing the hash using `match` version 1.0.0 is appropriate. However, the current VL compiler lacks mechanisms to express such compatibility in constraint resolution. The workaround involves using **`unversion`**, risking an MD5 hash's use with `match` version 2.0.0.

One promising approach to convey compatibilities is integrating semantic versioning [22] into the type system. If we introduce semantics into version labels, the hash generated in version 1.0.1 is backward compatible with version 1.0.0. Thus, by constructing a type system that respects explicitly defined version compatibilities, we can improve VL to accept a broader range of programs.

It is important to get reliable versions to achieve this goal. Lam et al. [14] emphasize the need for tool support to manage package modifications and the importance of analyzing compatibility through program analysis. *Delta-oriented programming* [24–26] could complement this approach by facilitating the way modularizing addition, overriding, and removal of programming elements and include application conditions for those modifications. This could result in a sophisticated package system that provides granular compatibility information.

Such a language could be an alternative to existing technologies for automatic update, collectively known as *adoptation.* These methods generate replacement rules based on structural similarities [5,33] and extract API replacement patterns from migrated code bases [27]. Some techniques involve library maintainers recording refactorings [7,12] and providing annotations [4] to describe how to update client code. However, the reported success rate of these techniques is less than 20% on average [6].

Supporting Type Incompatibility. One of the apparent problems with the current VL does not support *type incompatibilities.* VL forces terms of different versions to have the same type, both on the theoretical (typing rules in λ_{VL})

and implementation (bundling in VLMini) aspects. Supporting type incompatibility is important because type incompatibility is one of the top reasons for error-causing incompatibilities [23]. The current VL is designed in such a way because it retains the principle that equates the types of promotions and versioned records in λ_{VL}, easing the formalization of the semantics.

A promising approach to address this could be to decouple version inference from type inference and develop a version inference system on the polymorphic record calculus [19]. The idea stems from the fact that versioned types $\square_{\{l_1,l_2\}}A$ are structurally similar to record types $\{l_1 : A,\, l_2 : A\}$ of $\Lambda^{\forall,\bullet}$. Since $\Lambda^{\forall,\bullet}$ allows different record-element types for different labels and has concrete inference algorithms with polymorphism, implementing version inference on top of $\Lambda^{\forall,\bullet}$ would also make VL more expressive.

Adequate Version Polymorphism. In the current VL, there is an issue that the version label of top-level symbols in imported modules must be specified one, whereas users can select specific versions of external variables using `unversion` within the importing module. Consider using a generic function like `List.concat` in Fig. 7. If it is used in one part of the program within the context of **`Matrix`** version 1.0.0, the solution of the resource variable of `List.concat` version 1.0.0 becomes confined to {**`Matrix`** = 1.0.0, **`List`** = ...}. As a result, it is impossible to utilize `List.concat` version 1.0.0 with **`Matrix`** version 2.0.0 elsewhere in the program. This problem becomes apparent when we define a generic module like a standard library.

It is necessary to introduce full-version polymorphism in the core calculus instead of duplication to address this problem. The idea is to generate a type scheme by solving constraints for each module during bundling and instantiate each type and resource variable at each occurrence of an external variable. Such resource polymorphism is similar to that already implemented in Gr [20]. However, unlike Gr, VLMini provides a type inference algorithm that collects constraints on a per-module basis, so we need the well-defined form of the principal type. This extension is future work.

Conclusion. This paper proposes a method for dependency analysis and version control at the expression level by incorporating versions into language semantics, which were previously only identifiers of packages. This enables the simultaneous use of multiple versions and identifies programs violating version consistency at the expression level, which is impossible with conventional languages.

Our next step is to extend the version label, which currently only identifies versions, to *semantic versions* and to treat the notion of compatibility with language semantics. Like automatic updates by modern build tools based on semantic versioning, it would be possible to achieve incremental updates, which would be done step-by-step at the expression level. Working with existing package managers to collect compatibility information at the expression level would be more feasible to realize the goal.

References

1. Barrett, C., Stump, A., Tinelli, C., et al.: The SMT-LIB standard: version 2.0. In: Proceedings of the 8th International Workshop on Satisfiability Modulo Theories (Edinburgh, UK), vol. 13, p. 14 (2010)
2. Bavota, G., Canfora, G., Di Penta, M., Oliveto, R., Panichella, S.: How the apache community upgrades dependencies: an evolutionary study. Empir. Softw. Eng. **20**(5), 1275–1317 (2015). https://doi.org/10.1007/s10664-014-9325-9
3. Brunel, A., Gaboardi, M., Mazza, D., Zdancewic, S.: A core quantitative coeffect calculus. In: Shao, Z. (ed.) ESOP 2014. LNCS, vol. 8410, pp. 351–370. Springer, Heidelberg (2014). https://doi.org/10.1007/978-3-642-54833-8_19
4. Chow, Notkin: Semi-automatic update of applications in response to library changes. In: 1996 Proceedings of International Conference on Software Maintenance, pp. 359–368. IEEE, New York, USA (1996). https://doi.org/10.1109/ICSM.1996.565039
5. Cossette, B., Walker, R., Cottrell, R.: Using structural generalization to discover replacement functionality for API evolution (2014). https://doi.org/10.11575/PRISM/10182, https://prism.ucalgary.ca/handle/1880/49996
6. Cossette, B.E., Walker, R.J.: Seeking the ground truth: a retroactive study on the evolution and migration of software libraries. In: Proceedings of the ACM SIGSOFT 20th International Symposium on the Foundations of Software Engineering. FSE 2012, Association for Computing Machinery, New York, NY, USA (2012). https://doi.org/10.1145/2393596.2393661
7. Dig, D., Johnson, R.: How do APIs evolve? A story of refactoring. J. Softw. Maint. Evol. Res. Pract. **18**(2), 83–107 (2006). https://doi.org/10.1002/smr.328, https://onlinelibrary.wiley.com/doi/abs/10.1002/smr.328
8. Dunfield, J., Krishnaswami, N.R.: Complete and easy bidirectional typechecking for higher-rank polymorphism. SIGPLAN Not. **48**(9), 429–442 (2013). https://doi.org/10.1145/2544174.2500582
9. Dunfield, J., Krishnaswami, N.R.: Sound and complete bidirectional typechecking for higher-rank polymorphism with existentials and indexed types. In: Proceedings of ACM Programming Language, vol. 3(POPL) (2019). https://doi.org/10.1145/3290322
10. Durham Goode: Facebook Engineering: Scaling Mercurial at Facebook (2014). https://code.fb.com/core-data/scaling-mercurial-at-facebook/
11. Girard, J.Y.: Linear logic. Theor. Comput. Sci. **50**(1), 1–102 (1987). https://doi.org/10.1016/0304-3975(87)90045-4
12. Henkel, J., Diwan, A.: Catchup! Capturing and replaying refactorings to support API evolution. In: Proceedings. 27th International Conference on Software Engineering, 2005. ICSE 2005, pp. 274–283. IEEE, New York, USA (2005). https://doi.org/10.1109/ICSE.2005.1553570
13. Hughes, J., Vollmer, M., Orchard, D.: Deriving distributive laws for graded linear types. In: Dal Lago, U., de Paiva, V. (eds.) Proceedings Second Joint International Workshop on Linearity & Trends in Linear Logic and Applications, Online, 29–30 June 2020. Electronic Proceedings in Theoretical Computer Science, vol. 353, pp. 109–131. Open Publishing Association (2021). https://doi.org/10.4204/EPTCS.353.6
14. Lam, P., Dietrich, J., Pearce, D.J.: Putting the Semantics into Semantic Versioning, pp. 157–179. Association for Computing Machinery, New York, NY, USA (2020). https://doi.org/10.1145/3426428.3426922

15. Lubis, L.A., Tanabe, Y., Aotani, T., Masuhara, H.: Batakjava: an object-oriented programming language with versions. In: Proceedings of the 15th ACM SIGPLAN International Conference on Software Language Engineering, pp. 222–234. SLE 2022, Association for Computing Machinery, New York, NY, USA (2022). https://doi.org/10.1145/3567512.3567531
16. McDonnell, T., Ray, B., Kim, M.: An empirical study of API stability and adoption in the Android ecosystem. In: 2013 IEEE International Conference on Software Maintenance, ICSM, pp. 70–79. IEEE, New York, USA (2013). https://doi.org/10.1109/ICSM.2013.18
17. Merkel, D.: Docker: lightweight Linux containers for consistent development and deployment. Linux J. **239**, 2 (2014)
18. de Moura, L., Bjørner, N.: Z3: an efficient SMT solver. In: Ramakrishnan, C.R., Rehof, J. (eds.) Tools and Algorithms for the Construction and Analysis of Systems, pp. 337–340. Springer, Heidelberg (2008)
19. Ohori, A.: A polymorphic record calculus and its compilation. ACM Trans. Program. Lang. Syst. **17**(6), 844–895 (1995). https://doi.org/10.1145/218570.218572
20. Orchard, D., Liepelt, V.B., Eades, H., III.: Quantitative program reasoning with graded modal types. Proc. ACM Program. Lang. **3(ICFP)**, 1–30 (2019). https://doi.org/10.1145/3341714
21. Potvin, R., Levenberg, J.: Why google stores billions of lines of code in a single repository. Commun. ACM **59**(7), 78–87 (2016). https://doi.org/10.1145/2854146
22. Preston-Werner, T.: Semantic versioning 2.0.0 (2013). http://semver.org
23. Raemaekers, S., van Deursen, A., Visser, J.: Semantic versioning and impact of breaking changes in the maven repository. J. Syst. Softw. **129**, 140–158 (2017). https://doi.org/10.1016/j.jss.2016.04.008, http://www.sciencedirect.com/science/article/pii/S0164121216300243
24. Schaefer, I., Bettini, L., Damiani, F.: Compositional type-checking for delta-oriented programming. In: Proceedings of the Tenth International Conference on Aspect-Oriented Software Development, pp. 43–56. AOSD 2011, Association for Computing Machinery, New York, NY, USA (2011). https://doi.org/10.1145/1960275.1960283, https://doi.org/10.1145/1960275.1960283
25. Schaefer, I., Bettini, L., Bono, V., Damiani, F., Tanzarella, N.: Delta-oriented programming of software product lines. In: Bosch, J., Lee, J. (eds.) SPLC 2010. LNCS, vol. 6287, pp. 77–91. Springer, Heidelberg (2010). https://doi.org/10.1007/978-3-642-15579-6_6
26. Schaefer, I., Damiani, F.: Pure delta-oriented programming. In: Proceedings of the 2nd International Workshop on Feature-Oriented Software Development, pp. 49–56. FOSD 2010, Association for Computing Machinery, New York, NY, USA (2010). https://doi.org/10.1145/1868688.1868696
27. Schäfer, T., Jonas, J., Mezini, M.: Mining framework usage changes from instantiation code. In: Proceedings of the 30th International Conference on Software Engineering, pp. 471–480. ICSE 2008, Association for Computing Machinery, New York, NY, USA (2008). https://doi.org/10.1145/1368088.1368153
28. Tanabe, Y., Aotani, T., Masuhara, H.: A context-oriented programming approach to dependency hell. In: Proceedings of the 10th International Workshop on Context-Oriented Programming: Advanced Modularity for Run-time Composition, pp. 8–14. COP 2018, ACM, New York, NY, USA (2018). https://doi.org/10.1145/3242921.3242923

29. Tanabe, Y., Lubis, L.A., Aotani, T., Masuhara, H.: A functional programming language with versions. Art, Sci. Eng. Programm. **6**(1), 5:1–5:30 (2021). https://doi.org/10.22152/programming-journal.org/2022/6/5, https://doi.org/10.22152%2Fprogramming-journal.org%2F2022%2F6%2F5
30. Tanabe, Y., Lubis, L.A., Aotani, T., Masuhara, H.: Compilation semantics for a programming language with versions (2023). https://doi.org/10.48550/arXiv.2310.00298
31. Tanabe, Y., Lubis, L.A., Aotani, T., Masuhara, H.: A step toward programming with versions in real-world functional languages. In: Proceedings of the 14th ACM International Workshop on Context-Oriented Programming and Advanced Modularity, pp. 44–51. COP 2022, Association for Computing Machinery, New York, NY, USA (2022). https://doi.org/10.1145/3570353.3570359
32. Tolnay, D.: The semver trick (2017). https://github.com/dtolnay/semver-trick
33. Wu, W.: Modeling framework API evolution as a multi-objective optimization problem. In: 2011 IEEE 19th International Conference on Program Comprehension, pp. 262–265. IEEE, New York, USA (2011). https://doi.org/10.1109/ICPC.2011.43

What Types Are Needed for Typing Dynamic Objects? A Python-Based Empirical Study

Ke Sun[1], Sheng Chen[2], Meng Wang[3], and Dan Hao[1(✉)]

[1] Key Lab of HCST (PKU), MOE; SCS, Peking University, Beijing, China
sunke@stu.pku.edu.cn, haodan@pku.edu.cn
[2] The Center for Advanced Computer Studies, UL Lafayette, Lafayette, USA
sheng.chen@louisiana.edu
[3] University of Bristol, Bristol, UK
meng.wang@bristol.ac.uk

Abstract. Dynamic object-oriented languages, such as Python, Ruby, and Javascript are widely used nowadays. A distinguishing feature of dynamic object-oriented languages is that objects, the fundamental runtime data representation, are highly dynamic, meaning that a single constructor may create objects with different types and objects can evolve freely after their construction. While such dynamism facilitates fast prototyping, it brings many challenges to program understanding. Many type systems have been developed to aid programming understanding, and they adopt various types and techniques to represent and track dynamic objects. However, although many types and techniques have been proposed, it is unclear which one suits real dynamic object usages best. Motivated by this situation, we perform an empirical study on 50 mature Python programs with a focus on object dynamism and object type models. We found that (1) object dynamism is highly prevalent in Python programs, (2) class-based types are not precise to handle dynamic behaviors, as they introduce type errors for 52% of the evaluated polymorphic attributes, (3) typestate-based types, although mostly used in static languages, matches the behaviors of dynamic objects faithfully, and (4) some well-designed but still lightweight techniques for object-based types, such as argument type separation and recency abstraction can precisely characterize dynamic object behaviors. Those techniques are suitable for building precise but still concise object-based types.

Keywords: Type System · Empirical Study · Python

1 Introduction

Dynamic object-oriented languages, such as Python, Ruby, and Javascript are commonly used across many domains. They use dynamic typing to increase reusability and flexibility, facilitating fast prototyping (development) not provided by most static languages. In particular, unlike in static object-oriented languages where objects have mostly fixed attributes and their types [25], objects

C.-K. Hur (Ed.): APLAS 2023, LNCS 14405, pp. 24–45, 2023.
https://doi.org/10.1007/978-981-99-8311-7_2

in dynamic languages are highly dynamic. Both the attributes and types of an object may be changed freely over its life cycle.

To illustrate, consider the Python program in Fig. 1, which is adapted from *Rich*, a terminal beautification tool [34]. This program defines two instance objects (shorted as objects) of `Panel`: `panel1` and `panel2`. However, the types of the two objects are not stipulated by class definition and can be set and changed freely. We refer to this phenomenon as *object dynamism.*

Behaviors Causing Object Dynamism. Object dynamism originates from two sources: constructor polymorphism and object evolution [42,54]. With **constructor polymorphism**, objects of different types can be made from the same constructor. Lines 17-18 show such an example. Specifically, although `panel1` and `panel2` are created from the same `__init__`, `panel1` has the type $\tau_1 = \{\texttt{title} : \texttt{Text}, \texttt{width} : \texttt{int}, \texttt{height} : \texttt{int}\}$, while `panel2` has the type $\tau_2 = \{\texttt{title} : \texttt{str}, \texttt{width} : \texttt{NoneType}\}$[1]. In particular, two attributes (`title` and `width`) are shared but with different types, and one attribute (`height`) appears only in τ_1. After the construction phase, objects can dynamically evolve, making the types continue to change, denoted as **object evolution**. Lines 19-20 present such an example, which changes the `width` attribute of `panel2` from `NoneType` to `int` and adds the attribute `height`.

```
1  class Panel:
2      def __init__(self, title, width):
3          self.title = title
4          self.width = width
5          if self.width is not None:
6              self.height = self.width
7      def _title(self):
8          if isinstance(self.title, str):
9              return Text.from_markup(self.title)
10         else:
11             return self.title.copy()
12     def setheight(self, height):
13         self.height = height
14     def measure(self):
15         return self.width * self.height
16
17 panel1 = Panel(Text(), 42)
18 panel2 = Panel("Example Table", None)
19 panel2.width = 5 # modification
20 panel2.setheight(42) # extension
```

Fig. 1. An example Python program

An Empirical Study on Dynamic Objects for Type Systems. As dynamic languages are being used to build more and more important and large software systems, many type systems [10,23,30,33] have been developed to aid program comprehension and early programming error detection. Those type systems come up with special object types for representing dynamic objects. The most widely adopted design choice is to augment the class-based types, which assign a single type to all objects created from the same class, with features such as union types [9], and the ability to reason about type tests [28,48] and local type

[1] We refer the constructed types of `panel1`/`panel2` by τ_1/τ_2 in the rest of this paper.

assignments [3]. Due to their performance superiority and annotating convenience, class-based types have been extensively used in industrial and academic type systems [10,19,22,30,40,53]. However, it is not clear whether they provide dynamic objects with type representations that are precise enough.

On the other hand, many object-based type systems [8,17,45,55] have also been proposed, which assign a unique type to each object, according to its abstract address and evolution processes. Since those techniques provide dynamic objects with more precise representations, it is clear that they produce fewer type errors compared with class-based types. However, the actual improvement has not been investigated on a large scale. Meanwhile, the contributions of individual aspects of object-based types to the improvements are not understood.

To help understand the prevalence and characteristics of dynamic object behaviors, as well as the effectiveness of existing object types, we present an empirical study based on a dynamic analysis of 50 mature Python programs with over 3.76 million LOC. There have been several studies [4,24,42,54] that also consider the dynamic object behaviors. However, their analysis is not focused on types, and thus their implications on type systems are limited.

Some of our significant findings include: (1) Both constructor polymorphism and object evolution are very prevalent. The average proportions of classes exposing them are both higher than 20%, and they often occur at the same time. (2) Class-based types can be a practical choice, especially when paired with the ability to reason about type tests and local assignments. Although false type errors are reported for 52% of the polymorphic attributes when experimenting with them, those type errors are largely due to attribute absence, which is notoriously hard to detect statically [32]. (3) Typestate-based types, as already utilized extensively to represent object evolution in static languages [6,29,46], can be promising to be adopted to dynamic languages, considering the large proportion of attribute-absences-related errors, which turn out to be introduced mainly by object evolution. (4) Object-based types are found to be effective in representing dynamic objects. In particular, the ability to perform strong updates [8,23] is critical to increase the precision.

In summary, this paper makes the following contributions.

1. A large corpus composed of 50 mature Python projects with over 3.76 million LOC and a well-designed dynamic analysis infrastructure capable of analyzing precise and detailed object behaviors.
2. An empirical study of object dynamism in Python with findings and advice for evaluating current type systems and inspiring future type systems.

The artifact of this paper, containing the analysis infrastructure and the experiment scripts, can be accessed via https://github.com/ksun212/Python-objects.

2 Background

In this section, we introduce dynamic object behaviors in detail and review related studies on dynamic behaviors.

2.1 Dynamic Object Behaviors in Python

Constructor Polymorphism. We name the behavior that objects of different types are made from a single constructor as constructor polymorphism. In Python, a constructor is a normal member method that initializes attributes. In our example, different objects are constructed in a functional way, i.e., object types are solely decided by argument types. However, as an imperative language, the program's state can also influence the behaviors of constructors. For example, an attribute may be set when a global variable holds a specific value.

Object Evolution. We name the behavior that an object changes its type after being constructed as object evolution. Based on the action, object evolution can be classified into (1) extension (i.e., adding new attributes), (2) modification (i.e., modifying types of attributes), and (3) deletion (i.e., deleting attributes).

2.2 Existing Studies on Dynamic Behaviors

Although object dynamic behaviors are significant for building type systems and other static analyses for dynamic languages, only a few studies have been done to study their actual prevalence. In particular, Richards et al. [42] and Wei et al. [54] conducted empirical studies on the dynamic behaviors in JavaScript programs. However, the former did not distinguish between changes of attribute types (changes that lead to object evolution) and attribute values (changes do not lead to object evolution), and the latter measured constructor polymorphism via the number of runtime instances instead of object types that matter more to type system design. Only two pieces of work [4,24] investigated the dynamic behavior of Python objects. However, they mainly focus on object evolution, without investigating constructor polymorphism. Meanwhile, neither of the above studies analyzes the effectiveness of existing object types.

Several studies investigated other features of dynamic languages, such as eval expressions [41], callsite polymorphism [5,27], and dynamic variables [14]. These studies are not from type systems' perspective, the focus of this work.

3 Types for Dynamic Objects

In this section, we present a type syntax for class-based types and discuss local type refinements. Then, we review important aspects for object-based types.

3.1 Class-Based Types

Type Syntax. To consolidate the notion of class-based types in this paper, we propose a type syntax, which mostly coincides with the definition of class-based types in existing class-based type systems [10,19,

$$
\begin{aligned}
\tau &::= cls | \tau \vee \tau | abs \\
CT &::= cls : \{\overline{attr : \tau}\}, CT \mid \emptyset \\
\Gamma &::= x : cls, \Gamma \mid \emptyset \\
x &\in Program\ Variables \\
attr &\in Attribute\ Names \\
cls &\in Class\ Names
\end{aligned}
$$

Fig. 2. Syntax for class-based types.

22,30,40,53]. The only difference is that we model attribute absence using a constant type *abs*, while other systems provide type qualifiers [31] or simply omit it [19,30,53] (Fig. 2).

Under this syntax, the type environment (Γ) maps from variables to class names. The class table (CT) maps from class names to object types, which is a record labeled by attribute names with values ranging over attribute types (τ). τ can be another class name (such as builtin classes `int`, `str`, and user-defined classes `Panel`, `Text`), a special constant type *abs* to signify that the attribute is absent or a union of two attribute types. For the example in Fig. 1, a type system using this syntax gives type environment {`panel1` : `Panel`, `panel2` : `Panel`}, and class table {`Panel` : {`title` : `Text` ∨ `str`, `width` : `int` ∨ `NoneType`, `height` : `int` ∨ `abs`}}.

Polymorphic Attributes Cause Type Errors. Although class-based types provide a natural way to express object dynamism, they often introduce type errors. To see this, consider type-checking the method `measure`, which results in a type error, since `width` can be `NoneType` while `height` can be *abs*, both invalidating the addition operation. Those type errors are caused by polymorphic attributes, i.e., the attributes holding union types, when not all components of the union type can be used in any access-site of the attribute.

Local Type Refinements. To eliminate suspicious type errors, *local type refinements* [3,28,48] are often used to refine the union types. The core observation is that developers tend to use type tests and local assignments to refine the type of polymorphic attributes, which can be utilized to refine the union types to a smaller range thus eliminating type errors. For example, consider type-checking the method `_title`, in the first branch, the type of `title` is refined to be `str` by the type test `isinstance(self.title,str)`. For an example of local assignments, consider inserting `if self.width is None: self.width=42` into the beginning of the method `measure`, which refines the type of `width` to be only `int`.

3.2 Object-Based Types

Class-based type systems assign all objects belonging to the same class with the same type. We have discussed that this design choice introduces spurious type errors. Although local type refinements can be used to eliminate type errors, they rely on type tests or local assignments, which are unavailable in many cases. To eliminate the type errors, another idea is to assign more precise types to dynamic objects, by exposing more fine-grained object addresses and performing strong updates for object evolution as much as possible [1,8,17,44,45,52,55]. In the following of this paper, we name this kind of typing discipline as object-based types, whose effectiveness will be discussed in our study.

Store Abstraction. Each dynamic object receives a unique address from the heap (store). While types of objects may be identified by their addresses, few type systems support this, since addresses are allocated at runtime while the type systems we are investigating perform static checking. Instead, type systems often use abstractions of store to denote object types. In class-based type systems, each object uses the class name as its address. All objects of the same class share the same address. To keep sound, the types of all those objects, along their life cycles, must be merged. This is the reason that many attributes in class-based type systems are polymorphic, causing spurious type errors.

Using class names as addresses often leads to imprecision. A prominent approach is extending the class name with the construction location. Construction location can be annotated [16,45] or inferred [19,23,36]. In our example, we can separate the types of `panel1` and `panel2` using this approach, yielding $\Gamma = \{\texttt{panel1} : \mathit{Panel}@17, \texttt{panel2} : \mathit{Panel}@18\}$ and $CT = \{\mathit{Panel}@17 : \{\texttt{title} : \texttt{Text}, \texttt{width} : \texttt{int}, \texttt{height} : \texttt{int}\}, \mathit{Panel}@18 : \{\texttt{title} : \texttt{str}, \texttt{width} : \texttt{int} \vee \texttt{NoneType}, \texttt{height} : \texttt{int} \vee \texttt{abs}\}\}$. Note that $\mathit{Panel}@18$ must cover all the types of `panel2` in its life cycle. Suppose the method `measure` is called on `panel1`, this type system would correctly accept it but still reject the call on `panel2`.

Sometimes, using the construction locations is not precise enough, since many construction-sites can be called many times (e.g., occurring inside a function that is repeatedly called.). To handle this, location polymorphism [16] and k-callsite [36] have been proposed. We evaluate the help of k-callsites in our study.

Flow Sensitivity. As we discussed earlier, to keep sound, the types in the life cycle of an object must be merged. The reason is that the store abstraction (i.e., CT) must over-approximate the store at any time of the program execution. One common approach to relax this constraint is *flow-sensitive store abstraction* [2,16,36,43], which allows each program location to be associated with a different store abstraction. In our example, this yields $CT = \{..., \mathit{Panel}@18 : \{\texttt{title} : \texttt{str}, \texttt{width} : \texttt{NoneType}, \texttt{height} : \texttt{abs}\}\}$, $CT' = \{.., \mathit{Panel}@18 : \{\texttt{title} : \texttt{str}, \texttt{width} : \texttt{int} \vee \texttt{NoneType}, \texttt{height} : \texttt{abs}\}\}$, and $CT'' = \{.., \mathit{Panel}@18 : \{\texttt{title} : \texttt{str}, \texttt{width} : \texttt{int} \vee \texttt{NoneType}, \texttt{height} : \texttt{int} \vee \texttt{abs}\}\}$, where $CT/CT'/CT''$ denote the store abstraction associated with Line 18/19/20. Suppose that an access of `width` is inserted before Line 19, which requires it to have the type `NoneType`, then flow sensitivity allows this access to be accepted since the system knows that `width` can only be `NoneType` before Line 19. In a flow-insensitive system, this access would be incorrectly rejected. However, the method `measure` still cannot be called on `panel2`, even after Line 20. This is because, due to the potential existence of aliases, one attribute must be typed with all the types that are previously assigned to the attribute, a methodology often called "weak updates" [8].

Strong Updates. A type system that is able to replace the old type for an attribute with a new type when an object evolves is said to be able to perform "strong updates". Strong updates have to be performed on the top of flow-sensitive store abstraction. With strong updates, the type system knows $CT'' = \{..., \mathit{Panel}@18 : \{\texttt{title} : \texttt{Text}, \texttt{width} : \texttt{int}, \texttt{height} : \texttt{int}\}\}$, and subsequently, allows `measure` be called on `panel2` after Line 20.

Due to the alias problem, strong updates can not be performed arbitrarily [8]. It is widely known that strong updates can be applied to linear addresses [2,16,43], i.e., the addresses that refer to only one object. In our example, we have seen that the class name extended with construction locations linearly refer to the two objects. In general, more precise techniques like location polymorphism [16] and k-callsite [36] make more addresses linear. However, those

Table 1. Statistics and Categories of Experiment Subjects

Category	Subjects	LOC
Scientific Computing (SCI)	networkx, pinyin, sklearn, nltk, altair, kornia, stanza, featuretools, dvc, torch, pandas, seaborn, statsmodels, pyod, spacy, snorkel	2.29M
Programming (PRG)	pydantic, typer, bandit, isort, arrow, jedi, black, yapf, mypy	0.46M
Web (WEB)	requests, flask, impacket, routersploit, itsdangerous, pelican, sphinx	0.24M
Terminal (TER)	rich, thefuck, cookiecutter, click, prompt_toolkit	0.14M
Formating (FMT)	jinja, pypdf, markdown, weasyprint	0.12M
Utility (UTL)	pywhat, icecream, pendulum, pre_commit, faker	0.34M
Others (OTH)	newspaper, wordcloud, pyro, pyecharts	0.14M
All (ALL)	50 projects	3.76M

techniques have been witnessed to significantly increase running overhead [36] or incur excessive annotation burden [16]. Another widely adopted solution is recency abstraction [8,23]. Recency abstraction splits one address into two, one for the most recently constructed object and one for all previously constructed objects. Supposing just use the class name as addresses, recency abstraction gives $\Gamma = \{\texttt{panel1} : Panel_s, \texttt{panel2} : Panel_r\}$. For the most recently constructed object, since it is the only object referred to by the address, strong updates can be performed, while all previously constructed objects can only be updated weakly[2]. The assumption of recency abstraction is object evolution usually happens to the most recent object, instead of the previously constructed objects. Our example obeys this assumption since only `panel2` evolves.

4 Experimental Design

This study investigates the following questions around object dynamism in Python.
RQ1. Are dynamic object behaviors prevalent in the wild?
RQ2. How effective are class-based types and object-based types?

4.1 Subjects

In this experiment, we use 50 Python projects from Github. In particular, we select the top 50 popular Python projects on Github whose testing framework is *pytest*, after removing the ones that need to be run on multiprocessing mode (which causes potential races of the log file) or have special requirements (e.g., network or peripheral devices). By requiring *pytest* to be the testing framework, we can run all the subjects under a unified interface, simplifying the experiment setup. Due to space limitations, when presenting and analyzing the results, we

[2] In our example, only `panel1` is not recent. However, in general, there can be many.

divide these 50 subjects into 7 categories and present the results for each category. Table 1 presents these categories, the subjects they contain, and their total LOC. We present the details of these 50 subjects on the artifact.

To learn the dynamic behaviors of these Python projects, we run the test suite of each subject. In order to facilitate the analysis, we prune the test suites until they can be executed within 12 h and produce a trace file of less than 20G. The details of the used tests are also presented on the artifact.

4.2 Tracing and Analysis Infrastructure

Overview of the Infrastructure. Our infrastructure consists of a tracing module and an analysis module. The tracing module is based on CPython 3.9[3]. The tracing module traces the execution of a subject and records the events related to Python objects, such as the start/end of object construction, and assigning/deleting object attributes. The events are recorded with the necessary information to conduct our analysis, such as where the event happens (program location), and which object is related to the event. The analysis module analyzes the events to construct and evaluate class-based types and object-based types.

Constructing Types. We construct class-based types and object-based types from the traces. To construct class-based types for a class c, if one of its objects is observed to be assigned with an attribute a and type c' in the trace, we add a to the attribute set of c, and add c' to the types of $c.a$. If one attribute a is owned by one object of the class, but is not owned by another, we add abs to the types of $c.a$. We also add abs if the attribute is added/deleted in the evolution phase, since the attribute is absent before/after the extension/deletion. For class-based types, all objects of the same class share the same type. The construction of object-based types is similar, the only difference is that all objects of the same object address (instead of class) share the same type. For object-based types, we simulate flow-sensitive store abstraction by constructing different stores for different locations. On top of flow-sensitive store abstraction, We simulate strong updates by performing strong updates whenever the condition is met (i.e., the object address is linear or obeys recency abstraction).

Note that when constructing types, we construct for all classes observed in the traces. However, when evaluating the types, we focus on the objects whose classes are defined directly in the program, ignoring the objects defined in built-in or third-party libraries, to better reflect the nature of the analyzed programs.

Evaluating Types. We evaluate the effectiveness of class-based types and object-based types against the access-sites. To illustrate, consider the class-based type of `panel1`, namely, $\{\texttt{title} : \texttt{Text} \vee \texttt{str}, \texttt{width} : \texttt{int} \vee \texttt{NoneType}, \texttt{height} : \texttt{int} \vee \texttt{abs}\}$. Supposing we observe that the attribute `title` of `panel1` is accessed at Line 11, we evaluate this access-site in two steps. The first step performs local type refinements based on the type tests [28,48] and local assignments [3]. In our example, the polymorphic attribute `title` holds two classes, i.e., `str` and `Text`.

[3] https://github.com/python/cpython/tree/3.9.

However, for the access-site at Line 11, only `Text` is valid, while `str` is ruled out at Line 8. The second step judges if the types after refinement (i.e., `Text`) can be used in the access-site, i.e., satisfy the constraints of the access-site.

The complete constraints in one access-site can not be collected without building a complicated analysis. In our study, we utilize a substantial subset of the complete constraints, named *local constraints*. The major generation rules of local constraints are presented in Fig. 3. In this figure, *obj.a* denotes the access expression, T denotes the set of all types of the attribute a after refinement ($\{\texttt{Text}\}$ for `title` in our example). *Attr* is the function to extract the attribute set of one object type. In our example, since we have `self.title.copy`, we can generate the constraint $abs \notin \{\texttt{Text}\} \wedge copy \in Attr(\texttt{Text})$, which is true by examining the type set ($\{Text\}$) and the type of `Text`.

Similarly, consider another access-site of `title`, at Line 9. We can refine the type of `title` to `str` this time. However, since `title` is directly passed to another function, we cannot collect any local constraints, and thus we do not evaluate this access-site. So far, we have examined all the access-sites of `title`. Since it satisfies all examined access-sites, it is determined to be safe. For object types to be precise, they should make as many polymorphic attributes safe, since unsafe polymorphic attributes are very likely to be false alarms, due to the fact that the access-sites are collected dynamically without witnessing runtime type errors.

$$
\begin{array}{rcl@{\qquad}rcl}
obj.a & \Longrightarrow & abs \notin T & obj.a + e & \Longrightarrow & \forall \tau \in T, \_\_\text{add}\_\_ \in Attr(\tau) \\
obj.a() & \Longrightarrow & \forall \tau \in T, \_\_\text{call}\_\_ \in Attr(\tau) & obj.a.f & \Longrightarrow & \forall \tau \in T, f \in Attr(\tau) \\
obj.a[e] & \Longrightarrow & \forall \tau \in T, \_\_\text{getitem}\_\_ \in Attr(\tau) & len(obj.a) & \Longrightarrow & \forall \tau \in T, \_\_\text{len}\_\_ \in Attr(\tau)
\end{array}
$$

Fig. 3. Local Constraint Generation Rules

5 Results and Analysis

In this section, we answer the two research questions in two subsections.

5.1 Prevalence of Dynamic Behaviors

In this section, we study the prevalence of dynamic behaviors, as well as several important aspects of them, to help characterize the difficulty of analyzing them.

Constructor Polymorphism. Table 2 presents the statistics of classes that expose constructor polymorphism, where the second column presents the total number of classes in a specific category and in all subjects. The third and fourth columns present statistics on these classes, which we refer to as ratio results and subject-wise median results, respectively. To obtain ratio results (given by column "Ratio"), we divide the total number of classes that expose constructor polymorphism in one category by the total number of classes in that category. To obtain the subject-wise median results (given by column "Median"), we calculate the proportion of classes exposing constructor polymorphism for each subject in

Table 2. Prevalence of constructor polymorphism. Class shows the number of classes. Ratio and Median show the proportion of classes.

Category	Class	Ratio	Median
SCI	1773	0.24	0.28
PRG	360	0.32	0.20
WEB	643	0.12	0.14
TER	214	0.27	0.20
FMT	258	0.30	0.40
UTL	28	0.18	0.20
OTH	266	0.17	0.23
ALL	3542	0.23	0.20

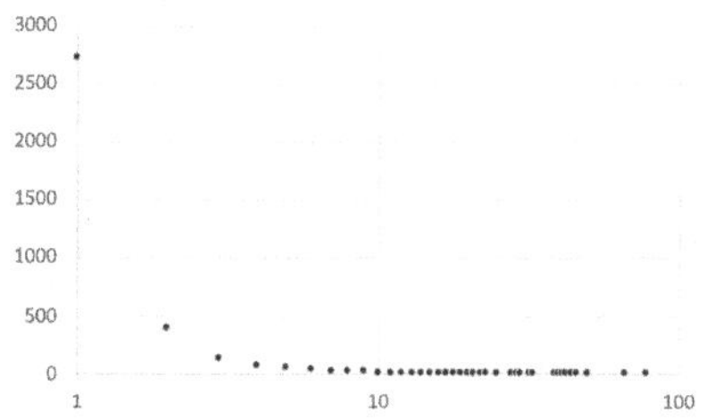

Fig. 4. Degree of constructor polymorphism. The X-axis/Y-axis denotes the number of distinct object types/classes.

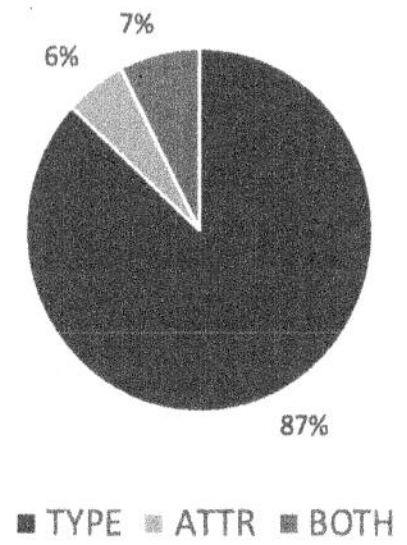

Fig. 5. Overall Relation among Object Types.

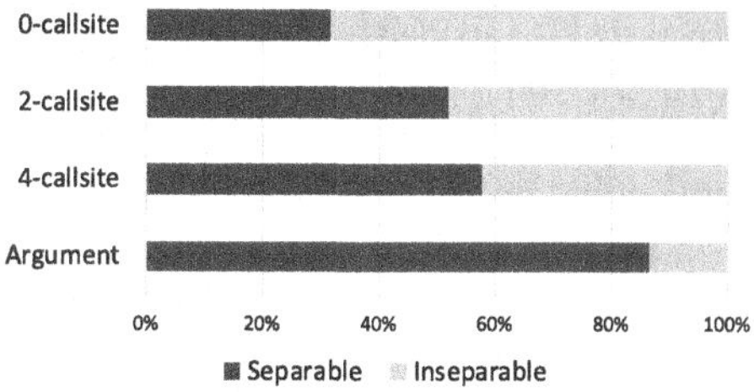

Fig. 6. Separability of Different Construction Contexts.

one category and take the median. Ratio results emphasize the overall proportion, while subject-wise median results emphasize the subject-wise differences. Due to space limitations, we present the results for each category and a summary of all subjects. The results of individual subjects are given on the artifact.

From this figure, the ratio and median proportion of classes that expose constructor polymorphism are both over 20%, indicating that constructor polymorphism is **prevalent**. Besides, we can also notice the differences among categories, e.g., *UTL*, *WEB* and *OTH* have fewer classes that expose constructor polymorphism. Many classes belonging to those categories have relatively simple functionality and do not need constructor polymorphism.

Now we know that constructor polymorphism is prevalent. But how polymorphic are polymorphic constructors, and how difficult it is to analyze them?

How Polymorphic. Figure 4 shows the degree of constructor polymorphism, that is, the number of distinct object types made out of polymorphic constructors. According to Fig. 4, most of the polymorphic constructors have a relative **low degree** (less than 5), indicating that typically only a few object types are made.

Table 3. Prevalence of object evolution. RO/MO presents the ratio/median for objects, while RC/MC presents that for classes.

Category	Object	RO	MO	Class	RC	MC
SCI	3×10^6	0.31	0.21	1773	0.36	0.28
PRG	1×10^6	0.11	0.02	360	0.11	0.15
WEB	2×10^5	0.28	0.40	643	0.31	0.43
TER	5×10^4	0.08	0.07	214	0.18	0.23
FMT	1×10^6	0.46	0.49	258	0.47	0.61
UTL	1×10^5	0.02	0.02	28	0.25	0.20
OTH	3×10^5	0.17	0.21	266	0.42	0.38
ALL	6×10^6	0.27	0.12	3542	0.33	0.28

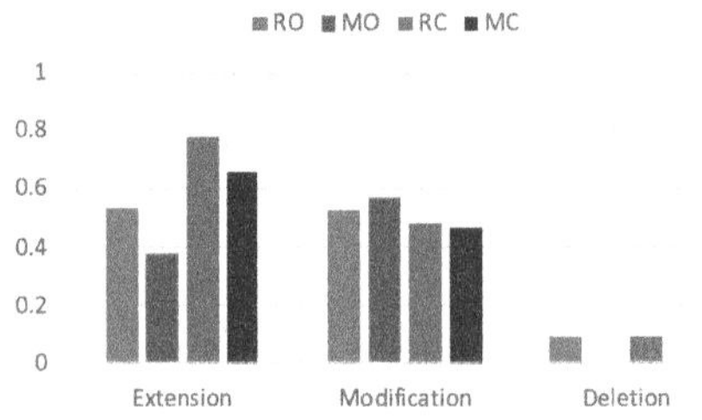

Fig. 7. Actions of Object Evolution

Polymorphic constructor constructs objects of different types. But, how different are these types? To answer this question, we divide the polymorphic constructors into three kinds, according to whether they construct object types with inconsistent attribute types (labeled *TYPE* in Fig. 5, e.g., $\{attr : int\}$ and $\{attr : str\}$), inconsistent attribute sets (*ATTR*, e.g., $\{attr : int\}$ and $\{attr : int, attr2 : int\}$), or both (*BOTH*, e.g., $\{attr : int\}$ and $\{attr : str, attr2 : int\}$). Figure 5 shows the proportion of those three kinds, which shows that most (87%) polymorphic constructors construct object types with consistent attribute sets but inconsistent attribute types. This suggests that polymorphic attribute types, instead of attribute sets, are contributed by constructor polymorphism. Thus, if the main cause of false type errors is attribute sets (we will see that it is), constructor polymorphism should be generally innocent.

Separability. Constructors in Python are just normal functions. To precisely analyze functions, context sensitivity is the prominent technique used in static analysis and type systems [21,26,37,52]. Context sensitivity relies on function call contexts to separate the return types of different function calls. The most widely used function call contexts are k-callsites [21,26,37] and argument types [1,52], namely k-length call stacks and types of arguments of call-sites. Figure 6 shows the proportion of polymorphic constructors that can be separated by argument types or k-callsite contexts. For a polymorphic constructor, if given an argument type/k-callsite of the constructor, only one object type is observed to be constructed under the argument type/k-callsite, we mark the constructor as *separable* by argument types/k-callsites. Otherwise, it is *inseparable.* According to Fig. 6, **argument types** effectively separate more than 80% of polymorphic constructors, implying the high dependency of constructed object types on the argument types. However, k-callsites are not as effective as argument types, although the separability increases with a longer callsite.

Object Evolution. Table 3 shows the prevalence of object evolution. Its second, third, and fourth columns present the total number of objects, the ratio, and the median proportion of objects that expose object evolution. The last three columns of this table present the total number of classes, the ratio, and the median proportion of classes that expose object evolution. Note that if any object of one class exposes object evolution, we regard the class as exposing object evolution. From the table, a large number of objects/classes (27%/33%) expose object evolution, indicating the **prevalence** of object evolution. Besides, *SCI*, *FMT*, and *WEB* have more objects/classes exposing object evolution and we suspect the reason to be the specific functionalities of these categories. For example, objects of class `DecisionTree` of the subject *sklearn* in the *SCI* category are extended with new attributes after they are trained.

Now we know that object evolution happens frequently. But how do the objects evolve, and how difficult it is to analyze the evolution?

How. Fig. 7 presents the statistics of evolution action. It shows the ratio and median proportion of objects and classes that expose extension, modification, and deletion, among all the **evolving** objects and classes. From this table, extension and modification are dominant. Meanwhile, deletion seldom occurs: although the ratio of deletion is around 10%, the median proportion is zero.

Furthermore, we analyze the pattern of evolution and find that most of the evolution processes are monotonic. Monotonicity is a property that has been used extensively in previous studies on object evolution [7,11,47]. Different from the types described in Sect. 3, types based on monotonicity allow object evolution to be soundly analyzed without the need for store abstraction [39]. In this study, following previous studies, we define monotonic evolution as the evolution in which attributes are only added but not deleted, and when the type of one attribute is changed, it only changes from a type to its subtype (we only consider nominal subtype). We calculate the ratio of evolving objects that evolve monotonically and find the ratio very high (85%). We believe that although monotonicity has not been widely spread around the techniques for dynamic languages, it is promising to propose systems utilizing it.

Function. The function where one evolution action happens significantly influences the difficulty of analyzing it. As shown in Fig. 8, we divide the functions where evolution actions happen into three kinds: *Local* means the evolution action happens in the same function as the construction-site. *Method* means the evolution action happens in one of the member methods of the evolving objects. Those two kinds generally allow modular reasoning to be performed [30,51,55] and are easier to analyze; *Others* denotes other functions. From the figure, we can see that most functions are member methods of the object. There are also some (23%) functions belonging to *Local*. Those findings indicate modular techniques for analyzing object evolution should be able to cover most cases.

Condition. Figure 9 shows the conditions under which object evolution happens. More precisely, this figure shows the distribution of evolution locations (evolution-sites), based on the **intra**procedural preconditions. The intraprocedural precondition of one evolution-site is the condition that must be satisfied to reach the evolution-site from the function entry. While in actual systems, **inter**procedural preconditions (i.e., the condition to reach the function callsite) must also be considered, collecting them requires a complicated infrastructure. Thus, we use intraprocedural preconditions to speculate the difficulty of analyzing the conditions. We split the intraprocedural preconditions into four major

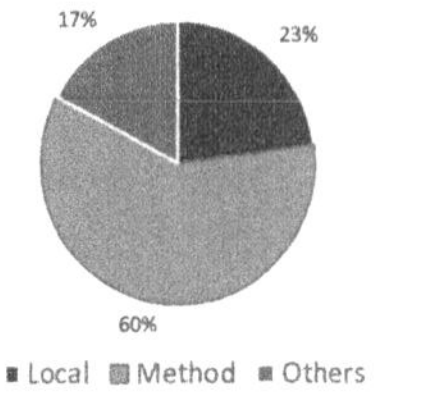

Fig. 8. Functions of Object Evolution

Table 4. Overall Dynamism

Category	Ratio		Median	
	Static	Hybrid	Static	Hybrid
SCI	0.54	0.14	0.59	0.11
PRG	0.60	0.03	0.67	0.02
WEB	0.61	0.05	0.50	0.05
TER	0.64	0.09	0.69	0.08
FMT	0.46	0.23	0.53	0.27
UTL	0.64	0.07	0.60	0.00
OTH	0.52	0.11	0.54	0.14
ALL	0.56	0.11	0.56	0.06

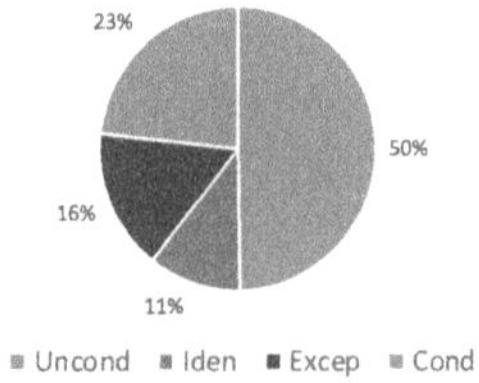

Fig. 9. Condition of Evolution

Table 5. Results of the Evaluation of Class-based Types

Category	Attributes		Access-site Evaluation							Absences	
	ALL	POL	EVA	UNI	TES	LOC	RN	RA	RB	ABS	CABS
SCI	18127	3802	1127	0.12	0.36	0.50	0.54	0.87	0.93	2623	239
PRG	2143	360	100	0.50	0.62	0.72	0.76	0.77	0.82	23	2
WEB	3842	957	217	0.13	0.26	0.41	0.59	0.74	0.95	572	58
TER	1126	187	36	0.36	0.78	0.83	0.92	0.86	0.94	12	0
FMT	1832	746	245	0.15	0.19	0.26	0.28	0.92	0.95	460	39
UTL	146	21	2	0.00	0.00	0.50	0.50	0.50	0.50	6	1
OTH	2145	231	31	0.42	0.55	0.55	0.65	0.87	0.97	114	6
ALL	29361	6304	1758	0.16	0.35	0.48	0.53	0.86	0.93	3810	345

kinds: (1) *Uncond*, where the precondition is simply *True*; (2) *Iden*, where the precondition is not *True*, but all branches conduct evolution identically[4]; (3) *Excep*, where the precondition is just to exclude the exceptional execution path (e.g., `if cond then raise exception else evolve`); (4) *Cond*, where the precondition does not belong to the previous three cases. From the figure, we can see most (77%) of the evolution-sites fall into *Uncound*, *Iden*, or *Excep*. Meanwhile, the proportion of *Cond* is still non-negligible (23%). This kind of evolution can be precisely analyzed only by path-sensitive type systems. However, most existing type systems for dynamic objects are not path-sensitive; instead, they merge the different types of one object in different branches. Although there do exist path-sensitive systems based on dependent and intersection types [16], or abstract interpretation [36], those systems suffer from performance issues, and complex type annotations [50]. To this end, we argue that more advanced techniques should proposed, maybe by making better use of the potential correspondence between conditional evolution and conditional accesses.

Overall Dynamism. Table 4 shows the overall dynamism of evaluated projects. The **second** and **fourth** columns show the ratio and median proportion of classes that do not expose any dynamic behaviors (i.e., static classes). The **third** and **fifth** columns show the metrics of classes that expose both kinds of dynamic

[4] In such cases, there is no need to precisely distinguish the branches.

behaviors (i.e., hybrid classes). From the table, the proportions of static classes in all classes and within a project are both 56%. Since static objects are ideal for performing program optimization [15,49], we believe that their high proportion encourages more optimization for them. Also, the infrastructure of this paper is a good start for identifying static objects/classes.

On the other hand, the ratio of classes that expose both behaviors is non-negligible (11%). This implies that two behaviors are sometimes utilized simultaneously because they may serve different purposes. Thus, we believe it is promising to develop unified techniques to handle both dynamic behaviors.

5.2 Effectiveness of the Types

In this section, we analyze the effectiveness of class-based types and object-based types. We start with the analysis of class-based types.

Class-Based Types. As discussed, polymorphic attributes are a good indicator of the effectiveness of class-based types. Thus, we first analyze polymorphic attributes, followed by an evaluation of the effectiveness of class-based types.

Polymorphic Attributes. Recall that an attribute is **polymorphic** if it holds a union type. In other words, it is assigned with multiple classes or *abs*. The second and third columns of Table 5 present the number of all attributes and polymorphic attributes. We observe that the proportion of polymorphic attributes is high (6304/29361 = 21.4%), indicating their prevalence in dynamic languages.

To understand how types held by polymorphic attributes are related, we classify polymorphic attributes into six kinds in Fig. 10. These six kinds include: (a) *ABS*, where each attribute (e.g., `height`) holds a single class or *abs*, (b) *OPT*, where each attribute (e.g., `width`) holds a single class or `NoneType`, after removing *abs*, (c) *NOM*, where each attribute holds multiple classes that, after removing `NoneType` and *abs*, have nominal relation (i.e., the nominal join is not `Object`), (d) *NUM*, where each attribute holds multiple classes that, after removing `NoneType` and *abs*, are all numeric (i.e., builtin numeric classes, `int` and `float`, and user-defined numeric classes, e.g., `numpy.float32`), (e) *STRU*, where each attribute holds multiple classes that, after removing `NoneType` and *abs*, have structural relation (i.e., the structural join is not `Object`), and (f) *OTHE*: the polymorphic attributes not belonging to previous kinds. When a polymorphic attribute belongs to more than one kind, we classify it into the earlier appeared kind because it is more specific. For example, the polymorphic attribute holding `int` and `float` belongs to both *NUM* and *STRU*. We classify it into *NUM* since all attributes belonging to *NUM* belong to *STRU*, but not vice versa.

From Fig. 10, we observe that a large proportion (53%+21%) of polymorphic attributes are *ABS* and *OPT*, meaning that most attributes are polymorphic because of *abs* or `NoneType`. Nevertheless, a significant proportion (26%) of polymorphic attributes are actually assigned with multiple classes even after removing *abs* and `NoneType`. Luckily, we find that most of those attributes do not belong to *OTHE*, indicating that a supertype (in the sense of nominal, numeric, or structural) is likely to be the intended type of each such attribute. Those

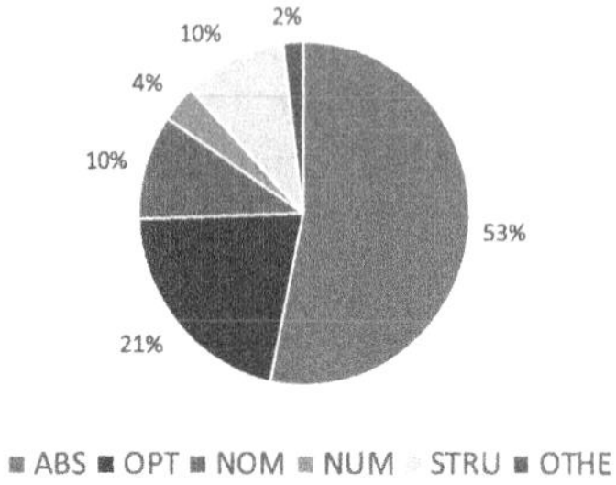

Fig. 10. Classification

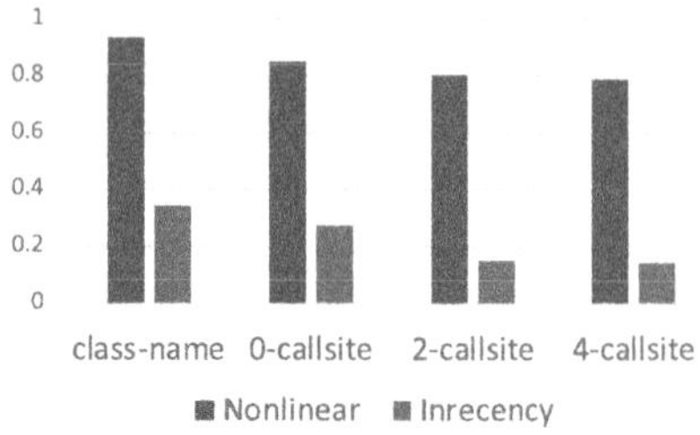

Fig. 11. Object Addresses

attributes are likely to be used without precisely distinguishing their actual types.

Evaluation. We will next evaluate the safety of accessing polymorphic attributes, as specified in Sect. 4.2. In this study, we evaluate only the polymorphic attributes for which at least one access-site exposes local constraints since constraints are necessary for the evaluation. Column *EVA* of Table 5 gives the ratio of evaluated attributes, i.e., 27% (1758/6304). The reason that many polymorphic attributes are not evaluated is twofold. First, there are 27% (1711/6304) attributes that we observe no access-site. The other attributes have access-sites observed, but those access-sites expose constraints that can not be collected by our local constraint generation rules. For example, the attributes may be passed into another function, put into a global container, or directly returned.

Columns *UNI* through *LOC* of Table 5 show the ratio of evaluated attributes that are determined to be safe. According to Sect. 4.2, an attribute is safe if it satisfies the local constraints of all evaluated access-sites. Also, local type refinements (i.e., type tests and local assignments) can be used to refine the types of the evaluated attribute and make the accesses safe. To analyze the effectiveness of local type refinements, we show the ratio of safe attributes with and without local type refinements. **First**, Column *UNI* shows the ratio of safe attributes without local type refinements. In this case, all access-sites of an attribute have to be safe for all its classes. Overall, *UNI* attributes are about 16%. The *UNI* is much higher in some categories, such as *PRG* and *OTH*, indicating that though polymorphic, attributes may be used uniformly without distinguishing their types. **Second**, the attribute may be type-tested against how it will be used, as illustrated in Sect. 3.1. The ratio of attributes that are safe due to such tests or the previous reason is shown in Column *TES*. **Third**, accessing polymorphic attributes may be safe thanks to local assignments [3] before the access, as illustrated also in Sect. 3.1. The ratio of attributes whose accesses are safe due to local assignments or previous reasons is shown in Column *LOC*. The *TES* and *LOC* results for all subjects are 35% and 48%, respectively, and are much higher in some categories (e.g., *PRG*, *TER*), meaning that local type refinements can significantly increase the effectiveness of class-based types.

Threats to Validity. There are three threats to the validity. **First**, since we only evaluate 27% of all polymorphic attributes, it is possible that the findings cannot be generalized to all polymorphic attributes. We do believe that the results are generalizable, however, since the difficulty in collecting constraints is due to the surrounding contexts which do not affect typing in general. To test this assumption, we sampled 300 polymorphic attributes from the 73% unevaluated attributes and conducted a manual analysis of them. We provided the necessary annotations to calculate *LOC* and *RB* for those attributes. The results are very close to the ones in Table 5, with *LOC* = 50%, and *RB* = 97%. **Second**, since we do not consider interprocedural constraints, it is possible that the types are actually unsafe to use in the access-site, but we report them to be safe. To this end, we manually investigate 100 safe attributes from the attributes belonging to *LOC*, and analyze if they are actually safe. Among the 100 attributes, we find no unsafe attributes. Thus, we believe that local constraints are effective in determining the safety of polymorphic attributes. **Third**, our interpretation of type tests is not complete. We only consider built-in type tests such as `isinstance` and `hasattr` and their boolean combinations, and ignore user-defined type tests and value tests. It is possible that the attributes considered unsafe by our approach are actually safe if we consider more complete type tests. To this end, we additionally classify all attributes "mentioned" in the type tests as safe. In this setting, *LOC* reaches 51%, only 3% higher than the original *LOC* results. Thus, we believe that our interpretation of type tests covers most cases.
Attribute Absences. For the 52% of attributes whose accesses are deemed unsafe, we manually investigate them and find the main reason is that attributes may hold *abs* or `NoneType` but are used without type tests or local assignments. Combined with our observation that a large proportion of attributes are *ABS* or *OPT*, we conduct an additional experiment to evaluate the connection between those two types and type safety. Specifically, for each attribute deemed as unsafe, we discard `NoneType`, *abs*, and both of them and rerun the experiment. For example, when evaluating `width`/`height` against their access-sites in `measure`, we remove `NoneType` and *abs* from their types and evaluate `int` only. We show the results of removing `NoneType`, *abs*, and both in columns *RN*, *RA*, and *RB*, respectively. According to the results, removing `NoneType` helps increase the proportion (48% to 53%), while removing absences helps significantly (48% to 86%), implying that attribute absences are the main cause of the type errors.

Since attribute absences are the main cause of the type errors, we conduct a specialized analysis of their sources, as shown in Columns *ABS* and *CABS*. *ABS* shows the number of polymorphic attributes holding *abs*, while *CABS* shows the same number when we only consider just-constructed objects. It can be observed from the results that construction contributes a little (345/3810 = 9%) to attribute absences, which implies that evolution is the main source of absences.

Object-Based Types. As discussed earlier, object addresses play an important role in object-based types. In this section, we first investigate several object addresses and then the effectiveness of object-based types.

Table 6. Results of the Evaluation of Object-based Types

CAT	Flow-insensi				Flow-sensi				Strong Updates (wo/w Recency)			
	CLS	L0	L2	L4	CLS	L0	L2	L4	CLS	L0	L2	L4
SCI	0.50	0.55	0.55	0.56	0.51	0.55	0.56	0.56	0.52/0.65	0.58/0.72	0.61/0.94	0.62/0.94
PRG	0.72	0.78	0.85	0.85	0.74	0.79	0.86	0.86	0.74/0.78	0.79/0.84	0.87/0.91	0.87/0.91
WEB	0.41	0.44	0.46	0.46	0.41	0.45	0.46	0.46	0.48/0.83	0.55/0.91	0.57/0.93	0.57/0.93
TER	0.83	0.86	0.92	0.92	0.83	0.86	0.92	0.92	0.86/0.89	0.89/0.92	0.94/0.97	0.94/0.97
FMT	0.26	0.27	0.27	0.27	0.26	0.27	0.27	0.27	0.26/0.35	0.27/0.37	0.27/0.37	0.28/0.37
UTL	0.50	0.50	0.50	0.50	0.50	0.50	0.50	0.50	1.00/1.00	1.00/1.00	1.00/1.00	1.00/1.00
OTH	0.55	0.58	0.58	0.58	0.55	0.58	0.58	0.58	0.65/0.77	0.77/0.97	0.77/0.97	0.77/0.97
ALL	0.48	0.51	0.53	0.53	0.49	0.52	0.53	0.53	0.50/0.65	0.55/0.71	0.58/0.86	0.59/0.86

Object Addresses. Recall that an address is nonlinear if it refers to multiple objects. Nonlinear addresses prevent strong updates. There are two solutions to this problem: more precise addresses or recency abstraction. To measure the effectiveness of more precise addresses, we compare four kinds of addresses, including class names and class names extended with 0/2/4-callsite of construction-sites (the 0-callsite case is simply construction location and so on for the rest). In Fig. 11, *Nonlinear* results measure the proportion of evolving classes that have at least two objects referred to by a single address. To measure the effectiveness of recency abstraction, we compare object addresses with and without recency abstraction. For an address with recency abstraction, strong updates cannot be performed when it refers to *inrecent*, evolving objects. *Inrecency* measures the proportion of evolving classes that have at least one address witnessing such a problem. From the figure, we can observe that the class name can easily be nonlinear, as 93% of the class names are nonlinear. More precise addresses help insignificantly. However, recency abstraction helps significantly. Even with the most imprecise object address (class name), only 34% of evolving classes belong to *Inrecency.* With 2-callsite only 15% of the evolving classes belong to *Inrecency.* In other words, with 2-callsite, most (85%) classes support strong updates.

Evaluation. We now extend the evaluation of class-based types to object-based types. The results are shown in Table 6. Columns under "Flow-insensi" show the proportion of safe polymorphic attributes when typed under flow-insensitive store abstraction with the four kinds of object addresses. *CLS* shows the proportion when class names are used as object addresses. This column is the same as the *LOC* column of Table 5. *L0*, *L2*, and *L4* show the proportions when 0/2/4 callsite of the construction-sites are used to extend the class names. Note that to keep the comparison with class-based types straightforward, we enable local refinements and use the same polymorphic attributes as in the evaluation of class-based types. It is possible that one attribute (e.g., `title`) is not polymorphic anymore when typed under more precise addresses. Even so, we still include it. It can be observed that using more precise object addresses increases the precision. However, the improvement is not significant. Columns under "Flow-sensi" show the same metrics but with flow-sensitive store abstraction. It can be shown that flow-sensitivity alone cannot improve the precision much. Flow-sensitivity alone (i.e., without strong updates) is effective only if one object can do something before taking some evolution actions, but not after. We can observe that such conditions should be rare since flow-sensitivity alone is not effective. This observation also aligns with our previous finding that object evolution is mostly monotonic, which means that objects gain new abilities as the evolution goes on, but never lose old abilities.

Columns under "Strong Updates" show the same metrics, but strong updates are performed for linear addresses/addresses that obey recency abstraction. Overall, we can find that the ability to perform strong updates significantly improves precision. This finding conforms to our previous finding that most errors are caused by attribute absences, which are themselves caused by object evolution. Strong updates make it possible to distinguish the object type before and after the evolution, and thus eliminate attribute absences and increase precision. Meanwhile, it can be observed that only performing strong updates for linear addresses is not sufficient, and using recency abstraction helps significantly, especially when used together with *L2* or more precise addresses.

Note that our evaluation of object-based types only reveals the upper bound of the precision. The precision of object-based types is also influenced by other factors such as the analysis of function calls/control flows (which determines whether the effects of different function calls/control flows are precisely separated). As the results in Sect. 5.1 suggest, the analysis of them is not a trivial task. However, since we want to focus on the factors that are specific to object types, while those factors influence the typing of the whole program, we do not conduct a detailed analysis of them and assume them to be precisely analyzed[5]. In other words, our aim is not to conduct a systematic evaluation of object-based types, but to derive observations on some important and representative factors.

Discussion. Now, we summarize the observations gained from our analysis and make suggestions on real-world type systems.

Class-Based Types. As can be observed from our experiment, class-based types can handle many polymorphic attributes. The effectiveness of class-based types is contributed significantly by local type refinement techniques, especially the ability to interpret type tests (a feature typically referred to as occurrence typing [13,28,48]). Moreover, since we find that our relatively simple "occurrence typing" covers most cases, we believe that the technique for occurrence typing needs not be very complicated to fulfill practical uses.

On the other hand, many polymorphic attributes cannot be handled by class-based types yet, especially when they hold *abs*. To make this insight more concrete, we check the polymorphic attributes with Pyright [35], a widely-used class-based type checker for Python, using class-based types similar to ours. More specifically, we randomly sample 100 polymorphic attributes from the 52% of the polymorphic attributes thought as unsafe in our study. We provide neces-

[5] As a dynamic analysis, we can naturally simulate the precision analysis of them.

sary type annotations for those polymorphic attributes and their related code and check the code with Pyright. We found that type errors are reported for 95 of the attributes. The reason that errors are not reported for some attributes is due to the unsound aspects of Pyright. For example, Pyright does not raise any error for the attribute whose corresponding class overrides the `getattr` method.

Object-Based Types. It is obvious from the results that object-based types are much more precise than class-based types. However, we want to emphasize that although our results are in favor of object-based types to a large extent, we do not mean that class-based types are useless since most of the spurious type errors related to class-based types are just caused by attribute absences, which are normally not expected to be excluded statically[6]. What's more, type checking/inference of class-based types is faster, and annotating class-based types is much easier than object-based types [38]. Thus, we suggest using these two kinds of types accordingly. In the scenarios where errors such as type mismatches are emphasized, and attribute absences matter less, we recommend class-based types. Meanwhile, in the scenarios where more rigorous verification is expected [12,18], we believe that object-based types are more suitable. In particular, in dependent type systems [16,50], object-based types with strong updates should be preferred, since they can help dependent type systems prove stronger properties.

Typestate-Based Types. At last, we discuss typestates [6,46]. By modeling evolution processes as finite state machines, typestates allow fine-grained representation of classes whose instances evolve. Typically, users must provide typestate annotations to use such types. However, recent studies [12,20] have proposed an inference algorithm for typestate annotations, when only attribute absences are concerned and evolution happens only inside member methods. Since we have found that attribute absences are the main cause of type errors and evolution does happen mainly inside member methods, we believe that it is promising to utilize typestate-based types. Future work in this direction should carefully differentiate among three states of an attribute, that is, absent, uninitialized (holding `None`), and initialized. What's more, adopting typestate-based types also requires some kind of strong update mechanism and can benefit from the monotonicity, which some findings in our study should help.

6 Conclusion and Future Work

In this paper, we conduct a systematic evaluation of object dynamism and object types. Our results reveal the prevalence of dynamic object behaviors. We also evaluate the widely used types for handling object dynamism and draw important implications for them. Although our study is set on Python, we expect the main findings to be transferable to other dynamic languages, since they share the same core semantics. For future work, we plan to build a type system for dynamic object-oriented languages based on the insights gained in this study.

[6] Even some static languages such as Java do not exclude them.

References

1. Agesen, O.: The Cartesian product algorithm. In: Tokoro, M., Pareschi, R. (eds.) ECOOP 1995. LNCS, vol. 952, pp. 2–26. Springer, Heidelberg (1995). https://doi.org/10.1007/3-540-49538-X_2
2. Ahmed, A., Fluet, M., Morrisett, G.: L^3: a linear language with locations. Fundamenta Informaticae **77**(4), 397–449 (2007)
3. Aiken, A., Foster, J.S., Kodumal, J., Terauchi, T.: Checking and inferring local non-aliasing. In: Proceedings of the ACM SIGPLAN 2003 Conference on Programming Language Design and Implementation, pp. 129–140 (2003)
4. Åkerblom, B., Stendahl, J., Tumlin, M., Wrigstad, T.: Tracing dynamic features in python programs. In: Proceedings of the 11th Working Conference on Mining Software Repositories, pp. 292–295 (2014)
5. Åkerblom, B., Wrigstad, T.: Measuring polymorphism in python programs. In: Proceedings of the 11th Symposium on Dynamic Languages, pp. 114–128 (2015)
6. Aldrich, J., Sunshine, J., Saini, D., Sparks, Z.: Typestate-oriented programming. In: Proceedings of the 24th ACM SIGPLAN Conference Companion on Object Oriented Programming Systems Languages and Applications, pp. 1015–1022 (2009)
7. Anderson, C., Giannini, P., Drossopoulou, S.: Towards type inference for JavaScript. In: Black, A.P. (ed.) ECOOP 2005. LNCS, vol. 3586, pp. 428–452. Springer, Heidelberg (2005). https://doi.org/10.1007/11531142_19
8. Balakrishnan, G., Reps, T.: Recency-abstraction for heap-allocated storage. In: Yi, K. (ed.) SAS 2006. LNCS, vol. 4134, pp. 221–239. Springer, Heidelberg (2006). https://doi.org/10.1007/11823230_15
9. Barbanera, F., Dezaniciancaglini, M., Deliguoro, U.: Intersection and union types: syntax and semantics. Inf. Comput. **119**(2), 202–230 (1995)
10. Bierman, G., Abadi, M., Torgersen, M.: Understanding TypeScript. In: Jones, R. (ed.) ECOOP 2014. LNCS, vol. 8586, pp. 257–281. Springer, Heidelberg (2014). https://doi.org/10.1007/978-3-662-44202-9_11
11. Blaudeau, C., Liu, F.: A conceptual framework for safe object initialization: a principled and mechanized soundness proof of the celsius model. Proc. ACM Program. Lang. **6**(OOPSLA2), 729–757 (2022)
12. Bravetti, M., et al.: Behavioural types for memory and method safety in a core object-oriented language. In: Oliveira, B.C.S. (ed.) APLAS 2020. LNCS, vol. 12470, pp. 105–124. Springer, Cham (2020). https://doi.org/10.1007/978-3-030-64437-6_6
13. Castagna, G., Laurent, M., Nguyen, K., Lutze, M.: On type-cases, union elimination, and occurrence typing. Proc. ACM Program. Lang. **6**(POPL), 1–31 (2022)
14. Chen, Z., Li, Y., Chen, B., Ma, W., Chen, L., Xu, B.: An empirical study on dynamic typing related practices in python systems. In: Proceedings of the 28th International Conference on Program Comprehension, pp. 83–93 (2020)
15. Choi, W., Chandra, S., Necula, G., Sen, K.: SJS: a type system for JavaScript with fixed object layout. In: Blazy, S., Jensen, T. (eds.) SAS 2015. LNCS, vol. 9291, pp. 181–198. Springer, Heidelberg (2015). https://doi.org/10.1007/978-3-662-48288-9_11
16. Chugh, R., Herman, D., Jhala, R.: Dependent types for JavaScript. In: Proceedings of the ACM International Conference on Object Oriented Programming Systems Languages and Applications, pp. 587–606 (2012)
17. Eifrig, J., Smith, S., Trifonov, V.: Sound polymorphic type inference for objects. In: Proceedings of the Tenth Annual Conference on Object-Oriented Programming Systems, Languages, and Applications, pp. 169–184 (1995)

18. Fähndrich, M., Leino, K.R.M.: Declaring and checking non-null types in an object-oriented language. In: Proceedings of the 18th Annual ACM SIGPLAN Conference on Object-Oriented Programing, Systems, Languages, and Applications, pp. 302–312 (2003)
19. Furr, M., An, J.h., Foster, J.S., Hicks, M.: Static type inference for ruby. In: Proceedings of the 2009 ACM Symposium on Applied Computing, pp. 1859–1866 (2009)
20. Golovanov, I., Jakobsen, M.S., Kettunen, M.K.: Typestate inference for mungo: Algorithm and implementation. Online Material (2020)
21. Google: Pytype, a static type analyzer for python code. Online Material (2023)
22. Hassan, M., Urban, C., Eilers, M., Müller, P.: MaxSMT-based type inference for Python 3. In: Chockler, H., Weissenbacher, G. (eds.) CAV 2018, Part II. LNCS, vol. 10982, pp. 12–19. Springer, Cham (2018). https://doi.org/10.1007/978-3-319-96142-2_2
23. Heidegger, P., Thiemann, P.: Recency types for analyzing scripting languages. In: D'Hondt, T. (ed.) ECOOP 2010. LNCS, vol. 6183, pp. 200–224. Springer, Heidelberg (2010). https://doi.org/10.1007/978-3-642-14107-2_10
24. Holkner, A., Harland, J.: Evaluating the dynamic behaviour of python applications. In: Proceedings of the Thirty-Second Australasian Conference on Computer Science, vol. 91, pp. 19–28 (2009)
25. Igarashi, A., Pierce, B.C., Wadler, P.: Featherweight Java: a minimal core calculus for Java and GJ. ACM Trans. Program. Lang. Syst. (TOPLAS) **23**(3), 396–450 (2001)
26. Jensen, S.H., Møller, A., Thiemann, P.: Type analysis for JavaScript. In: Palsberg, J., Su, Z. (eds.) SAS 2009. LNCS, vol. 5673, pp. 238–255. Springer, Heidelberg (2009). https://doi.org/10.1007/978-3-642-03237-0_17
27. Kaleba, S., Larose, O., Jones, R., Marr, S.: Who you gonna call: analyzing the run-time call-site behavior of ruby applications. In: Proceedings of the 18th ACM SIGPLAN International Symposium on Dynamic Languages, pp. 15–28 (2022)
28. Kent, A.M., Kempe, D., Tobin-Hochstadt, S.: Occurrence typing modulo theories. ACM SIGPLAN Not. **51**(6), 296–309 (2016)
29. Kouzapas, D., Dardha, O., Perera, R., Gay, S.J.: Typechecking protocols with Mungo and StMungo. In: Proceedings of the 18th International Symposium on Principles and Practice of Declarative Programming, pp. 146–159 (2016)
30. Lehtosalo, J.: Optional static typing for python. Online Material (2023)
31. Lerner, B.S., Politz, J.G., Guha, A., Krishnamurthi, S.: TeJaS: retrofitting type systems for JavaScript. ACM SIGPLAN Not. **49**(2), 1–16 (2013)
32. Madhavan, R., Komondoor, R.: Null dereference verification via over-approximated weakest pre-conditions analysis. ACM Sigplan Not. **46**(10), 1033–1052 (2011)
33. Maia, E., Moreira, N., Reis, R.: A static type inference for python. Proc. DYLA **5**(1), 1 (2012)
34. McGugan, W.: Rich, a python library for rich text and beautiful formatting in the terminal. Online Material (2023)
35. Microsoft: Pyright, a static type checker for python. Online Material (2023)
36. Monat, R., Ouadjaout, A., Miné, A.: Static type analysis by abstract interpretation of python programs. In: 34th European Conference on Object-Oriented Programming (ECOOP 2020). Schloss Dagstuhl-Leibniz-Zentrum für Informatik (2020)
37. Oxhøj, N., Palsberg, J., Schwartzbach, M.I.: Making type inference practical. In: Madsen, O.L. (ed.) ECOOP 1992. LNCS, vol. 615, pp. 329–349. Springer, Heidelberg (1992). https://doi.org/10.1007/BFb0053045

38. Pierce, B.C.: Types and Programming Languages. MIT Press, Cambridge (2002)
39. Pilkiewicz, A., Pottier, F.: The essence of monotonic state. In: Proceedings of the 7th ACM SIGPLAN Workshop on Types in Language Design and Implementation, pp. 73–86 (2011)
40. Rastogi, A., Swamy, N., Fournet, C., Bierman, G., Vekris, P.: Safe & efficient gradual typing for typescript. In: Proceedings of the 42nd Annual ACM SIGPLAN-SIGACT Symposium on Principles of Programming Languages, pp. 167–180 (2015)
41. Richards, G., Hammer, C., Burg, B., Vitek, J.: The eval that men do. In: Mezini, M. (ed.) ECOOP 2011. LNCS, vol. 6813, pp. 52–78. Springer, Heidelberg (2011). https://doi.org/10.1007/978-3-642-22655-7_4
42. Richards, G., Lebresne, S., Burg, B., Vitek, J.: An analysis of the dynamic behavior of JavaScript programs. In: Proceedings of the 31st ACM SIGPLAN Conference on Programming Language Design and Implementation, pp. 1–12 (2010)
43. Rondon, P.M., Kawaguchi, M., Jhala, R.: Low-level liquid types. ACM Sigplan Not. **45**(1), 131–144 (2010)
44. Salib, M.: Starkiller: a static type inferencer and compiler for Python. Ph.D. thesis, Massachusetts Institute of Technology (2004)
45. Smith, F., Walker, D., Morrisett, G.: Alias types. In: Smolka, G. (ed.) ESOP 2000. LNCS, vol. 1782, pp. 366–381. Springer, Heidelberg (2000). https://doi.org/10.1007/3-540-46425-5_24
46. Strom, R.E., Yemini, S.: Typestate: a programming language concept for enhancing software reliability. IEEE Trans. Softw. Eng. **SE-12**(1), 157–171 (1986). https://doi.org/10.1109/TSE.1986.6312929
47. Summers, A.J., Müller, P.: Freedom before commitment: a lightweight type system for object initialisation. In: Proceedings of the 2011 ACM International Conference on Object Oriented Programming Systems Languages and Applications, pp. 1013–1032 (2011)
48. Tobin-Hochstadt, S., Felleisen, M.: Logical types for untyped languages. In: Proceedings of the 15th ACM SIGPLAN International Conference on Functional Programming, pp. 117–128 (2010)
49. Van Rossum, G., Drake, F.L., Jr.: The Python Language Reference. Python Software Foundation, Wilmington (2014)
50. Vekris, P., Cosman, B., Jhala, R.: Refinement types for typescript. In: Proceedings of the 37th ACM SIGPLAN Conference on Programming Language Design and Implementation, pp. 310–325 (2016)
51. Vitousek, M.M., Kent, A.M., Siek, J.G., Baker, J.: Design and evaluation of gradual typing for python. In: Proceedings of the 10th ACM Symposium on Dynamic languages, pp. 45–56 (2014)
52. Wang, T., Smith, S.F.: Precise constraint-based type inference for Java. In: Knudsen, J.L. (ed.) ECOOP 2001. LNCS, vol. 2072, pp. 99–117. Springer, Heidelberg (2001). https://doi.org/10.1007/3-540-45337-7_6
53. Wang, Y.: PySonar2: an advanced semantic indexer for python. Online Material (2019)
54. Wei, S., Xhakaj, F., Ryder, B.G.: Empirical study of the dynamic behavior of JavaScript objects. Softw. Pract. Exper. **46**(7), 867–889 (2016)
55. Zhao, T.: Polymorphic type inference for scripting languages with object extensions. In: Proceedings of the 7th Symposium on Dynamic Languages, pp. 37–50 (2011)

Types and Semantics for Extensible Data Types

Cas van der Rest(✉) and Casper Bach Poulsen

Delft University of Technology, Delft, The Netherlands
{c.r.vanderrest,c.b.poulsen}@tudelft.nl

Abstract. Developing and maintaining software commonly requires (1) adding new data type constructors to existing applications, but also (2) adding new functions that work on existing data. Most programming languages have native support for defining data types and functions in a way that supports either (1) or (2), but not both. This lack of native support makes it difficult to use and extend libraries. A theoretically well-studied solution is to define data types and functions using *initial algebra semantics*. While it is possible to encode this solution in existing programming languages, such encodings add syntactic and interpretive overhead, and commonly fail to take advantage of the map and fold fusion laws of initial algebras which compilers could exploit to generate more efficient code. A solution to these is to provide native support for initial algebra semantics. In this paper, we develop such a solution and present a type discipline and core calculus for a language with native support for initial algebra semantics.

Keywords: Type systems · Modularity · Programming Language Design · Categorical Semantics

1 Introduction

A common litmus test for a programming language's capability for modularity is whether a programmer is able to extend existing data with new ways to construct it as well as to add new functionality for this data. All in a way that preserves static type safety; a conundrum which Wadler [38] dubbed the *expression problem*. When working in pure functional programming languages, another modularity question is how to model side effects modularly using, e.g., *monads* [28]. Ideally, we would keep the specific monad used to model the effects of a program abstract and program against an *interface* of effectful operations instead, defining the syntax and implementation of such interfaces separately and in a modular fashion.

The traditional approach for tackling these modularity questions in pure functional programming languages is by embedding the *initial algebra semantics* [18] of inductive data types in the language's type system. By working with such embeddings in favor of the language's built-in data types we gain modularity without

C.-K. Hur (Ed.): APLAS 2023, LNCS 14405, pp. 46–66, 2023.
https://doi.org/10.1007/978-981-99-8311-7_3

sacrificing type safety. This approach was popularized by Swierstra's *Data Types à la Carte* [36] as a solution to the expression problem, where it was used to derive modular interpreters for a small expression language. In later work, similar techniques were applied to define the syntax and implementation of a large class of monads using (algebraic) effects and handlers based on different flavors of inductively defined *free monads*. This was shown to be an effective technique for modularizing both first order [23] and higher order [7,31,40] effectful computations.

The key idea that unifies these techniques is the use of *signature functors*, which act as a de facto syntactic representation of an inductive data type or inductively defined free monad. Effectively, this defines a generic inductive data type or free monad that takes its constructors as a parameter. The crucial benefit of this setup is that we can compose data types and effects by taking the coproduct of signature functors, and we can compose function cases defined over these signature functors in a similarly modular way. Inductive data types and functions in mainstream functional programming languages generally do not support these kinds of composition.

While embedding signature functors has proven itself as a tremendously useful technique for enhancing functional languages with a higher degree of type safe modularity, the approach has some downsides:

- Encodings of a data type's initial algebra semantics lack the syntactic convenience of native data types, especially when it comes to constructing and pattern matching on values. Further overhead is introduced by their limited interoperability, which is typically relies on user-defined isomorphisms.
- The connection between initial algebra semantics encodings of data types, and the mathematical concepts that motivate them remains implicit. This has two drawbacks: (1) the programmer has to write additional code witnessing that their definitions possess the required structure (e.g., by defining instances of the `Functor` typeclass), and (2) a compiler cannot leverage the properties of this structure, such as by implementing (provably correct) optimizations based on the well-known map and fold fusion laws.

In this paper, we explore an alternative perspective that makes type-safe modularity part of the language's design, by including built-in primitives for the functional programmer's modularity toolkit—e.g., functors, folds, fixpoints, etc. We believe that this approach has the potential to present the programmer with more convenient syntax for working with extensible data types (see, for example, the language design proposed by Van der Rest and Bach Poulsen [32]). Furthermore, by supporting type-safe modularity through dedicated language primitives, we open the door for compilers to benefit from their properties, for example by applying fusion based optimizations.

1.1 Contributions

The semantics of (nested) algebraic data types has been studied extensively in the literature (e.g., by Johann et al. [20–22], and Abel et al. [2–4]) resulting in the development of various calculi with the purpose of studying different aspects of programming with algebraic data types. In this paper, we build on these works to develop a core calculus that seeks to distill the essential language features needed for developing programming languages with built-in support for type-safe modularity, while retaining the same formal foundations. Although the semantic ideas that we build on to develop our calculus are generally well-known, their application to improving the design of functional programming languages has yet to be explored in depth. It is still future work to leverage the insights gained by developing this calculus in the design of programming language that provide better ergonomics for working with extensible data types, but we believe the development of a core calculus capturing the essentials of programming with extensible data types to be a key step for achieving this goal. To bridge from the calculus presented in this paper to a practical language design, features such as *smart constructors*, *row types*, and *(functor) subtyping* (as employed, for example, by Morris and McKinna [29] and Hubers and Morris [19]) would be essential. We make the following technical contributions:

- We show (in Sect. 2) how modular functions over algebraic data types in the style of Data Types à la Carte and modular definitions of first-order and higher-order (algebraic) effects and handlers based on inductively defined free monads can be captured in the calculus.
- We present (in Sect. 3) a formal definition of the syntax and type system.
- We sketch (in Sect. 4) a categorical semantics for our calculus.
- We present (in Sect. 5) an operational semantics for our calculus, and discuss how it relates to the categorical semantics.

Section 6 discusses related work, and Sect. 7 concludes. An extended version of the paper [33] disucusses the categorical semantics in more detail.

2 Programming with Extensible Data Types, by Example

The basis of our calculus is the polymorphic λ-calculus extended with kinds, restricted to rank-1 polymorphism. We can define many familiar polymorphic functions, such as $(\mathit{id} : \forall\alpha.\alpha \Rightarrow \alpha) = \lambda x.x$ or $(\mathit{const} : \forall\alpha.\forall\beta.\alpha \Rightarrow \beta \Rightarrow \alpha) = \lambda x.\lambda y.x$. Types are closed under products and coproducts, with the unit type ($\mathbb{1}$) and empty type ($\mathbb{0}$) as their respective units. Furthermore, we include a type-level fixpoint (μ), which can be used to encode many well-known algebraic data types. For example, the type of lists is defined as $\mathit{List} \triangleq \lambda\alpha.\mu(\lambda X.\mathbb{1} + (\alpha \times X))$. A key feature of the calculus is that all higher-order types (i.e., that have one or more type argument) are, by construction, functorial in all their arguments. While this imposes some restrictions on the types we can define, it also means that the programmer gets access to primitive mapping and folding operations that they would otherwise have to define themselves. For the type *List*, for example, this means that we get both the usual mapping operation transforming its elements, as well as an operation corresponding to Haskell's *foldr*, for free.

Although the mapping and folding primitives for first-order type constructors (i.e., of kind $\star \rightsquigarrow \star$) are already enough to solve the expression problem for many algebraic data types (Sect. 2.1) and to encode modular algebraic effects (Sect. 2.2), they generalize to higher-order type constructors. The benefit of this generalization is that our calculus can also capture the definition of so-called *nested data types* [8], which arise as the fixpoint of a *higher-order functor*. We make essential use of the calculus' higher-order capabilities in Sect. 2.3 to define modular handlers for scoped effects [41] and modular elaborations for higher-order effects [31], as in both cases effect trees that represents monadic programs with higher-order operations is defined as a nested data type.

Notation. The examples in this section correspond to programs in our calculus, but we take some notational liberty to simplify the exposition. Abstraction and application of type variables is omitted, just as rank-1 universal qualifiers. By convention, variables bound by type-level λ-abstraction are denoted by capital letters (e.g., X), and universally quantified variables by Greek letters (e.g., α,β).

2.1 Modular Interpreters in the Style of Data Types à la Carte

We consider how to define a modular interpreter for a small expression language of simple arithmetic operations. For starters, we just include literals and addition. The corresponding BNF equation and signature functor are given below:

$$e ::= \mathbb{N} \mid e + e \qquad\qquad Expr \triangleq \lambda X.\mathbb{N} + (X \times X)$$

Now, we can define an *eval* that maps expressions—given by the fixpoint of *Expr*—to their result:

$$\begin{aligned} &expr : \mathbb{N} + (\mathbb{N} \times \mathbb{N}) \Rightarrow \mathbb{N} && eval : \mu(Expr) \Rightarrow \mathbb{N} \\ &expr = (\lambda x.x) \blacktriangledown (\lambda x.\boldsymbol{\pi_1}\ x + \boldsymbol{\pi_2}\ x) && eval = (\!|\ expr\ |\!)^{Expr} \end{aligned}$$

Terms typeset in **purple** are built-in operations. $\boldsymbol{\pi_1}$ and $\boldsymbol{\pi_2}$ are the usual projection functions for products, and $- \blacktriangledown -$ is an eliminator for coproducts. Following Meijer et al. [27], we write $(\!|\ alg\ |\!)^\tau$ (i.e., "banana brackets") to denote a fold over the type $\mu(\tau)$ with an *algebra* of type $alg : \tau\ \tau' \Rightarrow \tau'$. The calculus does not include a general term level fixpoint; the only way to write a function that recurses on the substructures of a μ-type is by using the built-in folding operation. While this limits the operations we can define for a given type, it also ensures that all well-typed terms in the calculus have a well-defined semantics.

Now, we can extend this expression language with support for a multiplication operation as follows, where $Mul \triangleq \lambda X.X \times X$:

$$\begin{aligned} &mul : \mathbb{N} \times \mathbb{N} \Rightarrow \mathbb{N} && eval : \mu(Expr + Mul) \Rightarrow \mathbb{N} \\ &mul = \lambda x.\boldsymbol{\pi_1}\ x * \boldsymbol{\pi_2}\ x && eval = (\!|\ expr \blacktriangledown mul\ |\!)^{Expr+Mul} \end{aligned}$$

2.2 Modular Algebraic Effects Using the Free Monad

As our second example we consider how to define modular algebraic effects and handlers [30] in terms of the free monad following Swierstra [36]. First, we define the *Free* type which constructs a free monad for a given signature functor f. We can think of a term with type $\mathit{Free}\ f\ \alpha$ as a syntactic representation of a monadic program producing a value of type α with f describing the operations which we can use to interact with the monadic context.

$$\mathit{Free} : (\star \rightsquigarrow \star) \rightsquigarrow \star \rightsquigarrow \star \quad \triangleq \quad \lambda f.\lambda\alpha.\mu(\lambda X.\alpha + f X)$$

Note that *Free* is a functor in both its arguments, and thus there are two ways to "map over" a value of type $\mathit{Free}\ f\ \alpha$; we can transform the values at the leaves using a function $\alpha \Rightarrow \beta$, or the shape of the nodes using a natural transformation $\forall\alpha.f\ \alpha \Rightarrow g\ \alpha$. The higher order map can be used, for example, for defining function that reorders the operations of effect trees with a composite signature.

$$\begin{aligned}&\mathit{reorder} : \mathit{Free}\ (f + g)\ \alpha \Rightarrow \mathit{Free}\ (g + f)\ \alpha\\&\mathit{reorder} = \mathsf{map}\langle \iota_2 \blacktriangledown \iota_1 \rangle^{\mathit{Free}}\end{aligned}$$

Here, we use the higher-order instances of the coproduct eliminator $- \blacktriangledown -$, the injections ι_1, ι_2, and the functorial map operation $\mathsf{map}\langle - \rangle^{-}$.

Effect handlers can straightforwardly be implemented as folds over *Free*. In fact, the behavior of a handler is entirely defined by the algebra that we use to fold over the effect tree, allowing us write a generic *handle* function:

$$\begin{aligned}&\mathit{handle} : (\alpha \Rightarrow \beta) \Rightarrow (f\ (\mathit{Free}\ g\ \beta) \Rightarrow \mathit{Free}\ g\ \beta) \Rightarrow \mathit{Free}\ (f + g)\ \alpha \Rightarrow \mathit{Free}\ g\ \beta\\&\mathit{handle} = \lambda h.\lambda i.(\!|\ (\mathsf{in} \circ \iota_1 \circ h) \blacktriangledown i \blacktriangledown (\mathsf{in} \circ \iota_2)\ |\!)^{\alpha+(fX)+(gX)}\end{aligned}$$

Here, in is the constructor of a type-level fixpoint (μ). The fold above distinguishes three cases: (1) pure values, in which case we return it again using the function h; (2) an operation of the signature f which is handled using the function i; or (3) an operation of the signature g which is preserved by reconstructing the effect tree and doing nothing.

As an example, we consider how to implement a handler for the *Abort* effect, which has a single operation indicating abrupt termination of a computation. We define its signature functor as follows:

$$\mathit{Abort} : \star \rightsquigarrow \star \quad \triangleq \quad \lambda X.\mathbb{1}$$

The definition of *Abort* ignores its argument, X, which is the type of the continuation. After aborting a computation, there is no continuation, thus the *Abort* effect does not need to store one. A handler for *Abort* is then defined like so, invoking the generic *handle* function defined above:

$$\begin{aligned}&\mathit{hAbort} : \mathit{Free}\ (\mathit{Abort} + f)\ \alpha \Rightarrow \mathit{Free}\ f\ (\mathit{Maybe}\ \alpha)\\&\mathit{hAbort} = \mathit{handle}\ \mathit{Just}\ (\lambda x.\mathsf{in}\ (\iota_1\ \mathit{Nothing}))\end{aligned}$$

2.3 Modular Higher-Order Effects

To describe the syntax of computations that interact with their monadic context through higher-order operations—that is, operations that may have monadic computations as arguments—we need to generalize the free monad as follows.

$$Prog : ((\star \rightsquigarrow \star) \rightsquigarrow \star \rightsquigarrow \star) \rightsquigarrow \star \rightsquigarrow \star \quad \triangleq \quad \lambda f.\mu(\lambda X.\lambda \alpha.\alpha + (f\ X\ \alpha))$$

Note that, unlike the *Free* type, *Prog* is defined as the fixpoint of a higher-order functor. This generalization allows for signature functors to freely choose the return type of continuations. Following Yang et al. [41], we use this additional expressivity to describe the syntax of higher-order operations by nesting continuations. For example, the following defines the syntax of an effect for exception catching, that we can interact with by either throwing an exception, or by declaring an exception handler that first executes its first argument, and only runs the second computation if an exception was thrown.

$$Catch : (\star \rightsquigarrow \star) \rightsquigarrow \star \rightsquigarrow \star \quad \triangleq \quad \lambda X.\lambda \alpha.\mathbb{1} + (X(X\alpha) \times (X(X\alpha))$$

A value of type *Prog Catch* α is then a syntactic representation of a monadic program that can both throw and catch exceptions. From this syntactic representation we can proceed in two different ways. The first option is to replace exception catching with an application of the *hAbort* handler, in line with Plotkin and Pretnar's [30] original strategy for capturing higher-order operations. In recent work, Bach Poulsen and Van der Rest [31] demonstrated how such abbreviations can be made modular and reusable by implementing them as algebras over the *Prog* type. Following their approach, we define the following elaboration of exception catching into a first-order effect tree.

$$\begin{aligned}
&eCatch : Prog\ Catch\ \alpha \Rightarrow Free\ Abort\ \alpha \\
&eCatch = (\!|\ (\mathsf{in} \circ \iota_1)\ \blacktriangledown\ (\mathsf{in} \circ \iota_2) \\
&\qquad\qquad \blacktriangledown\ (\lambda X.hAbort\ (\pi_1\ X) \gg\!= maybe\ (join\ (\pi_2\ X))\ id)\ |\!)^{\alpha + Catch\ X\ \alpha}
\end{aligned}$$

Here, the use of bind ($\gg\!=$) and *join* refer to the monadic structure of *Free*. Alternatively, we can define a handler for exception catching directly by folding over the *Prog* type, following the *scoped effects* approach by Wu et al. [40]:

$$\begin{aligned}
&hCatch : Prog\ (Catch + h)\ \alpha \Rightarrow Prog\ h\ (Maybe\ \alpha) \\
&hCatch = (\!|\ (\mathsf{in} \circ \iota_1 \circ Just) \\
&\qquad\qquad \blacktriangledown\ (\lambda x.\mathsf{in}\ (\iota_1\ Nothing)) \\
&\qquad\qquad \blacktriangledown\ (\lambda x.\pi_1\ x \gg\!= maybe\ (\pi_2\ x \gg\!= fwd)\ id)) \\
&\qquad\qquad \blacktriangledown\ (\mathsf{in} \circ \iota_2)\ |\!)^{\alpha + (Catch\ X\ \alpha) + (h\ X\ \alpha)}
\end{aligned}$$

Where the function *fwd* establishes that *Maybe* commutes with the *Prog* type in a suitable way:

$$fwd : Maybe\ (Prog\ h\ (Maybe\ \alpha)) \Rightarrow Prog\ h\ (Maybe\ \alpha)$$

That is, we show that *Prog h* is a *modular carrier* for *Maybe* [35].

$$\alpha, \beta, \gamma, X, Y \in \text{String}$$

$$\begin{array}{lcl}
\textit{Kind} & \ni & k ::= \star \mid k \rightsquigarrow k \\
\textit{KindEnv} & \ni & \Delta, \Phi ::= \emptyset \mid \Delta, \alpha : k \\
\\
\textit{Type} & \ni & \tau ::= \alpha \mid X \mid \tau\ \tau \mid \lambda X.\tau \mid \mu(\tau) \mid \tau \Rightarrow \tau \\
& & \quad \mid \mathbb{0} \mid \mathbb{1} \mid \tau \times \tau \mid \tau + \tau \\
\textit{Scheme} & \ni & \sigma ::= \forall \alpha.\sigma \mid \tau
\end{array}$$

Fig. 1. Type syntax

As demonstrated, our calculus supports defining higher-order effects and their interpretations. To conveniently sequence higher-order computations we typically also want to use monadic bind—i.e., $\gg\!= : \textit{Prog}\ h\ \alpha \to (\alpha \to \textit{Prog}\ h\ \beta) \to \textit{Prog}\ h\ \beta$. While it is possible to define monadic bind for *Free* from Sect. 2.2 in terms of a fold, defining the monadic bind for *Prog* requires a *generalized fold* [9,41]. Adding this and other recursion principles [27] to our calculus is future work.

3 The Calculus

The previous section demonstrated how a language with built-in support for functors, folds, and fixpoints provides support for defining and working with state-of-the-art techniques for type safe modular programming. In this section we present a core calculus for such a language. The basis of our calculus is the first-order fragment of System F^{ω}—i.e., the polymorphic λ-calculus with kinds, where universal quantification is limited to prenex normal form à la Hindley-Milner. Additionally, the syntax of types, defined in Fig. 1, includes primitives for constructing recursive types ($\mu(-)$), products ($\times$) and coproducts ($+$), as well as a unit type ($\mathbb{1}$) and empty type ($\mathbb{0}$). In the definition of the syntax of types, the use of $\forall$-types is restricted by stratifying the syntax into two layers, types and type schemes. Consequently, our calculus is, by design, *predicative*: $\forall$-types can quantify over types but not type schemes.

The motivation for this predicative design is that it permits a relatively straightforward categorical interpretation of $\forall$-types in terms of *ends* [33, §4.2]. Whereas the restriction of universal quantification to prenex normal form is usually imposed to facilitate type inference, our calculus does not support inference in its current form due to the structural treatment of data types. In a structural setting, inference requires the reconstruction of (recursive) data type definitions from values, which is, in general, not possible.

We remark that the current presentation of the type system is *declarative*, meaning that algorithmic aspects crucial to type checking, such as normalization and equality checking of types, are not covered by the current exposition. Our system is a subset of System F_{ω}, whose Church-style formulation is decidable while its Curry-style formulation is not. As such, we expect our type system to inherit these properties. Since we are restricting ourselves to a predicative subset of F_ω, we are optimistic that the Curry-style formulation of our type system will be decidable too, but verifying this expectation is future work.

$$\boxed{\Delta \mid \Phi \vdash \tau : k}$$

$$\textsc{K-Var}\ \frac{k : \alpha \in \Delta}{\Delta \mid \Phi \vdash \alpha : k} \qquad \textsc{K-Fvar}\ \frac{\Phi(X) \mapsto k}{\Delta \mid \Phi \vdash X : k} \qquad \textsc{K-App}\ \frac{\Delta \mid \Phi \vdash \tau_1 : k_1 \rightsquigarrow k_2 \qquad \Delta \mid \Phi \vdash \tau_2 : k_1}{\Delta \mid \Phi \vdash \tau_1\ \tau_2 : k_2}$$

$$\textsc{K-Abs}\ \frac{\Delta \mid \Phi, (X \mapsto k_1) \vdash \tau : k_2}{\Delta \mid \Phi \vdash \lambda X.\tau : k_1 \rightsquigarrow k_2} \qquad \textsc{K-Fix}\ \frac{\Delta \mid \Phi \vdash \tau : k \rightsquigarrow k}{\Delta \mid \Phi \vdash \mu(\tau) : k} \qquad \textsc{K-Fun}\ \frac{\Delta \mid \emptyset \vdash \tau_1 : \star \qquad \Delta \mid \Phi \vdash \tau_2 : \star}{\Delta \mid \Phi \vdash \tau_1 \Rightarrow \tau_2 : \star}$$

$$\textsc{K-Empty}\ \frac{}{\Delta \mid \Phi \vdash \mathbb{0} : k} \qquad \textsc{K-Unit}\ \frac{}{\Delta \mid \Phi \vdash \mathbb{1} : k} \qquad \textsc{K-Product}\ \frac{\Delta \mid \Phi \vdash \tau_1 : k \qquad \Delta \mid \Phi \vdash \tau_2 : k}{\Delta \mid \Phi \vdash \tau_1 \times \tau_2 : k}$$

$$\textsc{K-Sum}\ \frac{\Delta \mid \Phi \vdash \tau_1 : k \qquad \Delta \mid \Phi \vdash \tau_2 : k}{\Delta \mid \Phi \vdash \tau_1 + \tau_2 : k}$$

$$\boxed{\Delta \vdash \sigma}$$

$$\textsc{SC-Forall}\ \frac{\Delta, \alpha : k \vdash \sigma}{\Delta \vdash \forall \alpha.\sigma} \qquad \textsc{SC-Type}\ \frac{\Delta \mid \emptyset \vdash \tau : \star}{\Delta \vdash \tau}$$

Fig. 2. Well-formedness rules for types and type schemes

3.1 Well-Formed Types

Types are well-formed with respect to a kind k, describing the arity of a type's parameters, if it has any. Well-formedness of types is defined using the judgment $\Delta \mid \Phi \vdash \tau : k$, stating that the type τ has kind k under contexts Δ and Φ. Similarly, well-formedness of type schemes is defined by the judgment $\Delta \vdash \sigma$, stating that the type scheme σ is well-formed with respect to the context Δ.

Following Johann et al. [21], well-formedness of types is defined with respect to two contexts, one containing functorial variables (Φ), and one containing variables with mixed variance (Δ). Specifically, the variables in the context Φ are restricted to occur only in *strictly positive* [1,13] positions (i.e., they can never appear to the left of a function arrow), while the variables in Δ can have mixed variance. This restriction on the occurrence of the variables in Φ is enforced in the well-formedness rule for function types, K-Fun, which requires that its domain is typed under an empty context of functorial variables, preventing the domain type from dereferencing any functorial variables bound in the surrounding context. While it may seem overly restrictive to require type expressions to be strictly positive—rather than merely positive—in Φ, this is necessary to ensure that

μ-types, as well as its introduction and elimination forms, have a well-defined semantics. Variables in Φ are bound by type-level λ-abstraction, meaning that any type former with kind $k_1 \rightsquigarrow k_2$ is functorial in its argument. In contrast, the variables in Δ are bound by $\forall$-quantification.

Products ($\times$), coproducts ($+$), units ($\mathbb{1}$) and empty types ($\mathbb{0}$) can be constructed at any kind, reflecting the fact that the corresponding categorical (co)limits can be lifted from SET to its functor categories by computing them pointwise. This pointwise lifting of these (co)limits to functor categories is reflected in the β equalities for these type formers (shown in Fig. 5), which allow an instance at kind $k_1 \rightsquigarrow k_2$, when applied with a type argument, to be replaced with an instance at kind k_2.

The well-formed judgements for types effectively define a (simply typed) type level λ-calculus with base "type" $\star$. Consequently, the same type has multiple equivalent representations in the presence of β-redexes, raising the question of how we should deal with type normalization. The approach we adopt here is to add a non-syntactic conversion rule to the definition of our type system that permits any well-formed term to be typed under an equivalent type scheme. Section 3.3 discusses type equivalence in more detail.

3.2 Well-Typed Terms

Figure 3 shows the term syntax of our calculus. Along with the standard syntactic forms of the polymorphic λ-calculus we include explicit type abstraction and application, as well as introduction and elimination forms for recursive types (**in**/**unin**), products ($\pi_1/\pi_2/- \blacktriangle -$), coproducts ($\iota_1/\iota_2/- \blacktriangledown -$), and the unit (**tt**) and empty (**absurd**) types. Furthermore, the calculus includes dedicated primitives for mapping ($\mathsf{map}\langle - \rangle^-$) and folding ($(\!| - |\!)^-$) over a type.

Figure 3 also includes the definition of *arrow types*. In spirit of the syntactic notion of natural transformations used by Abel et al. [2–4] to study generalized (Mendler) iteration, an arrow type of the form $\tau_1 \xrightarrow{k} \tau_2$ (where $\tau_1, \tau_2 : k$) defines the type of *morphisms* between the objects that interpret τ_1 and τ_2. Arrow types are defined by induction over k, since the precise meaning of morphism for any pair of types depends on their kind. If $k = \star$, then a morphism between τ_1 and τ_2 is simply a function type. However, if τ_1 and τ_2 have one or more type argument, they are to be interpreted as objects in a suitable functor category, meaning that their morphisms are natural transformations. This is reflected in the definition of arrow types, by unfolding an arrow $\tau_1 \xrightarrow{k} \tau_2$ to a $\forall$-type that closes over all type arguments of τ_1 and τ_2, capturing the intuition that polymorphic functions cor respond to natural transformations.[1] For instance, we would type the inorder traversal of binary trees as $\mathit{inorder} : \mathit{Tree} \xrightarrow{\star \rightsquigarrow \star} \mathit{List}$ ($\triangleq \forall \alpha. \mathit{Tree}\ \alpha \Rightarrow \mathit{List}\ \alpha$), describing a natural transformation between the *Tree* and *List* functors.

[1] This intuition is made formal in the extended version [33, Theorem 1].

$$x, y \in \text{String}$$

$$
\begin{array}{lll}
\mathit{Env} & \ni & \Gamma ::= \emptyset \mid \Gamma, x : \sigma \\
\mathit{Term} & \ni & M, N ::= x \mid M\ N \mid \lambda x.M \mid \textsf{let}\ (x : \sigma) = M\ \textsf{in}\ N \\
& & \quad \mid \Lambda\alpha.M \mid M\ @\tau \mid \textsf{in} \mid \textsf{unin} \mid \textsf{map}\langle M \rangle^{\tau} \mid (\!|\ M\ |\!)^{\tau} \\
& & \quad \mid \pi_1 \mid \pi_2 \mid M \blacktriangle N \mid \iota_1 \mid \iota_2 \mid M \blacktriangledown N \mid \textsf{tt} \mid \textsf{absurd}
\end{array}
$$

$$
\begin{array}{rl}
\tau_1 \xrightarrow{\star} \tau_2 \triangleq \tau_1 \Rightarrow \tau_2 & \text{(Arrow Types)} \\
\tau_1 \xrightarrow{(k_1 \rightsquigarrow k_2)} \tau_2 \triangleq \forall \alpha.\ \tau_1\ \alpha \xrightarrow{k_2} \tau_2\ \alpha & \\
\textit{where} \quad \Delta \vdash \tau_1 \xrightarrow{k} \tau_2 \quad \textit{if} \quad \Delta \mid \emptyset \vdash \tau_1, \tau_2 : k &
\end{array}
$$

Fig. 3. Term syntax

The typing rules are shown in shown in Fig. 4. The rules rely on arrow types for introduction and elimination forms. For example, Products can be constructed at any kind (following rule K-PRODUCT in Fig. 2), so the rules for terms that operate on these (i.e., T-FST, T-Snd, and T-FORK) use arrow types at any kind k. Consequently, arrow types should correspond to morphisms in a suitable category, such that the semantics of a product type and its introduction/elimination forms can be expressed as morphisms in this category.

3.3 Type Equivalence

In the presence of type level λ-abstraction and application, the same type can have multiple representations. For this reason, the type system defined in Fig. 4 includes a non-syntactic conversion rule that allows a well-typed term to be re-typed under any equivalent type scheme. The relevant equational theory for types is defined in Fig. 5, and includes the customary β and η equivalences for λ-terms, as well as β rules for product, sum, unit, and empty types. The equations shown in Fig. 5 are motivated by the semantic model we discuss in Sect. 4, in the sense that equivalent types are interpreted to naturally isomorphic functors. The relation is also reflexive and transitive, motivated by respectively the identity and composition of natural isomorphisms. Viewing the equalities in Fig. 5 left-to-right provides us with a basis for a normalization strategy for types, which would be required for implementing the type system.

4 Categorical Semantics

In this section, we consider how to define a categorical semantics for our calculus, drawing inspiration from the semantics defined by Johann and Polonsky [22] and Johann et al. [20,21]. To define this semantics, we must show that each type in our calculus corresponds to a functor, and that all such functors have initial algebras. In the extended version of this paper [33] we discuss the requirements

$$\boxed{\Gamma \vdash M : \sigma}$$

$$\textsc{T-Var}\ \frac{x : \sigma \in \Gamma}{\Gamma \vdash x : \sigma} \qquad \textsc{T-App}\ \frac{\Gamma \vdash M : \tau_1 \Rightarrow \tau_2 \qquad \Gamma \vdash N : \tau_1}{\Gamma \vdash MN : \tau_2} \qquad \textsc{T-Abs}\ \frac{\Gamma, (x : \tau_1) \vdash M : \tau_2}{\Gamma \vdash \lambda x.M : \tau_1 \Rightarrow \tau_2}$$

$$\textsc{T-Let}\ \frac{\Gamma \vdash M : \sigma_1 \qquad \Gamma, x : \sigma_1 \vdash N : \sigma_2}{\Gamma \vdash \mathsf{let}\ (x : \sigma_1) = M\ \mathsf{in}\ N : \sigma_2} \qquad \textsc{T-TypeAbs}\ \frac{\Gamma \vdash M : \sigma \qquad \alpha \notin \mathsf{freevars}(\Gamma)}{\Gamma \vdash \Lambda \alpha.M : \forall \alpha.\sigma}$$

$$\textsc{T-TypeApp}\ \frac{\Gamma \vdash M : \forall \alpha.\sigma}{\Gamma \vdash M\ @\tau : \sigma[\tau/\alpha]} \qquad \textsc{T-In}\ \frac{}{\Gamma \vdash \mathsf{in} : \tau\ \mu(\tau) \xrightarrow{k} \mu(\tau)} \qquad \textsc{T-Out}\ \frac{}{\Gamma \vdash \mathsf{unin} : \mu(\tau) \xrightarrow{k} \tau\ \mu(\tau)}$$

$$\textsc{T-Map}\ \frac{\Gamma \vdash M : \tau_1 \xrightarrow{k_1} \tau_2}{\Gamma \vdash \mathsf{map}\langle M \rangle^{\tau} : \tau\ \tau_1 \xrightarrow{k_2} \tau\ \tau_2} \qquad \textsc{T-Fold}\ \frac{\Gamma \vdash M : \tau_1\ \tau_2 \xrightarrow{k} \tau_2}{\Gamma \vdash (\!|\ M\ |\!)^{\tau_1} : \mu(\tau_1) \xrightarrow{k} \tau_2}$$

$$\textsc{T-Fst}\ \frac{}{\Gamma \vdash \pi_1 : \tau_1 \times \tau_2 \xrightarrow{k} \tau_1} \qquad \textsc{T-Snd}\ \frac{}{\Gamma \vdash \pi_2 : \tau_1 \times \tau_2 \xrightarrow{k} \tau_2}$$

$$\textsc{T-Fork}\ \frac{\Gamma \vdash M : \tau \xrightarrow{k} \tau_1 \qquad \Gamma \vdash N : \tau \xrightarrow{k} \tau_2}{\Gamma \vdash M \blacktriangle N : \tau \xrightarrow{k} \tau_1 \times \tau_2} \qquad \textsc{T-Inl}\ \frac{}{\Gamma \vdash \iota_1 : \tau_1 \xrightarrow{k} \tau_1 + \tau_2}$$

$$\textsc{T-Inr}\ \frac{}{\Gamma \vdash \iota_2 : \tau_2 \xrightarrow{k} \tau_1 + \tau_2} \qquad \textsc{T-Join}\ \frac{\Gamma \vdash M : \tau_1 \xrightarrow{k} \tau \qquad \Gamma \vdash M : \tau_2 \xrightarrow{k} \tau}{\Gamma \vdash M \blacktriangledown N : \tau_1 + \tau_2 \xrightarrow{k} \tau} \qquad \textsc{T-Unit}\ \frac{}{\Gamma \vdash \mathsf{tt} : \mathbb{1}}$$

$$\textsc{T-Empty}\ \frac{}{\Gamma \vdash \mathsf{absurd} : \mathbb{0} \xrightarrow{k} \tau} \qquad \textsc{T-Conv}\ \frac{\Gamma \vdash M : \sigma_1 \qquad \sigma_1 \equiv \sigma_2}{\Gamma \vdash M : \sigma_2}$$

Fig. 4. Well-formed terms

for these initial algebras to exist, and argue informally why they should exist for the functors interpreting our types. Although Johann and Polonsky [22] present a detailed argument for the existence of initial algebras of the functors underlying nested data types, it is still future work to adapt this argument to our setting.

4.1 Semantic Setup

The general setup is as follows: kinds and kind contexts are associated with a category; i.e., an object in the category of categories, and the semantics of well-formed types are functors between the category associated with its context to the category associated with its kind. Crucially, these functors are both a morphisms

$$
\begin{aligned}
(\lambda X.\tau_1)\ \tau_2 &\equiv \tau_1[\tau_2/X] \\
(\lambda X.\tau\ X) &\equiv \tau \\
(\tau_1 \times \tau_2)\ \tau &\equiv (\tau_1\ \tau) \times (\tau_2\ \tau) \\
(\tau_1 + \tau_2)\ \tau &\equiv (\tau_1\ \tau) + (\tau_2\ \tau) \\
\mathbb{1}\ \tau &\equiv \mathbb{1} \\
\mathbb{0}\ \tau &\equiv \mathbb{0}
\end{aligned}
\qquad
\begin{array}{l}
T := [] \mid T\ \tau \mid \tau\ T \mid \mu(T) \mid T \Rightarrow \tau \mid \tau \Rightarrow T \\
\quad \mid\ T \times \tau \mid \tau \times T \mid T + \tau \mid \tau + T \\[1em]
\dfrac{\tau_1 \equiv \tau_2}{T[\ \tau_1\ ] \equiv T[\ \tau_2\ ]}
\end{array}
$$

Fig. 5. Equational theory for types

in the category of categories, and objects in a *functor category*. Well-typed terms map to a natural transformation between the functors interpreting respectively its context and its type. Formally, we define the semantics of kinds as follows:

$$[\![\star]\!] = \textsc{Set} \qquad [\![k_1 \rightsquigarrow k_2]\!] = [[\![k_1]\!], [\![k_2]\!]]$$

Where $\textsc{Set}$ denotes the category of sets and total functions, and $[\mathcal{C}, \mathcal{D}]$ the category of functors between $\mathcal{C}$ and $\mathcal{D}$.[2] By interpreting the function kind as objects in a functor category, we give formal grounds to our intention that all types of kind $k_1 \rightsquigarrow k_2$ define a functor. Indeed, if every type of kind $k_1 \rightsquigarrow k_2$ can be interpreted as a functor between the categories $[\![k_1]\!]$ and $[\![k_2]\!]$, this automatically entails that there is a corresponding action on morphisms that we can use to define the semantics of the $\mathsf{map}\langle - \rangle^-$ primitive for that type. The motivation for the folding ($(\!| - |\!)^-$) primitive is more involved, as it requires us to show that the functors interpreting type level functions have an initial algebra. We argue the existence of initial algebras for these endofunctors by appealing to Adámek's theorem [5]; the extended version [33, §4] discusses this in more detail.

4.2 Interpreting Types and Type Schemes

Following the general setup described above, the interpretation of a well-formed type (or type scheme) should be a functor from the category interpreting its context to the category interpreting its kind. Unlike the type variables in Φ, which are syntactically restricted to covariant occurrences, the variables in Δ have mixed variance. For this reason, we adopt a *difunctorial semantics*,[3] interpreting judgments as functors over the product category $[\![\Delta]\!]^{\mathsf{op}} \times [\![\Delta]\!]$:

$$[\![\ \Delta \mid \Phi \vdash \tau : k\ ]\!] : ([\![\Delta]\!]^{\mathsf{op}} \times [\![\Delta]\!]) \times [\![\Phi]\!] \to [\![k]\!]$$

Similarly, well-formed type schemes are also interpreted as a difunctor over $[\![\Delta]\!]$:

$$[\![\ \Delta \vdash \sigma\ ]\!] : [\![\Delta]\!]^{\mathsf{op}} \times [\![\Delta]\!] \to \textsc{Set}$$

[2] For presentational purposes, we omit some necessary restrictions on sizes here. The extended version [33, §4] defines these restrictions and the precise semantics.

[3] Similar models of type expressions with mixed variance appear, for example, when considering Mendler-style inductive types [37], or in the object calculus semantics by Glimming and Ghani [17].

The extended version [33, Fig.6] defines a full semantics of types and type schemes. To interpret the fragment of well-formed types that corresponds to the simply-typed λ-calculus, we appeal to the cartesian closed structure of the category of categories [26, p. 98]. Products, sums, unit types, empty types, and μ-types, are interpreted as their respective (co)limits in $\textsc{Set}$, which are preserved by its functor categories by computing objects pointwise, and universal quantifications are interpreted as an *end*.

Defining the semantics of function types requires slightly more care. The existence of exponentials in $\textsc{Set}$ induces a functor $(-)^{-} : \textsc{Set} \to \textsc{Set}^{\mathsf{op}} \to \textsc{Set}$, which, due to contravariance of the exponent, cannot be lifted to functor categories in the same way. However, by typing the domain of a function type under an empty context of functorial variables, we circumvent this problem. This, together with the fact that constructing the opposite category of the product category $[\![\Delta]\!]^{\mathsf{op}} \times [\![\Delta]\!]$ is an idempotent operation (up to isomorphism), ensures that we can construct a functor of the form $([\![\Delta]\!]^{\mathsf{op}} \times [\![\Delta]\!]) \times [\![\Phi]\!] \to \textsc{Set}$ from the denotations of the sub-derivations by computing exponentials pointwise.

4.3 Interpreting Arrow Types

The intuition of terms typed by an arrow type of the form $\tau_1 \xrightarrow{k} \tau_2$ is that they describe a morphism between the objects $[\![\tau_1]\!]$ and $[\![\tau_2]\!]$ in the category $[\![k]\!]$. However, the definition of arrow types unfolds to a type scheme, and thus their semantics is an object in $\textsc{Set}$. Informally speaking, this object should internalize the morphisms between $[\![\tau_1]\!]$ and $[\![\tau_2]\!]$ in $[\![k]\!]$. We make this intuition formal by establishing a form of *currying* for arrow types:

$$[\![k]\!](F(\boldsymbol{\delta}) \times [\![\tau_1]\!](\boldsymbol{\delta}^{\circ}), [\![\tau_2]\!](\boldsymbol{\delta})) \quad \simeq \quad \textsc{Set}(F(\boldsymbol{\delta}), [\![\tau_1 \xrightarrow{k} \tau_2]\!](\boldsymbol{\delta}))$$

Here, $F : [\![\Delta]\!]^{\mathsf{op}} \times [\![\Delta]\!] \to \textsc{Set}$ is a functor that interprets type environments, and $\boldsymbol{\delta}, \boldsymbol{\delta}^{\circ} \in [\![\Delta]\!]^{\mathsf{op}} \times [\![\Delta]\!]$ are objects interpreting the kind environment respectively its opposite. In the extended version [33, Theorem 1] we derive the isomorphism above, which is crucial for describing the semantics of well-typed terms. We write $\uparrow(-)/\downarrow(-)$ for the functions that transport along this isomorphism.

4.4 Interpreting Terms

The semantics of a well-typed term is a natural transformation between the functors interpreting its type environment its type. The semantics of type environment is defined component-wise in terms of the semantics for type schemes.

$$[\![\ \Gamma \vdash M : \sigma\ ]\!] : \mathit{Nat}([\![\Gamma]\!], [\![\sigma]\!])$$

$$
\begin{aligned}
[\![\Gamma \vdash x : \sigma]\!]_{\delta} &= \mathsf{lookup}^{\Gamma}_{x} \\
[\![\Gamma \vdash M\ N : \tau_2]\!]_{\delta} &= \mathsf{eval} \circ \langle [\![\Gamma \vdash M : \tau_1 \Rightarrow \tau_2]\!]_{\delta}, [\![\Gamma \vdash N : \tau_1]\!]_{\delta} \rangle \\
[\![\Gamma \vdash \lambda x.M : \tau_1 \Rightarrow \tau_2]\!]_{\delta} &= \mathsf{curry}([\![\Gamma, x : \tau_1 \vdash M : \tau_2]\!]_{\delta}) \\
[\![\Gamma \vdash \mathbf{let}\ (x : \sigma_1) = M\ \mathbf{in}\ N : \sigma_2]\!]_{\delta} &= \mathsf{eval} \circ \langle \mathsf{curry}([\![\Gamma, x : \sigma_1 \vdash N : \sigma_2]\!]_{\delta}), [\![\Gamma \vdash N : \sigma_1]\!]_{\delta} \rangle \\
[\![\Gamma \vdash \Lambda\alpha.M : \forall\alpha.\sigma]\!]_{\delta} &= [\![\Gamma \vdash M : \sigma]\!]_{\delta} \quad \text{(isomorphic per [26, p.255 eq.4])} \\
[\![\Gamma \vdash M @ \tau : \sigma[\tau/\alpha]]\!]_{\delta} &= \pi_{[\![\tau]\!]} \circ [\![\Gamma \vdash M : \forall\alpha.\sigma]\!]_{\delta} \\
[\![\Gamma \vdash \mathbf{in} : \tau\ \mu(\tau) \xrightarrow{k} \mu(\tau)]\!]_{\delta} &= \Uparrow(\mathsf{in} \circ \pi_2) \\
[\![\Gamma \vdash \mathbf{unin} : \mu(\tau) \xrightarrow{k} \tau\ \mu(\tau)]\!]_{\delta} &= \Uparrow(\mathsf{unin} \circ \pi_2) \\
[\![\Gamma \vdash \mathbf{map}\langle M \rangle^{\tau} : \tau\ \tau_1 \xrightarrow{k_2} \tau\ \tau_2]\!]_{\delta} &= \Uparrow(\lambda(\gamma, x).[\![\tau]\!](\delta)(\lambda y.\ \Downarrow([\![\Gamma \vdash M : \tau_1 \xrightarrow{k_1} \tau_2]\!]_{\delta})(\gamma, y))) \\
[\![\Gamma \vdash (\!| M |\!)^{\tau_1} : \mu(\tau_1) \xrightarrow{k} \tau_2]\!]_{\delta} &= \Uparrow(\lambda(\gamma, x).\mathsf{cata}(\lambda y.\ \Downarrow([\![\Gamma \vdash M : \tau_1\ \tau_2 \xrightarrow{k} \tau_2]\!]_{\delta})(\gamma, y))) \\
[\![\Gamma \vdash \pi_1 : \tau_1 \times \tau_2 \xrightarrow{k} \tau_1]\!]_{\delta} &= \Uparrow(\pi_1 \circ \pi_2) \\
[\![\Gamma \vdash \pi_2 : \tau_1 \times \tau_2 \xrightarrow{k} \tau_2]\!]_{\delta} &= \Uparrow(\pi_2 \circ \pi_2) \\
[\![\Gamma \vdash M \blacktriangle N : \tau \xrightarrow{k} \tau_1 \times \tau_2]\!]_{\delta} &= \Uparrow(\ \langle\ \Downarrow([\![\Gamma \vdash M : \tau \xrightarrow{k} \tau_1]\!]_{\delta})\ ,\ \Downarrow([\![\Gamma \vdash N : \tau \xrightarrow{k} \tau_2]\!]_{\delta})\ \rangle\ ) \\
[\![\Gamma \vdash \iota_1 : \tau_1 \xrightarrow{k} \tau_1 + \tau_2]\!]_{\delta} &= \Uparrow(\iota_1 \circ \pi_2) \\
[\![\Gamma \vdash \iota_2 : \tau_2 \xrightarrow{k} \tau_1 + \tau_2]\!]_{\delta} &= \Uparrow(\iota_2 \circ \pi_2) \\
[\![\Gamma \vdash M \blacktriangledown N : \tau_1 + \tau_2 \xrightarrow{k} \tau]\!]_{\delta} &= \Uparrow(\ [\ \Downarrow([\![\Gamma \vdash M : \tau_1 \xrightarrow{k} \tau]\!]_{\delta})\ ,\ \Downarrow([\![\Gamma \vdash N : \tau_2 \xrightarrow{k} \tau]\!]_{\delta})\ ]\ ) \\
[\![\Gamma \vdash \mathbf{tt} : \mathbb{1}]\!]_{\delta} &= !\quad \text{(the unique morphism to the terminal object)} \\
[\![\Gamma \vdash \mathbf{absurd} : \mathbb{0} \Rightarrow \tau]\!]_{\delta} &= \mathsf{curry}(h \circ \pi_2)
\end{aligned}
$$

Fig. 6. Semantics of Well-Typed Terms.

Fig. 6 shows how this natural transformation is defined. Both the denotation function $[\![-]\!]$ as well as the function it computes are total. Consequently, a well-typed value can be computed from every well-typed term. In this sense, the categorical model provides us with a sound computational model of the calculus, which we could implement by writing a definitional interpreter [34]. In the next section, we will discuss how a more traditional small-step operational semantics can be derived from the same categorical model.

5 Operational Semantics

The previous section gave an overview of a categorical semantics of our calculus. In this section, we define a small-step operational semantics for our calculus, and discuss how it relates to the categorical model.

$$v ::= \lambda x.M \mid \Lambda\alpha.M \mid \textsf{in}\ \overline{\tau}\ v \mid \textsf{unin}\ \overline{\tau}\ v \mid (v_1 \blacktriangle v_2)\ \overline{\tau}\ v \qquad \text{(Values)}$$
$$\mid\ \iota_1\ \overline{\tau}\ v \mid \iota_2\ \overline{\tau}\ v \mid \textsf{map}\langle v\rangle^{\tau'}\ \overline{\tau} \mid (\!|\ v\ |\!)^{\tau'}\ \overline{\tau} \mid \pi_1\ \overline{\tau} \mid \pi_2\ \overline{\tau}$$
$$\mid\ (v_1 \blacktriangledown v_2)\ \overline{\tau} \mid \textsf{tt}\ \overline{\tau} \mid \textsf{absurd}\ \overline{\tau}\ v$$

$$E ::= [] \mid E\ M \mid v\ E \mid E\ \tau \mid \textsf{let}\ (x : \sigma) = E\ \textsf{in}\ M \mid \textsf{let}\ (x : \sigma) = v\ \textsf{in}\ E \qquad \text{(Contexts)}$$
$$\mid\ \textsf{map}\langle E\rangle^{\tau} \mid (\!|\ E\ |\!)^{\tau} \mid E \blacktriangle M \mid v \blacktriangle E \mid E \blacktriangledown M \mid v \blacktriangledown E$$

Fig. 7. Values and Evaluation Contexts. Highlights indicate optional occurrences of (type) arguments

5.1 Reduction Rules

We define our operational semantics as a reduction semantics in the style of Felleisen and Hieb [16]. Figure 7 shows the definition of values and evaluation contexts. In our definition of values, we must account for the fact that language primitives can exist at any kind. For example, the primitive ι_1 by itself is a value of type $\tau_1 \xrightarrow{k} \tau_1 + \tau_2$. Simultaneously, applying ι_1 with a value and/or a sequence of type arguments (the number of which depends on the kind of its arrow type), also yields a value. In fact, all the *partial applications* of ι_1 with only some of its type arguments, or all type arguments but no value argument, are also values. We use gray highlights to indicate such an optional application with type and/or value arguments in the definition of values.

Figure 8 defines the reduction rules. We split the rules in two categories: the first set describes β-reduction[4] for the various type formers, while the second set determines how the **map**$\langle - \rangle^{-}$ primitive computes. Similar to the definition of values and contexts in Fig. 7, we use the notation $\overline{\tau}$ to depict a sequence of zero or more type applications. Unlike for values, these type arguments are not optional; terms typed by an arrow types must be fully applied with all their type arguments before they reduce. The notation $N \bullet M$ is used as a syntactic shorthand for the composition of two arrow types, which is defined through η-expansion of all its type arguments and the term argument. The reduction rules for the **map**$\langle\tau\rangle^{M}$ primitive are type directed, in the sense that the selected reduction depends on τ. This is necessary, because in an application of **map**$\langle - \rangle^{-}$ to a value, there is no way to decide whether to apply the function or to push the **map**$\langle - \rangle^{-}$ further inwards by only looking at the value.

5.2 Relation to the Denotational Model

The reduction rules shown in Fig. 8 define a computational model for our calculus. We now discuss how this model arises from the denotational model discussed in Sect. 4 and the extended version [33]. Informally speaking, reducing a term

[4] Here, we mean "β-reduction" in the more general sense of simplifying an application of an elimination form to an introduction form.

$$
\begin{aligned}
((\lambda x.M)\ v &\longrightarrow M[v/x] && (1)\\
\mathsf{let}\ (x:\sigma) = v\ \mathsf{in}\ M &\longrightarrow M[v/x] && (2)\\
(\Lambda\alpha.M)\ \tau &\longrightarrow M[\tau/\alpha] && (3)\\
\mathsf{unin}\ \overline{\tau}\ (\mathsf{in}\ \overline{\tau}\ v) &\longrightarrow v && (4)\\
\llparenthesis\ v_1\ \rrparenthesis^{\tau'}\ \overline{\tau}\ (\mathsf{in}\ \overline{\tau}\ v_2) &\longrightarrow v_1\ \overline{\tau}\ (\mathsf{map}\langle \llparenthesis\ v_1\ \rrparenthesis^{\tau'} \rangle^{\tau'}\ \overline{\tau}\ v_2) && (5)\\
\pi_1\ \overline{\tau}\ ((v_1 \blacktriangle v_2)\ \overline{\tau}\ v) &\longrightarrow v_1\ \overline{\tau}\ v && (6)\\
\pi_2\ \overline{\tau}\ ((v_1 \blacktriangle v_2)\ \overline{\tau}\ v) &\longrightarrow v_2\ \overline{\tau}\ v && (7)\\
(v_1 \blacktriangledown v_2)\ \overline{\tau}\ (\iota_1\ \overline{\tau}\ v)) &\longrightarrow v_1\ \overline{\tau}\ v && (8)\\
(v_1 \blacktriangledown v_2)\ \overline{\tau}\ (\iota_2\ \overline{\tau}\ v)) &\longrightarrow v_2\ \overline{\tau}\ v && (9)
\end{aligned}
$$

$$
\begin{aligned}
\mathsf{map}\langle v_1\rangle^{(\lambda X.X)}\ \overline{\tau}\ v_2 &\longrightarrow v_1\ \overline{\tau}\ v_2 && (10)\\
\mathsf{map}\langle v_1\rangle^{\mu(\tau')}\ \overline{\tau}\ (\mathsf{in}\ \overline{\tau}\ v_2) &\longrightarrow \mathsf{in}\ \overline{\tau}\ (\mathsf{map}\langle v_1\rangle^{(\tau'\ \mu(\tau'))}\ \overline{\tau}\ v_2) && (11)\\
\mathsf{map}\langle v\rangle^{\tau_1\times\tau_2}\ \overline{\tau}\ ((v_1 \blacktriangle v_2)\ \overline{\tau}\ v_3) &\longrightarrow ((\mathsf{map}\langle v\rangle^{\tau_1} \bullet v_1) \blacktriangle (\mathsf{map}\langle v\rangle^{\tau_2} \bullet v_2))\ \overline{\tau}\ v_3 && (12)\\
\mathsf{map}\langle v_1\rangle^{\tau_1+\tau_2}\ \overline{\tau}\ (\iota_1\ \overline{\tau}\ v_2) &\longrightarrow \iota_1\ \overline{\tau}\ (\mathsf{map}\langle v_1\rangle^{\tau_1}\ \overline{\tau}\ v_2) && (13)\\
\mathsf{map}\langle v_1\rangle^{\tau_1+\tau_2}\ \overline{\tau}\ (\iota_2\ \overline{\tau}\ v_2) &\longrightarrow \iota_2\ \overline{\tau}\ (\mathsf{map}\langle v_1\rangle^{\tau_2}\ \overline{\tau}\ v_2) && (14)\\
\mathsf{map}\langle v\rangle^{\mathbf{1}}\ \overline{\tau}\ (\mathsf{tt}\ \overline{\tau}) &\longrightarrow \mathsf{tt}\ \overline{\tau} && (15)
\end{aligned}
$$

$$N \bullet M \triangleq \overline{\Lambda\alpha}.\lambda x.N\ \overline{\alpha}\ (M\ \overline{\alpha}\ x)$$

Fig. 8. Reduction rules

should not change its meaning. This intuition is reflected by the following implication, which states if M reduces N, their semantics should be equal.[5]

$$M \longrightarrow N \implies [\![M]\!] = [\![N]\!] \qquad (1)$$

While we do not give a formal proof of the implication above, by relying on the categorical model to inform how terms compute we can be reasonably confident that our semantics does not contain any reductions that violate this property. That is, all the reductions shown in Fig. 8 are supported by an equality of morphisms in the categorical model.

What does this mean, specifically? The semantics of well-typed terms is given by a natural transformation, so if $M \longrightarrow N$, M and N should be interpreted as the same natural transformation. Equivalence of natural transformations is defined pointwise in terms of the equality relation for morphisms in the underlying category. In our case, this is the category SET, as terms are interpreted as natural transformations between functors into SET. By studying the properties—expressed as equalities between morphisms—of the constructions that give a semantics to the different type formers, and reifying these equalities as syntactic reduction rules, we obtain an operational model that we conjecture respects the denotational model by construction.

Let us illustrate this principle with a concrete example. The semantics of a sum type $\tau_1 + \tau_2 : k$ is given by a coproduct in the category $[\![k]\!]$. The universal

[5] This property implies what Devesas Campos and Levy [15] call *soundness* of the denotational model with respect to the operational model. Their soundness property is about a big-step relation; ours is small-step.

property of coproducts tells us that $[f, g] \circ \iota_1 = f$ and $[f, g] \circ \iota_2 = g$, or in other words, constructing and then immediately deconstructing a coproduct is the same as doing nothing. Rules (8) and (9) in Fig. 8 reflect these equations. That is, since the $\boldsymbol{\iota_1}$, $\boldsymbol{\iota_2}$, and $- \blacktriangledown -$ primitives are interpreted as the injections ι_1, ι_2, and unique morphism $[-, -]$ respectively, the universal property of coproducts tells us that the left-hand side and right-hand side of rule (8) and (9) in Fig. 8 are interpreted to equal morphism in the categorical domain.

The remaining reduction rules are justified by the categorical model in a similar fashion. More specifically:

- Rules (1,2) follow from the β-law for exponential objects, which states that $\mathsf{eval} \circ \langle \mathsf{curry}(f), id \rangle = f$.
- Rule (3) holds definitionally, assuming type substitution is appropriately defined such that it corresponds to functor application.
- Rule (4) follows from Lambek's lemma, which states that the structure map of an initial algebra is always an isomorphism. That is, there exists a morphism unin such that $\mathsf{unin} \circ \mathsf{in} = id$.
- Rule (5) reflects the universal property of folds, i.e., $\mathsf{cata}(f) \circ \mathsf{in} = f \circ F(\mathsf{cata}(f))$.
- Rules (6,7) follow from the universal property of products, which states that $\pi_1 \circ \langle f, g \rangle = f$ and $\pi_2 \circ \langle f, g \rangle = g$.
- Rule (10) mirrors the identity law for functors, i.e. $F(id) = id$.
- Rule (11) is derived from naturality of the component of the initial algebra of higher-order functors, which states that $\boldsymbol{\mu}(F)(f) \circ \mathsf{in} = \mathsf{in} \circ F(\boldsymbol{\mu}(F))(f)$.
- Rule (12,13,14,15) are derived from the way (co)-limits are computed pointwise in functor categories. For example, the morphism action of the product of two functors F and G is defined as $(F \times G)(f) = \langle F(f) \circ \pi_1, G(f) \circ \pi_2 \rangle$, which gives rise to rule (12).

6 Related Work

The problem of equipping functional languages with better support for modularity as been studied extensively in the literature. One of the earlier instances is the *Algebraic Design Language* (ADL) by Kieburtz and Lewis [24], which features language primitives for specifying computable functions in terms of algebras. ADL overlaps to a large extent with the first-order fragment of our calculus, but lacks support for defining nested data types. Zhang et al. [42] recently proposed a calculus and language for *compositional programming*, called CP. Their language design is inspired by *object algebras*, which in turn is based on the *tagless final* approach [11,25] and *final algebra semantics* [39], which, according to Wand [39, §7], is an extension of *initial algebra semantics*. These lines of work thus provide similar modularity as initial algebra semantics, but in a way that does not require *tagged values*. While the categorical foundations of Zhang et al.'s CP language seems to be an open question, the language provides flexible support for modular programming, in part due to its powerful notion of subtyping. We are not aware of attempts to model (higher-order) effects and handlers using CP. In contrast, our calculus is designed to have a clear categorical semantics. This semantics makes it straightforward to define state of the art type safe modular (higher-order) effects and handlers. Morris and McKinna [29] define a language that has built-in support for *row types*, which supports both extensible records and variants. While their language captures many known flavors of extensibility, due to parameterizing the type system over a so-called *row theory* describing how row types behave under composition, rows are restricted to first order types. Consequently, they cannot describe any modularity that hinges on the composition of (higher-order) signature functors.

The question of including nested data types in a language's support for modularity has received some attention as well. For example, Cai et al. [10] develop an extension of F_ω with equirecursive types tailored to describe patterns from datatype generic programming. Their calculus is expressive enough to capture the modularity abstractions discussed in this paper, including those defined as nested types, but lacks a denotational model. The interpretation of a subset of types in their calculus and (traversable) functors is discussed informally. Similarly, Abel et al. [4] consider an operational perspective of traversals over nested datatypes by studying several extensions of F_ω with primitives for *(generalized) Mendler iteration and coiteration.* Although these are expressive enough to describe modular higher-order effects and handlers, their semantic foundation is very different from the semantics of the primitive fold operation in our calculus.

A major source of inspiration for the work in this paper are recent works by Johann and Polonsky [22], Johann et al. [21], and Johann and Ghiorzi [20], which respectively study the semantics and parametricity of nested data types and GADTs. For the latter, the authors develop a dedicated calculus with a design and semantics that is very similar to ours. Still, there are some subtle but key differences between the designs; for example, their calculus does not include general notions of $\forall$-types and function types, but rather integrates these into a single type representing natural transformations between type constructors. While their setup does not require the same stratification of the type syntax we adopt here, it is also slightly less expressive, as the built-in type of transformations is restricted to closing over 0-arity arguments.

Data type generic programming commonly uses a *universe of descriptions* [6], which is a data type whose inhabitants correspond to a signature functor. Generic functions are commonly defined by induction over these descriptions, ranging over a semantic reflection of the input description in the type system of a dependently-typed host language [14]. In fact, Chapman et al. [12] considered the integration of descriptions in a language's design by developing a type theory with native support for generic programming. We are, however, not aware of any notion of descriptions that corresponds to our syntax of well-formed types.

7 Conclusion and Future Work

In this paper, we presented the design and semantics of a calculus with support for modularity. We demonstrated it can serve as a basis for capturing several well-known programming patterns for retrofitting type-safe modularity to functional languages, such as modular interpreters in the style of Data Types à la Carte, and modular (higher-order) algebraic effects. The formal semantics associates these patterns with their motivating concepts, creating the possibility for a compiler to benefit from their properties such as by performing fusion-based optimizations.

Acknowledgements. This research was partially funded by the NWO VENI Composable and Safe-by-Construction Programming Language Definitions project (VI.Veni.192.259).

References

1. Abbott, M.G., Altenkirch, T., Ghani, N.: Containers: constructing strictly positive types. Theor. Comput. Sci. **342**(1), 3–27 (2005). https://doi.org/10.1016/j.tcs.2005.06.002
2. Abel, A., Matthes, R.: (Co-)Iteration for higher-order nested datatypes. In: Geuvers, H., Wiedijk, F. (eds.) TYPES 2002. LNCS, vol. 2646, pp. 1–20. Springer, Heidelberg (2003). https://doi.org/10.1007/3-540-39185-1_1
3. Abel, A., Matthes, R., Uustalu, T.: Generalized iteration and coiteration for higher-order nested datatypes. In: Gordon, A.D. (ed.) FoSSaCS 2003. LNCS, vol. 2620, pp. 54–69. Springer, Heidelberg (2003). https://doi.org/10.1007/3-540-36576-1_4
4. Abel, A., Matthes, R., Uustalu, T.: Iteration and coiteration schemes for higher-order and nested datatypes. Theor. Comput. Sci. **333**(1–2), 3–66 (2005)
5. Adámek, J.: Free algebras and automata realizations in the language of categories. Comment. Math. Univ. Carol. **15**(4), 589–602 (1974)
6. Benke, M., Dybjer, P., Jansson, P.: Universes for generic programs and proofs in dependent type theory. Nord. J. Comput. **10**(4), 265–289 (2003)
7. van den Berg, B., Schrijvers, T., Poulsen, C.B., Wu, N.: Latent effects for reusable language components. In: Oh, H. (ed.) APLAS 2021. LNCS, vol. 13008, pp. 182–201. Springer, Cham (2021). https://doi.org/10.1007/978-3-030-89051-3_11
8. Bird, R., Meertens, L.: Nested datatypes. In: Jeuring, J. (ed.) MPC 1998. LNCS, vol. 1422, pp. 52–67. Springer, Heidelberg (1998). https://doi.org/10.1007/BFb0054285
9. Bird, R.S., Paterson, R.: Generalised folds for nested datatypes. Formal Aspects Comput. **11**(2), 200–222 (1999). https://doi.org/10.1007/s001650050047
10. Cai, Y., Giarrusso, P.G., Ostermann, K.: System f-omega with equirecursive types for datatype-generic programming. In: Bodík, R., Majumdar, R. (eds.) Proceedings of the 43rd Annual ACM SIGPLAN-SIGACT Symposium on Principles of Programming Languages, POPL 2016, St. Petersburg, FL, USA, 20–22 January 2016, pp. 30–43. ACM (2016). https://doi.org/10.1145/2837614.2837660
11. Carette, J., Kiselyov, O., Shan, C.: Finally tagless, partially evaluated: tagless staged interpreters for simpler typed languages. J. Funct. Program. **19**(5), 509–543 (2009). https://doi.org/10.1017/S0956796809007205
12. Chapman, J., Dagand, P., McBride, C., Morris, P.: The gentle art of levitation. In: Hudak, P., Weirich, S. (eds.) Proceeding of the 15th ACM SIGPLAN international conference on Functional programming, ICFP 2010, Baltimore, Maryland, USA, 27–29 September 2010, pp. 3–14. ACM (2010), https://doi.org/10.1145/1863543.1863547

13. Coquand, T., Paulin, C.: Inductively defined types. In: Martin-Löf, P., Mints, G. (eds.) COLOG 1988. LNCS, vol. 417, pp. 50–66. Springer, Heidelberg (1990). https://doi.org/10.1007/3-540-52335-9_47
14. Dagand, P.: A cosmology of datatypes: reusability and dependent types. Ph.D. thesis, University of Strathclyde, Glasgow, UK (2013). https://oleg.lib.strath.ac.uk/R/?func=dbin-jump-full&object_id=22713
15. Devesas Campos, M., Levy, P.B.: A syntactic view of computational adequacy. In: Baier, C., Dal Lago, U. (eds.) FoSSaCS 2018. LNCS, vol. 10803, pp. 71–87. Springer, Cham (2018). https://doi.org/10.1007/978-3-319-89366-2_4
16. Felleisen, M., Hieb, R.: The revised report on the syntactic theories of sequential control and state. Theor. Comput. Sci. 103(2), 235–271 (1992). https://doi.org/10.1016/0304-3975(92)90014-7
17. Glimming, J., Ghani, N.: Difunctorial semantics of object calculus. In: Bono, V., Bugliesi, M., Drossopoulou, S. (eds.) Proceedings of the Second Workshop on Object Oriented Developments, WOOD 2004, London, UK, 30 August 2004. ENTCS, vol. 138, pp. 79–94. Elsevier (2004). https://doi.org/10.1016/j.entcs.2005.09.012
18. Goguen, J.A.: An intial algebra approach to the specification, correctness and implementation of abstract data types. IBM Research Report 6487 (1976)
19. Hubers, A., Morris, J.G.: Generic programming with extensible data types: Or, making ad hoc extensible data types less ad hoc. Proc. ACM Program. Lang. **7**(ICFP) (2023). https://doi.org/10.1145/3607843
20. Johann, P., Ghiorzi, E.: Parametricity for nested types and gadts. Log. Methods Comput. Sci. **17**(4) (2021). https://doi.org/10.46298/lmcs-17(4:23)2021
21. Johann, P., Ghiorzi, E., Jeffries, D.: Parametricity for primitive nested types. In: FOSSACS 2021. LNCS, vol. 12650, pp. 324–343. Springer, Cham (2021). https://doi.org/10.1007/978-3-030-71995-1_17
22. Johann, P., Polonsky, A.: Higher-kinded data types: syntax and semantics. In: 34th Annual ACM/IEEE Symposium on Logic in Computer Science, LICS 2019, Vancouver, BC, Canada, 24–27 June 2019, pp. 1–13. IEEE (2019), https://doi.org/10.1109/LICS.2019.8785657
23. Kammar, O., Lindley, S., Oury, N.: Handlers in action. In: Morrisett, G., Uustalu, T. (eds.) ACM SIGPLAN International Conference on Functional Programming, ICFP 2013, Boston, MA, USA, 25–27 September 2013, pp. 145–158. ACM (2013). https://doi.org/10.1145/2500365.2500590
24. Kieburtz, R.B., Lewis, J.: Programming with algebras. In: Jeuring, J., Meijer, E. (eds.) AFP 1995. LNCS, vol. 925, pp. 267–307. Springer, Heidelberg (1995). https://doi.org/10.1007/3-540-59451-5_8
25. Kiselyov, O.: Typed tagless final interpreters. In: Gibbons, J. (ed.) Generic and Indexed Programming. LNCS, vol. 7470, pp. 130–174. Springer, Heidelberg (2012). https://doi.org/10.1007/978-3-642-32202-0_3
26. Mac Lane, S.: Categories for the Working Mathematician. GTM, vol. 5. Springer, New York (1978). https://doi.org/10.1007/978-1-4757-4721-8
27. Meijer, E., Fokkinga, M., Paterson, R.: Functional programming with bananas, lenses, envelopes and barbed wire. In: Hughes, J. (ed.) FPCA 1991. LNCS, vol. 523, pp. 124–144. Springer, Heidelberg (1991). https://doi.org/10.1007/3540543961_7
28. Moggi, E.: Notions of computation and monads. Inf. Comput. **93**(1), 55–92 (1991). https://doi.org/10.1016/0890-5401(91)90052-4
29. Morris, J.G., McKinna, J.: Abstracting extensible data types: or, rows by any other name. Proc. ACM Program. Lang. **3**(POPL), 12:1–12:28 (2019). https://doi.org/10.1145/3290325

30. Plotkin, G., Pretnar, M.: Handlers of algebraic effects. In: Castagna, G. (ed.) ESOP 2009. LNCS, vol. 5502, pp. 80–94. Springer, Heidelberg (2009). https://doi.org/10.1007/978-3-642-00590-9_7
31. Poulsen, C.B., van der Rest, C.: Hefty algebras: modular elaboration of higher-order algebraic effects. Proc. ACM Program. Lang. **7**(POPL), 1801–1831 (2023). https://doi.org/10.1145/3571255
32. van der Rest, C., Poulsen, C.B.: Towards a language for defining reusable programming language components - (project paper). In: Swierstra, W., Wu, N. (eds.) Trends in Functional Programming - 23rd International Symposium, TFP 2022, Virtual Event, March 17–18, 2022, Revised Selected Papers. LNCS, vol. 13401, pp. 18–38. Springer, Cham (2022). https://doi.org/10.1007/978-3-031-21314-4_2
33. van der Rest, C., Poulsen, C.B.: Types and semantics for extensible data types (extended version) (2023)
34. Reynolds, J.C.: Definitional interpreters for higher-order programming languages. High. Order Symb. Comput. **11**(4), 363–397 (1998). https://doi.org/10.1023/A:1010027404223
35. Schrijvers, T., Piróg, M., Wu, N., Jaskelioff, M.: Monad transformers and modular algebraic effects: what binds them together. In: Eisenberg, R.A. (ed.) Proceedings of the 12th ACM SIGPLAN International Symposium on Haskell, Haskell@ICFP 2019, Berlin, Germany, 18–23 August 2019, pp. 98–113. ACM (2019). https://doi.org/10.1145/3331545.3342595
36. Swierstra, W.: Data types à la carte. J. Funct. Program. **18**(4), 423–436 (2008). https://doi.org/10.1017/S0956796808006758
37. Uustalu, T., Vene, V.: Mendler-style inductive types, categorically. Nord. J. Comput. **6**(3), 343 (1999)
38. Wadler, P.: The expression problem. https://homepages.inf.ed.ac.uk/wadler/papers/expression/expression.txt (1998), Accessed 1 Jul 2020
39. Wand, M.: Final algebra semantics and data type extensions. J. Comput. Syst. Sci. **19**(1), 27–44 (1979). https://doi.org/10.1016/0022-0000(79)90011-4
40. Wu, N., Schrijvers, T., Hinze, R.: Effect handlers in scope. In: Swierstra, W. (ed.) Proceedings of the 2014 ACM SIGPLAN symposium on Haskell, Gothenburg, Sweden, 4–5 September 2014, pp. 1–12. ACM (2014), https://doi.org/10.1145/2633357.2633358
41. Yang, Z., Paviotti, M., Wu, N., van den Berg, B., Schrijvers, T.: Structured handling of scoped effects. In: ESOP 2022. LNCS, vol. 13240, pp. 462–491. Springer, Cham (2022). https://doi.org/10.1007/978-3-030-99336-8_17
42. Zhang, W., Sun, Y., d. S. Oliveira, B.C.: Compositional programming. ACM Trans. Program. Lang. Syst. **43**(3), 9:1–9:61 (2021). https://doi.org/10.1145/3460228

Functional Languages

A Diamond Machine for Strong Evaluation

Beniamino Accattoli[1(✉)] and Pablo Barenbaum[2,3]

[1] Inria & LIX, École Polytechnique, UMR 7161, Palaiseau, France
beniamino.accattoli@inria.fr
[2] Universidad Nacional de Quilmes (CONICET), Bernal, Argentina
[3] CONICET-Universidad de Buenos Aires, Instituto de Ciencias de la Computación, Rosario, Argentina

Abstract. Abstract machines for strong evaluation of the λ-calculus enter into arguments and have a set of transitions for backtracking out of an evaluated argument. We study a new abstract machine which avoids backtracking by splitting the run of the machine in smaller *jobs*, one for argument, and that jumps directly to the next job once one is finished.

Usually, machines are also deterministic and implement deterministic strategies. Here we weaken this aspect and consider a light form of non-determinism, namely the *diamond property*, for both the machine and the strategy. For the machine, this introduces a modular management of jobs, parametric in a scheduling policy. We then show how to obtain various strategies, among which leftmost-outermost evaluation, by instantiating in different ways the scheduling policy.

Keywords: Lambda calculus · abstract machines · strong evaluation

1 Introduction

An abstract machine for the λ-calculus, or for one of its extensions, is an implementation schema for a fixed evaluation strategy $\rightarrow_{\mathtt{str}}$ with sufficiently atomic operations (accounting for the *machine* part) and without too many implementative details (accounting for the *abstract* part). An abstract machine for $\rightarrow_{\mathtt{str}}$, ideally, refines the reduction of $\rightarrow_{\mathtt{str}}$-redexes realizing the following three tasks:

1. *Search*: searching for $\rightarrow_{\mathtt{str}}$-redexes;
2. *Names*: avoiding variable captures through some mechanism implementing α-conversion, or allowing one to avoid α-conversion altogether;
3. *Substitution*: refining meta-level substitution with an approximation based on delaying the substitution, which boils down to adopting a form of sharing, and replacing one variable occurrence at a time, in a demand-driven fashion.

These tasks are usually left to *meta-level operations* in λ-calculi, meaning that they happen outside the syntax of the calculus itself, in a black-box manner. The role of abstract machines is to explicitly take care of these aspects, or at least of

C.-K. Hur (Ed.): APLAS 2023, LNCS 14405, pp. 69–90, 2023.
https://doi.org/10.1007/978-981-99-8311-7_4

some of them, reifying them from the meta-level to the object-level. Concretely, this is obtained by enriching the specification of the operational semantics with dedicated data structures. Additionally, such a specification is usually designed as to be efficient, and usually the evaluation strategy $\rightarrow_{\mathtt{str}}$ is deterministic.

Search, Backtracking, and Jumping. A first motivation of this paper is obtaining a better understanding of the search mechanism of abstract machines. When pushed at the meta-level, search is usually specified via deduction rules or via a grammar of evaluation contexts, assuming that, at each application of a rewriting rule, the term is correctly split into an evaluation context and a redex. The meta-level aspect is the fact that the process of splitting the term (or applying the deductive rules) is not taken into account as an operation of the calculus.

For simple evaluation strategies such as, for instance, weak call-by-name in the pure λ-calculus (also known as *weak head reduction*), abstract machines (such as the Krivine or the Milner abstract machine) have one search transition for every production of the evaluation contexts for the meta-level definition of search. For less simple strategies, the searching for redexes by the machine often also accounts for the further mechanism of *backtracking search*, that is not visible in the operational semantics, not even at meta-level. Such a form of search—which is completely unrelated to *backtracking-as-in-classical-logic*—happens when the machine has finished evaluating a sub-term and needs to backtrack to retrieve the next sub-term to inspect. Typically, this happens when implementing strategies that evaluate arguments, and in particular for strategies evaluating to *strong* normal form (that is, also under abstraction), the paradigmatic and simplest example of which is leftmost(-outermost[1]) evaluation.

As an example, let f be a strong normal form and consider executing a machine for leftmost evaluation on $\lambda x.xft$. The machine would go under $\lambda x.$, find the head variable x and then start searching for a β-redex in f. Since there are none, the machine arrives at the end of f and then it usually *backtracks* through the structure of f, as to exit it and then start searching inside t. Backtracking search is natural when one sees the searching process as a *walk* over the code, moving only between *adjacent* constructors. This is the dominating approach in the design of abstract machines for λ-calculi, since the entirety of the (small) literature on machines for strong evaluation adopts it [4,8,12,14–16,20,23,24].

There is, however, a natural alternative approach which is *saving* the position where one would next backtrack, and then directly *jumping* to that position, instead of walking back to it. In this paper, we explore how to avoid backtracking search by adopting a form of *jumping search.* The idea is embarrassingly simple: creating a new *job* when an argument ready to be evaluated is found, adding it to a pool of jobs; then when the active job terminates, jumping to another job in the pool, without backtracking out of the terminated one.

Diamond Non-determinism. A second motivation of the paper is to understand how to deal with diamond non-determinism at the level of machines. It

[1] To ease the language, in the paper we shorten *leftmost-outermost* to *leftmost.*

is often the case that a deterministic strong strategy can be relaxed as to be non-deterministic. For instance, on the head normal form $x\,t\,u\,r$ leftmost evaluation would first evaluate t, then u, and then r. But the evaluations of t, u, and r are in fact independent, so that one could evaluate them in any order. One could even interleave their evaluations, as it is done for instance by the least level strategy, a non-deterministic strong strategy coming from the linear logic literature, introduced—we believe—by Girard [25] and studied for instance by de Carvalho et al. [19] on proof nets and by Accattoli et al. [9] on the λ-calculus.

Such a form of non-determinism is benign, as it does not affect the result, nor the length of the evaluation. Abstractly, it is captured by the *diamond property* (here defined following Dal Lago and Martini [21], while Terese [32] defines it more restrictively, without requiring $u_1 \neq u_2$), the strongest form of confluence:

$$\begin{array}{ccc} t & \longrightarrow & u_1 \\ \downarrow & & \\ u_2 & & \end{array} \quad \text{and } u_1 \neq u_2 \text{ imply } \exists r \text{ s.t.} \quad \begin{array}{ccc} t & \longrightarrow & u_1 \\ \downarrow & & \vdots \\ u_2 & \dashrightarrow & r \end{array}$$

What makes it stronger than confluence is that both the opening span from t and the closing one to r are made of *single* steps, not of sequences of steps.

The diamond property can be seen as a liberal form of determinism, because—when it holds—all reductions to normal form have the same length, and if one such reduction exists then there are no diverging reductions.

External Strategy and Machine. Here we introduce a relaxed, diamond version of the leftmost strategy, which we deem *external strategy*. We are inspired by Accattoli et al. [8], who study a similar strategy for strong call-by-value.

Diamond strategies can be seen as uniform frameworks capturing different deterministic strategies (for instance the leftmost and the least level strategy). Accordingly, a non-deterministic machine implementing a diamond strategy would factor out the commonalities of different deterministic machines.

We then design a machine for the external strategy, the *EXternal Abstract Machine* (EXAM) by building over the jumping search explained above. The idea, again, is very simple. It amounts to relaxing the scheduling of jobs from the pool, by allowing the machine to non-deterministically select whatever unfinished job at each step, instead of having to terminate the active job and then having to move to the next one in the pool.

In fact, we go one step further. We define a *pool interface* and the definition of the EXAM is *abstract* in that it only refers to the interface. Then one can define different *pool templates* that implement various scheduling policies for jobs. The external strategy is implemented when adopting the most general, non-deterministic template. By only replacing the template, we show how the same machine can also implement the leftmost strategy. At the end of the paper, we also quickly overview a template for the least level strategy, as well as one for a fair strategy.

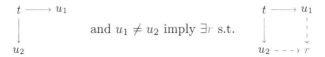

Related Work. This work adopts terminologies and techniques from the work on abstract machines by Accattoli and coauthors [1,3–5,7,8,10], and in particular refines their machine for leftmost evaluation [4]. They focus on the complexity of machines, while here we focus on *search* and ignore complexity, since their work shows that search has *linear* cost (in the time cost model, i.e. the number of β-steps) and thus it does not affect the asymptotic behavior, which is instead linked to how the machine realizes the orthogonal *substitution* task. The study of machines for strong evaluation is a blind spot of the field, despite the relevance for the implementation of proof assistants. The few studies in the literature have all been cited above. Search for abstract machines is related to Danvy and Nielsen's (generalized) *refocusing* [17,22], which however has never dealt with the jumping search introduced here. General non-deterministic machines are studied by Biernacka et al. [13], but the setting is different as they are not diamond.

Proofs. Proofs are in the technical report [2].

2 Normal Forms and the Importance of Being External

Basics of λ. The set $\mathcal{T}$ of untyped λ-terms is defined by $t ::= x \mid \lambda x.t \mid t\,t$. The capture-avoiding substitution of x by u in t is written $t\{x := u\}$. The relation of β-reduction at the root $\mapsto_\beta \subseteq \mathcal{T} \times \mathcal{T}$ is defined by $(\lambda x.t)\,u \mapsto_\beta t\{x := u\}$.

We shall use various notions of contexts, which are terms with a single occurrence of a free variable $\langle\cdot\rangle$, called a *hole*. If C is a context, $C\langle t\rangle$ denotes the *plugging* of t in C which is the textual substitution of $\langle\cdot\rangle$ by t in C. Plugging might capture variables, for instance if $C = \lambda x.\lambda y.\langle\cdot\rangle$ then $C\langle xy\rangle = \lambda x.\lambda y.xy$. Note that instead one would have $(\lambda x.\lambda y.z)\{z := xy\} = \lambda x'.\lambda y'.xy$.

The relation of β-reduction $\rightarrow_\beta \subseteq \mathcal{T} \times \mathcal{T}$ is the context closure of $\mapsto_\beta$, i.e. $C\langle t\rangle \rightarrow_\beta C\langle u\rangle$ if $t \mapsto_\beta u$, compactly noted also as $\rightarrow_\beta := C\langle\mapsto_\beta\rangle$. An evaluation $e : t \rightarrow_\beta{}^* u$ is a possibly empty sequence of β-steps.

Proposition 1 (Normal forms). *β-Normal forms are described by:*

NEUTRAL TERMS $n ::= x \mid nf$ NORMAL FORMS $f ::= n \mid \lambda x.f$

Weak Head Reduction and External Redexes. The simplest evaluation strategy is weak head reduction $\rightarrow_{wh}$, which is obtained as the closure $A\langle\mapsto_\beta\rangle$ of the root β-rule $\mapsto_\beta$ by the following notion of applicative contexts:

APPLICATIVE CONTEXTS $A ::= \langle\cdot\rangle \mid A\,t$.

Example: $(\lambda x.t)ur \rightarrow_{wh} t\{x \leftarrow u\}r$. Weak head reduction is deterministic. It fails to compute β-normal forms because it does not reduce arguments nor abstraction bodies, indeed $r((\lambda x.t)u) \not\rightarrow_{wh} r(t\{x \leftarrow u\})$ and $\lambda y.((\lambda x.t)u) \not\rightarrow_{wh} \lambda y.t\{x \leftarrow u\}$.

The key property of the weak head redex is that it is *external*, a key concept from the advanced rewriting theory of the λ-calculus studied by many authors [6,11,18,26–32]. Following Accattoli et al. [6], the intuition is that a redex R of a term t is *external* if:

1. *Action constraint*: no other redex in t can act on (that is, can erase or duplicate) R, and
2. *Hereditary clause*: the same it is true, hereditarily, for all the residuals of R after any other redex.

In $\delta(\mathtt{I}x)$, where $\delta := \lambda y.yy$ is the duplicator combinator and $\mathtt{I} := \lambda z.z$ is the identity combinator, the redex $\mathtt{I}x$ can be duplicated by δ, so it is not external because the action constraint is not respected. In $\mathtt{I}\delta(\mathtt{I}x)$, instead, the redex $\mathtt{I}x$ respects the action constraint, because $\mathtt{I}x$ is an outermost redex, and yet $\mathtt{I}x$ is not external because it does not validate the hereditary clause: its only residual after the step $\mathtt{I}\delta(\mathtt{I}x) \rightarrow_\beta \delta(\mathtt{I}x)$ can be duplicated by δ.

Defining external redexes requires the introduction of the theory of residuals, which is heavy and beyond the scope of this paper. The intuition behind it however guides the study in this paper, and we consider it a plus—rather than a weakness—that this can be done circumventing the theory of residuals.

Leftmost Reduction. One way to extend weak head reduction to compute β-normal forms as to always reduce external redexes is provided by *leftmost-outermost reduction* $\rightarrow_{lo}$ (shortened to *leftmost*). The definition relies on the notion of neutral term n used to describe normal forms, and it is given by the closure $L\langle\mapsto_\beta\rangle$ of root β by the following notion of leftmost contexts, defined by mutual induction with neutral contexts:

$$\text{NEUTRAL CTXS} \quad N ::= \langle\cdot\rangle \mid nL \mid Nt \qquad \text{LEFTMOST CTXS } L ::= N \mid \lambda x.L$$

Some examples: $y((\lambda x.t)u) \rightarrow_{lo} y(t\{x{\leftarrow}u\})$ and $\lambda y.((\lambda x.t)u) \rightarrow_{lo} \lambda y.t\{x{\leftarrow}u\}$ but $\mathtt{I}y((\lambda x.t)u) \not\rightarrow_{lo} \mathtt{I}y(t\{x{\leftarrow}u\})$. Leftmost reduction is deterministic and *normalizing*, that is, if t has a reduction to normal form f then leftmost reduction reaches f. Formally, if $t \rightarrow_\beta{}^* f$ with f normal then $t \rightarrow_{lo}^* f$—for a recent simple proof of this classic result see Accattoli et al. [9]. The normalization property can be seen as a consequence of the fact that the strategy reduces only external redexes. Note that the outermost strategy (that reduces redexes not contained in any other redex) is instead not normalizing, as the following Ω redex is outermost (but not leftmost), where $\Omega := \delta\delta$ is the paradigmatic looping λ-term:

$$(\lambda x.\, \lambda y.\, x)\, z\, \Omega \rightarrow_\beta (\lambda x.\, \lambda y.\, x)\, z\, \Omega \rightarrow_\beta \ldots \tag{1}$$

The key point is that the outermost strategy does reduce redexes that cannot be acted upon, but it does not satisfy the hereditary clause in the intuitive definition of external redex given above, for which one also needs an additional requirement such as selecting the leftmost redex among the outermost ones.

External Reduction. It is possible to define a strategy relaxing leftmost reduction, still reducing only external redexes, what we call *external reduction*. The definition uses the auxiliary notions of rigid terms and contexts, plus the applicative contexts A used for weak head reduction. The terminology is inspired by Accattoli et al.'s similar strategy for strong call-by-value evaluation [8].

Definition 1. *The following categories of terms and contexts are defined mutually inductively by the grammar:*

$$\textsc{Rigid terms} \quad r ::= x \mid r\,t$$
$$\textsc{Rigid ctxs} \quad R ::= \langle\cdot\rangle \mid r\,E \mid R\,t \qquad \textsc{External ctxs} \quad E ::= R \mid \lambda x.\,E$$

External reduction *is the rewriting relation* $\rightarrow_{\mathtt{x}} \subseteq \mathcal{T} \times \mathcal{T}$ *on* λ*-terms defined as the closure of root* β*-reduction under external contexts, that is,* $\rightarrow_{\mathtt{x}} := E\langle\mapsto_\beta\rangle$.

Alternative streamlined definitions for these notions are:

$$r \;::= x\,t_1 \ldots t_n$$
$$R ::= \langle\cdot\rangle\,t_1 \ldots t_n \mid x\,u_1 \ldots u_m\,E\,t_1 \ldots t_n \qquad E ::= \lambda x_1 \ldots x_k.\,R$$

As proved below, the leftmost strategy is a special case of the external one. The converse does *not* hold: $t = x(\mathtt{I}y)(\mathtt{I}z) \rightarrow_{\mathtt{x}} x(\mathtt{I}y)z = u$ but $t \not\rightarrow_{lo} u$. Instead, $t \rightarrow_{lo} xy(\mathtt{I}z) = r$. Note also a case of diamond: $t \rightarrow_{\mathtt{x}} r$ and $r \rightarrow_{\mathtt{x}} xyz \;{}_{\mathtt{x}}\!\leftarrow u$.

Proposition 2 (Properties of external reduction).

1. Leftmost is external*: if* $t \rightarrow_{lo} u$ *then* $t \rightarrow_{\mathtt{x}} u$.
2. External diamond*: if* $u \;{}_{\mathtt{x}}\!\leftarrow \cdot \rightarrow_{\mathtt{x}} r$ *with* $u \neq r$ *then* $u \rightarrow_{\mathtt{x}} \cdot \;{}_{\mathtt{x}}\!\leftarrow r$.

3 Preliminaries: Abstract Machines

Abstract Machines Glossary. Abstract machines manipulate *pre-terms*, that is, terms without implicit α-renaming. In this paper, an *abstract machine* is a quadruple $\mathtt{M} = (\mathtt{States}, \rightsquigarrow, \cdot \lhd \cdot, \underline{\cdot})$ the component of which are as follows.

- *States.* A state $s \in \mathtt{States}$ is composed by the *active term* t, and some data structures. Terms in states are actually pre-terms.
- *Transitions.* The pair $(\mathtt{States}, \rightsquigarrow)$ is a transition system with transitions $\rightsquigarrow$ partitioned into β*-transitions* $\rightsquigarrow_\beta$ (usually just one), that are meant to correspond to β-steps, and *overhead transitions* $\rightsquigarrow_{\mathtt{o}}$, that take care of the various tasks of the machine (searching, substituting, and α-renaming).
- *Initialization.* The component $\lhd \subseteq \Lambda \times \mathtt{States}$ is the *initialization relation* associating λ-terms to initial states. It is a *relation* and not a function because $t \lhd s$ maps a λ-term t (considered modulo α) to a state s having a *pre-term representant* of t (which is not modulo α) as active term. Intuitively, any two states s and s' such that $t \lhd s$ and $t \lhd s'$ are α-equivalent. A state s is *reachable* if it can be reached starting from an initial state, that is, if $s' \rightsquigarrow^* s$ where $t \lhd s'$ for some t and s', which we abbreviate using $t \lhd s' \rightsquigarrow^* s$.
- *Read-back.* The read-back function $\underline{\cdot} : \mathtt{States} \rightarrow \Lambda$ turns reachable states into λ-terms and satisfies the *initialization constraint*: if $t \lhd s$ then $\underline{s} =_\alpha t$.

Further Terminology and Notations. A state is *final* if no transitions apply. A *run* $\rho : s \rightsquigarrow^* s'$ is a possibly empty finite sequence of transitions, the length of which is noted $|\rho|$; note that the first and the last states of a run are not necessarily initial and final. If a and b are transitions labels (that is, $\rightsquigarrow_a \subseteq \rightsquigarrow$ and $\rightsquigarrow_b \subseteq \rightsquigarrow$) then $\rightsquigarrow_{a,b} := \rightsquigarrow_a \cup \rightsquigarrow_b$ and $|\rho|_a$ is the number of a transitions in ρ.

Well-Namedness and Renaming. For the machines at work in this paper, the preterms in initial states shall be *well-named*, that is, they have pairwise distinct bound names; for instance $(\lambda x.x)(\lambda y.yy)$ is well-named while $(\lambda x.x)(\lambda x.xx)$ is not. We shall also write $t^{\mathtt{R}}$ in a state s for a *fresh well-named renaming* of t, *i.e.* $t^{\mathtt{R}}$ is α-equivalent to t, well-named, and its bound variables are fresh with respect to those in t and in the other components of s.

Implementation Theorem, Abstractly. We now formally define the notion of a machine implementing a strategy.

Definition 2 (Machine implementation). *A machine* $\mathtt{M} = (\mathtt{States}, \leadsto, \cdot\triangleleft\cdot, \underline{\cdot})$ implements a strategy $\rightarrow_{\mathtt{str}}$ *when given a* λ*-term* t *the following holds:*

1. Runs to evaluations*: for any* $\mathtt{M}$*-run* $\rho : t \triangleleft s \leadsto_{\mathtt{M}}^{*} s'$ *there exists a* $\rightarrow_{\mathtt{str}}$*-evaluation* $e : t \rightarrow_{\mathtt{str}}^{*} \underline{s'}$.
2. Evaluations to runs*: for every* $\rightarrow_{\mathtt{str}}$*-evaluation* $e : t \rightarrow_{\mathtt{str}}^{*} u$ *there exists a* $\mathtt{M}$*-run* $\rho : t \triangleleft s \leadsto_{\mathtt{M}}^{*} s'$ *such that* $\underline{s'} = u$.
3. β-Matching*: in both previous points the number* $|\rho|_{\beta}$ *of* β*-transitions in* ρ *is exactly the length* $|e|$ *of the evaluation* e, i.e. $|e| = |\rho|_{\beta}$.

Next, we give sufficient conditions that a machine and a strategy have to satisfy in order for the former to implement the latter, what we call *an implementation system.* In the literature, strategies and machines are usually assumed to be deterministic. In Accattoli et al. [8], there is the case of a deterministic machine implementing a diamond strategy. Here we shall have a diamond machine implementing a diamond strategy, which is why the requirements are a bit different than for previous notion of implementation systems in the literature [7,8,10].

Definition 3 (Implementation system). *A machine* $\mathtt{M} = (\mathtt{States}, \leadsto, \cdot\triangleleft\cdot, \underline{\cdot})$ *and a strategy* $\rightarrow_{\mathtt{str}}$ *form an* implementation system *if:*

1. Overhead transparency*:* $s \leadsto_{\mathtt{o}} s'$ *implies* $\underline{s} = \underline{s'}$*;*
2. β-projection*:* $s \leadsto_{\beta} s'$ *implies* $\underline{s} \rightarrow_{\mathtt{str}} \underline{s'}$*;*
3. Overhead termination*:* $\leadsto_{\mathtt{o}}$ *terminates;*
4. β-reflection*: if* s *is* $\leadsto_{\mathtt{o}}$*-normal and* $\underline{s} \rightarrow_{\mathtt{str}} u$ *then there exists* s' *such that* $s \leadsto_{\beta} s'$ *and* $\underline{s'} = u$.

The first two properties guarantee that the *runs to evaluations* part of the implementation holds, the third and fourth properties instead induce the *evaluation to runs* part, which is slightly more delicate. In the deterministic case, such a second part usually follows from a weaker notion of implementation system, where β-reflection is replaced by the weaker *halt property*, stating that *if* s *is final then* $\underline{s}$ *is normal.* The diamond aspect of our study requires the stronger β-reflection property, which actually subsumes the halt one. Indeed, if $\underline{s}$ is not normal then by β-reflection s is not final.

Thanks to a simple lemma for the *evaluation to runs* part (in the technical report [2]), we obtain the following abstract implementation theorem.

Theorem 1 (Sufficient condition for implementations). *Let* $\mathtt{M}$ *be a machine and* $\rightarrow_{\mathtt{str}}$ *be a strategy forming an implementation system. Then,* $\mathtt{M}$ *implements* $\rightarrow_{\mathtt{str}}$. *More precisely, β-projection and overhead transparency imply the* runs to evaluations *part (plus β-matching), and overhead termination and β-reflection imply the* evaluations to runs *part (plus β-matching).*

DATA STRUCTURES, STATES, AND INITIALIZATION

STACKS	$S, S' ::= \epsilon \mid t : S$	ENVIRONMENTS	$E, E' ::= \epsilon \mid [x{\leftarrow}t] : E$
STATES	$s, s' ::= (t \mid S \mid E)$	INITIALIZATION	$t \lhd s$ if $s = (t^{\mathtt{R}} \mid \epsilon \mid \epsilon)$

TRANSITIONS

ACTIVE TERM	STACK	ENV		ACTIVE TERM	STACK	ENV
tu	S	E	$\rightsquigarrow_{\mathtt{sea}_@}$	t	$u : S$	E
$\lambda x.t$	$u : S$	E	$\rightsquigarrow_{\beta}$	t	S	$[x{\leftarrow}u] : E$
x	S	E	$\rightsquigarrow_{\mathtt{sub}}$	$E(x)^{\mathtt{R}}$	S	E
						If $x \in \mathtt{dom}\, E$

Fig. 1. Definition of the Milner Abstract Machine (MAM).

4 Preliminaries: The Milner Abstract Machine

The new machine for the external strategy that we are about to introduce builds on the Milner Abstract Machine (shortened to MAM) for weak head reduction by Accattoli et al. [3], that is probably the simplest abstract machine for the λ-calculus in the literature. In this section, we overview the MAM, the data structures and transitions of which are defined in Fig. 1.

Data Structures. The MAM has two data structures, the stack S and the environment E, which are lists. We use ':' for consing a single element onto a list, but also for list concatenation, so for instance $S : S'$ stands for the concatenation of stacks. The set of variables bound by an environment $E = [x_1{\leftarrow}t_1] \ldots [x_k{\leftarrow}t_k]$ is $\{x_1, \ldots, x_k\}$ and it is noted $\mathtt{dom}\, E$.

Transitions of the MAM. A term t is initialized into an initial state $t \lhd s$ by simply using an arbitrary well-named renaming $t^{\mathtt{R}}$ as active term together with empty stack and environment. The MAM *searches* for β-redexes in the active term by descending on the left of applications via transition $\rightsquigarrow_{\mathtt{sea}_@}$, while accumulating arguments on the (applicative) *stack*, which is simply a stack of terms. If it finds an abstraction $\lambda x.t$ and the stack has u on top, then it performs the machine analogous of a β-redex, that is a $\rightsquigarrow_{\beta}$ transition, which adds the entry $[x{\leftarrow}u]$ on top of the *environment*, to be understood as a delayed, explicit substitution. If the MAM finds a variable x, then it looks up in the environment E if it finds an associated entry $[x{\leftarrow}t]$, and replaces x with an α-renamed $t^{\mathtt{R}}$ copy of t.

Transitions $\rightsquigarrow_{\mathtt{sea_@}}$ and $\rightsquigarrow_{\mathtt{sub}}$ are the overhead transitions of the MAM, that is, $\rightsquigarrow_{\mathtt{o}}:=\rightsquigarrow_{\mathtt{sea_@},\mathtt{sub}}$, and $\rightsquigarrow_{\beta}$ is its only β-transition. The MAM is deterministic.

Read-Back. The read-back of MAM states to terms can be defined in at least two ways, by either first reading back the environment or the stack. Here we give an environment-first definition, which shall be used also for the EXAM.

Definition 4 (MAM read-back). *The read-back $\underline{t}_E$ and $\underline{S}_E$ of terms and stack with respect to an environment E are the terms and stacks given by:*

$$\begin{array}{lll} \textsc{Terms} & \underline{t}_{\epsilon} := t & \underline{t}_{[x\leftarrow u]:E} := \underline{(t\{x := u\})}_E \\ \textsc{Stacks} & \underline{\epsilon}_E := \epsilon & \underline{t : S}_E := \underline{t}_E : \underline{S}_E \end{array}$$

The read-back $\underline{t}_S$ of t with respect to a stack S is the term given by:

$$\underline{t}_{\epsilon} := t \qquad \underline{t}_{u:S} := \underline{(t\,u)}_S$$

Finally, the read-back of a state is defined as $\underline{(t \mid S \mid E)} := \underline{\underline{t}_E}_{\underline{S}_E}$.

Theorem 2 ([3]). *The MAM implements weak head reduction $\rightarrow_{wh}$.*

Environments are defined as *lists* of entries, but they are meant to be concretely implemented as a store, without a rigid list structure. The idea is that variables are implemented as memory locations, as to obtain constant-time access to the right entry of the environment via the operation $E(x)$. It is nonetheless standard to define environments as lists, as it helps one stating invariants concerning them. For more implementative details, see Accattoli and Barras [5].

Comparison with the KAM. For the reader acquainted with the famous Krivine Abstract Machine (KAM), the difference is that the stack and the environment of the MAM contain *codes*, not *closures* as in the KAM, and that there is a single *global* environment instead of many *local* environments. A global environment indeed circumvents the complex mutually recursive notions of *local environment* and *closure*, at the price of the explicit α-renaming $t^{\mathtt{R}}$ which is applied *on the fly* in $\rightsquigarrow_{\mathtt{sub}}$. The price however is negligible, at least theoretically, as the asymptotic complexity of the machine is not affected, see Accattoli and co-authors [3,5] (the same can be said of variable names vs de Bruijn indexes/levels).

5 The External Abstract Machine

In this section, we define the EXternal Abstract Machine (EXAM), an abstract machine for the external strategy $\rightarrow_{\mathtt{x}}$, by using the MAM as a sort of building block. The EXAM is given in Fig. 2 and explained in the following paragraphs. An example of run is given at the end of this section.

Data Structures. The EXAM has three data structures, two of which are new with respect to the MAM:

- The *approximant* (of the normal form) $\mathbb{A}$, which collects the parts of the normal form already computed by the run of the EXAM. The approximant is a *named multi-context*, defined below, that is, a context with zero, one, or more named holes $\langle\cdot\rangle_\alpha$, each one identified by a distinct name α, β, etc.
- The *pool* P, which is a data structure containing a set of named MAM *jobs*, providing operations for scheduling the execution of these jobs. Each named job j_α has shape $(t, S)_\alpha$, that is, it contains a term and a stack. The idea is that the job $j_\alpha = (t, S)_\alpha$ of name α is executing the term corresponding to (t, S) and that the result of such execution shall be plugged in the approximant $\mathbb{A}$, replacing the hole $\langle\cdot\rangle_\alpha$. Pools are discussed in detail below.
- The *environment* E, which is as for the MAM except that it is shared among all the jobs in the pool.

DATA STRUCTURES, STATES, AND INITIALIZATION

APPROX.	$\mathbb{A} ::= \langle\cdot\rangle_\alpha \mid \mathbb{R} \mid \lambda x.\mathbb{A}$	RIGID APPROX.	$\mathbb{R} ::= x \mid \mathbb{R}\,\mathbb{A}$
JOBS	$j_\alpha ::= (t, S)_\alpha$	STATES	$s ::= [\![\mathbb{A} \mid P \mid E]\!]$ with P a pool
		INITIALIZATION	$t \lhd s$ if $s = [\![\langle\cdot\rangle_\alpha \mid \mathtt{new}((t^{\mathtt{R}}, \epsilon)_\alpha) \mid \epsilon]\!]$

TRANSITIONS

AP.	POOL	ENV		AP.	POOL	ENV
$\mathbb{A}$	$(t\,u, S)_\alpha \overset{\mathtt{sel}}{\leftharpoondown} P$	E	$\rightsquigarrow_{\mathtt{sea}_@}$	$\mathbb{A}$	$(t, u : S)_\alpha \overset{\mathtt{dro}}{\rightharpoondown} P$	E
$\mathbb{A}$	$(\lambda x.t, u : S)_\alpha \overset{\mathtt{sel}}{\leftharpoondown} P$	E	$\rightsquigarrow_\beta$	$\mathbb{A}$	$(t, S)_\alpha \overset{\mathtt{dro}}{\rightharpoondown} P$	$[x{\leftarrow}u] : E$
$\mathbb{A}$	$(x, S)_\alpha \overset{\mathtt{sel}}{\leftharpoondown} P$	E	$\rightsquigarrow_{\mathtt{sub}}$	$\mathbb{A}$	$(E(x)^{\mathtt{R}}, S)_\alpha \overset{\mathtt{dro}}{\rightharpoondown} P$	E
				If $x \in \mathtt{dom}\,E$ and $t^{\mathtt{R}}$ is a fresh renaming of t		
$\mathbb{A}$	$(\lambda x.t, \epsilon)_\alpha \overset{\mathtt{sel}}{\leftharpoondown} P$	E	$\rightsquigarrow_{\mathtt{sea}_\lambda}$	$\mathbb{A}'$	$(t, \epsilon)_\alpha \overset{\mathtt{dro}}{\rightharpoondown} P$	E
					With $\mathbb{A}' := \mathbb{A}\langle\lambda x.\langle\cdot\rangle_\alpha\rangle_\alpha$	
$\mathbb{A}$	$(x, t_1 : .. : t_n)_\alpha \overset{\mathtt{sel}}{\leftharpoondown} P$	E	$\rightsquigarrow_{\mathtt{sea}_\mathcal{V}}$	$\mathbb{A}'$	$(t_1, \epsilon)_{\beta_1} : .. : (t_n, \epsilon)_{\beta_n} \overset{\mathtt{add}}{\rightharpoondown} P$	E
	If $x \notin \mathtt{dom}\,E$, and with $n \geq 0$, $\mathbb{A}' := \mathbb{A}\langle x\,\langle\cdot\rangle_{\beta_1}..\langle\cdot\rangle_{\beta_n}\rangle_\alpha$, and $\beta_1, .., \beta_n$ fresh					

Fig. 2. Definition of the EXternal Abstract Machine (EXAM).

Transitions and Functioning of the EXAM. A term t is initialized into an initial state $t \lhd s$ by creating a pool with a single named job $(t^{\mathtt{R}}, \epsilon)_\alpha$ (having a well-named $t^{\mathtt{R}}$ version of t and an empty stack) and pairing it with the approximant $\mathbb{A} = \langle\cdot\rangle_\alpha$ and empty environment. The EXAM proceeds as the MAM until it reaches a MAM final state. Let us consider the normal forms for weak head reduction and the corresponding final states of the MAM, which are of two kinds:

1. *Abstractions (with no arguments)*: the $\to_{wh}$ normal form is $\lambda x.u$ which is the read-back of a final MAM state $(\lambda x.t, \epsilon, E)$ with empty stack (that is, $u = \underline{t}_E$). In this case, the EXAM performs a $\rightsquigarrow_{\mathtt{sea}_\lambda}$ transition, storing $\lambda x.\langle\cdot\rangle_\alpha$ into the approximant $\mathbb{A}$ at α, and adding a named job $(t, \epsilon)_\alpha$ to the pool P.

2. *Possibly applied variables (with no substitution)*: the $\to_{wh}$ normal form is $xu_1 \ldots u_n$ with $n \geq 0$, which is the read-back of a final state $(x, t_1 : \ldots : t_n, E)$ with $x \notin \mathtt{dom}\, E$ (that is, $u_i = \underline{t_i}_E$). In this case, the EXAM performs a $\rightsquigarrow_{\mathtt{sea}_\mathcal{V}}$ transition. If $n = 0$ then $\rightsquigarrow_{\mathtt{sea}_\mathcal{V}}$ simply adds x into the approximant $\mathbb{A}$ at α. If $n > 0$ then $\rightsquigarrow_{\mathtt{sea}_\mathcal{V}}$ adds n new named jobs $(t_1, \epsilon)_{\beta_1}, .., (t_n, \epsilon)_{\beta_n}$ to the pool P and adds $x\langle\cdot\rangle_{\alpha_1} .. \langle\cdot\rangle_{\alpha_1}$ into the approximant $\mathbb{A}$ at α.

Transitions $\rightsquigarrow_{\mathtt{sea}_@}$, $\rightsquigarrow_{\mathtt{sea}_\lambda}$, and $\rightsquigarrow_{\mathtt{sea}_\mathcal{V}}$ are the search transitions of the EXAM. Together with $\rightsquigarrow_{\mathtt{sub}}$, they are the overhead transitions of the EXAM, that is, $\rightsquigarrow_{\mathtt{o}} := \rightsquigarrow_{\mathtt{sea}_@, \mathtt{sub}, \mathtt{sea}_\lambda, \mathtt{sea}_\mathcal{V}}$, and $\rightsquigarrow_\beta$ is its only β-transition. The transition relation of the EXAM is the union of all these relations, *i.e.* $\rightsquigarrow_{\mathtt{EXAM}} := \rightsquigarrow_{\mathtt{sea}_@, \beta, \mathtt{sub}, \mathtt{sea}_\lambda, \mathtt{sea}_\mathcal{V}}$.

Pool Interface and Templates. The EXAM selects at each step a (named) job from the pool—the one performing the step—according to a possibly non-deterministic policy, and drops it back in the pool after the transition, unless the job is over, which happens in transition $\rightsquigarrow_{\mathtt{sea}_\mathcal{V}}$. In general, *dropping a job back into a pool* and *adding a job to a pool* are not the same operation, since the former applies to jobs that were in the pool before being selected, while addition is reserved to new jobs. We actually abstract away from a job scheduling policy and from the details of the pool data structure: the pool is an abstract *interface* which can be realized by various concrete data structures called *pool templates.*

Definition 5 (Pool templates). *A pool template is a data structure P coming with the following five operations of the* pool interface*:*

- Names, support, and new*: there are a name function* $\mathtt{names}(P) = \{\alpha_1, .., \alpha_n\}$ *providing the finite and possibly empty set of the names of the jobs in the pool ($\mathbb{N} \ni n \geq 0$), a support function* $\mathtt{supp}(P) = \{j_{\alpha_1}, .., j_{\alpha_n}\}$ *providing the set of jobs in the pool (indexed by* $\mathtt{names}(P)$*), and a function* $\mathtt{new}(j_\alpha)$ *creating a pool containing j_α, that is, such that* $\mathtt{supp}(\mathtt{new}(j_\alpha)) = \{j_\alpha\}$.
- Selection*: there is a selection relation $\overset{\mathtt{sel}}{\leftarrow} (P, j_\alpha, P')$ such that $j_\alpha \in$* $\mathtt{supp}(P)$ *and* $\mathtt{supp}(P') = \mathtt{supp}(P) \setminus \{j_\alpha\}$. *The intuition is that P' is P without j_α, which has been selected and removed from P. There is a* choice constraint*: if P is non-empty then $\overset{\mathtt{sel}}{\leftarrow} (P, j_\alpha, P')$ holds for some j_α and P'. We write $j_\alpha \overset{\mathtt{sel}}{\leftarrow} P'$ for a pool P such that $\overset{\mathtt{sel}}{\leftarrow} (P, j_\alpha, P')$.*
- Dropping*: there is a dropping function $\overset{\mathtt{dro}}{\rightarrow} (j_\alpha, P) = P'$ defined when $\alpha \notin$* $\mathtt{names}(P)$ *and such that* $\mathtt{supp}(P') = \mathtt{supp}(P) \cup \{j_\alpha\}$. *Dropping is meant to add a job j_α back to a pool P from which j_α was previously selected. It is not necessarily the inverse of selection. We write $j_\alpha \overset{\mathtt{dro}}{\rightarrow} P$ for the pool $\overset{\mathtt{dro}}{\rightarrow} (j_\alpha, P)$.*
- Adding*: similarly, there is an adding function $\overset{\mathtt{add}}{\rightarrow} (j_\alpha, P) = P'$ defined when $\alpha \notin$* $\mathtt{names}(P)$ *and such that* $\mathtt{supp}(P') = \mathtt{supp}(P) \cup \{j_\alpha\}$. *Adding is meant to add a new job j_α to a pool P, that is, a job that has never been in P. We write $j_\alpha \overset{\mathtt{add}}{\rightarrow} P$ for $\overset{\mathtt{add}}{\rightarrow} (j_\alpha, P) = P'$, and extend it to lists as follows: $\epsilon \overset{\mathtt{add}}{\rightarrow} P := P$, and $j_{\alpha_1} : .. : j_{\alpha_n} \overset{\mathtt{add}}{\rightarrow} P := j_{\alpha_n} \overset{\mathtt{add}}{\rightarrow} \left(j_{\alpha_1} : .. : j_{\alpha_{n-1}} \overset{\mathtt{add}}{\rightarrow} P\right)$.*

Set EXAM. The simplest pool template is the *set template* where pools P are sets of named jobs, the support is the pool itself (and the name set is as expected), $\mathtt{new}(j_\alpha)$ creates a singleton with j_α, selection is the relation $\{(P, j_\alpha, P \setminus \{j_\alpha\}) \mid j_\alpha \in P\}$, and both dropping and adding are the addition of an element. The set template models the most general behavior, as *any* job of the pool can then be selected for the next step. The EXAM instantiated on the set template is called *Set EXAM.* Other templates shall be considered at the end of the paper, motivating in particular the distinction between dropping and adding.

Approximants and Named Multi-Contexts. The definition of the EXAM rests on approximants, which are stable prefixes of normal forms, that is, normal forms from which some sub-terms have been removed and replaced with named holes. In fact, we are going to introduce more general *(named) multi-contexts* to give a status to approximants in which some but not all holes have been replaced by an *arbitrary term*—which shall be needed in proofs (when manipulating the read-back)—thus losing their "normal prefix" property.

Definition 6 (Named multi-contexts). *A* (named) multi-context $\mathbb{C}$ *is a* λ*-term in which there may appear free occurrences of (named) holes,* i.e.*:*

$$\text{(NAMED) MULTI-CONTEXTS} \quad \mathbb{C} ::= x \mid \langle\cdot\rangle_\alpha \mid \lambda x.\mathbb{C} \mid \mathbb{C}\,\mathbb{C}$$

The plugging $\mathbb{C}\langle\mathbb{C}'\rangle_\alpha$ *of* α *by* $\mathbb{C}'$ *in* $\mathbb{C}$*, is the capture-allowing substitution of* $\langle\cdot\rangle_\alpha$ *by* $\mathbb{C}'$ *in* $\mathbb{C}$*. We write* $\mathtt{names}(\mathbb{C})$ *for the set of names that occur in* $\mathbb{C}$*. We shall use only multi-contexts where named holes have pairwise* distinct names.

Note that a multi-context $\mathbb{C}$ without holes is simply a term, thus the defined notion of plugging subsumes the plugging $\mathbb{C}\langle t\rangle_\alpha$ of terms in multi-contexts.

Approximants $\mathbb{A}$ are defined in Fig. 2 by mutual induction with rigid approximants $\mathbb{R}$, and are special cases of multi-contexts. Alternative streamlined definitions for (rigid) approximants are (possibly $y = x_i$ for some $i \in \{1, \ldots, n\}$):

$$\mathbb{R} ::= x\,\mathbb{A}_1..\mathbb{A}_n \qquad\qquad \mathbb{A} ::= \lambda x_1..x_n.\,\langle\cdot\rangle_\alpha \mid \lambda x_1..x_n.\,y\,\mathbb{A}_1..\mathbb{A}_n$$

Note that in $\mathbb{A}$ and $\mathbb{R}$ holes are never applied, that is, they are *non-applying* multi-contexts. For the sake of readability, in the paper we only give statements about approximants, which are then reformulated in the technical report [2] by pairing them with a similar statement about rigid approximants, and proving the two of them simultaneously by mutual induction.

We prove two properties of approximants. Firstly, to justify that transitions $\rightsquigarrow_{\mathtt{sea}_\lambda}$ and $\rightsquigarrow_{\mathtt{sea}_\mathcal{V}}$ are well-defined, we show that the first component of the state on their right-hand side is indeed an approximant. Secondly, we relate approximants with normal forms, to justify the terminology.

Lemma 1 (Inner extension of approximants). *If* $\mathbb{A}$ *is an approximant and* $\beta_1, \ldots, \beta_n \notin \mathtt{names}(\mathbb{A})$ *then* $\mathbb{A}\langle \lambda x. \langle\cdot\rangle_\alpha\rangle_\alpha$ *and* $\mathbb{A}\langle x\, \langle\cdot\rangle_{\beta_1}..\langle\cdot\rangle_{\beta_n}\rangle_\alpha$ *are approximants.*

Lemma 2. *An approximant* $\mathbb{A}$ *without named holes is a normal form.*

Read-Back. To give a notion of read-back that is independent of the pool template, we define the read-back using a set X of uniquely named jobs—standing for the support $\mathtt{supp}(P)$ of the pool—rather than the pool P itself. Moreover, we need a way of applying the substitution induced by an environment to named jobs and sets of named jobs, which is based on the notions $\underline{t}_E$ and $\underline{S}_E$ for terms and stacks given for the MAM, from which we also borrow the definition of $\underline{t}_S$.

Definition 7 (EXAM read-back). *Applying an environment* E *to jobs and job sets is defined as follows:*

$$\text{JOBS/JOBS SETS} \quad \underline{(t,S)_\alpha}_E := (\underline{t}_E, \underline{S}_E)_\alpha \qquad \underline{\{j_{\alpha_1}, .., j_{\alpha_n}\}}_E := \{\underline{j_{\alpha_1}}_E, .., \underline{j_{\alpha_n}}_E\}$$

The read-back of jobs, and of a multi context $\mathbb{C}$ *with respect to a set of uniquely named jobs* $\{j_{\alpha_1}, .., j_{\alpha_n}\}$ *are defined as follows:*

$$\underline{(t,S)_\alpha} := \underline{t}_S \qquad \underline{\mathbb{C}}_{\{j_{\alpha_1}, .., j_{\alpha_n}\}} := \mathbb{C}\langle \underline{j_{\alpha_1}}\rangle_{\alpha_1}..\langle \underline{j_{\alpha_n}}\rangle_{\alpha_n}$$

An EXAM state s *is read-back as a multi-context setting* $\underline{[\![\mathbb{A} \mid P \mid E]\!]} := \underline{\mathbb{A}_{\mathtt{supp}(P)}}_E$.

Diamond. Since the selection operation is non-deterministic, the EXAM in general is non-deterministic. The most general case is given by the *Set EXAM*, which is the EXAM instantiated with the set template for pools described after Definition 5. As for the external strategy, the Set EXAM has the diamond property up to a slight glitch: swapping the order of two β-transitions on two different jobs, adds entries to the environment in different orders.

Let $\approx$ be the minimal equivalence relation on environments containing the following relation:

$$E : [x{\leftarrow}t] : [y{\leftarrow}u] : E' \quad \sim \quad E : [y{\leftarrow}u] : [x{\leftarrow}t] : E' \quad \text{if } x \notin u \text{ and } y \notin t$$

Let $\equiv$ be the relation over states s. t. $[\![\mathbb{A} \mid P \mid E_1]\!] \equiv [\![\mathbb{A} \mid P \mid E_2]\!]$ if $E_1 \approx E_2$.

Proposition 3. *The Set EXAM is diamond up to* $\equiv$, *i.e., if* $s \rightsquigarrow_{\mathtt{EXAM}} s_1$ *and* $s \rightsquigarrow_{\mathtt{EXAM}} s_2$ *then* $\exists s_1'$ *and* s_2' *such that* $s_1 \rightsquigarrow_{\mathtt{EXAM}} s_1'$, $s_2 \rightsquigarrow_{\mathtt{EXAM}} s_2'$, *and* $s_1' \equiv s_2'$.

Example 1. The following is a possible run of the Set EXAM—that is, the EXAM with the set template for pools—on the term $t := x(\mathtt{I}_y z)(\delta_w z)$ where $\mathtt{I}_y = \lambda y.y$ and $\delta_w = \lambda w.ww$, ending in a final state.

Approx.	Pool	Env	Tran.	Selected Job
$\langle\cdot\rangle_\alpha$	$\{(x(\mathtt{I}_y z)(\delta_w z), \epsilon)_\alpha\}$	ϵ	$\rightsquigarrow_{\mathtt{sea}_@}$	α
$\langle\cdot\rangle_\alpha$	$\{(x(\mathtt{I}_y z), \delta_w z)_\alpha\}$	ϵ	$\rightsquigarrow_{\mathtt{sea}_@}$	α
$\langle\cdot\rangle_\alpha$	$\{(x, \mathtt{I}_y z : \delta_w z)_\alpha\}$	ϵ	$\rightsquigarrow_{\mathtt{sea}_\mathcal{V}}$	α
$x\langle\cdot\rangle_\beta\langle\cdot\rangle_\gamma$	$\{(\mathtt{I}_y z, \epsilon)_\beta, (\delta_w z, \epsilon)_\gamma\}$	ϵ	$\rightsquigarrow_{\mathtt{sea}_@}$	γ
$x\langle\cdot\rangle_\beta\langle\cdot\rangle_\gamma$	$\{(\mathtt{I}_y z, \epsilon)_\beta, (\delta_w, z)_\gamma\}$	ϵ	$\rightsquigarrow_\beta$	γ
$x\langle\cdot\rangle_\beta\langle\cdot\rangle_\gamma$	$\{(\mathtt{I}_y z, \epsilon)_\beta, (ww, \epsilon)_\gamma\}$	$[w{\leftarrow}z]$	$\rightsquigarrow_{\mathtt{sea}_@}$	β
$x\langle\cdot\rangle_\beta\langle\cdot\rangle_\gamma$	$\{(\mathtt{I}_y, z)_\beta, (ww, \epsilon)_\gamma\}$	$[w{\leftarrow}z]$	$\rightsquigarrow_{\mathtt{sea}_@}$	γ
$x\langle\cdot\rangle_\beta\langle\cdot\rangle_\gamma$	$\{(\mathtt{I}_y, z)_\beta, (w, w)_\gamma\}$	$[w{\leftarrow}z]$	$\rightsquigarrow_\beta$	β
$x\langle\cdot\rangle_\beta\langle\cdot\rangle_\gamma$	$\{(y, \epsilon)_\beta, (w, w)_\gamma\}$	$[y{\leftarrow}z] : [w{\leftarrow}z]$	$\rightsquigarrow_{\mathtt{sub}}$	β
$x\langle\cdot\rangle_\beta\langle\cdot\rangle_\gamma$	$\{(z, \epsilon)_\beta, (w, w)_\gamma\}$	$[y{\leftarrow}z] : [w{\leftarrow}z]$	$\rightsquigarrow_{\mathtt{sub}}$	γ
$x\langle\cdot\rangle_\beta\langle\cdot\rangle_\gamma$	$\{(z, \epsilon)_\beta, (z, w)_\gamma\}$	$[y{\leftarrow}z] : [w{\leftarrow}z]$	$\rightsquigarrow_{\mathtt{sea}_\mathcal{V}}$	γ
$x\langle\cdot\rangle_\beta(x\langle\cdot\rangle_{\gamma'})$	$\{(z, \epsilon)_\beta, (w, \epsilon)_{\gamma'}\}$	$[y{\leftarrow}z] : [w{\leftarrow}z]$	$\rightsquigarrow_{\mathtt{sub}}$	γ'
$x\langle\cdot\rangle_\beta(x\langle\cdot\rangle_{\gamma'})$	$\{(z, \epsilon)_\beta, (z, \epsilon)_{\gamma'}\}$	$[y{\leftarrow}z] : [w{\leftarrow}z]$	$\rightsquigarrow_{\mathtt{sea}_\mathcal{V}}$	β
$xz(x\langle\cdot\rangle_{\gamma'})$	$\{(z, \epsilon)_{\gamma'}\}$	$[y{\leftarrow}z] : [w{\leftarrow}z]$	$\rightsquigarrow_{\mathtt{sea}_\mathcal{V}}$	γ'
$xz(zz)$	$\emptyset$	$[y{\leftarrow}z] : [w{\leftarrow}z]$		

6 Runs to Evaluations

In this section, we develop the projection of EXAM runs on external evaluations, and then instantiates it with a deterministic pool template obtaining runs corresponding to leftmost evaluations.

Overhead Transparency. By the abstract recipe for implementation theorems in Sect. 3, to project runs on evaluations we need to prove *overhead transparency* and *β-projection.* Overhead transparency is simple, it follows from the definition of read-back plus some of its basic properties (in the technical report [2]).

Proposition 4 (Overhead transparency). *If $s \rightsquigarrow_{\mathrm{o}} s'$ then $\underline{s} = \underline{s'}$.*

Invariants. To prove the β-projection property, we need some invariants of the EXAM. We have a first set of invariants concerning variable names, hole names, and binders. A notable point is that their proofs use only properties of the pool interface, and are thus valid for every pool template instantiation of the EXAM.

Terminology: a *binding occurrence* of a variable x is an occurrence of $\lambda x.\, t$ in $\mathbb{A}$, P or E, or an occurrence of $[x{\leftarrow}t]$ in E, for some t.

Lemma 3 (EXAM Invariants). *Let $s = [\![\mathbb{A} \mid P \mid E]\!]$ be an EXAM reachable state reachable. Then:*

1. Uniqueness. *There are no repeated names in $\mathbb{A}$.*
2. Freshness. *Different binding occurrences in s refer to different variable names.*
3. Bijection. *The set of names in $\mathbb{A}$ is in 1–1 correspondence with the set of names in P, that is,* $\mathtt{names}(\mathbb{A}) = \mathtt{names}(P)$.
4. Freeness. *The free variables of $\mathbb{A}$ are globally free, that is,* $\mathtt{fv}(\mathbb{A}) \cap \mathtt{dom}\, E = \emptyset$.

5. Local scope. *For every sub-term of the form* $\lambda x.t$ *in a job in* $\mathtt{supp}(P)$ *or in* E*, there are no occurrences of* x *outside of* t*. Moreover, in the environment* $[x_1{\leftarrow}t_1] : .. : [x_n{\leftarrow}t_n]$*, there are no occurrences of* x_i *in* t_j *if* $i \leq j$*.*

The read-back of an EXAM state is defined as a multi-context, but for reachable states it is a term, as stated by Point 2 of the next lemma, proved by putting together the bijection invariant for reachable states (Lemma 3.3) and Point 1.

Lemma 4 (Reachable states read back to terms).

1. *Let* $\mathbb{A}$ *be an approximant and let* X *be a set of uniquely named jobs such that* $\mathtt{names}(\mathbb{A}) \subseteq \mathtt{names}(X)$*. Then* $\underline{\mathbb{A}}_X$ *is a term.*
2. *Let* s *be a reachable state. Then its read-back* $\underline{s}$ *is a term.*

Contextual Read-Back. The key point of the β-projection property is proving that the read-back of the data structures of a reachable state without the active term/job is an evaluation context—an external context in our case. This is ensured by the following lemma. It has a simple proof (using Lemma 4) because we can state it about approximants without mentioning reachable state, given that we know that the first component of a reachable state is always an approximant (because of Lemma 1). The lemma is then used in the proof of β-projection.

Lemma 5 (External context read-back). *Let* X *be a set of uniquely named jobs and* $\mathbb{A}$ *be an approximant with no repeated names such that* $\mathtt{names}(\mathbb{A}) \setminus \mathtt{names}(X) = \{\alpha\}$*. Then* $\underline{\mathbb{A}}_X\langle\langle\cdot\rangle\rangle_\alpha$ *is an external context.*

Theorem 3 (β-projection). *If* $s \rightsquigarrow_\beta s'$ *then* $\underline{s} \rightarrow_{\mathtt{x}} \underline{s'}$*.*

Now, we obtain the *runs to evaluations* part of the implementation theorem, which by the theorem about sufficient conditions for implementations (Theorem 1) follows from overhead transparency and β-projection.

Corollary 1 (EXAM runs to external evaluations). *For any EXAM run* $\rho : t \lhd s \rightsquigarrow^*_{\mathtt{EXAM}} s'$ *there exists a* $\rightarrow_{\mathtt{x}}$*-evaluation* $e : t \rightarrow^*_{\mathtt{x}} \underline{s'}$*. Moreover,* $|e| = |\rho|_\beta$*.*

Last, we analyze final states.

Proposition 5 (Characterization of final states). *Let* s *be a reachable final state. Then there is a normal form* f *such that* $s = [\![f \mid \emptyset \mid E]\!]$ *and* $\underline{s} = f$*. Moreover, if* $s \equiv s'$ *then* s' *is final and* $\underline{s'} = f$*.*

6.1 Leftmost Runs to Leftmost Evaluations

Now, we instantiate the EXAM with the stack template for pools, obtaining a machine implementing leftmost evaluation.

Leftmost EXAM. Let the *Leftmost EXAM* be the deterministic variant of the EXAM adopting the stack template for pools, that is, such that:

- Pools are lists $j_{\alpha_1} : .. : j_{\alpha_n}$ of named jobs, $\mathtt{new}(j_\alpha)$ creates the list containing only j_α, and the support of a pool is the set of jobs in the list;
- Selection pops from the pool, that is, if $P = j_{\alpha_1} : .. : j_{\alpha_n}$ then $j_\alpha \overset{\mathtt{sel}}{\leftharpoondown} P$ pops j_α from the list $j_\alpha : j_{\alpha_1} : .. : j_{\alpha_n}$;
- Both dropping and adding push on the list, and are inverses of selection.

Example 2. The Leftmost EXAM run on the same term $t := x(\mathtt{I}_y z)(\delta_w z)$ used for the Set EXAM in Example 1 follows (excluding the first three transitions, that are the same for both machines, as they are actually steps of the MAM).

Approx.	Pool	Env	Trans.	Selected Job
$x\langle\cdot\rangle_\beta\langle\cdot\rangle_\gamma$	$(\mathtt{I}_y z, \epsilon)_\beta : (\delta_w z, \epsilon)_\gamma$	ϵ	$\rightsquigarrow_{\mathtt{sea}_@}$	β
$x\langle\cdot\rangle_\beta\langle\cdot\rangle_\gamma$	$(\mathtt{I}_y, z)_\beta : (\delta_w z, \epsilon)_\gamma$	ϵ	$\rightsquigarrow_\beta$	β
$x\langle\cdot\rangle_\beta\langle\cdot\rangle_\gamma$	$(y, \epsilon)_\beta : (\delta_w z, \epsilon)_\gamma$	$[y\leftarrow z]$	$\rightsquigarrow_{\mathtt{sub}}$	β
$x\langle\cdot\rangle_\beta\langle\cdot\rangle_\gamma$	$(z, \epsilon)_\beta : (\delta_w z, \epsilon)_\gamma$	$[y\leftarrow z]$	$\rightsquigarrow_{\mathtt{sea}_\mathcal{V}}$	β
$xz\langle\cdot\rangle_\gamma$	$(\delta_w z, \epsilon)_\gamma$	$[y\leftarrow z]$	$\rightsquigarrow_{\mathtt{sea}_@}$	γ
$xz\langle\cdot\rangle_\gamma$	$(\delta_w, z)_\gamma$	$[y\leftarrow z]$	$\rightsquigarrow_\beta$	γ
$xz\langle\cdot\rangle_\gamma$	$(ww, \epsilon)_\gamma$	$[w\leftarrow z] : [y\leftarrow z]$	$\rightsquigarrow_{\mathtt{sea}_@}$	γ
$xz\langle\cdot\rangle_\gamma$	$(w, w)_\gamma$	$[w\leftarrow z] : [y\leftarrow z]$	$\rightsquigarrow_{\mathtt{sub}}$	γ
$xz\langle\cdot\rangle_\gamma$	$(z, w)_\gamma$	$[w\leftarrow z] : [y\leftarrow z]$	$\rightsquigarrow_{\mathtt{sea}_\mathcal{V}}$	γ
$xz(z\langle\cdot\rangle_{\gamma'})$	$(w, \epsilon)_{\gamma'}$	$[w\leftarrow z] : [y\leftarrow z]$	$\rightsquigarrow_{\mathtt{sub}}$	γ'
$xz(z\langle\cdot\rangle_{\gamma'})$	$(z, \epsilon)_{\gamma'}$	$[w\leftarrow z] : [y\leftarrow z]$	$\rightsquigarrow_{\mathtt{sea}_\mathcal{V}}$	γ'
$xz(zz)$	ϵ	$[w\leftarrow z] : [y\leftarrow z]$		

Proving that Leftmost EXAM runs read back to leftmost evaluations requires a new β-projection property. Its proof is based on the following quite complex invariant about instantiations of the approximants computed by the Leftmost EXAM. *Terminology*: a context C is *non-applying* if $C \neq D\langle\langle\cdot\rangle t\rangle$ for all D and t, that is, it does not apply the hole to an argument.

Proposition 6 (Leftmost context invariant). *Let*

- $s = [\![\mathbb{A} \mid j_{\alpha_1} : .. : j_{\alpha_n} \mid E]\!]$ *be a reachable Leftmost EXAM state with* $n \geq 1$*;*
- f_j *be a normal form for all* j *such that* $1 \leq j < n$*,*
- t_j *be a term for all* j *such that* $1 < j \leq n$*, and*
- L *be a non-applying leftmost context.*

Then $C^s_{f_1,..,f_{i-1}|L|t_{i+1},..,t_n} := \mathbb{A}\langle f_1\rangle_{\alpha_1}..\langle f_{i-1}\rangle_{\alpha_{i-1}}\langle L\rangle_{\alpha_i}\langle t_{i+1}\rangle_{\alpha_{i+1}}..\langle t_n\rangle_{\alpha_n}$ *is a non-applying leftmost context for every* $i \in \{1, \ldots, n\}$*.*

From the invariant, it follows that a reachable state less the first job reads back to a leftmost context, which implies the leftmost variant of β-projection, in turn allowing us to project Leftmost EXAM runs on leftmost evaluations.

Lemma 6 (Leftmost context read-back). *Let* $s = [\![\mathbb{A} \mid j_{\alpha_1} : .. : j_{\alpha_n} \mid E]\!]$ *be a reachable Leftmost EXAM state with* $n \geq 1$ *and* $s_\bullet := [\![\mathbb{A} \mid j_{\alpha_2} : .. : j_{\alpha_n} \mid E]\!]$. *Then* $\underline{s_\bullet}\langle\langle\cdot\rangle\rangle_{\alpha_1}$ *is a non-applying leftmost context.*

Proposition 7 (Leftmost β-projection). *Let* s *be a reachable Leftmost EXAM state. If* $s \rightsquigarrow_\beta s'$ *then* $\underline{s} \rightarrow_{lo} \underline{s'}$.

Corollary 2 (Leftmost EXAM runs to leftmost evaluations). *For any Leftmost EXAM run* $\rho : t \lhd s \rightsquigarrow^*_{\mathtt{EXAM}} s'$ *there exists a* $\rightarrow_{lo}$*-evaluation* $e : t \rightarrow^*_{lo} \underline{s'}$. *Moreover,* $|e| = |\rho|_\beta$.

7 Evaluations to Runs

Here, we develop the reflection of external evaluations to EXAM runs. By the abstract recipe for implementation theorems in Sect. 3, one needs to prove *overhead termination* and *β-reflection*. At the level of non-determinism, the external strategy is matched by the most permissive scheduling of jobs, that is, the set template. Therefore, we shall prove the result with respect to the Set EXAM.

Overhead Termination. To prove overhead termination, we define a measure. The measure does not depend on job names nor bound variable names, which is why the definition of the measure replaces them with underscores (and it is well defined even if it uses the renaming $E(x)^{\mathtt{R}}$).

Definition 8 (Overhead measure). *Let* j_α *be a job and* E *be an environment satisfying the freshness name property (together) of Lemma 3, and* s *be a reachable state. The overhead measures* $|j_\alpha, E|_\circ$ *and* $|s|_\circ$ *are defined as follows:*

$$\begin{aligned}
|(\lambda_.t, u : S)__, E|_\circ &:= 0 \\
|(\lambda_.t, \epsilon)__, E|_\circ &:= 1 + |(t, \epsilon)__, E|_\circ \\
|(tu, S)__, E|_\circ &:= 1 + |(t, u : S)__, E|_\circ \\
|(x, \epsilon)__, E|_\circ &:= 1 + |(E(x)^{\mathtt{R}}, \epsilon)__, E|_\circ && \text{if } x \in \mathtt{dom}\, E \\
|(x, t_1 : .. : t_n)__, E|_\circ &:= 1 + \textstyle\sum_{i=1}^{n} |(t_i, \epsilon)__, E|_\circ \text{ with } n \geq 0, && \text{if } x \notin \mathtt{dom}\, E \\
|[\![\mathbb{A} \mid P \mid E]\!]|_\circ &:= \textstyle\sum_{j_\alpha \in \mathtt{supp}(P)} |j_\alpha, E|_\circ
\end{aligned}$$

Proposition 8 (Overhead termination). *Let* s *be a Set EXAM reachable state. Then* $s \rightsquigarrow_\circ^{|s|_\circ} s'$ *with* s' $\rightsquigarrow_\circ$*-normal.*

Addresses and β-Reflection. For the β-reflection property, we need a way to connect external redexes on terms with β-transitions on states. We use *addresses*.

Definition 9 (Address and sub-term at an address). *An* address $\mathbb{a}$ *is a string over the alphabet* $\{l, r, \lambda\}$. *The sub-term* $t|_{\mathbb{a}}$ *of a term* t *at address* $\mathbb{a}$ *is the following partial function (the last case of which means that in any case not covered by the previous ones* $t|_{\mathbb{a}}$ *is undefined):*

$$t|_\epsilon := t \qquad (tu)|_{l:\mathbb{a}} := t|_\mathbb{a} \qquad (tu)|_{r:\mathbb{a}} := u|_\mathbb{a} \qquad (\lambda x.t)|_{\lambda:\mathbb{a}} := t|_\mathbb{a}$$
$$-|_{c:\mathbb{a}} := \bot \quad \text{if } c \in \{l, r, \lambda\}$$

The sub-term $\mathbb{C}|_\mathbb{a}$ at $\mathbb{a}$ of a multi-context is defined analogously. An address $\mathbb{a}$ is defined in t (resp. $\mathbb{C}$) if $t|_\mathbb{a} \neq \bot$ (resp. $\mathbb{C}|_\mathbb{a} \neq \bot$), and undefined otherwise.

There is a strong relationship between addresses in the approximant of a state and in the read-back of the state, as expressed by the following lemma. The lemma is then used to prove β-reflection, from which the *evaluation to runs* part of the implementation theorem follows.

Lemma 7. *Let $s = [\![\mathbb{A} \mid P \mid E]\!]$ be a state and $\mathbb{a}$ a defined address in $\mathbb{A}$. Then $\mathbb{a}$ is a defined address in $\underline{s}$, and $\underline{s}|_\mathbb{a}$ starts with the same constructor of $\mathbb{A}|_\mathbb{a}$ unless $\mathbb{A}|_\mathbb{a}$ is a named hole.*

Proposition 9 (β-reflection). *Let s be a $\leadsto_o$-normal reachable state. If $\underline{s} \to_\mathtt{x} u$ then there exists s' such that $s \leadsto_\beta s'$ and $\underline{s'} = u$.*

Corollary 3 (Evaluations to runs). *For every $\to_\mathtt{x}$-evaluation $e : t \to_\mathtt{x}^* u$ there exists a Set EXAM run $\rho : t \lhd s \leadsto_{\mathtt{EXAM}}^* s'$ such that $\underline{s'} = u$.*

A similar result for leftmost evaluation and the Leftmost EXAM follows more easily from the characterization of final states (Proposition 5), overhead termination (Proposition 8), and determinism of the Leftmost EXAM—this is the standard pattern for deterministic strategies and machines, used for instance by Accattoli et al. for their machine for leftmost evaluation [4].

Names and Addresses. It is natural to wonder whether one can refine the EXAM by using addresses $\mathbb{a}$ as a more precise form of names for jobs. It is possible, it is enough to modify the EXAM as to extend at each step the name/address. For instance, transition $\leadsto_{\mathtt{sea}_@}$ would become:

Ap. | Pool | Env		Ap. | Pool | Env
$\mathbb{A} \mid (t\,u, S)_\mathbb{a} \overset{\mathtt{sel}}{\leftharpoondown} P \mid E$	$\leadsto_{\mathtt{sea}_@}$	$\mathbb{A} \mid (t, u : S)_{l:\mathbb{a}} \overset{\mathtt{dro}}{\rightharpoondown} P \mid E$

Then a β-transition of address $\mathbb{a}$ in a reachable state s corresponds exactly to a β-redex of address $\mathbb{a}$ in $\underline{s}$. We refrained from adopting addresses as names, however, because this is only useful for proving the β-reflection property of the EXAM, the machine does not need such an additional structure for its functioning.

8 Further Pool Templates

Least Level. Another sub-strategy of external reduction that computes β-normal forms is provided by *least level reduction* $\to_{\ell\ell}$, a notion from the linear logic literature. Picking a redex of minimal level, where the level is the number of arguments in which the redex is contained, is another predicate (similarly to the leftmost one) that ensures externality of an outermost redex. Note that the

Ω redex in (1) (page 5) is not of minimal level (it has level 1 while the redex involving z has level 0). Least level reduction is non-deterministic but diamond. For instance the two redexes (of level 1) in $x(\mathtt{I}y)(\mathtt{I}z)$ are both least level. Note that the leftmost redex might not be least level, as in $x(x(\mathtt{I}y))(\mathtt{I}z)$, where the leftmost redex is $\mathtt{I}y$ and has level 2, while $\mathtt{I}z$ has level 1.

By replacing the stack template with a queue one, the Leftmost EXAM turns into a machine for least level evaluation. The key point is that when new jobs are created, which is done only by transition $\rightsquigarrow_{\mathtt{sea}_{\mathcal{V}}}$, they all have level $n+1$ where n is the level of the active job. To process jobs by increasing levels, then, it is enough to add the new jobs *at the end of the pool*, rather than at the beginning. This is an example where dropping (which pushes an element on top of the list of jobs) and adding (which adds at the end) are *not* the same operation.

Fair Template. Another interesting template is the one where pools are lists and dropping always adds at the end of the list. In this way the EXAM is *fair*, in the sense that even when it diverges, it keeps evaluating all jobs. This kind of strategies are of interest for infinitary λ-calculi, where one wants to compute all branches of an infinite normal form, instead of being stuck on one.

9 Conclusions

This paper studies two simple ideas and applies them to the paradigmatic case of strong call-by-name evaluation. Firstly, avoiding *backtracking on the search for redexes* by introducing *jobs* for each argument and jumping to the next job when one is finished. Secondly, modularizing the scheduling of jobs via a *pool interface* that can be instantiated by various concrete schedulers, called *pool templates.*

The outcome of the study is a compact, modular, and—we believe—elegant abstract machine for strong evaluation. In particular, we obtain the simplest machine for leftmost evaluation in the literature. Our study also gives a computational interpretation to the diamond non-determinism of strong call-by-name.

For the sake of simplicity, our study extends the MAM, which implements weak head reduction using global environments. Our technique, however, is reasonably modular in the underlying machine/notion of environment. One can, indeed, replace the MAM with Krivine abstract machine (KAM), which instead uses local environments, by changing only the fact that the jobs of the EXAM have to carry their own local environment. Similarly, the technique seems to be adaptable to the CEK or other machines for weak evaluation. It would be interesting to compare the outcome of these adaptations with existing machines for strong call-by-value [8,14,15] or strong call-by-need [12,16].

References

1. Accattoli, B.: The useful MAM, a reasonable implementation of the strong λ-calculus. In: Väänänen, J., Hirvonen, Å., de Queiroz, R. (eds.) WoLLIC 2016. LNCS, vol. 9803, pp. 1–21. Springer, Heidelberg (2016). https://doi.org/10.1007/978-3-662-52921-8_1
2. Accattoli, B., Barenbaum, P.: A diamond machine for strong evaluation. CoRR abs/2309.12515 (2023). https://arxiv.org/abs/2309.12515
3. Accattoli, B., Barenbaum, P., Mazza, D.: Distilling abstract machines. In: Proceedings of the 19th ACM SIGPLAN International Conference on Functional Programming, Gothenburg, Sweden, September 1–3, 2014, pp. 363–376 (2014). https://doi.org/10.1145/2628136.2628154
4. Accattoli, B., Barenbaum, P., Mazza, D.: A strong distillery. In: Feng, X., Park, S. (eds.) APLAS 2015. LNCS, vol. 9458, pp. 231–250. Springer, Cham (2015). https://doi.org/10.1007/978-3-319-26529-2_13
5. Accattoli, B., Barras, B.: Environments and the complexity of abstract machines. In: Vanhoof, W., Pientka, B. (eds.) Proceedings of the 19th International Symposium on Principles and Practice of Declarative Programming, Namur, Belgium, October 09–11, 2017, pp. 4–16. ACM (2017). https://doi.org/10.1145/3131851.3131855
6. Accattoli, B., Bonelli, E., Kesner, D., Lombardi, C.: A nonstandard standardization theorem. In: Jagannathan, S., Sewell, P. (eds.) The 41st Annual ACM SIGPLAN-SIGACT Symposium on Principles of Programming Languages, POPL '14, San Diego, CA, USA, January 20–21, 2014, pp. 659–670. ACM (2014). https://doi.org/10.1145/2535838.2535886
7. Accattoli, B., Condoluci, A., Guerrieri, G., Sacerdoti Coen, C.: Crumbling abstract machines. In: Komendantskaya, E. (ed.) Proceedings of the 21st International Symposium on Principles and Practice of Programming Languages, PPDP 2019, Porto, Portugal, October 7–9, 2019, pp. 4:1–4:15. ACM (2019). https://doi.org/10.1145/3354166.3354169
8. Accattoli, B., Condoluci, A., Sacerdoti Coen, C.: Strong Call-by-Value is Reasonable, Implosively. In: 36th Annual ACM/IEEE Symposium on Logic in Computer Science, LICS 2021, Rome, Italy, June 29 - July 2, 2021, pp. 1–14. IEEE (2021). https://doi.org/10.1109/LICS52264.2021.9470630
9. Accattoli, B., Faggian, C., Guerrieri, G.: Factorization and normalization, essentially. In: Lin, A.W. (ed.) APLAS 2019. LNCS, vol. 11893, pp. 159–180. Springer, Cham (2019). https://doi.org/10.1007/978-3-030-34175-6_9
10. Accattoli, B., Guerrieri, G.: Abstract machines for open call-by-value. Sci. Comput. Program. **184** (2019). https://doi.org/10.1016/j.scico.2019.03.002
11. Barendregt, H.P., Kennaway, R., Klop, J.W., Sleep, M.R.: Needed reduction and spine strategies for the lambda calculus. Inf. Comput. **75**(3), 191–231 (1987). https://doi.org/10.1016/0890-5401(87)90001-0
12. Biernacka, M., Biernacki, D., Charatonik, W., Drab, T.: An abstract machine for strong call by value. In: Oliveira, B.C.S. (ed.) APLAS 2020. LNCS, vol. 12470, pp. 147–166. Springer, Cham (2020). https://doi.org/10.1007/978-3-030-64437-6_8
13. Biernacka, M., Biernacki, D., Lenglet, S., Schmitt, A.: Non-deterministic abstract machines. In: Klin, B., Lasota, S., Muscholl, A. (eds.) 33rd International Conference on Concurrency Theory, CONCUR 2022, September 12–16, 2022, Warsaw, Poland. LIPIcs, vol. 243, pp. 7:1–7:24. Schloss Dagstuhl - Leibniz-Zentrum für Informatik (2022). https://doi.org/10.4230/LIPIcs.CONCUR.2022.7

14. Biernacka, M., Charatonik, W.: Deriving an abstract machine for strong call by need. In: Geuvers, H. (ed.) 4th International Conference on Formal Structures for Computation and Deduction, FSCD 2019, June 24–30, 2019, Dortmund, Germany. LIPIcs, vol. 131, pp. 8:1–8:20. Schloss Dagstuhl - Leibniz-Zentrum für Informatik (2019). https://doi.org/10.4230/LIPIcs.FSCD.2019.8
15. Biernacka, M., Charatonik, W., Drab, T.: A derived reasonable abstract machine for strong call by value. In: Veltri, N., Benton, N., Ghilezan, S. (eds.) PPDP 2021: 23rd International Symposium on Principles and Practice of Declarative Programming, Tallinn, Estonia, September 6–8, 2021, pp. 6:1–6:14. ACM (2021). https://doi.org/10.1145/3479394.3479401
16. Biernacka, M., Charatonik, W., Drab, T.: A simple and efficient implementation of strong call by need by an abstract machine. Proc. ACM Program. Lang. **6**(ICFP), 109–136 (2022). https://doi.org/10.1145/3549822
17. Biernacka, M., Charatonik, W., Zielinska, K.: Generalized refocusing: from hybrid strategies to abstract machines. In: 2nd International Conference on Formal Structures for Computation and Deduction, FSCD 2017, September 3–9, 2017, Oxford, UK, pp. 10:1–10:17 (2017). https://doi.org/10.4230/LIPIcs.FSCD.2017.10
18. Boudol, G.: Computational semantics of term rewriting systems. In: Algebraic Methods in Semantics, pp. 169–236. Cambridge University Press (1986)
19. de Carvalho, D., Pagani, M., Tortora de Falco, L.: A semantic measure of the execution time in linear logic. Theor. Comput. Sci. **412**(20), 1884–1902 (2011). https://doi.org/10.1016/j.tcs.2010.12.017
20. Crégut, P.: Strongly reducing variants of the Krivine abstract machine. High. Order Symb. Comput. **20**(3), 209–230 (2007). https://doi.org/10.1007/s10990-007-9015-z
21. Dal Lago, U., Martini, S.: The weak lambda calculus as a reasonable machine. Theor. Comput. Sci. **398**(1–3), 32–50 (2008). https://doi.org/10.1016/j.tcs.2008.01.044
22. Danvy, O., Nielsen, L.R.: Refocusing in Reduction Semantics. Tech. Rep. RS-04-26, BRICS (2004)
23. García-Pérez, Á., Nogueira, P.: The full-reducing Krivine abstract machine KN simulates pure normal-order reduction in lockstep: a proof via corresponding calculus. J. Funct. Program. **29**, e7 (2019). https://doi.org/10.1017/S0956796819000017
24. García-Pérez, Á., Nogueira, P., Moreno-Navarro, J.J.: Deriving the full-reducing Krivine machine from the small-step operational semantics of normal order. In: 15th International Symposium on Principles and Practice of Declarative Programming, PPDP'13, pp. 85–96. ACM (2013). https://doi.org/10.1145/2505879.2505887
25. Girard, J.: Light linear logic. Inf. Comput. **143**(2), 175–204 (1998). https://doi.org/10.1006/inco.1998.2700
26. Gonthier, G., Lévy, J.J., Melliès, P.A.: An abstract standardisation theorem. In: Proceedings of the Seventh Annual Symposium on Logic in Computer Science (LICS '92), Santa Cruz, California, USA, June 22–25, 1992, pp. 72–81. IEEE Computer Society (1992). https://doi.org/10.1109/LICS.1992.185521
27. Huet, G.P., Lévy, J.J.: Computations in orthogonal rewriting systems, I. In: Lassez, J., Plotkin, G.D. (eds.) Computational Logic - Essays in Honor of Alan Robinson, pp. 395–414. The MIT Press (1991)
28. Huet, G.P., Lévy, J.J.: Computations in orthogonal rewriting systems, II. In: Lassez, J., Plotkin, G.D. (eds.) Computational Logic - Essays in Honor of Alan Robinson, pp. 415–443. The MIT Press (1991)

29. Maranget, L.: Optimal derivations in weak lambda-calculi and in orthogonal terms rewriting systems. In: Wise, D.S. (ed.) Conference Record of the Eighteenth Annual ACM Symposium on Principles of Programming Languages, Orlando, Florida, USA, January 21–23, 1991, pp. 255–269. ACM Press (1991). https://doi.org/10.1145/99583.99618
30. Melliès, P.A.: Description Abstraite de système de réécriture. PhD thesis, Paris 7 University (1996)
31. Oostrom, V.: Normalisation in weakly orthogonal rewriting. In: Narendran, P., Rusinowitch, M. (eds.) RTA 1999. LNCS, vol. 1631, pp. 60–74. Springer, Heidelberg (1999). https://doi.org/10.1007/3-540-48685-2_5
32. Terese: Term rewriting systems. Cambridge tracts in theoretical computer science, vol. 55. Cambridge University Press (2003)

Proofs as Terms, Terms as Graphs

Jui-Hsuan Wu(✉)

LIX, Institut Polytechnique de Paris, Palaiseau, France
jwu@lix.polytechnique.fr

Abstract. Starting from an encoding of untyped λ-terms with sharing, defined using synthetic inference rules based on a focused proof system for Gentzen's LJ, we introduce the positive λ-calculus, a call-by-value calculus with explicit substitutions. This calculus is closely related to Accattoli and Paolini's value substitution calculus but has a different style of reduction rules that provides a good notion of sharing along the reduction. We also propose a graphical representation in order to capture the structural equivalence on terms that can be described using rule permutations. On one hand, this graphical representation provides a way to remove redundancy in the syntax, and on the other hand, it allows implementing basic operations such as substitution and reduction in a straightforward way.

Keywords: Proof theory · Term representation · λ-calculus · Sharing · Graphical representation

1 Introduction

Terms (or expressions) are essential in different settings: mathematical proofs, programming languages, proof assistants, etc. To prevent redundancy in these systems, a canonical and compact syntactic structure is needed. Proof theory has been broadly used in the studies of term representation. There have been several different approaches to address the question of the canonicity of proofs, such as proof nets [20], expansion trees [25], focusing [7], combinatorial proofs [22], etc.

Focusing and Synthetic Inference Rules. In this paper, we choose to use focusing as our main tool. Andreoli introduced the first focused proof system to describe proofs in linear logic in a more structured way. Inference rules are organized into two different phases: *positive* and *negative* phases. Andreoli [8] and Chaudhuri [11] suggested that phases should be viewed as large-scale rules for proof construction. In [24], Marin et al. defined another version of large-scale rules, called *synthetic inference rule*, which is essentially composed of a negative phase and a positive phase, in order to provide more high-level descriptions of proof systems. The invention of synthetic inference rules also provides a systematic way to extend proof systems such as LJ and LK.

C.-K. Hur (Ed.): APLAS 2023, LNCS 14405, pp. 91–111, 2023.
https://doi.org/10.1007/978-981-99-8311-7_5

Various focused proof systems have been proposed for *LJ* [18,21,23] and *LK* [15,23]. Several authors also designed term calculi for *LJT* [21], *LJQ* [18], and *LJF* [10]. In [27], Miller and Wu use synthetic inference rules built using the focused proof system *LJF* to study term structures. In *LJF*, formulas are polarized and different polarity assignments yield different forms of proofs and thus provide different styles of term representation. In this paper, we are interested in their encoding of untyped λ-terms defined by giving the positive polarity to every atomic formula. Unlike the usual syntax of untyped λ-terms, this encoding constructs terms in a *bottom-up* style and allows sharing within a term using *named structures*, or *explicit substitutions*. This term representation is, however, not compact, in the sense that a lot of named structures can be permuted or put in parallel. These permutations correspond, in fact, to phase permutations in focused proof systems, and to rule permutations in terms of synthetic inference rules.

Focusing and Graphical Structures. Several authors have proposed *multi-focused* proof systems to illustrate this phenomenon for *MALL* [13,16,26], *LK* [12], and *LJ* [28]. Moreover, in each of [12,13], an isomorphism has been established between the multi-focused proof system and a graphical representation of proofs (proof nets and expansion trees, respectively). This is where our *graphical representation* for terms comes in. Though inspired by these works on multi-focusing, we choose to put our focus on terms, i.e. (single-)focused proofs, and define the structural equivalence that can also be justified by rule permutations. Also, note that the structural equivalence considered in this paper does not cover all the possible permutations that are captured by multi-focused proof systems.

Explicit Substitution and Proof Nets. Historically, there have been several attempts to connect λ-calculus with sharing, or explicit substitution [1], to proof nets. This connection was first proposed by Di Cosmo and Kesner [17] to study cut-elimination. Recently, proof nets have also been connected to calculi such as the call-by-value λ-calculus [2] and the linear substitution calculus [3]. In this paper, like in each of [2,3], we show that the structural equivalence on terms is exactly the same as the one captured by the graphical representation. In contrast to these works that often introduce boxes to deal with sharing, we decide to use the notion of *bodies*, which is closely related to the notion of *level* in these works. This choice does not make a huge difference in our theoretical results, but it provides a clear way to establish the correspondence between the usual syntax and the graphical one.

Graphs and Sharing. Graphs have been widely used in the studies of sharing. Since Wadsworth [29], several authors have proposed different graphical structures to study full laziness (see [9] for an overview), a concept related to evaluation based on the call-by-need mechanism. Another aspect about sharing, called *sharing equality*, whose goal is to decide whether the unfoldings of two terms with sharing are equal, has also been discovered in recent years. A linear algorithm was proposed in [14] based on a graphical representation called λ-*graphs* for untyped λ-terms. This graphical representation is close to the one studied in our work, which allows us to apply the algorithm without any difficulty.

Contribution.

1. We propose a rewrite system for the encoding of untyped λ-terms proposed in [27], called the *positive λ-calculus.* Note that it is *inspired* by proof theory but does not follow the usual "redex = cut" paradigm. This rewrite system follows a call-by-value discipline and is closely related to the value substitution calculus [6] and the linear substitution calculus [4].
2. We propose a graphical representation, called λ-graphs with bodies, for this encoding of untyped λ-terms and provide a one-to-one correspondence between λ-graphs with bodies and terms up to permutations of independent named structures (Theorem 5).
3. We describe how substitution and reduction can be easily implemented on λ-graphs with bodies.

Proofs. Most proofs are ignored and can be found in the full version, available at https://hal.inria.fr/hal-04222527.

2 Preliminaries: The Focused Proof System LJF and Synthetic Inference Rules

Fix a set ATOM of *atomic formulas. Formulas* are built with implications and atomic formulas. An *atomic bias assignment* is a map δ from ATOM to $\{+, -\}$. A *polarized formula* (resp. *polarized theory*) is a formula (resp. multiset of formulas) together with an atomic bias assignment. Implications are negative and atomic formulas can be either positive or negative following the atomic bias assignment. In *LJF*, there are two kinds of sequents: $\Uparrow$-sequents $\Gamma \Uparrow \Theta \vdash \Delta \Uparrow \Delta'$ and $\Downarrow$-sequents $\Gamma \Downarrow \Theta \vdash \Delta \Downarrow \Delta'$. Here, $\Gamma, \Theta, \Delta, \Delta'$ are multisets of formulas. Γ and Δ' are called *storage zones* and Θ and Δ are called *staging zones.* In a $\Downarrow$-sequent, exactly one of Θ and Δ can be non-empty and contains exactly one formula. To simplify the notation, we drop an arrow whenever its corresponding staging zone is empty. As a result, sequents without any arrow are $\Uparrow$-sequents as any $\Downarrow$-sequent has exactly one non-empty staging zone. Furthermore, $\Delta \cup \Delta'$ is a singleton, as we are in an intuitionistic setting. The rules of the implicational fragment of *LJF* are presented in Fig. 1. *LJF* proofs have a two-phase structure: $\Uparrow$-phases and $\Downarrow$-phases.

Definition 1 (Synthetic inference rules, [24]**).** *A synthetic inference rule is a rule of the form*

$$\frac{\Gamma_1 \vdash A_1 \quad \cdots \quad \Gamma_n \vdash A_n}{\Gamma \vdash A}\,N \qquad \text{justified by an LJF derivation of the form} \qquad \dfrac{\begin{array}{c}\Gamma_1 \vdash A_1 \quad \cdots \quad \Gamma_n \vdash A_n\\ \Pi \\ \Gamma \Downarrow N \vdash A\end{array}}{\Gamma \vdash A}\,D_l$$

Here, N is a negative formula that appears in Γ, $n \geq 0$, and within Π, a $\Downarrow$-sequent never occurs above an $\Uparrow$-sequent. The structure of LJF proofs implies $N \in \Gamma_i$ for all $1 \leq i \leq n$. This rule is called the synthetic inference rule for N.

Decide, Release, and Store Rules

$$\frac{N,\Gamma \Downarrow N \vdash A}{N,\Gamma \vdash A}\,D_l \qquad \frac{\Gamma \vdash P \Downarrow}{\Gamma \vdash P}\,D_r \qquad \frac{\Gamma \Uparrow P \vdash A}{\Gamma \Downarrow P \vdash A}\,R_l \qquad \frac{\Gamma \vdash N \Uparrow}{\Gamma \vdash N \Downarrow}\,R_r$$

$$\frac{\Gamma, C \Uparrow \Theta \vdash \Delta \Uparrow \Delta'}{\Gamma \Uparrow \Theta, C \vdash \Delta \Uparrow \Delta'}\,S_l \qquad \frac{\Gamma \Uparrow \Theta \vdash A}{\Gamma \Uparrow \Theta \vdash A \Uparrow}\,S_r$$

Initial Rules

$$\frac{\delta(A) = +}{A,\Gamma \vdash A \Downarrow}\,I_r \qquad \frac{\delta(A) = -}{\Gamma \Downarrow A \vdash A}\,I_l$$

Introduction Rules for implication

$$\frac{\Gamma \vdash B \Downarrow \qquad \Gamma \Downarrow B' \vdash A}{\Gamma \Downarrow B \supset B' \vdash A}\supset L \qquad \frac{\Gamma \Uparrow \Theta, B \vdash B' \Uparrow}{\Gamma \Uparrow \Theta \vdash B \supset B' \Uparrow}\supset R$$

Fig. 1. The implicational fragment of the focused proof system LJF. Here, P is positive, N is negative, A is atomic, and B, B' and C are arbitrary formulas.

$$\dfrac{\dfrac{\dfrac{}{\Gamma \vdash D \Downarrow}\,I_r \qquad \dfrac{\dfrac{}{\Gamma \vdash D \Downarrow}\,I_r \qquad \dfrac{\Gamma, D \vdash D}{\Gamma \Downarrow D \vdash D}\,S_l/R_l}{\Gamma \Downarrow D \supset D \vdash D}\supset L}{\Gamma \Downarrow D \supset D \supset D \vdash D}\supset L}{\Gamma \vdash D}\,D_l$$

$$\dfrac{\dfrac{\dfrac{\dfrac{\dfrac{\Gamma, D \vdash D}{\Gamma \Uparrow D \vdash D \Uparrow}\,S_l/S_r}{\Gamma \vdash D \supset D \Uparrow}\supset R}{\Gamma \vdash D \supset D \Downarrow}\,R_r \qquad \dfrac{\Gamma, D \vdash D}{\Gamma \Downarrow D \vdash D}\,S_l/R_l}{\Gamma \Downarrow (D \supset D) \supset D \vdash D}\supset L}{\Gamma \vdash D}\,D_l$$

Fig. 2. Two derivations justifying synthetic inference rules (D is atomic and polarized positively).

Synthetic inference rules show how a formula can be *used* in a proof and they can be used to extend sequent systems such as LJ. Since the synthetic inference rules for atomic formulas are exactly the same as the initial rule of LJ, we will only consider synthetic inference rules for non-atomic formulas. We give in Fig. 2 two LJF derivations justifying synthetic inference rules for two different formulas. In [24], it is shown that the synthetic inference rules for certain formulas are particularly simple and can be easily used to extend LJ with a (polarized) theory. To express this, we first define the order of a formula.

Definition 2. *The order of a formula B, written $ord(B)$, is defined as follows: $ord(A) = 0$ if A is atomic and $ord(B_1 \supset B_2) = max(ord(B_1) + 1, ord(B_2))$.*

Definition 3 (Extensions of LJ by polarized theories, [24]). *Let $\mathcal{T}$ be a finite multiset of formulas of order one or two, and let δ be an atomic bias assignment. We define the extension $LJ\lfloor \mathcal{T}, \delta \rfloor$ of LJ by the polarized theory $(\mathcal{T}, \delta)$ to be the two-sided proof system built as follows. The only sequents in the $LJ\lfloor \mathcal{T}, \delta \rfloor$ proof system are of the form $\Gamma \vdash A$ where A is atomic and Γ is a multiset of atomic formulas. The inference rules of $LJ\lfloor \mathcal{T}, \delta \rfloor$ include the initial rule of LJ and for every synthetic inference rule*

$$\frac{N, \Gamma_1 \vdash A_1 \quad \ldots \quad N, \Gamma_n \vdash A_n}{N, \Gamma \vdash A}\,N$$

where $N \in \mathcal{T}$, then the rule

$$\frac{\Gamma_1 \vdash A_1 \quad \dots \quad \Gamma_n \vdash A_n}{\Gamma \vdash A} N$$

is included in $LJ\lfloor \mathcal{T}, \delta \rfloor$.

Note that in the original version proposed in [24], $\mathcal{T}$ is a set instead of a multiset. In fact, each formula in $\mathcal{T}$ corresponds to a combinator in annotated proofs. Different occurrences of the same formula define different combinators. This is why we consider multisets instead of sets of formulas.

The following theorem justifies Definition 3.

Theorem 1. *Let $\mathcal{T}$ be a finite multiset of formulas of order one or two, and let δ be an atomic bias assignment. Then for any atomic formula A and Γ containing atomic formulas only, $\Gamma, \mathcal{T} \vdash A$ is provable in LJ if and only if $\Gamma \vdash A$ is provable in $LJ\lfloor \mathcal{T}, \delta \rfloor$.*

$$x : D \in \Gamma \ \frac{}{\Gamma \vdash x : D}\ nvar \qquad \frac{\Gamma \vdash s : D \quad \Gamma \vdash t : D}{\Gamma \vdash st : D}\ napp \qquad \frac{\Gamma, x : D \vdash t : D}{\Gamma \vdash \lambda x.t : D}\ nabs$$

$$x : D \in \Gamma \ \frac{}{\Gamma \vdash x : D}\ pvar \qquad \{y : D, z : D\} \subseteq \Gamma \ \frac{\Gamma, x : D \vdash t : D}{\Gamma \vdash t[x \leftarrow yz] : D}\ papp \qquad \frac{\Gamma, y : D \vdash s : D \quad \Gamma, x : D \vdash t : D}{\Gamma \vdash t[x \leftarrow \lambda y.s] : D}\ pabs$$

Fig. 3. Annotated inference rules of the systems $LJ\lfloor \Gamma_0, \delta^- \rfloor$ (left) and $LJ\lfloor \Gamma_0, \delta^+ \rfloor$ (right) where $\delta^-(D) = -$, $\delta^+(D) = +$ and $\Gamma_0 = \{D \supset D \supset D, (D \supset D) \supset D\}$.

3 The positive λ-calculus

The notion of terms, which is usually a primitive notion in most of the literature, is a derived notion here: they are annotations of proofs. By annotating inference rules in the proof system $LJ\lfloor \mathcal{T}, \delta \rfloor$, we obtain rules for various combinators, each one of which corresponds to a formula in $\mathcal{T}$. In [27], Miller and Wu give an encoding of untyped λ-terms by considering the theory $\Gamma_0 = \{D \supset D \supset D, (D \supset D) \supset D\}$ where D is an atomic formula. If D is given the negative polarity, we get the negative bias syntax, i.e., the usual tree structure for untyped λ-terms. If D is given the positive polarity, we get the positive bias syntax, a structure where explicit sharing is possible. The annotated inference rules obtained using both polarity assignments are shown in Fig. 3. As an example, the *papp* and *pabs* rules are obtained from the two derivations given in Fig. 2. Note that the branches ended with I_r rule become a side condition on the schema variable Γ.

In the following, we introduce a calculus called *positive λ-calculus* based on terms built using the positive bias syntax. Since the sequents and inference rules considered only involve the atomic formula D, we often replace the annotated formula $x : D$ (resp. $t : D$) with simply its annotation x (resp. t).

Terms. Fix a set NAME $= \{x, y, z, \ldots\}$ of *names* (or *variables*). The set TERM of terms, denoted by $s, t, u, \ldots$, is generated by the following grammar:

$$\text{TERMS} \quad s, t := x \mid t[x \leftarrow yz] \mid t[x \leftarrow \lambda y.s]$$

A term is essentially a list of constructs $[x \leftarrow p]$, called *explicit substitutions* or *named structures*, preceded by a name, which we call the output of the term.

The set $fv(t)$ of *free variables* of a term t is given by: $fv(x) = \{x\}$, $fv(t[x \leftarrow yz]) = (fv(t) \setminus \{x\}) \cup \{y, z\}$ and $fv(t[x \leftarrow \lambda y.s]) = (fv(s) \setminus \{y\}) \cup (fv(t) \setminus \{x\})$. Note that every name x introduced by the construct $[x \leftarrow p]$ is bound. We should consider terms up to α-equivalence and assume that all bound names are distinct from each other and from any free variables.

A *signature* is a finite subset Σ of NAME. We write Σ, x for $\Sigma \cup \{x\}$ and this also implies that $x \notin \Sigma$. We say that t is a Σ-term if $\Sigma \vdash t$ using the *pvar*, *papp*, and *pabs* rules in Fig. 3.

Contexts. We define *contexts* and *left contexts* by the following grammar:

$$\begin{array}{rl} \text{CONTEXTS} & C := \Box \mid C[x \leftarrow yz] \mid C[x \leftarrow \lambda y.s] \mid t[x \leftarrow \lambda y.C] \\ \text{LEFT CONTEXTS} & L := \Box \mid L[x \leftarrow yz] \mid L[x \leftarrow \lambda y.s] \end{array}$$

The *plugging* $C\langle t \rangle$ (resp. $L\langle t \rangle$) of t in the context C (resp. left context L) is obtained from C (resp. L) by replacing the placeholder $\Box$ with t. Every term can be written uniquely as $L\langle x \rangle$ for some left context L and variable x. Note that we allow plugging in a context to capture variables. A *congruence* on terms is an equivalence relation that is closed by context.

Structural Equivalence. Named structures can be seen as intermediate definitions within a term. If two definitions are independent of each other, we should be able to permute them. By defining $fv(yz) = \{y, z\}$ and $fv(\lambda y.s) = fv(s) \setminus \{y\}$, this can be expressed using the equation:

$$t[x_1 \leftarrow p_1][x_2 \leftarrow p_2] \sim_{\texttt{str}} t[x_2 \leftarrow p_2][x_1 \leftarrow p_1] \qquad \text{if } x_1 \notin fv(p_2) \text{ and } x_2 \notin fv(p_1)$$

Definition 4 (Structural equivalence). *We define an equivalence relation* $\equiv_{\texttt{str}}$ *on terms, called the structural equivalence, as the smallest congruence containing* $\sim_{\texttt{str}}$.

Note that the structural equivalence can also be justified by rule permutations.

Substitution. In [27], there is a big-step (atomic) cut-elimination procedure for proofs built using synthetic inference rules. This procedure provides a definition of substitution for terms.

Definition 5 (Substitution on terms, [27]). *Let t, u be terms and x a name such that $x \notin fv(u)$. We define the result of substituting u for x in t, written $t[x/u]$, as follows:*

$$t[x/s[y \leftarrow zw]] = t[x/s][y \leftarrow zw] \qquad t[x/s[y \leftarrow \lambda z.u]] = t[x/s][y \leftarrow \lambda z.u]$$

Here, $t[x/y]$ is obtained from t by renaming x to y. Note that by expressing the term u uniquely as $L\langle y\rangle$, we have $t[x/u] = L\langle t[x/y]\rangle$ by a straightforward induction.

Unfolding and Reduction. Term reduction is often related to cut-elimination in the literature. However, terms considered here correspond to cut-free proofs. A natural question to ask is: How should we evaluate them? Of course, we could *unfold* all the named structures of a term and get its corresponding untyped λ-term.

Definition 6. *The unfolding $\underline{t}$ of a term t is the untyped λ-term defined as follows:*

$$\underline{x} = x \qquad \underline{t[x \leftarrow yz]} = \underline{t}\{x/yz\} \qquad \underline{t[x \leftarrow \lambda y.s]} = \underline{t}\{x/\lambda y.\underline{s}\}$$

where $\{\cdot/\cdot\}$ is the meta-level substitution of untyped λ-terms.

For example, we have $\underline{y[y \leftarrow fz][f \leftarrow \lambda x.x]} = (\lambda x.x)z$. This definition provides a way to translate from the positive bias syntax to the negative bias syntax. Note that the unfolding of a term is not necessarily a β-normal untyped λ-term. For a term t, we could refer to the β-normal form of its unfolding as its *meaning*. However, computing unfoldings of terms might require exponential costs.

TOP-LEVEL RULES

$$C\langle t[z \leftarrow xw]\rangle[x \leftarrow \lambda y.L\langle y'\rangle] \mapsto_{\mathtt{beta}} C\langle L\langle t\{z/y'\}\rangle\{y/w\}\rangle[x \leftarrow \lambda y.L\langle y'\rangle]$$

$$t[x \leftarrow \lambda y.s] \mapsto_{\mathtt{gc}} t \qquad \text{if } x \notin fv(t)$$

REWRITE RULES

$$C\langle t\rangle \to_{\mathtt{beta}} C\langle u\rangle \qquad \text{if } t \mapsto_{\mathtt{beta}} u$$

$$C\langle t\rangle \to_{\mathtt{gc}} C\langle u\rangle \qquad \text{if } t \mapsto_{\mathtt{gc}} u$$

$$t \to_{\mathtt{pos}} u \qquad \text{if } t \to_{\mathtt{beta}} u \text{ or } t \to_{\mathtt{gc}} u$$

Fig. 4. Rewrite rules of the positive λ-calculus.

Therefore, we proceed in a different way here: we look for a reduction procedure that only involves the positive bias syntax and is compatible with the β-reduction in the negative bias syntax (a reduction step should not change the meaning of a term). We now define `beta`-redexes and the `beta`-rule. Consider the following annotated proof:

$$\dfrac{\dfrac{\Pi_1}{\Sigma, y : D \vdash s : D} \qquad \dfrac{\dfrac{\dfrac{\Pi_2}{\Sigma', x : D, z : D \vdash t : D}}{\Sigma', x : D \vdash t[z \leftarrow xw] : D}\,papp}{\vdots \atop \Sigma, x : D \vdash C\langle t[z \leftarrow xw]\rangle : D}}{\Sigma \vdash C\langle t[z \leftarrow xw]\rangle[x \leftarrow \lambda y.s] : D}\,pabs$$

with $w : D \in \Sigma', x : D$ and C a context. In the term annotating the conclusion, the name x is used to introduce an abstraction $\lambda y.s$ and is later applied to an argument w. We call the named application pattern xw here a beta-redex. To eliminate this beta-redex, we shall consider the following proof:

$$\dfrac{\dfrac{\Pi_1'}{\Sigma', x : D \vdash s\{y/w\} : D} \qquad \dfrac{\Pi_2}{\Sigma', x : D, z : D \vdash t : D}}{\Sigma', x : D \vdash Cut(z.t, s\{y/w\}) : D}\,cut$$

where Π_1' is obtained from Π_1 by variable renaming and weakening. By eliminating this cut, we obtain a cut-free proof of the conclusion $\Sigma', x : D \vdash t[z/s\{y/w\}] : D$. This gives the following beta-rule:

$$C\langle t[z \leftarrow xw]\rangle[x \leftarrow \lambda y.s] \mapsto_{\texttt{beta}} C\langle t[z/s\{y/w\}]\rangle[x \leftarrow \lambda y.s]$$

that can also be expressed using left contexts as shown in Fig. 4. We also consider a garbage collection rule for named abstractions. This rule can be justified by the fact that if a formula is never used in a proof, then we can remove the rule that introduces it.

Intuitively, to eliminate a beta-redex, it suffices to make a copy of the abstraction body, make a variable renaming within this copy and a variable renaming in the rest of the term. We illustrate these steps in the following example:

$$\begin{array}{ll}
x_2[x_2 \leftarrow fx_1][x_1 \leftarrow fx_0][f \leftarrow \lambda x.z[z \leftarrow yy][y \leftarrow xx]] & \rightarrow_{\texttt{beta}} \\
x_2[x_2 \leftarrow fz_1][z_1 \leftarrow y_1y_1][y_1 \leftarrow x_0x_0][f \leftarrow \lambda x.z[z \leftarrow yy][y \leftarrow xx]] & \rightarrow_{\texttt{beta}} \\
z_2[z_2 \leftarrow y_2y_2][y_2 \leftarrow z_1z_1][z_1 \leftarrow y_1y_1][y_1 \leftarrow x_0x_0][f \leftarrow \lambda x.z[z \leftarrow yy][y \leftarrow xx]] & \rightarrow_{\texttt{gc}} \\
z_2[z_2 \leftarrow y_2y_2][y_2 \leftarrow z_1z_1][z_1 \leftarrow y_1y_1][y_1 \leftarrow x_0x_0] &
\end{array}$$

Like the VSC, the positive λ-calculus enjoys the confluence property.

Theorem 2. *The positive λ-calculus is confluent.*

The $\rightarrow_{\texttt{pos}}$ is not terminating as shown by the term $w[w \leftarrow xx][x \leftarrow \lambda y.z[z \leftarrow yy]]$.

The following proposition shows that $\rightarrow_{\texttt{pos}}$ does not affect the meaning of a term.

Proposition 1. *Let s and t be terms such that $s \rightarrow_{\texttt{pos}} t$. Then $\underline{s} \rightarrow_\beta^* \underline{t}$.*

It is easy to see that, for every named application $[x \leftarrow yz]$ in a normal term t, y is not a name introducing an abstraction. We have thus the following proposition.

Proposition 2. *If s is a normal term, then $\underline{s}$ is β-normal.*

The converse is however not true as shown by the term $t = z'[z \leftarrow wx][x \leftarrow \lambda y.s]$. $\underline{t} = z'$ is β-normal but t is normal if and only if s is normal.

This rewrite system follows a call-by-value discipline that can be observed in the example above as there is no way to remove the named application $[z \leftarrow wx]$. Also, note that it is a *strong* calculus as we allow reduction under an abstraction.

The positive λ-calculus is closely related to the value substitution calculus (VSC) of [6], presented in Fig. 5, and the linear substitution calculus (LSC) of [4], presented in Fig. 6. In both systems, $\mathtt{m}$ stands for multiplicative and e stands for exponential (these terms come from the literature on linear logic). On one hand, the positive λ-calculus has a call-by-value behavior similar to that of the VSC, and on the other hand, it admits a micro-step exponential rule (for named abstractions) as in the LSC. Another difference between the positive λ-calculus and the VSC is that in the positive λ-calculus, a named abstraction is only duplicated when it is applied to an argument in a named application. This is also connected to an optimization sometimes called *substituting abstractions on-demand.* For example, consider the term

$$t = w[w \leftarrow fx][f \leftarrow \lambda z_0.z_3[z_3 \leftarrow G(z_2)][z_2 \leftarrow G(z_1)][z_1 \leftarrow G(z_0)]][x \leftarrow \lambda y.s].$$

where $G(t) = \lambda w_0.w_3[w_3 \leftarrow w_1 w_2][w_2 \leftarrow gt][w_1 \leftarrow gt]$ with g a fixed name and s a normal term in positive λ-calculus. In the positive λ-calculus, after one $\mathtt{beta}$-step and one $\mathtt{gc}$-step, we obtain

$$z_3'[z_3' \leftarrow G(z_2')][z_2' \leftarrow G(z_1')][z_1' \leftarrow G(x)][x \leftarrow \lambda y.s].$$

which is a normal term in the positive λ-calculus. However, in the VSC, we have

$$\begin{array}{ll}
z_3'[z_3' \leftarrow G(z_2')][z_2' \leftarrow G(z_1')][z_1' \leftarrow G(x)][x \leftarrow \lambda y.s] & \rightarrow_{\mathsf{e}} \\
z_3'[z_3' \leftarrow G(z_2')][z_2' \leftarrow G(z_1')][z_1' \leftarrow G(\lambda y.s)] & \rightarrow_{\mathsf{e}} \\
z_3'[z_3' \leftarrow G(z_2')][z_2' \leftarrow G(G(\lambda y.s))] & \rightarrow_{\mathsf{e}} \\
z_3'[z_3' \leftarrow G(G(G(\lambda y.s)))] & \rightarrow_{\mathsf{e}} \\
G(G(G(\lambda y.s))) &
\end{array}$$

which contains $2^3 = 8$ copies of $\lambda y.s$. From this example, we can see that the positive λ-calculus allows more sharing and avoids some possible exponential blow-ups that can occur in the VSC. Also, note that one has $\underline{s} = \underline{t}$ for $s \rightarrow_{\mathsf{e}} t$. As a result, these e-steps can be seen as redundant since they do not create any redex and can be ignored with the positive λ-calculus.

More formally, we can consider a variant of the VSC that treats substitutions in a linear style. That is, the e-rule is replaced by the following two rules:

$$\begin{array}{rll}
C\langle x\rangle[x \leftarrow L\langle v\rangle] \mapsto_{\mathsf{e}'} L\langle C\langle v\rangle[x \leftarrow v]\rangle & \\
t[x \leftarrow L\langle v\rangle] \mapsto_{\mathsf{gc}'} t & \text{if } x \notin fv(t)
\end{array}$$

Then the beta-rule can be expressed as a sequence of m, e′, and gc′-steps.

$$\begin{array}{rl} C\langle t[z \leftarrow xw]\rangle[x \leftarrow \lambda y.L\langle y'\rangle] & \to_{\mathtt{e'}} \\ C\langle t[z \leftarrow (\lambda y.L\langle y'\rangle)w]\rangle[x \leftarrow \lambda y.L\langle y'\rangle] & \to_{\mathtt{m}} \\ C\langle t[z \leftarrow L\langle y'\rangle[y \leftarrow w]]\rangle[x \leftarrow \lambda y.L\langle y'\rangle] & \to^*_{\mathtt{e'}}\to_{\mathtt{gc'}} \\ C\langle t[z \leftarrow L\langle y'\rangle\{y/w\}]\rangle[x \leftarrow \lambda y.L\langle y'\rangle] & \to^*_{\mathtt{e'}}\to_{\mathtt{gc'}} \\ C\langle L\langle t\{z/y'\}\rangle\{y/w\}\rangle[x \leftarrow \lambda y.L\langle y'\rangle] & \end{array}$$

This shows that the reduction in the positive λ-calculus can be seen as a reduction strategy in the VSC that only applies *useful* substitutions to abstractions (a substitution is useful if it creates new redexes) and thus allows more sharing within a term. Therefore, we can say that the reduction of the positive λ-calculus works better than that of the VSC in terms of sharing on terms of the positive λ-calculus. However, we cannot say that the positive λ-calculus is better in general as the VSC contains more terms.

$$\begin{array}{rl} L\langle \lambda x.t\rangle u & \mapsto_{\mathtt{m}} L\langle t[x \leftarrow u]\rangle \\ t[x \leftarrow L\langle v\rangle] & \mapsto_{\mathtt{e}} L\langle t\{x/v\}\rangle \end{array}$$

Fig. 5. Reduction rules of the value substitution calculus [2]. Here, v is either a variable or an abstraction.

$$\begin{array}{rll} L\langle \lambda x.t\rangle u & \mapsto_{\mathtt{m'}} L\langle t[x \leftarrow u]\rangle & \\ C\langle x\rangle[x \leftarrow u] & \mapsto_{\mathtt{e'}} C\langle u\rangle[x \leftarrow u] & \\ t[x \leftarrow u] & \mapsto_{\mathtt{gc'}} t & \text{if } x \notin fv(t) \end{array}$$

Fig. 6. Reduction rules of the linear substitution calculus [3].

Furthermore, $\equiv_{\mathtt{str}}$ is a bisimulation with respect to $\to_{\mathtt{pos}}$.

Theorem 3. *Let t and u be two terms. If $t \equiv_{\mathtt{str}} u$ and $t \to_{\mathtt{pos}} t'$, then there exists u' such that $u \to_{\mathtt{pos}} u'$ and $t' \equiv_{\mathtt{str}} u'$.*

Proof. It suffices to see that $\sim_{\mathtt{str}}$ never creates or removes redexes.

A few more comments on the positive λ-calculus:

1. The positive bias syntax resembles the A-normal form [19]. A similar representation called *crumbled forms* has also been adapted in [5] to build an abstract machine for strong call-by-value. One issue common to calculi with explicit substitutions is the need for commutation rules to preserve specific syntactic forms. Terms in the positive bias syntax or crumbled forms can, however, be evaluated without using these rules.

2. While the beta-step keeps the sharing structure used to define the argument, there are still some redundancies in the positive λ-calculus. Consider the term $x_2[x_2 \leftarrow fx_1][x_1 \leftarrow fx_0][f \leftarrow \lambda x.z[z \leftarrow xy][y \leftarrow aa]]$. To eliminate the two beta-redexes fx_0 and fx_1, we have to make two copies of the abstraction body. Thus, the structure aa is introduced twice. To solve this redundancy, a possible solution is to *lift* the named structure $[y \leftarrow aa]$ to top-level before evaluation and obtain $x_2[x_2 \leftarrow fx_1][x_1 \leftarrow fx_0][f \leftarrow \lambda x.z[z \leftarrow xy]][y \leftarrow aa]$. This observation is often related to *full laziness* [29], a concept that has been widely studied in call-by-need settings, often using some graphical structures. However, we do not explore this aspect in this paper, and we leave it as a future work.

4 A Graphical Representation for Terms: λ-graphs with bodies

In this section, we introduce a graphical representation for terms, called λ-graphs with bodies, that will be proved to capture the structural equivalence on Σ-terms given in Sect. 3. The definition of λ-graphs with bodies is split into two parts: we first define pre-graphs, and then define λ-graphs with bodies by giving additional structures and properties to deal with abstractions.

Definition 7. *A pre-graph is a directed acyclic graph built with the following three kinds of nodes:*

- *Application: an application node is labeled with @ and has two incoming edges (left and right). An application node is also called an @-node.*
- *Abstraction: an abstraction node is labeled with λ and has one incoming edge. Its only direct predecessor is called the output of the abstraction node. An abstraction node is also called a λ-node.*
- *Variable: a variable node has no incoming edge.*

A direct predecessor of a node is also called a child of the node.

Internal nodes (application and abstraction) of a pre-graph are used to represent intermediate expressions defined using constructs $[x \leftarrow p]$ within a term. We orient edges in such a way that there is an edge from n to m if and only if the definition of m requires the definition of n. In other words, nodes are defined in a *bottom-up* fashion.

In the following, we denote by $\mathcal{N}_\mathcal{G}$ and $\mathcal{E}_\mathcal{G} \subseteq \mathcal{N}_\mathcal{G} \times \mathcal{N}_\mathcal{G}$, respectively, the set of nodes and the set of edges of a graph $\mathcal{G}$.

Definition 8. *An unlabeled λ-graph with bodies is a pre-graph $\mathcal{G}$ together with two functions $bv : \Lambda_\mathcal{G} \rightarrow \mathcal{V}_\mathcal{G}$ and $body : \Lambda_\mathcal{G} \rightarrow 2^{\mathcal{N}_\mathcal{G} \setminus \mathcal{V}_\mathcal{G}}$ where $\Lambda_\mathcal{G}$ is the set of abstraction nodes of $\mathcal{G}$ and $\mathcal{V}_\mathcal{G}$ is the set of variable nodes of $\mathcal{G}$:*

1. *$body(l) \cap body(l') = \emptyset$ for $l \neq l'$.*

2. *The graph* $\mathcal{B}_{\mathcal{G}} = (\Lambda_{\mathcal{G}}, \{(l, l') \mid l, l' \in \Lambda_{\mathcal{G}}, l \in body(l')\})$, *called the scope graph of* $\mathcal{G}$, *is a DAG.*
3. *If a node* n *is* $bv(l)$ *or is in* $body(l)$ *and there is an edge* $(n, m) \in \mathcal{E}_{\mathcal{G}}$, *then we have*
   - $m = l$, *or*
   - $m \in body(l')$ *such that there is a path from* l' *to* l *in* $\mathcal{B}_{\mathcal{G}}$. *Note that this path is unique.*

We call $bv(l)$ *the bound variable node and* $body(l)$ *the body of the abstraction node* l. *A node that does not belong to any body is called body-free and we denote by* $body(\mathcal{G})$ *the set of body-free non-variable nodes in* $\mathcal{G}$. *A free variable node is a variable node that is not a bound variable node and a global node is a body-free node that is not a bound variable node.*

Intuitively, Point 3. of Definition 8 checks that every definition in a term is used in a valid scope: a name introduced in an abstraction can only be used within the abstraction.

Definition 9. *A well-labeled* λ*-graph with bodies, or simply a* λ*-graph with bodies, is an unlabeled* λ*-graph with bodies with a unique label assigned to each free variable node, and with a global node chosen, called the output of the* λ*-graph with bodies. A* Σ*-*λ*-graph with bodies is a* λ*-graph with bodies with a free variable node labeled by each element of a signature* Σ.

In order to visualize the maps $bv(\cdot)$ and $body(\cdot)$, we color the labels of abstraction nodes to distinguish them and color the frame of the nodes in their bodies with the same color. We proceed similarly for bound variables. In particular, a global node has its frame colored in black. Figure 7(a) shows a λ-graph with bodies, while Fig. 7(b) shows an example that breaks Point 3. of Definition 8. In Fig. 7(b), n belongs to the red body, m belongs to the blue body and there is an edge (n, m). m is not the red λ-node and there is no path from the blue λ-node to the red λ-node in the scope graph.

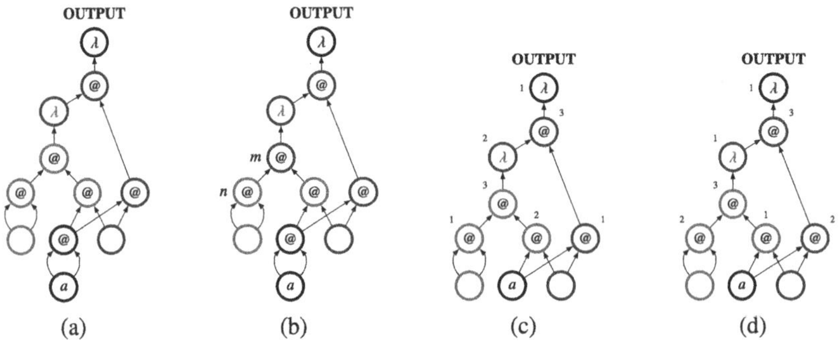

Fig. 7. Various figures.

5 Σ-λ-graphs with bodies and Σ-terms

In this section, we prove that there is a one-to-one correspondence between Σ-λ-graphs with bodies and Σ-terms up to $\equiv_{\mathtt{str}}$. In order to establish such a correspondence, we first establish a one-to-one correspondence between ordered Σ-λ-graphs with bodies and Σ-terms where ordered Σ-λ-graphs with bodies are refinements of Σ-λ-graphs with bodies with some additional structure.

Dependency. Terms are expressed in a linear style. In other words, all the intermediate expressions within a term are defined in some (linear) order. However, graphs do not usually have this kind of structure. In order to establish the correspondence between terms and graphs, we have to give some more structure to our graphical representation. To do that, we first define dependency relations on nodes.

Definition 10. *Let $\mathcal{G}$ be a λ-graph with bodies and l an abstraction node. We define a relation $\prec_l$, called the dependency relation of l, on the set $body(l)$ of nodes as follows:*

- *$n \prec_l m$ if $(n, m) \in \mathcal{E}_{\mathcal{G}}$.*
- *$n \prec_l m$ if $(n, m') \in \mathcal{E}_{\mathcal{G}}$ for some $m' \in body(l')$ with $l' \neq l$, and there is a path from l' to m in $\mathcal{B}_{\mathcal{G}}$.*

Definition 11. *Let $\mathcal{G}$ be a λ-graph with bodies. We define the dependency relation $\prec_{\mathcal{G}}$ of $\mathcal{G}$ on the set $body(\mathcal{G})$ of body-free non-variable nodes of $\mathcal{G}$ as follows:*

- *$n \prec_{\mathcal{G}} m$ if $(n, m) \in \mathcal{E}_{\mathcal{G}}$.*
- *$n \prec_{\mathcal{G}} m$ if $(n, m') \in \mathcal{E}_{\mathcal{G}}$ for some $m' \in body(l)$, and there is a path from l to m in $\mathcal{B}_{\mathcal{G}}$.*

Definition 12. *Let $\mathcal{G}$ be a λ-graph with bodies. We define*

- *the dependency graph of $\mathcal{G}$, as the graph $\mathcal{D}_{\mathcal{G}} = (body(\mathcal{G}), \{(n, m) \mid n \prec_{\mathcal{G}} m\})$, and*
- *for all abstraction node l, the dependency graph of l, as the graph $\mathcal{D}_l = (body(l), \{(n, m) \mid n \prec_l m\})$.*

Proposition 3. *Let $\mathcal{G}$ be a λ-graph with bodies. Then we have:*

- *$\mathcal{D}_{\mathcal{G}}$ is a DAG, and*
- *for all abstraction node l of $\mathcal{G}$, $\mathcal{D}_l$ is a DAG.*

For example, for the λ-graph with bodies $\mathcal{G}$ in Fig. 7(a), the dependency graph of the red (resp. blue) λ-node is the subgraph of $\mathcal{G}$ induced by its body, while the dependency graph $\mathcal{D}_{\mathcal{G}}$ of $\mathcal{G}$ has an edge from the application node to the blue λ-node.

As mentioned previously, our graphical representation should be equipped with some linear orderings on internal nodes. Moreover, these orderings should be compatible with the dependency relations defined above: they should be topological sorts of their corresponding dependency graphs.

Definition 13. *A topological sort of a directed graph $\mathcal{G}$ is a sequence containing each of its vertices such that for every edge (n, m), n appears before m in the sequence.*

Definition 14. *An ordered λ-graph with bodies $\hat{\mathcal{G}}$ is a λ-graph with bodies $\mathcal{G}$ together with a topological sort $T_{\mathcal{G}}$ of the graph $\mathcal{D}_{\mathcal{G}}$ and a topological sort T_l of the graph $\mathcal{D}_l$, for each l.*

Figures 7(c) and 7(d) show two ordered λ-graphs with bodies whose underlying λ-graphs with bodies are the same. As an example, the term corresponding to 7(c) is

$$x[x \leftarrow \lambda b_0.b_3[b_3 \leftarrow b_2 b_1][b_2 \leftarrow \lambda r_0.r_3[r_3 \leftarrow r_1 r_2][r_2 \leftarrow ab_0][r_1 \leftarrow r_0 r_0]][b_1 \leftarrow ab_0]].$$

Before giving a one-to-one correspondence between ordered λ-graphs with bodies and terms, we give a notion of *boxes* that is useful in the following.

Definition 15. *Let $\mathcal{G}$ be a λ-graph with bodies and l an abstraction node. We define the box of l as the union of bodies together with their bound variable nodes* below *l:*

$$box(l) = \bigcup_{l' \rightsquigarrow l \text{ in } \mathcal{B}_{\mathcal{G}}} (body(l') \cup \{bv(l')\})$$

where $l' \rightsquigarrow l$ in $\mathcal{B}_{\mathcal{G}}$ means that there is a path from l' to l in $\mathcal{B}_{\mathcal{G}}$.

In 7(a), the box of the red λ-node contains all the red-framed nodes while the box of the blue λ-node contains all the blue-framed and red-framed nodes.

Intuitively, for a λ-node l of a λ-graph with bodies $\mathcal{G}$, the graph obtained from the subgraph of $\mathcal{G}$ induced by $box(l)$ corresponds to the abstraction it introduces.

Ordered λ-graphs with bodies can actually be defined inductively as terms. We first give the following useful definitions.

Definition 16. *Let Σ be a signature and $x \in \Sigma$. We define $(x)_\Sigma$ as the ordered Σ-λ-graph with bodies that contains a free variable node labeled by each element of Σ and has the one labeled by x as the output.*

Definition 17. *Let Σ and Σ' be signatures, x, y, x_1, x_2 be names such that $\{x_1, x_2\} \subseteq \Sigma$, $x \notin \Sigma$ and $y \notin \Sigma'$, $\hat{\mathcal{G}}$ an ordered (Σ, x)-λ-graph with bodies and $\hat{\mathcal{G}}'$ an ordered (Σ', y)-λ-graph with bodies. Then*

- $\hat{\mathcal{G}}\{\mathbf{nd}\ x \leftarrow x_1@x_2\}$ *is defined as the graph* $\hat{\mathcal{H}}$ *obtained from* $\hat{\mathcal{G}}$ *by replacing the free variable node labeled by* x *with an @-node whose left (resp. right) child is the variable node labeled by* x_1 *(resp.* x_2*). We then extend the topological sort* $T_{\mathcal{G}}$ *by having this application node as the minimal node. It is clear that* $\hat{\mathcal{H}}$ *is also an ordered* Σ*-*λ*-graph with bodies.*
- $\hat{\mathcal{G}}\{\mathbf{nd}\ x \leftarrow \lambda y.\hat{\mathcal{G}}'\}$ *is defined as the graph* $\hat{\mathcal{H}}$ *obtained from by merging* $\mathcal{G}$ *and* $\mathcal{G}'$ *and by replacing the free variable node labeled by* x *with a new abstraction node* l *constructed as follows:*
  - *its only child is the output of* $\mathcal{G}'$*,*
  - *its bound variable is the free variable node labeled by* y *in* $\mathcal{G}'$ *(we erase the label* y*),*
  - *its body contains all the body-free non-variable nodes of* $\mathcal{G}'$*, and*
  - *its topological sort* T_l *is that of* $\hat{\mathcal{G}}'$*.*

  Note that $\mathcal{G}$ *and* $\mathcal{G}'$ *can share some free variable nodes: they are merged so that there is only one free variable node labeled by each element of* $\Sigma \cap \Sigma'$*. In the end, we extend the topological sort* $T_{\mathcal{G}}$ *by having this new abstraction node as the minimal node. It is not difficult to see that* $\hat{\mathcal{H}}$ *is an ordered* $(\Sigma \cup \Sigma')$*-*λ*-graph with bodies.*

Note that we can also use these definitions for λ*-graphs with bodies by forgetting topological sorts.*

Proposition 4. *Let* Σ *be a signature. Then* $\hat{\mathcal{G}}$ *is an ordered* Σ*-*λ*-graph with bodies if and only if* $\Sigma \vdash \hat{\mathcal{G}}$ *where* $\Sigma \vdash \hat{\mathcal{G}}$ *is defined by the following rules.*

$$x \in \Sigma\ \frac{}{\Sigma \vdash (x)_\Sigma}\ var \qquad \{y,z\} \subseteq \Sigma\ \frac{\Sigma, x \vdash \hat{\mathcal{G}}}{\Sigma \vdash \hat{\mathcal{G}}\{\mathbf{nd}\ x \leftarrow y@z\}}\ @ \qquad \frac{\Sigma, y \vdash \hat{\mathcal{G}}' \quad \Sigma, x \vdash \hat{\mathcal{G}}}{\Sigma \vdash \hat{\mathcal{G}}\{\mathbf{nd}\ x \leftarrow \lambda y.\hat{\mathcal{G}}'\}}\ \lambda$$

Proof. $(\Rightarrow)$ Immediate from Definition 16 and Definition 17.

$(\Leftarrow)$ Let $\hat{\mathcal{G}} = (\mathcal{G}, T_{\mathcal{G}}, \{T_l \mid l \in \Lambda_{\mathcal{G}}\})$ be an ordered Σ-λ-graph with bodies. We proceed by induction on the number of non-variable nodes and consider each time the minimal node with respect to $T_{\mathcal{G}}$. Details can be found in the full version.

Note that the rules defining terms (*pvar*, *papp*, *pabs*) have the same structure as those in Proposition 4.

Theorem 4. *Let* Σ *be a signature. Then there is a one-on-one correspondence between ordered* Σ*-*λ*-graphs with bodies and* Σ*-terms.*

Proof. We can define translations $[\![\cdot]\!]_\Sigma$ from Σ-terms to ordered Σ-λ-graphs with bodies and $[\,\cdot\,]_\Sigma$ from ordered Σ-λ-graphs with bodies to Σ-terms by induction on the rules *pvar*, *papp*, *pabs* and those in Proposition 4. For the base cases, let $[\![x]\!]_\Sigma = (x)_\Sigma$ and $[(x)_\Sigma]_\Sigma = x$. We then have $[[\![t]\!]_\Sigma]_\Sigma = t$ and $[\![[\hat{\mathcal{G}}]_\Sigma]\!]_\Sigma = \hat{\mathcal{G}}$ for all Σ-term t and ordered Σ-λ-graph with bodies $\hat{\mathcal{G}}$.

We have established an isomorphism between Σ-terms and ordered Σ-λ-graphs with bodies. In Sect. 3, terms are considered equivalent up to $\equiv_{\texttt{str}}$. How about ordered λ-graphs with bodies? It is natural to consider that ordered λ-graphs with bodies are equivalent if they share the same underlying λ-graph with bodies. The following proposition shows that topological sorts of a DAG can be connected to each other via *swaps*, similar to permutations of named structures for terms.

Proposition 5. *Let $\mathcal{G}$ be a DAG and S a topological sort of $\mathcal{G}$. We call swapping two non-adjacent nodes of $\mathcal{G}$ in a sequence of nodes a valid swap. Then a sequence of nodes can be obtained from S by a sequence of valid swaps if, and only if, it is a topological sort of $\mathcal{G}$.*

The following theorem is a consequence of Theorem 4 and Proposition 5. Details can be found in the full version.

Theorem 5. *We have a one-to-one correspondence between Σ-λ-graphs with bodies and Σ-terms up to $\equiv_{\mathtt{str}}$.*

In the following, we also use $[\![\cdot]\!]_\Sigma$ (resp. $[\,\cdot\,]_\Sigma$) to denote the (bijective) map from the set of Σ-terms to the set of Σ-λ-graphs with bodies.

6 Substitution and Reduction on λ-graphs with bodies

In this section, we show how substitution and reduction can be easily implemented on λ-graphs with bodies.

Substitution. Note that variable renaming, which is required in the case of terms, is not needed as internal nodes do not come with a label.

Definition 18 (Substitution on λ-graphs with bodies). *Let $\mathcal{G}$ be a Σ-λ-graph with bodies and $\mathcal{G}'$ a Σ'-λ-graph with bodies with $x \notin \Sigma'$. We define the substitution of x for $\mathcal{G}'$ in $\mathcal{G}$, written $\mathcal{G}[x/\mathcal{G}']$, as the $((\Sigma \setminus \{x\}) \cup \Sigma')$-$\lambda$-graph with bodies obtained from by merging $\mathcal{G}'$ into $\mathcal{G}$ and, if $x \in \Sigma$ by replacing the free variable node labeled by x with the output node of $\mathcal{G}'$. Note that we have to merge common free variable nodes labeled by elements of $(\Sigma \setminus \{x\}) \cap \Sigma'$ and the output node of $\mathcal{G}[x/\mathcal{G}']$ is that of $\mathcal{G}$.*

In Fig. 8, we present an example for the substitution on λ-graphs with bodies. From this example, we can clearly see that the structure of bodies is kept under substitution.

The substitution on λ-graphs with bodies implements indeed the substitution on terms.

Theorem 6. *Let t be a Σ-term and u a Σ'-term such that $x \notin \Sigma'$. Then $[\![t[x/u]]\!]_{(\Sigma\setminus\{x\})\cup\Sigma'} = [\![t]\!]_\Sigma[x/[\![u]\!]_{\Sigma'}]$.*

Proof. A straightforward induction on u.

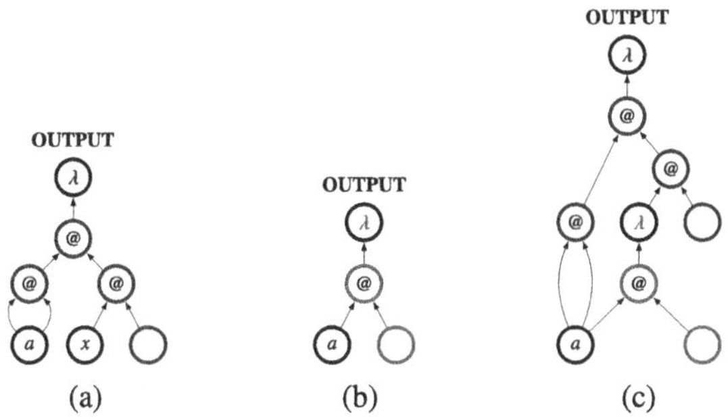

Fig. 8. An example for the substitution on λ-graphs with bodies: (c) is the result of substituting the free variable node x for (b) in (a).

Reduction. We now show how to implement the two rewrite rules on λ-graphs with bodies. We first define *contexts* for λ-graphs with bodies using the following grammar:

$$\mathcal{C} := \Box \mid \mathcal{C}[\mathbf{nd}\ x \leftarrow y@z] \mid \mathcal{C}[\mathbf{nd}\ x \leftarrow \lambda y.\mathcal{G}] \mid \mathcal{G}[\mathbf{nd}\ x \leftarrow \lambda y.\mathcal{C}]$$

The *plugging* $\mathcal{C}\langle\mathcal{G}\rangle$ of a λ-graph with bodies $\mathcal{G}$ in the context $\mathcal{C}$ is defined inductively by:

$$\begin{aligned}\Box\langle\mathcal{G}\rangle &= \mathcal{G}\\ \mathcal{C}[\mathbf{nd}\ x \leftarrow y@z]\langle\mathcal{G}\rangle &= \mathcal{C}\langle\mathcal{G}\rangle\{\mathbf{nd}\ x \leftarrow y@z\}\\ \mathcal{C}[\mathbf{nd}\ x \leftarrow \lambda y.\mathcal{G}']\langle\mathcal{G}\rangle &= \mathcal{C}\langle\mathcal{G}\rangle\{\mathbf{nd}\ x \leftarrow \lambda y.\mathcal{G}'\}\\ \mathcal{G}'[\mathbf{nd}\ x \leftarrow \lambda y.\mathcal{C}]\langle\mathcal{G}\rangle &= \mathcal{G}'\{\mathbf{nd}\ x \leftarrow \lambda y.\mathcal{C}\langle\mathcal{G}\rangle\}.\end{aligned}$$

The `gc`-rule can be defined by erasing an abstraction node with no parent and its box. A `beta`-redex is simply an @-node that has a λ-node as its left child. To eliminate it, it suffices to duplicate the *box* of the λ-node, replace the @-node with the copy of the output node of λ-node, and then replace the bound variable in this copy with the argument, i.e., the right child of the @-node. One should be careful about the structure of bodies: in this copy, all the nodes that were in the body of the λ-node should be moved to the same body as the argument or to the corresponding body if the argument is a bound variable. Figure 9 shows a `beta`-reduction step on λ-graphs with bodies. We denote by $\rightarrow_{\mathtt{G}}$ the contextual closure of these two steps (`gc` and `beta`).

The translation $[\![\cdot]\!]_\Sigma$ is a strong bisimulation between the positive λ-calculus and λ-graphs with bodies with $\rightarrow_{\mathtt{G}}$.

Theorem 7. *Let s and t be two Σ-terms. Then $s \rightarrow_{\mathtt{pos}} t$ if and only if $[\![s]\!]_\Sigma \rightarrow_{\mathtt{G}} [\![t]\!]_\Sigma$.*

Proof. This is a consequence of Theorem 6.

In general, strong bisimulations preserve confluence quotient by the translation. Here, the quotient induced by the translation $[\![\cdot]\!]_\Sigma$ on Σ-λ-graphs with

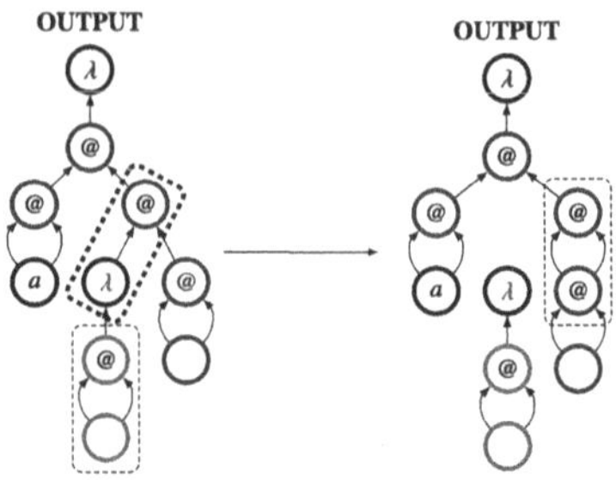

Fig. 9. An example of beta-reduction on λ-graphs with bodies. The thick dashed box is a beta-redex and the two thin dashed boxes in the λ-graphs with bodies correspond to the box of the red λ-node and its copy, respectively. (Color figure online)

bodies is the identity, so the confluence coincides with the confluence modulo quotient by $[\![\cdot]\!]_\Sigma$. Hence, we have the confluence of $\rightarrow_{\mathsf{G}}$ from that of $\rightarrow_{\mathsf{pos}}$.

Theorem 8. $\rightarrow_{\mathsf{G}}$ *is confluent.*

Proof. Straightforward from Theorem 2, Theorem 3 and Theorem 7.

Relations with Other Graphical Representations. In [2], Accattoli revealed a close relationship between the proof nets and the value substitution calculus. As mentioned earlier, the VSC is equipped with a small-step but not a micro-step e-rule. By replacing the e-rule by its micro-step variant, one is actually able to simulate the positive λ-calculus in the VSC. This is also true on the graphical side. However, we have a slightly different treatment of free variables here: free variable nodes are considered shared between all the bodies, so no free variable node is explicitly included in any body. This approach is suggested by the rules *papp* and *pabs* where the left hand side of the conclusion is entirely included in those of the premises (this is actually a feature of *LJF*, where weakenings are delayed and only allowed in initial rules I_l and I_r). Due to this choice, the content of a box is no longer a λ-graph with bodies (one has to include all the free variable nodes), which makes induction arguments a bit more complicated. However, it provides us a clear way to *sequentialize* λ-graphs with bodies.

In [14], λ-graphs are used to study the sharing equality. As the name suggests, λ-graphs with bodies can be (almost) seen as an extension of λ-graphs with bodies. They only differ in the following points:

- λ-graphs are not pointed: there is no unique output assigned to a λ-graph as their goal is to study if two terms have the same encoding *under the same context*.
- There is no *useless* node under an abstraction in λ-graphs: an abstraction node has a unique child (output). Without the notion of bodies, there is no way to define nodes that are under an abstraction but not used to define the output. This is not a drawback as these useless nodes do not affect the unfoldings of terms.

7 Generalization

In this section, we explain briefly how this graphical representation can be generalized using *LJF* and different polarized theories.

In Definition 3, *LJ* can be extended by any polarized theory of order one or two. In our study of untyped λ-terms, we use exactly one formula of order one $(D \supset D \supset D)$ and one formula of order two $((D \supset D) \supset D)$. Our graphical representation can be generalized to any *positively polarized* theory of order one or two in the following way.

Each node comes with a *type* which is an atomic formula. A formula of order one or two can be written as $B_1 \supset \cdots \supset B_n \supset A$ with $n \geq 1$, B_i of order at most one and A atomic. This formula corresponds to a node *of type* A that has n incoming edges, each of which corresponds to one B_i. For $1 \leq i \leq n$, if B_i is atomic, then it corresponds to simply a node of type B_i, and if B_i is of order one, then it comes with a notion of *body*.

A similar notion of reduction can also be defined: a redex is simply a group of nodes that follow a certain pattern, and reduction rules can be defined using the children (or boxes) of these nodes.

8 Conclusion

We propose the positive λ-calculus based on the encoding of untyped λ-terms defined using the positive bias assignment in [27]. This calculus features a call-by-value rewrite system and is closely related to the value substitution calculus.

We introduce a graphical representation for terms of the positive λ-calculus, called λ-graphs with bodies and show how operations such as substitution and reduction can be implemented on this structure.

Using the focused proof system *LJF* as a framework to build term structures makes it possible to generalize the results in this paper to other kinds of term calculi.

Future Work. We plan to explore at least the following directions in the future:

- Fully lazy sharing: As mentioned, the reduction procedure of the positive λ-calculus is not perfect since all the named structures within an abstraction are duplicated. We hope to explore the possibilities of allowing more sharing along the reduction and works on full laziness can surely provide more insights.
- Mixing positive and negative term structures: An important feature of *LJF* is *polarization*. This paper focuses on the case that atoms are all given the positive polarity. What if we consider atoms of different polarities? Will this allow expressing more term structures while having a good notion of sharing? These are the questions we hope to answer in our follow-up study.
- Connections with the VSC: The VSC has been applied to study the call-by-value λ-calculus and various topics related to it: abstract machines, sharing, etc. Also, a correspondence between VSC-terms and proof nets has been established. In this paper, we show how these two calculi are similar but different at the same time. It seems natural and interesting to look for more

connections between these two calculi and to see if the positive λ-calculus can provide a different perspective on the topics mentioned above.

Acknowledgement. I would like to thank Dale Miller and Beniamino Accattoli for their valuable discussions and suggestions. I am also grateful to the anonymous reviewers for their helpful comments.

References

1. Abadi, M., Cardelli, L., Curien, P.L., Lévy, J.J.: Explicit substitutions. J. Funct. Program. **1**(4), 375–416 (1991)
2. Accattoli, B.: Proof nets and the call-by-value λ-calculus. J. Theor. Comput. Sci. (TCS) (2015). https://doi.org/10.1016/j.tcs.2015.08.006
3. Accattoli, B.: Proof nets and the linear substitution calculus. In: Fischer, B., Uustalu, T. (eds.) ICTAC 2018. LNCS, vol. 11187, pp. 37–61. Springer, Cham (2018). https://doi.org/10.1007/978-3-030-02508-3_3
4. Accattoli, B., Bonelli, E., Kesner, D., Lombardi, C.: A nonstandard standardization theorem. In: Proceedings of the 41st ACM SIGPLAN-SIGACT Symposium on Principles of Programming Languages, pp. 659–670 (2014)
5. Accattoli, B., Condoluci, A., Coen, C.S.: Strong call-by-value is reasonable, implosively. In: 2021 36th Annual ACM/IEEE Symposium on Logic in Computer Science (LICS), pp. 1–14. IEEE (2021)
6. Accattoli, B., Paolini, L.: Call-by-value solvability, revisited. In: Schrijvers, T., Thiemann, P. (eds.) FLOPS 2012. LNCS, vol. 7294, pp. 4–16. Springer, Heidelberg (2012). https://doi.org/10.1007/978-3-642-29822-6_4
7. Andreoli, J.M.: Logic programming with focusing proofs in linear logic. J. Logic Comput. **2**(3), 297–347 (1992). https://doi.org/10.1093/logcom/2.3.297
8. Andreoli, J.M.: Focussing and proof construction. Ann. Pure Appl. Logic **107**(1), 131–163 (2001)
9. Balabonski, T.: A unified approach to fully lazy sharing. In: Proceedings of the 39th Annual ACM SIGPLAN-SIGACT Symposium on Principles of Programming Languages, pp. 469–480 (2012)
10. Brock-Nannestad, T., Guenot, N., Gustafsson, D.: Computation in focused intuitionistic logic. In: Falaschi, M., Albert, E. (eds.) Proceedings of the 17th International Symposium on Principles and Practice of Declarative Programming, Siena, Italy, 14–16 July 2015. pp. 43–54. ACM (2015). https://doi.org/10.1145/2790449.2790528
11. Chaudhuri, K.: Focusing strategies in the sequent calculus of synthetic connectives. In: Cervesato, I., Veith, H., Voronkov, A. (eds.) LPAR 2008. LNCS (LNAI), vol. 5330, pp. 467–481. Springer, Heidelberg (2008). https://doi.org/10.1007/978-3-540-89439-1_33
12. Chaudhuri, K., Hetzl, S., Miller, D.: A multi-focused proof system isomorphic to expansion proofs. J. Log. Comput. **26**(2), 577–603 (2016)
13. Chaudhuri, K., Miller, D., Saurin, A.: Canonical sequent proofs via multi-focusing. In: Ausiello, G., Karhumäki, J., Mauri, G., Ong, L. (eds.) TCS 2008. IIFIP, vol. 273, pp. 383–396. Springer, Boston, MA (2008). https://doi.org/10.1007/978-0-387-09680-3_26
14. Condoluci, A., Accattoli, B., Coen, C.S.: Sharing equality is linear. In: Proceedings of the 21st International Symposium on Principles and Practice of Declarative Programming, pp. 1–14 (2019). https://doi.org/10.1145/3354166.3354174

15. Danos, V., Joinet, J.B., Schellinx, H.: LKT and LKQ: sequent calculi for second order logic based upon dual linear decompositions of classical implication. In: Girard, J.Y., Lafont, Y., Regnier, L. (eds.) Advances in Linear Logic, pp. 211–224. No. 222 in London Mathematical Society Lecture Note Series, Cambridge University Press (1995). https://doi.org/10.1017/CBO9780511629150
16. Delande, O., Miller, D.: A neutral approach to proof and refutation in MALL. In: Pfenning, F. (ed.) 23th Symposium on Logic in Computer Science, pp. 498–508. IEEE Computer Society Press (2008). https://doi.org/10.1016/j.apal.2009.07.017
17. Di Cosmo, R., Kesner, D.: Strong normalization of explicit substitutions via cut elimination in proof nets. In: Proceedings of Twelfth Annual IEEE Symposium on Logic in Computer Science, pp. 35–46 (1997). https://doi.org/10.1109/LICS.1997.614927
18. Dyckhoff, R., Lengrand, S.: LJQ: a strongly focused calculus for intuitionistic logic. In: Beckmann, A., Berger, U., Löwe, B., Tucker, J.V. (eds.) CiE 2006. LNCS, vol. 3988, pp. 173–185. Springer, Heidelberg (2006). https://doi.org/10.1007/11780342_19
19. Flanagan, C., Sabry, A., Duba, B.F., Felleisen, M.: The essence of compiling with continuations. In: Proceedings of the ACM SIGPLAN 1993 Conference on Programming Language Design and Implementation, pp. 237–247 (1993)
20. Girard, J.Y.: Linear logic. Theoret. Comput. Sci. **50**(1), 1–102 (1987). https://doi.org/10.1016/0304-3975(87)90045-4
21. Herbelin, H.: A λ-calculus structure isomorphic to Gentzen-style sequent calculus structure. In: Pacholski, L., Tiuryn, J. (eds.) CSL 1994. LNCS, vol. 933, pp. 61–75. Springer, Heidelberg (1995). https://doi.org/10.1007/BFb0022247
22. Hughes, D.J.D.: Proofs without syntax. Ann. Math. **143**(3), 1065–1076 (2006)
23. Liang, C., Miller, D.: Focusing and polarization in linear, intuitionistic, and classical logics. Theor. Comput. Sci. **410**(46), 4747–4768 (2009). https://doi.org/10.1016/j.tcs.2009.07.041, abstract Interpretation and Logic Programming: In honor of professor Giorgio Levi
24. Marin, S., Miller, D., Pimentel, E., Volpe, M.: From axioms to synthetic inference rules via focusing. Ann. Pure Appl. Logic **173**(5), 1–32 (2022). https://doi.org/10.1016/j.apal.2022.103091
25. Miller, D.: A compact representation of proofs. Stud. Logica. **46**(4), 347–370 (1987). https://doi.org/10.1007/BF00370646
26. Miller, D., Saurin, A.: From proofs to focused proofs: a modular proof of focalization in linear logic. In: Duparc, J., Henzinger, T.A. (eds.) CSL 2007. LNCS, vol. 4646, pp. 405–419. Springer, Heidelberg (2007). https://doi.org/10.1007/978-3-540-74915-8_31
27. Miller, D., Wu, J.H.: A positive perspective on term representations. In: Klin, B., Pimentel, E. (eds.) 31st EACSL Annual Conference on Computer Science Logic (CSL 2023). Leibniz International Proceedings in Informatics (LIPIcs), vol. 252, pp. 3:1–3:21. Schloss Dagstuhl-Leibniz-Zentrum fuer Informatik, Dagstuhl, Germany (2023). https://doi.org/10.4230/LIPIcs.CSL.2023.3
28. Pimentel, E., Nigam, V., Neto, J.: Multi-focused proofs with different polarity assignments. In: Benevides, M., Thiemann, R. (eds.) Proceedings of the Tenth Workshop on Logical and Semantic Frameworks, with Applications (LSFA 2015), ENTCS, vol. 323, pp. 163–179, July 2016. https://doi.org/10.1016/j.entcs.2016.06.011
29. Wadsworth, C.P.: Semantics and Pragmatics of the Lambda Calculus. Ph.D. thesis, University of Oxford (1971)

Typed Non-determinism in Functional and Concurrent Calculi

Bas van den Heuvel[1], Joseph W. N. Paulus[1,2], Daniele Nantes-Sobrinho[3,4], and Jorge A. Pérez[1(✉)]

[1] University of Groningen, Groningen, The Netherlands
j.a.perez@rug.nl
[2] University of Oxford, Oxford, UK
[3] University of Brasília, Brasília, Brazil
[4] Imperial College London, London, UK

Abstract. We study functional and concurrent calculi with non-determinism, along with type systems to control resources based on linearity. The interplay between non-determinism and linearity is delicate: careless handling of branches can discard resources meant to be used exactly once. Here we go beyond prior work by considering non-determinism in its standard sense: once a branch is selected, the rest are discarded. Our technical contributions are three-fold. First, we introduce a π-calculus with non-deterministic choice, governed by session types. Second, we introduce a resource λ-calculus, governed by intersection types, in which non-determinism concerns fetching of resources from bags. Finally, we connect our two typed non-deterministic calculi via a correct translation.

1 Introduction

In this paper, we present new formulations of typed programming calculi with *non-determinism.* A classical ingredient of models of computation, non-determinism brings flexibility and generality in specifications. In process calculi such as CCS and the π-calculus, one source of non-determinism is choice, which is typically *non-confluent*: that is, given $P + Q$, we have either $P + Q \longrightarrow P$ or $P + Q \longrightarrow Q$. Thus, committing to a branch entails discarding the rest.

We study non-determinism as a way of increasing the expressivity of typed calculi in which resource control is based on *linearity.* The interplay between non-determinism and linearity is delicate: a careless discarding of branches can jeopardize resources meant to be used exactly once. On the concurrent side, we consider the π-calculus, the paradigmatic model of concurrency [27]. We focus on π-calculi with *session types* [14,15], in which linear logic principles ensure communication correctness: here the resources are names that perform session protocols; they can be *unrestricted* (used multiple times) and *linear* (used exactly once). To properly control resources, non-confluent non-determinism is confined to unrestricted names; linear names can only perform deterministic choices.

In this context, considering *confluent* forms of non-determinism can be appealing. Intuitively, such formulations allow all branches to proceed independently: given $P_1 \longrightarrow Q_1$ and $P_2 \longrightarrow Q_2$, then $P_1 + P_2 \longrightarrow Q_1 + P_2$ and

C.-K. Hur (Ed.): APLAS 2023, LNCS 14405, pp. 112–132, 2023.
https://doi.org/10.1007/978-981-99-8311-7_6

$P_1 + P_2 \longrightarrow P_1 + Q_2$. Because confluent non-determinism does not discard branches, it is compatible with a resource-conscious view of computation.

Confluent non-determinism has been studied mostly in the functional setting; it is present, e.g., in Pagani and Ronchi della Rocca's resource λ-calculus [21] and in Ehrhard and Regnier's differential λ-calculus [10]. In [21], non-determinism resides in the application of a term M to a *bag* of available resources C; a β-reduction applies M to a resource *non-deterministically fetched* from C. Confluent non-deterministic choice is also present in the session-typed π-calculus by Caires and Pérez [5], where it expresses a choice between different implementations of the same session protocols, which are all *non-deterministically available*—they may be available but may also *fail*. In their work, a Curry-Howard correspondence between linear logic and session types ('*propositions-as-sessions*' [6,31]) ensures confluence, protocol fidelity, and deadlock-freedom. Paulus et al. [22] relate functional and concurrent calculi with confluent non-determinism: they give a translation of a resource λ-calculus into the session π-calculus from [5], in the style of Milner's '*functions-as-processes*' [17].

Although results involving confluent non-determinism are most significant, usual (non-confluent) non-determinism remains of undiscussed convenience in formal modeling; consider, e.g., specifications of distributed protocols [2,20] in which commitment is essential. Indeed, non-confluent non-deterministic choice is commonplace in verification frameworks such as mCRL2 [12]. It is also relevant in functional calculi; a well-known framework is De'Liguoro and Piperno's (untyped) non-deterministic λ-calculus [8] (see also [9] and references therein).

To further illustrate the difference between confluent and non-confluent non-determinism, we consider an example adapted from [5]: a movie server that offers a choice between buying a movie or watching its trailer. In $\mathsf{s}\pi^+$, the typed π-calculus that we present in this paper, this server can be specified as follows:

$$\mathsf{Server}_s = s.\mathtt{case}\begin{Bmatrix} \mathsf{buy} : s(\mathit{title}); s(\mathit{paym}); \overline{s}[\mathtt{movie}]; \overline{s}[\,] \ , & -\mathsf{Server}_s^{\mathsf{buy}} \\ \mathsf{peek} : s(\mathit{title}); \overline{s}[\mathtt{trailer}]; \overline{s}[\,] & -\mathsf{Server}_s^{\mathsf{peek}} \end{Bmatrix}$$

where $s(-)$ and $\overline{s}[-]$ denote input and output prefixes on a name/channel s, respectively, and '`movie`' and '`trailer`' denote references to primitive data. Also, the free names of a process are denoted with subscripts. Process Server_s offers a choice on name s ($s.\mathtt{case}\{-\}$) between labels buy and peek. If buy is received, process $\mathsf{Server}_s^{\mathsf{buy}}$ is launched: it receives the movie's title and a payment method, sends the movie, and closes the session on s ($\overline{s}[\,]$). If peek is received, it proceeds as $\mathsf{Server}_s^{\mathsf{peek}}$: the server receives the title, sends the trailer, and closes the session.

Using the non-deterministic choice operator of $\mathsf{s}\pi^+$, denoted '$+\!\!\!\!+$', we can specify a process for a client Alice who is interested in the movie 'Jaws' but is undecided about buying the film or just watching its trailer for free:

$$\begin{aligned} \mathsf{Alice}_s := \quad & \overline{s}.\mathsf{buy};\ \overline{s}[\mathtt{Jaws}]; \overline{s}[\mathtt{mcard}]; s(\mathit{movie}); s(); \mathbf{0} \ -\mathsf{Alice}_s^{\mathsf{buy}} \\ +\!\!\!\!+\ & \overline{s}.\mathsf{peek};\ \overline{s}[\mathtt{Jaws}]; s(\mathit{trailer}); s(); \mathbf{0} \qquad\quad -\mathsf{Alice}_s^{\mathsf{peek}} \end{aligned}$$

If Alice_s selects the label buy ($\overline{s}.\mathsf{buy}$), process $\mathsf{Alice}_s^{\mathsf{buy}}$ is launched: it sends title and payment method, receives the movie, waits for the session to close ($s()$), and then terminates ($\mathbf{0}$). If Alice_s selects peek, process $\mathsf{Alice}_s^{\mathsf{peek}}$ is launched: it sends a title, receives the trailer, waits for the session to close, and terminates. Then, process $\mathsf{Sys} := (\boldsymbol{\nu} s)(\mathsf{Server}_s \mid \mathsf{Alice}_s)$ denotes the composition of client and server, connected along s (using $(\boldsymbol{\nu} s)$). Our semantics for $\mathsf{s}\pi^+$, denoted $\rightsquigarrow$, enforces non-confluent non-determinism, as Sys can reduce to separate processes, as expected:

$$\mathsf{Sys} \rightsquigarrow (\boldsymbol{\nu} s)(\mathsf{Server}_s^{\mathsf{buy}} \mid \mathsf{Alice}_s^{\mathsf{buy}}) \qquad \text{and} \qquad \mathsf{Sys} \rightsquigarrow (\boldsymbol{\nu} s)(\mathsf{Server}_s^{\mathsf{peek}} \mid \mathsf{Alice}_s^{\mathsf{peek}})$$

In contrast, the confluent non-deterministic choice from [5], denoted '$\oplus$', behaves differently: in their confluent semantics, Sys reduces to a *single* process including *both alternatives*, i.e., $\mathsf{Sys} \longrightarrow (\boldsymbol{\nu} s)(\mathsf{Server}_s^{\mathsf{buy}} \mid \mathsf{Alice}_s^{\mathsf{buy}}) \oplus (\boldsymbol{\nu} s)(\mathsf{Server}_s^{\mathsf{peek}} \mid \mathsf{Alice}_s^{\mathsf{peek}})$.

Contributions. We study new concurrent and functional calculi with usual (non-confluent) forms of non-determinism. Framed in the typed (resource-conscious) setting, we strive for definitions that do not exert a too drastic discarding of branches (as in the non-confluent case) but also that do not exhibit a lack of commitment (as in the confluent case). Concretely, we present:

(Section 2) $\mathsf{s}\pi^+$, a variant of the session-typed π-calculus in [5], now with non-confluent non-deterministic choice. Its semantics adapts to the typed setting the usual semantics of non-deterministic choice in the untyped π-calculus [27]. Well-typed processes enjoy type preservation and deadlock-freedom (Theorems 1 and 2).

(Section 3) $\lambda_{\mathtt{C}}^{\ell}$, a resource λ-calculus with non-determinism, enhanced with constructs for expressing resource usage and failure. Its non-idempotent intersection type system provides a quantitative measure of the need/usage of resources. Well-typed terms enjoy subject reduction and subject expansion (Theorems 3 and 4).

(Section 4) A typed translation of $\lambda_{\mathtt{C}}^{\ell}$ into $\mathsf{s}\pi^+$, which provides further validation for our non-deterministic calculi, and casts them in the context of 'functions-as-processes'. We prove that our translation is *correct*, i.e., it preserves types and satisfies tight operational correspondences (Theorems 5 and 6).

Moreover, Sect. 5 closes by discussing related works. Omitted technical material can be found in the full version of the paper [13].

2 A Typed π-calculus with Non-deterministic Choice

We introduce $\mathsf{s}\pi^+$, a session-typed π-calculus with non-deterministic choice. Following [5], session types express protocols to be executed along channels. These protocols can be *non-deterministic*: sessions may succeed but also fail. The novelty in $\mathsf{s}\pi^+$ is the non-deterministic choice operator '$P \mathbin{+\!\!\!+} Q$', whose *lazily committing semantics* is compatible with linearity. We prove that well-typed processes satisfy two key properties: *type preservation* and *deadlock-freedom.*

$P, Q ::= \mathbf{0}$	inaction	$\mid [x \leftrightarrow y]$	forwarder
$\mid (\boldsymbol{\nu} x)(P \mid Q)$	connect	$\mid P \mathbin{+\!\!\!\!\parallel} Q$	non-determinism
$\mid \overline{x}[y]; (P \mid Q)$	output	$\mid x(y); P$	input
$\mid \overline{x}.\ell; P$	select	$\mid x.\mathtt{case}\{i : P\}_{i \in I}$	branch
$\mid \overline{x}[]$	close	$\mid x(); P$	wait
$\mid x.\mathtt{some}_{w_1,\ldots,w_n}; P$	expect	$\mid \overline{x}.\mathtt{some}; P$	available
$\mid P \mid Q$	parallel	$\mid \overline{x}.\mathtt{none}$	unavailable

$$P \equiv P' \; [P \equiv_\alpha P'] \qquad [x \leftrightarrow y] \equiv [y \leftrightarrow x] \qquad P \mid \mathbf{0} \equiv P$$

$$(P \mid Q) \mid R \equiv P \mid (Q \mid R) \qquad P \mid Q \equiv Q \mid P \qquad (\boldsymbol{\nu} x)(P \mid Q) \equiv (\boldsymbol{\nu} x)(Q \mid P)$$

$$P \mathbin{+\!\!\!\!\parallel} P \equiv P \qquad P \mathbin{+\!\!\!\!\parallel} Q \equiv Q \mathbin{+\!\!\!\!\parallel} P \qquad (P \mathbin{+\!\!\!\!\parallel} Q) \mathbin{+\!\!\!\!\parallel} R \equiv P \mathbin{+\!\!\!\!\parallel} (Q \mathbin{+\!\!\!\!\parallel} R)$$

$$(\boldsymbol{\nu} x)((P \mid Q) \mid R) \equiv (\boldsymbol{\nu} x)(P \mid R) \mid Q \qquad [x \notin \mathit{fn}(Q)]$$

$$(\boldsymbol{\nu} x)((\boldsymbol{\nu} y)(P \mid Q) \mid R) \equiv (\boldsymbol{\nu} y)((\boldsymbol{\nu} x)(P \mid R) \mid Q) \qquad [x \notin \mathit{fn}(Q), y \notin \mathit{fn}(R)]$$

Fig. 1. $\mathsf{s}\pi^+$: syntax (top) and structural congruence (bottom).

2.1 Syntax and Semantics

We use $P, Q, \ldots$ to denote processes, and $x, y, z, \ldots$ to denote *names* representing channels. Figure 1 (top) gives the syntax of processes. $P\{y/z\}$ denotes the capture-avoiding substitution of y for z in P. Process $\mathbf{0}$ denotes inaction, and $[x \leftrightarrow y]$ is a forwarder: a bidirectional link between x and y. Parallel composition appears in two forms: while the process $P \mid Q$ denotes communication-free concurrency, process $(\boldsymbol{\nu} x)(P \mid Q)$ uses restriction $(\boldsymbol{\nu} x)$ to express that P and Q implement complementary behaviors on x and do not share any other names.

Process $P \mathbin{+\!\!\!\!\parallel} Q$ denotes the non-deterministic choice between P and Q: intuitively, if one choice can perform a synchronization, the other option may be discarded if it cannot. Since $\mathbin{+\!\!\!\!\parallel}$ is associative, we often omit parentheses. Also, we write $\mathop{+\!\!\!\!\parallel}_{i \in I} P_i$ for the non-deterministic choice between each P_i for $i \in I$.

Our output construct integrates parallel composition and restriction: process $\overline{x}[y]; (P|Q)$ sends a fresh name y along x and then continues as $P|Q$. The type system will ensure that behaviors on y and x are implemented by P and Q, respectively, which do not share any names—this separation defines communication-free concurrency and is key to ensuring deadlock-freedom. The input process $x(y); P$ receives a name z along x and continues as $P\{z/y\}$, which does not require the separation present in the output case. Process $x.\mathtt{case}\{i : P_i\}_{i \in I}$ denotes a branch with labeled choices indexed by the finite set I: it awaits a choice on x with continuation P_j for each $j \in I$. The process $\overline{x}.\ell; P$ selects on x the choice labeled ℓ before continuing as P. Processes $\overline{x}[]$ and $x(); P$ are dual actions for closing the session on x. We omit replicated servers $!x(y); P$ and corresponding client requests $?\overline{x}[y]; P$, but they can be easily added (cf. [13]).

The remaining constructs define non-deterministic sessions which may provide a protocol or fail, following [5]. Process $\overline{x}.\texttt{some}; P$ confirms the availability of a session on x and continues as P. Process $\overline{x}.\texttt{none}$ signals the failure to provide the session on x. Process $x.\texttt{some}_{w_1,\ldots,w_n}; P$ specifies a dependency on a non-deterministic session on x (names $w_1, \ldots, w_n$ implement sessions in P). This process can either (i) synchronize with a '$\overline{x}.\texttt{some}$' and continue as P, or (ii) synchronize with a '$\overline{x}.\texttt{none}$', discard P, and propagate the failure to $w_1, \ldots, w_n$. To reduce eye strain, in writing $x.\texttt{some}$ we freely combine names and sets of names. This way, e.g., we write $x.\texttt{some}_{y,fn(P),fn(Q)}$ rather than $x.\texttt{some}_{\{y\}\cup fn(P)\cup fn(Q)}$.

Name y is bound in $(\boldsymbol{\nu} y)(P \mid Q)$, $\overline{x}[y]; (P \mid Q)$, and $x(y); P$. The set $fn(P)$ includes the names in P that are not bound. We adopt Barendregt's convention.

Structural Congruence. Reduction defines the steps that a process performs on its own. It relies on *structural congruence* ($\equiv$), the least congruence relation on processes induced by the rules in Fig. 1 (bottom). Like the syntax of processes, the definition of $\equiv$ is aligned with the type system (defined next), such that $\equiv$ preserves typing (subject congruence, cf. Theorem 1). Differently from [5], we do not allow distributing non-deterministic choice over parallel and restriction. As shown in [13], the position of a non-deterministic choice in a process determines how it may commit, so changing its position affects commitment.

Reduction: Intuitions and Prerequisites. Barring non-deterministic choice, our reduction rules arise as directed interpretations of proof transformations in the underlying linear logic. We follow Caires and Pfenning [6] and Wadler [31] in interpreting cut-elimination in linear logic as synchronization in $\mathsf{s}\pi^+$.

Before delving into our reduction rules (Fig. 2), it may be helpful to consider the usual reduction axiom for the (untyped) π-calculus (e.g., [19,27]):

$$(\overline{x}[z]; P_1 + M_1) \mid (x(y); P_2 + M_2) \longrightarrow P_1 \mid P_2\{z/y\} \tag{1}$$

This axiom captures the interaction of two (binary) choices: it integrates the commitment of choice in synchronization; after the reduction step, the two branches not involved in the synchronization, M_1 and M_2, are discarded. Our semantics of $\mathsf{s}\pi^+$ is defined similarly: when a prefix within a branch of a choice synchronizes with its dual, that branch reduces and the entire process commits to it.

The key question at this point is: when and to which branches should we commit? In (1), a communication commits to a single branch. For $\mathsf{s}\pi^+$, we define a *lazy semantics* that minimizes commitment as much as possible.

The intuitive idea is that multiple branches of a choice may contain the same prefix, and so all these branches represent possibilities for synchronization ("possible branches"). Other branches with different prefixes denote different possibilities ("impossible branches"). When one synchronization is chosen, the possible branches are maintained while the impossible ones are discarded.

Example 1. To distinguish possible and impossible branches, consider:

$$P := (\boldsymbol{\nu} s)\big(s.\mathsf{case}\{\mathsf{buy} : \ldots, \mathsf{peek} : \ldots\} \mid (\overline{s}.\mathsf{buy}; \ldots \mathbin{+\!\!\!+} \overline{s}.\mathsf{buy}; \ldots \mathbin{+\!\!\!+} \overline{s}.\mathsf{peek}; \ldots)\big)$$

The branch construct (case) provides the context for the non-deterministic choice. When the case synchronizes on the 'buy' label, the two branches prefixed by '$\overline{s}$.buy' are possible, whereas the branch prefixed by '$\overline{s}$.peek' becomes impossible, and can be discarded. The converse occurs when the 'peek' label is selected. $\triangledown$

To formalize these intuitions, our reduction semantics (Fig. 2) relies on some auxiliary definitions. First, we define contexts.

Definition 1. *We define* ND-contexts $(\mathtt{N}, \mathtt{M})$ *as follows:*

$$\mathtt{N}, \mathtt{M} ::= [\cdot] \mid \mathtt{N} \mid P \mid (\boldsymbol{\nu} x)(\mathtt{N} \mid P) \mid \mathtt{N} \mathbin{+\!\!\!\!+} P$$

The process obtained by replacing $[\cdot]$ *in* $\mathtt{N}$ *with* P *is denoted* $\mathtt{N}[P]$. *We refer to ND-contexts that do not use the clause '*$\mathtt{N} \mathbin{+\!\!\!\!+} P$*' as* D-contexts, *denoted* $\mathtt{C}, \mathtt{D}$.

Using D-contexts, we can express that, e.g., $\mathop{+\!\!\!\!+}_{i\in I} \mathtt{C}_\mathtt{i}[\overline{x}[]]$ and $\mathop{+\!\!\!\!+}_{j\in J} \mathtt{D}_\mathtt{j}[x(); Q_j]$ should match. To account for reductions with impossible branches, we define a precongruence on processes, denoted $\succeq_S$, where the parameter S denotes the subject(s) of the prefix in the possible branches. Our semantics is closed under $\succeq_S$. Hence, e.g., anticipating a reduction on x, the possible branch $\mathtt{C}_1[x(y); P]$ can be extended with an impossible branch to form $\mathtt{C}_1[x(y); P] \mathbin{+\!\!\!\!+} \mathtt{C}_2[z(); Q]$.

Before defining $\succeq_S$ (Definition 3), we first define prefixes (and their subjects). Below, we write $\widetilde{x}$ to denote a finite tuple of names $x_1, \ldots, x_k$.

Definition 2. *Prefixes are defined as follows:*

$$\alpha, \beta ::= \overline{x}[y] \mid x(y) \mid \overline{x}.\ell \mid x.\mathtt{case} \mid \overline{x}[] \mid x() \mid \overline{x}.\mathtt{some} \mid \overline{x}.\mathtt{none} \mid x.\mathtt{some}_{\widetilde{w}} \mid [x \leftrightarrow y]$$

The subjects of α*, denoted* $subj\{\alpha\}$*, are* $\{x, y\}$ *in case of* $[x \leftrightarrow y]$*, or* $\{x\}$*. By abuse of notation, we write* $\alpha; P$ *even when* α *takes no continuation (as in* $\overline{x}[]$*,* $\overline{x}.\mathtt{none}$*, and* $[x \leftrightarrow y]$*) and for* $\overline{x}[y]$ *which takes a parallel composition as continuation.*

Definition 3. *Let* $\bowtie$ *denote the least relation on prefixes (Definition 2) defined by:*
(i) $\overline{x}[y] \bowtie \overline{x}[z]$*, (ii)* $x(y) \bowtie x(z)$*, and (iii)* $\alpha \bowtie \alpha$ *otherwise.*

Given a non-empty set $S \subseteq \{x, y\}$*, the precongruence* $P \succeq_S Q$ *holds when both following conditions hold:*

1. $S = \{x\}$ *implies*
   $P = \left(\mathop{+\!\!\!\!+}_{i\in I} \mathtt{C}_\mathtt{i}[\alpha_i; P_i]\right) \mathbin{+\!\!\!\!+} \left(\mathop{+\!\!\!\!+}_{j\in J} \mathtt{C}_\mathtt{j}[\beta_j; Q_j]\right)$ *and* $Q = \mathop{+\!\!\!\!+}_{i\in I} \mathtt{C}_\mathtt{i}[\alpha_i; P_i]$*, where*
   (i) $\forall i, i' \in I.\, \alpha_i \bowtie \alpha_{i'}$ *and* $subj\{\alpha_i\} = \{x\}$*, and*
   (ii) $\forall i \in I.\, \forall j \in J.\, \alpha_i \not\bowtie \beta_j \wedge x \in fn(\beta_j; Q_j)$*;*
2. $S = \{x, y\}$ *implies*
   $P = \left(\mathop{+\!\!\!\!+}_{i\in I} \mathtt{C}_\mathtt{i}[[x \leftrightarrow y]]\right) \mathbin{+\!\!\!\!+} \left(\mathop{+\!\!\!\!+}_{j\in J} \mathtt{C}_\mathtt{j}[[x \leftrightarrow z_j]]\right) \mathbin{+\!\!\!\!+} \left(\mathop{+\!\!\!\!+}_{k\in K} \mathtt{C}_\mathtt{k}[\alpha_k; P_k]\right)$
   and $Q = \mathop{+\!\!\!\!+}_{i\in I} \mathtt{C}_\mathtt{i}[[x \leftrightarrow y]]$*, where*
   (i) $\forall j \in J.\, z_j \neq y$*, and (ii)* $\forall k \in K.\, x \in fn(\alpha_k; P_k) \wedge \forall z.\, \alpha_k \not\bowtie [x \leftrightarrow z]$*.*

$$[\rightsquigarrow_{\mathrm{ID}}]\ (\boldsymbol{\nu} x)\Big(\mathop{+\!\!\!\!+}_{i\in I}\mathsf{C}_i\big[[x \leftrightarrow y]\big] \mid Q\Big) \rightsquigarrow_{x,y} \mathop{+\!\!\!\!+}_{i\in I}\mathsf{C}_i[Q\{y/x\}]$$

$$[\rightsquigarrow_{\otimes\parr}]\ (\boldsymbol{\nu} x)\Big(\mathop{+\!\!\!\!+}_{i\in I}\mathsf{C}_i[\overline{x}[y_i];(P_i \mid Q_i)] \mid \mathop{+\!\!\!\!+}_{j\in J}\mathsf{D}_j[x(z);R_j]\Big)$$

$$\rightsquigarrow_x \mathop{+\!\!\!\!+}_{i\in I}\mathsf{C}_i\Big[(\boldsymbol{\nu} x)(Q_i \mid (\boldsymbol{\nu} w)(P_i\{w/y_i\} \mid \mathop{+\!\!\!\!+}_{j\in J}\mathsf{D}_j[R_j\{w/z\}]))\Big]$$

$$[\rightsquigarrow_{\oplus\&}]\ (\boldsymbol{\nu} x)\Big(\mathop{+\!\!\!\!+}_{i\in I}\mathsf{C}_i[\overline{x}.k';P_i] \mid \mathop{+\!\!\!\!+}_{j\in J}\mathsf{D}_j[x.\mathtt{case}\{k:Q_j^k\}_{k\in K}]\Big)$$

$$\rightsquigarrow_x (\boldsymbol{\nu} x)\Big(\mathop{+\!\!\!\!+}_{i\in I}\mathsf{C}_i[P_i] \mid \mathop{+\!\!\!\!+}_{j\in J}\mathsf{D}_j[Q_j^{k'}]\Big) \qquad [k' \in K]$$

$$[\rightsquigarrow_{\mathbf{1}\bot}]\ (\boldsymbol{\nu} x)\Big(\mathop{+\!\!\!\!+}_{i\in I}\mathsf{C}_i[\overline{x}[]] \mid \mathop{+\!\!\!\!+}_{j\in J}\mathsf{D}_j[x();Q_j]\Big) \rightsquigarrow_x \mathop{+\!\!\!\!+}_{i\in I}\mathsf{C}_i[\mathbf{0}] \mid \mathop{+\!\!\!\!+}_{j\in J}\mathsf{D}_j[Q_j]$$

$$[\rightsquigarrow_{\mathtt{some}}]\ (\boldsymbol{\nu} x)\Big(\mathop{+\!\!\!\!+}_{i\in I}\mathsf{C}_i[\overline{x}.\mathtt{some};P_i] \mid \mathop{+\!\!\!\!+}_{j\in J}\mathsf{D}_j[x.\mathtt{some}_{w_1,\ldots,w_n};Q_j]\Big)$$

$$\rightsquigarrow_x (\boldsymbol{\nu} x)\Big(\mathop{+\!\!\!\!+}_{i\in I}\mathsf{C}_i[P_i] \mid \mathop{+\!\!\!\!+}_{j\in J}\mathsf{D}_j[Q_j]\Big)$$

$$[\rightsquigarrow_{\mathtt{none}}]\ (\boldsymbol{\nu} x)\Big(\mathop{+\!\!\!\!+}_{i\in I}\mathsf{C}_i[\overline{x}.\mathtt{none}] \mid \mathop{+\!\!\!\!+}_{j\in J}\mathsf{D}_j[x.\mathtt{some}_{w_1,\ldots,w_n};Q_j]\Big)$$

$$\rightsquigarrow_x \mathop{+\!\!\!\!+}_{i\in I}\mathsf{C}_i[\mathbf{0}] \mid \mathop{+\!\!\!\!+}_{j\in J}\mathsf{D}_j[\overline{w_1}.\mathtt{none} \mid \ldots \mid \overline{w_n}.\mathtt{none}]$$

$$[\rightsquigarrow_{\succeq_S}]\ \frac{x \in S \qquad P \succeq_S P' \qquad Q \succeq_S Q' \qquad (\boldsymbol{\nu} x)(P' \mid Q') \rightsquigarrow_S R}{(\boldsymbol{\nu} x)(P \mid Q) \rightsquigarrow_S R}$$

$$[\rightsquigarrow_{\nu +\!\!\!\!+}]\ \frac{(\boldsymbol{\nu} x)(P \mid \mathsf{N}[\mathsf{C}[Q_1] +\!\!\!\!+ \mathsf{C}[Q_2]]) \rightsquigarrow_S R}{(\boldsymbol{\nu} x)(P \mid \mathsf{N}[\mathsf{C}[Q_1 +\!\!\!\!+ Q_2]]) \rightsquigarrow_S R}$$

$$[\rightsquigarrow_{\equiv}]\ \frac{P \equiv P' \qquad P' \rightsquigarrow_S Q' \qquad Q' \equiv Q}{P \rightsquigarrow_S Q} \qquad [\rightsquigarrow_{\nu}]\ \frac{P \rightsquigarrow_S P'}{(\boldsymbol{\nu} x)(P \mid Q) \rightsquigarrow_S (\boldsymbol{\nu} x)(P' \mid Q)}$$

$$[\rightsquigarrow_{|}]\ \frac{P \rightsquigarrow_S P'}{P \mid Q \rightsquigarrow_S P' \mid Q} \qquad [\rightsquigarrow_{+\!\!\!\!+}]\ \frac{P \rightsquigarrow_S P'}{P +\!\!\!\!+ Q \rightsquigarrow_S P' +\!\!\!\!+ Q}$$

Fig. 2. Reduction semantics for $\mathsf{s}\pi^+$.

Intuitively, $\bowtie$ allows us to equate output/input prefixes with the same subject (but different object). The rest of Definition 3 accounts for two kinds of reduction, using S to discard "impossible" branches. In case S is $\{x\}$ (Item 1), it concerns a synchronization on x; in case S is $\{x, y\}$, it concerns forwarding on x and y (Item 2). In both cases, P and Q contain matching prefixes on x, while P may contain additional branches with different or blocked prefixes on x; x must appear in the hole of the contexts in the additional branches in P (enforced with $x \in \mathit{fn}(\ldots)$), to ensure that no matching prefixes are discarded.

Example 2. Recall process P from Example 1. To derive a synchronization with the 'buy' alternative of the case, we can use $\succeq_S$ to discard the 'peek' alternative, as follows: $\overline{\mathsf{s}}.\mathsf{buy};\ldots +\!\!\!\!+ \overline{\mathsf{s}}.\mathsf{buy};\ldots +\!\!\!\!+ \overline{\mathsf{s}}.\mathsf{peek};\ldots \succeq_s \overline{\mathsf{s}}.\mathsf{buy};\ldots +\!\!\!\!+ \overline{\mathsf{s}}.\mathsf{buy};\ldots$ ▽

Reduction Rules. Figure 2 gives the rules for the (lazy) reduction semantics, denoted $\rightsquigarrow_S$, where the set S contains the names involved in the interaction. We omit the curly braces in this annotation; this way, e.g., we write '$\leadsto_{x,y}$' instead of '$\leadsto_{\{x,y\}}$'. Also, we write $\leadsto_S^k$ to denote a sequence of $k \geq 0$ reductions.

The first six rules in Fig. 2 formalize forwarding and communication: they are defined on choices containing different D-contexts (cf. Definition 1), each with the same prefix but possibly different continuations; these rules preserve the non-deterministic choices. Rule $[\leadsto_{\text{ID}}]$ fixes S to the forwarder's two names, and the other rules fix S to the one involved name. In particular, Rule $[\leadsto_{\otimes\invamp}]$ formalizes name communication: it involves multiple senders and multiple receivers (grouped in choices indexed by I and J, respectively). Because they proceed in lock-step, reduction leads to substitutions involving the same (fresh) name w; also, the scopes of the choice and the contexts enclosing the senders is extended.

Rule $[\leadsto_{\succeq_S}]$ is useful to derive a synchronization that discards groups of choices. Rule $[\leadsto_{\nu \mathbin{+\!\!\!+}}]$ allows inferring reductions when non-deterministic choices are not top-level: e.g., $(\boldsymbol{\nu}x)(\overline{x}[] \mid (\boldsymbol{\nu}y)((x(); Q_1 \mathbin{+\!\!\!+} x(); Q_2) \mid R)) \leadsto_x (\boldsymbol{\nu}y)(Q_1 \mid R) \mathbin{+\!\!\!+} (\boldsymbol{\nu}y)(Q_2 \mid R)$. The last four rules formalize that reduction is closed under structural congruence, restriction, parallel composition, and non-deterministic choice.

As mentioned earlier, a key motivation for our work is to have non-deterministic choices that effectively enforce commitment, without a too drastic discarding of alternatives. Next we illustrate this intended form of *gradual commitment.*

Example 3. (A Modified Movie Server). Consider the following variant of the movie server from the introduction, where the handling of the payment is now modeled as a branch:

$$\mathsf{NewServer}_s := s(\mathit{title}); s.\mathsf{case}\left\{\begin{array}{l}\mathsf{buy} : s.\mathsf{case}\left\{\begin{array}{l}\mathsf{card} : s(\mathit{info}); \overline{s}[\mathtt{movie}]; \overline{s}[],\\ \mathsf{cash} : \overline{s}[\mathtt{movie}]; \overline{s}[]\end{array}\right\},\\ \mathsf{peek} : \overline{s}[\mathtt{trailer}]; \overline{s}[]\end{array}\right\}$$

Consider a client, Eve, who cannot decide between buying 'Oppenheimer' or watching its trailer. In the former case, she has two options for payment method:

$$\mathsf{Eve}_s := \overline{s}[\mathtt{Oppenheimer}]; \left(\begin{array}{l}\quad \overline{s}.\mathsf{buy}; \overline{s}.\mathsf{card}; \overline{s}[\mathtt{visa}]; s(\mathit{movie}); s(); \mathbf{0}\\ \mathbin{+\!\!\!+} \overline{s}.\mathsf{buy}; \overline{s}.\mathsf{cash}; s(\mathit{movie}); s(); \mathbf{0}\\ \mathbin{+\!\!\!+} \overline{s}.\mathsf{peek}; s(\mathit{link}); s(); \mathbf{0}\end{array}\right)$$

Let $\mathsf{Sys}^* := (\boldsymbol{\nu}s)(\mathsf{NewServer}_s \mid \mathsf{Eve}_s)$. After sending the movie's title, Eve's choice (buying or watching the trailer) enables gradual commitment. We have:

$$\mathsf{Sys}^* \leadsto_s^2 (\boldsymbol{\nu}s)\big(s.\mathsf{case}\{\mathsf{card} : \ldots, \mathsf{cash} : \ldots\} \mid (\overline{s}.\mathsf{card}; \ldots \mathbin{+\!\!\!+} \overline{s}.\mathsf{cash}; \ldots)\big) =: \mathsf{Sys}_1^*$$

$$\text{and} \qquad \mathsf{Sys}^* \leadsto_s^2 (\boldsymbol{\nu}s)(\overline{s}[\mathtt{trailer}]; \ldots \mid s(\mathit{trailer}); \ldots) =: \mathsf{Sys}_2^*$$

Process Sys_1^* represents the situation for Eve after selecting buy, in which case the third alternative ($\overline{s}.\mathsf{peek}; \ldots$) can be discarded as an impossible branch. Process Sys_2^* represents the dual situation. From Sys_1^*, the selection of payment method completes the commitment to one alternative; we have: $\mathsf{Sys}_1^* \leadsto_s (\boldsymbol{\nu}s)(s(\mathit{info}); ... \mid \overline{s}[\mathtt{visa}]; ...)$ and $\mathsf{Sys}_1^* \leadsto_s (\boldsymbol{\nu}s)(\overline{s}[\mathtt{movie}]; ... \mid s(\mathit{movie}); ...)$. ▽

$$[\textsc{Tcut}]\ \frac{P \vdash \Gamma, x{:}A \qquad Q \vdash \Delta, x{:}\overline{A}}{(\nu x)(P \mid Q) \vdash \Gamma, \Delta} \qquad [\textsc{Tmix}]\ \frac{P \vdash \Gamma \qquad Q \vdash \Delta}{P \mid Q \vdash \Gamma, \Delta}$$

$$[\mathrm{T}\nplus]\ \frac{P \vdash \Gamma \qquad Q \vdash \Gamma}{P \nplus Q \vdash \Gamma} \qquad [\textsc{Tempty}]\ \frac{}{\mathbf{0} \vdash \emptyset} \qquad [\textsc{Tid}]\ \frac{}{[x \leftrightarrow y] \vdash x{:}A, y{:}\overline{A}}$$

$$[\mathrm{T}\mathbf{1}]\ \frac{}{\overline{x}[] \vdash x{:}\mathbf{1}} \qquad [\mathrm{T}\bot]\ \frac{P \vdash \Gamma}{x(); P \vdash \Gamma, x{:}\bot} \qquad [\mathrm{T}\otimes]\ \frac{P \vdash \Gamma, y{:}A \qquad Q \vdash \Delta, x{:}B}{\overline{x}[y]; (P \mid Q) \vdash \Gamma, \Delta, x{:}A \otimes B}$$

$$[\mathrm{T}⅋]\ \frac{P \vdash \Gamma, y{:}A, x{:}B}{x(y); P \vdash \Gamma, x{:}A ⅋ B} \qquad [\mathrm{T}\oplus]\ \frac{P \vdash \Gamma, x{:}A_j \qquad j \in I}{\overline{x}.j; P \vdash \Gamma, x{:}\oplus\{i : A_i\}_{i \in I}}$$

$$[\mathrm{T}\&]\ \frac{\forall i \in I.\ P_i \vdash \Gamma, x{:}A_i}{x.\mathtt{case}\{i : P_i\}_{i \in I} \vdash \Gamma, x{:}\&\{i : A_i\}_{i \in I}} \qquad [\mathrm{T}\&\mathtt{some}]\ \frac{P \vdash \Gamma, x{:}A}{\overline{x}.\mathtt{some}; P \vdash \Gamma, x{:}\&A}$$

$$[\mathrm{T}\&\mathtt{none}]\ \frac{}{\overline{x}.\mathtt{none} \vdash x{:}\&A} \qquad [\mathrm{T}\oplus\mathtt{some}]\ \frac{P \vdash \&\Gamma, x{:}A}{x.\mathtt{some}_{dom(\Gamma)}; P \vdash \&\Gamma, x{:}\oplus A}$$

Fig. 3. Typing rules for $s\pi^+$.

2.2 Resource Control for $s\pi^+$ via Session Types

We define a session type system for $s\pi^+$, following 'propositions-as-sessions' [6, 31]. As already mentioned, in a session type system, resources are names that perform protocols: the *type assignment* $x : A$ says that x should conform to the protocol specified by the session type A. We give the syntax of types:

$$A, B ::= \mathbf{1} \mid \bot \mid A \otimes B \mid A ⅋ B \mid \oplus\{i : A\}_{i \in I} \mid \&\{i : A\}_{i \in I} \mid \&A \mid \oplus A$$

The units $\mathbf{1}$ and $\bot$ type closed sessions. $A \otimes B$ types a name that first outputs a name of type A and then proceeds as B. Similarly, $A ⅋ B$ types a name that inputs a name of type A and then proceeds as B. Types $\oplus\{i : A_i\}_{i \in I}$ and $\&\{i : A_i\}_{i \in I}$ are given to names that can select and offer a labeled choice, respectively. Then, $\&A$ is the type of a name that *may produce* a behavior of type A, or fail; dually, $\oplus A$ types a name that *may consume* a behavior of type A.

For any type A we denote its *dual* as $\overline{A}$. Intuitively, dual types serve to avoid communication errors: the type at one end of a channel is the dual of the type at the opposite end. Duality is an involution, defined as follows:

$$\overline{\mathbf{1}} = \bot \qquad \overline{A \otimes B} = \overline{A} ⅋ \overline{B} \qquad \overline{\oplus\{i : A_i\}_{i \in I}} = \&\{i : \overline{A_i}\}_{i \in I} \qquad \overline{\&A} = \oplus\overline{A}$$

$$\overline{\bot} = \mathbf{1} \qquad \overline{A ⅋ B} = \overline{A} \otimes \overline{B} \qquad \overline{\&\{i : A_i\}_{i \in I}} = \oplus\{i : \overline{A_i}\}_{i \in I} \qquad \overline{\oplus A} = \&\overline{A}$$

Judgments are of the form $P \vdash \Gamma$, where P is a process and Γ is a context, a collection of type assignments. In writing $\Gamma, x : A$, we assume $x \notin dom(\Gamma)$. We write $dom(\Gamma)$ to denote the set of names appearing in Γ. We write $\&\Gamma$ to denote that $\forall x : A \in \Gamma.\ \exists A'.\ A = \&A'$.

Figure 3 gives the typing rules: they correspond to the rules in Curry-Howard interpretations of classical linear logic as session types (cf. Wadler [31]), with the rules for $\&A$ and $\oplus A$ extracted from [5], and the additional Rule $[T\#]$ for non-confluent non-deterministic choice, which modifies the confluent rule in [5].

Most rules follow [31], so we focus on those related to non-determinism. Rule [T$\&$some] types a process with a name whose behavior can be provided, while Rule [T$\&$none] types a name whose behavior cannot. Rule [T$\oplus$some] types a process with a name x whose behavior may not be available. If the behavior is not available, all the sessions in the process must be canceled; hence, the rule requires all names to be typed under the $\&A$ monad.

Rule $[T\#]$ types our new non-deterministic choice operator; the branches must be typable under the same typing context. Hence, all branches denote the same sessions, which may be implemented differently. In context of a synchronization, branches that are kept are able to synchronize, whereas the discarded branches are not; nonetheless, the remaining branches still represent different implementations of the same sessions. Compared to the rule for non-determinism in [5], we do not require processes to be typable under the $\&A$ monad.

Example 4. Consider again process Eve_s from Example 3. The three branches of the non-deterministic choice give *different implementations of the same session*: assuming primitive, self-dual data types $\mathtt{C}$, $\mathtt{M}$, and $\mathtt{L}$, all three branches on s are typable by $\oplus\{\mathsf{buy} : \oplus\{\mathsf{card} : \mathtt{C} \otimes \mathtt{M} \parr \bot, \mathsf{cash} : \mathtt{M} \parr \bot\}, \mathsf{peek} : \mathtt{L} \parr \bot\}$. ▽

Example 5 (Unavailable Movies). Consider now a modified movie server, which offers movies that may not be yet available. We specify this server using non-deterministic choice and non-deterministically available sessions:

$$\mathsf{BuyServ}_s := s(\mathit{title}); (\overline{s}.\mathtt{none} \# \overline{s}.\mathtt{some}; s(\mathit{paym}); \overline{s}[\mathtt{movie}]; \overline{s}[]) \vdash s : \mathtt{T} \parr (\&(\mathtt{P} \parr \mathtt{M} \otimes \mathbf{1})),$$

where $\mathtt{T}, \mathtt{P}, \mathtt{M}$ denote primitive, self-dual data-types. While the branch '$\overline{s}.\mathtt{none}$' signals that the movie is not available, the branch '$\overline{s}.\mathtt{some}; \ldots$' performs the expected protocol. We now define a client Ada who buys a movie for Tim, using session s; Ada only forwards it to him (using session u) if it is actually available:

$$\begin{aligned}\mathsf{Ada}_{s,u} &:= \overline{s}[\mathtt{Barbie}]; s.\mathtt{some}_u; \overline{s}[\mathtt{visa}]; s(\mathit{movie}); s(); \overline{u}.\mathtt{some}; \overline{u}[\mathit{movie}]; \overline{u}[] \\ &\quad \vdash s : \mathtt{T} \otimes (\oplus(\mathtt{P} \otimes \mathtt{M} \parr \bot)), u : \&(\mathtt{M} \otimes \mathbf{1}) \\ \mathsf{Tim}_u &:= u.\mathtt{some}; u(\mathit{movie}); u(); \mathbf{0} \vdash u : \oplus(\mathtt{M} \parr \mathbf{1})\end{aligned}$$

Let $\mathsf{BuySys} := (\boldsymbol{\nu} s)(\mathsf{BuyServ}_s \mid (\boldsymbol{\nu} u)(\mathsf{Ada}_{s,u} \mid \mathsf{Tim}_u))$. Depending on whether the server has the movie "Barbie" available, we have the following reductions:

$$\mathsf{BuySys} \rightsquigarrow_s^2 (\boldsymbol{\nu} u)(\overline{u}.\mathtt{none} \mid \mathsf{Tim}_u) \quad \text{or} \quad \mathsf{BuySys} \rightsquigarrow_s^5 (\boldsymbol{\nu} u)(\overline{u}.\mathtt{some}; \ldots \mid \mathsf{Tim}_u)$$

▽

Our type system ensures *session fidelity* and *communication safety*, but not confluence: the former says that processes correctly follow their ascribed session protocols, and the latter that no communication errors/mismatches occur. Both properties follow from the fact that typing is consistent across structural congruence and reduction. See [13] for details.

$M, N, L ::= x$	variable	$\mid M\langle\langle C/x \rangle\rangle$	intermediate subst.
$\mid (M\ C)$	application	$\mid M \langle\!\!\!\langle C/\widetilde{x} \rangle\!\!\!\rangle$	explicit subst.
$\mid \lambda x.M$	abstraction	$\mid \mathtt{fail}^{\widetilde{x}}$	failure
$\mid M[\widetilde{x} \leftarrow x]$	sharing		
$C, D ::= \mathtt{1} \mid \wr M \int \cdot C$			bag
$\mathcal{C} ::= [\cdot] \mid \mathcal{C}[\widetilde{x} \leftarrow x] \mid (\mathcal{C}\ C) \mid \mathcal{C}\langle\!\!\!\langle C/\widetilde{x} \rangle\!\!\!\rangle$			context

Fig. 4. Syntax of $\lambda^{\ell}_{\mathtt{C}}$: terms, bags, and contexts.

Theorem 1 (Type Preservation). *If $P \vdash \Gamma$, then both $P \equiv Q$ and $P \leadsto_S Q$ (for any Q and S) imply $Q \vdash \Gamma$.*

Another important, if often elusive, property in session types is *deadlock-freedom*, which ensures that processes can reduce as long as they are not inactive. Our type system satisfies deadlock-freedom for processes with fully connected names, i.e., typable under the empty context. See [13] for details.

Theorem 2 (Deadlock-freedom). *If $P \vdash \emptyset$ and $P \not\equiv \mathbf{0}$, then there are Q and S such that $P \leadsto_S Q$.*

3 A Non-deterministic Resource λ-calculus

We present $\lambda^{\ell}_{\mathtt{C}}$, a resource λ-calculus with non-determinism and lazy evaluation. In $\lambda^{\ell}_{\mathtt{C}}$, non-determinism is non-confluent and *implicit*, as it arises from the fetching of terms from bags of *linear* resources. This is different from $\mathsf{s}\pi^{+}$, where the choice operator '$+\!\!\!\!+$' specifies non-determinism *explicitly*. A mismatch between the number of variable occurrences and the size of the bag induces *failure*.

In $\lambda^{\ell}_{\mathtt{C}}$, the *sharing* construct $M[x_1, \ldots, x_n \leftarrow x]$, expresses that x may be used in M under "aliases" $x_1, \ldots, x_n$. Hence, it atomizes n occurrences of x in M, via an explicit pointer to n variables. This way, e.g., the λ-term $\lambda x.(x\ x)$ is expressed in $\lambda^{\ell}_{\mathtt{C}}$ as $\lambda x.(x_1 \wr x_2 \int [x_1, x_2 \leftarrow x])$, where $\wr x_2 \int$ is a bag containing x_2.

3.1 Syntax and Reduction Semantics

Syntax. We use $x, y, z, \ldots$ for variables, and write $\widetilde{x}$ to denote a finite sequence of pairwise distinct x_i's, with length $|\widetilde{x}|$. Figure 4 gives the syntax of terms (M, N, L) and bags (C, D). The empty bag is denoted $\mathtt{1}$. We use C_i to denote the i-th term in C, and $\mathsf{size}(C)$ denotes the number of elements in C. To ease readability, we often write, e.g., $\wr N_1, N_2 \int$ as a shorthand notation for $\wr N_1 \int \cdot \wr N_2 \int$.

In $M[\widetilde{x} \leftarrow x]$, we say that $\widetilde{x}$ are the *shared variables* and that x is the *sharing variable*. We require for each $x_i \in \widetilde{x}$: (i) x_i occurs exactly once in M; (ii) x_i is not a sharing variable. The sequence $\widetilde{x}$ can be empty: $M[\leftarrow x]$ means that x does not share any variables in M. Sharing binds the shared variables in the term.

$$\texttt{[RS:Beta]}\ \frac{}{(\lambda x.M)C \longrightarrow M\langle\langle C/x\rangle\rangle} \qquad \texttt{[RS:Ex-Sub]}\ \frac{\mathsf{size}(C) = |\widetilde{x}| \quad M \neq \mathtt{fail}^{\widetilde{y}}}{(M[\widetilde{x} \leftarrow x])\langle\langle C/x\rangle\rangle \longrightarrow M\langle\!| C/\widetilde{x} |\!\rangle} \qquad \texttt{[RS : TCont]}\ \frac{M \longrightarrow N}{\mathcal{C}[M] \longrightarrow \mathcal{C}[N]}$$

$$\texttt{[RS:Fetch}^{\ell}\texttt{]}\ \frac{\mathsf{head}(M) = x_j \quad 0 < i \leq \mathsf{size}(C)}{M\langle\!| C/\widetilde{x}, x_j |\!\rangle \longrightarrow M\{C_i/x_j\}\langle\!| (C \setminus C_i)/\widetilde{x} |\!\rangle}$$

$$\texttt{[RS:Fail}^{\ell}\texttt{]}\ \frac{\mathsf{size}(C) \neq |\widetilde{x}| \quad \widetilde{y} = (\mathsf{fv}(M) \setminus \{\widetilde{x}\}) \cup \mathsf{fv}(C)}{(M[\widetilde{x} \leftarrow x])\langle\langle C/x\rangle\rangle \longrightarrow \mathtt{fail}^{\widetilde{y}}} \qquad \texttt{[RS:Cons}_1\texttt{]}\ \frac{\widetilde{y} = \mathsf{fv}(C)}{\mathtt{fail}^{\widetilde{x}}\ C \longrightarrow \mathtt{fail}^{\widetilde{x} \cup \widetilde{y}}}$$

$$\texttt{[RS:Cons}_2\texttt{]}\ \frac{\mathsf{size}(C) = |\widetilde{x}| \quad \widetilde{z} = \mathsf{fv}(C)}{(\mathtt{fail}^{\widetilde{x} \cup \widetilde{y}}[\widetilde{x} \leftarrow x])\langle\langle C/x\rangle\rangle \longrightarrow \mathtt{fail}^{\widetilde{y} \cup \widetilde{z}}} \qquad \texttt{[RS:Cons}_3\texttt{]}\ \frac{\widetilde{z} = \mathsf{fv}(C)}{\mathtt{fail}^{\widetilde{y} \cup \widetilde{x}}\langle\!| C/\widetilde{x} |\!\rangle \longrightarrow \mathtt{fail}^{\widetilde{y} \cup \widetilde{z}}}$$

where $\mathsf{head}(M)$ is defined as follows:

$$\mathsf{head}(x) = x \qquad \mathsf{head}(\lambda x.M) = \lambda x.M \qquad \mathsf{head}((M\ C)) = \mathsf{head}(M)$$

$$\mathsf{head}(\mathtt{fail}^{\widetilde{x}}) = \mathtt{fail}^{\widetilde{x}} \quad \mathsf{head}(M\langle\langle C/x\rangle\rangle) = M\langle\langle C/x\rangle\rangle \quad \mathsf{head}(M\langle\!| C/\widetilde{x} |\!\rangle) = \mathsf{head}(M)$$

$$\mathsf{head}(M[\widetilde{x} \leftarrow x]) = \begin{cases} x & \mathsf{head}(M) = y \text{ and } y \in \widetilde{x} \\ \mathsf{head}(M) & \text{otherwise} \end{cases}$$

Fig. 5. Reduction rules for $\lambda^{\ell}_{\mathsf{C}}$.

An abstraction $\lambda x.M$ binds occurrences of x in M. Application $(M\ C)$ is as usual. The term $M\langle\!| C/\widetilde{x} |\!\rangle$ is the *explicit substitution* of a bag C for $\widetilde{x}$ in M. We require $\mathsf{size}(C) = |\widetilde{x}|$ and for each $x_i \in \widetilde{x}$: (i) x_i occurs in M; (ii) x_i is not a sharing variable; (iii) x_i cannot occur in another explicit substitution in M. The term $M\langle\langle C/x\rangle\rangle$ denotes an intermediate explicit substitution that does not (necessarily) satisfy the conditions for explicit substitutions.

The term $\mathtt{fail}^{\widetilde{x}}$ denotes failure; the variables in $\widetilde{x}$ are "dangling" resources, which cannot be accounted for after failure. We write $\mathsf{fv}(M)$ to denote the free variables of M, defined as expected. Term M is *closed* if $\mathsf{fv}(M) = \emptyset$.

Semantics. Figure 5 gives the reduction semantics, denoted $\longrightarrow$, and the *head variable* of term M, denoted $\mathsf{head}(M)$. Rule [RS : Beta] induces an intermediate substitution. Rule [RS : Ex-Sub] reduces an intermediate substitution to an explicit substitution, provided the size of the bag equals the number of shared variables. In case of a mismatch, the term evolves into failure via Rule [RS : Fail$^{\ell}$].

An explicit substitution $M\langle\!| C/\widetilde{x} |\!\rangle$, where the head variable of M is $x_j \in \widetilde{x}$, reduces via Rule [R : Fetch$^{\ell}$]. The rule extracts a C_i from C (for some $0 < i \leq \mathsf{size}(C)$) and substitutes it for x_j in M; this is how fetching induces a non-deterministic choice between $\mathsf{size}(C)$ possible reductions. Rules $[\mathtt{RS} : \mathtt{Cons_j}]$ for $j \in \{1, 2, 3\}$ consume terms when they meet failure. Finally, Rule $[\mathtt{RS} : \mathtt{TCont}]$ closes reduction under contexts. The following example illustrates reduction.

Example 6. Consider the term $M_0 = (\lambda x.x_1 \wr x_2 \wr x_3\ \mathtt{1} \int \int[\widetilde{x} \leftarrow x]) \wr \mathtt{fail}^{\emptyset}, y, I \int$, where $I = \lambda x.(x_1[x_1 \leftarrow x])$ and $\widetilde{x} = x_1, x_2, x_3$. First, M_0 evolves into an intermediate substitution (2). The bag can provide for all shared variables, so it then evolves into an explicit substitution (3):

$$M_0 \longrightarrow (x_1 \wr x_2 \wr x_3\ \mathtt{1} \int \int[\widetilde{x} \leftarrow x])\langle\!\langle \wr \mathtt{fail}^{\emptyset}, y, I \int / x \rangle\!\rangle \tag{2}$$

$$\longrightarrow (x_1 \wr x_2 \wr x_3\ \mathtt{1} \int \int) \langle\!| \wr \mathtt{fail}^{\emptyset}, y, I \int / \widetilde{x} |\!\rangle = M \tag{3}$$

Since $\mathsf{head}(M) = x_1$, one of the three elements of the bag will be substituted. M represents a non-deterministic choice between the following three reductions:

$$M \begin{cases} \nearrow (\mathtt{fail}^{\emptyset} \wr x_2 \wr x_3\ \mathtt{1} \int \int) \langle\!| \wr y, I \int / x_2, x_3 |\!\rangle = N_1 \\ \longrightarrow (y \wr x_2 \wr x_3\ \mathtt{1} \int \int) \langle\!| \wr \mathtt{fail}^{\emptyset}, I \int / x_2, x_3 |\!\rangle = N_2 \\ \searrow (I \wr x_2 \wr x_3\ \mathtt{1} \int \int) \langle\!| \wr \mathtt{fail}^{\emptyset}, y \int / x_2, x_3 |\!\rangle = N_3 \end{cases}$$

▽

3.2 Resource Control for $\lambda^{\ell}_{\mathsf{C}}$ via Intersection Types

Our type system for $\lambda^{\ell}_{\mathsf{C}}$ is based on non-idempotent intersection types. As in prior works [4,21], intersection types account for available resources in bags, which are unordered and have all the same type. Because we admit the term $\mathtt{fail}^{\tilde{x}}$ as typable, we say that our system enforces *well-formedness* rather than *well-typedness*. As we will see, well-typed terms form the sub-class of well-formed terms that does not include $\mathtt{fail}^{\tilde{x}}$ (see the text after Theorem 3).

Strict types (σ, τ, δ) and multiset types (π, ζ) are defined as follows:

$$\sigma, \tau, \delta ::= \ \mathbf{unit} \mid \pi \rightarrow \sigma \qquad \pi, \zeta ::= \bigwedge_{i \in I} \sigma_i \mid \omega$$

Given a non-empty I, multiset types $\bigwedge_{i \in I} \sigma_i$ are given to bags of size $|I|$. This operator is associative, commutative, and non-idempotent (i.e., $\sigma \wedge \sigma \neq \sigma$), with identity ω. Notation σ^k stands for $\sigma \wedge \cdots \wedge \sigma$ (k times, if $k > 0$) or ω (if $k = 0$).

Judgments have the form $\Gamma \vDash M : \tau$, with contexts defined as follows:

$$\Gamma, \Delta ::= \text{-} \mid \Gamma, x : \pi \mid \Gamma, x : \sigma$$

where - denotes the empty context. We write $dom(\Gamma)$ for the set of variables in Γ. For $\Gamma, x : \pi$, we assume $x \notin dom(\Gamma)$. To avoid ambiguities, we write $x : \sigma^1$ to denote that the assignment involves a multiset type, rather than a strict type. Given Γ, its *core context* $\Gamma^{\downarrow}$ concerns variables with types different from ω; it is defined as $\Gamma^{\downarrow} = \{x : \pi \in \Gamma \mid \pi \neq \omega\}$.

$$\frac{}{x:\sigma \models x:\sigma}\ [\texttt{FS:var}^{\ell}] \qquad \frac{}{- \models \mathtt{1}:\omega}\ [\texttt{FS:1}^{\ell}] \qquad \frac{\Gamma \models N:\sigma \quad \Delta \models C:\sigma^{k}}{\Gamma,\Delta \models \{\!| N |\!\}\cdot C:\sigma^{k+1}}\ [\texttt{FS:bag}^{\ell}] \qquad \frac{dom(\Gamma^{\downarrow}) = \widetilde{x}}{\Gamma^{\downarrow} \models \mathtt{fail}^{\widetilde{x}}:\tau}\ [\texttt{FS:fail}]$$

$$\frac{\Gamma \models M:\tau}{\Gamma, x:\omega \models M[\leftarrow x]:\tau}\ [\texttt{FS:weak}] \qquad \frac{\Gamma, x_1:\sigma,\ldots,x_k:\sigma \models M:\tau \quad k\neq 0}{\Gamma, x:\sigma^{k} \models M[x_1,\ldots,x_k \leftarrow x]:\tau}\ [\texttt{FS:shar}]$$

$$\frac{\Gamma, x:\sigma^{k} \models M[\widetilde{x}\leftarrow x]:\tau}{\Gamma \models \lambda x.(M[\widetilde{x}\leftarrow x]):\sigma^{k}\to\tau}\ [\texttt{FS:abs-sh}] \qquad \frac{\Gamma \models M:\sigma^{j}\to\tau \quad \Delta \models C:\sigma^{k}}{\Gamma,\Delta \models M\,C:\tau}\ [\texttt{FS:app}]$$

$$\frac{\Gamma, x:\sigma^{j} \models M[\widetilde{x}\leftarrow x]:\tau \quad \Delta \models C:\sigma^{k}}{\Gamma,\Delta \models (M[\widetilde{x}\leftarrow x])\langle\!\langle C/x\rangle\!\rangle:\tau}\ [\texttt{FS:Esub}] \qquad \frac{\Gamma, x_1:\sigma,\cdots,x_k:\sigma \models M:\tau \quad \Delta \models C:\sigma^{k}}{\Gamma,\Delta \models M\langle\!| C/x_1,\cdots,x_k |\!\rangle:\tau}\ [\texttt{FS:Esub}^{\ell}]$$

Fig. 6. Well-Formedness Rules for $\lambda^{\ell}_{\mathtt{C}}$.

Definition 4 (Well-formedness in $\lambda^{\ell}_{\mathtt{C}}$). *A term M is* well-formed *if there exists a context Γ and a type τ such that the rules in Fig. 6 entail $\Gamma \models M:\tau$.*

In Fig. 6, Rule [$\texttt{FS}:\texttt{var}^{\ell}$] types variables. Rule [$\texttt{FS}:\texttt{1}^{\ell}$] types the empty bag with ω. Rule [$\texttt{FS}:\texttt{bag}^{\ell}$] types the concatenation of bags. Rule [$\texttt{FS}:\texttt{fail}$] types the term $\mathtt{fail}^{\widetilde{x}}$ with a strict type τ, provided that the domain of the core context coincides with $\widetilde{x}$ (i.e., no variable in $\widetilde{x}$ is typed with ω). Rule [$\texttt{FS}:\texttt{weak}$] types $M[\leftarrow x]$ by weakening the context with $x:\omega$. Rule [$\texttt{FS}:\texttt{shar}$] types $M[\widetilde{x}\leftarrow x]$ with τ, provided that there are assignments to the shared variables in $\widetilde{x}$.

Rule [$\texttt{FS}:\texttt{abs-sh}$] types an abstraction $\lambda x.(M[\widetilde{x}\leftarrow x])$ with $\sigma^{k}\to\tau$, provided that $M[\widetilde{x}\leftarrow x]:\tau$ can be entailed from an assignment $x:\sigma^{k}$. Rule [$\texttt{FS}:\texttt{app}$] types $(M\ C)$, provided that M has type $\sigma^{j}\to\tau$ and C has type σ^{k}. Note that, unlike usual intersection type systems, j and k may differ. Rule [$\texttt{FS}:\texttt{Esub}$] types the intermediate substitution of a bag C of type σ^{k}, provided that x has type σ^{j}; again, j and k may differ. Rule [$\texttt{FS}:\texttt{Esub}^{\ell}$] types $M\langle\!| C/\widetilde{x} |\!\rangle$ as long as C has type $\sigma^{|\widetilde{x}|}$, and each $x_i \in \widetilde{x}$ is of type σ.

Well-formed terms satisfy subject reduction (SR), whereas *well-typed* terms, defined below, satisfy also subject expansion (SE). See [13] for details.

Theorem 3 (SR in $\lambda^{\ell}_{\mathtt{C}}$). *If $\Gamma \models M:\tau$ and $M \longrightarrow M'$, then $\Gamma \models M':\tau$.*

From our system for well-formedness we can extract a system for *well-typed* terms, which do not include $\mathtt{fail}^{\widetilde{x}}$. Judgments for well-typedness are denoted $\Gamma \vdash M:\tau$, with rules copied from Fig. 6 (the rule name prefix FS is replaced with TS), with the following modifications: (i) Rule [TS:fail] is removed; (ii) Rules [TS:app] and [TS:Esub] are modified to disallow a mismatch between

$$
\begin{aligned}
\llbracket x \rrbracket_u &= \overline{x}.\texttt{some}; [x \leftrightarrow u] \\
\llbracket \lambda x.M \rrbracket_u &= \overline{u}.\texttt{some}; u(x); \llbracket M \rrbracket_u \\
\llbracket (M\, C) \rrbracket_u &= (\boldsymbol{\nu} v)(\llbracket M \rrbracket_v \mid v.\texttt{some}_{u,\mathsf{lfv}(C)}; \overline{v}[x]; (\llbracket C \rrbracket_x \mid [v \leftrightarrow u])) \\
\llbracket M \langle\!\langle C/x \rangle\!\rangle \rrbracket_u &= (\boldsymbol{\nu} x)(\llbracket M \rrbracket_u \mid \llbracket C \rrbracket_x) \\
\llbracket \wr N \int \cdot\, C \rrbracket_x &= x.\texttt{some}_{\mathsf{fv}(C),\mathsf{fv}(N)}; x(y_i); x.\texttt{some}_{y_i,\mathsf{fv}(C),\mathsf{fv}(N)}; \overline{x}.\texttt{some}; \overline{x}[z_i]; \\
&\qquad (z_i.\texttt{some}_{\mathsf{fv}(N)}; \llbracket N \rrbracket_{z_i} \mid \llbracket C \rrbracket_x \mid \overline{y_i}.\texttt{none}) \\
\llbracket \mathtt{1} \rrbracket_x &= x.\texttt{some}_{\emptyset}; x(y_n); (\overline{y_n}.\texttt{some}; \overline{y_n}[\,] \mid x.\texttt{some}_{\emptyset}; \overline{x}.\texttt{none}) \\
\llbracket M \langle\!| \wr N_1, N_2 \int / x_1, x_2 |\!\rangle \rrbracket_u &= (\boldsymbol{\nu} z_1)(z_1.\texttt{some}_{\mathsf{fv}(N_1)}; \llbracket N_1 \rrbracket_{z_1} \mid (\boldsymbol{\nu} z_2)(z_2.\texttt{some}_{\mathsf{fv}(N_2)}; \llbracket N_2 \rrbracket_{z_2} \\
&\qquad \mid \textstyle\sum\!\!\!\!+_{x_i \in \{x_1,x_2\}} \sum\!\!\!\!+_{x_j \in \{x_1,x_2 \setminus x_i\}} \llbracket M \rrbracket_u \{z_1/x_i\}\{z_2/x_j\})) \\
\llbracket M[\leftarrow x] \rrbracket_u &= \overline{x}.\texttt{some}; \overline{x}[y_i]; (y_i.\texttt{some}_{u,\mathsf{fv}(M)}; y_i(); \llbracket M \rrbracket_u \mid \overline{x}.\texttt{none}) \\
\llbracket M[\widetilde{x} \leftarrow x] \rrbracket_u &= \overline{x}.\texttt{some}; \overline{x}[y_i]; \big(y_i.\texttt{some}_{\emptyset}; y_i(); \mathbf{0} \mid \overline{x}.\texttt{some}; x.\texttt{some}_{u,\mathsf{fv}(M)\setminus\widetilde{x}}; \\
&\qquad \textstyle\sum\!\!\!\!+_{x_i \in \widetilde{x}} x(x_i); \llbracket M[(\widetilde{x} \setminus x_i) \leftarrow x] \rrbracket_u\big) \\
\llbracket \mathtt{fail}^{x_1,\ldots,x_k} \rrbracket_u &= \overline{u}.\texttt{none} \mid \overline{x_1}.\texttt{none} \mid \ldots \mid \overline{x_k}.\texttt{none}
\end{aligned}
$$

Fig. 7. Translation of $\lambda^{\ell}_{\mathsf{C}}$ into $\mathsf{s}\pi^+$.

variables and resources, i.e., multiset types should match in size. Well-typed terms are also well-formed, and thus satisfy SR. Moreover, as a consequence of adopting (non-idempotent) intersection types, they also satisfy SE:

Theorem 4 (SE in $\lambda^{\ell}_{\mathsf{C}}$). *If $\Gamma \vdash M' : \tau$ and $M \longrightarrow M'$, then $\Gamma \vdash M : \tau$.*

4 A Typed Translation of $\lambda^{\ell}_{\mathsf{C}}$ into $\mathsf{s}\pi^+$

While $\mathsf{s}\pi^+$ features non-deterministic choice, $\lambda^{\ell}_{\mathsf{C}}$ is a prototypical programming language in which implicit non-determinism implements fetching of resources. Resources are controlled using different type systems (session types in $\mathsf{s}\pi^+$, intersection types in $\lambda^{\ell}_{\mathsf{C}}$). To reconcile these differences and illustrate the potential of $\mathsf{s}\pi^+$ to precisely model non-determinism as found in realistic programs/protocols, we give a translation of $\lambda^{\ell}_{\mathsf{C}}$ into $\mathsf{s}\pi^+$. This translation preserves types (Theorem 5) and respects well-known criteria for dynamic correctness [11,23,24] (Theorem 6).

The Translation. Given a $\lambda^{\ell}_{\mathsf{C}}$-term M, its translation into $\mathsf{s}\pi^+$ is denoted $\llbracket M \rrbracket_u$ and given in Fig. 7. As usual, every variable x in M becomes a name x in process $\llbracket M \rrbracket_u$, where name u provides the behavior of M. A peculiarity is that, to handle failures in $\lambda^{\ell}_{\mathsf{C}}$, u is a non-deterministically available session: the translated term can be available or not, as signaled by prefixes $\overline{u}.\texttt{some}$ and $\overline{u}.\texttt{none}$, respectively. As a result, reductions from $\llbracket M \rrbracket_u$ include synchronizations that codify M's behavior but also synchronizations that confirm a session's availability.

At its core, our translation follows Milner's. This way, e.g., the process $\llbracket (\lambda x.M)\ C \rrbracket_u$ enables synchronizations between $\llbracket \lambda x.M \rrbracket_v$ and $\llbracket C \rrbracket_x$ along name v,

$$\llbracket \mathbf{unit} \rrbracket = \&\mathbf{1} \qquad \llbracket \sigma^k \to \tau \rrbracket = \&(\overline{\llbracket \sigma^k \rrbracket_{(\sigma,i)}} \parr \llbracket \tau \rrbracket)$$
$$\llbracket \sigma \wedge \pi \rrbracket_{(\tau,i)} = \oplus((\&\mathbf{1}) \parr (\oplus\&((\oplus\llbracket \sigma \rrbracket) \otimes (\llbracket \pi \rrbracket_{(\tau,i)}))))$$
$$\llbracket \omega \rrbracket_{(\sigma,i)} = \begin{cases} \oplus((\&\mathbf{1}) \parr (\oplus\&\mathbf{1})) & \text{if } i = 0 \\ \oplus((\&\mathbf{1}) \parr (\oplus\&((\oplus\llbracket \sigma \rrbracket) \otimes (\llbracket \omega \rrbracket_{(\sigma,i-1)})))) & \text{if } i > 0 \end{cases}$$

Fig. 8. Translation of intersection types into session types (cf. Definition 5).

resulting in the translation of an intermediate substitution. The *key novelty* is the role and treatment of non-determinism. Accommodating non-confluent non-determinism is non-trivial, as it entails translating explicit substitutions and sharing in $\lambda_{\mathsf{C}}^{\ell}$ using the non-deterministic choice operator $\mathbin{+\!\!\!+}$ in $\mathsf{s}\pi^{+}$. Next we discuss these novel aspects, while highlighting differences with respect to a translation by Paulus et al. [22], which is given in the confluent setting (see Section 5).

In Fig. 7, non-deterministic choices occur in the translations of $M\langle\!|C/\widetilde{x}|\!\rangle$ (explicit substitutions) and $M[\widetilde{x} \leftarrow x]$ (non-empty sharing). Roughly speaking, the position of $\mathbin{+\!\!\!+}$ in the translation of $M\langle\!|C/\widetilde{x}|\!\rangle$ represents the most desirable way of mimicking the fetching of terms from a bag. This use of $\mathbin{+\!\!\!+}$ is a central idea in our translation: as we explain below, it allows for appropriate commitment in non-deterministic choices, but also for *delayed* commitment when necessary.

For simplicity, we consider explicit substitutions $M\langle\!|C/\widetilde{x}|\!\rangle$ where $C = \wr N_1, N_2 \int$ and $\widetilde{x} = x_1, x_2$. The translation $\llbracket M\langle\!|C/\widetilde{x}|\!\rangle \rrbracket_u$ uses the processes $\llbracket N_i \rrbracket_{z_i}$, where each z_i is fresh. First, each bag item confirms its behavior. Then, a variable $x_i \in \widetilde{x}$ is chosen non-deterministically; we ensure that these choices consider all variables. Note that writing $\mathbin{+\!\!\!+}_{x_i \in \{x_1,x_2\}} \mathbin{+\!\!\!+}_{x_j \in \{x_1,x_2\} \setminus x_i}$ is equivalent to non-deterministically assigning x_i, x_j to each permutation of x_1, x_2. The resulting choice involves $\llbracket M \rrbracket_u$ with x_i, x_j substituted by z_1, z_2. Commitment here is triggered only via synchronizations along z_1 or z_2; synchronizing with $z_i.\mathtt{some}_{\mathsf{fv}(N_i)}; \llbracket N_i \rrbracket_{z_i}$ then represents fetching N_i from the bag. The size of the translated term $\llbracket M\langle\!|C/\widetilde{x}|\!\rangle \rrbracket_u$ is exponential with respect to the size of C.

The process $\llbracket M[\widetilde{x} \leftarrow x] \rrbracket_u$ proceeds as follows. First, it confirms its behavior along x. Then it sends a name y_i on x, on which a failed reduction may be handled. Next, the translation confirms again its behavior along x and non-deterministically receives a reference to an $x_i \in \widetilde{x}$. Each branch consists of $\llbracket M[(\widetilde{x} \setminus x_i) \leftarrow x] \rrbracket_u$. The possible choices are permuted, represented by $\mathbin{+\!\!\!+}_{x_i \in \widetilde{x}}$. Synchronizations with $\llbracket M[(\widetilde{x} \setminus x_i) \leftarrow x] \rrbracket_u$ and bags delay commitment in this choice (we return to this point below). The process $\llbracket M[\leftarrow x] \rrbracket_u$ is similar but simpler: here the name x fails, as it cannot take further elements to substitute.

In case of a failure (i.e., a mismatch between the size of the bag C and the number of variables in M), our translation ensures that the confirmations of C will not succeed. This is how failure in $\lambda_{\mathsf{C}}^{\ell}$ is correctly translated to failure in $\mathsf{s}\pi^{+}$.

Translation Correctness. The translation is typed: intersection types in $\lambda^{\ell}_{\mathsf{C}}$ are translated into session types in $\mathsf{s}\pi^{+}$ (Fig. 8). This translation of types abstractly describes how non-deterministic fetches are codified as non-deterministic session protocols. It is worth noting that this translation of types is the same as in [22]. This is not surprising: as we have seen, session types effectively abstract away from the behavior of processes, as all branches of a non-deterministic choice use the same typing context. Still, it is pleasant that the translation of types remains unchanged across different translations with our (non-confluent) non-determinism (in Fig. 7) and with confluent non-determinism (in [22]).

To state *static* correctness, we require the following definition:

Definition 5. *Let* $\Gamma = x_1 : \sigma_1, ..., x_m : \sigma_m, v_1 : \pi_1, ..., v_n : \pi_n$ *be a context. The translation* $[\![\cdot]\!]_{\_}$ *in Fig. 8 extends to contexts as follows:*

$$[\![\Gamma]\!] = x_1 : \&\overline{[\![\sigma_1]\!]}, \cdots, x_m : \&\overline{[\![\sigma_m]\!]}, v_1 : \overline{[\![\pi_1]\!]_{(\sigma,i_1)}}, \cdots, v_n : \overline{[\![\pi_n]\!]_{(\sigma,i_n)}}$$

Well-formed terms translate into well-typed processes:

Theorem 5. *If* $\Gamma \models M : \tau$*, then* $[\![M]\!]_u \vdash [\![\Gamma]\!], u : [\![\tau]\!]$.

To state *dynamic* correctness, we rely on established notions that (abstractly) characterize *correct translations.* A language $\mathcal{L} = (L, \to)$ consists of a set of terms L and a reduction relation $\to$ on L. Each language $\mathcal{L}$ is assumed to contain a success constructor ✓. A term $T \in L$ has *success*, denoted $T \Downarrow$ ✓, when there is a sequence of reductions (using $\to$) from T to a term satisfying success criteria.

Given $\mathcal{L}_1 = (L_1, \to_1)$ and $\mathcal{L}_2 = (L_2, \to_2)$, we seek translations $[\![\cdot]\!] : L_1 \to L_2$ that are correct: they satisfy well-known correctness criteria [11,23,24]. We state the set of correctness criteria that determine the correctness of a translation.

Definition 6 (Correct Translation). *Let* $\mathcal{L}_1 = (\mathcal{M}, \to_1)$ *and* $\mathcal{L}_2 = (\mathcal{P}, \to_2)$ *be two languages. Let* $\asymp_2$ *be an equivalence over* $\mathcal{L}_2$*. We use* M, M' *(resp.* P, P'*) to range over terms in* $\mathcal{M}$ *(resp.* $\mathcal{P}$*). Given a translation* $[\![\cdot]\!] : \mathcal{M} \to \mathcal{P}$*, we define:*

> ***Completeness:*** *For every* M, M' *such that* $M \to_1^* M'$*, there exists* P *such that* $[\![M]\!] \to_2^* P \asymp_2 [\![M']\!]$.
> ***Weak Soundness:*** *For every* M *and* P *such that* $[\![M]\!] \to_2^* P$*, there exist* M'*,* P' *such that* $M \to_1^* M'$ *and* $P \to_2^* P' \asymp_2 [\![M']\!]$.
> ***Success Sensitivity:*** *For every* M*, we have* $M \Downarrow$ ✓ *if and only if* $[\![M]\!] \Downarrow$ ✓.

Let us write Λ to denote the set of well-formed $\lambda^{\ell}_{\mathsf{C}}$ terms, and Π for the set of all well-typed $\mathsf{s}\pi^{+}$ processes, both including ✓. We have our final result:

Theorem 6 (Translation correctness under $\rightsquigarrow$). *The translation* $[\![\cdot]\!]_{\_} : (\Lambda, \longrightarrow) \to (\Pi, \rightsquigarrow)$ *is correct (cf. Definition 6) using equivalence* $\equiv$ *(Fig. 1).*

The proof of Theorem 6 involves instantiating/proving each of the parts of Definition 6. Among these, *weak soundness* is the most challenging to prove. Prior work on translations of typed λ into π with confluent non-determinism [22] rely critically on confluence to match a behavior in π with a corresponding behavior in λ. Because in our setting confluence is lost, we must resort to a different proof.

As already discussed, our translation makes the implicit non-determinism in a $\lambda_{\mathsf{C}}^{\ell}$-term M explicit by adding non-deterministic choices in key points of $[\![M]\!]_u$. Our reduction $\rightsquigarrow$ preserves those branches that simultaneously have the same prefix available (up to $\bowtie$). In proving weak soundness, we exploit the fact that reduction entails delayed commitment. To see this, consider the following terms:

$$(\boldsymbol{\nu}x)((\alpha_1; P_1 \mathbin{+\!\!\!\!\!+} \alpha_2; P_2) \mid Q) \tag{4}$$

$$(\boldsymbol{\nu}x)(\alpha_1; P_1 \mid Q) \mathbin{+\!\!\!\!\!+} (\boldsymbol{\nu}x)(\alpha_2; P_2 \mid Q) \tag{5}$$

In (4), commitment to a choice relies on whether $\alpha_1 \bowtie \alpha_2$ holds (cf. Definition 3). If $\alpha_1 \not\bowtie \alpha_2$, a choice is made; otherwise, commitment is delayed, and depends on P_1 and P_2. Hence, in (4) the possibility of committing to either branch is kept open. In contrast, in (5) commitment to a choice is independent of $\alpha_1 \bowtie \alpha_2$.

Our translation exploits the delayed commitment of non-determinism illustrated by (4) to mimic commitment to non-deterministic choices in $\lambda_{\mathsf{C}}^{\ell}$, which manifests in fetching resources from bags. The fact that this delayed commitment preserves information about the different branches (e.g., P_1 and P_2 in (4)) is essential to establish weak soundness, i.e., to match a behavior in $\mathsf{s}\pi^+$ with a corresponding step in $\lambda_{\mathsf{C}}^{\ell}$. In contrast, forms of non-determinism in $[\![N]\!]_u$ that resemble (5) are useful to characterize behaviors different from fetching.

5 Summary and Related Work

We studied the interplay between resource control and non-determinism in typed calculi. We introduced $\mathsf{s}\pi^+$ and $\lambda_{\mathsf{C}}^{\ell}$, two calculi with non-confluent non-determinism, both with type systems for resource control. Inspired by the untyped π-calculus, non-determinism in $\mathsf{s}\pi^+$ is lazy and explicit, with session types defined following 'propositions-as-sessions' [5]. In $\lambda_{\mathsf{C}}^{\ell}$, non-determinism arises in the fetching of resources, and is regulated by intersection types. A correct translation of $\lambda_{\mathsf{C}}^{\ell}$ into $\mathsf{s}\pi^+$ precisely connects their different forms of non-determinism.

Related Work. Integrating (non-confluent) non-determinism within session types is non-trivial, as carelessly discarding branches would break typability. Work by Caires and Pérez [5], already mentioned, develops a confluent semantics by requiring that non-determinism is only used inside the monad $\&A$; our non-confluent semantics drops this requirement. This allows us to consider non-deterministic choices not possible in [5], such as, e.g., selections of different labels. We stress that linearity is not jeopardized: the branches of '$\mathbin{+\!\!\!\!\!+}$' do not represent *different sessions*, but *different implementations* of the same sessions.

Atkey et al. [1] and Kokke et al. [16] extend 'propositions-as-sessions' with non-determinism. Their approaches are very different (conflation of the additives and bounded linear logic, respectively) and support non-determinism for unrestricted names only. Also, [1,16] do not connect with typed λ-calculi, as we do.

Rocha and Caires also consider non-determinism, relying on confluence in [25] and on unrestricted names in [26]. Casal et al. [7,30] develop a type system for *mixed sessions* (sessions with mixed choices), which can express non-determinism but does not ensure deadlock-freedom. Ensuring deadlock-freedom by typing is a key feature of the 'propositions-as-sessions' approach that we adopt for $s\pi^+$.

Our language $\lambda_{\mathsf{C}}^{\ell}$ is most related to calculi by Boudol [3], Boudol and Laneve [4], and by Pagani and Ronchi Della Rocca [21]. Non-determinism in the calculi in [3,4] is committing and implicit; their linear resources can be consumed *at most* once, rather than *exactly* once. The work [21] considers non-committing non-determinism that is both implicit (as in $\lambda_{\mathsf{C}}^{\ell}$) and explicit (via a sum operator on terms). Both [3,21] develop (non-idempotent) intersection type systems to regulate resources. In our type system, all terms in a bag have the same type; the system in [21] does not enforce this condition. Unlike these type systems, our system for well-formedness can type terms with a lack or an excess of resources.

Boudol and Laneve [4] and Paulus et al. [22] give translations of resource λ-calculi into π. The translation in [4] is used to study the semantics induced upon λ-terms by a translation into π; unlike ours, it does not consider types. As already mentioned in Sect. 4, Paulus et al. [22] relate calculi with *confluent* non-determinism: a resource λ-calculus with sums on terms, and the session π-calculus from [5]. Our translation of terms and that in [22] are very different: while here we use non-deterministic choice to mimic the sharing construct, the translation in [22] uses it to translate bags. Hence, our Theorem 6 cannot be derived from [22].

The last decade of work on 'propositions-as-sessions' has delivered insightful connections with typed λ-calculi—see, e.g., [28,29,31]. Excepting [22], already discussed, none of these works consider non-deterministic λ-calculi.

Acknowledgments. We are grateful to the anonymous reviewers for useful comments on previous versions of this paper. We are also grateful to Mariangiola Dezani for her encouragement and suggestions. This research has been supported by the Dutch Research Council (NWO) under project No. 016.Vidi.189.046 ('Unifying Correctness for Communicating Software') and the EPSRC Fellowship 'VeTSpec: Verified Trustworthy Software Specification' (EP/R034567/1).

References

1. Atkey, R., Lindley, S., Morris, J.G.: Conflation confers concurrency. In: Lindley, S., McBride, C., Trinder, P., Sannella, D. (eds.) A List of Successes That Can Change the World. LNCS, vol. 9600, pp. 32–55. Springer, Cham (2016). https://doi.org/10.1007/978-3-319-30936-1_2
2. Berger, M., Honda, K.: The two-phase commitment protocol in an extended pi-calculus. In: Aceto, L., Victor, B. (eds.) 7th International Workshop on Expressiveness in Concurrency, EXPRESS 2000, Satellite Workshop of CONCUR 2000, State College, PA, USA, 21 August 2000. Electronic Notes in Theoretical Computer Science, vol. 39, pp. 21–46. Elsevier (2000). https://doi.org/10.1016/S1571-0661(05)82502-2

3. Boudol, G.: The lambda-calculus with multiplicities. In: Best, E. (ed.) CONCUR 1993. LNCS, vol. 715, pp. 1–6. Springer, Heidelberg (1993). https://doi.org/10.1007/3-540-57208-2_1
4. Boudol, G., Laneve, C.: Lambda-calculus, multiplicities, and the pi-calculus. In: Proof, Language, and Interaction, Essays in Honour of Robin Milner, pp. 659–690 (2000)
5. Caires, L., Pérez, J.A.: Linearity, control effects, and behavioral types. In: Yang, H. (ed.) ESOP 2017. LNCS, vol. 10201, pp. 229–259. Springer, Heidelberg (2017). https://doi.org/10.1007/978-3-662-54434-1_9
6. Caires, L., Pfenning, F.: Session types as intuitionistic linear propositions. In: Gastin, P., Laroussinie, F. (eds.) CONCUR 2010. LNCS, vol. 6269, pp. 222–236. Springer, Heidelberg (2010). https://doi.org/10.1007/978-3-642-15375-4_16
7. Casal, F., Mordido, A., Vasconcelos, V.T.: Mixed sessions. Theor. Comput. Sci. **897**, 23–48 (2022). https://doi.org/10.1016/j.tcs.2021.08.005
8. de'Liguoro, U., Piperno, A.: Non deterministic extensions of untyped lambda-calculus. Inf. Comput. **122**(2), 149–177 (1995). https://doi.org/10.1006/inco.1995.1145
9. Dezani-Ciancaglini, M.: Logical semantics for concurrent lambda-calculus. Ph.D. thesis, Nijmegen University (1996). https://www.di.unito.it/~dezani/papers/tesi.ps
10. Ehrhard, T., Regnier, L.: The differential lambda-calculus. Theor. Comput. Sci. **309**(1–3), 1–41 (2003). https://doi.org/10.1016/S0304-3975(03)00392-X
11. Gorla, D.: Towards a unified approach to encodability and separation results for process calculi. Inf. Comput. **208**(9), 1031–1053 (2010). https://doi.org/10.1016/j.ic.2010.05.002
12. Groote, J.F., Mousavi, M.R.: Modeling and Analysis of Communicating Systems. MIT Press (2014). https://mitpress.mit.edu/books/modeling-and-analysis-communicating-systems
13. van den Heuvel, B., Paulus, J.W.N., Nantes-Sobrinho, D., Pérez, J.A.: Typed non-determinism in functional and concurrent calculi (extended version). CoRR abs/2205.00680 (2022). https://doi.org/10.48550/arXiv.2205.00680
14. Honda, K.: Types for dyadic interaction. In: Best, E. (ed.) CONCUR 1993. LNCS, vol. 715, pp. 509–523. Springer, Heidelberg (1993). https://doi.org/10.1007/3-540-57208-2_35
15. Honda, K., Vasconcelos, V.T., Kubo, M.: Language primitives and type discipline for structured communication-based programming. In: Hankin, C. (ed.) ESOP 1998. LNCS, vol. 1381, pp. 122–138. Springer, Heidelberg (1998). https://doi.org/10.1007/BFb0053567
16. Kokke, W., Morris, J.G., Wadler, P.: Towards races in linear logic. Log. Meth. Comput. Sci. **16**(4) (2020). https://doi.org/10.23638/LMCS-16(4:15)2020
17. Milner, R.: Functions as processes. Research Report 1154, INRIA, Sophia Antipolis (1990). Final version appeared as [18]
18. Milner, R.: Functions as processes. Math. Struct. Comput. Sci. **2**(2), 119–141 (1992). https://doi.org/10.1017/S0960129500001407
19. Milner, R., Parrow, J., Walker, D.: A calculus of mobile processes. I. Inf. Comput. **100**(1), 1–40 (1992). https://doi.org/10.1016/0890-5401(92)90008-4
20. Nestmann, U., Fuzzati, R., Merro, M.: Modeling consensus in a process calculus. In: Amadio, R., Lugiez, D. (eds.) CONCUR 2003. LNCS, vol. 2761, pp. 399–414. Springer, Heidelberg (2003). https://doi.org/10.1007/978-3-540-45187-7_26

21. Pagani, M., della Rocca, S.R.: Solvability in resource lambda-calculus. In: Ong, L. (ed.) FoSSaCS 2010. LNCS, vol. 6014, pp. 358–373. Springer, Heidelberg (2010). https://doi.org/10.1007/978-3-642-12032-9_25
22. Paulus, J.W.N., Nantes-Sobrinho, D., Pérez, J.A.: Non-deterministic functions as non-deterministic processes. In: Kobayashi, N. (ed.) 6th International Conference on Formal Structures for Computation and Deduction, FSCD 2021, Buenos Aires, Argentina (Virtual Conference), 17–24 July 2021. LIPIcs, vol. 195, pp. 21:1–21:22. Schloss Dagstuhl - Leibniz-Zentrum für Informatik (2021). https://doi.org/10.4230/LIPIcs.FSCD.2021.21, Extended version on https://arxiv.org/abs/2104.14759
23. Peters, K.: Translational expressiveness. Comparing process calculi using encodings. Ph.D. thesis, Berlin Institute of Technology (2012). https://doi.org/10.14279/depositonce-3416
24. Peters, K.: Comparing process calculi using encodings. In: Pérez, J.A., Rot, J. (eds.) Proceedings Combined 26th International Workshop on Expressiveness in Concurrency and 16th Workshop on Structural Operational Semantics, EXPRESS/SOS 2019, Amsterdam, The Netherlands, 26th August 2019. EPTCS, vol. 300, pp. 19–38 (2019). https://doi.org/10.4204/EPTCS.300.2
25. Rocha, P., Caires, L.: Propositions-as-types and shared state. Proc. ACM Program. Lang. **5**(ICFP), 79:1–79:30 (2021). https://doi.org/10.1145/3473584
26. Rocha, P., Caires, L.: Safe session-based concurrency with shared linear state. In: Wies, T. (ed.) Programming Languages and Systems. LNCS, vol. 2072, pp. 421–450. Springer, Cham (2023). https://doi.org/10.1007/978-3-031-30044-8_16
27. Sangiorgi, D., Walker, D.: The Pi-Calculus - A Theory of Mobile Processes. Cambridge University Press, Cambridge (2001)
28. Toninho, B., Caires, L., Pfenning, F.: Functions as session-typed processes. In: Birkedal, L. (ed.) FoSSaCS 2012. LNCS, vol. 7213, pp. 346–360. Springer, Heidelberg (2012). https://doi.org/10.1007/978-3-642-28729-9_23
29. Toninho, B., Yoshida, N.: On polymorphic sessions and functions. In: Ahmed, A. (ed.) ESOP 2018. LNCS, vol. 10801, pp. 827–855. Springer, Cham (2018). https://doi.org/10.1007/978-3-319-89884-1_29
30. Vasconcelos, V.T., Casal, F., Almeida, B., Mordido, A.: Mixed sessions. In: ESOP 2020. LNCS, vol. 12075, pp. 715–742. Springer, Cham (2020). https://doi.org/10.1007/978-3-030-44914-8_26
31. Wadler, P.: Propositions as sessions. In: Thiemann, P., Findler, R.B. (eds.) ACM SIGPLAN International Conference on Functional Programming, ICFP 2012, Copenhagen, Denmark, 9–15 September 2012, pp. 273–286. ACM (2012). https://doi.org/10.1145/2364527.2364568

Interactive Theorem Proving

A Fresh Look at Commutativity: Free Algebraic Structures via Fresh Lists

Clemens Kupke, Fredrik Nordvall Forsberg, and Sean Watters(✉)

University of Strathclyde, Glasgow, UK
{clemens.kupke,fredrik.nordvall-forsberg,sean.watters}@strath.ac.uk

Abstract. We show how types of free idempotent commutative monoids and free commutative monoids can be constructed in ordinary dependent type theory, without the need for quotient types or setoids, and prove that these constructions realise finite sets and multisets, respectively. Both constructions arise as generalisations of C. Coquand's data type of fresh lists. We also show how many other free structures also can be realised by other instantiations. All of our results have been formalised in Agda.

Keywords: Free algebraic structures · Dependent Type theory

1 Introduction

The type of lists is one of the most elementary inductive data types. It has been studied and used extensively by computer scientists and programmers for decades. Two conceptually similar structures are those of finite sets and multisets, which can be thought of as unordered analogues to lists. However, capturing unordered structures in a data type while maintaining desirable properties such as decidable equality and the correct equational theory is challenging.

The usual approach to formalise unordered structures in mathematics is to represent them as functions (with finite support): finite sets as $X \to 2$, and finite multisets as $X \to \mathbb{N}$, respectively. However, these representations do not enjoy decidable equality, even if the underlying type X does.

The approach taken in most programming languages is to pretend — one uses a list (or another ordered structure for efficiency) internally, but hides it and any invariants behind a layer of abstraction provided by an API. However, each set or multiset can then be represented by many different lists, meaning that the equational theory might not be correct. This is a problem in a dependently typed setting, where having equality as a first-class type allows us to distinguish between different representations of the same set.

The analogous approach in dependent type theory is to encode these invariants in an equivalence relation on lists, and define finite sets and multisets as setoids of lists plus the appropriate equivalence relation [4]. However, this merely side-steps the issue; we may still have two distinct lists which represent the same finite (multi)set. Thus, we are forced to work with the equivalence relation at all times instead of the identity type.

C.-K. Hur (Ed.): APLAS 2023, LNCS 14405, pp. 135–154, 2023.
https://doi.org/10.1007/978-981-99-8311-7_7

In the setting of homotopy type theory [30] (HoTT), we can use higher inductive types (HITs) to define the identities on an inductive type simultaneously with its elements. This allows us to bridge the gap from the setoid approach to obtain a data type which enjoys both decidable equality and the right equational theory, as demonstrated by Choudhury and Fiore [9].

However, it may not always be possible to work in HoTT; thus, the main question we set out to answer in this work is whether it is possible in ordinary dependent type theory to define data types of finite sets and multisets, which:

(i) have decidable equality iff the underlying set has decidable equality; and
(ii) satisfy the equational theories of finite sets and multisets.

For the latter, we take as our success criteria the facts that the type of finite sets is the free idempotent commutative monoid [13] and that finite multisets are the free commutative monoid. Thus, we are really aiming to find data types for the free idempotent commutative monoid and free commutative monoid, which satisfy the above property (i). We accomplish this by restricting our attention to only those sets with decidable equality that can be totally ordered. We can then form a type of sorted lists over such a set. Provided we treat the existence of the ordering data carefully, this type turns out to give us exactly finite sets when the order is strict, and finite multisets when it is non-strict.

We show that our constructions satisfy universal properties, in the sense that they are left adjoints to forgetful functors — this is the standard way to state freeness in the language of category theory. However, note that the notion of freeness is with respect to e.g. totally ordered monoids, rather than all monoids. For proving the universal properties and for defining the categories involved, we need function extensionality. Nevertheless the constructions themselves work in ordinary dependent type theory.

Related Work. Fresh lists, the key inductive data type of this work, were first introduced by C. Coquand to represent contexts in the simply typed lambda calculus [11], and then highlighted as an example of an inductive-recursive definition by Dybjer [12]. The particular notion of fresh list discussed here is a minor variation of the version found in the Agda standard library [2], which generalises the notion of freshness to an arbitrary relation.

In Sect. 4 we discuss sorted lists and finite sets, both of which have been extensively investigated in the past. Sorted lists are one of the archetypal examples of a dependent type, with one particularly elegant treatment of them being given by McBride [21]. Meanwhile, Appel and Leroy [3] recently introduced canonical binary tries as an extensional representation of finite *maps*. These can be used to construct finite sets with elements from the index type (positive natural numbers for Appel and Leroy). The use of tries allows for significantly improved lookup performance compared to lists, and with more work, it is conceivable that finite sets with elements from an arbitrary but fixed first-order data type could be extensionally represented this way [16]. Our representation using sorted lists is not as efficient, but on the other hand works uniformly in the element type, as long as it is equipped with a total order.

In the setting of HoTT, there is a significant body of existing work. Choudhury and Fiore [9] give a treatment of finite multisets, showing how they can be constructed using HITs. Joram and Veltri [19] continue this thread with a treatment of the final coalgebra of the finite multiset functor. Earlier, Piceghello's PhD thesis [24] investigated coherence for symmetric monoidal groupoids, showing an equivalence between free symmetric monoidal groupoids and sorted lists. Building on this, Choudhury et al. [10] investigated the relationship between sorting algorithms and the symmetric group S_n, as part of a study of the groupoid semantics of reversible programming languages.

Contributions. We make the following contributions:

- We show how finite sets and multisets can be constructed in ordinary dependent type theory, without using quotient types or working with setoids.
- We prove that, assuming function extensionality, our finite sets construction forms a free-forgetful adjunction between the category of sets equipped with an order relation, and the category of idempotent, commutative monoids equipped with an order relation. Similarly our finite multisets construction form an adjunction between sets equipped with an order relation and the category of commutative monoids equipped with an order relation.
- We show how the above constructions arise from instantiations of the data type of fresh lists, and how other instantiations give free left-regular band monoids, free reflexive partial monoids, free monoids, and free pointed sets.

All our constructions and results are formalised in the proof assistant Agda, using the `--safe` and `--cubical-compatible` flags. The development [31] builds on the Agda standard library, contains around 5,300 lines of code, and typechecks in around 35 s on an Intel i5-1145G7 laptop with 16 GiB of RAM. An HTML listing of the Agda code can be found at https://seanwatters.uk/agda/fresh-lists/. Each result also has a clickable hyperlink ⚙ to the corresponding formalised statement.

2 Preliminaries and Setting

We work in the mathematical setting of Martin-Löf type theory, for example as realised by Agda [23]. We write $(x : A) \to B\,x$ for the dependent function type, and use curly braces $\{x : A\} \to B\,x$ when we wish to leave the argument x implicit. We write $a = b$ for the identity type, and $a := b$ for definitions.

We say that a type A is *propositional* if all its elements are equal, that is, if $(x, y : A) \to x = y$ is provable. A type is a *set* if its identity type is propositional. Many of the types we work with will turn out to be sets (indeed, at times we take this as a prerequisite), but we do *not* assume Streicher's Axiom K [27] at the meta level, which states that every type is a set. On the other hand, we also do not assume any features from homotopy type theory, but aim to stay compatible with it. We write Type for the universe of all types, and Set and Prop for the appropriate restrictions to sets and propositions, respectively.

3 Fresh Lists

In this section we introduce the key notion of fresh lists. As we will see later, depending on the notion of freshness, fresh lists can represent various data types such as lists consisting of repetitions of one element, or lists where all elements are distinct. For us the most important example of fresh lists will be sorted lists. We will use these in Sects. 4 and 5 as representations of the free (idempotent) commutative monoid over a set equipped with an order relation.

In technical terms, the type of fresh lists is a parameterised data type similar to the type of ordinary lists, with the additional requirement that in order to adjoin a new element x to a list xs, that element x must be "fresh" with respect to all other elements already present in the list xs. For convenience, we use an inductive-inductive [22] simultaneous definition of the freshness predicate; the Agda standard library instead uses an inductive-recursive definition.

Definition 1 (⚙). *Given a type A and a binary relation $R : A \to A \to \mathsf{Type}$, we mutually inductively define a type $\mathit{FList}(A, R)$, together with a relation $\#_R : A \to \mathit{FList}(A, R) \to \mathsf{Type}$, by the following constructors:*

$$\begin{aligned} \mathit{nil} &: \mathit{FList}(A, R) \\ \mathit{cons} &: (x : A) \to (xs : \mathit{FList}(A, R)) \to x \#_R\ xs \to \mathit{FList}(A, R) \end{aligned}$$

$$\begin{aligned} \mathit{nil}_\# &: \{a : A\} \to a \#_R\ \mathit{nil} \\ \mathit{cons}_\# &: \{a : A\} \to \{x : A\} \to \{xs : \mathit{FList}(A, R)\} \to \{p : x \#_R\ xs\} \to \\ &\qquad\qquad R\ a\ x \to a \#_R\ xs \to a \#_R\ (\mathit{cons}\ x\ xs\ p\ ) \end{aligned}$$

For $a, x : A$, and $xs : \mathit{FList}(A, R)$, we say that a is fresh for x when we have $R\ a\ x$, and that a is fresh for xs when we have $a \#_R\ xs$.

Our presentation of fresh lists internalises the proof data in the cons constructor. One alternative "externalised" approach is to define the type of fresh lists as the type of pairs of an ordinary list, together with a single freshness proof for the whole list. This externalised presentation is isomorphic to ours, but we do not make further use of it in this work as we find it more convenient to enforce our invariants at the level of the constructors.

Proposition 2 (⚙). *For any $R : A \to A \to \mathsf{Type}$, we have $\mathit{FList}(A, R) \cong \Sigma(xs : \mathit{List}\ A).\mathit{is\text{-}fresh}_R\ xs$, where $\mathit{is\text{-}fresh}_R : \mathit{List}\ A \to \mathsf{Type}$ is defined by*

$$\begin{aligned} \mathit{is\text{-}fresh}_R\ \mathit{nil} &:= \top \\ \mathit{is\text{-}fresh}_R\ (\mathit{cons}\ x\ xs) &:= (\mathit{All}\ (R\ x)\ xs) \times (\mathit{is\text{-}fresh}_R\ xs) \end{aligned}$$

□

The definition of the type of fresh lists makes no explicit assumptions about the properties of the relation R. Note in particular that $R\ x\ y$ may or may not be propositional. However, in practice, we would like to have that two fresh lists are equal if and only if their heads and tails are equal. For this, we need to require $x \#_R xs$ to be propositional for all $x : A$ and $xs : \mathsf{FList}(A, R)$. This is the case exactly when $R\ x\ y$ is propositional for all $x, y : A$.

Proposition 3 (⚙). *Let $R : A \to A \to \mathsf{Type}$. The type $R\,x\,y$ is propositional for all $x, y : A$ if and only if $x \#_R xs$ is propositional for all $x : A$ and $xs : \mathsf{FList}(A, R)$.*

Proof. If R is propositional, then any two $p, q : x \#_R xs$ are equal by induction over p and q. In the other direction, if $p, q : R\,x\,y$, then $\mathsf{cons}_\# \ p \ \mathsf{nil}_\#, \mathsf{cons}_\# \ q \ \mathsf{nil}_\# : x \#_R [y]$, hence $p = q$ by assumption, and injectivity of $\mathsf{cons}_\#$. □

This gives us the expected characterisation of equality of fresh lists:

Corollary 4 (⚙). *Assume R is propositional. We have $\mathsf{cons}\ x\ xs\ p = \mathsf{cons}\ y\ ys\ q$ for any freshness proofs p and q if and only if $x = y$ and $xs = ys$. In particular, if A has decidable equality, then so does $\mathsf{FList}(A, R)$.* □

The following lemma tells us that when the freshness relation R is transitive, then $a \#_R xs$ can be established by a single proof that a is related to the head of xs. It follows by a straightforward induction on xs.

Lemma 5 (⚙). *If R is transitive, then for any $a, x : A$ and $xs : \mathsf{FList}(A, R)$, if $R\,a\,x$ and $x \#_R xs$ then $a \#_R xs$.* □

We next define the standard $\mathsf{Any}\ P$ predicate on fresh lists, which holds if the predicate P is satisfied by some element of the list.

Definition 6 (⚙). *Let $P : A \to \mathsf{Type}$. The family $\mathsf{Any}\ P : \mathsf{FList}(A, R) \to \mathsf{Type}$ is defined inductively by the following constructors:*

$$\mathsf{here} : \{x : A\}\{xs : \mathsf{FList}(A, R)\}\{p : x \#_R xs\} \to P\ x \to \mathsf{Any}\ P\ (\mathsf{cons}\ x\ xs\ p)$$
$$\mathsf{there} : \{x : A\}\{xs : \mathsf{FList}(A, R)\}\{p : x \#_R xs\} \to \mathsf{Any}\ P\ xs \to \mathsf{Any}\ P\ (\mathsf{cons}\ x\ xs\ p)$$

Using this construction, we can now define the membership relation $\in$ on fresh lists, i.e., the type of proofs $x \in xs$ that some element of xs is equal to x.

Definition 7 (⚙). *For $x : A$ and $xs : \mathsf{FList}(A, R)$, let*

$$x \in xs := \mathsf{Any}\ (\lambda(a : A).\, x = a)\ xs\ .$$

The following lemma relates freshness and the membership relation: a is fresh for xs if and only if a is related to every element in xs.

Lemma 8 (⚙). *Let $a : A$ and $xs : \mathsf{FList}(A, R)$. We have $a \#_R xs$ if and only if $R\,a\,b$ holds for every $b : A$ such that $b \in xs$.* □

Although the freshness proofs are essential when *building* a list, if we want to do recursion on a given list, we frequently only care about the elements, not the proofs (regardless of whether the freshness relation is propositional or not). As such, we can define right fold in the same manner as for ordinary lists, and show that it is the universal way to define functions which ignore freshness proofs.

Proposition 9 (⚙). *For types X and Y, there is a function*

$$\mathsf{foldr} : (X \to Y \to Y) \to Y \to \mathsf{FList}(X, R) \to Y$$

satisfying $\mathsf{foldr}\ f\ e\ \mathsf{nil} = e$ *and* $\mathsf{foldr}\ f\ e\ (\mathsf{cons}\ x\ xs\ p) = f\ x\ (\mathsf{foldr}\ f\ e\ xs)$, *and* foldr *is universal in the following sense: For all functions* $h : \mathsf{FList}(X, R) \to Y$, *if there is* $e : Y$ *and* $f : X \to Y \to Y$ *such that* $h\ \mathsf{nil} = e$ *and* $h\ (\mathsf{cons}\ x\ xs\ p) = f\ x\ (h\ xs)$, *then* $h\ xs = \mathsf{foldr}\ f\ e\ xs$ *for all* $xs : \mathsf{FList}(X, R)$. □

The proof is identical to the analogous one for ordinary lists [17].

4 Free Idempotent Commutative Monoids via Sorted Lists

The important mathematical concept of a (finite) set is also a useful abstract data structure for programmers. In circumstances where we are only concerned with whether a particular element is present or not, it is advantageous to represent data in an unordered form. However, the details of exactly how to do this in a programming context are not straightforward. Inductive data types such as lists and trees, for example, are inherently ordered.

In this section, we unify the two notions of finite sets and sorted lists. We instantiate fresh lists with a strict total order as the freshness relation, giving a data type for sorted lists which cannot contain duplicates, and use this as our representation of finite sets. The key idea is that instead of working with ordinary lists quotiented by permutations (as Choudhury and Fiore [9] do), we force every collection of elements to have exactly one permissible permutation via our lists being sorted-by-construction. As a direct consequence, this type admits an extensionality principle analogous to that of sets — two sorted lists are equal if and only if they have the same elements.

4.1 Sorted Lists

We begin by defining the type $\mathsf{SList}(A, <)$ of sorted duplicate-free lists over A as an instance of FList.

Definition 10 (⚙). *Let A be a type, and* $<: A \to A \to \mathsf{Prop}$ *a propositional strict total order, i.e.,* $<$ *is propositional, transitive, and trichotomous: for every* $x, y : A$, *exactly one of* $x < y$ *or* $x = y$ *or* $y < x$ *holds. Then let* $\mathsf{SList}(A, <) := \mathsf{FList}(A, <)$.

We write $\#$ for $\#_<$, for simplicity. Note that with this exclusive-disjunction presentation of trichotomy, having a constructive witness that $<$ is trichotomous immediately implies decidable equality on A. This makes intuitive sense as we would like the question of whether an element can be appended to a list to be decidable. By Hedberg's theorem, having decidable equality also means that A is a set [15].

We now define the binary operation which merges two sorted lists together, suggestively named $\cup$, with a view towards showing that $(\mathsf{SList}(A, <),\ \cup,\ \mathsf{nil})$ is an idempotent commutative monoid. We initially define the monoid multiplication only on elements, without heed to whether any appropriate freshness proofs exist that validate the definition. We then show that such proofs do exist for all inputs.

Proposition 11 (⚙). *There is* $\cup : \mathsf{SList}(A,<) \to \mathsf{SList}(A,<) \to \mathsf{SList}(A,<)$ *with*

$$\begin{aligned} \mathsf{nil} \cup ys &:= ys \\ xs \cup \mathsf{nil} &:= xs \end{aligned}$$

$$(\mathsf{cons}\ x\ xs\ p) \cup (\mathsf{cons}\ y\ ys\ q) := \begin{cases} \mathsf{cons}\ x\ (xs \cup (\mathsf{cons}\ y\ ys\ q))\ r & \text{if } x < y \\ \mathsf{cons}\ x\ (xs \cup ys)\ s & \text{if } x = y \\ \mathsf{cons}\ y\ ((\mathsf{cons}\ x\ xs\ p) \cup ys)\ t & \text{if } x > y \end{cases}$$

for freshness proofs r, s, *and* t *of the following types, which can be computed mutually with the definition of* $\cup$*:*

$$\begin{aligned} r &: x \# (xs \cup (\mathsf{cons}\ y\ ys\ q)) \\ s &: x \# (xs \cup ys) \\ t &: y \# ((\mathsf{cons}\ x\ xs\ p) \cup ys) \end{aligned}$$

Proof. Mutually with the definition of $\cup$, we prove that for all $a : A$ and $xs, ys : \mathsf{SList}(A,<)$, if a is fresh for both xs and ys, then a is fresh for $xs \cup ys$. The freshness proofs r, s, and t required can then be constructed from p and q. The proof follows by induction on both lists. If either list is nil, then the proof is trivial. Now consider the case where we must show that a is fresh for $(\mathsf{cons}\ x\ xs\ p) \cup (\mathsf{cons}\ y\ ys\ q)$, for some $x, y : A$, $xs, ys : \mathsf{SList}(A,<)$, $p : x \# xs$, and $q : y \# ys$. By trichotomy, we have three cases to consider; either $x < y$, $x = y$, or $x > y$. If $x < y$, then we must show that $a \# \mathsf{cons}\ x\ (xs \cup (\mathsf{cons}\ y\ ys\ q))$. By assumption, $a < x$, and $a \# (xs \cup (\mathsf{cons}\ y\ ys\ q))$ by the induction hypothesis. The cases for $x = y$ and $x > y$ follow by similar arguments. □

4.2 Sorted Lists Form an Idempotent Commutative Monoid

We now prove that $(\mathsf{SList}(A,<), \cup, \mathsf{nil})$ is an idempotent commutative monoid. The main tool we use for this proof is an *extensionality principle* for sorted lists, which is analogous to the axiom of extensionality for sets. In order to prove the extensionality principle, we require the following lemma. Its proof follows straightforwardly from the properties of $<$.

Lemma 12 (⚙). *Let* $a, x : A$, $xs : \mathsf{SList}(A,<)$, *and* $p : x \# xs$.

(i) If $a < x$, *then* $a \notin (\mathsf{cons}\ x\ xs\ p)$.
(ii) If $a \# xs$, *then* $a \notin xs$. □

We are now ready to prove the extensionality principle, which characterises the identity type of SList.

Theorem 13 (⚙ Extensionality Principle for SList). *Given sorted lists $xs, ys : \mathsf{SList}(A, <)$, we have $(a \in xs) \longleftrightarrow (a \in ys)$ for all $a : A$ iff $xs = ys$.*

Proof. The direction from right to left is obvious. For the other direction, we proceed by induction on both lists. The case where both are nil is trivial. The cases where one is nil and the other is cons are trivially impossible.

We focus on the case where we must show $(\mathsf{cons}\ x\ xs\ p) = (\mathsf{cons}\ y\ ys\ q)$, for some $x, y : A$, $xs, ys : \mathsf{SList}(A, <)$, $p : x \# xs$ and $q : y \# ys$. Assume $(a \in \mathsf{cons}\ x\ xs\ p) \longleftrightarrow (a \in \mathsf{cons}\ y\ ys\ q)$. By trichotomy, either $x < y$, $x > y$, or $x = y$. The former two cases are impossible by Lemma 12. Therefore, $x = y$. By Corollary 4, since $<$ is proof irrelevant, it now suffices to show $xs = ys$. By the induction hypothesis, this will be the case if $(a \in xs) \longleftrightarrow (a \in ys)$. For the forward direction, assume $u : a \in xs$. Applying there u to our initial assumption, we get $a \in (\mathsf{cons}\ y\ ys\ q)$. Either $a = y$, or $a \in ys$. The former case is impossible; if $a = y$, then $a = x$ by transitivity, so by Lemma 12, $a \notin xs$. But $a \in xs$ by assumption. Contradiction. The other direction follows the same argument. □

Using the extensionality principle, it is now not hard to prove that sorted lists form an idempotent commutative monoid.

Proposition 14 (⚙). *$(\mathsf{SList}(A, <),\ \cup,\ \mathsf{nil})$ is an idempotent commutative monoid. That is, the following equations hold for all $xs, ys, zs : \mathsf{SList}(A, <)$:*

- *unit:* $(\mathsf{nil} \cup xs) = xs = (xs \cup \mathsf{nil})$
- *associativity:* $((xs \cup ys) \cup zs) = (xs \cup (ys \cup zs))$
- *commutativity:* $(xs \cup ys) = (ys \cup xs)$
- *idempotence:* $(xs \cup xs) = xs$

Proof. The unit laws are trivial. For associativity, commutativity, and idempotence, we first prove that $a \in (xs \cup ys)$ if and only if $a \in xs$ or $a \in ys$. The equations then follow more or less directly using Theorem 13. □

4.3 A Free-Forgetful Adjunction

Since singleton lists are always sorted, they clearly give an inclusion of the underlying type A into the type of sorted lists. We might thus hope that $\mathsf{SList}(A, <)$ can be characterised by the universal property of being the smallest idempotent commutative monoid generated by A, i.e., that it is the free idempotent commutative monoid. However, in order to form the type of sorted lists over some type A, we must already have a strict total order on A. And we cannot assume that we would be able to find such an order for any set; this is a weak form of the Axiom of Choice, called the Ordering Principle (OP) (see e.g. [18, §2.3]), which implies excluded middle, as proven by Swan [28]. As such, in our constructive setting, the domain of the SList functor cannot be Set, as it lacks the required data to form sorted lists. Instead of Set, we must consider a category whose objects are linearly ordered sets (in the same sense as we have used thus far, which implies decidable equality on the elements).

We also require a forgetful functor from our category of idempotent commutative monoids into this category of linearly ordered sets, which intuitively needs to retain this ordering data — we only want to forget the monoid structure. As such, instead of the category of idempotent commutative monoids, we must consider a category of such structures equipped with their own linear orders. There are some design decisions to be made in defining these categories, regarding how much structure the morphisms ought to preserve. Specifically, we must decide whether they should be monotone with respect to the ordering data of the objects. We argue that the correct decision here is (perhaps counter-intuitively) to *not* preserve the order, a choice that we will motivate more fully in Sect. 4.4.

Definition 15 (⚙). *Let* STO *denote the category whose objects are strictly totally ordered types, and whose morphisms are (not necessarily monotone) functions on the underlying types. That is:*

- *Objects are pairs* $(X, \ <_X)$ *of a type* X *together with a propositional strict total order* $<_X \colon X \to X \to \mathsf{Prop}$.
- *Morphisms from* $(X, \ <_X)$ *to* $(Y, \ <_Y)$ *are functions* $X \to Y$.

As previously remarked, the trichotomy property of $<_X$ implies that X has decidable equality, which in turn means that X is a set, by Hedberg's theorem [15].

Definition 16 (⚙). *Let* OICMon *denote the category whose objects are strictly totally ordered idempotent commutative monoids (where the monoid multiplication does not necessarily preserve ordering), and whose morphisms are (not necessarily monotone) monoid homomorphisms. That is:*

- *Objects are 4-tuples* $(X, \ <_X, \ \cdot_X, \ \epsilon_X)$ *of a set* X*, a propositional strict total order* $<_X \colon X \to X \to \mathsf{Prop}$*, a binary operation* $\cdot_X : X \to X \to X$*, and an object* $\epsilon_X : X$*, such that* $(X, \ \cdot_X, \ \epsilon_X)$ *is an idempotent commutative monoid.*
- *Morphisms from* $(X, \ <_X, \ \cdot_X, \ \epsilon_X)$ *to* $(Y, \ <_Y, \ \cdot_Y, \ \epsilon_Y)$ *are functions* $f : X \to Y$ *which preserve units and multiplication.*

Since morphisms in OICMon formally carry witnesses that the underlying functions preserve unit and multiplication, this could potentially make proofs of equality between such morphisms troublesome. Thankfully, because the underlying types are sets, these troubles do not materialise, as long as we have function extensionality. This is recorded in the following lemma.

Lemma 17 (⚙). *Assuming function extensionality, two morphisms of* OICMon *are equal if and only if their underlying set functions are (pointwise) equal.* □

We must now show that as well as being idempotent commutative monoids, our sorted lists also come equipped with strict total orders. We do this by defining a lifting of orders on a type to orders on sorted lists over that type, using the lexicographic order. Note that while we require the existence of an order to have an object in OICMon, the exact choice of order does not matter; any two objects in the category with the same underlying set will be isomorphic.

Proposition 18 (⚙). *Let $<$ be a propositional strict total order on a type A. Then the lexicographic order $<_L$ on $\mathsf{SList}(A,<)$, defined inductively below, is also a propositional strict total order.*

$$\begin{aligned}
\mathit{nil}_{<_L} &: \{y : A\}\ \{ys : \mathit{SList}(A,<)\}\ \{q : y \# ys\} \\
&\quad \to \mathit{nil} <_L \mathit{cons}\ y\ ys\ q \\
\mathit{here}_{<_L} &: \{x, y : A\}\ \{xs, ys : \mathit{SList}(A,<)\}\ \{p : x \# xs\}\ \{q : y \# ys\} \\
&\quad \to x < y \to \mathit{cons}\ x\ xs\ p <_L \mathit{cons}\ y\ ys\ q \\
\mathit{there}_{<_L} &: \{x, y : A\}\ \{xs, ys : \mathit{SList}(A,<)\}\ \{p : x \# xs\}\ \{q : y \# ys\} \\
&\quad \to x = y \to xs <_L ys \to \mathit{cons}\ x\ xs\ p <_L \mathit{cons}\ y\ ys\ q
\end{aligned}$$

□

We can now show that SList is a functor STO → OICMon, with action on objects given by $\mathsf{SList}(A,<_A) := (\mathsf{SList}(A,<_A), <_L, \cup, \mathsf{nil})$. We define the action on morphisms on the underlying sets, and then show that it preserves the monoid structure, and hence is a morphism in OICMon. Our implementation of map for sorted lists is essentially insertion sort; we take a function on the underlying set, apply it to each element, and insert the result into the output list.

Definition 19 (⚙). *Given two types A and B with strict total orders $<_A : A \to A \to \mathsf{Prop}$ and $<_B : B \to B \to \mathsf{Prop}$, let:*

$$\begin{aligned}
&\mathit{map} : (A \to B) \to \mathit{SList}(A,<_A) \to \mathit{SList}(B,<_B) \\
&\mathit{map}\ f\ \mathit{nil} := \mathit{nil} \\
&\mathit{map}\ f\ (\mathit{cons}\ x\ xs\ p) := \mathit{insert}\ (f\ x)\ (\mathit{map}\ f\ xs)
\end{aligned}$$

where $\mathit{insert}\ x\ xs := (\mathit{cons}\ x\ \mathit{nil}\ \mathit{nil}_{\#}) \cup xs$.

We now show that map preserves the monoid structure, and hence is a morphism in OICMon. The proof uses Theorem 13.

Lemma 20 (⚙). *For all functions $f : A \to B$ and $xs, ys : \mathit{SList}(A,<)$, we have*

$$\mathit{map}\ f\ (xs \cup ys) = (\mathit{map}\ f\ xs) \cup (\mathit{map}\ f\ ys)$$

□

Similarly, assuming function extensionality and using Lemma 17, we can show that map preserves identity and composition, and hence is a functor.

Theorem 21 (⚙). *Assuming function extensionality, SList : STO → OICMon forms a functor which is left adjoint to the forgetful functor $\mathcal{U}$: OICMon → STO defined by $\mathcal{U}(X,<,\cdot,\epsilon) := (X,<)$.*

Proof. The bijection on homsets sends a monoid morphism $f : \mathsf{SList}(A,<_A) \to (B,<,\cdot,\epsilon)$ to the function $\hat{f} : A \to B$ defined by $\hat{f} := \lambda(x : A).\ f\ (\mathsf{cons}\ x\ \mathsf{nil}\ \mathsf{nil}_{\#})$, and a function $g : A \to B$ to the monoid morphism $\check{g} : \mathsf{SList}(A,<_A) \to (B,<,\cdot,\epsilon)$ defined by $\check{g} := \mathsf{foldr}\ (\lambda(a : A)(b : B).\ (g\ a) \cdot_B b)\ \epsilon_B$. The fact that $\check{\hat{f}} = f$ follows from Proposition 9. The proofs of $\hat{\check{g}} = g$ and naturality follow by unfolding the definitions and Lemma 17 — hence the assumption of function extensionality.

□

4.4 Motivating the Lack of Monotonicity

We now return to our decision to not require monotonicity for the morphisms of STO and OICMon. That we require our objects to have ordering information at all could be seen as an implementation detail; the ordering is needed to form the type of sorted lists, but thereafter we would like to treat them as finite sets.

For an illustrative example, consider the different notions of map that we obtain with and without monotonicity (recall Definition 19 for the latter). With monotonicity, we would obtain a functorial action which applies a monotone function to each element in place, such that map is also monotone. However, in practice we do not find much value in respecting whichever arbitrary order was chosen; we would rather have the freedom to lift any function to act on sorted lists, and have the implementation of map handle the details. In practice, we are mostly interested in finite sets over first order inductive data types anyway, and these can always be totally ordered. More provocatively: since we work on a computer, all of our data ought to be represented by a bit pattern in the end anyway, and by considering not necessarily monotone functions, we ensure that the particular choice of ordering derived from these bit patterns play no role.

In the same spirit, one could wonder if there is actually any difference between the categories STO and Set. After all, since morphisms are not monotone, all objects in STO with the same underlying type are actually isomorphic. The following proposition makes clear what kind of choice principle is needed in order to choose a canonical representative for these isomorphism classes. Recall that the Ordering Principle states that every set can be totally ordered: for every set X, there is a strict total order on X. This principle is weaker than the Axiom of Choice, but not provable in ZF set theory [25]; in the context of Homotopy Type Theory, Swan proved that the Ordering Principle implies Excluded Middle [28].

Proposition 22 (⚙). *The Ordering Principle holds if and only if both forgetful functors* $\mathcal{U}_{\mathsf{STO}} : \mathsf{STO} \to \mathsf{Set}$ *and* $\mathcal{U}_{\mathsf{OICMon}} : \mathsf{OICMon} \to \mathsf{ICMon}$ *are equivalences.*

Proof. If the Ordering Principle holds, then each type can be equipped with an strict total order, which gives an inverse to each forgetful functor. Conversely, an inverse to the forgetful functors equips each set with a strict total order. □

Thus, in the presence of the non-constructive Ordering Principle, sorted lists are the free idempotent commutative monoid over sets. However we prefer to stay constructive and ask for more input data in the form of an order instead.

5 Free Commutative Monoids via Sorted Lists with Duplicates

Finite multisets have long been applied across computer science, particularly in database theory [6]. However their unordered nature again makes representing them in a data type challenging. We have seen that when we consider fresh lists with a strict total order as the freshness relation, we obtain a data type for sorted lists which contain no duplicate elements. If we drop the requirement that the order is irreflexive, we obtain a type $\mathsf{SListD}(A, \leqslant)$ of sorted lists where repetitions are allowed. The corresponding notion of trichotemy in this setting is totality of the order (i.e., for all x and y, either $x \leqslant y$ or $y \leqslant x$), together with decidability of both the order and the equality on the underlying type.

Definition 23 (⚙). *Let A be a type with decidable equality, and $\leqslant : A \to A \to$ Prop a propositional, decidable total order. Then let $\mathsf{SListD}(A, \leqslant) := \mathsf{FList}(A, \leqslant)$.*

Again we write $\#$ for $\#_{\leqslant}$. Using the decidability of the order, we can now again define the merge operation on sorted lists.

Proposition 24 (⚙). *There is $\cup : \mathsf{SListD}(A, \leqslant) \to \mathsf{SListD}(A, \leqslant) \to \mathsf{SListD}(A, \leqslant)$ with*

$$\mathsf{nil} \cup ys := ys$$
$$xs \cup \mathsf{nil} := xs$$
$$(\mathsf{cons}\ x\ xs\ p) \cup (\mathsf{cons}\ y\ ys\ q) := \begin{cases} \mathsf{cons}\ x\ (xs \cup (\mathsf{cons}\ y\ ys\ q))\ r & \text{if } x \leqslant y \\ \mathsf{cons}\ y\ ((\mathsf{cons}\ x\ xs\ p) \cup ys)\ s & \text{otherwise} \end{cases}$$

where freshness proofs r and s with the following types exist by the same argument as in Proposition 11:

$$r : x \# (xs \cup (\mathsf{cons}\ y\ ys\ q))$$
$$s : y \# ((\mathsf{cons}\ x\ xs\ p) \cup ys)$$

□

Just as SList corresponds to finite sets and free idempotent commutative monoids, SListD corresponds to finite multisets and free commutative monoids. Our proof strategy follows the same structure as for Theorem 13, with one notable exception — the extensionality principle as stated for SList is not true for SListD, where for example $[a, a]$ and $[a]$ have the same elements, but with different multiplicity. Put differently: as Gylterud noted, the membership relation is prop-valued for sets, but set-valued for multisets [14, § 3.5]. As such, the extensionality principle for multisets uses isomorphism rather than logical equivalence: multisets xs and ys are equal if and only if $(a \in xs) \simeq (a \in ys)$ for every element a.

However, isomorphisms can be onerous to work with formally, and we can do better. Note that there will be a function $\mathsf{count} : \mathsf{SListD}(A, \leqslant) \to A \to \mathbb{N}$ which, given a sorted list and some element of A, returns the number of occurrences of that element in the list. We can also think of this function as converting a sorted list to its multiplicity function. The extensionality principle that we will prove is the following: two sorted list with duplicates are equal if and only if their multiplicity functions are pointwise equal. We stress that we do not need to assume function extensionality for this result.

We prove the non-trivial "if" direction in two stages: pointwise equality of multiplicity functions implies isomorphism of membership relations, which in turn implies equality of sorted lists. First, we define the count function:

Definition 25 (⚙). *Let* $\mathsf{count} : \mathsf{SListD}(A, \leqslant) \to A \to \mathbb{N}$, *where:*

$$\mathsf{count}\ \mathsf{nil}\ x := 0$$

$$\mathsf{count}\ (\mathsf{cons}\ y\ ys\ p)\ x := \begin{cases} 1 + (\mathsf{count}\ ys\ x) & \text{if } x = y \\ \mathsf{count}\ ys\ x & \text{otherwise} \end{cases}$$

We collect some basic properties of the count function.

Lemma 26 (⚙).

(i) For any $x : A$ *and* $ys : \mathsf{SListD}(A, \leqslant)$, *if* $x \notin ys$ *then* $\mathsf{count}\ ys\ x = 0$.
(ii) If for all $a : A$ *we have* $\mathsf{count}\ (\mathsf{cons}\ x\ xs\ p)\ a = \mathsf{count}\ (\mathsf{cons}\ y\ ys\ q)\ a$, *then for all* $a : A$ *also* $\mathsf{count}\ xs\ a = \mathsf{count}\ ys\ a$.

Proof. Part (i) follows by induction on ys. For (ii), by decidable equality of A, either $x = y$, or $x \neq y$, and by decidability of $\leqslant$, either $x \leqslant y$, or $y \leqslant x$. Without loss of generality, assume $x \leqslant y$.

If $x = y$, then peeling away the heads will either preserve the number of as on both sides, or decrement each count by one; in either case, the conclusion follows.

If $x \neq y$, we consider the four cases where each of x and y are either equal to a or not. The case where $x \neq a \neq y$ follows by the same argument as when $x = y$. The case where $x = a = y$ is impossible since $x \neq y$. Finally, also the case where $x = a \neq y$ (or the other way around) is impossible: we have $a = x \leqslant y$ and $y \# ys$, hence $a \notin \mathsf{cons}\ y\ ys\ q$, hence $\mathsf{count}\ (\mathsf{cons}\ y\ ys\ q)\ a = 0$ by (i). But since $a = x$, we have that $\mathsf{count}\ (\mathsf{cons}\ x\ xs\ p)\ a \geqslant 1$, contradicting the assumption. □

We are now ready to prove the first step towards the extensionality principle.

Proposition 27 (⚙). *Let* $xs, ys : \mathsf{SListD}(A, \leqslant)$. *If* $\mathsf{count}\ xs\ a = \mathsf{count}\ ys\ a$ *for all* $a : A$, *then we have isomorphisms* $(a \in xs) \cong (a \in ys)$ *for all* $a : A$.

Proof. The proof proceeds by induction on both lists. The case where both lists are nil holds trivially. Both cases where one is nil and the other is not are trivially impossible. When the lists are of the form $\mathsf{cons}\ x\ xs\ p$ and $\mathsf{cons}\ y\ ys\ q$, we can apply Lemma 26 to obtain that $\mathsf{count}\ xs\ a = \mathsf{count}\ ys\ a$ for all $a : A$. Then by the induction hypothesis, there is $f : (a \in xs) \cong (a \in ys)$. We now apply decidable equality of A to make a case distinction between $x = y$ and $x \neq y$. If $x = y$, we extend the isomorphism f by sending $\mathsf{here}\, p$ to $\mathsf{here}\, p$ and shifting the old proofs of membership by there. The other case $x \neq y$ is impossible, which we now show. By Lemma 26, we have $\mathsf{count}\ xs\ x = \mathsf{count}\ ys\ x$ for all $a : A$. Hence by instantiating the hypothesis with x, we have, since $x \neq y$,

$$\mathsf{count}\ (\mathsf{cons}\ x\ xs\ p)\ x = \mathsf{count}\ (\mathsf{cons}\ y\ ys\ q)\ x = \mathsf{count}\ ys\ x = \mathsf{count}\ xs\ x$$

but also $\mathsf{count}\ (\mathsf{cons}\ x\ xs\ p)\ x = 1 + \mathsf{count}\ xs\ x$, which is a contradiction. □

We now prove the second step: sorted lists are equal if and only if they have isomorphic membership relations. We first show that we can "peel off" the same head and still have isomorphic membership relations for the tails of the lists.

Lemma 28 (⚙). *For all $b : A$, $xs, ys : \mathsf{SListD}(A, \leqslant)$, and freshness proofs p and q, if we have an isomorphism $(a \in \mathsf{cons}\ b\ xs\ p) \cong (a \in \mathsf{cons}\ b\ ys\ q)$ for every $a : A$, then we also have an isomorphism $(a \in xs) \cong (a \in ys)$ for every $a : A$.*

Proof. Given an isomorphism $f : (a \in \mathsf{cons}\ b\ xs\ p) \to (a \in \mathsf{cons}\ b\ ys\ q)$, we construct a function $g_{xs,ys} : a \in xs \to a \in ys$, and show that $g_{ys,xs}$ is the inverse of $g_{xs,ys}$. Given $u : (a \in xs)$, we have $a \in (\mathsf{cons}\ b\ ys\ q)$, by $f\ (\mathsf{there}\ u)$. There are two possible cases: if $f\ (\mathsf{there}\ u) = \mathsf{there}\ v$ for some $v : a \in ys$, then we take $g(u) = v$. Otherwise if $f\ (\mathsf{there}\ u) = \mathsf{here}\ v$ for some $v : a = b$, then we can apply f again. If $f\ (\mathsf{here}\ v) = \mathsf{there}\ w$ for some $w : a \in ys$, then we take $g(u) = w$. If $f\ (\mathsf{here}\ v) = \mathsf{here}\ w$ for some $w : a = b$, then we can derive a contradiction: since equality on A is propositional, $v = w$, and hence $f\ (\mathsf{here}\ v) = f\ (\mathsf{there}\ u)$, and applying the inverse of f to both sides, we get $\mathsf{here}\ v = \mathsf{there}\ u$. However, different constructors of an inductive type are never equal. □

Using this lemma, we can now prove the extensionality principle for sorted lists with duplicates up to isomorphism of membership. Note that this theorem is not true for ordinary lists — it relies on the lists being sorted.

Proposition 29 (⚙). *Let $xs, ys : \mathsf{SListD}(A, \leqslant)$. If for all $a : A$ we have isomorphisms $(a \in xs) \cong (a \in ys)$, then $xs = ys$.*

Proof. By induction on xs and ys; the only non-trivial case is when the lists are of the form $\mathsf{cons}\ x\ xs\ p$ and $\mathsf{cons}\ y\ ys\ q$, in which case they are equal if $x = y$ and $xs = ys$ by Corollary 4. We have $xs = ys$ by Lemma 28 and the induction hypothesis. To prove $x = y$, note that $x \in \mathsf{cons}\ y\ ys\ q$ and $y \in \mathsf{cons}\ x\ xs\ p$ by the assumed isomorphism. Thus either $x = y$, or $x \in ys$ and $y \in xs$. In the former case, we are done, and in the latter case, since also $x \# xs$ and $y \# ys$, we then have both $x \leqslant y$ and $y \leqslant x$ by Lemma 8, so that indeed $x = y$ by antisymmetry. □

Combining Propositions 27 and 29, we get a convenient characterisation of the identity type for sorted lists with duplicates.

Theorem 30 (⚙ Extensionality Principle for SListD). *For sorted lists $xs, ys : \mathsf{SListD}(A, \leqslant)$, if $\mathsf{count}\ xs\ a = \mathsf{count}\ ys\ a$ for all $a : A$, then $xs = ys$.* □

We can now put this principle to use in order to prove that sorted lists with duplicates satisfies the axioms of a commutative monoid. This is very direct, after proving that $\mathsf{count}\ (xs \cup ys)\ a = \mathsf{count}\ xs\ a + \mathsf{count}\ ys\ a$ for all $a : A$.

Proposition 31 (⚙). *$(\mathsf{SListD}(A, \leqslant), \cup, \mathsf{nil})$ is a commutative monoid.* □

From here, we can define a category DTO of propositional decidable total orders with decidable equality, whose morphisms are not necessarily monotone functions between the underlying sets, and a category OCMon of ordered commutative monoids. By using the lexicographic order $\leqslant_L$ on sorted lists, SListD can be extended to a functorial mapping DTO → OCMon, which is left adjoint to the forgetful functor from OCMon to DTO. This exhibits SListD$(A, \leqslant)$ as the free commutative monoid over A. The proofs are similar to the ones in Sect. 4, so we simply state the main result:

Proposition 32 (⚙). *Let A be a type with decidable equality and $\leqslant : A \to A \to$ Prop a propositional decidable total order. Assuming function extensionality, (SListD$(A, \leqslant), \leqslant_L, \cup$, nil) is the free commutative monoid over A, i.e., SListD : DTO → OCMon forms a functor which is left adjoint to the forgetful functor $\mathcal{U}$: OCMon → DTO defined by $\mathcal{U}(X, \leqslant, \cdot, \epsilon) := (X, \leqslant)$.* □

Again we can get rid of the order relations if and only if we accept a little non-constructivity: The Ordering Principle holds if and only if both forgetful functors $\mathcal{U}_{\mathsf{DTO}}$: DTO → Set and $\mathcal{U}_{\mathsf{OCMon}}$: OCMon → CMon are equivalences.

6 Notions of Freshness for Other Free Structures

There are other notions of freshness relations that one can consider. These give rise to many other familiar free structures, some of which we consider here.

6.1 Free Monoids

It is well known that free monoids can be represented as ordinary lists, with list concatenation as multiplication, and the empty list as the unit. A moment's thought gives that lists are the same thing as fresh lists with the constantly true relation as the freshness relation, i.e., when everything is fresh. Further, the category of sets equipped with their constantly true relation is isomorphic to the category of sets. We thus achieve the following theorem:

Proposition 33 (⚙). *Let $R_\top$ denote the complete relation on A. Then List A is isomorphic to FList$(A, R_\top)$, and hence, assuming function extensionality, FList$(A, R_\top)$ is the free monoid over the set A, i.e., FList$(-, R_\top)$: Set → Mon forms a functor which is left adjoint to the forgetful functor $\mathcal{U}$: Mon → Set defined by $\mathcal{U}(X, \cdot, \epsilon) := X$.* □

6.2 Free Pointed Sets

If we instead choose the constantly false relation, then we can only construct lists of lengths at most 1: creating a two-element list would require a proof that the first element is "fresh" for the second, i.e., a proof of falsity. This means that fresh lists for this relation gives rise to free pointed sets: elements can be included as singleton lists, and there is a new canonical point, namely the empty list. This is nothing but the *Maybe monad* in disguise! The category of sets equipped with their constantly false relation is again isomorphic to the category of sets, and writing $\mathsf{Set}_\bullet$ for the category of pointed sets, we have:

Proposition 34 (⚙). *Let $R_\bot$ denote the empty relation on A. Then* $\mathsf{Maybe}\ A$ *is isomorphic to* $\mathsf{FList}(A, R_\bot)$*, and hence, assuming function extensionality,* $\mathsf{FList}(A, R_\bot)$ *is the free pointed set over the set A, i.e.,* $\mathsf{FList}(-, R_\bot) : \mathsf{Set} \to \mathsf{Set}_\bullet$ *forms a functor which is left adjoint to the forgetful functor* $\mathcal{U} : \mathsf{Set}_\bullet \to \mathsf{Set}$ *defined by* $\mathcal{U}(X, x) := X$. □

6.3 Free Left-Regular Band Monoids

What kind of free structure do we get if we consider C. Coquand's original use of fresh lists for the inequality relation, or, more generally, for an apartness relation? Recall that an apartness relation $\not\approx : A \to A \to \mathsf{Prop}$ is a binary propositional relation satisfying axioms dual to those of an equivalence relation:

- *irreflexivity*: for all $x : A$, we do not have $x \not\approx x$;
- *symmetry*: for all $x, y : A$, if $y \not\approx x$ then $x \not\approx y$; and
- *cotransitivity*: for all $x, y, z : A$, if $x \not\approx y$, then $x \not\approx z$ or $z \not\approx y$.

An apartness relation $\not\approx$ is *tight*, if $\neg x \not\approx y \to x = y$. For any type X, there is a canonical "denial inequality" apartness relation $\neq : X \to X \to \mathsf{Type}$ given by $x \neq y := \neg(x = y)$ (which is tight if X has decidable equality), but there are often other more informative apartness relations for specific types.

In a fresh list where the notion of freshness is given by an apartness relation, it is thus indeed the case that if $x \#_{\not\approx} xs$, then x does not occur in xs due to the irreflexivity axiom. One might think that this should give rise to idempotent monoids, but in fact an even stronger axiom is satisfied, which allows to cancel a second occurrence of the same element also when there is an arbitrary number of elements between the occurrences. Such monoids are known as *left regular band monoids* [7] (and also as graphic monoids [20]).

Definition 35 (⚙). *A left-regular band monoid is a monoid $(X, \cdot, \epsilon)$, such that for any $x, y : X$, we have $x \cdot y \cdot x = x \cdot y$.*

Of course, a left-regular band monoid is in particular idempotent, since

$$x \cdot x = x \cdot \epsilon \cdot x \overset{\text{LR}}{=} x \cdot \epsilon = x$$

for any $x : X$. We will now show that fresh lists for a decidable tight apartness relation gives rises to left-regular band monoids, again equipped with a decidable tight apartness relation. An apartness relation $\not\approx$ is tight and decidable if and only if for any $x, y : A$, we have either $x = y$ or $x \not\approx y$ — we will need this property to be able to remove elements from lists. Types equipped with a decidable tight apartness relation form a category $\mathsf{Type}_{\text{dec-apart}}$, whose morphisms are functions between the underlying types. Note that due to the decidability of the apartness relation, the underlying type also has decidable equality, and hence is in fact a set. Similarly, left-regular monoids equipped with apartness relations form a category $\mathsf{LRMon}_{\text{apart}}$, whose morphisms are monoid homomorphisms.

Proposition 36 (⚙). *Let A be a type and $\not\approx$: $A \to A \to$ Prop a decidable tight apartness relation. Assuming function extensionality, ($\mathsf{FList}(A, \not\approx), \neq$) is the free left regular band monoid with a decidable tight apartness relation over the apartness type $(A, \not\approx)$, i.e., $\mathsf{FList} : \mathsf{Type}_{dec\text{-}apart} \to \mathsf{LRMon}_{apart}$ forms a functor which is left adjoint to the forgetful functor $\mathcal{U} : \mathsf{LRMon}_{apart} \to \mathsf{Type}_{dec\text{-}apart}$ defined by $\mathcal{U}(X, \cdot, \epsilon, \not\approx) := (X, \not\approx)$.*

Proof. To construct a monoid operation on $\mathsf{FList}(A, \not\approx)$, we first use tightness and decidability of $\not\approx$ to define element removal $-\backslash\{-\} : \mathsf{FList}(A, \not\approx) \to A \to \mathsf{FList}(A, \not\approx)$, with $\mathsf{nil}\backslash\{x\} = \mathsf{nil}$, and

$$(\mathsf{cons}\, y\, ys\, p)\backslash\{x\} = \begin{cases} ys & \text{if } x = y \\ \mathsf{cons}\, y\, (ys\backslash\{x\})\, (\backslash\text{-fresh}(p)) & \text{if } x \not\approx y \end{cases}$$

where $\backslash\text{-fresh} : y \#_{\not\approx} ys \to y \#_{\not\approx} (ys\backslash\{x\})$ is defined simultaneously. For each $zs : \mathsf{FList}(A, \not\approx)$ and $y : A$, we then prove $\backslash\text{-removes}(zs, y) : y \#_{\not\approx} (zs\backslash\{y\})$ by induction on zs. We define the monoid multiplication on $\mathsf{FList}(A, \not\approx)$ as follows:

$$\begin{aligned} \mathsf{nil} \cup ys &:= ys \\ (\mathsf{cons}\ x\ xs\ p) \cup ys &:= \mathsf{cons}\ x\ ((xs \cup ys)\backslash\{x\})\ (\backslash\text{-removes}(xs \cup ys, x)) \end{aligned}$$

Associativity and the left regular band identity $xs \cup ys \cup zs = xs \cup ys$ are proven by induction on the lists involved. Finally the adjunction is proven similarly to the other fresh lists adjunctions. □

6.4 Free Reflexive Partial Monoids

Next we consider fresh lists for the equality relation on a set A. After forming a singleton list, we can only extend it by adding more copies of the already existing element in the list. Such a fresh list is thus either the empty list, or consists of $n > 0$ copies of some element in A:

Lemma 37 (⚙). *Let A be a set. Fresh lists for the equality relation $\mathsf{FList}(A, =)$ are isomorphic to structures of the form $1 + (A \times \mathbb{N}^{>0})$.* □

All our previous instantiations have been, at the very least, monoids. But what is the correct notion of multiplication for $\mathsf{FList}(A, =)$? In particular, how should we define it for lists which contain different elements, for example $[a, a] \cdot [b]$? There is no sensible way to combine these lists to produce a fresh list — we would like the monoid multiplication to be undefined in such cases. This leads us to consider the notion of partial monoids [26] (also called pre-monoids [5]): monoid-like structures that come with a "definedness" predicate which tells us when two elements may be multiplied.

Definition 38 (⚙). *A partial monoid is a set X : Set together with a propositional relation $\_ \cdot \_ \downarrow: X \to X \to$ Prop, a dependent function $\mathsf{op} : (x, y : X) \to (x \cdot y \downarrow) \to X$, and an element $\epsilon : X$, such that the following axioms hold, where we write $x \cdot_p y$ for $\mathsf{op}\ x\ y\ p$.*

- identity*: For all* $x : X$, *we have* $\iota_{x,\epsilon} : (x \cdot \epsilon \downarrow)$ *and* $\iota_{\epsilon,x} : (\epsilon \cdot x \downarrow)$, *and* $x \cdot_{\iota_{x,\epsilon}} \epsilon = x = \epsilon \cdot_{\iota_{\epsilon,x}} x$*;*
- associativity*: For all* $x, y, z : X$,

$$(\Sigma(p : (y \cdot z \downarrow)).(x \cdot (y \cdot_p z) \downarrow)) \longleftrightarrow (\Sigma(q : (x \cdot y \downarrow)).((x \cdot_q y) \cdot z \downarrow))$$

and for all $p : (y \cdot z \downarrow)$, $p' : (x \cdot (y \cdot_p z) \downarrow)$, $q : (x \cdot y \downarrow)$, $q' : ((x \cdot_q y) \cdot z \downarrow)$, *we have* $x \cdot_{p'} (y \cdot_p z) = (x \cdot_q y) \cdot_{q'} z$.

A partial monoid is reflexive *if* $(x \cdot x \downarrow)$ *for all* $x : X$.

Using Lemma 37, it is now not hard to show that $\mathsf{FList}(A, =)$ is a reflexive partial monoid with $\mathsf{inl} *$ as unit, and $((\mathsf{inr}\,(x, n)) \cdot (\mathsf{inr}\,(y, m)) \downarrow)$ holding exactly when $x = y$, with $\mathsf{inr}\,(x, n) \cdot_{\mathsf{refl}} \mathsf{inr}\,(x, m) = \mathsf{inr}\,(x, n{+}m)$. To show that $\mathsf{FList}(A, =)$ is the *free* reflexive partial monoid, we need to be able to construct powers x^n in arbitrary reflexive partial monoids. For example, $x^3 = x \cdot (x \cdot x)$ is defined because $(x \cdot x) \cdot (x \cdot x)$ is defined by reflexivity, hence by associativity also $x \cdot (x \cdot (x \cdot x))$ is defined, and in particular $x^3 = x \cdot (x \cdot x)$ is defined. In the general case, we define x^n by induction on $n : \mathbb{N}$, and simultaneously prove that both $(x \cdot x^k \downarrow)$ and $(x^m \cdot x \downarrow)$ for all $k, m : \mathbb{N}$, as well as that $x \cdot x^\ell = x^\ell \cdot x$ for all $\ell : \mathbb{N}$.

A morphism between partial monoids is a function between the carriers that preserves definedness and operations. Reflexive partial monoids and their morphisms form a category RPMon, and we again obtain a free-forgetful adjunction:

Proposition 39 (⚙). *Let* A *be a set. Assuming function extensionality, the set* $\mathit{FList}(A, =)$ *with definedness relation and operations as described above is the free reflexive partial monoid over* A*, i.e.,* $\mathit{FList} : \mathsf{Set} \to \mathsf{RPMon}$ *forms a functor which is left adjoint to the forgetful functor* $\mathcal{U} : \mathsf{RPMon} \to \mathsf{Set}$. □

7 Conclusions and Future Work

We have shown how finite sets and multisets can be realised as fresh lists in plain dependent type theory, resulting in a well-behaved theory with good computational properties such as decidable equality, and without resorting to setoids or higher inductive types. Our only requirement is that the type we start with can be equipped with an order relation — a strict total order for finite sets, and a non-strict one for finite multisets. However, as suggested by a reviewer, relative adjunctions [29] can perhaps be used to formulate a universal property also over unordered structures. We have also shown how many other free structures can be understood in this unifying framework, such as free monoids, free pointed sets, and free left-regular band monoids. Measuring the efficiency of for example deciding equality in our free structures is left as future work.

There are many more algebraic structures that could be studied from the point of view of fresh lists, such as Abelian groups. Free algebraic structures without associativity tend to correspond to variations on binary trees [8]; as such, it would make sense to also investigate notions of "fresh trees", or perhaps a general notion of freshness for containers [1]. It would also be interesting to pin down exactly in which sense SList realises a predicative finite power set functor in type theory. One future use for this could be a constructive framework for modal logics supporting verification algorithms that are correct by construction.

Acknowledgements. We thank Guillaume Allais for interesting suggestions, Ezra Schoen for the idea to consider reflexive partial monoids in Sect. 6.4, and the referees for insightful comments and improvements. This work was supported by the Engineering and Physical Sciences Research Council [EP/W52394X/1]; the National Physical Laboratory; and the Leverhulme Trust [RPG-2020-232].

References

1. Abbott, M., Altenkirch, T., Ghani, N.: Categories of containers. In: Gordon, A.D. (ed.) FoSSaCS 2003. LNCS, vol. 2620, pp. 23–38. Springer, Heidelberg (2003). https://doi.org/10.1007/3-540-36576-1_2
2. The Agda Community: Agda standard library (2023). https://github.com/agda/agda-stdlib
3. Appel, A.W., Leroy, X.: Efficient extensional binary tries. J. Autom. Reason. **67**(1), 8 (2023). https://doi.org/10.1007/s10817-022-09655-x
4. Barthe, G., Capretta, V., Pons, O.: Setoids in type theory. J. Funct. Program. **13**(2), 261–293 (2003). https://doi.org/10.1017/S0956796802004501
5. Bessis, D.: The dual braid monoid. Annales scientifiques de l'Ecole normale supérieure **36**(5), 647–683 (2003). https://doi.org/10.1016/j.ansens.2003.01.001
6. Blizard, W.D.: The development of multiset theory. Modern Logic **1**(4), 319–352 (1991)
7. Brown, K.S.: Semigroups, rings, and Markov chains. J. Theor. Probab. **13**(3), 871–938 (2000). https://doi.org/10.1023/a:1007822931408
8. Bunkenburg, A.: The Boom hierarchy. In: O'Donnell, J.T., Hammond, K. (eds.) Proceedings of the 1993 Glasgow Workshop on Functional Programming, pp. 1–8. Springer (1994). https://doi.org/10.1007/978-1-4471-3236-3_1
9. Choudhury, V., Fiore, M.: Free commutative monoids in Homotopy Type Theory. In: Hsu, J., Tasson, C. (eds.) Mathematical Foundations of Programming Semantics (MFPS '22). Electronic Notes in Theoretical Informatics and Computer Science, vol. 1 (2023). https://doi.org/10.46298/entics.10492
10. Choudhury, V., Karwowski, J., Sabry, A.: Symmetries in reversible programming: From symmetric rig groupoids to reversible programming languages. In: Proceedings of the ACM on Programming Languages 6(POPL), pp. 1–32 (2022). https://doi.org/10.1145/3498667
11. Coquand, C.: A formalised proof of the soundness and completeness of a simply typed lambda-calculus with explicit substitutions. Higher Order Symbol. Comput. **15**(1), 57–90 (2002). https://doi.org/10.1023/A:1019964114625
12. Dybjer, P.: A general formulation of simultaneous inductive-recursive definitions in type theory. J. Symb. Log. **65**(2), 525–549 (2000). https://doi.org/10.2307/2586554
13. Frumin, D., Geuvers, H., Gondelman, L., Weide, N.v.d.: Finite sets in homotopy type theory. In: International Conference on Certified Programs and Proofs (CPP '18), pp. 201–214. Association for Computing Machinery (2018). https://doi.org/10.1145/3167085

14. Gylterud, H.R.: Multisets in type theory. Math. Proc. Cambridge Philos. Soc. **169**(1), 1–18 (2020). https://doi.org/10.1017/S0305004119000045
15. Hedberg, M.: A coherence theorem for Martin-Löf's type theory. J. Funct. Program. **8**(4), 413–436 (1998). https://doi.org/10.1017/s0956796898003153
16. Hinze, R.: Generalizing generalized tries. J. Funct. Program. **10**(4), 327–351 (2000). https://doi.org/10.1017/S0956796800003713
17. Hutton, G.: A tutorial on the universality and expressiveness of fold. J. Funct. Program. **9**(4), 355–372 (1999). https://doi.org/10.1017/s0956796899003500
18. Jech, T.: The Axiom of Choice. North-Holland (1973)
19. Joram, P., Veltri, N.: Constructive final semantics of finite bags. In: Naumowicz, A., Thiemann, R. (eds.) Interactive Theorem Proving (ITP '23). Leibniz International Proceedings in Informatics (LIPIcs), vol. 268, pp. 20:1–20:19. Schloss Dagstuhl - Leibniz-Zentrum für Informatik, Dagstuhl, Germany (2023). https://doi.org/10.4230/LIPIcs.ITP.2023.20
20. Lawvere, F.W.: Display of graphics and their applications, as exemplified by 2-categories and the Hegelian "taco". In: Proceedings of the First International Conference on Algebraic Methodology and Software Technology, pp. 51–74 (1989)
21. McBride, C.: How to keep your neighbours in order. In: Jeuring, J., Chakravarty, M.M.T. (eds.) International conference on Functional programming (ICFP '14), pp. 297–309. Association for Computing Machinery (2014). https://doi.org/10.1145/2628136.2628163
22. Nordvall Forsberg, F.: Inductive-inductive definitions. Ph.D. thesis, Swansea University (2013)
23. Norell, U.: Towards a practical programming language based on dependent type theory. Ph.D. thesis, Chalmers University of Technology (2007)
24. Piceghello, S.: Coherence for Monoidal and Symmetric Monoidal Groupoids in Homotopy Type Theory. Ph.D. thesis, The University of Bergen (2021)
25. Pincus, D.: The dense linear ordering principle. J. Symb. Log. **62**(2), 438–456 (1997). https://doi.org/10.2307/2275540
26. Poinsot, L., Duchamp, G., Tollu, C.: Partial monoids: associativity and confluence. J. Pure Appl. Math. Adv. Appl. **3**(2), 265–285 (2010)
27. Streicher, T.: Investigations into intensional type theory. Habilitation thesis (1993)
28. Swan, A.: If every set has some irreflexive, extensional order, then excluded middle follows. Agda formalisation by Tom De Jong available at https://www.cs.bham.ac.uk/~mhe/TypeTopology/Ordinals.WellOrderingTaboo.html
29. Ulmer, F.: Properties of dense and relative adjoint functors. J. Algebra **8**(1), 77–95 (1968). https://doi.org/10.1016/0021-8693(68)90036-7
30. The Univalent Foundations Program: Homotopy Type Theory: Univalent Foundations of Mathematics. Institute for Advanced Study (2013). https://homotopytypetheory.org/book/
31. Watters, S., Nordvall Forsberg, F., Kupke, C.: Agda formalisation of "A Fresh Look at Commutativity: Free Algebraic Structures via Fresh Lists". https://doi.org/10.5281/zenodo.8357335 (2023)

Oracle Computability and Turing Reducibility in the Calculus of Inductive Constructions

Yannick Forster[1(✉)], Dominik Kirst[2,3], and Niklas Mück[3]

[1] Inria, LS2N, Université Nantes, Nantes, France
yannick.forster@inria.fr
[2] Ben-Gurion University of the Negev, Beer-Sheva, Israel
kirst@cs.bgu.ac.il
[3] Saarland University and MPI-SWS, Saarland Informatics Campus, Saarbrücken, Germany
mueck@mpi-sws.org

Abstract. We develop synthetic notions of oracle computability and Turing reducibility in the Calculus of Inductive Constructions (CIC), the constructive type theory underlying the Coq proof assistant. As usual in synthetic approaches, we employ a definition of oracle computations based on meta-level functions rather than object-level models of computation, relying on the fact that in constructive systems such as CIC all definable functions are computable by construction. Such an approach lends itself well to machine-checked proofs, which we carry out in Coq.

There is a tension in finding a good synthetic rendering of the higher-order notion of oracle computability. On the one hand, it has to be informative enough to prove central results, ensuring that all notions are faithfully captured. On the other hand, it has to be restricted enough to benefit from axioms for synthetic computability, which usually concern first-order objects. Drawing inspiration from a definition by Andrej Bauer based on continuous functions in the effective topos, we use a notion of sequential continuity to characterise valid oracle computations.

As main technical results, we show that Turing reducibility forms an upper semilattice, transports decidability, and is strictly more expressive than truth-table reducibility, and prove that whenever both a predicate p and its complement are semi-decidable relative to an oracle q, then p Turing-reduces to q.

Keywords: Type theory · Logical foundations · Synthetic computability theory · Coq proof assistant

Yannick Forster received funding from the European Union's Horizon 2020 research and innovation programme under the Marie Skłodowska-Curie grant agreement No. 101024493. Dominik Kirst is supported by a Minerva Fellowship of the Minerva Stiftung Gesellschaft fuer die Forschung mbH.

C.-K. Hur (Ed.): APLAS 2023, LNCS 14405, pp. 155–181, 2023.
https://doi.org/10.1007/978-981-99-8311-7_8

1 Introduction

In recent years, synthetic computability theory [1,2,5,37] has gained increasing attention in the fields of constructive mathematics and interactive theorem proving [10,12,16,24,39,40]. In contrast to the usual analytic approach based on describing the functions considered computable by means of a model like Turing machines, μ-recursive functions, or the λ-calculus, the synthetic approach exploits that in a constructive setting no non-computable functions can be defined in the first place, making a later description of the computable fragment obsolete. This idea enables much more compact definitions and proofs, for instance decidability of sets over $\mathbb{N}$ can be expressed by equivalence to functions $f : \mathbb{N} \to \mathbb{B}$ without any further computability requirement regarding f, simplifying a formal mathematical development.

Furthermore, synthetic computability is the only approach to computability enabling a feasible mechanisation using a proof assistant. The general value of machine-checking important foundational results, for instance to obtain a library of mathematics and theoretical computer science, has become more appreciated in more and more subcommunities, up to the point that some mechanisations of results reach cutting edge research. However, even though machine-checked mathematics has a long history, computability theory, and even more so relative computability theory based on oracles, have not been tackled to a substantial amount past basic results such as Rice's theorem before the use of synthetic computability. This is because there is a big amount of "invisible" mathematics [4] that has to be made explicit in proof assistants, due to the use of the informal Church Turing thesis on paper that cannot be formally replicated. Filling in these missing details is infeasible, to the amount that textbook computability theory based on models of computations and the informal Church Turing thesis is not really formalisable to a reasonable extent.

The synthetic perspective remedies these issues and has been fruitfully used to describe basic concepts in computability theory in proof assistants. The approach is especially natural in constructive type theories such as the Calculus of Inductive Constructions (CIC) [6,34] underlying the Coq proof assistant [41]: as CIC embodies a dependently-typed functional programming language, every definable function conveys its own executable implementation.

However, the synthetic characterisation of oracle computations in general (i.e. algorithms relative to some potentially non-computable subroutine) and Turing reductions in particular (i.e. decision procedures relative to some oracle giving answer to a potentially non-decidable problem) has turned out to be more complicated. First, a Turing reduction cannot naively be described by a transformation of computable decision procedures $\mathbb{N} \to \mathbb{B}$ as this would rule out the intended application to oracles for problems that can be proved undecidable using usual axioms of synthetic computability such as Church's thesis (CT). Secondly, when instead characterising Turing reductions by transformations of possibly non-computable decision procedures represented as binary relations $\mathbb{N} \to \mathbb{B} \to \mathbb{P}$, one has to ensure that computability is preserved in the sense that computable oracles induce computable reductions in order to enable intended properties like the transport of (un-)decidability. Thirdly, to rule out exotic reductions whose behaviour on non-computable oracles differs substantially from their action on computable oracles, one needs to impose a form of continuity.

The possible formulations of continuity of functionals on partial spaces such as $\mathbb{N} \to \mathbb{B} \to \mathbb{P}$ are numerous: Bauer [3], who gave the first synthetic definition of oracle computability we draw our inspiration from, employs the order-theoretic variant of functionals preserving suprema in directed countable partial orders. The first author of this paper [11] describes a reformulation in CIC in joint work with the second author, using a modified variant of modulus continuity where every terminating oracle computation provides classical information about the information accessed from the oracle. We have suggested a more constructive formulation of modulus continuity in past work [15] and established Post's theorem connecting the arithmetical hierarchy with Turing degrees for this definition [22,30]. However, this proof assumes an enumeration of all (higher-order) oracle computations defined via modulus continuity, which seems not to follow from CT, therefore leaving the consistency status of the assumption unclear.

As a remedy to this situation, we propose an alternative synthetic characterisation of oracle computability based on a stricter notion of sequential continuity, loosely following van Oosten [33]. Concretely, a sequentially continuous function with input type I and output type O with an oracle expecting questions of type Q and giving answers of type A can be represented by a partial function $\tau : I \to A^* \rightharpoonup Q + O$, where τi can be seen as a (potentially infinite) tree. Concretely, τi is a function that maps paths of type A^* (i.e. edges are labeled by elements of type A) to inner nodes labeled by Q and leafs labeled by O.

While this concept naturally describes the functionals considered computable by emphasising the sequence of computation steps interleaved with oracle interactions, it immediately yields the desired enumeration from CT by reducing higher-order functionals on partial spaces to partial first-order functions.

In this paper we develop the theory of oracle computability as far as possible without any axioms for synthetic computability: we show that Turing reducibility forms an upper semilattice, transports decidability, and is strictly more expressive than truth-table reducibility, and prove that whenever both a predicate p and its complement are semi-decidable relative to an oracle q, then p Turing-reduces to q.[1] All results are mechanised in Coq, both to showcase the feasibility of the synthetic approach and as base for future related mechanisation projects.

For easy accessibility, the Coq development[2] is seamlessly integrated with the text presentation: every formal statement in the PDF version of this paper is hyperlinked with HTML documentation of the Coq code. To further improve

[1] The non-relativised form of the latter statement also appears under the name of "Post's theorem" in the literature [42], not to be confused with the mentioned theorem regarding the arithmetical hierarchy, see the explanation in Sect. 9.

[2] https://github.com/uds-psl/coq-synthetic-computability/tree/code-paper-oracle-computability.

fluid readability, we introduce most concepts and notations in passing, but hyperlink most definitions in the PDF with the glossary in Appendix A.

Contribution. We give a definition of synthetic oracle computability in constructive type theory and derive notions of Turing reducibility and relative semi-decidability. We establish basic properties of all notions, most notably that Turing reducibility forms an upper semi-lattice, transports decidability if and only if Markov's principle holds, and is strictly more general than truth-table reducibility. We conclude by a proof of Post's theorem relating decidability with semi-decidability of a set and its complement.

Outline. We begin by introducing the central notion of synthetic oracle computability in Sect. 2, employed in Sect. 3 to derive synthetic notions of Turing reducibility and oracle semi-decidability. Before we discuss their respective properties (Sects. 6 and 7) and show that Turing reducibility is strictly weaker than a previous synthetic rendering of truth-table reducibility (Sect. 8), we develop the basic theory of synthetic oracle computations by establishing their closure properties (Sect. 4) and by capturing their computational behaviour (Sect. 5). Some of these closure properties rely on a rather technical alternative characterisation of oracle computability described in Appendix B, which will also be used to establish the main result relating oracle semi-decidability with Turing reducibility discussed in Sect. 9. We conclude in Sect. 10 with remarks on the Coq formalisation as well as future and related work.

2 Synthetic Oracle Computability

The central notion of this paper is the synthetic definition of oracle computability. Historically, oracle computability was introduced as an extension of Turing machines in Turing's PhD thesis [43], but popularised by Post [35]. Various analytic definitions of oracle computability exist, all having in common that computations can ask questions and retrieve answers from an oracle.

For our synthetic definition, we specify concretely when a higher-order functional $F\colon (Q \to A \to \mathbb{P}) \to (I \to O \to \mathbb{P})$ is considered (oracle-)computable. Such a functional takes as input a possibly non-total binary relation $R\colon Q \to A \to \mathbb{P}$, an oracle relating questions $q\colon Q$ to answers $a\colon A$, and yields a computation relating inputs $i\colon I$ to outputs $o\colon O$. For special cases like Turing reductions, we will instantiate $Q, I := \mathbb{N}$ and $A, O := \mathbb{B}$. Note that we do not require oracles R to be deterministic, but if they are, then so are the resulting relations FR (cf. Lemma 11).

We define oracle computability by observing that a terminating computation with oracles has a sequential form: in any step of the sequence, the oracle computation can ask a question to the oracle, return an output, or diverge. Informally, we can enforce such sequential behaviour by requiring that every terminating computation $FR\,i\,o$ can be described by (finite, possibly empty) lists $qs\colon Q^*$ and $as\colon A^*$ such that from the input i the output o is eventually obtained after a finite sequence of steps, during which the questions in qs are asked to the oracle one-by-one, yielding corresponding answers in as. This computational data can be captured by a partial[3] function of type $I \to A^* \rightharpoonup Q + O$, called the (computation) tree of F, that on some input and list of previous answers either returns the next question to the oracle, returns the final output, or diverges.

So more formally, we call $F\colon (Q \to A \to \mathbb{P}) \to (I \to O \to \mathbb{P})$ an (oracle-)computable functional if there is a tree $\tau\colon I \to A^* \rightharpoonup Q + O$ such that

$$\forall R\,i\,o.\ F R\,i\,o \leftrightarrow \exists qs\ as.\ \tau i\,;R \vdash qs\,;as \wedge \tau\,i\,as \triangleright \mathsf{out}\ o$$

with the interrogation relation $\sigma; R \vdash qs; as$ being defined inductively by

$$\frac{}{\sigma\,;R \vdash [\,]\,;[\,]} \qquad \frac{\sigma\,;R \vdash qs\,;as \qquad \sigma\,as \triangleright \mathsf{ask}\ q \qquad Rqa}{\sigma\,;R \vdash qs +\!\!+ [q]\,;as +\!\!+ [a]}$$

where A^* is the type of lists over a, $l +\!\!+ l'$ is list concatenation, where we use the suggestive shorthands $\mathsf{ask}\ q$ and $\mathsf{out}\ o$ for the respective injections into the sum type $Q + O$, and where $\sigma\colon A^* \rightharpoonup Q + O$ denotes a tree at a fixed input i.

To provide some further intuition and visualise the usage of the word "tree", we discuss the following example functional in more detail:

$$\begin{aligned} F &: (\mathbb{N} \to \mathbb{B} \to \mathbb{P}) \to (\mathbb{N} \to \mathbb{B} \to \mathbb{P}) \\ F R\,i\,o &:= o = \mathsf{true} \wedge \forall q < i.\ R\,q\,\mathsf{true} \end{aligned}$$

Intuitively, the functional can be computed by asking all questions q for $q < i$ to the oracle. If the oracle does not return any value, F does not return a value. If the oracle returns false somewhere, F also does not return a value – i.e. runs forever. If the oracle indeed returns true for all $q < i$, F returns true.

In the case of $i = 3$, this process may be depicted by

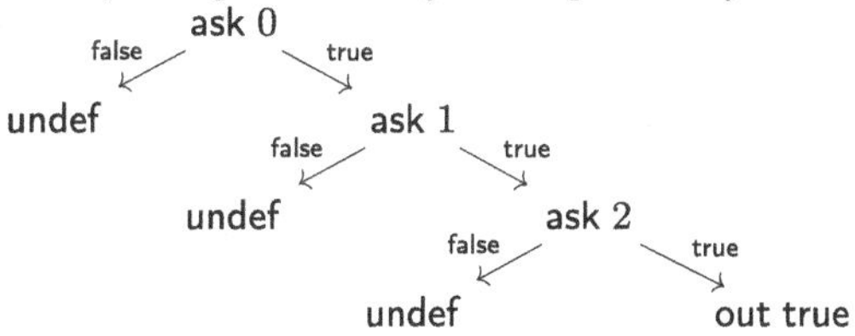

where the paths along labelled edges represent the possible answer lists as while the nodes represent the corresponding actions of the computation: the paths along inner nodes denote the question lists qs and the leafs the output behaviour. Note that $\mathsf{ret} : X \rightharpoonup X$ is the return of partial functions, turning a value into an always defined partial value, while undef denotes the diverging partial value. Formally, a tree $\tau\colon \mathbb{N} \to \mathbb{B}^* \rightharpoonup \mathbb{N} + \mathbb{B}$ computing F can be defined by

$$\tau\,i\,as := \begin{cases} \mathsf{undef} & \text{if } \mathsf{false} \in as \\ \mathsf{ret}\ (\mathsf{ask}\ |as|) & \text{if } \mathsf{false} \notin as \wedge |as| < i \\ \mathsf{ret}\ (\mathsf{out}\ \mathsf{true}) & \text{if } \mathsf{false} \notin as \wedge |as| \geq i \end{cases}$$

[3] There are many ways how semi-decidable partial values can be represented in CIC, for instance via step-indexing. Since the actual implementation does not matter, we abstract over any representation providing the necessary operations, see Appendix A.

where here and later on we use such function definitions by cases to represent (computable) pattern matching.

As usual in synthetic mathematics, the definition of a functional F as being computable if it can be described by a tree is implicitly relying on the fact that all definable (partial) functions in CIC could also be shown computable in the analytic sense. Describing oracle computations via trees in stages goes back to Kleene [25], cf. also the book by Odifreddi [31]. Our definition can be seen as a more explicit form of sequential continuity due to van Oosten [32,33], or as a partial, extensional form of a dialogue tree due to Escardó [9]. Our definition allows us to re-prove the theorem by Kleene [26] and Davis [7] that computable functionals fulfill the more common definition of continuity with a modulus:

Lemma 1. *Let F be a computable functional. If $F R\, i\, o$, then there exists a list $qs : Q^*$, the so-called modulus of continuity, such that $\forall q \in qs.\ \exists a.\ Rqa$ and for all R' with $\forall q \in qs. \forall a.\ Rqa \leftrightarrow R'qa$ we also have that $F R'\, i\, o$.*

Proof. Given $F R\, i\, o$ and F computable by τ we have $\tau i\ ;\ R \vdash qs\ ;\ as$ and $\tau\, i\, as \triangleright \mathsf{out}\ o$. It suffices to prove both $\forall q \in qs.\ \exists a.\ Rqa$ and $\tau i\ ;\ R' \vdash qs\ ;\ as$ by induction on the given interrogation, which is trivial. □

Nevertheless, our notion of computable functionals is strictly stronger than modulus continuity as stated, while we are unaware of a proof relating it to a version where the moduli are computed by a partial function.

Lemma 2. *There are modulus-continuous functionals that are not computable.*

Proof. Consider the functional $F : (\mathbb{N} \to \mathbb{B} \to \mathbb{P}) \to (I \to O \to \mathbb{P})$ defined by

$$F Rio \ := \ \exists q.\, R\, q\, \mathsf{true}.$$

Clearly, F is modulus-continuous since from a terminating run $F Rio$ we obtain q with $R\, q\, \mathsf{true}$ and therefore can choose $qs := [q]$ as suitable modulus.

However, suppose $\tau : I \to \mathbb{B}^* \rightharpoonup \mathbb{N} + O$ were a tree for F, then given some input i we can inspect the result of $\tau\, i\, []$ because $F\, R_\top\, i\, o$ holds for all i, o, and the full oracle $R_\top\, q\, a := \top$. However, the result cannot be $\mathsf{out}\ o$ for any output o, as this would yield $F R_\bot$ for the empty oracle $R_\bot\, q\, a := \bot$, violating the definition of F. Thus $\tau\, i\, [] \triangleright \mathsf{ask}\ q_0$, conveying an initial question q_0 independent of the input oracle. But then employing the oracle R_0 defined by $R_0\, q_0\, a := \bot$ and $R_0\, q\, a := \top$ for all $q \neq q_0$ we certainly have $F\, R_0\, i\, o$ by definition but no interrogation $\tau i\ ;\ R_0 \vdash qs\ ;\ as$ with $\tau\, i\, as \triangleright \mathsf{out}\ o$, as this would necessarily include an answer a with $R_0\, q_0\, a$ as first step, contradicting the construction of R_0. □

The advantage of using the stricter notion of sequential continuity over modulus continuity is that by their reduction to trees, computable functionals are effectively turned into flat first-order functions on data types. Thus one directly obtains an enumeration of all oracle computations, as needed in most advanced scenarios, from an enumeration of first-order functions, which itself could be obtained by assuming usual axioms for synthetic computability.

3 Turing Reducibility and Oracle Semi-decidability

Using our synthetic notion of oracle computability, we can directly derive synthetic formulations of two further central notions of computability theory: Turing reducibility – capturing when a predicate is decidable relative to a given predicate – and oracle semi-decidability – capturing when a predicate can be recognised relative to a given predicate. To provide some intuition first, we recall that in the synthetic setting a predicate $p : X \to \mathbb{P}$ over some type X is decidable if there is a function $f : X \to \mathbb{B}$ such that $\forall x.\ px \leftrightarrow fx = \mathsf{true}$, i.e. f acts as a decider of p. This definition is standard in synthetic computability [1,16] and relies on the fact that constructively definable functions $f : X \to \mathbb{B}$ are computable.

To relativise the definition of a decider to an oracle, we first define the characteristic relation $\hat{p} : X \to \mathbb{B} \to \mathbb{P}$ of a predicate $p : X \to \mathbb{P}$ by

$$\hat{p} \ := \ \lambda xb. \begin{cases} px & \text{if } b = \mathsf{true} \\ \neg px & \text{if } b = \mathsf{false}. \end{cases}$$

Employing $\hat{p}$, we can now equivalently characterise a decider f for p by requiring that $\forall xb.\ \hat{p}xb \leftrightarrow fx = b$. Relativising this exact pattern, we then define Turing reducibility of a predicate $p : X \to \mathbb{P}$ to $q : Y \to \mathbb{P}$ by a computable functional F transporting the characteristic relation of q to the characteristic relation of p:

$$p \preceq_{\mathsf{T}} q \ := \ \exists F.\ F \textit{ is computable} \wedge \forall xb.\ \hat{p}xb \leftrightarrow F\hat{q}xb$$

Note that while we do not need to annotate a decider f with a computability condition because we consider all first-order functions of type $\mathbb{N} \to \mathbb{N}$ or $\mathbb{N} \to \mathbb{B}$ as computable, a Turing reduction is not first-order, and thus needs to be enriched with a tree to rule out unwanted behaviour. In fact, without this condition, we would obtain $p \preceq_{\mathsf{T}} q$ for every p and q by simply setting $F\,R := \hat{p}$.

Next, regarding semi-decidability, a possible non-relativised synthetic definition is to require a partial function $f : X \rightharpoonup \mathbb{1}$ such that $\forall x.\ px \leftrightarrow fx \triangleright \star$, where $\mathbb{1}$ is the inductive unit type with singular element $\star$. That is, the semi-decider f terminates on elements of p and diverges on the complement $\overline{p}$ of p (cf. [11]).

Again relativising the same pattern, we say that $p : X \to \mathbb{P}$ is (oracle-)semi-decidable relative to $q : Y \to \mathbb{P}$ if there is a computable functional F mapping relations $R : Y \to \mathbb{B} \to \mathbb{P}$ to relations of type $X \to \mathbb{1} \to \mathbb{P}$ such that $F\hat{q}$ accepts p:

$$\mathcal{S}_q(p) \ := \ \exists F.\ F \textit{ is computable} \wedge \forall x.\ px \leftrightarrow F\hat{q}x\star$$

As in the case of Turing reductions, the computability condition of an oracle semi-decider is crucial: without the restriction, we would obtain $\mathcal{S}_q(p)$ for every p and q by setting $F\,R\,x\,\star := p\,x$.

While we defer developing the theory of synthetic Turing reducibility and oracle semi-decidability to later sections, we can already record here that the fact that decidability implies semi-decidability also holds in relativised form:

Lemma 3. *If $p \preceq_{\mathsf{T}} q$ then $\mathcal{S}_q(p)$ and $\mathcal{S}_q(\overline{p})$.*

Proof. Let F witnesses $p \preceq_{\mathsf{T}} q$, then $F' \, R \, x \, \star := F \, R \, x \, \mathsf{true}$ witnesses $\mathcal{S}_q(p)$. In particular, if $\tau : X \to \mathbb{B}^* \rightharpoonup \mathbb{N} + \mathbb{B}$ computes F, then $\tau' : X \to \mathbb{B}^* \rightharpoonup \mathbb{N} + \mathbb{1}$, constructed by running τ and returning $\mathsf{out} \star$ whenever τ returns $\mathsf{out\ true}$, computes F'. The proof of $\mathcal{S}_q(\overline{p})$ is analogous, simply using false in place of true. □

4 Closure Properties of Oracle Computations

In this section we collect some examples of computable functionals and show how they can be composed, yielding a helpful abstraction for later computability proofs without need for constructing concrete computation trees. Note that the last statements of this section depend on a rather technical intermediate construction using a more flexible form of interrogations. We refer to the Coq code and to Appendix B, where we will also deliver the proofs left out.

First, we show that composition with a transformation of inputs preserves computability and that all partial functions are computable, ignoring the input oracle. The latter also implies that total, constant, and everywhere undefined functions are computable.

Lemma 4. *The following functionals mapping relations $R : Q \to A \to \mathbb{P}$ to relations of type $I \to O \to \mathbb{P}$ are computable:*

1. $\lambda R \, i \, o. \, F R \, (g i) \, o$ *for* $g : I \to I'$ *and computable* $F : (Q \to A \to \mathbb{P}) \to (I' \to O \to \mathbb{P})$,
2. $\lambda R \, i \, o. \, f i \triangleright o$ *given* $f : I \rightharpoonup O$,
3. $\lambda R \, i \, o. \, f i = o$ *given* $f : I \to O$,
4. $\lambda R \, i \, o. \, o = v$ *given* $v : O$,
5. $\lambda R \, i \, o. \, \bot$.

Proof. For 1, let τ compute F and define $\tau' \, i \, l := \tau \, (g i) \, l$. For 2, define $\tau' \, i \, l := f i \gg\!= \lambda o. \, \mathsf{ret} \, (\mathsf{out} \, o)$, where $\gg\!=$ is the bind operation of partial functions. All others follow by using (2). □

Next, if $Q = I$ and $A = O$, then the identity functional is computable:

Lemma 5. *The functional mapping $R : Q \to A \to \mathbb{P}$ to R itself is computable.*

Proof. Define

$$\tau \, q \, l := \begin{cases} \mathsf{ret} \, (\mathsf{ask} \, q) & \text{if } l = [] \\ \mathsf{ret} \, (\mathsf{out} \, a) & \text{if } l = (q, a) :: l'. \end{cases}$$

□

Moreover, given two functionals and a boolean test on inputs, the process calling either of the two depending on the test outcome is computable:

Lemma 6. *Let F_1 and F_2 both map relations $R : Q \to A \to \mathbb{P}$ to relations of type $I \to O \to \mathbb{P}$ and $f : I \to \mathbb{B}$. Then F mapping R to the following relation of type $I \to O \to \mathbb{P}$ is computable:*

$$\lambda io. \begin{cases} F_1 \, R \, i \, o & \text{if } f i = \mathsf{true} \\ F_2 \, R \, i \, o & \text{if } f i = \mathsf{false} \end{cases}$$

Proof. Let τ_1 and τ_2 compute F_1 and F_2 respectively and define

$$\tau\, i\, l := \begin{cases} \tau_1\, i\, l & \text{if } f i = \mathsf{true} \\ \tau_2\, i\, l & \text{if } f i = \mathsf{false}. \end{cases}$$

□

Taken together, the previous three lemmas yield computability proofs for functionals consisting of simple operations like calling functions, taking identities, and branching over conditionals. The next three lemmas extend to partial binding, function composition, and linear search, so in total we obtain an abstraction layer accommodating computability proofs for the most common ingredients of algorithms. As mentioned before, we just state the last three lemmas without proof here and refer to the Coq development and Appendix B for full detail.

Lemma 7. *Let F_1 map relations $R\colon Q {\to} A {\to} \mathbb{P}$ to relations of type $I {\to} O' {\to} \mathbb{P}$, F_2 map relations $R\colon Q {\to} A {\to} \mathbb{P}$ to relations of type $(I \times O') {\to} O {\to} \mathbb{P}$, and both be computable. Then F mapping $R\colon Q {\to} A {\to} \mathbb{P}$ to $\lambda io.\, \exists o'\colon O'.\, F_1\, R\, i\, o' \wedge F_2\, R\, (i, o')\, o$ of type $I {\to} O {\to} \mathbb{P}$ is computable.*

Lemma 8. *Let F_1 map relations $R\colon Q {\to} A {\to} \mathbb{P}$ to relations $X {\to} Y {\to} \mathbb{P}$, F_2 map relations $R\colon X {\to} Y {\to} \mathbb{P}$ to relations $I {\to} O {\to} \mathbb{P}$, and both be computable. Then F mapping $R\colon Q {\to} A {\to} \mathbb{P}$ to $\lambda io.\ F_2\ (F_1 R)\ i\ o$ of type $I {\to} O {\to} \mathbb{P}$ is computable.*

Lemma 9. *The functional mapping $R\colon (I \times \mathbb{N}) {\to} \mathbb{B} {\to} \mathbb{P}$ to the following relation of type $I {\to} \mathbb{N} {\to} \mathbb{P}$ is computable: $\lambda in\ R\ (i, n)\ \mathsf{true} \wedge \forall m < n.\ R\ (i, m)\ \mathsf{false}$.*

5 Computational Cores of Oracle Computations

In this section, we prove that if F maps $R\colon Q {\to} A {\to} \mathbb{P}$ to a relation $I {\to} O {\to} \mathbb{P}$ and F is computable, then there is a higher-order function $f\colon (Q {\rightharpoonup} A) {\to} (I {\rightharpoonup} O)$ such that for any $r\colon Q {\rightharpoonup} A$ with graph R, the graph of fr agrees with FR. This means that every computable functional possesses an explicit computational core, mapping (partially) computable input to (partially) computable output, needed for instance to justify that decidability is transported backwards along Turing reductions (Lemma 26).

In preparation, the following two lemmas state simple properties of interrogations regarding concatenation and determinacy. Given $\sigma\colon A^* {\rightharpoonup} Q + O$ and $l\colon A^*$ we write $\sigma@l$ for the sub-tree of σ starting at path l, i.e. for the tree $\lambda l'.\ \sigma(l +\!\!+ l')$.

Lemma 10. *We have interrogations $\sigma\,;R \vdash qs_1\,;as_1$ and $\sigma@as_1\,;R \vdash qs_2\,;as_2$ if and only if $|qs_2| = |as_2|$ and $\sigma\,;R \vdash qs_1 +\!\!+ qs_2\,;as_1 +\!\!+ as_2$.*

Lemma 11. *Let R be functional and $\sigma\,;R \vdash qs_1\,;as_1$ as well as $\sigma\,;R \vdash qs_2\,;as_2$. Then if $|qs_1| \le |qs_2|$, then qs_1 is a prefix of qs_2 and as_1 is a prefix of as_2.*

Now conveying the main idea, we first define an evaluation function $\delta\ \sigma\ f : \mathbb{N} \rightharpoonup Q + O$ which evaluates $\sigma : A^* \rightharpoonup Q + O$ on $f : Q \rightharpoonup A$ for at most n questions.

$$\delta\ \sigma\ f\ n := \sigma[\,] \ggg= \lambda x. \begin{cases} \mathsf{ret}\ (\mathsf{out}\ o) & \text{if } x = \mathsf{out}\ o \\ \mathsf{ret}\ (\mathsf{ask}\ q) & \text{if } x = \mathsf{ask}\ q, n = 0 \\ fq \ggg= \lambda a.\ \delta\ (\sigma@[a])\ f\ n' & \text{if } x = \mathsf{ask}\ q, n = \mathsf{S}\ n'. \end{cases}$$

The intuition is that δ always reads the initial node of the tree σ by evaluating $\sigma[\,]$. If $\sigma[\,] \triangleright \mathsf{out}\ o$, then δ returns this output. Otherwise, if $\sigma[\,] \triangleright \mathsf{ask}\ q$ and δ has to evaluate no further questions ($n = 0$), it returns $\mathsf{ask}\ q$. If δ has to evaluate $\mathsf{S}\ n$ questions, it evaluates $fq \triangleright a$ and recurses on the subtree of σ with answer a, i.e. on $\sigma@[a]$. We first verify that δ composes with interrogations by induction on the interrogation:

Lemma 12. *If $\sigma\ ;(\lambda qa.\ fq \triangleright a) \vdash qs\ ;\ as$ and $\delta(\tau@as)fn \triangleright v$ then $\delta\tau fn \triangleright v$.*

Conversely, every evaluation of δ yields a correct interrogation:

Lemma 13. *If $\delta\ \sigma\ f\ n \triangleright \mathsf{out}\ o$ then there are qs and as with $|qs| \leq n$ and $\sigma\ ;(\lambda qa.\ fq \triangleright a) \vdash qs\ ;\ as$, and $\sigma\ as \triangleright \mathsf{out}\ o$.*

Proof. By induction on n, using Lemma 10. □

Put together, a computable functional is fully captured by δ for oracles described by partial functions:

Lemma 14. *Given a functional F computed by τ we have that*

$$F(\lambda qa.\ fq \triangleright a)io \leftrightarrow \exists n.\ \delta\ (\tau i)\ f\ n \triangleright \mathsf{out}\ o.$$

This is enough preparation to describe the desired computational core of computable functionals:

Theorem 15. *If F maps $R : Q \to A \to \mathbb{P}$ to a relation $I \to O \to \mathbb{P}$ and F is computable, then there is a partial function $f : (Q \rightharpoonup A) \to I \rightharpoonup O$ such that if R is computed by a partial function $r : Q \rightharpoonup A$, then FR is computed by fr.*

Proof. Let F be computed by τ. We define fri to search for n such that $\delta\ (\tau i)\ f\ n$ returns $\mathsf{out}\ o$, and let it return this o. The claim then follows straightforwardly by the previous lemma and Lemma 11. □

6 Properties of Oracle Semi-decidability

In the following two sections we establish some standard properties of our synthetic renderings of oracle semi-decidability and Turing reducibility, respectively. All proofs are concise but precise, given that in the synthetic setting they just amount to the essence of the computational manipulations often described just informally for a concrete model of computation in the analytic approach to computability employed e.g. in textbooks.

We first establish the connection to non-relative semi-decidability.

Lemma 16. *If p is semi-decidable, then $\mathcal{S}_q(p)$ for any q.*

Proof. Let $f : X \rightharpoonup \mathbb{1}$ be a semi-decider for p. With Lemma 4 (2) the functional mapping R to $\lambda xo.\ fx \triangleright o$ is computable, and it is easily shown to be a semi-decider for p relative to q. □

Lemma 17. *If $\mathcal{S}_q(p)$ and q is decidable, then p is semi-decidable.*

Proof. Let g decide q and let F be a semi-decider of p relative to q. Let f be the function from Theorem 15 that transports computable functions along F. Now $f(\lambda y.\ \mathsf{ret}(gy))$ is a semi-decider for p. □

We next establish closure properties of oracle semi-decidability along reductions. First, we can replace the oracle by any other oracle it reduces to:

Lemma 18. *If $\mathcal{S}_q(p)$ and $q \preceq_{\mathsf{T}} q'$, then also $\mathcal{S}_{q'}(p)$.*

Proof. Straightforward using Lemma 8. □

Secondly, if we can semi-decide a predicate p relative to q, then also simpler predicates should be semi-decidable relative to q. This however requires a stricter notion of reduction, for instance many-one reductions that rule out complementation. As in [16], we say that $p' : X \to \mathbb{P}$ many-one reduces to $p : Y \to \mathbb{P}$ if there is a function $f : X \to Y$ embedding p' into p:

$$p' \preceq_m p \ := \ \exists f : X \to Y.\ \forall x.\ p'x \leftrightarrow p(fx)$$

Now the sought after property can be stated as follows:

Lemma 19. *If $\mathcal{S}_q(p)$ and $p' \preceq_m p$, then also $\mathcal{S}_q(p')$.*

Proof. Straightforward using Lemma 4 (1,4) and Lemma 7. □

7 Properties of Turing Reducibility

We continue with similarly standard properties of Turing reducibility. Again, all proofs are concise but precise. As a preparation, we first note that Turing reducibility can be characterised without the relational layer.

Lemma 20. *$p \preceq_{\mathsf{T}} q$ if and only if there is τ such that for all x and b we have*

$$\hat{p}xb \leftrightarrow \exists qs\, as.\ \tau x \,;\, q \vdash qs \,;\, as \wedge \tau\, x\, as \triangleright \mathsf{out}\ b.$$

Now to begin, we show that Turing reducibility is a preorder.

Theorem 21. *Turing reducibility is reflexive and transitive.*

Proof. Reflexivity follows directly by the identity functional being computable via Lemma 4. Transitivity follows with Lemma 8. □

In fact, Turing reducibility is an upper semilattice:

Theorem 22. *Let $p{:}X\to\mathbb{P}$ and $q{:}Y\to\mathbb{P}$. Then there is a lowest upper bound $p+q{:}X+Y\to\mathbb{P}$ w.r.t. $\preceq_{\mathsf{T}}$: Let $(p+q)(\mathsf{inl}\ x) := px$ and $(p+q)(\mathsf{inr}\ y) := qy$. then $p+q$ is the join of p and q w.r.t $\preceq_{\mathsf{T}}$, i.e. $p\preceq_{\mathsf{T}} p+q$, $q\preceq_{\mathsf{T}} p+q$, and for all r if $p\preceq_{\mathsf{T}} r$ and $q\preceq_{\mathsf{T}} r$ then $p+q\preceq_{\mathsf{T}} r$.*

Proof. The first two claims follow by Lemma 4 (1) and Lemma 5. For the third, let F_1 reduce p to r and be computed by τ_1 and F_2 reduce q to r computed by τ_2. Define

$$F\,R\,z\,o := \begin{cases} F_1 R\,x\,o & \text{if } z = \mathsf{inl}\ x \\ F_2 R\,x\,o & \text{if } z = \mathsf{inr}\ y \end{cases} \qquad\qquad \tau zl := \begin{cases} \tau_1 xl & \text{if } z = \mathsf{inl}\ x \\ \tau_2 yl & \text{if } z = \mathsf{inr}\ y \end{cases}$$

τ computes F, and F reduces $p+q$ to r. □

We continue by establishing properties analogous to the ones concerning oracle semi-decidability discussed in Sect. 6. First, analogously to Lemma 16, the non-relativised notion of decidability implies Turing reducibility:

Lemma 23. *If p and $\overline{p}$ are semi-decidable, then $p\preceq_{\mathsf{T}} q$ for any q. In particular, if p is decidable, then $p\preceq_{\mathsf{T}} q$ for any q.*

Proof. Let f semi-decide p and g semi-decide $\overline{p}$. Define $F\,R\,x\,b := \hat{p}xb$ and let τxl ignore l and find the least n such that either $fxn = \mathsf{true}$ or $gxn = \mathsf{true}$ and then return $\mathsf{out}\ (fxn)$. □

Secondly, Lemmas 18 and 19 correspond to the transitivity of Turing reducibility, the latter relying on the fact that many-one reductions induce Turing reductions:

Lemma 24. *If $p\preceq_m q$ then $p\preceq_{\mathsf{T}} q$.*

Proof. Let f be the many-one reduction. Define $F\,R\,x\,b := R\,(fx)\,b$. □

Thirdly, in connection to Lemma 17, we prove the more involved result that Turing reducibility reflects decidability if and only if Markov's principle holds. Markov's principle is an axiom in constructive mathematics stating that satisfiability of functions $\mathbb{N}\to\mathbb{B}$ is stable under double negation, i.e.:

$$\mathsf{MP} := \forall f{:}\mathbb{N}\to\mathbb{B}.\ \neg\neg(\exists n.\ fn = \mathsf{true}) \to \exists n.\ fn = \mathsf{true}$$

Concretely, MP will be needed as it corresponds to the termination of non-diverging partial functions:

Lemma 25. MP *if and only if $\forall XY.\forall f{:}X\rightharpoonup Y.\forall x.\neg\neg(\exists y.\ fx\triangleright Y)\to\exists y.\ fx\triangleright Y$.*

Another ingredient is that total partial function $X\rightharpoonup Y$ induce functions $X\to Y$, as stated here for the specific case of deciders $X\to\mathbb{B}$:

Lemma 26. *Let* $f\colon X \rightharpoonup \mathbb{B}$ *and* $p\colon X \to \mathbb{P}$. *If* $\forall x.\ px \leftrightarrow fx \triangleright \mathsf{true}$ *and* $\forall x. \exists b.\ fx \triangleright b$, *then* p *is decidable, i.e. there is a function* $g\colon X \to \mathbb{B}$ *such that* $\forall x.\ px \leftrightarrow gx = \mathsf{true}$.

Now assuming $p \preceq_{\mathsf{T}} q$ for q decidable, we can derive a non-diverging partial decider for p, which is turned into a total partial decider with Lemma 25 and then into an actual decider with Lemma 26:

Theorem 27. *Given* MP, *if* q *is decidable and* $p \preceq_{\mathsf{T}} q$, *then* p *is decidable.*

Proof. Let F be the reduction relation and let f transport computability along it as in Theorem 15. Let g decide q. It is straightforward that $\forall xb.\ \hat{p}xb \leftrightarrow f(\lambda y.\mathsf{ret}\,(gy))x \triangleright b$ (*). It suffices to prove that $\forall x. \exists b.\ f(\lambda y.\mathsf{ret}\,(gy))x \triangleright b$ to obtain the claim from Lemma 26.

Using Lemma 25 and MP, given x it suffices to prove $\neg\neg\exists b.\ f(\lambda y.\mathsf{ret}\,(gy))x \triangleright b$. Because the goal is negative and we can prove $\neg\neg(px \vee \neg px)$, we are allowed to do a case analysis on px. In both cases we can prove termination using (*). □

As hinted above, the previous theorem could be stated without MP by using a notion of decidability via a non-diverging partial decider $f\colon X \rightharpoonup \mathbb{B}$, i.e. with $\forall x. \neg\neg\exists b.\ fx \triangleright b$. However, in the stated form, it is in fact equivalent to MP:

Lemma 28. *If* p *is decidable if there is decidable* q *with* $p \preceq_{\mathsf{T}} q$, *then* MP *holds.*

Proof. By [16, Theorem 2.20] it suffices to prove that whenever $p\colon \mathbb{N} \to \mathbb{P}$ and $\overline{p}$ are semi-decidable, then also p is decidable, which follows by Lemma 23 and the assumption for some choice of a decidable predicate q. □

Lastly, we prove that using classical logic, predicates are Turing-equivalent to their complement, providing evidence for the inherent classicality:

Lemma 29. *For double-negation stable* p, $p \preceq_{\mathsf{T}} \overline{p}$ *and* $\overline{p} \preceq_{\mathsf{T}} p$.

Proof. Assume $\forall x.\ \neg\neg px \to px$. For both reductions, take $F R\, x\, b := R\, x\, (\neg_{\mathbb{B}} b)$, which is computable by Lemma 7, Lemma 5, and Lemma 4 (1,3). □

Lemma 30. *Let* X *be some type with* $x_0\colon X$. *If* $p \preceq_{\mathsf{T}} \overline{p}$ *for all* $p\colon X \to \mathbb{P}$, *then* MP *implies the law of excluded middle* ($\mathsf{LEM} := \forall P : \mathbb{P}.\, P \vee \neg P$).

Proof. Assume MP, X with $x_0 : X$, and that $p \preceq_{\mathsf{T}} \overline{p}$ for all $p : X \to \mathbb{P}$. It suffices to prove that for every proposition P we have $\neg\neg P \to P$. So assume $\neg\neg P$.

By MP and Theorem 27, we have that whenever $\lambda x. \neg P$ is decidable, then so is $\lambda x. P$. Now since $\neg\neg P$ holds, $\lambda x.\mathsf{false}$ decides $\lambda x. \neg P$. Thus we have a decider f for $\lambda x. P$. A case analysis on $f x_0$ yields either P and we are done – or $\neg P$, which is ruled out by $\neg\neg P$. □

The last lemma ensures that some amount of classical logic is necessary to prove that Turing reducibility is closed under complements, since it is well-known that MP does not imply LEM.

8 Turing Reducibility and Truth-Table Reducibility

As a further expectable property, we establish the well-known connection of Turing reducibility to truth-table reducibility [35], namely that every truth-table reduction induces a Turing reduction while the converse does not hold. Note that the proofs in this section have a classical flavour where explicitly mentioned.

Intuitively, a truth-table reduction can be seen as a restricted form of a Turing reduction: to reduce a predicate $p: X \to \mathbb{P}$ to a predicate $q: Y \to \mathbb{P}$, on input x, it has to compute a list of oracle queries of type Y^* and provide a truth-table mapping the list of answers of the oracle for q to an output of the reduction. Consequently, questions can not depend on answers of the oracle, and no non-termination is permitted. See also the explanations by Rogers [38, §8.3] or Odifreddi [31, III.3].

Concretely, we use the synthetic definition of truth-table reducibility from Forster and Jahn [13]. We model truth-tables as lists $\mathbb{B}^*$, but just work with a boolean evaluation predicate $l \vDash T$ and refer to the Coq code for its definition.

$$p \preceq_{\mathtt{tt}} q := \exists f: X \to Y^* \times \mathbb{B}^*. \forall x: X. \forall l: \mathbb{B}^*. \, \mathsf{Forall}_2 \, \hat{q} \, (\pi_1(fx)) \, l \to (px \leftrightarrow l \vDash \pi_2(fx))$$

where Forall_2 lifts binary predicates to lists pointwise by conjunction.

We first show that truth-table reducibility implies Turing reducibility.

Theorem 31. *If q is classical (i.e. $\forall y.\, qy \vee \neg qy$), then $p \preceq_{tt} q$ implies $p \preceq_{\mathsf{T}} q$.*

Proof. Let f be the truth-table reduction. Define F to map $R: Y \to \mathbb{B} \to \mathbb{P}$ to

$$\lambda xb.\ \exists l: \mathbb{B}^*. \ \mathsf{Forall}_2 \ R \ (\pi_1(fx)) \ l \wedge l \vDash \pi_2(fx))$$

which can be computed by the tree

$$\tau x l := \begin{cases} \mathsf{ret}\ (\mathsf{ask}\ a) & \text{if } \pi_1(fx) \text{ at position } |l| \text{ is } a \\ \mathsf{ret}\ (\mathsf{out}\ (l \vDash \pi_2(fx))) & \text{otherwise.} \end{cases}$$

The direction from right to left is straightforward. For the direction from left to right, it suffices to prove the existence of l with $\mathsf{Forall}_2\ \hat{q}\ \pi_1(fx)\ l$, following by induction on $\pi_1(fx)$, using the assumption that q is classical to construct l. □

We now prove that the inclusion of truth-table reducibility in Turing reducibility is strict. Forster and Jahn [13] introduce a hypersimple predicate $H_I: \mathbb{N} \to \mathbb{P}$ as the deficiency predicate of a strongly enumerable predicate $I: \mathbb{N} \to \mathbb{P}$ [8]: Given an injective, strong enumerator E_I of I ($\forall x.\ Ix \leftrightarrow \exists n. E_I n = x$), they set

$$H_I x \ := \ \exists x_0 > x.\ E_I x_0 < E_I x.$$

They prove that I does not truth-table reduce to H_I assuming axioms for synthetic computability, and in particular that the halting problem fulfills the preconditions for I. Thus, to separate truth-table from Turing reducibility, it suffices to give a Turing reduction $I \preceq_{\mathsf{T}} H_I$ (without having to assume axioms for synthetic computability).

Algorithmically, one can decide Iz given a partial function $f{:}\,\mathbb{N} \rightharpoonup \mathbb{B}$ deciding H_I as follows: We search for x such that $fx \triangleright \mathsf{false}$ and $E_I x > z$, i.e. $\neg H_I x$. Such an x does (not not) exists because the complement of H_I is non-finite. Then Iz holds if and only if $z \in [E_I 0, \dots E_I(x+1)]$.

Formally, we first establish the classical existence of such x in the more general situation of arbitrary non-finite predicates and injections.

Lemma 32. *If $p{:}\,X \to \mathbb{P}$ is non-finite and $f{:}\,X \to \mathbb{N}$ is injective, then for $z{:}\,\mathbb{N}$*

$$\neg\neg\exists x.\, px \land fx \geq z \land \forall y.\, py \to fy \geq z \to fx \leq fy.$$

Next, we verify the resulting characterisation of I via list membership.

Lemma 33. *If $\neg H_I x$ and $E_I x > z$, then $Iz \leftrightarrow [E_I 0, \dots, E_I(x+1)]$.*

Put together, we can describe the desired Turing reduction.

Theorem 34. *Assuming* LEM, *if I is strongly enumerable, then $I \preceq_{\mathsf{T}} H_I$.*

Proof. We define F to map relations R to the relation

$$\lambda zb.\, \exists x.\, R\,x\,\mathsf{false} \;\land\; E_I x > z \;\land\; (b = \mathsf{true} \leftrightarrow z \in [E_I 0, \dots, E_I(x+1)]) \\ \land\; (\forall x' < x.\, (R\,x'\,\mathsf{true} \lor (R\,x'\,\mathsf{false} \land E_I x' \leq z)))$$

which is straightforward to show computable.

Regarding $F(\hat{H}_I)zb \leftrightarrow \hat{I}zb$, the direction from left to right is immediate from Lemma 33. For the direction from right to left, assume $\hat{I}zb$. Let x be obtained for H_I and E_I from Lemma 32. Then x fulfils the claim by Lemma 33. □

Since in this paper we do not assume axioms for synthetic computability that imply $I \not\preceq_{\mathsf{tt}} H_I$, we keep the conclusion that truth-table reducibility is strictly stronger than Turing reducibility implicit.

9 Post's Theorem (PT)

There are various results (rightly) called "Post's theorem" in the literature. Here, we are concerned with the result that if both a predicate and its complement are semi-decidable, the predicate is decidable. This theorem was proved by Post in 1944 [35], and is not to be confused with Post's theorem relating the arithmetical hierarchy and Turing jumps from 1948 [36]. We thus simply refer to the result we consider as PT_0, and use PT for its relativised version.

It is well-known that PT_0 is equivalent to Markov's principle [1,16,42]. We here prove that the relativised version PT is fully constructive, and that in fact the equivalence proof of MP and PT_0 can be given using PT and the already proven equivalence between MP and the statement that Turing reducibility transports decidability backwards given in Sect. 7.

As an auxiliary notion, we introduce an equivalent but a priori more expressive form of interrogations which maintains an internal state of the computation and can "stall", i.e. trees do not have to either ask a question or produce an output, but can alternatively choose to just update the state. Such trees are of type $S \to A^* \rightharpoonup (S \times Q^?) + O$, where $Q^?$ is the inductive option type with elements None and $\mathsf{Some}\ q$ for $q{:}\,Q$.

A stalling tree is a partial function $\sigma{:}\, S \to A^* \rightharpoonup (S \times Q^?) + O$. We define a stalling interrogation predicate $\sigma\,;R \vdash qs\,;as\,;s \succ s'$ inductively by:

$$\frac{}{\sigma\,;R \vdash [\,]\,;[\,]\,;s \succ s} \qquad \frac{\sigma\,;R \vdash qs\,;as\,;s \succ s'' \qquad \sigma\ \ ;s''\ \ ;as \triangleright \mathsf{ask}\,(s', \mathsf{None})}{\sigma\,;R \vdash qs\,;as\,;s \succ s'}$$

$$\frac{\sigma\,;R \vdash qs\,;as\,;s \succ s'' \qquad \sigma\ \ ;s''\ \ ;as \triangleright \mathsf{ask}\,(s', \mathsf{Some}\ q) \qquad Rqa}{\sigma\,;R \vdash qs +\!\!+ [q]\,;as +\!\!+ [a]\,;s \succ s'}$$

The first and third rule are not significantly different from before, apart from also threading a state s. The second rule allows the tree to stall by only updating the state to s', but without asking an actual question. Intuitively, we can turn a stalling tree τ into a non-stalling one τ' by having τ' compute on input as first all results of τ on all prefixes of as, starting from a call $\tau\, i\, s_0\ as$ for a given initial state s_0. We give this construction in full detail in Appendix B.

A functional F mapping $R{:}\, Q \to A \to \mathbb{P}$ to a relation of type $I \to O \to \mathbb{P}$ is computable via stalling interrogations if there are a type S, an element $s_0{:}\, S$, and a function $\tau{:}\, I \to S \to A^* \rightharpoonup (S \times Q^?) + O$ such that

$$\forall R\,i\,o.\ F R\,i\,o \leftrightarrow \exists qs\ as\ s.\ \tau i\,;R \vdash qs\,;as\,;s_0 \succ s\ \wedge\ \tau\, i\, s\ as \triangleright \mathsf{out}\ o.$$

We prove that the two definitions of computability are equivalent in Appendix B and immediately move on to the proof of PT.

Theorem 35. (PT) *If $\mathcal{S}_q(p)$ and $\mathcal{S}_q(\overline{p})$, then $p \preceq_{\mathsf{T}} q$.*

Proof. Let $p{:}\, X \to \mathbb{P}$ and $q{:}\, Y \to \mathbb{P}$ as well as F_1 and F_2 be the functionals representing the semi-deciders, computed respectively by τ_1 and τ_2. The intuition is, on input x and as, to execute $\tau_1\ x$ and $\tau_2\ x$ in parallel and ensure that both their questions are asked. The interrogation can finish with true if $\tau_1\ x$ outputs a value, and with false if $\tau_2\ x$ does.

There are two challenges in making this intuition formal as an oracle computation: Only answers from as that τ_1 and τ_2 asked for have to be actually passed to it, respectively, and both τ_1 and τ_2 need to be allowed to ask all of their questions and eventually produce an output fairly, even though only one of them ever will.

Using Lemma 20, we define the Turing reduction without providing the relational layer and instead directly construct a tree τ based on stalling interrogations with state type $S := Y^? \times \mathbb{N} \times (\mathbb{B} \times Y)^*$. The first argument is used to remember a question that needs to be asked next, arising from cases where both τ_1 and τ_2 want to ask a question. The second argument is a step-index n

used to evaluate both τ_1 and τ_2 for n steps. The third argument records which question was asked by τ_1 and which by τ_2. To then construct τ compactly, we define helper functions $\mathsf{getas}_{1,2}\colon (\mathbb{B} \times Y)^* \to \mathbb{B}^* \to Y^*$ which choose answers from the second list according to the respective boolean in the first list.

We then define

$$\tau(\mathsf{Some}\ q, n, t)\,as := \mathsf{ret}\ (\mathsf{ask}\ (\mathsf{None}, n, t +\!\!+ [(\mathsf{false}, q)], \mathsf{Some}\ q))$$

$$\tau(\mathsf{None}, n, t)\,as := \begin{cases} \mathsf{ret}\ (\mathsf{out}\ \mathsf{true}) & \text{if } x_1 = \mathsf{Some}\ (\mathsf{out}\ o) \\ \mathsf{ret}\ (\mathsf{out}\ \mathsf{false}) & \text{if } x_2 = \mathsf{Some}\ (\mathsf{out}\ o) \\ \mathsf{ret}\ (\mathsf{ask}\ (\mathsf{Some}\ q', \mathsf{S}\ n, t +\!\!+ [(\mathsf{true}, q)], \mathsf{Some}\ q)) & \text{if } x_1 = \mathsf{Some}\ (\mathsf{ask}\ q) \\ & \quad \text{and } x_2 = \mathsf{Some}\ (\mathsf{ask}\ q') \\ \mathsf{ret}\ (\mathsf{ask}\ (\mathsf{None}, \mathsf{S}\ n, t +\!\!+ [(\mathsf{true}, q)], \mathsf{Some}\ q)) & \text{if } x_1 = \mathsf{Some}\ (\mathsf{ask}\ q) \\ \mathsf{ret}\ (\mathsf{ask}\ (\mathsf{None}, \mathsf{S}\ n, t +\!\!+ [(\mathsf{false}, q)], \mathsf{Some}\ q)) & \text{if } x_2 = \mathsf{Some}\ (\mathsf{ask}\ q) \\ \mathsf{ret}\ (\mathsf{ask}\ (\mathsf{None}, \mathsf{S}\ n, t, \mathsf{None})) & \text{otherwise} \end{cases}$$

where $x_1 = \rho^n\ (\tau_1\, x\, (\mathsf{getas}_1\, t\ as))$ and $x_2 = \rho^n\ (\tau_2\, x\, (\mathsf{getas}_2\, t\ as))$, with ρ being a step-indexed evaluation function for partial values.

This means that whenever τ_1 returns an output, then true is returned and whenever τ_2 returns an output, then false is returned while no question is ever missed and the interrogation stalls if n does not suffice to evaluate either τ_1 or τ_2. The invariants to prove that this indeed yields the wanted Turing reduction are technical but pose no major hurdles, we refer to the Coq code for details. □

Corollary 36. *The following are equivalent:*

1. MP
2. *Termination of partial functions is double negation stable.*
3. *Turing reducibility transports decidability backwards.*
4. PT_0

Proof. Implications (1) → (2) and (4) → (1) are well-known. We have already proved implication (2) → (3). It suffices to prove (3) → (4), which is almost direct using PT: Assume that for all X, Y, $p\colon X \to \mathbb{P}$, and $q\colon Y \to \mathbb{P}$ we have that if q is decidable and $p \preceq_{\mathsf{T}} q$, then p is decidable. Let furthermore p and its complement be semi-decidable. We prove that p is decidable. Clearly, it suffices to prove that $p \preceq_{\mathsf{T}} q$ for a decidable predicate q (e.g. $\lambda n\colon \mathbb{N}.\top$). Using PT, it suffices to prove p and its complement semi-decidable in q, which in turn follows from the assumption that they are semi-decidable and Lemma 16. □

10 Discussion

Mechanisation in Coq. The Coq mechanisation accompanying this paper closely follows the structure of the hyperlinked mathematical presentation and spans roughly 2500 lines of code for the novel results, building on a library of basic synthetic computability theory. It showcases the feasibility of mechanising ongoing research with reasonable effort and illustrates the interpretation of synthetic oracle computations as a natural notion available in dependently-typed programming languages. In fact, using Coq helped us a lot with finding the proofs concerning constructive reverse mathematics (Lemmas 28 and 30 and Corollary 36) in the first place, where subtleties like double negations need to be tracked over small changes in the definitions.

On top of the usual proof engineering, we used three notable mechanisation techniques. First, we generalise over all possible implementations of partial functions, so our code is guaranteed to just rely on the abstract interface described in Appendix A. Secondly, we devised a custom tactic `psimpl` that simplifies goals involving partial functions by strategically rewriting with the specifications of the respective operations. Thirdly, to establish computability of composed functionals, instead of constructing a complicated tree at once, we postpone the construction with the use of existential variables and apply abstract lemmas such as the ones described in Sect. 4 to obtain the trees step by step.

Related Work. Synthetic computability was introduced by Richman [37] and popularised by Richman, Bridges, and Bauer [1–3,5]. In synthetic computability, one assumes axioms such as CT ("Church's thesis" [28,42]), postulating that *all* functions are μ-recursive. CT is proved consistent for univalent type theory by Swan and Uemura [39]. Since univalent type theory proves unique choice, using it as the basis for computability theory renders CT inconsistent with already the weak principle of omniscience [10], and consequently with the law of excluded middle, precluding interesting results in constructive reverse mathematics.

Forster [12] identifies that working in CIC allows assuming CT and its consequences even under the presence of the law of excluded middle. This approach has been used to develop the theory of many-one and truth-table reducibility [13], to give a proof of the Myhill isomorphism theorem [14] and a more general treatment of computational back-and-forth arguments [21], to show that random numbers defined using Kolmogorov complexity form a simple set [17], to analyse Tennenbaum's theorem regarding its constructive content [20], to give computational proofs of Gödel's first incompleteness theorem [23,24], and to develop an extensive Coq library of undecidability proofs [18].

The first synthetic definition of oracle computability is due to Bauer [3], based on continuous functionals in the effective topos. The first author introduced a classically equivalent definition in his PhD thesis [11] based on joint work with the second author. Subsequently, we have adapted this definition into one constructively equivalent to Bauer's definition [15]. All these previous definitions however have in common that it is unclear how to derive an enumeration of all oracle computable functionals from CT as used in [22,30], because they do not reduce higher-order functionals to first-order functions. Recently, Swan has suggested a definition of oracle computability based on modalities in univalent type theory [40].

Future Work. With the present paper, we lay the foundation for several future investigations concerning synthetic oracle computability in the context of axioms like CT, both by improving on related projects and by tackling new challenges. First, a rather simple test would be the Kleene-Post theorem [27], establishing incomparable Turing degrees as already approximated in [22], assuming an enumeration of all oracle computations of their setting. Similarly, we plan to establish Post's theorem [36], connecting the arithmetical hierarchy with Turing degrees. An interesting challenge would be a synthetic proof of the Friedberg-Muchnik theorem [19,29], solving Post's problem [35] concerning the existence of undecidable Turing degrees strictly below the halting problem.

Acknowledgements. We want to thank Felix Jahn, Gert Smolka, Dominique Larchey-Wendling, and the participants of the TYPES '22 conference for many fruitful discussions about Turing reducibility, as well as Martin Baillon, Yann Leray, Assia Mahboubi, Pierre-Marie Pédrot, and Matthieu Piquerez for discussions about notions of continuity. The central inspiration to start working on Turing reducibility in type theory is due to Andrej Bauer's talk at the Wisconsin logic seminar in February 2021.

A Glossary of Definitions

We collect some basic notations and definitions:

- $\mathbb{P}$ is the (impredicative) universe of propositions.
- *Natural numbers:* $n : \mathbb{N} ::= 0 \mid \mathsf{S}\, n$
- *Booleans:* $b : \mathbb{B} ::= \mathsf{true} \mid \mathsf{false}$
- *Unit type:* $\mathbb{1} ::= \star$
- *Sum type:* $X + Y ::= \mathsf{inl} x \mid \mathsf{inr} y \quad (x : X, y : Y)$
- *Option type:* $o : X^? ::= \mathsf{None} \mid \mathsf{Some}\, x \quad (x : X)$
- *Lists:* $l : X^* ::= [\,] \mid x :: l \quad (x : X)$

List operations. We often rely on concatenation of of two lists $l_1 +\!\!+ l_2$:

$$[\,] +\!\!+ l_2 := l_2 \qquad\qquad (x :: l_1) +\!\!+ l_2 := x :: (l_1 +\!\!+ l_2)$$

Also, we use an inductive predicate $\mathsf{Forall}_2 : (X \to Y \to \mathbb{P}) \to X^* \to Y^* \to \mathbb{P}$

$$\frac{}{\mathsf{Forall}_2\, p\, [\,]\, [\,]} \qquad\qquad \frac{pxy \qquad \mathsf{Forall}_2\, p\, l_1\, l_2}{\mathsf{Forall}_2\, p\, (x :: l_1)\, (y :: l_2)}$$

Characteristic Relation. The characteristic relation $\hat{p} : X \to \mathbb{B} \to \mathbb{P}$ of a predicate $p : X \to \mathbb{P}$ is introduced in Sect. 3 as

$$\hat{p} \;:=\; \lambda xb. \begin{cases} px & \text{if } b = \mathsf{true} \\ \neg px & \text{if } b = \mathsf{false}. \end{cases}$$

Reducibility. $\preceq_m$ is many-one reducibility, introduced in Sect. 6. $\preceq_{\mathtt{tt}}$ is truth-table reducibility, introduced in Sect. 8. $\preceq_{\mathsf{T}}$ is Turing reducibility, introduced in Sect. 3.

Interrogations. The interrogation predicate $\sigma\,;R\vdash qs\,;as$ is introduced in Sect. 2. It works on a tree $\sigma\colon A^*\to Q+O$. We often also use trees taking an input, i.e. $\tau\colon I\to A^*\to Q+O$. Given σ, we denote the subtree starting at path $l\colon A^*$ with $\sigma@l := \lambda l'.\,\sigma(l +\!\!+ l')$.

Partial Functions. We use an abstract type of partial values over X, denoted as $\mathcal{P}X$, with evaluation relation $\triangleright\colon\mathcal{P}X\to X\to\mathbb{P}$. We set $X\rightharpoonup Y := X\to\mathcal{P}Y$ and use

- $\mathsf{ret} : X\rightharpoonup X$ with $\mathsf{ret}\; x\triangleright x$,
- $\gg\!=\colon\mathcal{P}X\to(X\to\mathcal{P}Y)\to\mathcal{P}Y$ with $x\gg\!= f\triangleright y \leftrightarrow \exists v.\; x\triangleright v\wedge f v\triangleright y$,
- $\mu\colon(\mathbb{N}\to\mathcal{P}\mathbb{B})\to\mathcal{P}\mathbb{N}$ with $\mu f\triangleright n\leftrightarrow f n\triangleright\mathsf{true}\wedge\forall m<n.\; f m\triangleright\mathsf{false}$, and
- $\mathsf{undef}\colon\mathcal{P}X$ with $\forall v.\;\mathsf{undef}\not\triangleright v$.

One can for instance implement $\mathcal{P}X$ as monotonic sequences $f:\mathbb{N}\to X^?$, i.e. with $f n=\mathsf{Some}\;x\to\forall m\ge n.\; f m=\mathsf{Some}\;x$ and $f\triangleright x := \exists n.\; f n=\mathsf{Some}\;x$. For any implementation it is only crucial that the graph relation $\lambda xy.fx\triangleright y$ for $f\colon\mathbb{N}\rightharpoonup\mathbb{N}$ is semi-decidable but cannot be proved decidable. Semi-decidability induces a function $\rho\colon\mathcal{P}X\to\mathbb{N}\to X^?$, which we write as $\rho^n x$ with the properties that $x\triangleright v\leftrightarrow\exists n.\;\rho^n x=\mathsf{Some}\;v$ and $\rho^n x=\mathsf{Some}\;v\to\forall m\ge n.\;\rho^m x=\mathsf{Some}\;v$.

B Extended Forms of Interrogations

B.1 Extended Interrogations with State

As an auxiliary notion, before introducing the stalling interrogations, we first introduce extended interrogations with a state argument, but without stalling. An extended tree is a function $\sigma : S\to A^*\rightharpoonup(S\times Q)+O$. We define an inductive extended interrogation predicate $\sigma\,;R\vdash qs\,;as\,;s\succ s'$ by:

$$\frac{}{\sigma\,;R\vdash[\,]\,;[\,]\,;s\succ s}\qquad\frac{\sigma\,;R\vdash qs\,;as\,;s\succ s''\qquad \sigma\;s''\;as\triangleright\mathsf{ask}\;(s',q)\qquad Rqa}{\sigma\,;R\vdash qs +\!\!+ [q]\,;as +\!\!+ [a]\,;s\succ s'}$$

A functional F mapping $R\colon Q\to A\to\mathbb{P}$ to a relation of type $I\to O\to\mathbb{P}$ is computable via extended interrogations if there are a type S, an element $s_0 : S$, and a function $\tau\colon I\to S\to A^*\rightharpoonup(S\times Q)+O$ such that

$$\forall R\,i\,o.\; F R\,i\,o\leftrightarrow\exists qs\;as\;s.\;\tau i\,;R\vdash qs\,;as\,;s_0\succ s\;\wedge\;\tau\,i\,s\;as\triangleright\mathsf{out}\;o.$$

Note that we do not pass the question history to the function here, because if necessary it can be part of the type S.

Lemma 37. *Computable functionals are computable via extended interrogations.*

Proof. Let F be computable by τ. Set S to be any inhabited type with element s_0 and define

$$\tau'\ i\ s\ l := \tau\ i\ l \gg\!= \lambda x.\ \begin{cases} \mathsf{ret}\ (\mathsf{ask}\ (s, q)) & \text{if } x = \mathsf{ask}\ q \\ \mathsf{ret}\ o & \text{if } x = \mathsf{out}\ o. \end{cases}.$$

Then τ' computes F via extended interrogations. □

Lemma 38. *Functionals computable via extended interrogations are computable.*

Proof. Let $\tau : I \to S \to A^* \rightharpoonup (S \times Q) + O$ compute F via extended interrogations. Define $\tau' : S \to A^* \to I \to A^* \rightharpoonup Q + O$ as

$$\tau'\ s\ l\ i\ [] := \tau\ i\ s\ l \gg\!= \begin{cases} \mathsf{ret}\ (\mathsf{ask}\ q) & \text{if } x = \mathsf{ask}\ (e, q) \\ \mathsf{ret}\ (\mathsf{out}\ o) & \text{if } x = \mathsf{out}\ o, \end{cases}$$

$$\tau'\ s\ l\ i\ (a :: as) := \tau\ s\ l\ i \gg\!= \lambda x.\ \begin{cases} \tau'\ s'\ (l +\!\!+ [a])\ i\ as & \text{if } x = \mathsf{ask}\ (s', q) \\ \mathsf{ret}\ (\mathsf{out}\ o) & \text{if } x = \mathsf{out}\ o. \end{cases}$$

Then $\tau'\ s_0\ []$ computes F. □

B.2 Stalling Interrogations

We here give the left out proofs that stalling interrogations as described in Sect. 9 and interrogations are equivalent.

Lemma 39. *Functionals computable via extended interrogations are computable via stalling interrogations.*

Proof. Let F be computable using a type S and element s_0 by τ via extended interrogations. We use the same type S and element s_0 and define τ' to never use stalling:

$$\tau'\ i\ s\ l := \tau\ i\ s\ l \gg\!= \lambda x.\ \begin{cases} \mathsf{ret}\ (\mathsf{ask}\ (s', \mathsf{Some}\ q)) & \text{if } x = \mathsf{ask}\ (s', q) \\ \mathsf{ret}\ (\mathsf{out}\ o) & \text{if } x = \mathsf{out}\ o. \end{cases}$$

Then τ' computes F via stalling interrogations. □

Lemma 40. *Functionals computable via stalling interrogations are computable via extended interrogations.*

Proof. Take $\tau : I \to S \to A^* \rightharpoonup (S \times Q^?) + O$ computing F via stalling interrogations. We construct $\tau'\ i\ s\ as$ to iterate the function $\lambda s'.\ \tau\ i\ s'\ as$ of type $S \rightharpoonup (S \times Q^?) + O$. If $\mathsf{ask}\ (s'', \mathsf{None})$ is returned, the iteration continues with s''. If $\mathsf{ask}\ (s, \mathsf{Some}\ q)$ is returned, $\tau'\ i\ s\ as$ returns $\mathsf{ask}\ (s, q)$. If $\mathsf{out}\ o$ is returned, $\tau'\ i\ s\ as$ returns $\mathsf{out}\ o$ as well.

We omit the technical details how to implement this iteration process using unbounded search $\mu : (\mathbb{N} \rightharpoonup \mathbb{B}) \rightharpoonup \mathbb{N}$. □

B.3 Proofs of Closure Properties

We here give the proofs that executing two computable functionals one after the other, composing computable functionals, and performing an unbounded search on a computable functional are all computable operations as stated in Sect. 4. We explain the tree constructions, which are always the core of the argument. The verification of the trees are then tedious but relatively straightforward inductions, we refer to the Coq code for full detail.

Proof (of Lemma 7). Let τ_1 compute F_1 maping relations $R\colon Q{\to}A{\to}\mathbb{P}$ to relations of type $I{\to}O'{\to}\mathbb{P}$, and τ_2 compute F_2 mapping relations $R\colon Q{\to}A{\to}\mathbb{P}$ to relations of type $(I \times O'){\to}O{\to}\mathbb{P}$.

To compute the functional mapping an oracle $R\colon Q{\to}A{\to}\mathbb{P}$ to a computation $\lambda io.\, \exists o'{:}\,O'.\, F_1\, R\, i\, o' \wedge F_2\, R\,(i, o')\, o$ of type $I{\to}O{\to}\mathbb{P}$ we construct a stalling tree with state type $(O' \times \mathbb{N})^?$ and starting state None. The intuition is that the state s remains None as long as τ_1 asks questions, and once an output o' is produced we save it and the number of questions that were asked until then in the state, which remains unchanged after. Then, τ_2 can ask questions, but since as contains also answers to questions of τ_1, we drop the first n before passing it to τ_2.

Formally, the tree takes as arguments the input i, state s ans answer list as, and returns

$$\begin{cases} \mathsf{ret}\,(\mathsf{ask}\,(\mathsf{None}, \mathsf{Some}\; q)) & \text{if } s = \mathsf{None}, \tau_1\, i\; as \rhd \mathsf{Some}\,(\mathsf{ask}\; q) \\ \mathsf{ret}\,(\mathsf{ask}\,(\mathsf{Some}\,(o', |as|), \mathsf{None})) & \text{if } s = \mathsf{None}, \tau_1\, i\; as \rhd \mathsf{Some}\,(\mathsf{out}\; o') \\ \mathsf{ret}\,(\mathsf{ask}\,(\mathsf{Some}\,(o', n), \mathsf{Some}\; q)) & \text{if } s = \mathsf{Some}\,(o', n), \tau_2\,(i, o')\,(as \uparrow_n) \rhd \mathsf{Some}\,(\mathsf{ask}\; q) \\ \mathsf{ret}\,(\mathsf{ask}\,(\mathsf{Some}\,(o', n), \mathsf{Some}\; q)) & \text{if } s = \mathsf{Some}\,(o', n), \tau_2\,(i, o')\,(as \uparrow_n) \rhd \mathsf{Some}\,(\mathsf{out}\; o) \end{cases}$$

where $as \uparrow_n$ drops the first n elements of as. Note that formally, we use bind to analyse the values of τ_1 and τ_2, but just write a case analysis on paper. □

Proof (of Lemma 8). Let τ_1 compute F_1 mapping relations $R\colon Q{\to}A{\to}\mathbb{P}$ to relations $X{\to}Y{\to}\mathbb{P}$, and τ_1 compute F_2 mapping relations $R\colon X{\to}Y{\to}\mathbb{P}$ to relations $I{\to}O{\to}\mathbb{P}$. We construct a stalling tree τ computing a functional mapping $R\colon Q{\to}A{\to}\mathbb{P}$ to $\lambda io.\; F_2\,(F_1 R)\, i\, o$ of type $I{\to}O{\to}\mathbb{P}$.

Intuitively, we want to execute τ_2. Whenever it asks a question x, we record it and execute $\tau_1\, x$ to produce an answer. Since the answer list as at any point will also contain answers of the oracle produces for any earlier question x' of τ_2, we record furthermore how many questions were already asked to the oracle to compute $\tau_1 x$.

As state type, we thus use $(X \times Y)^* \times (X \times \mathbb{N})^?$, where the first component remembers questions and answers for τ_2, and the second component indicates whether we are currently executing τ_2 (then it is None), or τ_1, when it is $\mathsf{Some}\,(x, n)$ to indicate that on answer list as we need to run $\tau_1\, x\,(as \downarrow^n)$, where $as \downarrow^n$ contains the last n elements of as. The initial state is $([\,], \mathsf{None})$.

We define τ to take as arguments an input i, a state (t, z), and an answer list as and return

$$\begin{cases} \mathsf{out}\ o & \text{if } x = \mathsf{None}, \tau_2\, i\, (\mathsf{map}\, \pi_2\, t) \rhd \mathsf{out}\ o \\ \mathsf{ask}\ (t, \mathsf{Some}\ (x, 0), \mathsf{None}) & \text{if } x = \mathsf{None}, \tau_2\, i\, (\mathsf{map}\, \pi_2\, t) \rhd \mathsf{ask}\ x \\ \mathsf{ask}\ (t, \mathsf{Some}\ (x, \mathsf{S}\ n), \mathsf{Some}\ q) & \text{if } x = \mathsf{Some}\ (x, n), \tau_1\, x\, (as \uparrow^n) \rhd \mathsf{ask}\ q \\ \mathsf{ask}\ (t +\!\!+ [(x, y)], \mathsf{None}, \mathsf{None}) & \text{if } x = \mathsf{Some}\ (x, n), \tau_1\, x\, (as \uparrow^n) \rhd \mathsf{out}\ y \end{cases}$$

Intuitively, when we are in the mode to execute τ_2 and it returns an output, we return the output. If it returns a question x, we change mode and stall. When we are in the mode to execute τ_1 to produce an answer for x, taking the last n given answers into account and it asks a question q, we ask the question and indicate that now one more answer needs to be taken into account. If it returns an output y, we add the pair $[(x, y)]$ to the question answer list for τ_1, change the mode back to execute τ_2, and stall. □

Proof (of Lemma 9). We define a tree τ computing the functional mapping R: $(I \times \mathbb{N}) \rightarrow \mathbb{B} \rightarrow \mathbb{P}$ to the following relation of type $I \rightarrow \mathbb{N} \rightarrow \mathbb{P}$: $\lambda in.\ R\,(i, n)\, \mathsf{true} \wedge \forall m < n.\ R\,(i, m)\, \mathsf{false}$.

$$\tau\ i\ as := \begin{cases} \mathsf{ret}\ (\mathsf{out}\ i) & \text{if } as[i] = \mathsf{true} \\ \mathsf{ret}\ (\mathsf{ask}\ (i, |as|)) & \text{if } \forall j.\ as[j] = \mathsf{false} \end{cases}$$

Note that a function $\mathsf{find}\ as$ computing the smallest i such that as at position i is true, and else returning None is easy to implement.

Intuitively, we just ask all natural numbers as questions in order. On answer list l with length n, this means we have asked $[0, \ldots, n-1]$. We check whether for one of these the oracle returned true, and else ask $n = |l|$. □

C Relation to Bauer's Turing Reducibility

We show the equivalence of the modulus continuity as defined in Lemma 1 with the order-theoretic characterisation used by Bauer [3]. The latter notion is more sensible for functionals acting on functional relations, so we fix some

$$F : (Q \rightsquigarrow A) \rightarrow (I \rightsquigarrow O)$$

where $X \rightsquigarrow Y$ denotes the type of functional relations $X \rightarrow Y \rightarrow \mathbb{P}$. To simplify proofs and notation, we assume extensionality in the form that we impose $R = R'$ for all $R, R' : X \rightsquigarrow Y$ with $Rxy \leftrightarrow R'xy$ for all $x : X$ and $y : Y$.

To clarify potential confusion upfront, note that Bauer does not represent oracles on $\mathbb{N}$ as (functional) relations but as pairs (X, Y) of disjoint sets with $X, Y : \mathbb{N} \rightarrow \mathbb{P}$, so his oracle computation operate on such pairs. However, since such a pair (X, Y) gives rise to a functional relation $R : \mathbb{N} \rightsquigarrow \mathbb{B}$ by setting $R\,n\,b := (X\,n \wedge b = \mathsf{true}) \vee (Y\,n \wedge b = \mathsf{false})$ and, conversely, $R : \mathbb{N} \rightsquigarrow \mathbb{B}$ induces a pair (X, Y) via $X\,n := R\,n\,\mathsf{true}$ and $Y\,n := R\,n\,\mathsf{false}$, Bauer's oracle functionals correspond to our specific case of functionals $(\mathbb{N} \rightsquigarrow \mathbb{B}) \to (\mathbb{N} \rightsquigarrow \mathbb{B})$. He then describes the computable behaviour of an oracle functional by imposing continuity and a computational core operating on disjoint pairs (X, Y) of enumerable sets that the original oracle functional factors through, which in our chosen approach correspond to the existence of computation trees. So while the overall setup of our approach still fits to Bauer's suggestion, we now show that our notion of continuity is strictly stronger than his by showing the latter equivalent to modulus continuity.

Informally, Bauer's notion of continuity requires that F preserves suprema, which given a non-empty directed set : $(Q \rightsquigarrow A) \to \mathbb{P}$ of functional relations requires that $F\,(\bigcup_{R \in S} R) = \bigcup_{R \in S} F\,R$, i.e. that the F applied to the union of S should be the union of F applied to each R in S. Here directedness of S means that for every $R_1, R_2 \in S$ there is also $R_3 \in S$ with $R_1, R_2 \subseteq R_3$, which ensures that the functional relations included in S are compatible so that the union of S is again a functional relation.

Lemma 41. *If F is modulus-continuous, then it preserves suprema.*

Proof. First, we observe that F is monotone, given that from $F\,R\,i\,o$ we obtain some modulus $L : Q^*$ that directly induces $F\,R'\,i\,o$ for every R' with $R \subseteq R'$.

So now S be directed and non-empty, we show both inclusions separately. First $\bigcup_{R \in S} F\,R \subseteq F\,(\bigcup_{R \in S} R)$ follows directly from monotonicity, since if $F\,R\,i\,o$ for some $R \in S$ we also have $F\,(\bigcup_{R \in S} R)\,i\,o$ given $R \subseteq \bigcup_{R \in S} R$.

Finally assuming $F\,(\bigcup_{R \in S} R)\,i\,o$, let $L : Q^*$ be a corresponding modulus, so in particular $L \subseteq \mathsf{dom}(\bigcup_{R \in S} R)$. Using directedness (and since S is non-empty), by induction on L we can find $R_L \in S$ such that already $L \subseteq \mathsf{dom}(R_L)$. But then also $F\,R_L\,i\,o$ since L is a modulus and R_L agrees with $\bigcup_{R \in S} R)$ on L. □

Lemma 42. *If F is preserves suprema, then it is modulous continuous.*

Proof. Again, we first observe that F is monotone, given that for $R \subseteq R'$ the (non-empty) set $S := \{R, R'\}$ is directed and hence if $F\,R\,i\,o$ we obtain $F\,R'\,i\,o$ since $R' = \bigcup_{R \in S} R$.

Now assuming $F\,R\,i\,o$ we want to find a corresponding modulus. Consider

$$S := \{R_L \mid L \subseteq \mathsf{dom}(R)\}$$

where $R_L\,q\,a := q \in L \land R\,q\,a$, so S contains all terminating finite subrelations of R. So by construction, we have $R = \bigcup_{R \in S} R$ and hence $F\,(\bigcup_{R \in S} R)\,i\,o$, thus since F preserves suprema we obtain $L \subseteq \mathsf{dom}(R)$ such that already $F\,R_L\,i\,o$. The remaining part of L being a modulus for $F\,R\,i\,o$ follows from monotonicity. □

References

1. Bauer, A.: First steps in synthetic computability theory. Electron. Not. Theoret. Comput. Sci. **155**, 5–31 (2006). https://doi.org/10.1016/j.entcs.2005.11.049
2. Bauer, A.: On fixed-point theorems in synthetic computability. Tbilisi Math. J. **10**(3), 167–181 (2017). https://doi.org/10.1515/tmj-2017-0107
3. Bauer, A.: Synthetic mathematics with an excursion into computability theory (slide set). University of Wisconsin Logic seminar (2020). http://math.andrej.com/asset/data/madison-synthetic-computability-talk.pdf
4. Bauer, A.: Formalizing invisible mathematics. In: Workshop on Machine Assisted Proofs, Institute for Pure and Applied Mathematics (IPAM) at the University of California in Los Angeles (UCLA), 13–17 February 2023 (2023). https://www.youtube.com/watch?v=wZSvuCJBaFU
5. Bridges, D., Richman, F.: Varieties of Constructive Mathematics, vol. 97. Cambridge University Press (1987). https://doi.org/10.1017/CBO9780511565663
6. Coquand, T., Huet, G.P.: The calculus of constructions. Inf. Comput. **76**(2/3), 95–120 (1988). https://doi.org/10.1016/0890-5401(88)90005-3
7. Davis, M.D.: Computability and Unsolvability. McGraw-Hill Series in Information Processing and Computers. McGraw-Hill (1958)
8. Dekker, J.C.E.: A theorem on hypersimple sets. Proc. Am. Math. Soc. **5**, 791–796 (1954). https://doi.org/10.1090/S0002-9939-1954-0063995-6
9. Escardo, M.: Continuity of Gödel's system T definable functionals via effectful forcing. Electron. Not. Theoret. Comput. Sci. **298**, 119–141 (2013). https://doi.org/10.1016/j.entcs.2013.09.010
10. Forster, Y.: Church's thesis and related axioms in Coq's type theory. In: Baier, C., Goubault-Larrecq, J. (eds.) 29th EACSL Annual Conference on Computer Science Logic (CSL 2021). Leibniz International Proceedings in Informatics (LIPIcs), vol. 183, pp. 21:1–21:19. Schloss Dagstuhl-Leibniz-Zentrum für Informatik, Dagstuhl, Germany (2021). https://doi.org/10.4230/LIPIcs.CSL.2021.21. https://drops.dagstuhl.de/opus/volltexte/2021/13455
11. Forster, Y.: Computability in constructive type theory. Ph.D. thesis, Saarland University (2021). https://doi.org/10.22028/D291-35758
12. Forster, Y.: Parametric Church's thesis: synthetic computability without choice. In: Artemov, S., Nerode, A. (eds.) LFCS 2022. LNCS, vol. 13137, pp. 70–89. Springer, Cham (2022). https://doi.org/10.1007/978-3-030-93100-1_6
13. Forster, Y., Jahn, F.: Constructive and synthetic reducibility degrees: post's problem for many-one and truth-table reducibility in Coq. In: Klin, B., Pimentel, E. (eds.) 31st EACSL Annual Conference on Computer Science Logic (CSL 2023). Leibniz International Proceedings in Informatics (LIPIcs), vol. 252, pp. 21:1–21:21. Schloss Dagstuhl - Leibniz-Zentrum für Informatik, Dagstuhl, Germany (2023). https://doi.org/10.4230/LIPIcs.CSL.2023.21. https://drops.dagstuhl.de/opus/volltexte/2023/17482
14. Forster, Y., Jahn, F., Smolka, G.: A computational cantor-Bernstein and Myhill's isomorphism theorem in constructive type theory. In: CPP 2023–12th ACM SIGPLAN International Conference on Certified Programs and Proofs, pp. 1–8. ACM, Boston, United States, January 2023. https://doi.org/10.1145/3573105.3575690. https://inria.hal.science/hal-03891390
15. Forster, Y., Kirst, D.: Synthetic Turing reducibility in constructive type theory. In: 28th International Conference on Types for Proofs and Programs (TYPES 2022) (2022). https://types22.inria.fr/files/2022/06/TYPES_2022_paper_64.pdf

16. Forster, Y., Kirst, D., Smolka, G.: On synthetic undecidability in Coq, with an application to the Entscheidungsproblem. In: Proceedings of the 8th ACM SIGPLAN International Conference on Certified Programs and Proofs - CPP 2019. ACM Press (2019). https://doi.org/10.1145/3293880.3294091. https://doi.org/10.1145/3293880.3294091
17. Forster, Y., Kunze, F., Lauermann, N.: Synthetic kolmogorov complexity in Coq. In: Andronick, J., de Moura, L. (eds.) 13th International Conference on Interactive Theorem Proving (ITP 2022). Leibniz International Proceedings in Informatics (LIPIcs), vol. 237, pp. 12:1–12:19. Schloss Dagstuhl - Leibniz-Zentrum für Informatik, Dagstuhl, Germany (2022). https://doi.org/10.4230/LIPIcs.ITP.2022.12. https://drops.dagstuhl.de/opus/volltexte/2022/16721
18. Forster, Y., et al.: A Coq library of undecidable problems. In: The Sixth International Workshop on Coq for Programming Languages (CoqPL 2020) (2020). https://github.com/uds-psl/coq-library-undecidability
19. Friedberg, R.M.: Two recursively enumerable sets of incomparable degrees of unsovlability (solution of Post's problem), 1944. Proc. Nat. Acad. Sci. **43**(2), 236–238 (1957). https://doi.org/10.1073/pnas.43.2.236. https://doi.org/10.1073/pnas.43.2.236
20. Hermes, M., Kirst, D.: An analysis of Tennenbaum's theorem in constructive type theory. In: Felty, A.P. (ed.) 7th International Conference on Formal Structures for Computation and Deduction, FSCD 2022, 2–5 August 2022, Haifa, Israel. LIPIcs, vol. 228, pp. 9:1–9:19. Schloss Dagstuhl - Leibniz-Zentrum für Informatik (2022). https://doi.org/10.4230/LIPIcs.FSCD.2022.9
21. Kirst, D.: Computational back-and-forth arguments in constructive type theory. In: Andronick, J., de Moura, L. (eds.) 13th International Conference on Interactive Theorem Proving (ITP 2022). Leibniz International Proceedings in Informatics (LIPIcs), vol. 237, pp. 22:1–22:12. Schloss Dagstuhl - Leibniz-Zentrum für Informatik, Dagstuhl, Germany (2022). https://doi.org/10.4230/LIPIcs.ITP.2022.22. https://drops.dagstuhl.de/opus/volltexte/2022/16731
22. Kirst, D., Forster, Y., Mück, N.: Synthetic versions of the kleene-post and post's theorem. In: 28th International Conference on Types for Proofs and Programs (TYPES 2022) (2022). https://types22.inria.fr/files/2022/06/TYPES_2022_paper_65.pdf
23. Kirst, D., Hermes, M.: Synthetic undecidability and incompleteness of first-order axiom systems in Coq: extended version. J. Autom. Reason. **67**(1), 13 (2023). https://doi.org/10.1007/s10817-022-09647-x
24. Kirst, D., Peters, B.: Gödel's theorem without tears - essential incompleteness in synthetic computability. In: Klin, B., Pimentel, E. (eds.) 31st EACSL Annual Conference on Computer Science Logic, CSL 2023, 13–16 February 2023, Warsaw, Poland. LIPIcs, vol. 252, pp. 30:1–30:18. Schloss Dagstuhl - Leibniz-Zentrum für Informatik (2023). https://doi.org/10.4230/LIPIcs.CSL.2023.30
25. Kleene, S.C.: Recursive functionals and quantifiers of finite types I. Trans. Am. Math. Soc. **91**(1), 1 (1959). https://doi.org/10.2307/1993145. https://www.jstor.org/stable/1993145?origin=crossref
26. Kleene, S.C.: Introduction to Metamathematics, vol. 483. Van Nostrand, New York (1952)
27. Kleene, S.C., Post, E.L.: The upper semi-lattice of degrees of recursive unsolvability. Ann. Math. **59**(3), 379 (1954). https://doi.org/10.2307/1969708
28. Kreisel, G.: Mathematical logic. Lect. Mod. Math. **3**, 95–195 (1965). https://doi.org/10.2307/2315573

29. Muchnik, A.A.: On strong and weak reducibility of algorithmic problems. Sibirskii Matematicheskii Zhurnal **4**(6), 1328–1341 (1963)
30. Mück, N.: The arithmetical hierarchy, oracle computability, and Post's theorem in synthetic computability. Bachelor's thesis, Saarland University (2022). https://ps.uni-saarland.de/~mueck/bachelor.php
31. Odifreddi, P.: Classical Recursion Theory: The Theory of Functions and Sets of Natural Numbers. Elsevier (1992)
32. van Oosten, J.: A combinatory algebra for sequential functionals of finite type. In: Models and Computability, pp. 389–406. Cambridge University Press, June 1999. https://doi.org/10.1017/cbo9780511565670.019
33. van Oosten, J.: Partial combinatory algebras of functions. Notre Dame J. Formal Logic **52**(4), 431–448 (2011). https://doi.org/10.1215/00294527-1499381
34. Paulin-Mohring, C.: Inductive definitions in the system Coq rules and properties. In: Bezem, M., Groote, J.F. (eds.) TLCA 1993. LNCS, vol. 664, pp. 328–345. Springer, Heidelberg (1993). https://doi.org/10.1007/BFb0037116
35. Post, E.L.: Recursively enumerable sets of positive integers and their decision problems. Bull. Am. Math. Soc. **50**(5), 284–316 (1944). https://doi.org/10.1090/S0002-9904-1944-08111-1
36. Post, E.L.: Degrees of recursive unsolvability - preliminary report. Bull. Am. Math. Soc. **54**(7), 641–642 (1948)
37. Richman, F.: Church's thesis without tears. J. Symbolic Logic **48**(3), 797–803 (1983). https://doi.org/10.2307/2273473
38. Rogers, H.: Theory of Recursive Functions and Effective Computability (1987)
39. Swan, A., Uemura, T.: On Church's thesis in cubical assemblies. arXiv preprint arXiv:1905.03014 (2019)
40. Swan, A.W.: Oracle modalities. In: Second International Conference on Homotopy Type Theory (HoTT 2023) (2023). https://hott.github.io/HoTT-2023/abstracts/HoTT-2023_abstract_35.pdf
41. The Coq Development Team: The Coq proof assistant, June 2023. https://doi.org/10.5281/zenodo.8161141
42. Troelstra, A.S., van Dalen, D.: Constructivism in Mathematics. Studies in Logic and the Foundations of Mathematics, vol. i, 26 (1988)
43. Turing, A.M.: Systems of logic based on ordinals. Proc. Lond. Math. Soc. **2**(1), 161–228 (1939). https://doi.org/10.1112/plms/s2-45.1.161

Experimenting with an Intrinsically-Typed Probabilistic Programming Language in Coq

Ayumu Saito[1,2] and Reynald Affeldt[2(✉)]

[1] Department of Mathematical and Computing Science, Tokyo Institute of Technology, Tokyo, Japan
[2] National Institute of Advanced Industrial Science and Technology, Tokyo, Japan
reynald.affeldt@aist.go.jp

Abstract. Although the formalization of probabilistic programs already has several applications in the fields of security proofs and artificial intelligence, formal verification experiments are still underway to support the many features of probabilistic programming. We report on the formalization in the Coq proof assistant of a syntax and a denotational semantics for a probabilistic programming language with sampling, scoring, and normalization. We use dependent types in a crucial way since our syntax is intrinsically-typed and since the semantic values are essentially dependent records. Thanks to the features of Coq, we can use notations that hide the details of type inference when writing examples. The resulting formalization is usable to reason about simple probabilistic programs.

1 Introduction

The formalization of probabilistic programs [9] already has several applications in security (e.g., [8]) or artificial intelligence (e.g., [7]). However, the support to formalize all the features of probabilistic programs is still lacking. For example, the formalization of equational reasoning by Heimerdinger and Shan [14] is axiomatized; the study of nested queries and recursion by Zhang and Amin [30] relies on a partially axiomatized formalization of measure theory. Efforts are underway to improve the formal foundations of probabilistic programming languages. For example, Affeldt et al. have been formalizing in the Coq proof [29] assistant *s-finite kernels* (which are essentially families of measures that lend themselves well to composition [23,24]) to represent the semantics of a first-order probabilistic programming language [4]. Hirata et al. have been formalizing quasi-Borel spaces in Isabelle/HOL to handle higher-order features [15,16].

In this paper, we address the problem of the formalization of the syntax and the denotational semantics of a probabilistic programming language, to reason about programs with sampling, scoring, and normalization, in a proof assistant based on dependent type theory. In such programs, semantic values are typically measurable functions or s-finite kernels. However, a mere formalization of s-finite kernels (such as [4]) does not provide a practical mean to reason about programs

C.-K. Hur (Ed.): APLAS 2023, LNCS 14405, pp. 182–202, 2023.
https://doi.org/10.1007/978-981-99-8311-7_9

in the absence of syntax. Indeed, criteria that are easily thought of as syntactic (e.g., the fact that a variable is not free in an expression) need to be recast into semantic terms [4, Sect. 7.1.2]. The evaluation of variables needs to be expressed semantically as measurable functions that access the execution environment by indices akin to de Bruijn indices (see [4, Sections 7.1.2 and 7.2.2]). This situation calls for more formalization experiments of syntax and semantics of probabilistic programming languages.

In the following we provide a formal syntax and denotational semantics for sfPPL, a probabilistic programming language based on s-finite kernels. For syntax formalization, we choose *intrinsic typing* by which the typing rules of the language are embedded into the syntax. This guarantees that one can only write well-typed programs but requires a proof assistant based on dependent type theory such as Coq or Agda. The idea of intrinsic-typing is well-known but has not been applied to a probabilistic programming language as far as we know. Besides syntax, we also use dependent types in a crucial way to represent semantic values of sfPPL, which are either a measurable function (a dependent pair of a function and a proof that it is measurable) or an s-finite kernel. In addition to dependent types, we exploit other features of Coq to provide a concrete syntax by using bidirectional hints [28], canonical structures [13], and custom entries [27]. This provides a generic approach to represent a programming language inside Coq with intrinsic-typing and a user-friendly syntax. Using this approach, we eventually investigate the formalization of reusable lemmas for the verification of probabilistic programs with sfPPL.

Outline. We complete our review of related work in Sect. 2. Section 3 is for preliminaries on measure theory and its formalization in Coq. Section 4 is an overview of the syntax, the typing rules, and the semantics of sfPPL. We split the formalization of the syntax of sfPPL by first explaining the idea of *intrinsically-typed concrete syntax* using a toy language in Sect. 5. We then explain the formalization of the syntax of sfPPL in Sect. 6 and its denotational semantics in Sect. 7. We experiment with the resulting framework by verifying simple programs in Sect. 8 and conclude in Sect. 9.

2 Related Work

To the best of our knowledge, our experiment is the first formalization of a probabilistic programming language using an intrinsically-typed syntax.

The formalization of probabilistic programs in proof assistants is a long-standing topic. In seminal work in HOL, Hurd verifies the Miller-Rabin probabilistic primality test [17]. In Coq, Audebaud and Paulin-Mohring verify randomized algorithms [6] but the measure theory they rely on has some limitations (discrete distributions only, etc.). More recent applications have been targeting artificial intelligence. Bagnall and Stewart encode in Coq a denotational semantics in which a program is interpreted as the expected value of a real number-valued valuation function w.r.t. the distribution of its results [7]; this work is limited to discrete distributions. In Lean, Tassarotti et al. represent stochastic procedures using the Giry monad to formalize PAC learnability for decision stumps [26]. These pieces of work do not feature the combined use of sampling and scoring. We already mentioned in Sect. 1 formalization work in Coq partly relying on axiomatization [14,30]. To address this problem, Affeldt et al. formalize s-finite kernels in Coq, allowing for the support of sampling, scoring, and normalization, without being limited to discrete distributions [4]. They apply their formalization to the encoding of the semantics of a probabilistic programming language. One practical limitation is that they use ad hoc Coq notations to represent variables as De Bruijn indices. In Isabelle/HOL, Hirata et al. formalize quasi-Borel spaces to handle sampling and higher-order features [15], to which they recently add scoring [16]. These last pieces of work do not provide an encoding of syntax.

The encoding of intrinsically-typed syntax in proof assistants based on dependent type theory has also attracted much interest. Benton et al. provide an historical account [10, Sect. 1] along with applications in Coq to a simply-typed language and to the polymorphic lambda calculus. Indeed, this technique is often applied to foundational calculi, e.g., system F in Agda [12]. In Coq, Affeldt and Sakaguchi apply it to a subset of the C programming language [5]. Intrinsically-typed syntax allows for a succinct handling of the many integral types of C. While the encoding of well-formed type contexts in C is a source of difficulty, the absence of let-in expressions simplifies the encoding of an intrinsically-typed syntax for C. Poulsen et al. propose to use intrinsically-typed syntax to write in Agda definitional interpreters for imperative languages. They explain how to deal with mutable state and apply this approach to a subset of Java [20]. Besides encoding of semantics, intrinsically-typed syntax also has other applications such as compiler calculation [18]. We are however not aware of related work applying intrinsically-typed syntax to a probabilistic programming language.

3 Preliminaries: Measure Theory in MathComp-Analysis

3.1 Reminder About Measure Theory

A σ-algebra on a set X is a collection of subsets of X that contains $\emptyset$ and that is closed under complement and countable union. We note Σ_X for such a σ-algebra and call *measurable sets* the sets in Σ_X. For example, the standard σ-algebra on $\mathbb{R}$ is the smallest σ-algebra containing the intervals: the Borel sets. A *measurable space* is a set together with the σ-algebra defining the measurable sets. Given two σ-algebras Σ_X and Σ_Y, the product σ-algebra is the smallest σ-algebra generated by $\{A \times B \mid A \in \Sigma_X, B \in \Sigma_Y\}$.

A (non-negative) *measure* is a function $\mu : \Sigma_X \to [0, \infty]$ such that $\mu(\emptyset) = 0$ and $\mu(\bigcup_i A_i) = \sum_i \mu(A_i)$ for pairwise-disjoint measurable sets A_i, where the sum is countable. This property is called σ-additivity. The Dirac measure δ_x is defined by $\delta_x(U) = [x \in U]$ (using the Iverson bracket notation). A *probability measure* on Σ_X is a measure μ such that $\mu(X) = 1$.

If Σ_X and Σ_Y are two σ-algebras, a *measurable function* $f : X \to Y$ is such that, for all measurable subsets $B \in \Sigma_Y$, the inverse image is a measurable subset $f^{-1}(B) \in \Sigma_X$. If Σ_D is a σ-algebra, we can integrate a measurable function $f : D \to [0, \infty]$ w.r.t. a measure μ over D to get an extended real number denoted by $\int_{x \in D} f\, x (\mathbf{d}\, \mu)$.

A *kernel* $X \rightsquigarrow Y$ is a function $k : X \to \Sigma_Y \to [0, \infty]$ such that for all x, $k\, x$ is a measure and for all measurable sets U, $x \mapsto k\, x\, U$ is a measurable function. A kernel $k : X \rightsquigarrow Y$ is a *finite kernel* when there is a finite bound r such that for all x, $k\, x\, Y < r$; this is a uniform upper bound, i.e., the same r for all x. When for all x, $k\, x\, Y = 1$, we talk about a *probability kernel.*

A kernel $k : X \rightsquigarrow Y$ is an *s-finite kernel* when there is a sequence s of finite kernels such that $k = \sum_{i=0}^{\infty} s_i$. Let us denote by $X \overset{\text{s-fin}}{\rightsquigarrow} Y$ the type of s-finite kernels. Given a kernel $l : X \rightsquigarrow Y$ and a kernel $k : X \times Y \rightsquigarrow Z$, the composition of the kernel l and of the kernel k is $x, U \mapsto \int_y k\,(x, y)\, U(\mathbf{d}\, l\, x)$.

3.2 Basics of MathComp-Analysis and Its Measure Theory

This paper relies on MathComp-Analysis [1], a library for classical analysis[1] in Coq that provides among others a formalization of measure theory including s-finite kernels.

The type `set T` is for sets of objects of type `T`. The set of all the objects of type `T` is denoted by `setT : set T`. The type `\bar R` is the type `R` extended with two infinity elements. It is typically used when `R` is a numeric type. In particular, the numeric type `realType` corresponds to real numbers, so that when the type of `R` is `realType`, `R` corresponds to $\mathbb{R}$ and `\bar R` corresponds to $\overline{\mathbb{R}} = \mathbb{R} \cup \{+\infty, -\infty\}$. The expression `%:R` injects a natural number into $\mathbb{R}$, `%:E` injects a real number into $\overline{\mathbb{R}}$. Non-negative numeric types are noted `{nonneg R}` where `R` is a numeric type. Given `e : {nonneg R}`, `e%:num` is the projection of type `R`. A function returning unconditionally `c` is represented by `cst c`.

σ-algebra's are represented by objects of type `measurableType d` where `d` is a "display parameter" [2, Sect. 3.2.1]. Given `T` of type `measurableType d` and `U` of type `set T`, `measurable U` asserts that `U` belongs to the σ-algebra corresponding to `T`. The parameter `d` controls the display of the `measurable` predicate, so that `measurable U` is printed as `d.-measurable U`. The display mechanism is useful to disambiguate goals with several σ-algebras [2, Sect. 3.4]. For example, the display of the product of two measurable types with displays `d1` and `d2` is a measurable type with display `(d1, d2).-prod`.

Given `T` of type `measurableType d`, a non-negative measure on `T` is denoted by `{measure set T -> \bar R}`, where `R` has type `realType`. The Dirac measure is denoted by `dirac a` with notation `\d_a`. The type of a `R`-valued probability measure over the measurable type `T` is `probability T R`. We write `measurable_fun D f` for a measurable function `f` with domain `D`. A kernel $f : X \rightsquigarrow Y$ (resp. an s-finite kernel $f : X \overset{\text{s-fin}}{\rightsquigarrow} Y$) is noted `R.-ker X ~> Y` (resp. `R.-sfker X ~> Y`) (`R` indicates the support type of extended real numbers).

[1] MathComp-Analysis adds to the constructive logic of Coq functional and propositional extensionality and the axiom of constructive indefinite description [3, Sect. 5].

4 Probabilistic Programming Language Using s-Finite Kernels

Before entering the details of formalization, we explain the syntax and the semantics of SFPPL, a probabilistic programming language based on s-finite kernels. The syntax corresponds to [25, Sect. 3] [23, Sect. 3.1] [24, Sect. 4.1, 4.3]. The semantics comes from [23,24]. It is a simplification because we do not formalize a generic notion of sum types.

The main specificity of SFPPL types is a type for probability distributions:

$$\mathbf{A} ::= \mathbf{U} \mid \mathbf{B} \mid \mathbf{R} \mid P(\mathbf{A}) \mid \mathbf{A}_1 \times \mathbf{A}_2$$

The syntax $\mathbf{U}$ is for a type with one element, $\mathbf{B}$ for boolean numbers, $\mathbf{R}$ for real numbers, $P(\mathbf{A})$ for distributions over $\mathbf{A}$, $\mathbf{A}_1 \times \mathbf{A}_2$ for the cartesian product.

The expressions of SFPPL extend the expressions of a first-order functional language with three instructions specific to probabilistic programming languages:

$$\begin{aligned} e ::= {} & \mathtt{tt} \mid b \mid r \mid f(e_1, \dots, e_n) \mid (e_1, e_2) \mid \pi_1(e) \mid \pi_2(e) \\ & \mathtt{if}\, e\, \mathtt{then}\, e_1\, \mathtt{else}\, e_2 \mid x \mid \mathtt{return}\, e \mid \mathtt{let}\ x := e_1\ \mathtt{in}\ e_2 \mid \\ & \mathtt{sample}(e) \mid \mathtt{score}(e) \mid \mathtt{normalize}(e) \end{aligned}$$

The syntax `tt` is for the element of type $\mathbf{U}$, b for boolean numbers, r for real numbers. All measurable functions (and arithmetic operations) can be introduced as constants with the syntax $f(e_1, \dots, e_n)$. Pairs are (e_1, e_2), π_1 and π_2 access their projections. If-then-else branching is self-explanatory. Variables are ranged over by x (y, z, etc.). Last we have return, let-in expressions, and the three instructions specific to probabilistic programming languages: sampling (from a probability measure), scoring (to record that a datum was observed as being drawn from a probability distribution, the parameter is the density of the probability distribution), and normalization (of a measure into a probability measure).

Typing judgments distinguish *deterministic* and *probabilistic* expressions. Typing environments (hereafter, contexts) are tuples $(x_1 : \mathbf{A}_1; \dots; x_n : \mathbf{A}_n)$ ranged over by Γ. The typing judgment is $\Gamma \vdash_{\mathsf{D}} e : \mathbf{A}$ for deterministic expressions and $\Gamma \vdash_{\mathsf{P}} e : \mathbf{A}$ for probabilistic ones. We reproduce here the typing rules for the basic datatypes, constants, products, projections, and variables.

$$\frac{}{\Gamma \vdash_{\mathsf{D}} \mathtt{tt} : \mathbf{U}} \quad \frac{b \in \mathbb{B}}{\Gamma \vdash_{\mathsf{D}} b : \mathbf{B}} \quad \frac{r \in \mathbb{R}}{\Gamma \vdash_{\mathsf{D}} r : \mathbf{R}} \quad \frac{\Gamma \vdash_{\mathsf{D}} e_i : \mathbf{A}_i}{\Gamma \vdash_{\mathsf{D}} f(e_1, \dots, e_n) : \mathbf{A}}\, f \text{ is measurable}$$

$$\frac{\Gamma \vdash_{\mathsf{D}} e_1 : \mathbf{A}_1 \quad \Gamma \vdash_{\mathsf{D}} e_2 : \mathbf{A}_2}{\Gamma \vdash_{\mathsf{D}} (e_1, e_2) : \mathbf{A}_1 \times \mathbf{A}_2} \qquad \frac{\Gamma \vdash_{\mathsf{D}} e : \mathbf{A}_1 \times \mathbf{A}_2}{\Gamma \vdash_{\mathsf{D}} \pi_i(e) : \mathbf{A}_i}$$

$$\frac{x \notin \mathrm{dom}(\Gamma')}{\Gamma, x : \mathbf{A}, \Gamma' \vdash_{\mathsf{D}} x : \mathbf{A}} \quad \frac{\Gamma, \Gamma' \vdash_z e : \mathbf{A}_0 \quad x \notin \mathrm{dom}(\Gamma), x \notin \mathrm{dom}(\Gamma')}{\Gamma, x : \mathbf{A}_1, \Gamma' \vdash_z e : \mathbf{A}_0}\, z \in \{\mathsf{D}, \mathsf{P}\}$$

These typing rules are mostly about deterministic expressions except the weakening rule that also applies to probabilistic expressions.

The typing rules for the other instructions illustrate the interplay between deterministic and probabilistic expressions. For example, `return` turns a deterministic expression into a probabilistic one. Note that we assume that `normalize` returns a default distribution when the normalization constant is 0 or ∞.

$$\frac{\Gamma \vdash_{\mathsf{D}} e : \mathbf{B} \quad \Gamma \vdash_z e_1 : \mathbf{A} \quad \Gamma \vdash_z e_2 : \mathbf{A}}{\Gamma \vdash_z \texttt{if}\, e\, \texttt{then}\, e_1\, \texttt{else}\, e_2 : \mathbf{A}} z \in \{\mathsf{D}, \mathsf{P}\}$$

$$\frac{\Gamma \vdash_{\mathsf{D}} e : \mathbf{A}}{\Gamma \vdash_{\mathsf{P}} \texttt{return}\, e : \mathbf{A}} \qquad \frac{\Gamma \vdash_{\mathsf{P}} e_1 : \mathbf{A}_1 \quad \Gamma, x : \mathbf{A}_1 \vdash_{\mathsf{P}} e_2 : \mathbf{A}_2}{\Gamma \vdash_{\mathsf{P}} \texttt{let}\ x := e_1\ \texttt{in}\ e_2 : \mathbf{A}_2}$$

$$\frac{\Gamma \vdash_{\mathsf{D}} e : P(\mathbf{A})}{\Gamma \vdash_{\mathsf{P}} \texttt{sample}(e) : \mathbf{A}} \quad \frac{\Gamma \vdash_{\mathsf{D}} e : \mathbf{R}}{\Gamma \vdash_{\mathsf{P}} \texttt{score}(e) : \mathbf{U}} \quad \frac{\Gamma \vdash_{\mathsf{P}} e : \mathbf{A}}{\Gamma \vdash_{\mathsf{D}} \texttt{normalize}(e) : P(\mathbf{A})}$$

Let us denote the denotational semantics of SFPPL by a function $[\![\cdot]\!]$ that interprets the syntax of types, of contexts, and of typing judgments resp. to measurable spaces, products of measurable spaces, and measurable functions or s-finite kernels. For example, the measurable space corresponding to $\mathbf{R}$ is $[\![\mathbf{R}]\!]$, the set $\mathbb{R}$ of real numbers with its Borel sets. A context $\Gamma = (x_1 : \mathbf{A}_1; \ldots; x_n : \mathbf{A}_n)$ is interpreted by the product space $[\![\Gamma]\!] \stackrel{\text{def}}{=} \prod_{i=1}^{n} [\![\mathbf{A}_i]\!]$. Deterministic expressions $\Gamma \vdash_{\mathsf{D}} e : \mathbf{A}$ are interpreted by measurable functions $[\![\Gamma]\!] \to [\![\mathbf{A}]\!]$ and probabilistic expressions $\Gamma \vdash_{\mathsf{P}} e : \mathbf{A}$ are interpreted by s-finite kernels $[\![\Gamma]\!] \overset{\text{s-fin}}{\rightsquigarrow} [\![\mathbf{A}]\!]$. In particular, the semantics of $[\![\texttt{let}\ x := e_1\ \texttt{in}\ e_2]\!]$ is the composition (see Sect. 3.1) of a kernel $[\![\Gamma]\!] \overset{\text{s-fin}}{\rightsquigarrow} [\![\mathbf{A}_1]\!]$ corresponding to e_1 and a kernel $[\![\Gamma]\!] \times [\![\mathbf{A}_1]\!] \overset{\text{s-fin}}{\rightsquigarrow} [\![\mathbf{A}_2]\!]$ corresponding to e_2; the result is a kernel of type $[\![\Gamma]\!] \overset{\text{s-fin}}{\rightsquigarrow} [\![\mathbf{A}_2]\!]$ [23].

5 Intrinsically-Typed Concrete Syntax for a Toy Language

We recall the notion of intrinsically-typed syntax and introduce the notion of *intrinsically-typed concrete syntax*. For this purpose, we use a subset of SFPPL (Sect. 4) where types are ranged over by $\mathbf{A} ::= \mathbf{U} \mid \mathbf{R}$ and expressions are ranged over by $e ::= \texttt{tt} \mid r \mid x \mid e_1 + e_2 \mid \texttt{let}\ x := e_1\ \texttt{in}\ e_2$. The symbol $+$ represents the addition of real numbers. Typing contexts and typing rules are defined as in Sect. 4 except that both $\vdash_{\mathsf{D}}$ and $\vdash_{\mathsf{P}}$ become $\vdash$ because there are no probabilistic expressions; the only difference is a typing rule for addition: $\Gamma \vdash e_1 : \mathbf{R} \wedge \Gamma \vdash e_2 : \mathbf{R} \to \Gamma \vdash e_1 + e_2 : \mathbf{R}$.

We explain an encoding of this toy language using intrinsically-typed syntax in Sect. 5.1. This syntax enforces the property that only well-typed expressions can be encoded but type-checking can only be automated for ground expressions. In Sect. 5.2, we show that we can solve this problem using COQ's canonical structures. In Sect. 5.3, we explain how to give our toy language a readable concrete syntax.

5.1 Intrinsically-Typed Syntax for a Toy Language

We formalize the basic types $\mathbf{U}$ and $\mathbf{R}$ as an inductive type and define a context as a list of pairs of a string and of a type:

```
Inductive typ := Unit | Real. Definition ctx := seq (string * typ).
```

With intrinsically-typed syntax, the expressions are defined by an inductive type indexed by a context and a type:

```
1 Inductive exp : ctx -> typ -> Type :=
2 | exp_unit g : exp g Unit
3 | exp_real g : R -> exp g Real
4 | exp_var g t str : t = lookup Unit g str -> exp g t
5 | exp_add g : exp g Real -> exp g Real -> exp g Real
6 | exp_letin g t1 t2 x : exp g t1 -> exp ((x, t1) :: g) t2 -> exp g t2.
```

The constructors `exp_unit` and `exp_real` build basic data structures. The constructor `exp_var` builds an expression `exp g t` where `t` is the type associated with the string `str` in the context, as proved by the equality at line 4. In particular, given a concrete type and a concrete context, this equality can be checked by the Coq's conversion rule using `erefl`. In the constructor `exp_letin`, a new bound variable is introduced and the context is extended; this is the reason why contexts appear as an index of `exp`. We observe here that intrinsically-typed syntax also means that expressions are well-scoped by construction.

We complete the encoding of the intrinsically-typed syntax by setting the context and type parameters of constructors as implicit (using curly brackets):

```
1 Arguments exp_unit {g}.
2 Arguments exp_real {g}.
3 Arguments exp_var {g t}.
4 Arguments exp_add {g} &.
5 Arguments exp_letin {g} & {t1 t2}.
```

The `&` mark at lines 4 and 5 is a bidirectionality hint: it indicates that Coq should first type-check `g` and propagate the information to type-check the remaining arguments [28].

For example, here is the abstract syntax for `let` $x := 1$ `in let` $y := 2$ `in` $x + y$:

```
1 Example letin_add : exp [::] _ :=
2   exp_letin "x" (exp_real 1) (exp_letin "y" (exp_real 2)
3    (exp_add (exp_var "x" erefl) (exp_var "y" erefl))).
```

As intended, we only need to pass the outermost context (here the empty context `[::]`) for this expression to type-check. Without bidirectionality hints, the above expression would fail to type-check with the following error message:

```
The term "exp_var "x" (erefl (lookup Unit ?g1 "x"))" has type "exp ?g1
(lookup Unit ?g1 "x")" while it is expected to have type "exp ?g1 Real".
```

In other words, type-checking gets stuck on a hole `?g1` corresponding to the context. This can be fixed by inserting an intermediate context, e.g., by replacing the syntax for the variable x at line 3 by `(@exp_var g _ "x" erefl)`[2] where `g` is

[2] In Coq, `@` disables implicit arguments.

the context `[:: ("y", Real); ("x", Real)]` but that somehow defeats the purpose of intrinsically-typed syntax. As a side node, we observe that in AGDA, `letin_add` type-checks using a similar encoding without explicit bidirectionality hints.

The intrinsically-typed syntax above allows for type-checking ground expressions but fails to type-check expressions where string identifiers are parameters, making it difficult to write generic statements about intrinsically-typed terms.

5.2 Canonical Structures for Intrinsically-Typed Syntax

We use canonical structures in the manner of Gonthier et al. [13, Sections 2.3 and 6.1] so that one can write easily generic statements about intrinsically-typed expressions. The idea is to provide an alternative way to construct program variables that triggers a search that builds the context along with type inference.

We define "tagged contexts" (`T` is a decidable type with an element `t0`):

```
Let ctx := seq (string * T). Structure tagged_ctx := Tag {untag : ctx}.
```

We define a structure `find`, parameterized by a string, that contains a tagged context and a proof that the string is associated with some datum:

```
Structure find str t := Find {
  ctx_of : tagged_ctx ;
  ctx_prf : t = lookup (untag ctx_of) str}.
```

Then, we define an alternative way to build variables that is parameterized by a `find` structure:

```
Definition exp_var' str {t : typ} (g : find str t) :=
  @exp_var (untag (ctx_of g)) t str (ctx_prf g).
```

The important point is the use of the projection `ctx_of` that will trigger a search for an appropriate `g : find str t`. We still need to tell COQ how to search for instances of `find`. There are two ways to instantiate this structure. The pair `(str, t)` can be the head of the context, in which case the following lemma provides a way to instantiate the second field of `find`:

```
Lemma ctx_prf_head str t g : t = lookup ((str, t) :: g) str.
```

Otherwise, the pair `(str, t)` might be in the tail of the context:

```
Lemma ctx_prf_tail str t g str' t' : str' != str ->
  t = lookup g str -> t = lookup ((str', t') :: g) str.
```

To account for these two situations, we introduce two definitions that unfold to `Tag`, the constructor for tagged contexts:

```
Definition recurse_tag h := Tag h.
Canonical found_tag h := recurse_tag h.
```

We associate the definition `found_tag` with the situation where the sought variable is in the head of the context and `recurse_tag` with the other situation:

```
Canonical found str t g : find str t :=
  @Find str t (found_tag ((str, t) :: g)) (@ctx_prf_head str t g).
Canonical recurse str t str' t' {H : infer (str' != str)}
    (g : find str t) : find str t :=
  @Find str t (recurse_tag ((str', t') :: untag (ctx_of g)))
    (@ctx_prf_tail str t (untag (ctx_of g)) str' t' H (ctx_prf g)).
```

(The identifier `infer` comes from MathComp-Analysis [1] and provides a proof that two strings are different automatically using type classes.) Since `found_tag` is canonical it will be searched for first, in case of success we will have inferred a correct context, otherwise Coq unfolds `found_tag` to reveal `recurse_tag` and tries to look for the variable in the tail of the context, recursively [13,31].

Using `exp_var'` instead of `exp_var`, we can rewrite the example of the previous section with just the assumption that the string identifiers are different:

```
Example letin_add (x y : string)
    (xy : infer (x != y)) (yx : infer (y != x)) : exp [::] _ :=
  exp_letin x (exp_real 1) (exp_letin y (exp_real 2)
    (exp_add (exp_var' x _) (exp_var' y _))).
```

We can therefore use `exp_var'` instead of `exp_var`; moreover the former can always be rewritten into the latter:

```
Lemma exp_var'E str t (g : find str t) H : exp_var' str g = exp_var str H.
```

5.3 Intrinsically-Typed Concrete Syntax with Custom Entries

Custom entries [27] are a feature of Coq to support autonomous grammars of terms. The definition of a grammar for our toy language starts by declaring an identifier for the custom entry: `Declare Custom Entry expr`. Then we introduce a notation (`[...]`) to delimit expressions written with the `expr` grammar and a notation (`{...}`) to delimit Coq terms that appear inside `expr` expressions:

```
Notation "[ e ]" := e (e custom expr at level 5).
Notation "{ x }" := x (in custom expr, x constr).
```

We can then write the grammar $e ::= \texttt{tt} \mid r \mid x \mid e_1 + e_2 \mid \texttt{let}\ x := e_1\ \texttt{in}\ e_2$:

```
Notation "x" := x (in custom expr at level 0, x ident).
Notation "x ':R'" := (exp_real x) (in custom expr at level 1).
Notation "e1 + e2" := (exp_add e1 e2)
  (in custom expr at level 2, left associativity).
Notation "'let' x ':=' e1 'in' e2" := (exp_letin x e1 e2)
  (in custom expr at level 3, x constr, e1 custom expr at level 2,
   e2 custom expr at level 3, left associativity).
```

Line 1 is to allow for the use of Coq identifiers inside `expr` expressions. The other lines are for real numbers, additions, and let-in expressions; they all use the constructors of the syntax. As for variables, we have a notation for `exp_var'`:

```
Notation "# x" := (exp_var' x%string _) (in custom expr at level 1).
```

Using these notations, our running example `let` $x := 1$ `in let` $y := 2$ `in` $x + y$ can be written succinctly and more generally:

```
Example letin_add (x y : string)
    (yx : infer (y != x)) (xy : infer (x != y)) : exp [::] _ :=
  [let x := {1}:R in let y := {2}:R in #x + #y].
```

6 Intrinsically-Typed Probabilistic Programming Language

We formalize an intrinsically-typed concrete syntax for sfPPL (Sect. 4) on the model of the previous section (Sect. 5).

6.1 Intrinsically-Typed Expressions

```
Inductive exp : flag -> ctx -> typ -> Type :=
| exp_unit g : exp D g Unit
| exp_bool g : bool -> exp D g Bool
| exp_real g : R -> exp D g Real
| exp_pair g t1 t2 : exp D g t1 -> exp D g t2 -> exp D g (Pair t1 t2)
| exp_proj1 g t1 t2 : exp D g (Pair t1 t2) -> exp D g t1
| exp_proj2 g t1 t2 : exp D g (Pair t1 t2) -> exp D g t2
| exp_var g str t : t = lookup Unit g str -> exp D g t
| exp_bernoulli g (r : {nonneg R}) (r1 : r%:num <= 1) :
    exp D g (Prob Bool)
| exp_poisson g : nat -> exp D g Real -> exp D g Real
| exp_normalize g t : exp P g t -> exp D g (Prob t)
| exp_letin g t1 t2 str : exp P g t1 -> exp P ((str, t1) :: g) t2 ->
    exp P g t2
| exp_sample g t : exp D g (Prob t) -> exp P g t
| exp_score g : exp D g Real -> exp P g Unit
| exp_return g t : exp D g t -> exp P g t
| exp_if z g t : exp D g Bool -> exp z g t -> exp z g t -> exp z g t
| exp_weak z g h t x : exp z (g ++ h) t ->
    x.1 \notin dom (g ++ h) -> exp z (g ++ x :: h) t.
```

Fig. 1. Expressions of sfPPL.

First, the Coq encoding of the syntax of the types of sfPPL is immediate:

```
Inductive typ := Unit | Bool | Real
  | Pair : typ -> typ -> typ | Prob : typ -> typ.
```

To distinguish between deterministic and probabilistic expressions, we use a flag: `Inductive flag := D | P`. It is better to use a flag than a mutually inductive type because we can have only one constructor for typing rules that do not depend on whether an expression is deterministic or probabilistic.

The constructors for basic datatypes (`exp_unit`, `exp_bool`, `exp_real`), pairs (`exp_pair`) and their projections (`exp_proj1`, `exp_proj2`) should read easily (Fig. 1, lines 2–7). The constructors for variables (`exp_var`, line 8) and for let-in expressions (`exp_letin`, line 13) are essentially the same as in Sect. 5.1. The constructors `exp_bernoulli` and `exp_poisson` (lines 9–11) provide two examples of measurable functions that we explain below. The constructors for return, sampling, scoring, and normalizing are as we explained in Sect. 4. The constructors `exp_if` and `exp_weak` accommodate both the deterministic and the probabilistic cases thanks to a flag. The rule `exp_weak` allows to change the type of an expression by inserting a fresh variable at an arbitrary position in the context.

The constructor `exp_bernoulli` represents a Bernoulli distribution that takes as parameters a non-negative real number `r` and a proof that `r` ≤ 1. Since it is a distribution of boolean numbers, the type of the corresponding expression is `exp D g (Prob Bool)`. Informally, the typing rule could be written:

$$\frac{r \in \mathbb{R} \quad 0 \leq r \leq 1}{\Gamma \vdash_{\mathsf{D}} \texttt{exp\_bernoulli}(r) : P(\mathbf{B})}$$

Given a natural number n and an expression e, the constructor `exp_poisson` represents the likelihood of n for a Poisson distribution with rate e:

$$\frac{n \in \mathbb{N} \quad \Gamma \vdash_{\mathsf{D}} e : \mathbf{R}}{\Gamma \vdash_{\mathsf{D}} \texttt{exp\_poisson}(n, e) : \mathbf{R}}$$

6.2 Intrinsically-Typed Concrete Syntax for sfPPL

We use custom entries as in Sect. 5.3 to provide a concrete syntax for SFPPL. Instead of reproducing the complete grammar that can be found online [21], we consider the following illustrative program from [24]:

$$\begin{array}{l}\texttt{normalize}(\ \texttt{let}\ x := \texttt{sample}(\mathit{bernoulli}(2/7))\ \texttt{in} \\ \qquad\qquad\ \texttt{let}\ r := \texttt{if}\ x\ \texttt{then}\ 3\ \texttt{else}\ 10\ \texttt{in} \\ \qquad\qquad\ \texttt{let}\ \_ := \texttt{score}(\mathit{poisson}(4, r))\ \texttt{in}\ \texttt{return}\ x\ )\end{array}$$

This program is about inferring whether today is the weekend according to the number of buses passing by. It selects a boolean number from a Bernoulli distribution to represent whether today is the weekend. The if-then-else expression models the fact that there are three buses per hour during the weekend and ten buses per hour otherwise. Scoring records the observation that four buses have been passing by in one hour, assuming buses arrive as a Poisson process with rate r. The resulting measure is eventually normalized. As a COQ term:

```
Definition staton_bus_syntax0 : exp _ [::] _ :=
  [let "x" := Sample {exp_bernoulli (2 / 7%:R)%:nng p27} in
   let "r" := if #{"x"} then return {3}:R else return {10}:R in
   let "_" := Score {exp_poisson 4 [#{"r"}]} in return #{"x"}].
Definition staton_bus_syntax := [Normalize {staton_bus_syntax0}].
```

We use the same delimiters to enter and exit the grammar and the same notation for constants as in Sect. 5.3. Other grammar entries should be intuitive. The Coq expression p27 is a proof that $2/7 \leq 1$.

7 Denotational Semantics of sfPPL

We formalize a denotational semantics for sfPPL that links the syntax of Sect. 6 to previous work [4]. Intuitively, this is the function $[\![\cdot]\!]$ of Sect. 4. Since the denotations are non-trivial objects (measurable functions and s-finite kernels), we formalize an evaluation function and show that it is a function.

7.1 Interpretation of Types and Contexts

We first provide Coq functions to interpret types, their sequences, and contexts to measurable spaces.

We interpret an object `t : typ` with the function `measurable_of_typ` that returns a measurable type (Sect. 3.2) together with its display in the form of a dependent pair `{d & measurableType d}`. The implementation is by recursion on the structure of `t` and uses the product spaces of MathComp-Analysis. The function `mtyp t` takes the second projection (using `projT2`) of `measurable_of_typ t`. We interpret a list `s : seq typ` with the function `measurable_of_seq` that essentially iterates the function `measurable_of_typ` over `s`. More precisely, given a list $[\mathbf{A}_1; \mathbf{A}_2; \cdots; \mathbf{A}_n]$, it returns a measurable space made of nested products $[\![\mathbf{A_1}]\!] \times ([\![\mathbf{A_2}]\!] \times \cdots ([\![\mathbf{A_n}]\!] \times [\![\mathbf{U}]\!]))$; we use $\mathbf{U}$ to avoid empty spaces. The result of `measurable_seq` is a dependent pair of type `{d & measurableType d}`. When applied to a context `g : ctx`, the function `mctx` returns the second projection of `measurable_seq (map snd g)`.

7.2 Evaluation Relation for sfPPL Expressions

The evaluation of sfPPL expressions takes the form of a mutually inductive relation. The relation `evalD` relates an expression `exp D g t` to a measurable function `f` such that the domain of `f` is the interpretation of `g` and the codomain of `f` is the interpretation of `t`, i.e., its type is `dval R g t := @mctx R g -> @mtyp R t`. The type of `evalD` is therefore:

```
forall g t, exp D g t ->
  forall f : dval R g t, measurable_fun setT f -> Prop.
```

The expression `forall f : dval R g t, measurable_fun setT f` is a dependent pair of a function with a measurability proof; hereafter, `evalD e f mf` stands for `e -D> f ; mf`. Similarly, `evalP` relates an expression `exp P g t` to an s-finite kernel of type `pval R g t := R.-sfker @mctx R g ~> @mtyp R t`. The type of `evalP` is therefore `forall g t, exp P g t -> pval R g t -> Prop` and we note `e -P> k` for `evalP e k`. Let us now explain the main constructors of `evalD` and `evalP`.

The constructors `eval_unit`, `eval_bool`, and `eval_real` (Fig. 2, lines 3–5) relates basic data structures to constant functions (`ktt`, `kb`, and `kr` are notations for the proof that constant functions are measurable).

The constructors for pairs and their projections use results from MathComp-Analysis to build measurability proofs for products (`measurable_fun_prod`, line 8) or to compose measurability proofs (`measurableT_comp`, lines 10, 12).

```
1  Inductive evalD : forall g t, exp D g t ->
2    forall f : dval R g t, measurable_fun setT f -> Prop :=
3  | eval_unit g   : ([TT] : exp D g _)  -D> cst tt ; ktt
4  | eval_bool g b : ([b:B] : exp D g _) -D> cst b ; kb b
5  | eval_real g r : ([r:R] : exp D g _) -D> cst r ; kr r
6  | eval_pair g t1 (e1 : exp D g t1) f1 mf1 t2 (e2 : exp D g t2) f2 mf2 :
7      e1 -D> f1 ; mf1  ->  e2 -D> f2 ; mf2 ->
8    [(e1, e2)] -D> fun x => (f1 x, f2 x) ; measurable_fun_prod mf1 mf2
9  | eval_proj1 g t1 t2 (e : exp D g (Pair t1 t2)) f mf : e -D> f ; mf ->
10   [\pi_1 e] -D> fst \o f ; measurableT_comp measurable_fst mf
11 | eval_proj2 g t1 t2 (e : exp D g (Pair t1 t2)) f mf : e -D> f ; mf ->
12   [\pi_2 e] -D> snd \o f ; measurableT_comp measurable_snd mf
13 | eval_var g x H : let i := index x (dom g) in
14   exp_var x H -D> acc_typ (map snd g) i ; measurable_acc_typ (map snd g) i
15 | eval_bernoulli g (r : {nonneg R}) (r1 : r%:num <= 1) :
16   (exp_bernoulli r r1 : exp D g _) -D> cst (bernoulli r1) ;
17                                            measurable_cst _
18 | eval_poisson g n (e : exp D g _) f mf : e -D> f ; mf ->
19   exp_poisson n e -D> poisson n \o f ;
20                       measurableT_comp (measurable_poisson n) mf
21 | eval_normalize g t (e : exp P g t) k : e -P> k ->
22   exp_normalize e -D> normalize_pt k ; measurable_normalize_pt k
23 | evalD_if g t e f mf (e1 : exp D g t) f1 mf1 e2 f2 mf2 :
24     e -D> f ; mf -> e1 -D> f1 ; mf1 -> e2 -D> f2 ; mf2 ->
25   [if e then e1 else e2] -D> fun x => if f x then f1 x else f2 x ;
26                              measurable_fun_ifT mf mf1 mf2
27 | evalD_weak g h t e x (H : x.1 \notin dom (g ++ h)) f mf : e -D> f ; mf ->
28   (exp_weak _ g h x e H : exp _ _ t) -D> weak g h x f ;
29                                          measurable_weak g h x f mf
```

Fig. 2. Evaluation relation for the deterministic expressions of sfPPL. See Fig. 3 for probabilistic expressions.

The constructor `eval_var` (line 13) defines the evaluation of a variable `x` by first finding its index `i` in the context `g` and produces a measurable function. The function `acc_typ` accesses the interpretation of `g` and returns the element corresponding to the `i`th measurable space of `g`:

```
Fixpoint acc_typ (s : seq typ) n : projT2 (@measurable_of_seq R s) ->
  projT2 (measurable_of_typ (nth Unit s n)) := (* See [21] *).
```

Since the interpretation of the context is a nested product, such a function is built out of projections and is therefore measurable (proof `measurable_acc_type`). This generic way to compute measurable functions that access the environment is an improvement over previous work [4] where accesses were performed using ad hoc Coq notations for just a handful of functions.

The constructor `eval_bernoulli` (line 15) yields a constant function that returns a Bernoulli distribution. This particular method of sampling does not depend on the execution but there is no fundamental limitation to extend `evalD` with nested queries, as long as one provides a proof of measurability.

The constructor `eval_poisson` (line 18) produces a function `poisson n \o f` where `n` is the observation recorded for scoring and `f` is a measurable function that evaluates to the rate of the Poisson process. The expression `poisson n` is the measurable function $\lambda r.\, r^{\mathrm{n}} e^{-r}/\mathrm{n}!$.

For an expression `e : exp P g t` corresponding to an s-finite kernel `k`, the constructor `eval_normalize` (line 21) yields a function `normalize_pt k` going from `mctx g` to a probability measure over `mtyp t`. This function works by lifting a function that normalizes measures using a default probability measure when normalization is not possible [21].

The constructor `evalD_weak` (Fig. 2, line 27) produces a function `weak g h x t` of type `dval R (g ++ h) t -> dval R (g ++ x :: h) t`. The probabilistic version `evalP_weak` (Fig. 3, line 15) is similar but of course evaluates to an s-finite kernel.

```
1  with evalP : forall g t, exp P g t -> pval R g t -> Prop :=
2  | eval_letin g t1 t2 str (e1 : exp _ g t1) (e2 : exp _ _ t2) k1 k2 :
3      e1 -P> k1 -> e2 -P> k2 ->
4      [let str := e1 in e2] -P> letin' k1 k2
5  | eval_sample g t (e : exp _ _ (Prob t))
6    (f : mctx g -> pprobability (mtyp t) R) mf :
7      e -D> f ; mf -> [Sample e] -P> sample f mf
8  | eval_score g (e : exp _ g _) f mf :
9      e -D> f ; mf -> [Score e] -P> kscore mf
10 | eval_return g t (e : exp D g t) f mf :
11     e -D> f ; mf -> [return e] -P> ret mf
12 | evalP_if g t e f mf (e1 : exp P g t) k1 e2 k2 :
13     e -D> f ; mf -> e1 -P> k1 -> e2 -P> k2 ->
14    [if e then e1 else e2] -P> ite mf k1 k2
15 | evalP_weak g h t (e : exp P (g ++ h) t) x
16   (H : x.1 \notin dom (g ++ h)) f :
17     e -P> f -> exp_weak _ g h x e H -P> kweak g h x f
```

Fig. 3. Evaluation relation for the probabilistic expressions of sfPPL. See Fig. 2 for deterministic expressions.

The constructor `eval_letin` evaluates a let-in expression by combining the s-finite kernels of the two sub-expressions (Fig. 3, line 4). The function `letin'` has type $X \overset{\text{s-fin}}{\rightsquigarrow} Y \to Y \times X \overset{\text{s-fin}}{\rightsquigarrow} Z \to X \overset{\text{s-fin}}{\rightsquigarrow} Z$ so that it keeps the nesting of measurable spaces in the same order as the contexts where new variables are added by list consing. It is defined by composing the composition of kernels (Sections 3.1 and 4, [4, Sect. 5.1]) with a kernel of type $X \times Y \overset{\text{s-fin}}{\rightsquigarrow} Z \to Y \times X \overset{\text{s-fin}}{\rightsquigarrow} Z$ that swaps the projections of a product space.

We briefly explain the last constructors of Fig. 3. The constructor `eval_sample` (line 5) produces a probability kernel given a measurable function of a type compatible with the functions yielded by the constructors `eval_bernoulli` and `eval_normalize`. The constructor `eval_score` (line 8) yields an s-finite kernel of type (`mctx g`)$\overset{\text{s-fin}}{\rightsquigarrow}$**U** where `g` is the context of the expression passed to the `Score` expression. The constructor `eval_return` (line 10) produces an s-finite kernel `ret mf` where `ret` is the functional $x \mapsto \delta_{\mathtt{f}(x)}$ formalized as `kdirac` in [4, Sect. 4.6].

7.3 From the Evaluation Relation to a Function

The evaluation relation of the previous section is actually a function because it is right-unique and left-total. Right-uniqueness can be proved by induction on the evaluation relation:

```
Lemma evalD_uniq g t (e : exp D g t) (u v : dval R g t) mu mv :
  e -D> u ; mu -> e -D> v ; mv -> u = v.
Lemma evalP_uniq g t (e : exp P g t) (u v : pval R g t) :
  e -P> u -> e -P> v -> u = v.
```

Left-totality can be proved by induction on the syntax:

```
Lemma eval_total z g t (e : exp z g t) : (match z with
  | D => fun e => exists f mf, e -D> f ; mf
  | P => fun e => exists k, e -P> k end) e.
```

Thanks to these properties, we can produce a pair of functions `execD` and `execP` written using the constructive indefinite description axiom `cid` of Coq:

```
Definition execD g t (e : exp D g t)
    : {f : dval R g t & measurable_fun setT f} :=
  let: exist _ H := cid (evalD_total e) in existT _ _ (projT1 (cid H)).
Definition execP g t (e : exp P g t) : pval R g t :=
  projT1 (cid (evalP_total e)).
```

Finally, we prove equations for `execD`/`execP` that associate to each expression of SFPPL its result according to `evalD`/`evalP`. In general these equations are recursive, e.g., the execution of a return expression:

```
Lemma execP_return g t (e : exp D g t) :
  execP [return e] = ret (projT2 (execD e)).
```

The proofs of these equations are manual but follow an easy pattern which is a direct application of the equivalence between `execD`/`execP` and `evalD`/`evalP` (see lemmas `execD_evalD`/`execP_evalP` in [21]).

8 Using sfPPL to Reason Formally about Programs

Pair of Samplings. The following program samples two values from Bernoulli distributions with parameters $1/2$ and $1/3$ and returns the pair (`p1S` n is a proof that $1/(n+1) \leq 1$):

```
Definition sample_pair_syntax0 : exp _ [::] _ :=
  [let "x" := Sample {exp_bernoulli (1 / 2)%:nng (p1S 1)} in
   let "y" := Sample {exp_bernoulli (1 / 3)%:nng (p1S 2)} in
   return (#{"x"}, #{"y"})].
```

We can verify that the pair `(true, true)` is returned with probability $1/6$:

```
Lemma exec_sample_pair0_TandT :
  @execP R [::] _ sample_pair_syntax0 tt [set (true, true)] = (1 / 6)%:E.
```

Since we compute a pair of boolean numbers and since the context is empty, the result of execution has type `R.-sfker unit ~> bool * bool`. This is why we pass `tt` and, as an event, the pair whose projections are `true`. The proof is by rewriting using equations such as `execP_return` (Sect. 7.3) and, once the semantics is revealed, by using generic lemmas from MathComp-Analysis.

Sampling and Scoring. The following program samples a value from a Bernoulli distributions with parameter $1/3$ and scores the output with $1/3$ or $2/3$:

```
Definition bernoulli13_score := [Normalize
  let "x" := Sample {@exp_bernoulli R [::] (1 / 3)%:nng (p1S 2)} in
  let "_" := if #{"x"} then Score {(1 / 3)}:R else Score {(2 / 3)}:R in
  return #{"x"}].
```

We can verify that the resulting probability measure is $\frac{1}{3} \times \frac{1}{3} : \frac{2}{3} \times \frac{2}{3} = 1 : 4$, i.e., the Bernoulli distribution with parameter $1/5$:

```
Lemma exec_bernoulli13_score :
  execD bernoulli13_score = execD (exp_bernoulli (1 / 5)%:nng (p1S 4)).
```

The proof is essentially by rewriting [21, file `lang_syntax_examples.v`].

Probabilistic Inference. We solve the probabilistic inference problem of Sect. 6.2 by computing the measure corresponding to the execution of `staton_bus_syntax0`. This measure corresponds to the probability measure `true` : `false` $= \frac{2}{7} \times \frac{3^4 e^{-3}}{4!} : \frac{5}{7} \times \frac{10^4 e^{-10}}{4!} \approx 0.78 : 0.22$. It can be defined in Coq as a sum of Dirac measures:

```
Let staton_bus_probability U := (2 / 7)%:E * (poisson4 3)%:E * \d_true U +
                                (5 / 7)%:E * (poisson4 10)%:E * \d_false U.
```

We state that execution of `staton_bus_syntax0` yields the expected measure:

```
Lemma exec_staton_bus0 (U : set bool) :
  execP staton_bus_syntax0 tt U = staton_bus_probability U.
```

The proof goes through the intermediate step of computing the semantics of `staton_bus_syntax0` and then shows that this semantics is the expected measure.

Program Transformation. We verify the equivalence between the program used just above (`staton_bus_syntax0`) and a slightly modified version in which we only change the associativity of let-in expressions:

```
[let "x" := Sample {exp_bernoulli (2 / 7%:R)%:nng p27} in
 let "_" :=
   let "r" := if #{"x"} then return {3}:R else return {10}:R in
   Score {exp_poisson 4 [#{"r"}]} in
 return #{"x"}].
```

This seemingly trivial modification is actually explained by a non-trivial lemma [23, Lemma 3]. The associativity of let-in expressions can be stated as follows [23, Sect. 4.2]: $[\![\texttt{let x} := \texttt{e}_1 \texttt{ in let y} := \texttt{e}_2 \texttt{ in e}_3]\!] = [\![\texttt{let y} := (\texttt{let x} := \texttt{e}_1 \texttt{ in e}_2) \texttt{ in e}_3]\!]$. To type-check an equivalent formal statement, we need to be careful about the type of $\texttt{e}_3$. The typing judgment for $\texttt{e}_3$ on the left-hand side is of the form $\texttt{y} : \mathbf{A}_2, \texttt{x} : \mathbf{A}_1, \Gamma \vdash \texttt{e}_3 : \mathbf{A}_3$ while on the right-hand side it is $\texttt{y} : \mathbf{A}_2, \Gamma \vdash \texttt{e}_3 : \mathbf{A}_3$. In our formalization, we use `exp_weak` (Sect. 6.1) to weaken $\texttt{e}_3$ of type `exp P [:: (y, t2) & g] t3` to the type `exp P [:: (y, t2); (x, t1) & g] t3`:

```
Lemma letinA g x y t1 t2 t3 (xyg : x \notin dom ((y, t2) :: g))
    (e1 : exp P g t1) (e2 : exp P [:: (x, t1) & g] t2)
    (e3 : exp P [:: (y, t2) & g] t3) :
  forall U, measurable U ->
  execP [let x := e1 in let y := e2 in
         {@exp_weak _ _ [:: (y, t2)] _ _ (x, t1) e3 xyg}] ^~ U =
  execP [let y := let x := e1 in e2 in e3] ^~ U.
```

The notation `f ^~ y` is for the function $\lambda x. f\, x\, y$. We can prove `letinA` using lemmas for `execP` (Sect. 7.3) and previous work [4], and use this lemma to prove the equivalence between the two versions of our probabilistic inference problem.

Commutativity. We formalize the commutativity example by Staton [24, Sect. 5.1]:

$$[\![\texttt{let x} := \texttt{e}_1 \texttt{ in let y} := \texttt{e}_2 \texttt{ in return}\,(\texttt{x}, \texttt{y})]\!] = [\![\texttt{let y} := \texttt{e}_2 \texttt{ in let x} := \texttt{e}_1 \texttt{ in return}\,(\texttt{x}, \texttt{y})]\!]$$

This kind of commutativity properties was the main motivation for the use of s-finite kernels; it relies on a version of Fubini's theorem for s-finite measures [23]. The property above holds under the condition that `x` is not free in $\texttt{e}_2$ and `y` is not free in $\texttt{e}_1$. We can specify these conditions by having $\texttt{e}_1$ and $\texttt{e}_2$ of types `exp P g t1` and `exp P g t2` with `x` and `y` not appearing in `dom g`. However, as in the associativity of let-in expressions, we need to weaken $\texttt{e}_1$ and $\texttt{e}_2$ appropriately:

```
Lemma letinC g t1 t2 (e1 : exp P g t1) (e2 : exp P g t2)
  (x y : string) (xy : infer (x != y)) (yx : infer (y != x))
  (xg : x \notin dom g) (yg : y \notin dom g) :
  forall U, measurable U ->
```

```
execP [let x := e1 in let y := {exp_weak _ [::] _ (x, t1) e2 xg} in
      return (#x, #y)] ^~ U =
execP [let y := e2 in let x := {exp_weak _ [::] _ (y, t2) e1 yg} in
      return (#x, #y)] ^~ U.
```

The proof of `letinC` relies on previous work [4, Sect. 7.1.2] and its generic statement relies on our use of canonical structures (Sect. 5.2).

9 Conclusions

To the best of our knowledge, we provide the first formalization of a probabilistic programming language with sampling, scoring, and normalization, using an intrinsically-typed syntax. Our work builds on top of an existing formalization of s-finite kernels [4] that we improve (we hinted at some technical improvements in Sect. 7.2) and, more importantly, that we extend with a syntax and a denotational semantics. We proposed a generic approach to encode intrinsically-typed syntax in Coq using bidirectional hints and canonical structures; combined with Coq's custom entries, this allows for the formalization of a user-friendly concrete syntax (Sect. 5). More specifically to probabilistic programming languages, we explained in Sect. 7 how to handle in the semantics nested product spaces (an important construct in probability theory) and measurable functions and s-finite kernels (which present themselves as dependent records). We formalized a denotational semantics in the form of a function derived from an evaluation relation. We showed that our formalization can be used to reason about simple probabilistic programs by rewriting, covering the examples from [4] and more.

Current and Future Work. We have recently added to our framework a formalization of iteration as proposed by Staton [23, Sect. 4.2]. It takes the form of an s-finite kernel **iterate** t **from** $x := u$ that calls t from $x = u$, repeats with $x = u'$ if t returns $u' : \mathbf{A}$ or stops if t returns in $\mathbf{B}$; see [21, file `prob_lang.v`] for the code. This makes it possible to extend SFPPL with loops. As a technical improvement, we are considering the use of deep-embedded binders [19] to avoid strings from the Coq standard library in the concrete syntax. It might also be worth testing whether type classes can be used instead of canonical structures to type-check intrinsically-typed syntax [13, Sect. 7] [19, Sect. 5]. Though not specifically designed for that purpose, MathComp-Analysis turned out to be a good match to formalize the denotational semantics of a probabilistic programming language, which raises the question of its application to the formalization of an operational semantics such as in [11]. We are now investigating application of our approach to more verification examples as a step towards the formalization of equational reasoning for probabilistic programs [14,22].

Acknowledgements. The authors would like to thank the members of the Programming Research Group of the Department of Mathematical and Computing Science at the Tokyo Institute of Technology for their input, and to the anonymous reviewers for many comments that substantially improved this paper. The authors acknowledge the support of the JSPS KAKENHI Grant Number 22H00520.

References

1. Affeldt, R., et al.: MathComp-Analysis: mathematical components compliant analysis library (2023). Since 2017. Version 0.6.4. https://github.com/math-comp/analysis
2. Affeldt, R., Cohen, C.: Measure construction by extension in dependent type theory with application to integration. J. Autom. Reason. **67**(3), 28:1–28:27 (2023). https://doi.org/10.1007/s10817-023-09671-5
3. Affeldt, R., Cohen, C., Rouhling, D.: Formalization techniques for asymptotic reasoning in classical analysis. J. Formaliz. Reason. **11**(1), 43–76 (2018). https://doi.org/10.6092/issn.1972-5787/8124
4. Affeldt, R., Cohen, C., Saito, A.: Semantics of probabilistic programs using s-finite kernels in Coq. In: 12th ACM SIGPLAN International Conference on Certified Programs and Proofs (CPP 2023), Boston, MA, USA, 16–17 January 2023, pp. 3–16. ACM (2023). https://doi.org/10.1145/3573105.3575691
5. Affeldt, R., Sakaguchi, K.: An intrinsic encoding of a subset of C and its application to TLS network packet processing. J. Formaliz. Reason. **7**(1), 63–104 (2014). https://doi.org/10.6092/issn.1972-5787/4317
6. Audebaud, P., Paulin-Mohring, C.: Proofs of randomized algorithms in Coq. Sci. Comput. Program. **74**(8), 568–589 (2009). https://doi.org/10.1016/j.scico.2007.09.002
7. Bagnall, A., Stewart, G.: Certifying the true error: machine learning in Coq with verified generalization guarantees. In: 33rd AAAI Conference on Artificial Intelligence, 31st Conference on Innovative Applications of Artificial Intelligence, 9th Symposium on Educational Advances in Artificial Intelligence, Honolulu, Hawaii, USA, 27 January–1 February 2019, pp. 2662–2669. AAAI Press (2019). https://doi.org/10.1609/aaai.v33i01.33012662
8. Barthe, G., Grégoire, B., Béguelin, S.Z.: Formal certification of code-based cryptographic proofs. In: 36th ACM SIGPLAN-SIGACT Symposium on Principles of Programming Languages (POPL 2009), Savannah, GA, USA, 21–23 January 2009, pp. 90–101. ACM (2009). https://doi.org/10.1145/1480881.1480894
9. Barthe, G., Katoen, J.P., Silva, A. (eds.): Foundations of Probabilistic Programming. Cambridge University Press, Cambridge (2020). https://doi.org/10.1017/9781108770750
10. Benton, N., Hur, C., Kennedy, A., McBride, C.: Strongly typed term representations in Coq. J. Autom. Reason. **49**(2), 141–159 (2012). https://doi.org/10.1007/s10817-011-9219-0
11. Borgström, J., Lago, U.D., Gordon, A.D., Szymczak, M.: A lambda-calculus foundation for universal probabilistic programming. In: 21st ACM SIGPLAN International Conference on Functional Programming (ICFP 2016), Nara, Japan, 18–22 September 2016, pp. 33–46. ACM (2016). https://doi.org/10.1145/2951913.2951942
12. Chapman, J., Kireev, R., Nester, C., Wadler, P.: System *F* in Agda, for fun and profit. In: Hutton, G. (ed.) MPC 2019. LNCS, vol. 11825, pp. 255–297. Springer, Cham (2019). https://doi.org/10.1007/978-3-030-33636-3_10
13. Gonthier, G., Ziliani, B., Nanevski, A., Dreyer, D.: How to make ad hoc proof automation less ad hoc. J. Funct. Program. **23**(4), 357–401 (2013). https://doi.org/10.1017/S0956796813000051
14. Heimerdinger, M., Shan, C.: Verified equational reasoning on a little language of measures. In: Workshop on Languages for Inference (LAFI 2019), Cascais, Portugal, 15 January 2019 (2019)

15. Hirata, M., Minamide, Y., Sato, T.: Program logic for higher-order probabilistic programs in Isabelle/HOL. In: Hanus, M., Igarashi, A. (eds.) FLOPS 2022. LNCS, vol. 13215, pp. 57–74. Springer, Cham (2022). https://doi.org/10.1007/978-3-030-99461-7_4
16. Hirata, M., Minamide, Y., Sato, T.: Semantic foundations of higher-order probabilistic programs in Isabelle/HOL. In: 14th International Conference on Interactive Theorem Proving (ITP 2023). LIPIcs, Białystok, Poland, 31 July–4 August 2023, vol. 268, pp. 18:1–18:18. Schloss Dagstuhl - Leibniz-Zentrum für Informatik (2023). https://doi.org/10.4230/LIPIcs.ITP.2023.18
17. Hurd, J.: Formal verification of probabilistic algorithms. Ph.D. thesis, Computer Laboratory, University of Cambridge (2001)
18. Pickard, M., Hutton, G.: Calculating dependently-typed compilers (functional pearl). Proc. ACM Program. Lang. **5**(ICFP), 1–27 (2021). https://doi.org/10.1145/3473587
19. Pit-Claudel, C., Bourgeat, T.: An experience report on writing usable DSLs in Coq. In: 7th International Workshop on Coq for Programming Languages (CoqPL 2021) (2021). https://popl21.sigplan.org/details/CoqPL-2021-papers/7/An-experience-report-on-writing-usable-DSLs-in-Coq
20. Poulsen, C.B., Rouvoet, A., Tolmach, A., Krebbers, R., Visser, E.: Intrinsically-typed definitional interpreters for imperative languages. Proc. ACM Program. Lang. **2**(POPL), 16:1–16:34 (2018). https://doi.org/10.1145/3158104
21. Saito, A., Affeldt, R.: Experimenting with an intrinsically-typed probabilistic programming language in Coq. Part of MathComp-Analysis Pull Request (2023). Application of s-finite kernels to program semantics (2023), formal development accompanying this paper. https://github.com/math-comp/analysis/pull/912
22. Shan, C.: Equational reasoning for probabilistic programming. POPL TutorialFest (2018)
23. Staton, S.: Commutative semantics for probabilistic programming. In: Yang, H. (ed.) ESOP 2017. LNCS, vol. 10201, pp. 855–879. Springer, Heidelberg (2017). https://doi.org/10.1007/978-3-662-54434-1_32
24. Staton, S.: Probabilistic programs as measures, pp. 43–74 (2020). https://doi.org/10.1017/9781108770750.003. Chapter in [9]
25. Staton, S., Yang, H., Wood, F.D., Heunen, C., Kammar, O.: Semantics for probabilistic programming: higher-order functions, continuous distributions, and soft constraints. In: 31st Annual ACM/IEEE Symposium on Logic in Computer Science (LICS 2016), New York, NY, USA, 5–8 July 2016, pp. 525–534. ACM (2016). https://doi.org/10.1145/2933575.2935313
26. Tassarotti, J., Vajjha, K., Banerjee, A., Tristan, J.: A formal proof of PAC learnability for decision stumps. In: 10th ACM SIGPLAN International Conference on Certified Programs and Proofs (CPP 2021), Virtual Event, Denmark, 17–19 January 2021, pp. 5–17. ACM (2021). https://doi.org/10.1145/3437992.3439917
27. The Coq Development Team: Custom entries. Inria (2019). Chapter Syntax extensions and notation scopes of [29]. direct link
28. The Coq Development Team: Bidirectionality hints. Inria (2020). Chapter Setting properties of a function's arguments of [29]. direct link
29. The Coq Development Team: The Coq Proof Assistant Reference Manual. Inria (2023). Version 8.17.1. https://coq.inria.fr/distrib/current/refman/

30. Zhang, Y., Amin, N.: Reasoning about "reasoning about reasoning": semantics and contextual equivalence for probabilistic programs with nested queries and recursion. Proc. ACM Program. Lang. **6**(POPL), 1–28 (2022). https://doi.org/10.1145/3498677
31. Ziliani, B., Sozeau, M.: A comprehensible guide to a new unifier for CIC including universe polymorphism and overloading. J. Funct. Program. **27**, e10 (2017). https://doi.org/10.1017/S0956796817000028

Verification

Towards a Framework for Developing Verified Assemblers for the ELF Format

Jinhua Wu[1], Yuting Wang[1(✉)], Meng Sun[1], Xiangzhe Xu[2], and Yichen Song[1]

[1] Shanghai Jiao Tong University, Shanghai, China
yuting.wang@sjtu.edu.cn
[2] Purdue University, West Lafayette, USA
xu1415@purdue.edu

Abstract. Most of the existing work on verified compilation leaves unverified the translation of assembly programs into binary code in object file formats (e.g., the Executable and Linkable Format or ELF). The challenges of developing verified assemblers come from the intrinsic complexities in low-level assembling processes caused by the need to support different computer architectures and their details, such as encoding a large number of instructions and verifying its correctness. We present a framework that overcomes the above challenges. It works as a template which may be instantiated to generate verified assemblers for different architectures targeting ELF object files. For this, it is parameterized over the implementation and verification of architecture-dependent assembling processes through well-defined interfaces. By plugging the architecture-dependent parts into the template, we get complete verified assemblers. To manage the complexity in developing and verifying encoding of instructions, we integrate into our framework the CSLED framework for automatically generating verified instruction encoders and decoders from declarative instruction specifications. To show the effectiveness of our framework, we have applied it to generate verified assemblers for the complete X86 and RISC-V assembly languages in CompCert.

1 Introduction

Although the formal development of compilers and their correctness proofs have been extensively studied (e.g. the state-of-the-art verified C compiler CompCert [7,8]), few of the existing work has completed the last mile, i.e., to verify the translation of assembly code into machine code. An obvious obstacle of developing verified assemblers is the potentially large amount of work to support different commercial architectures. Even for a single architecture, the details need to be taken care of during assembly are overwhelming. A typical example is the encoding of assembly instructions into machine instructions which may be hundreds or even thousands in number in any *instruction set architecture* (ISA).

To manage the high complexity in building assemblers that target different object files formats (e.g., PE/COFF, Mach-O and ELF) and architectures

C.-K. Hur (Ed.): APLAS 2023, LNCS 14405, pp. 205–224, 2023.
https://doi.org/10.1007/978-981-99-8311-7_10

(e.g., X86, RISC-V and ARM), the standard practice in industry is to separate the implementation of platform-independent parts of assemblers from the platform-dependent parts. The GNU assembler [18] follows this approach by employing Binary File Descriptor (BFD) to implement this separation. The same idea should also be applicable to verified assemblers. However, the existing work on assembler verification does not provide this flexibility as they are designed to work for ad-hoc machine code formats or for fixed architectures (see Sect. 6).

In this paper, we present our initial attempt to develop a framework for building verified assemblers that target the ELF format by following the above idea. In our framework, the architecture-independent parts of assemblers are developed separately from the architecture-dependent parts. The former is captured by a template of implementation and proofs which formalizes the assembly processes that transform the architecture-independent parts of assembly programs into constituents of ELF objects (e.g., generation of symbol tables). Furthermore, this template is parameterized over the architecture-dependent transformations (e.g., instruction encoding) through well-defined interfaces. To generate a verified assembler for a specific architecture, users instantiate the template with the implementation and proofs of the architecture-dependent components for this architecture through these interfaces. An immediate benefit of this approach is the ability to generate assemblers targeting different platforms by only switching the architecture-dependent instances, which significantly reduces the complexity in developing verified assemblers.

An essential architecture-dependent assembly pass is the encoding of assembly instructions into binary machine code. It is difficult to implement and even more difficult to prove correct because there are at least hundreds or sometimes even thousands of instructions in a common ISA. To tackle this difficulty, we adopt the CSLED framework [22]. In CSLED, one can write down an instruction format as a declarative specification, from which a pair of verified instruction encoder and decoder is automatically generated. However, the generated encoders and decoders work with a form of abstract assembly instructions different from our source assembly language. We address this problem by developing verified translators to connect the verified encoders with our assembly instructions.

Our framework is implemented in the Coq proof assistant [17] and utilizes CompCert's infrastructure [7]. To demonstrate its effectiveness, we apply it to generate verified assemblers for the complete X86 and RISC-V assembly languages used in CompCert. There are different challenges to apply our framework to X86 and RISC-V. For X86, we need to deal with the complex instruction format. For RISC-V, we improve the CSLED framework to overcome the limitation in CSLED for supporting RISC instructions. To examine their usefulness, we have connected them with the back-end of the newest version of Stack-Aware CompCert [19,21] to form a full compilation chain from C to ELF objects. We choose to connect with Stack-Aware CompCert instead of the regular CompCert because its target assembly languages are closer to realistic assembly languages (e.g., no pseudo instructions for stack manipulation). Note that this connection is not fully verified yet due to limitations in (Stack-Aware) CompCert (see Sect. 5.1).

We summarize our contributions as follows:

- Our key contribution is an approach to developing customizable verified assemblers targeting different ISAs by separating the architecture-independent and -dependent components of verified assemblers, such that the former are abstracted over the latter through well-defined interfaces. To generate concrete verified assemblers, users only need to provide instances of architecture-dependent components which meet the abstract interfaces. The design of such interfaces is a key challenge of this work. To reduce the effort for instantiating instruction encoders, we integrate the automation framework CSLED into our framework. Users only need to write down declarative specifications, from which verified encoders are automatically generated, and add glue code to integrate these encoders into verified assemblers.
- We demonstrate the effectiveness and flexibility of our approach by applying our framework to develop verified assemblers for the complete X86 and RISC-V assembly languages in CompCert. We have successfully replaced the unverified GNU assembler used by CompCert with our verified assemblers, therefore significantly reduce its TCB. These applications show that the complexity of implementing verified assemblers for different ISAs is confined in architecture-dependent components, and it takes a reasonable amount of effort to support representative CISC and RISC architectures.

The entire framework and their applications can be found at https://doi.org/10.5281/zenodo.8363543. In the rest of the paper, we first introduce necessary background in Sect. 2. We then present the design of our framework in Sect. 3. In Sect. 4, we discuss the application of our framework to X86 and RISC-V. We connect the instantiated assemblers to Stack-Aware CompCert and discuss evaluation in Sect. 5. Finally, we discuss the related work and conclude in Sect. 6.

2 Background

2.1 A Running Example

To provide a better understanding of the background knowledge, we introduce a running example which is a simple C program that gets compiled to X86-64 assembly code and finally translated into an ELF object file, as shown in Fig. 1. In the C program, `main` initializes the global variable `counter` and calls `incr` to increase it by one. The corresponding assembly code is in the AT&T X86 syntax, in which `incr` loads `counter` into the register `eax`, adds one to `eax` by using `leal` instruction, and then stores the modified value back to the `counter`. `counter` is labeled as a *common* symbol which is not initialized and not allocated in the object file. Note that we have omitted instructions not relevant to our discussion (e.g., for stack allocation). In the later sections, the running example will be used to explain the important concepts and components of our framework, such as generation of symbols and sections, generation of relocation information for linking, and encoding of instructions.

```c
int counter;

void incr(){
  counter++;
}

int main(){
  counter = 0;
  incr();
}
```

(a) C code

```
counter: # common symbol
incr:
  ...
  movl counter,%eax
  leal 1(%eax),%eax
  movl %eax,counter
  ...
main:
  ...
  call incr
  ...
```

(b) Assembly code

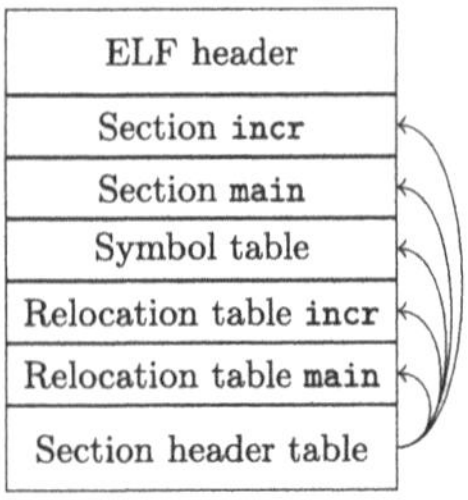

(c) ELF object file

Fig. 1. A Running Example

2.2 Compiler Verification Based on Simulation

Correctness of compilation is often described as preservation of program semantics. A common approach to semantics preservation is to model semantics in a small-step style as *labeled transition systems* (LTS) and to establish *simulation relations* between the source and target semantics. Our framework makes use of this approach, in particular, its realization in CompCert [7] which consists of a sequence of passes that successively translate a large subset of C into assembly languages. We discuss the essential concepts supporting this approach below.

CompCert provides a uniform abstraction of programs for all of its languages. In any language $\mathcal{L}$ of CompCert, a program P of type $P_{\mathcal{C}}$ consists of a mapping from identifiers to global definitions which are parameterized by the types of functions and information of variables (denoted by F and V, respectively):

$$G := \lambda(F\ V : \mathit{Type}).\langle \mathit{fun} : F,\ \mathit{var} : \mathit{Gv}\ V\rangle$$
$$P_{\mathcal{C}} := \lambda(F\ V : \mathit{Type}).\{\mathit{defs} : \mathit{List}\ (\mathit{id} * (G\ F\ V))\}.$$

Here, we use $\{\cdot\}$ to represent records and $\langle\cdot\rangle$ to represent variants. *id* is the type of identifiers. G is the type of global definitions, which may be either functions of type F or variables of type $\mathit{Gv}\ V$ where Gv provides information about variables such as their initial values. For instance, the formalized C program in the running example contains three global definitions: two functions and one variable.

Assembly programs are based on this uniform representation, albeit parameterized by the type of instructions to support different architectures:

$$\mathit{Fn} := \lambda(I : \mathit{Type}).\{\mathit{signature} : \mathit{Sig},\ \mathit{code} : \mathit{List}\ I\}$$
$$\mathit{Fd} := \lambda(I : \mathit{Type}).\langle \mathit{internal} : \mathit{Fn}\ I,\ \mathit{external} : \mathit{Ef}\rangle$$
$$P_{\mathcal{A}} := \lambda(I : \mathit{Type}).P_{\mathcal{C}}\ (\mathit{Fd}\ I)\ \mathit{Unit}.$$

Here, I is the type parameter of instructions. A function of type Fd is either internal or external, where an internal function (of type Fn) has a signature and consists of a list of assembly instructions. The type Unit denotes that there is no type information for global variables in assembly programs. For instance, the formalized assembly program in the running example again contains two functions and one variable where the functions are parameterized by an inductive definition of X86 instructions.

Memory models are essential components of program semantics. CompCert adopts a uniform memory model for all of its languages [9,10]. A memory state m consists of a finite set of memory blocks with distinct identifiers and with linear memory addresses such that (b, δ) denotes a pointer to block b at address δ. Such abstraction enables straightforward pointer arithmetic and memory isolation which are essential for low-level programming. With the uniform memory model, the semantics of a program P of type $(P_{\mathcal{C}}\ F\ V)$ is defined as an LTS derived from the following relations over program states which are pairs of memory states of type M and language-specific states of type St (e.g., register states in assembly programs). Moreover, Tc is the type of event traces, and $Prop$ is the type of propositions.

$$init : \lambda(F\ V : Type).(P_{\mathcal{C}}\ F\ V) \rightarrow (M \times St) \rightarrow Prop$$
$$step : (M \times St) \rightarrow Tc \rightarrow (M \times St) \rightarrow Prop.$$

Here, *init* establishes the initial program state as a result of loading P; *step* describes the effect of one-step execution which emits a list of events. The memory initialized by *init* contains a unique block for each global definition in P. In the remaining discussions, we denote the semantics of P in language $\mathcal{L}$ as $[\![P]\!]_{\mathcal{L}}$, or simply $[\![P]\!]$ if $\mathcal{L}$ can be inferred from the context.

For a given compiler pass $\mathbb{C}$ described as a partial function, if $\mathbb{C}(P) = \lfloor P' \rfloor$ (where $\lfloor \cdot \rfloor$ is the *some* constructor of the *option* type), CompCert establishes a *forward simulation* between $[\![P]\!]$ and $[\![P']\!]$ denoted by $[\![P]\!] \preccurlyeq [\![P']\!]$. A particular instance we will use in this paper is the *lock-step forward simulation*, for which an *invariant* (or simulation relation) $\sim$ between source and target program states is defined and satisfies the following conditions: *1)* $(m, s) \sim (m', s')$ holds for the initial states (m, s) and (m', s'), and *2)* $\sim$ is preserved during the execution. We write $[\![P]\!] \preccurlyeq_{\sim} [\![P']\!]$ when $\sim$ is explicitly given. Note that $\sim$ must capture the relation between source and target memory states which is represented by *memory injections* [9,10]. A memory injection j is a partial function which maps source memory blocks into target blocks. The values (e.g., pointers) stored in the source and target memory must be related according to the injection. A special case is when $\sim$ is equality, meaning that the injection is an identity function. We shall write $[\![P]\!] \preccurlyeq_{=} [\![P']\!]$ to denote simulations with the equality invariant.

With the above definitions, the correctness of $\mathbb{C}$ is formulated as follows:

$$\forall P\ P', \mathbb{C}(P) = \lfloor P' \rfloor \Longrightarrow [\![P]\!] \preccurlyeq [\![P']\!].$$

By vertically composing simulations established for every compiler pass, the semantics preservation of CompCert is proved.

2.3 Relocatable ELF Object Files

The verified assemblers we intend to develop target relocatable ELF object files, which represent open binary modules that may be linked into executable ELF programs. As shown in Fig. 1c, a relocatable ELF object consists of an ELF header which contains meta-information, a list of sections containing program data (including symbol and relocation tables), and section header tables that store the attributes of these sections (e.g., locations of sections in the object).

Sections are the key constituents of ELF objects. In this work, we are only concerned with four kinds of sections: code sections, data sections, symbol tables, and relocation tables. Code and data sections store the binary form of instructions and data. In our running example, the assembly program is complied to an object with two code sections for `incr` and `main`, respectively. It has no data section for `counter` as it is not needed for global variables with no initial value. Symbol tables are used to record references to global definitions. A symbol table consists of a list of *symbol entries*. Each entry contains the information extracted from a global definition in the program, including the type of the definition (e.g., function or data), the type of its binding (e.g., local or global), the section index which points to the section where the definition resides in (special indices are used for common or external symbols), its value (e.g., the offset into its section) and size. In Fig. 1c, there is a single symbol table containing three symbol entries for the global definitions, where `counter` is labeled as a common symbol.

A code or data section may refer to symbols whose addresses cannot be resolved at compile time (e.g., any reference to global definitions in a section whose memory location may be adjusted by the linker). In this case, there is a relocation table associated with this section which consists of *relocation entries*. Each relocation entry points to a location in the section that stores an unresolved symbol. During the linking, the linker would determine the concrete addresses of these symbols and overwrite this location with them. More specifically, a *relocation entry* contains the offset of the unresolved symbol in its section, the relocation type (e.g., relative or absolute addressing), the identifier of the unresolved symbol, and a constant addend for adjusting the symbol address. In our example, the addresses (or relative addresses) of `incr` and `counter` are unknown before linking. Therefore, there are two relocation tables for the sections for `incr` and `main`, respectively. The table for `incr` contains two relocation entries pointing to `counter` in `movl counter,%eax` and `movl %eax,counter`, and `main` contains one entry for `call incr`. The linker will determine the addresses of `incr` and `counter` and overwrite the locations pointed by the relocation entries.

2.4 Machine Instruction Formats

A main job of assemblers is to encode assembly instructions into their binary form. For this, we need to understand the binary format of instructions. In this paper, we are concerned with two representative CISC and RISC instruction formats, i.e., X86 and RISC-V instruction formats.

X86. Figure 2 shows the format of X86 instructions. An instruction consists of a sequence of binary tokens. The REX prefixes, when present, indicate the instructions are in 64-bit mode or in 32-bit mode and referring to extended

REX Prefix	Opcode	ModRM	SIB	Disp	Imms

Fig. 2. The Format of X86 Instructions

registers (`r8` to `r15`). An opcode is 1 to 3 bytes in length and determines the types of instructions. The ModRM byte indicates which addressing modes are used for the operands of this instruction. These addressing modes, which follow the ModRM byte, include SIB (Scale, Index, and Base) byte and a displacement of the address of the referred symbol. For an instruction operating on immediate values, a token of immediate data (Imms) must occur at the end of it.

We use the instruction `movl counter,%eax` in the running example and its variants `movq counter,%rax` and `movl counter,%r8` to demonstrate instruction encoding. For `movl counter,%eax`, its encoding in hexadecimal is `{Opcode:8B, ModRM:05, Disp:00 00 00 00}`. Here, `8B` is the opcode for move instructions that move memory contents to a register. `05` contains the encoding of `eax` and part of the addressing mode. `Disp` is the location that stores the address of `counter` which is currently zero and to be resolved by linking. The encoding of `movq counter,%rax` has an REX prefix `48` which indicates it is a 64-bit instruction. `movl counter,%r8` is 32-bit albeit refers to an extended register `r8`. It has an REX prefix `44` which contains one bit in the encoded `r8` because `r8` requires four bits to encode but there is only space for three bits in `ModRM`.

RISC-V. RISC-V instructions have a uniform size of 32-bit. Therefore, each instruction consists of a single token. RISC-V uses different formats for different types of instructions. Their encoding is straightforward because, given any instruction of a specific type, the positions of its operands are fixed by its format.

2.5 The CSLED Framework

To alleviate the difficulty of the instruction encoding, we employ the CSLED framework. CSLED [22] is a meta-programming framework for automatic generation of verified instruction encoders and decoders from declarative specifications of instruction formats. Given an instruction set, the user first writes down its specifications $\mathcal{S}$ in the CSLED instruction specification language, which capture the encoding format of the instruction set (e.g., the X86 format described in Sect. 2.4). Given $\mathcal{S}$, the framework generates an abstract syntax of instructions $\mathbb{A}$, an encoder $\mathbb{E} : \mathbb{A} \to \lfloor \mathit{List\ Byte} \rfloor$ and a decoder $\mathbb{D} : \mathit{List\ Byte} \to \lfloor \mathbb{A} \times \mathit{List\ Byte} \rfloor$ for these instructions. It also generates the proofs of the following properties asserting that the encoder and decoder are mutual inverses of each other. All the generated definitions and proofs are formalized in Coq.

Theorem 1 (Consistency of Encoders and Decoders).

$$\forall\, k\ l\ l', \mathbb{E}(k) = \lfloor l \rfloor \Longrightarrow \mathbb{D}(l{+}{+}l') = \lfloor (k, l') \rfloor.$$
$$\forall\, k\ l\ l', \mathbb{D}(l{+}{+}l') = \lfloor (k, l') \rfloor \Longrightarrow \mathbb{E}(k) = \lfloor l \rfloor.$$

```
token Opcode = (8);
token ModRM = (8);
field mod = ModRM(7:6);
field reg_op = ModRM(5:3);
field rm = ModRM(2:0);
token SIB = (8);
token Disp32 = (32);

token REX = (8);
field rmagic = REX(7:4);
field w = REX(3:3);
field r = REX(2:2);
field x = REX(1:1);
field b = REX(0:0);

class Addr =
  | constr addr_disp [Disp32]
  (mod=0x0 & rm=0x5; fld %1)
  ...
class Instruction =
  | constr mov_mr [reg_op, Addr]
    (Opcode=0x8B; fld %1 & cls %2)
  ...
```

Fig. 3. An Example of CSLED Specifications

As an example, we show a snippet of the specifications of X86 instructions in Fig. 3. An instruction is built from *tokens*. Each token has one or more bytes (multiple of 8 bits). A *field* occupies a segment of a token, representing an operand or a constant. The tokens and fields reflect the instruction formats as described in Sect. 2.4. A *class* can be viewed as a variant whose binary form occupies a list of tokens. It is used to describe either a collection of instructions or its operands such as the addressing modes. Each branch of the `Instruction` class relates constant or values of operands to their corresponding fields in tokens or other classes through a *pattern* (written inside the parentheses). Here, the names of operands are listed in the brackets. The references to the n-th operand in the patterns are represented by `fld %n` or `cls %n`, depending on whether the operand is a field or a class. For example, the specification of `movl counter,%eax` in CSLED makes use of the branch with the constructor `mov_mr`. Its pattern corresponds to its encoding discussed in Sect. 2.4, such that the operand `reg_op` and the addressing mode are mapped into their corresponding binary tokens according to the pattern after the opcode `0x8B`.

3 The Framework

3.1 An Overview

Our framework is shown in Fig. 4. It can be viewed as a template of verified assemblers parameterized over architecture-dependent components, as depicted in the left box. This parameterization is achieved by exposing interfaces for encapsulation of architecture-dependent assembly processes. The main interfaces are highlighted with colored boxes in the assembly passes ($\mathbb{C}_1^{\square}$ and $\mathbb{C}_2^{\square}$) and disassembly functions ($\mathbb{D}_1^{\square}$ and $\mathbb{D}_2^{\square}$). Here, boxes with the same color represent interfaces for the same pass. The implementation of architecture-dependent components is shown in the right dashed box. By plugging them into the template through its interfaces, we get complete verified assemblers. The concrete definitions of these interfaces will be discussed in Sect. 3.3.

The main constituent of the template is a verified assembly chain with four passes, i.e., $\mathbb{C}_i (0 \leq i \leq 3)$. The source program is called Realistic Assembly or RealAsm in which every formalized assembly instruction corresponds to an actual machine instruction. The assembly chain transforms RealAsm programs into relocatable ELF objects through an intermediate representation called *relocatable programs* which is an abstract representation of ELF objects. We write

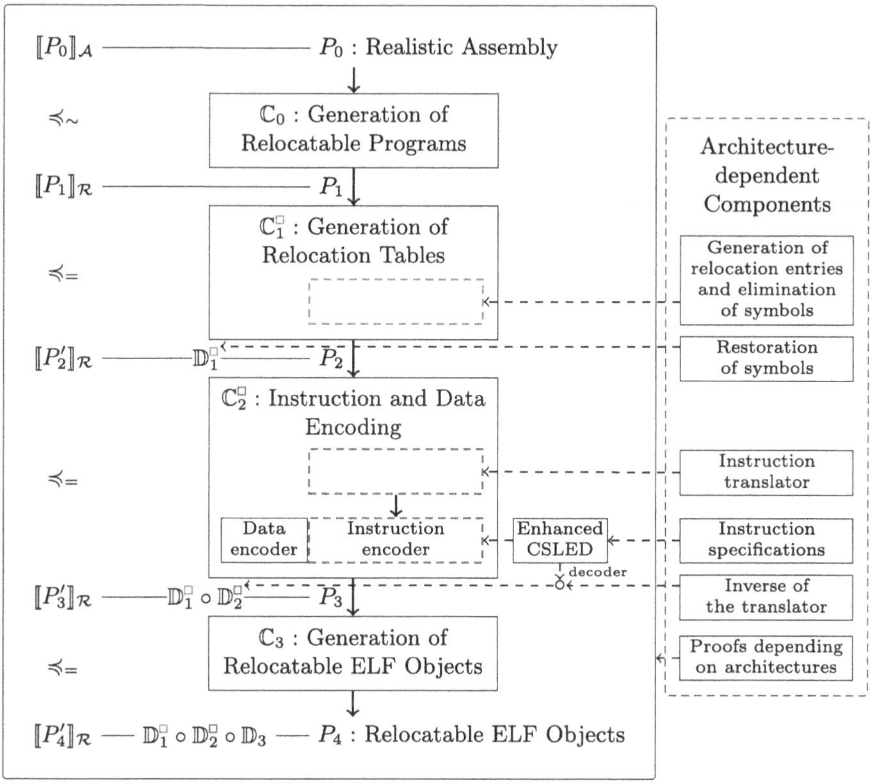

$\mathbb{C}_i$: the ith assembly pass, where $\mathbb{C}_1^\square$ and $\mathbb{C}_2^\square$ expose interfaces
P_i : the output of the $(i-1)$th pass
$\mathbb{D}_j$: disassembly functions used to define semantics (discussed in Sec. 3.2) where $\mathbb{D}_1^\square$ and $\mathbb{D}_2^\square$ expose interfaces to be instantiated
$\mathcal{A}$ and $\mathcal{R}$: realistic assembly languages and relocatable programs

Fig. 4. The Framework

$P_i (0 \leq i \leq 4)$ to represent these programs where P_0 is a RealAsm program, P_4 is an ELF object and the remaining ones are relocatable programs. Verification of the assembler is accomplished by proving lock-step forward simulation for every pass. To define the semantics for intermediate programs at different stages of assembly by reusing a single semantics of relocatable programs (denoted by $[\![\cdot]\!]_\mathcal{R}$), we define functions $\mathbb{D}_1^\square$, $\mathbb{D}_2^\square$, and $\mathbb{D}_3$ for reverting the assembly processes. The rationale for using such "disassembly" functions is given in Sect. 3.2. Another constituent of the template is the enhanced version of CSLED that supports both CISC and RISC instructions. It is used to automatically generate instruction encoders and decoders along with their consistency proofs from instruction specifications. In particular, the decoder is plugged into $\mathbb{D}_2^\square$ to implement the inversion of instruction encoding. In the rest of this section, we elaborate on the representations and semantics of programs and the implementation of assembly passes along with their verification.

3.2 Source, Intermediate and Target Programs

Memory Model. CompCert's assembly language treats the stack as an unbounded linked list of stack frames, therefore requires pseudo instruction for stack manipulation (e.g., `Pallocframe` and `Pfreeframe`). To define semantics for realistic assembly programs without pseudo instructions, we adopt Stack-Aware CompCert's memory model for all the languages of our assembler. It enhances CompCert's memory model with a single and continuous stack [19], thereby enabling stack manipulation using the stack pointer instead of pseudo instructions.

Realistic Assembly Programs. A realistic assembly (or RealAsm) program is an instance of the assembly program of the type $P_{\mathcal{A}}$ introduced in Sect. 2.2, where the instructions (of type I) only contain real machine instructions. Its semantic is defined as an LTS consisting of *init* and *step* relations as introduced in Sect. 2.2. The initial memory as a result of calling *init* consists of a finite and continuous stack block, a unique block with initialized data for each internal function or variable, and a unique empty block for each external function or variable. The *step* relation of RealAsm programs is similar to CompCert's assembly except that no transition for pseudo instructions is defined and that it makes use of Stack-Aware CompCert's memory model.

Relocatable Programs. The relocatable program is a uniform intermediate representation for the assembly passes. It is a record parameterized by the instructions and data types (I and D, respectively):

$$\begin{aligned} S &:= \lambda(I\ D : \mathit{Type}).\langle \mathit{code} : \mathit{List}\ I,\ \mathit{rwdata} : \mathit{List}\ D,\ \mathit{rodata} : \mathit{List}\ D\rangle \\ P_{\mathcal{R}} &:= \lambda(I\ D : \mathit{Type}).\{\mathit{sectbl} : \mathit{id} \rightarrow \lfloor S\ I\ D \rfloor,\ \mathit{symbtbl} : \mathit{id} \rightarrow \lfloor B \rfloor, \\ &\qquad\qquad \mathit{reloctbls} : \mathit{id} \rightarrow \lfloor \mathit{List}\ R \rfloor\}. \end{aligned}$$

Here, $P_{\mathcal{R}}$ encodes the four different kinds of ELF sections introduced in Sect. 2.3. It contains a table of sections (for code and data sections), a symbol table, and a mapping of relocation tables. They respectively map an identifier into a section (of type $S\ I\ D$), a symbol entry (of type B), and a relocation table (of type $\mathit{List}\ R$ where R is the type of relocation entries). An element in the section table is either a code section containing a list of elements of type I, or a read-write or read-only data section containing elements of type D. The formal definitions of symbol entries and relocation entries mirror their informal definitions in Sect. 2.3.

The semantics for relocatable programs denoted as $[\![\cdot]\!]_{\mathcal{R}}$ serves as the uniform foundation for describing other languages' semantics (except for RealAsm) in our framework. In this semantics, the order of memory blocks allocated during memory initialization is different from that for assembly or higher-level programs where memory blocks for global definitions are allocated in the same order as the definitions occurring in the program. In the definition of *init* in $[\![\cdot]\!]_{\mathcal{R}}$, the memory blocks for sections corresponding to internal definitions with non-empty initialization data or code are first allocated, then followed by the allocation of variable definitions with no initial values (corresponding to common symbols) and external definitions. The *step* relation is similar to RealAsm as it reuses the semantics of RealAsm's instructions. Note that $[\![\cdot]\!]_{\mathcal{R}}$ cannot be directly applied to P_2 and P_3 which, although also relocatable programs, are the results of further compilation by $\mathbb{C}_1^{\square}$ and $\mathbb{C}_2^{\square}$. To define their semantics by reusing $[\![\cdot]\!]_{\mathcal{R}}$, we first apply $\mathbb{D}_1^{\square}$ and $\mathbb{D}_2^{\square}$ to disassemble them and then apply $[\![\cdot]\!]_{\mathcal{R}}$. Therefore, their semantics are $[\![\mathbb{D}_1^{\square}(P_2)]\!]_{\mathcal{R}}$ and $[\![\mathbb{D}_1^{\square} \circ \mathbb{D}_2^{\square}(P_3)]\!]_{\mathcal{R}}$, respectively. The definitions of compilation and disassembly and their interfaces will be discussed in detail in Sect. 3.3.

Relocatable ELF Objects. Relocatable ELF objects (denoted by $\mathcal{E}$) formalize the ELF format introduced in Sect. 2.3. They are encoded as triples of the form (E_h, E_s, E_{sh}), where E_h formalizes the ELF header, E_s is a list of ELF sections in binary forms and E_{sh} is a list of section headers. To define the semantics of a relocatable ELF program P_4 (denoted as $[\![P_4]\!]_{\mathcal{E}}$), we first use a function $\mathbb{D}_3$ which models ELF loading to get a relocatable program in binary form and then apply $\mathbb{D}_2^{\square}$ and $\mathbb{D}_1^{\square}$. That is, $[\![P_4]\!]_{\mathcal{E}}$ is formulated as $[\![\mathbb{D}_1^{\square} \circ \mathbb{D}_2^{\square} \circ \mathbb{D}_3(P_4)]\!]_{\mathcal{R}}$.

Rationale Behind Disassembly. As we have discussed above, we use disassembly functions to describe program semantics so that we only need a uniform semantics for relocatable programs which in turn reuses the semantics of assembly instructions. This greatly simplifies the verification of assemblers. This reliance on disassembly is not a fundamental limitation for two reasons. First, some form of disassembly is unavoidable for describing semantics for binary programs. For example, to describe the semantics of ELF, it is necessary to model ELF loading and instruction decoding, which are encoded in $\mathbb{D}_3$ and $\mathbb{D}_2^{\square}$ in our framework, respectively. Second, the structure of our framework does not change even if we use a more realistic ISA or ELF semantics without disassembly (e.g., Sail [2]). The only difference is that the forward simulation $\preccurlyeq_{=}$ need to be generalized to $\preccurlyeq_{\sim}$. Except for that, the structure of proofs should remain the same. Therefore, our framework is still applicable with more realistic binary semantics. The discussion about verification below should make these points clear.

3.3 Assembly Passes

The four assembly passes ($\mathbb{C}_0$ to $\mathbb{C}_3$) build relocatable ELF objects step-by-step. $\mathbb{C}_0$ and $\mathbb{C}_1^{\square}$ build the relocatable programs, among which $\mathbb{C}_0$ constructs a collection of sections and a symbol table from a RealAsm program and $\mathbb{C}_1^{\square}$ iterates the sections to generate relocation entries and eliminate unresolved symbols. $\mathbb{C}_2^{\square}$ performs instruction and data encoding that converts the contents in sections into bytes. $\mathbb{C}_3$ generates relocatable ELF objects on a particular architecture (e.g., X86 or RISC-V). Their correctness are established as lock-step forward simulations as depicted in Fig. 4. The semantics of P_0 to P_4 have already been described in the last section. We use $\sim$ to denote the invariant for verifying $\mathbb{C}_0$ which relates the states of $P_{\mathcal{A}}$ and $P_{\mathcal{R}}$. For the remaining three passes, as the program semantics are defined by reverting the compilation, we use the equivalent relation $=$ as invariants. This in turn reduces lock-step simulation to proving correct that disassembly functions are exactly the inversion of compilation. Finally, by composing the correctness proofs of the four passes, we get the following semantics preservation theorem for our assembler:

Theorem 2 (Semantics Preservation of the Assembler).

$$\forall P\ P',\ \mathbb{C}_3 \circ \mathbb{C}_2^{\square} \circ \mathbb{C}_1^{\square} \circ \mathbb{C}_0(P) = \lfloor P' \rfloor \implies [\![P]\!]_{\mathcal{A}} \preccurlyeq [\![P']\!]_{\mathcal{E}}.$$

In the remaining section, we discuss how to implement and verify these passes.

Generation of Relocatable Programs. This pass ($\mathbb{C}_0$) transforms a RealAsm program into a relocatable program containing sections and a symbol table in two steps. First, for every internal global definition in the source program, a corresponding section is built by invoking a function called *gen_section* to extract code or data from the definition. Second, a symbol table is created by repeatedly invoking *gen_symbol_entry* on *all* global definitions to get the symbol entries and inserting them into the initially empty symbol table. The types of $\mathbb{C}_0$, *gen_section* and *gen_symbol_entry* are given as follows:

$$\begin{aligned} \mathit{gen\_section} &: \forall I, (G\ (Fd\ I)\ \mathit{Unit}) \rightarrow \lfloor S\ I\ \mathit{Data} \rfloor \\ \mathit{gen\_symbol\_entry} &: \forall I, (G\ (Fd\ I)\ \mathit{Unit}) \rightarrow B \\ \mathbb{C}_0 &: \forall I, (P_{\mathcal{A}}\ I) \rightarrow \lfloor P_{\mathcal{R}}\ I\ \mathit{Data} \rfloor. \end{aligned}$$

Here, *Data* is the type of initial values of global variables defined in CompCert. For our running example, $\mathbb{C}_0$ generates two sections for `incr` and `main` and a symbol table with three symbol entries for the three global definitions. Therefore, the generated relocatable program mirrors the structure of the ELF object as depicted in Fig. 1c (except for the relocation tables). Note that the implementation of $\mathbb{C}_0$ is ignorant of I, therefore independent of architectures.

Given $\mathbb{C}_0(P_0) = \lfloor P_1 \rfloor$, we need to prove $[\![P_0]\!]_{\mathcal{A}} \preccurlyeq_{\sim} [\![P_1]\!]_{\mathcal{R}}$. Following the ideas described in Sect. 2.2, we define an invariant $\sim$ and prove that it holds for the initial states and is preserved by lock-step execution. The only non-trivial component of $\sim$ is a memory injection between source memory blocks for global definitions and corresponding target blocks for sections and symbols. The main difficulty of the proof is to show this injection indeed holds after initialization. Once the invariant is established, lock-step simulation naturally follows from it. Establishing this initial injection has been easy for all of CompCert's passes: since the global definitions for source and target are initialized in the same order, the injection is proved to hold by starting from an empty injection and incrementally showing that it is preserved after adding memory blocks for each pair of corresponding source and target global definitions. However, this incremental approach no longer works for $\mathbb{C}_0$ because the order of initialization is changed. Consider our running example. In the source RealAsm program, the order of initialization is `counter`, `incr` and `main`. However, as described in Sect. 3.2, in relocatable programs memory blocks are first allocated for sections and then for the remaining symbols. As a result, the initialization order for the relocatable program of our example is `incr`, `main` and `counter`. Therefore, incremental pairing of definitions and growth of injection during initialization is no longer possible. To solve this problem, we directly prove that an injection between all source definitions and target blocks holds right after the initialization is completed. Because of its monolithic nature, this proof is considerably more complicated than the incremental proofs. Nevertheless, the initial injection can be directly established by observing that the source block initialized from a definition g is related to the target block initialized from $gen\_section(g)$ or $gen\_symbol\_entry(g)$.

Generation of Relocation Tables. $\mathbb{C}_1^{\square}$ generates relocation entries for instructions or data that refer to symbols whose addresses are not determined until linking. For each code or data section, it generates one relocation table. To facilitate encoding of instructions and data into binary forms, it also eliminates the symbols in them. Its type is:

$$\mathbb{C}_1^{\square} : \forall I, (Z \to I \to (\lfloor R \rfloor \times I)) \to (P_{\mathcal{R}}\ I\ Data) \to \lfloor P_{\mathcal{R}}\ I\ Data \rfloor.$$

The first argument of $\mathbb{C}_1^{\square}$ is a parameter named gen_reloc. As its color shows, it is part of the interfaces for encapsulating the architecture-dependent components. Given an instruction i and its offset o in i, $gen\_reloc\ o\ i$ produces a relocation entry for i if i contains a symbol and returns an updated instruction with the symbol replaced by the constant 0. For example, given `movl counter,%eax` and its offset inside the `incr` section, an instance of gen_reloc for the X86 architecture constructs a relocation entry for `counter` as described in Sect. 2.3. It also produces an updated instruction `movl 0,%eax` where `counter` is replaced by `0`. This makes the instruction independent of any symbol and hence can be encoded into bits.

Given $\mathbb{C}_1^{\square}(P_1) = \lfloor P_2 \rfloor$, we need to prove $[\![P_1]\!]_{\mathcal{R}} \preccurlyeq_{=} [\![\mathbb{D}_1^{\square}(P_2)]\!]_{\mathcal{R}}$. Note that, if we could show that $\mathbb{D}_1^{\square}$ reverts $\mathbb{C}_1^{\square}$, then the forward simulation holds trivially with an equality invariant. $\mathbb{D}_1^{\square}$ has the following type:

$$\mathbb{D}_1^{\square} : \forall I, (R \to I \to I) \to (P_{\mathcal{R}}\ I\ Data) \to (P_{\mathcal{R}}\ I\ Data).$$

Its first argument is called $restore\_symb$ and is also part of our framework's interfaces. Given an instruction i and its relocation entry r, $restore\_symb\ r\ i$ extracts the symbol stored in r and writes it back into i. For example, $restore\_symb$ converts `movl 0,%eax` back to `movl counter,%eax` given the generated relocation entry. The key to showing that $\mathbb{D}_1^{\square}$ reverts $\mathbb{C}_1^{\square}$ is to prove the following property, i.e., $restore\_symb$ reverts gen_reloc, whose proof is straightforward:

$$\forall\ i\ i'\ e\ o,\ gen\_reloc\ o\ i = (\lfloor e \rfloor, i') \Longrightarrow restore\_symb\ e\ i' = i.$$

The above verification process is also applicable to the remaining two passes.

Instruction and Data Encoding. $\mathbb{C}_2^{\square}$ encodes instructions and data sections into sections containing bytes. It has the following type:

$$\mathbb{C}_2^{\square} : \forall I\ I', (I \to \lfloor List\ I' \rfloor) \to (I' \to \lfloor List\ Byte \rfloor) \to (P_{\mathcal{R}}\ I\ Data) \to \lfloor P_{\mathcal{R}}\ Byte\ Byte \rfloor.$$

The first two arguments are called *translate_instr* and *csled_encode*, respectively. They are also part of our framework's interfaces. *translate_instr* is a hand-written instruction translator for converting RealAsm instructions into a list of abstract assembly instructions characterized by the inductive definition for instructions generated from CSLED specifications (i.e., $\mathbb{A}$ introduced in Sect. 2.5). These CSLED instructions are subsequently encoded into bytes by *csled_encode* which makes use of the encoder generated from CSLED specifications (i.e., $\mathbb{E}$ in Sect. 2.5). Unlike instruction encoding, data encoding is independent of architectures. The data encoder (of type $Data \to List\ Byte$) is directly embedded into $\mathbb{C}_2^{\square}$. It encodes data of different types (e.g. int, float, or double) into bytes by using appropriate encoders for scalar values.

Given $\mathbb{C}_2^{\square}(P_2) = \lfloor P_3 \rfloor$, we need to prove $[\![\mathbb{D}_1^{\square}(P_2)]\!]_{\mathcal{R}} \preccurlyeq_{=} [\![\mathbb{D}_1^{\square} \circ \mathbb{D}_2^{\square}(P_3)]\!]_{\mathcal{R}}$. It follows by showing that $\mathbb{D}_2^{\square}$ reverts $\mathbb{C}_2^{\square}$. $\mathbb{D}_2^{\square}$ decodes binary instructions back to RealAsm instructions. It has the following type:

$$\mathbb{D}_2^{\square} : \forall\ I\ I', (List\ Byte \to \lfloor I' \rfloor) \to (List\ I' \to \lfloor I \rfloor) \to (P_{\mathcal{R}}\ Byte\ Byte) \to \lfloor P_{\mathcal{R}}\ I\ Byte \rfloor.$$

The first two arguments are called *csled_decode* and *revert_translate* where *csled_decode* is the instruction decoder generated by CSLED (i.e., $\mathbb{D}$ in Sect. 2.5) and *revert_translate* further decodes CSLED instructions into RealAsm assembly instructions. To show instruction encoding is reverted by $\mathbb{D}_2^{\square}$, the key is to prove that *revert_translate* reverts *translate_instr* and *csled_decode* reverts *csled_encode*. The former is easily proved manually with certain automation scripts in Coq. The latter follows directly from Theorem 1 which is automatically generated by CSLED. Note that there is no need to show data encoding can be reverted: we can prove that the initial memory values (in bytes) obtained from data of type *Data* are equal to those initialized from data of type *Byte*.

Generation of Relocatable ELF Objects. $\mathbb{C}_3 : (P_{\mathcal{R}}\ Byte\ Byte) \to P_{\mathcal{E}}$ encodes the symbol table and relocation tables to a list of ELF sections, and generates headers for all the sections. As mentioned in Sect. 3.2, the ELF semantics is defined by employing an ELF loader $\mathbb{D}_3$. To verify this pass, we show that $\mathbb{D}_3$ reverts $\mathbb{C}_3$. We elide a discussion of this proof as it is straightforward.

4 Applications

We demonstrate the effectiveness of our framework by building assemblers for X86 and RISC-V that support all the 32 and 64-bit X86 and RISC-V instructions used by CompCert. By design, all we need to do is to provide instances for the interfaces exposed by our framework.

```
class Instruction =
  |constr rex [w,r,x,b] (rmagic=0x4 & fld %1 & fld %2 & fld %3 & fld %4)
  |constr mov_mr [reg_op, Addr] (Opcode=0x8B; fld %1 & cls %2)
  |...
```

Fig. 5. A Snippet of the X86 Specifications

4.1 Building an Assembler for X86

To obtain instances of the interfaces for supporting X86 instructions in CompCert, the most challenging task is to write down the CSLED specifications that capture the complex X86 instruction format. Instantiation of the remaining interfaces (e.g., *gen_reloc* and *translate_instr*) is straightforward.

As demonstrated in Sect. 2.5, CSLED is already sufficient for specifying 32-bit X86 instructions. However, it is more difficult to support 64-bit X86 instructions which can be viewed as 32-bit instructions prepended with an REX prefix which extends operands to 64 bits. An obvious solution is to write down two versions of CSLED specifications: one for 32-bit without the REX prefix and the other for 64-bit with the prefix. However, this duplication is not only tedious and error-prone, but also generates inefficient encoders and decoders with bloated proofs. To solve this problem, we treat REX as a new "instruction", as depicted in Fig. 5 where the first operand (bit) `w` denotes whether the instruction is in 32-bit or 64-bit mode and the remaining three operands (bits) are used to encode the extended registers referred by the instruction. The key observation that enables the treatment of REX as a separate instruction is that, by the design of the X86 64-bit extension, the binary form of REX does not overlap with any regular instruction. Therefore, unambiguous encoders and decoders can be generated from the CSLED specifications in Fig. 5.

4.2 Building an Assembler for RISC-V

RISC architectures have more consistent and much simpler instruction formats than CISC architectures. For instance, no REX prefix is needed to distinguish between 32-bit and 64-bit instructions. Therefore, it is conceptually more straightforward to build assemblers for RISC-V than for X86. However, to apply our framework, we still need to address a practical problem: the original CSLED cannot directly support encoding and decoding of RISC-V instructions. The original CSLED describes an instruction as a sequence of bytes such that a field cannot span over more than one byte. Therefore, CSLED is insufficient for encoding many RISC-V instructions with this characteristic.

The root cause of the above problem is that the algorithm for generating encoders and decoders in CSLED treats *byte* as the atomic unit for binary data. To support RISC instructions, we switched the atomic unit to *bit* and refactored the algorithm so that it can still correctly generate encoders and decoders, and their correctness proofs. After that, it is easy to write a RISC-V instruction specification for CompCert and to generate a verified RISC-V assembler.

Fig. 6. The End-to-end Compilation Chain

5 Evaluation

5.1 Connecting with Stack-Aware CompCert

To evaluate the effectiveness of our approach, we connect our verified assemblers with Stack-Aware CompCert [19,21]. The complete compilation chain is shown in Fig. 6. The pretty printers translate CompCert assembly code into RealAsm code by expanding all the pseudo instructions into real assembly instructions. This phase is the only part not yet formally verified. The difficulty in its verification is mainly caused by the discrepancy between the memory models used by (Stack-Aware) CompCert and our verified assemblers. In particular, pointer values and certain scalar values stored in CompCert's memory are abstract and cannot be directly interpreted as binary values. As a result, the source and target semantics of the pretty printer cannot be matched via simulation. To solve this problem, we will need a version of Stack-Aware CompCert with a more concrete memory model. This is a non-trivial task and left for future work.

5.2 Statistics and Comparison

To examine the efficiency of our assemblers, we have applied our X86 and RISC-V compilation chains to the test suite provided by CompCert. Initially, we observed a 2.6% slowdown on average by running the code generated by our compilation chains and comparing it with the performance of the code generated by CompCert which uses the GNU assembler `as`. By inspecting the code generated by `as`, we discovered that it runs more efficiently by choosing instructions operating on aligned data (especially for floating-point values). We then modified our pretty printer to generate the same instructions, which brought the slowdown down to 1.1%. We conjecture that our performance can be further improved by choosing instructions with smaller immediate values (e.g., 8-bit instead of 32-bit), which may reduce cache misses. Such experiments are left to future work.

The statistics of our Coq development are shown in Table 1, where the numbers are measured in lines of code (LoC) and obtained by using `coqwc`. Note that we count Coq specifications and proofs separately. The framework column displays LoC for architecture-independent components, while the applications column displays LoC for architecture-dependent components. The second to fourth rows show the statistics for the program representations in our framework. The subsequent four rows are for the assembly passes. In instruction and data encoding, we show LoC for the manually written translators and the CSLED specifications separately. The next row shows the statistics for the pretty printers which are developed for each architecture (but not verified). As shown in the

Table 1. Statistics of Our Development

Components	Framework		Applications			
			X86		RISC-V	
	Spec	Proof	Spec	Proof	Spec	Proof
Realistic Assembly	40	28	221	8	332	15
Relocatable Programs	1347	2165	797	48	423	38
Relocatable ELF	970	507	16	0	16	0
Generation of Relocatable Programs	685	1600	251	548	156	134
Generation of Relocation Tables	217	501	443	54	140	21
Instruction and Data Encoding	244	1016	0	0	0	0
• Instruction Translators	0	0	2178	469	2144	432
• CSLED Specifications	0	0	150	0	229	0
Generation of Relocatable ELF	605	1032	87	153	83	121
Pretty Printers	0	0	1005	0	1127	0
Total	4108	6849	5148	1280	4650	761

last row, a major part of the work for developing verified assemblers is isolated in the generic and architecture-independent framework. Note that a major part of the architecture-dependent development is for instruction translators (about 2.5k LoC each for X86 and RISC-V). However, we observe that these code and proofs are highly structured and may be simplified with further automation. The Coq proof scripts automatically generated by CSLED are quite large and may slow down the proof checking significantly when the number of instructions increases. We plan to solve this problem by dividing instructions into smaller categories which can be verified independently.

Finally, we compare our work with the most relevant existing work, i.e., CompCertELF [20] which also implements a verified assembler for the 32-bit X86 backend of CompCert. The main difference is that CompCertELF only supports a subset of X86-32 instructions and this support is hard-coded in its implementation. In particular, 89 X86-32 instructions of CompCert are implemented, out of which 24 are fully verified. This takes about 2300 LoC. As shown in Table 1 we only need 2647 LoC (2178 + 469) for the hand-written translator and 150 lines of the CSLED specifications to support the complete X86-32 and X86-64 backends of CompCert (a total of 146 instructions implemented and verified). Moreover, since CompCertELF does not separate the architecture-independent and -dependent implementation and proofs, it is unclear how it can be extended to support other architectures.

6 Related Work and Conclusion

Verified Assembly. To develop a verified assembler, it is necessary to precisely describe the semantics of assembly programs and object files. The semantics of assembly programs in CompCert [8] is not ideal as it is not based on a realistic machine model (e.g., pointers can not be represented as binary values) [9]. There has been work on fixing these problems [3,4,13]. CompCertS [3] uses a concrete memory model to map memory blocks to 32-bit integers. Kang et al. [4] combines the logical and concrete memory models to enable injection (casting) of pointers into integers. Mullen et al. [13] defines a new semantics for X86-32 assembly which models pointers as 32-bit integers by introducing a memory allocator to translate memory blocks to concrete addresses. The memory model we use is based on Stack-Aware CompCert [19,21]. It extends the memory with an abstract stack to support the finite and continuous stacks in assembly programs.

There exists a lot of work on formalizing generation of low-level code (e.g., proof carrying code [1,14] and typed assembly [11,12]). However, none of them formally proves the correctness of assemblers. Recent work on verified compilation tried to address this problem. CakeML [6,16] is a verified compiler for a subset of Standard ML. Its backend supports compilation to machine code on different architectures. However, it uses an internal representation called `LABLANG` to store the encoded data instead of a standard binary file format [16]. CompCertELF [20] supports verified compilation from C programs all the way to the relocatable ELF files. However, it only supports a small subset of X86-32 and is difficult to extend due to its hard-coded dependency on X86-32. A translation validator known as *Valex* has been developed for the PowerPC assembler in CompCert [5]. It checks the consistency between generated executable programs and abstract assembly code. However, it is not formally verified.

Instruction Encoding and Decoding. CSLED [22] is a framework for automatically generating verified encoders and decoders from instruction specifications. Its specification language is based on the instruction specification language SLED [15] which does not provide any formal guarantee.

Conclusion. We have presented a framework for developing verified assemblers. It takes the form of a template implementing the architecture-independent parts of the verified assemblers. To obtain a verified assembler targeting a specific architecture, users only need to instantiate the architecture-dependent components exposed as interfaces in our framework. To demonstrate its effectiveness, we have applied our framework to develop assemblers sufficient to support the X86 and RISC-V backends of CompCert. We have further connected them with Stack-Aware CompCert via pretty printers and experimented on CompCert's official test suite. Our work is an initial attempt to develop realistic assemblers and linkers for end-to-end compiler verification. In the future, we would like to formally verify the pretty printers by using a more realistic memory model, extend our work to support verified linkers and verified compositional compilation, and scale our approach to other compilers, optimizations and object file formats.

Acknowledgements. We thank the anonymous referees for their feedback which improved this paper significantly. This work was supported by the National Natural Science Foundation of China (NSFC) under Grant No. 62002217.

References

1. Appel, A.W.: Foundational proof-carrying code. In: Proceedings of 31st IEEE Symposium on Logic in Computer Science (LICS'16), pp. 247–256. IEEE Computer Society, Boston (2001). https://doi.org/10.1109/LICS.2001.932501
2. Armstrong, A., et al.: Isa semantics for armv8-a, risc-v, and cheri-mips. Proc. ACM Program. Lang. **3**(POPL), 71:1–71:31 (2019). https://doi.org/10.1145/3290384
3. Besson, F., Blazy, S., Wilke, P.: CompCertS: a memory-aware verified C compiler using pointer as integer semantics. In: Ayala-Rincón, M., Muñoz, C.A. (eds.) ITP 2017. LNCS, vol. 10499, pp. 81–97. Springer, Cham (2017). https://doi.org/10.1007/978-3-319-66107-0_6
4. Kang, J., Hur, C.K., Mansky, W., Garbuzov, D., Zdancewic, S., Vafeiadis, V.: A formal c memory model supporting integer-pointer casts. In: Proceedings of 2015 ACM Conference on Programming Language Design and Implementation (PLDI 2015), pp. 326–335. ACM, New York (2015). https://doi.org/10.1145/2737924.2738005
5. Kästner, D., et al.: Compcert: practical experience on integrating and qualifying a formally verified optimizing compiler. In: Proceedings of 9th European Congress Embedded Real-Time Software and Systems, pp. 1–9. SEE (2018)
6. Kumar, R., Myreen, M.O., Norrish, M., Owens, S.: Cakeml: a verified implementation of ml. In: Proceedings of 41st ACM Symposium on Principles of Programming Languages (POPL 2014), pp. 179–191. ACM, New York (2014). https://doi.org/10.1145/2535838.2535841
7. Leroy, X.: The CompCert Verified Compiler (2005-2023). http://compcert.inria.fr/
8. Leroy, X.: A formally verified compiler back-end. J. Autom. Reason. **43**(4), 363–446 (2009). https://doi.org/10.1007/s10817-009-9155-4
9. Leroy, X., Appel, A.W., Blazy, S., Stewart, G.: The CompCert Memory Model, Version 2. Research Report RR-7987, INRIA (2012). https://hal.inria.fr/hal-00703441
10. Leroy, X., Blazy, S.: Formal verification of a C-like memory model and its uses for verifying program transformation. J. Autom. Reason. **41**(1), 1–31 (2008). https://doi.org/10.1007/s10817-008-9099-0
11. Morrisett, G., et al.: TALx86: a realistic typed assembly language. In: 1999 ACM SIGPLAN Workshop on Compiler Support for System Software, pp. 25–35. Atlanta, GA, USA (1999)
12. Morrisett, J.G., Walker, D., Crary, K., Glew, N.: From system F to typed assembly language. ACM Trans. Program. Lang. Syst. **21**(3), 527–568 (1999). https://doi.org/10.1145/319301.319345
13. Mullen, E., Zuniga, D., Tatlock, Z., Grossman, D.: Verified peephole optimizations for compcert. In: Proceedings of 2016 ACM Conference on Programming Language Design and Implementation (PLDI 2016). pp. 448–461. ACM, New York (2016). https://doi.org/10.1145/2980983.2908109
14. Necula, G.: Proof-carrying code. In: Proceedings of 24th ACM Symposium on Principles of Programming Languages (POPL 1997), pp. 106–119. ACM, New York (1997). https://doi.org/10.1145/263699.263712

15. Ramsey, N., Fernández, M.F.: Specifying representations of machine instructions. ACM Trans. Program. Lang. Syst. **19**(3), 492–524 (1997). https://doi.org/10.1145/256167.256225
16. Tan, Y.K., Myreen, M.O., Kumar, R., Fox, A.C.J., Owens, S., Norrish, M.: The verified cakeml compiler backend. J. Funct. Program. **29**, e2 (2019). https://doi.org/10.1017/S0956796818000229
17. The Coq development team: The Coq proof assistant (1999 - 2023). http://coq.inria.fr
18. The GNU development team: GNU Binutils (2000 - 2023). https://sourceware.org/binutils/
19. Wang, Y., Wilke, P., Shao, Z.: An abstract stack based approach to verified compositional compilation to machine code. Proc. ACM Program. Lang. **3**(POPL), 62:1–62:30 (2019). https://doi.org/10.1145/3290375
20. Wang, Y., Xu, X., Wilke, P., Shao, Z.: Compcertelf: verified separate compilation of c programs into elf object files. Proc. ACM Program. Lang. 4(OOPSLA) **197**, 1–197:28 (2020). https://doi.org/10.1145/3428265
21. Wang, Y., Zhang, L., Shao, Z., Koenig, J.: Verified compilation of C programs with a nominal memory model. Proc. ACM Program. Lang. **6**(POPL), 1–31 (2022). https://doi.org/10.1145/3498686
22. Xu, X., Wu, J., Wang, Y., Yin, Z., Li, P.: Automatic generation and validation of instruction encoders and decoders. In: Silva, A., Leino, K.R.M. (eds.) CAV 2021. LNCS, vol. 12760, pp. 728–751. Springer, Cham (2021). https://doi.org/10.1007/978-3-030-81688-9_34

Transport via Partial Galois Connections and Equivalences

Kevin Kappelmann(✉)

Technical University of Munich, Boltzmannstrasse 3, Garching 85748, Germany
kevin.kappelmann@tum.de

Abstract. Multiple types can represent the same concept. For example, lists and trees can both represent sets. Unfortunately, this easily leads to incomplete libraries: some set-operations may only be available on lists, others only on trees. Similarly, subtypes and quotients are commonly used to construct new type abstractions in formal verification. In such cases, one often wishes to reuse operations on the representation type for the new type abstraction, but to no avail: the types are not the same. To address these problems, we present a new framework that transports programs via equivalences. Existing transport frameworks are either designed for dependently typed, constructive proof assistants, use univalence, or are restricted to partial quotient types. Our framework (1) is designed for simple type theory, (2) generalises previous approaches working on partial quotient types, and (3) is based on standard mathematical concepts, particularly Galois connections and equivalences. We introduce the notions of partial Galois connection and equivalence and prove their closure properties under (dependent) function relators, (co)datatypes, and compositions. We formalised the framework in Isabelle/HOL and provide a prototype.

Keywords: Galois connections · Equivalences · Relational parametricity

1 Introduction

Computer scientists often write programs and proofs in terms of representation types but provide their libraries in terms of different, though related, type abstractions. For example, the abstract type of finite sets may be represented by the type of lists: every finite set is related to every list containing the same elements and, conversely, every list is related to its set of elements. As such, every function on lists respecting this relation may be reused for a library on finite sets. To be more explicit, consider the following example in simple type theory:

Supplementary Information The online version contains supplementary material available at https://doi.org/10.1007/978-981-99-8311-7_11.

C.-K. Hur (Ed.): APLAS 2023, LNCS 14405, pp. 225–245, 2023.
https://doi.org/10.1007/978-981-99-8311-7_11

A Simple Example. Take the types of lists, $\alpha\,\mathsf{list}$, and finite sets, $\alpha\,\mathsf{fset}$. There is a function $\mathsf{to\_fset} : \alpha\,\mathsf{list} \Rightarrow \alpha\,\mathsf{fset}$ that turns a list into its set of elements. This allows us to define the relation $\mathsf{LFS}\,xs\,s := \mathsf{to\_fset}\,xs = s$ that identifies lists and finite sets, e.g. $\mathsf{LFS}\,[1,2,3]\,\{1,2,3\}$ and $\mathsf{LFS}\,[3,1,2]\,\{1,2,3\}$. Our goal is to use this identification to transport programs between these two types.

For instance, take the function $\mathsf{max\_list}\,xs := \mathsf{foldr}\,\mathsf{max}\,xs\,0$ of type $\mathbb{N}\,\mathsf{list} \Rightarrow \mathbb{N}$ that returns the maximum natural number contained in a list. After some thinking, one recognises that $\mathsf{max\_list}$ respects the relation LFS in the following sense: if two lists correspond to the same set, then applying $\mathsf{max\_list}$ to these lists returns equal results. Formally,

$$\forall xs\,ys.\, \mathsf{to\_fset}\,xs = \mathsf{to\_fset}\,ys \longrightarrow \mathsf{max\_list}\,xs = \mathsf{max\_list}\,ys. \tag{1}$$

Despite this insight, we still cannot directly compute the maximum of a finite set $s : \mathbb{N}\,\mathsf{fset}$ using $\mathsf{max\_list}$; the term $\mathsf{max\_list}\,s$ does not even typecheck (for good reasons). But there is an indirect way if we are also given an "inverse" of $\mathsf{to\_fset}$, call it $\mathsf{to\_list}^{\mathsf{fin}} : \alpha\,\mathsf{fset} \Rightarrow \alpha\,\mathsf{list}$, that returns an arbitrary list containing the same elements as the given set. The functions $\mathsf{to\_fset}$ and $\mathsf{to\_list}^{\mathsf{fin}}$ form an equivalence between $\alpha\,\mathsf{list}$ and $\alpha\,\mathsf{fset}$ that respects the relation LFS:

$$\forall xs.\, \mathsf{LFS}\,xs\,(\mathsf{to\_fset}\,xs) \qquad \text{and} \qquad \forall s.\, \mathsf{LFS}\,(\mathsf{to\_list}^{\mathsf{fin}}\,s)\,s. \tag{2}$$

Thanks to this equivalence, we can compute the maximum of s by simply transporting s along the equivalence:

$$\mathsf{max\_fset}\,s := \mathsf{max\_list}\,(\mathsf{to\_list}^{\mathsf{fin}}\,s). \tag{3}$$

The correctness of this transport is guaranteed by (1)–(3):

$$\forall xs\,s.\, \mathsf{LFS}\,xs\,s \longrightarrow \mathsf{max\_list}\,xs = \mathsf{max\_fset}\,s. \tag{4}$$

We can now readily replace any occurrence of $\mathsf{max\_fset}\,s$ by $\mathsf{max\_list}\,(\mathsf{to\_list}^{\mathsf{fin}}\,s)$ and, vice versa, any occurrence of $\mathsf{max\_list}\,xs$ by $\mathsf{max\_fset}\,(\mathsf{to\_fset}\,xs)$. This process can be extended to many other functions, such as map, filter, intersect, by introducing new terms map_fset, filter_fset, intersect_fset and proving their respectfulness theorems. Indeed, it is a very repetitive task begging for automation.

State of the Art. There are various frameworks to automate the transport of terms along equivalences. Most of them are designed for dependently typed, constructive proof assistants and are based on *type equivalences* [8,9,26,28,29], which play a central role in homotopy type theory. In a nutshell, type equivalences are pairs of functions f, g that are mutually inverse (i.e. $g\,(f\,x) = x$ and $f\,(g\,y) = y$) together with a compatibility condition. They cannot solve our problem since $\mathsf{to\_fset}$ and $\mathsf{to\_list}^{\mathsf{fin}}$ are not mutually inverse.

Angiuli et al. [1] note and address this issue in Cubical Agda [32]. Essentially, they first quotient both types and then obtain a type equivalence between the quotiented types. Their approach supports a restricted variant of *quasi-partial equivalence relations* [16] but also uses univalence [33], which is unavailable in major proof assistants like Isabelle/HOL [24] and Lean 3 [22]/Lean 4 [23].

Another existing framework is Isabelle's *Lifting package* [13], which transports terms via *partial quotient types*:

Definition 1. *A partial quotient type* (T, Abs, Rep) *is given by a right-unique and right-total relation* T *and two functions* Abs, Rep *respecting* T, *that is* $T\,x\,y \longrightarrow Abs\,x = y$ *and* $T\,(Rep\,y)\,y$, *for all* x, y.

In fact, $(\mathsf{LFS}, \mathsf{to\_fset}, \mathsf{to\_list}^{\mathsf{fin}})$ forms a partial quotient type. The Lifting package can thus transport our list library to finite sets[1]. However, the package also has its limitations:

Limitations of the Lifting Package. Consider the previous example with one modification: rather than transporting $\mathsf{max\_list}$ to finite sets, we want to transport it to the type of (potentially infinite) sets, $\alpha\,\mathsf{set}$. We cannot build a partial quotient type from $\alpha\,\mathsf{list}$ to $\alpha\,\mathsf{set}$ because the required relation $T : \alpha\,\mathsf{list} \Rightarrow \alpha\,\mathsf{set} \Rightarrow \mathsf{bool}$ is not right-total (we can only relate finite sets to lists). The Lifting package is stuck. But in theory, we can (almost) repeat the previous process: There is again a function $\mathsf{to\_set} : \alpha\,\mathsf{list} \Rightarrow \alpha\,\mathsf{set}$. We can define a relation $\mathsf{LS}\,xs\,s := \mathsf{to\_set}\,xs = s$. We can again prove that $\mathsf{max\_list}$ respects LS:

$$\forall xs\,ys.\,\mathsf{to\_set}\,xs = \mathsf{to\_set}\,ys \longrightarrow \mathsf{max\_list}\,xs = \mathsf{max\_list}\,ys. \tag{5}$$

There is a function $\mathsf{to\_list} : \alpha\,\mathsf{set} \Rightarrow \alpha\,\mathsf{list}$, and we obtain a *partial* equivalence:

$$\forall xs.\,\mathsf{LS}\,xs\,(\mathsf{to\_set}\,xs) \quad \text{and} \quad \forall s.\,\mathsf{finite}\,s \longrightarrow \mathsf{LS}\,(\mathsf{to\_list}\,s)\,s. \tag{6}$$

We can define the function $\mathsf{max\_set}\,s := \mathsf{max\_list}\,(\mathsf{to\_list}\,s)$. And we again obtain a correctness theorem: $\forall xs\,s.\,\mathsf{LS}\,xs\,s \longrightarrow \mathsf{max\_list}\,xs = \mathsf{max\_set}\,s$. While this process looks rather similar, there is one subtle change: the second part of Eq. (6) only holds conditionally. As a contribution of this paper, we show that these conditions are not showstoppers, and that we can transport via such partial equivalences in general.

Now one may argue that we could still use partial quotient types to transport from lists to sets: First obtain a right-unique, right-total relation T by building a subtype of the target type. Then transport to the new subtype and then inject to the original type. In spirit, this is close to the approach suggested by Angiuli et al. [1]. But the author finds this unsatisfactory from a practical and a conceptual perspective: From a practical perspective, it introduces unnecessary subtypes to our theory. And conceptually, the process for sets and lists was almost identical to the one for finite sets and lists – there was no detour via subtypes.

A second limitation of the Lifting package is that it does not support *inter-argument dependencies*. For example, take the types of natural numbers, $\mathbb{N}$,

[1] The Lifting package is indeed used pervasively for such purposes. At the time of writing, Isabelle/HOL and the *Archive of Formal Proofs* (https://www.isa-afp.org/) contain more than 2800 invocations of the package.

and integers, $\mathbb{Z}$. We can construct a partial quotient type $(\mathsf{ZN}, \mathsf{to\_nat}, \mathsf{to\_int})$, where $\mathsf{to\_int} : \mathbb{N} \Rightarrow \mathbb{Z}$ is the standard embedding, $\mathsf{to\_nat} : \mathbb{Z} \Rightarrow \mathbb{N}$ is its inverse (a partial function), and $\mathsf{ZN}\, i\, n := i = \mathsf{to\_int}\, n$. It then seems straightforward to transport subtraction $(-_{\mathbb{Z}}) : \mathbb{Z} \Rightarrow \mathbb{Z} \Rightarrow \mathbb{Z}$ from integers to natural numbers in the following way:

$$n_1 -_{\mathbb{N}} n_2 := \mathsf{to\_nat}\left(\mathsf{to\_int}\, n_1 -_{\mathbb{Z}} \mathsf{to\_int}\, n_2\right). \tag{7}$$

And of course, we expect a correctness theorem:

$$\forall i_1\, n_1\, i_2\, n_2.\, \mathsf{ZN}\, i_1\, n_1 \wedge \mathsf{ZN}\, i_2\, n_2 \longrightarrow \mathsf{ZN}\,(i_1 -_{\mathbb{Z}} i_2)\,(n_1 -_{\mathbb{N}} n_2). \tag{8}$$

But alas, the theorem does not hold: we need an extra dependency between the arguments of the respective subtractions, e.g. $i_1 \geq i_2$ or $n_1 \geq n_2$. Unfortunately, the Lifting package's theory [13] cannot account for such dependencies, and as such, the transport attempt for $(-_{\mathbb{Z}})$ fails.

In a similar way, the list index operator $(!!) : \alpha\, \mathsf{list} \Rightarrow \mathbb{N} \Rightarrow \alpha$ can only be transported to the type of arrays for indices that are in bounds (cf. Sect. 5, Example 2). While solutions for dependently typed environments [1,8,9,26,28,29] typically handle such examples by encoding the dependencies in a type, e.g. $(xs : \alpha\, \mathsf{list}) \Rightarrow \{0, \ldots, \mathsf{length}\, xs - 1\} \Rightarrow \alpha$, it is unclear how to support this in a simply typed environment. As a contribution of this paper, we show how to account for such dependencies with the help of *dependent function relators.*

Contributions and Outline. We introduce a new transport framework – simply called Transport. Our framework (1) is applicable to simple type theory, (2) is richer than previous approaches working on partial quotient types, and (3) is based on standard mathematical notions, particularly Galois connections and equivalences. In Sect. 2, we distil the essence of what we expect when we transport terms via equivalences. The derived set of minimal expectations motivates us to base our framework on Galois connections.

To meet these expectations, we introduce the notion of partial Galois connections, which generalise (standard) Galois connections and partial quotient types, in Sect. 3.4. We also introduce a generalisation of the well-known function relator that allows for dependent relations in Sect. 3.2.

Section 4 builds the technical core of the paper. We derive closure conditions for partial Galois connections and equivalences as well as typical order properties (reflexivity, transitivity, etc.). Specifically, we show closure properties under (dependent) function relators, relators for (co)datatypes, and composition. All these results are novel and formalised in Isabelle/HOL.

Based on our theory, we implemented a prototype for automated transports in Isabelle/HOL and illustrate its usage in Sect. 5. We conclude with related work in Sect. 6 and future work in Sect. 7.

This article's extended version [14] includes the formalisation and a guide linking all definitions, results, and examples to their formal counterpart in Isabelle/HOL.

2 The Essence of Transport

Existing frameworks, although beneficial in practical contexts, are unapplicable to our introductory examples. We hence first want to find *the essence of transport*[2]. To find this essence, we have to answer the following question:

What are the minimum expectations when we transport terms via equivalences?

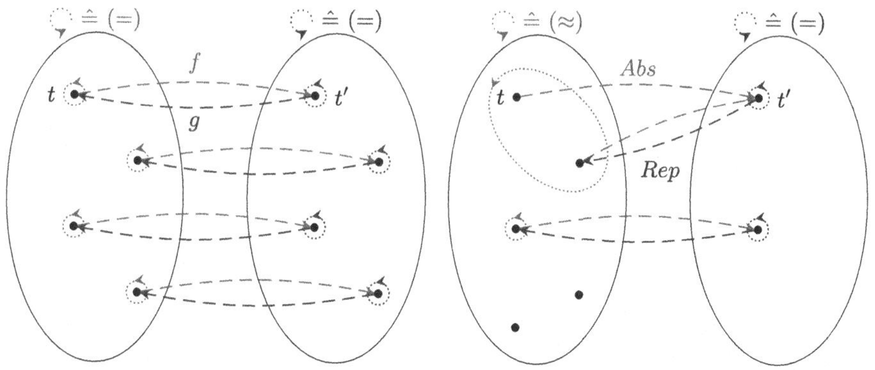

(a) Example of a type equivalence. Left and right-hand side relation are restricted to be equality.

(b) Example of a partial quotient type. The left relation can be an arbitrary partial equivalence relation. The right relation is restricted to be equality.

Fig. 1. Examples of equivalences used in prior work. Types are drawn solid, black. Transport functions are drawn dashed. Each equivalence gives rise to a number of equivalence classes on the left and right-hand side of the equivalence, which are drawn dotted. Arrows inside equivalence classes are omitted.

In this section, we argue that Galois connections are the right notion to cover this essence. Let us examine prior work to identify some guiding principles.

Type Equivalences. Much recent work is based on type equivalences [1,8,9,26, 28,29]. We denote a type equivalence between α and β with mutual inverses $f : \alpha \Rightarrow \beta$ and $g : \beta \Rightarrow \alpha$ by $(\alpha \simeq \beta)\, f\, g$. Then, on a high level, given a set of equivalences $(\alpha_i \simeq \beta_i)\, f_i\, g_i$ for $1 \leq i \leq n$ and two target types α, β that may include α_i, β_i, one tries to build an equivalence $(\alpha \simeq \beta)\, f\, g$. Given a term $t : \alpha$, we can then define $t' := f\, t$, satisfying $t = g\, t'$. Symmetrically, for a term $t' : \beta$, we can define $t := g\, t'$, satisfying $f\, t = t'$. This situation is depicted in Fig. 1(a).

[2] To avoid confusion, our work is not about the transport map from homotopy type theory [31, Chapter 2]. We focus on the general task of transporting a term t to another term t' along some notion of equivalence (not necessarily a type equivalence).

Partial Quotient Types. The Lifting package [13] is based on partial quotient types (T, Abs, Rep) (see Definition 1). Every partial quotient type induces a relation $(\approx) : \alpha \Rightarrow \alpha \Rightarrow \mathsf{bool}$ that identifies values in α that map to the same value in β:

$$x_1 \approx x_2 := \mathsf{in\_dom}\, T\, x_1 \wedge Abs\, x_1 = Abs\, x_2. \quad (9)$$

Given a set of partial quotient types $(T_i : \alpha_i \Rightarrow \beta_i \Rightarrow \mathsf{bool}, Abs_i, Rep_i)$ for $1 \leq i \leq n$ and two target types α, β that may include α_i, β_i, the Lifting package tries to build a partial quotient type $(T : \alpha \Rightarrow \beta \Rightarrow \mathsf{bool}, Abs, Rep)$. Given a term t in the domain of $(\approx)$, we can then define $t' := Abs\, t$, satisfying $t \approx Rep\, t'$. Symmetrically, for a term $t' : \beta$, we can define $t := Rep\, t'$, satisfying $Abs\, t = t'$. This situation is depicted in Fig. 1(b).

The Essence. Abstracting from these approaches, we note some commonalities:

- As input, they take base equivalences, which are then used to build more complex equivalences.
- The equivalences include a *left transport function* $l : \alpha \Rightarrow \beta$ and a *right transport function* $r : \beta \Rightarrow \alpha$. They can be used to move terms from one side of the equivalence to a "similar" term on the other side of the equivalence.
- Terms $t : \alpha$ and $t' : \beta$ that are "similar" stand in particular relations: in the case of type equivalences, $t = r\, t'$ and $l\, t = t'$; in the case of Lifting, $t \approx r\, t'$ and $l\, t = t'$. More abstractly, $L\, t\, (r\, t')$ and $R\, (l\, t)\, t'$ for some *left relation* $L : \alpha \Rightarrow \alpha \Rightarrow \mathsf{bool}$ and *right relation* $R : \beta \Rightarrow \beta \Rightarrow \mathsf{bool}$.[3]
- More generally, L and R specify how terms ought to be related in α and β and determine which terms can be meaningfully transported using l and r.
- L, R, l, r are compatible: if terms are related on one side (e.g. $L\, t_1\, t_2$), their transports are related on the other side (e.g. $R\, (l\, t_1)\, (l\, t_2)$).

Based on these commonalities, we can formulate six minimum expectations:

(1) We want to specify how terms in α and β are related using relations L, R.
(2) Transports should be possible by means of functions $l : \alpha \Rightarrow \beta, r : \beta \Rightarrow \alpha$.
(3) The notion of equivalence should be closed under common relators, particularly those for functions and (co)datatypes.
(4) Terms related on one side have transports that are related on the other side.
(5) Transporting a term should result in a term that is "similar" to its input.
(6) "Similar" terms $t : \alpha$ and $t' : \beta$ are related with each other's transports, i.e. $L\, t\, (r\, t')$ and $R\, (l\, t)\, t'$.

Applying Expectation (6) to Expectation (5) then yields the requirements

[3] The choice of $L\, t\, (r\, t'), R\, (l\, t)\, t'$ may seem arbitrary – why not pick $L\, t\, (r\, t'), R\, t'\, (l\, t)$ instead? In the end, the choice does not matter: While the former leads us to (monotone) Galois connections, the latter leads us to antitone Galois connections. Using that L, R form a Galois connection if and only if L, R^{-1} form an antitone Galois connection, every result in this paper can be transformed to its corresponding result on antitone Galois connections by an appropriate instantiation of the framework.

(a) $L\,t\,(r\,(l\,t))$, (b) $R\,(l\,(r\,t'))\,t'$.

At this point, one may notice the similarity to *Galois connections*. A Galois connection between two preorders $(\leq_L)$ and $(\leq_R)$ consists of two functions l and r such that

- l is monotone, that is $x_1 \leq_L x_2 \longrightarrow l\,x_1 \leq_R l\,x_2$ for all x_1, x_2,
- r is monotone, that is $y_1 \leq_R y_2 \longrightarrow r\,y_1 \leq_L r\,y_2$ for all y_1, y_2, and
- $x \leq_L r\,(l\,x)$ and $l\,(r\,y) \leq_R y$ for all x, y.[4]

The final conditions correspond to Requirements (a) and (b) above, while the monotonicity conditions on l and r correspond to Expectation (4).

Other Motivations. A second motivation to base our framework on Galois connections comes from category theory. There, an equivalence between two categories L, R is given by two functors $l : L \to R$ and $r : R \to L$ and two natural isomorphisms $\eta : Id_L \to r \circ l$ and $\epsilon : l \circ r \to Id_R$. Applied to preorders $(\leq_L), (\leq_R)$ and monotone functions l, r, this translates to the four conditions

(a) $x \leq_L r\,(l\,x)$, (b) $l\,(r\,y) \leq_R y$, (c) $r\,(l\,x) \leq_L x$, (d) $y \leq_R l\,(r\,y)$.

A related categorical concept is that of an *adjunction*. When applied to preorders and monotone functions, an adjunction is similar to an equivalence but is only required to satisfy Conditions (a) and (b). In fact, while Galois connections are not categorical equivalences, they are adjunctions. From this perspective, a Galois connection can be seen as a weak form of an (order) equivalence.

A final motivation is the applicability and wide-spread use of Galois connections. They are fundamental in the closely related field of abstract interpretation [5,7], where they are used to relate concrete to abstract domains. Moreover, they are pervasive throughout mathematics. In the words of Saunders Mac Lane:

> *The slogan is "Adjoint functors arise everywhere".*
>
> (Categories for the Working Mathematician)

We hope our exposition convinced the reader that Galois connections are a suitable notion to cover the essence of transport. The remaining challenges are

- to bring the notion of Galois connections to a partial world – the relations L, R may only be defined on a subset of α, β – and
- to check the closure properties of our definitions under common relators.

3 Partial Galois Connections, Equivalences, and Relators

In the previous section, we singled out Galois connections as a promising candidate for TRANSPORT. Now we want to bring our ideas to the formal world of proof assistants. In this section, we introduce the required background theory for this endeavour. In the following, we fix two relations $L : \alpha \Rightarrow \alpha \Rightarrow \mathsf{bool}$, $R : \beta \Rightarrow \beta \Rightarrow \mathsf{bool}$ and two functions $l : \alpha \Rightarrow \beta$, $r : \beta \Rightarrow \alpha$.

[4] These two conditions are equivalent to requiring $x \leq_L r\,y \longleftrightarrow l\,x \leq_R y$ for all x, y.

3.1 (Order) Basics

We work in a polymorphic, simple type theory [3], as employed, for example, in Isabelle/HOL [24]. In particular, our formalisation uses function extensionality. We assume basic familiarity with Isabelle's syntax. Here, we only recap the most important concepts for our work. A complete list of definitions can be found in [14, Appendix A.1].

A *predicate on a type* α is a function of type $\alpha \Rightarrow \mathsf{bool}$. A *relation on* α *and* β is a function of type $\alpha \Rightarrow \beta \Rightarrow \mathsf{bool}$. *Composition of two relations* R, S is defined as $(R \circ S)\, x\, y := \exists z.\, R\, x\, z \wedge S\, z\, y$. A *relation* R *is finer than a relation* S, written $R \leq S$, if $\forall x\, y.\, R\, x\, y \longrightarrow S\, x\, y$. It will be convenient to interpret relations as infix operators. For every relation R, we hence introduce an infix operator $(\leq_R) := R$, that is $x \leq_R y \longleftrightarrow R\, x\, y$. We also write $(\geq_R) := (\leq_R)^{-1}$. The *field predicate on a relation* is defined as $\mathsf{in\_field}\, R\, x := \mathsf{in\_dom}\, R\, x \vee \mathsf{in\_codom}\, R\, x$.

We use relativised versions of well-known order-theoretic concepts. For example, given a predicate P, we define *reflexivity on* P *and* R as $\mathsf{reflexive\_on}\, P\, R := \forall x.\, P\, x \longrightarrow R\, x\, x$. We proceed analogously for other standard order-theoretic concepts, such as transitivity, preorders, etc. (see [14, Appendix A.1]).

3.2 Function Relators and Monotonicity

We introduce a generalisation of the well-known function relator (see e.g. [25]). The slogan of the function relator is "related functions map related inputs to related outputs". Our generalisation – the *dependent function relator* – additionally allows its target relation to depend on both inputs:

$$([x\, y :: R] \Rrightarrow S)\, f\, g := \forall x\, y.\, R\, x\, y \longrightarrow S\, (f\, x)\, (g\, y), \tag{10}$$

where x, y may occur freely in S. The well-known *(non-dependent) function relator* is given as a special case: $(R \Rrightarrow S) := ([\_\ \_ :: R] \Rrightarrow S)$. A function is *monotone from* R *to* S if it maps R-related inputs to S-related outputs:

$$([x\, y :: R] \Rrightarrow_{\mathsf{m}} S)\, f := ([x\, y :: R] \Rrightarrow S)\, f\, f, \tag{11}$$

where x, y may occur freely in S. A *monotone function relator* is like a function relator but additionally requires its members to be monotone:

$$\begin{aligned}([x\, y :: R] \Rrightarrow^{\oplus} S)\, f\, g :=& ([x\, y :: R] \Rrightarrow S)\, f\, g \\ & \wedge ([x\, y :: R] \Rrightarrow_{\mathsf{m}} S)\, f \wedge ([x\, y :: R] \Rrightarrow_{\mathsf{m}} S)\, g,\end{aligned} \tag{12}$$

where x, y may occur freely in S. In some examples, we have to include conditionals in our relators. For this, we define the *relational if conditional* $\mathsf{rel\_if}\, B\, S\, x\, y := B \longrightarrow S\, x\, y$ and set the following notation:

$$([x\, y :: R \mid B] \Rrightarrow S) := ([x\, y :: R] \Rrightarrow \mathsf{rel\_if}\, B\, S), \tag{13}$$

where x, y may occur freely in B, S.

3.3 Galois Relator

In Expectation (6) of Sect. 2, we noted that "similar" terms t, t' are related with each other's transports, i.e. $L\, t\,(r\, t')$ and $R\,(l\, t)\, t'$. We now define this relation formally, calling it the *Galois relator*:

$$\mathsf{Galois}\,(\leq_L)\,(\leq_R)\, r\, x\, y := \mathsf{in\_codom}(\leq_R)\, y \wedge x \leq_L r\, y \tag{14}$$

When the parameters are clear from the context, we will use the infix notation $({}_L\lessapprox) := \mathsf{Galois}\,(\leq_L)\,(\leq_R)\, r$. It is easy to show that Galois relators generalise the transport relations of partial quotient types:

Lemma 1. *For every partial quotient type (T, l, r) with induced left relation $(\leq_L)$, we have $T = \mathsf{Galois}\,(\leq_L)\,(=)\, r$.*

3.4 Partial Galois Connections and Equivalences

In their standard form, Galois connections are defined on preorders $(\leq_L), (\leq_R)$, where every $x : \alpha$ is in the domain of $(\leq_L)$ and every $y : \beta$ is in the domain of $(\leq_R)$. But as we have seen, this is not generally the case when transporting terms.

We hence lift the notion of Galois connections to a partial setting. We also do not assume any order axioms on $(\leq_L), (\leq_R)$ a priori but add them as needed. In our formalisation, we moreover break the concept of Galois connections down into smaller pieces that, to our knowledge, do not appear as such in the literature. This allows us to obtain very precise results when deriving the closure properties for our definitions (Sect. 4). But for reasons of brevity, we only state the main definitions and results here. Details can be found in [14, Appendix A.4].

The *(partial) Galois property* is defined as:

$$\begin{aligned}((\leq_L) \trianglelefteq (\leq_R))\, l\, r :=& \forall x\, y.\, \mathsf{in\_dom}\,(\leq_L)\, x \wedge \mathsf{in\_codom}(\leq_R)\, y \longrightarrow \\ & (x \leq_L r\, y \longleftrightarrow l\, x \leq_R y).\end{aligned} \tag{15}$$

If l and r are also monotone, we obtain a *(partial) Galois connection*:

$$\begin{aligned}((\leq_L) \dashv (\leq_R))\, l\, r :=& ((\leq_L) \trianglelefteq (\leq_R))\, l\, r \\ & \wedge ((\leq_L) \Rrightarrow_{\mathsf{m}} (\leq_R))\, l \wedge ((\leq_R) \Rrightarrow_{\mathsf{m}} (\leq_L))\, r.\end{aligned} \tag{16}$$

We omit the qualifier "partial" when referring to these definitions, unless we want to avoid ambiguity. An example Galois connection can be found in Fig. 2(a).

As mentioned in Sect. 2, Galois connections can be seen as a weak form of an equivalence. Unfortunately, they are not in general closed under compositions (cf. Sect. 4.3), where we need a stronger form of an equivalence. We can obtain a suitable strengthening by requiring a two-sided Galois connection, which we call a *(partial) Galois equivalence*:

$$((\leq_L) \equiv_{\mathsf{G}} (\leq_R))\, l\, r := ((\leq_L) \dashv (\leq_R))\, l\, r \wedge ((\leq_R) \dashv (\leq_L))\, r\, l \tag{17}$$

An example of a Galois equivalence can be found in Fig. 2(b). It can be shown that Galois equivalences are, under mild conditions, equivalent to the traditional notion of (partial) order equivalences (see [14, Appendix A.4]).

In practice, the relations $(\leq_L), (\leq_R)$ are often preorders or partial equivalence relations (PERs). Given some $((\leq_L) \equiv_{\mathsf{G}} (\leq_R))\, l\, r$, we hence introduce the notations $((\leq_L) \equiv_{\mathsf{pre}} (\leq_R))\, l\, r$ and $((\leq_L) \equiv_{\mathsf{PER}} (\leq_R))\, l\, r$ in case both relations $(\leq_L), (\leq_R)$ are preorders and PERs on their domain, respectively. It is easy to show that Galois equivalences generalise partial quotient types:

Lemma 2. *(T, l, r) is a partial quotient type with induced left relation $(\leq_L)$ if and only if $((\leq_L) \equiv_{\mathsf{PER}} (=))\, l\, r$.*

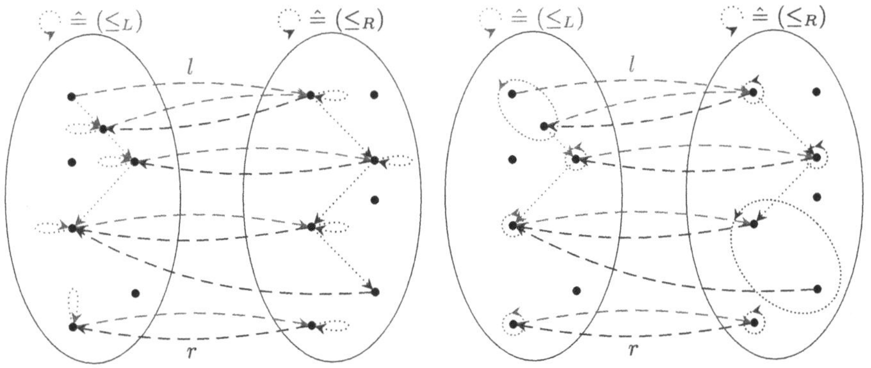

(a) A partial Galois connection. Note that unlike in Fig. 1, the relations may not decompose into equivalence classes.

(b) A partial Galois equivalence. The relations decompose into "strongly connected components", drawn as dotted circles. Any two members in such a component are connected. These arrows are omitted.

Fig. 2. Examples of partial equivalences as defined in (16), (17). Types are drawn solid, black, transport functions dashed, and left and right relations dotted.

4 Closure Properties

We now explore the closure properties of partial Galois connections and equivalences, as well as standard order properties, such as reflexivity and transitivity. We will derive closure conditions for the dependent function relator, relators for (co)datatypes, and composition. In each case, we will also derive conditions under which the Galois relator aligns with the context-dependent notion of "similarity".

For reasons of brevity, we only show that our framework is robust under Galois equivalences on preorders (and thus PERs) here. The results for Galois connections (and proof sketches) can be found in [14, Appendix B.1].

4.1 (Dependent) Function Relator

In the field of abstract interpretation, it is well-known that Galois connections, as usually defined in the literature, are closed under the non-dependent, monotone function relator (see for example [7]). We generalise this result to partial Galois connections and to dependent function relators.

Remark 1. The relations and functions we use are often non-dependent in practice. The following definitions and theorems are considerably simpler in this case. The reader hence might find instructive to first consult the results for this special case in [14, Appendix B.1].

The Setup. In Sect. 1, we highlighted the need of inter-argument dependencies when transporting functions. For example, we may only transport the index operator $(!!) : \alpha\,\mathsf{list} \Rightarrow \mathbb{N} \Rightarrow \alpha$ if a given index is not out of bounds for a given list. We can realise such dependencies with the help of the dependent function relator from Sect. 3.2. For this, we fix the following variables:

$$\begin{aligned}
&L_1 : \alpha_1 \Rightarrow \alpha_1 \Rightarrow \mathsf{bool}, && l_1 : \alpha_1 \Rightarrow \alpha_2,\\
&R_1 : \alpha_2 \Rightarrow \alpha_2 \Rightarrow \mathsf{bool}, && r_1 : \alpha_2 \Rightarrow \alpha_1,\\
&L_2 : \alpha_1 \Rightarrow \alpha_1 \Rightarrow \beta_1 \Rightarrow \beta_1 \Rightarrow \mathsf{bool}, && l_2 : \alpha_2 \Rightarrow \alpha_1 \Rightarrow \beta_1 \Rightarrow \beta_2,\\
&R_2 : \alpha_2 \Rightarrow \alpha_2 \Rightarrow \beta_2 \Rightarrow \beta_2 \Rightarrow \mathsf{bool}, && r_2 : \alpha_1 \Rightarrow \alpha_2 \Rightarrow \beta_2 \Rightarrow \beta_1.
\end{aligned}$$

Each variable L_2, R_2, l_2, r_2 takes parameters from α_1, α_2. These parameters enable the expression of inter-argument dependencies (cf. Sect. 5, Example 2). We hence call L_2, R_2, l_2, r_2 the *dependent variables*. Intuitively, we are in a situation where

(1) we are given an equivalence between $(\leq_{L_1})$ and $(\leq_{R_1})$, using l_1 and r_1,
(2) whenever $x \;{}_{L_1}\!\lessapprox x'$, we are given an equivalence between $(\leq_{L_2\, x\, (r_1\, x')})$ and $(\leq_{R_1\, (l_1\, x)\, x'})$, using the transport functions $l_2\, x'\, x$ and $r_2\, x\, x'$, and
(3) we want to construct an equivalence for functions between $\big([x_1\, x_2 :: (\leq_{L_1})] \Rrightarrow^{\oplus} (\leq_{L_2\, x_1\, x_2})\big)$ and $\big([x'_1\, x'_2 :: (\leq_{R_1})] \Rrightarrow^{\oplus} (\leq_{R_2\, x'_1\, x'_2})\big)$.

To define suitable transport functions, we use the *dependent function mapper*:

$$\big([x :: f]\!\rightarrow g\big)\, h\, x := g\,(f\,x)\,(h\,(f\,x)), \tag{18}$$

where x may occur freely in g. We can now define the target relations and transport functions:

$$\begin{aligned}
L &:= \big([x_1\, x_2 :: (\leq_{L_1})] \Rrightarrow^{\oplus} (\leq_{L_2\, x_1\, x_2})\big), & l &:= \big([x' :: r_1]\!\rightarrow l_2\, x'\big),\\
R &:= \big([x'_1\, x'_2 :: (\leq_{R_1})] \Rrightarrow^{\oplus} (\leq_{R_2\, x'_1\, x'_2})\big), & r &:= \big([x :: l_1]\!\rightarrow r_2\, x\big).
\end{aligned} \tag{19}$$

In particular, $l\, f\, x' = l_2\, x'\,(r_1\, x')\,\big(f\,(r_1\, x')\big)$ and $r\, g\, x = r_2\, x\,(l_1\, x)\,\big(g\,(l_1\, x)\big)$.

Closure Theorems. Checking the closure of order-theoretic concepts, such as reflexivity, transitivity, and symmetry, is fairly straightforward. Verifying the closure of Galois connections and equivalences, however, is nuanced, requiring careful alignment of the dependent variables' parameters. These alignments require the following *monotonicity conditions*, which, broadly speaking, say that (1) L_2, R_2 are antimonotone in their first and monotone in their second parameter, and (2) l_2, r_2 are monotone in both parameters:

(i) If $x_1 \leq_{L_1} x_2 \leq_{L_1} x_3 \leq_{L_1} x_4$ then $(\leq_{L_2\, x_2\, x_3}) \leq (\leq_{L_2\, x_1\, x_4})$.
(ii) If $x_1' \leq_{R_1} x_2' \leq_{R_1} x_3' \leq_{R_1} x_4'$ then $(\leq_{R_2\, x_2'\, x_3'}) \leq (\leq_{R_2\, x_1'\, x_4'})$.
(iii) If $x_1 \leq_{L_1} x_2 \ {}_{L_1}\lessapprox x_1' \leq_{R_1} x_2'$ and $\mathsf{in\_field}\, (\leq_{L_2\, x_1\, (r_1\, x_2')})\, y$ then $(l_2\, x_1'\, x_1\, y) \leq_{R_2\, (l_1\, x_1)\, x_2'} (l_2\, x_2'\, x_2\, y)$.
(iv) If $x_1 \leq_{L_1} x_2 \ {}_{L_1}\lessapprox x_1' \leq_{R_1} x_2'$ and $\mathsf{in\_field}\, (\leq_{R_2\, (l_1\, x_1)\, x_2'})\, y'$ then $(r_2\, x_1\, x_1'\, y') \leq_{L_2\, x_1\, (r_1\, x_2')} (r_2\, x_2\, x_2'\, y')$.

We are now ready to state our main result for Galois equivalences on preorders and PERs. The result for Galois connections (and a proof sketch) can be found in [14, Appendix B.1]. All other results can be found in our formalisation.

Theorem 1. *Let* $\star \in \{\equiv_{\mathsf{pre}}, \equiv_{\mathsf{PER}}\}$ *and assume*

(**1**) $((\leq_{L_1}) \star (\leq_{R_1}))\, l\, r$,
(**2**) *if* $x \ {}_{L_1}\lessapprox x'$ *then* $((\leq_{L_2\, x\, (r_1\, x')}) \star (\leq_{R_2\, (l_1\, x)\, x'}))\, (l_2\, x'\, x)\, (r_2\, x\, x')$,
(**3**) *Conditions (i)–(iv).*

Then $((\leq_L) \star (\leq_R))\, l\, r$.

"Similarity". Given the closure theorem, we can readily transport a function f from $(\leq_L)$ to a function g in $(\leq_R)$. Due to Expectations (4) and (6), we also know that $f \ {}_{L}\lessapprox g$, that is $([x_1\, x_2 :: (\leq_{L_1})] \Rrightarrow^{\oplus} (\leq_{L_2\, x_1\, x_2}))\, f\, (r\, g)$ and $([x_1'\, x_2' :: (\leq_{R_1})] \Rrightarrow^{\oplus} (\leq_{R_2\, x_1'\, x_2'}))\, (l\, f)\, r$. But arguably, this is not quite enough:

Remember the slogan of the function relator: "related functions map related inputs to related outputs". We know how to relate terms between $(\leq_{L_1})$ and $(\leq_{R_1})$: we can use $({}_{L_1}\lessapprox)$. Whenever $x \ {}_{L_1}\lessapprox x'$, we also know how to relate terms between $(\leq_{L_2\, x\, (r_1\, x')})$ and $(\leq_{R_2\, (l_1\, x)\, x'})$: we can use

$$({}_{L_2\, x\, x'}\lessapprox) := \mathsf{Galois}\, (\leq_{L_2\, x\, (r_1\, x')})\, (\leq_{R_2\, (l_1\, x)\, x'})\, (r_2\, x\, x'). \tag{20}$$

So when we say that "f and g are similar", we may actually desire that

$$([x\, x' :: ({}_{L_1}\lessapprox)] \Rrightarrow ({}_{L_2\, x\, x'}\lessapprox))\, f\, g. \tag{21}$$

The following theorem answers when $({}_{L}\lessapprox)$ aligns with this definition of similarity for preordered Galois equivalences. Preciser results can be found in [14, Appendix B.1] and the formalisation.

Theorem 2. *Assume*

(1) $((\leq_{L_1}) \equiv_{\mathsf{pre}} (\leq_{R_1}))\, l_1\, r_1$,
(2) *if* $x \;{}_{L_1}\!\lessapprox x'$ *then* $((\leq_{L_2\, x\, (r_1\, x')}) \equiv_{\mathsf{pre}} (\leq_{R_2\, (l_1\, x)\, x'}))\, (l_2\, x'\, x)(r_2\, x\, x')$,
(3) *Conditions (i) and (iv),*
(4) $\mathsf{in\_dom}\, (\leq_L)\, f$, *and* $\mathsf{in\_codom}\, (\leq_R)\, g$.

Then $f \;{}_{L}\!\lessapprox g \longleftrightarrow ([x\, x' :: ({}_{L_1}\!\lessapprox)] \Rrightarrow ({}_{L_2\, x\, x'}\!\lessapprox))\, f\, g$.

4.2 (Co)datatypes

Different proof assistants ground (co)datatypes in different ways. For instance, Coq and Lean introduce them axiomatically, whereas Isabelle/HOL proves their existence using the theory of *bounded natural functors* [30]. As our formalisation takes place in Isabelle/HOL, we use the latter theory. Nonetheless, the results presented in this section are relatively straightforward and can likely be adapted to other "reasonable" definitions of (co)datatypes.

In this section, we derive closure properties for arbitrary *natural functors.* A natural functor is a bounded natural functor without cardinality constraints. The exact axioms can be found elsewhere [30]. For our purposes, it suffices to say that natural functors are equipped with a *mapper* and a *relator.* More precisely, for every n-ary natural functor $(\alpha_1, \dots, \alpha_n)\, F$, there are two functions:

$$\begin{aligned}
\mathsf{map}_F &: (\alpha_1 \Rightarrow \beta_1) \Rightarrow \cdots \Rightarrow (\alpha_n \Rightarrow \beta_n) \Rightarrow (\alpha_1, \dots, \alpha_n)\, F \Rightarrow (\beta_1, \dots, \beta_n)\, F \\
\mathsf{rel}_F &: (\alpha_1 \Rightarrow \beta_1 \Rightarrow \mathsf{bool}) \Rightarrow \cdots \Rightarrow (\alpha_n \Rightarrow \beta_n \Rightarrow \mathsf{bool}) \Rightarrow \\
&\quad (\alpha_1, \dots, \alpha_n)\, F \Rightarrow (\beta_1, \dots, \beta_n)\, F \Rightarrow \mathsf{bool}
\end{aligned}$$

The former lifts functions on the functor's type arguments to the functorial structure, the latter lifts relations on the functor's type arguments to the functorial structure. Using the mapper and relator, it is straightforward to define appropriate target relations and transport functions. First we fix the following variables for $1 \leq i \leq n$:

$$L_i : \alpha_i \Rightarrow \alpha_i \Rightarrow \mathsf{bool}, \quad l_i : \alpha_i \Rightarrow \beta_i, \quad R_i : \beta_i \Rightarrow \beta_i \Rightarrow \mathsf{bool}, \quad r_i : \beta_i \Rightarrow \alpha_i.$$

Then we define the new target relations and transport functions as follows:

$$\begin{aligned}
L &:= \mathsf{rel}_F\, (\leq_{L_1})\, \dots\, (\leq_{L_n}), & l &:= \mathsf{map}_F\, l_1\, \dots\, l_n, \\
R &:= \mathsf{rel}_F\, (\leq_{R_1})\, \dots\, (\leq_{R_n}), & r &:= \mathsf{map}_F\, r_1\, \dots\, r_n.
\end{aligned} \tag{22}$$

The closure properties follow without any difficulty:

Theorem 3. *Let* $\star \in \{\dashv, \equiv_{\mathsf{G}}, \equiv_{\mathsf{pre}}, \equiv_{\mathsf{PER}}\}$ *and assume* $((\leq_{L_i}) \star (\leq_{R_i}))\, l_i\, r_i$ *for* $1 \leq i \leq n$. *Then* $((\leq_L) \star (\leq_R))\, l\, r$.

As in the previous section, we can ponder whether the relation $({}_{L}\!\lessapprox)$ adequately captures our desired notion of "similarity". Again, we already know how to relate terms between $(\leq_{L_i})$ and $(\leq_{R_i})$ for $1 \leq i \leq n$: we can use $({}_{L_i}\!\lessapprox)$. We also know how to relate two functors: we can use rel_F. We thus may desire that "t and t' are similar" when $\mathsf{rel}_F\, ({}_{L_1}\!\lessapprox)\, \dots\, ({}_{L_n}\!\lessapprox)\, t\, t'$. It is easy to show that $({}_{L}\!\lessapprox)$ aligns with this desire:

Theorem 4. $({}_{L}\lessapprox) = \mathsf{rel}_F\,({}_{L_1}\lessapprox)\ \dots\ ({}_{L_n}\lessapprox)$.

Proof details for this section can be found in our formalisation. The formalisation includes tactic scripts that are applicable to functors of arbitrary arity. Integrating them into Isabelle/HOL's datatype package is left as future work.

4.3 Compositions

It is well-known that Galois connections, as defined in the literature, are closed under composition in the following sense: given Galois connections between $(\leq_{L_1}), (\leq_{R_1})$ and $(\leq_{L_2}), (\leq_{R_2})$ with $(\leq_{R_1}) = (\leq_{L_2})$, we can build a Galois connection between $(\leq_{L_1}), (\leq_{R_2})$. This result readily generalises to our partial setting (see [14, Appendix B.2]). However, $(\leq_{R_1})$ and $(\leq_{L_2})$ usually do not coincide in our context. We need a more general result.

The Setup. Our goal is to define a notion of composition that works even if $(\leq_{R_1})$ and $(\leq_{L_2})$ do not coincide. For this, we fix the variables

$$\begin{array}{llll} L_1 : \alpha \Rightarrow \alpha \Rightarrow \mathsf{bool}, & l_1 : \alpha \Rightarrow \beta, & R_1 : \beta \Rightarrow \beta \Rightarrow \mathsf{bool}, & r_1 : \beta \Rightarrow \alpha, \\ L_2 : \beta \Rightarrow \beta \Rightarrow \mathsf{bool}, & l_2 : \beta \Rightarrow \gamma, & R_2 : \gamma \Rightarrow \gamma \Rightarrow \mathsf{bool}, & r_2 : \gamma \Rightarrow \beta. \end{array}$$

Intuitively, we are in a situation where

(1) we are given an equivalence between $(\leq_{L_1})$ and $(\leq_{R_1})$, using l_1 and r_1,
(2) we are given an equivalence between $(\leq_{L_2})$ and $(\leq_{R_2})$, using l_2 and r_2, and
(3) we want to construct an equivalence with transport functions $l_2 \circ l_1$ and $r_1 \circ r_2$ between those parts of $(\leq_{L_1})$ and $(\leq_{R_2})$ that can be made "compatible" with respect to these functions. This particularly means that we can apply the transport functions on these parts without leaving the domains of the input equivalences.

The question is: how do we find those parts and how can we make them compatible? The solution we propose is inspired by and generalises the approach of Huffman and Kunčar [13]. We provide details and intuitions for the constructions in [14, Appendix B.2]. The resulting target relations and transport functions are defined as follows (where $({}_{R_i}\lessapprox) := \mathsf{Galois}\,(\leq_{R_i})\,(\leq_{L_i})\,l_i$):

$$\begin{array}{ll} L := ({}_{L_1}\lessapprox) \circ (\leq_{L_2}) \circ ({}_{R_1}\lessapprox), & l := l_2 \circ l_1, \\ R := ({}_{R_2}\lessapprox) \circ (\leq_{R_1}) \circ ({}_{L_2}\lessapprox), & r := r_1 \circ r_2. \end{array} \tag{23}$$

Closure Theorems. Again, we only state our main result for Galois equivalences on preorders and PERs. Preciser results can be found in [14, Appendix B.2] (including a proof sketch) and in our formalisation.

Theorem 5. *Let* $\star \in \{\equiv_{\mathsf{pre}}, \equiv_{\mathsf{PER}}\}$ *and assume*

(1) $\forall i \in \{1, 2\}.\ ((\leq_{L_i}) \star (\leq_{R_i}))\ l_i\, r_i$,
(2) $((\leq_{R_1}) \circ (\leq_{L_2})) = ((\leq_{L_2}) \circ (\leq_{R_1}))$.

Then $((\leq_L) \star (\leq_R))\ l\, r$.

"Similarity". For a final time, we can ponder whether the relation $({}_{L}\lessapprox)$ is sufficient to capture our desired notion of "similarity": Again, we already know how to relate terms between $(\leq_{L_i})$ and $(\leq_{R_i})$ for $i \in \{1,2\}$: we can use $({}_{L_i}\lessapprox)$. We also have a natural way to combine these relations, namely composition. We thus may desire that "t and t' are similar" when $\big(({}_{L_1}\lessapprox) \circ ({}_{L_2}\lessapprox)\big)\, t\, t'$. The next theorem answers when $({}_{L}\lessapprox)$ aligns with this desire for Galois equivalences. Preciser results can be found in [14, Appendix B.2] and the formalisation.

Theorem 6. *Assume*

(1) $\forall i \in \{1,2\}.\ \big((\leq_{L_i}) \equiv_{\mathsf{pre}} (\leq_{R_i})\big)\, l_i\, r_i$,
(2) $\big((\leq_{R_1}) \circ (\leq_{L_2})\big) = \big((\leq_{L_2}) \circ (\leq_{R_1})\big)$,

Then $({}_{L}\lessapprox) = \big(({}_{L_1}\lessapprox) \circ ({}_{L_2}\lessapprox)\big)$.

5 Application Examples

As all our results are formalised in Isabelle/HOL, we can directly use them to manually transport terms in said environment. But that would be rather tiresome. We thus implemented a prototype in Isabelle/ML to automate transports.

The Prototype. The method **trprover** uses registered base equivalences, along with the closure theorems from Sect. 4, to construct more complex equivalences. The prototype is currently restricted to equivalences on partial equivalence relations (PERs) for pragmatic reasons: their closure theorems have fewer assumptions and are hence simpler to apply. Providing automation for weaker equivalences is future work. The current prototype also does not build composition closures (Sect. 4.3) and automates only a fragment of dependent function relators for simplicity reasons. Again, these extensions are future work.

The prototype provides a command **trp**. As input, it takes a term $t : \alpha$ (the term to be transported) and two optional target relations $L : \alpha \Rightarrow \alpha \Rightarrow \mathsf{bool}$, $R : \beta \Rightarrow \beta \Rightarrow \mathsf{bool}$. This is unlike other transport frameworks [9,13,26,29], which only take the term $t : \alpha$ and a target type β. This design decision is crucial since we can neither assume a unique correspondence between types and target relations in practice (cf. Example 3), nor can we express dependencies in types, but we express them using dependent relators (cf. Example 2). The command then opens two goals. The first one asks for an equivalence $\big((\leq_L) \equiv_{\mathsf{PER}} (\leq_R)\big)\, l\, r$, the second one for a proof that $\mathsf{in\_dom}\,(\leq_L)\, t$. On success, it registers a new term t' and a theorem that $t\ {}_{L}\lessapprox\ t'$. It also registers a second theorem where the relator $({}_{L}\lessapprox)$ has been rewritten to its desired form as described in Theorems 2,4, and 6.

The following examples are best explored interactively in our formalisation. We define the *restricted equality relation on predicates* as $x =_P y := P\,x \wedge x = y$ and the *restricted equality relation on sets* as $x =_S y := x \in S \wedge x = y$.

Example 1. It is easy to transport the list and set examples from Sect. 1. We just have to prove the equivalence between $\mathsf{LFS_L}\, xs\, xs' := \mathsf{LFS}\, xs\, (\mathsf{to\_fset}\, xs')$

and $(=) : \mathbb{N}\,\mathsf{fset} \Rightarrow \mathbb{N}\,\mathsf{fset} \Rightarrow \mathsf{bool}$ and invoke our prototype on max_list:

$$\textbf{lemma}\,[\texttt{per\_intro}]\!: (\mathsf{LFS_L} \equiv_{\mathsf{PER}} (=))\ \mathsf{to\_fset}\ \mathsf{to\_list^{fin}}$$
$$\textbf{trp}\ \mathsf{max\_fset} : \mathbb{N}\,\mathsf{fset} \Rightarrow \mathbb{N}\ \textbf{where}\ \mathsf{t} = \mathsf{max\_list}\ \textbf{by trprover}$$

The [per_intro] tag is used by **trprover** to discharge the closure theorems' side conditions. **trp** registers the theorem $(\mathsf{LFS} \Rrightarrow (=))\ \mathsf{max\_list}\ \mathsf{max\_fset}$ and the definition $\mathsf{max\_fset}\,s := \mathsf{max\_list}\,(\mathsf{to\_list^{fin}}\,s)$ as a result. We can also readily transport in the opposite direction or use sets rather than fsets if we define $\mathsf{LS_L}\,xs\,xs' := \mathsf{LS}\,xs\,(\mathsf{to\_set}\,xs')$:

$$\textbf{trp}\ \mathsf{max\_list'} : \mathbb{N}\,\mathsf{list} \Rightarrow \mathbb{N}\ \textbf{where}\ \mathsf{t} = \mathsf{max\_fset}\ \textbf{by trprover}$$
$$\textbf{lemma}\,[\texttt{per\_intro}]\!: (\mathsf{LS_L} \equiv_{\mathsf{PER}} (=_{\mathsf{finite}}))\ \mathsf{to\_set}\ \mathsf{to\_list}$$
$$\textbf{trp}\ \mathsf{max\_set} : \mathbb{N}\,\mathsf{set} \Rightarrow \mathbb{N}\ \textbf{where}\ \mathsf{t} = \mathsf{max\_list}\ \textbf{by trprover}$$

Example 2. As noted in Sect. 1, transporting subtractions $i_1 -_{\mathbb{Z}} i_2$ from $\mathbb{Z}$ to $\mathbb{N}$ requires a dependency $i_1 \geq i_2$. We model this dependency using dependent function relators. We first define $\mathsf{Zpos} := (=_{(\leq)0})$ and then proceed as usual:

$$\textbf{lemma}\,[\texttt{per\_intro}]\!: (\mathsf{Zpos} \equiv_{\mathsf{PER}} (=))\ \mathsf{to\_nat}\ \mathsf{to\_int}$$
$$\textbf{trp}\ (-_{\mathbb{N}}) : \mathbb{N} \Rightarrow \mathbb{N} \Rightarrow \mathbb{N}\ \textbf{where}\ \mathsf{t} = (-_{\mathbb{Z}})$$
$$\textbf{and}\ \mathsf{L} = ([i_1\,\_ :: \mathsf{Zpos}] \Rrightarrow [i_2\,\_ :: \mathsf{Zpos} \mid i_1 \geq i_2] \Rrightarrow \mathsf{Zpos})$$
$$\textbf{and}\ \mathsf{R} = ([n_1\,\_ :: (=)] \Rrightarrow [n_2\,\_ :: (=) \mid n_1 \geq n_2] \Rrightarrow (=))\ \textbf{by trprover}$$

Similarly, operations on datatypes may only conditionally be transportable. For example, we may only transport the index operator $(!!) : \alpha\,\mathsf{list} \Rightarrow \mathbb{N} \Rightarrow \alpha$ to the type of immutable arrays ($\alpha\,\mathsf{iarray}$) if the index is not out of bounds. In the following, let S be an arbitrary partial equivalence relation:

$$\textbf{lemma}\,[\texttt{per\_intro}]\!: (\mathsf{ListRel}\,S \equiv_{\mathsf{PER}} \mathsf{IArrRel}\,S)\ \mathsf{to\_iarr}\ \mathsf{to\_list}$$
$$\textbf{trp}\ \mathsf{iarr\_ind} : \alpha\,\mathsf{iarray} \Rightarrow \mathbb{N} \Rightarrow \alpha\ \textbf{where}\ \mathsf{t} = (!!)$$
$$\textbf{and}\ \mathsf{L} = ([xs\,\_ :: \mathsf{ListRel}\,S] \Rrightarrow [i\,\_ :: (=) \mid i < \mathsf{length}\,xs] \Rrightarrow S)$$
$$\textbf{and}\ \mathsf{R} = ([arr\,\_ :: \mathsf{IArrRel}\,S] \Rrightarrow [i\,\_ :: (=) \mid i < \mathsf{iarr\_length}\,arr] \Rrightarrow S)$$
$$\textbf{by trprover}$$

Example 3. Isabelle/Set [15] is a set-theoretic environment in Isabelle/HOL. Its type of sets is called set. Isabelle/Set provides a *set-extension* mechanism: As input, it takes two sets $A : \mathsf{set}$ and $B : \mathsf{set}$ and an injection from A to B. It then creates a new set $B' \supseteq A$ together with a bijection between B and B' with mutual inverses $l, r : \mathsf{set} \Rightarrow \mathsf{set}$. This mechanism is used to enforce subset relationships. For instance, it first uses a construction of the integers $\mathbb{Z} : \mathsf{set}$ where $\mathbb{N} \not\subseteq \mathbb{Z}$. It then uses the set-extension mechanism to create a copy $\mathbb{Z}' \supseteq \mathbb{N}$ with inverses l, r. Doing so necessitates a manual transport of all definitions from

$\mathbb{Z}$ to $\mathbb{Z}'$. Using TRANSPORT, it is possible to automate this process:

$$\textbf{lemma}\,[\texttt{per\_intro}]\colon ((=_{\mathbb{Z}}) \equiv_{\mathsf{PER}} (=_{\mathbb{Z}'}))\, l\, r$$
$$\textbf{trp}\,(+_{\mathbb{Z}'})\,\textbf{where}\,\mathtt{t} = (+_{\mathbb{Z}})\,\textbf{and}\,\mathtt{L} = \big((=_{\mathbb{Z}}) \Rrightarrow (=_{\mathbb{Z}}) \Rrightarrow (=_{\mathbb{Z}})\big)$$
$$\textbf{and}\,\mathtt{R} = \big((=_{\mathbb{Z}'}) \Rrightarrow (=_{\mathbb{Z}'}) \Rrightarrow (=_{\mathbb{Z}'})\big)\,\textbf{by trprover}$$
$$\textbf{trp}\,(-_{\mathbb{Z}'})\,\textbf{where}\,\mathtt{t} = (-_{\mathbb{Z}})\,\textbf{and}\,\mathtt{L} = \big((=_{\mathbb{Z}}) \Rrightarrow (=_{\mathbb{Z}}) \Rrightarrow (=_{\mathbb{Z}})\big)$$
$$\textbf{and}\,\mathtt{R} = \big((=_{\mathbb{Z}'}) \Rrightarrow (=_{\mathbb{Z}'}) \Rrightarrow (=_{\mathbb{Z}'})\big)\,\textbf{by trprover}$$

Note that all constants $(+_{\mathbb{Z}}), (+_{\mathbb{Z}'}), (-_{\mathbb{Z}}), (-_{\mathbb{Z}'})$ are of the same type $\mathsf{set} \Rightarrow \mathsf{set} \Rightarrow \mathsf{set}$. This stresses the point that users must be able to specify target relations and not just target types.

6 Related Work

Transport in Proof Assistants. Our work was chiefly inspired by Isabelle's Lifting package [13, 17], which transports terms via partial quotient types. All closure theorems in this work generalise the ones in [13]. Besides this source of inspiration, the theory of automated transports has seen prolific work in recent years:

Tabareau et al. [28] proved a strengthened relational parametricity result, called *univalent parametricity*, for the Calculus of Inductive Constructions. Their approach ensures that all relations are compatible with type equivalences. One can then use univalence [33] to seamlessly transport terms between related types. The framework is implemented using Coq's typeclass mechanism [27].

Tabareau et al. [29] extended their work to integrate what they call *"white-box transports"*. White-box transports structurally rewrite a term t to t' using user-specified correspondences. In contrast, *"black-box transports"* transport t without looking at its syntactic structure. For instance, given an equivalence between unary and binary numbers $(\mathbb{N} \simeq \mathsf{Bin})\, l\, r$, black-box transporting the term $0 +_{\mathbb{N}} 0$ results in $l\,(0 +_{\mathbb{N}} 0)$. In contrast, given correspondences between the functions $(+)_{\mathbb{N}}, (+)_{\mathsf{Bin}}$ and constants $0, 0_{\mathsf{Bin}}$, white-box transporting the term results in $0_{\mathsf{Bin}} +_{\mathsf{Bin}} 0_{\mathsf{Bin}}$. These modes can also be mixed: given just the equivalence $(\mathbb{N} \simeq \mathsf{Bin})\, l\, r$ and correspondence between $(+)_{\mathbb{N}}, (+)_{\mathsf{Bin}}$, we obtain $(l\,0) +_{\mathsf{Bin}} (l\,0)$. Isabelle's Lifting package also supports white-box transports via the **transfer** method [17]. While our work is concerned with black-box transports, our prototype also contains experimental support for white-box transports. This integration will be further polished in future work.

Angiuli et al. [1] establish representation independence results in Cubical Agda [32]. Their approach applies to a restricted variant of quasi-partial equivalence relations [16]. Essentially, they quotient two types by a given correspondence to obtain a type equivalence between the quotiented types.

Dagand et al. [8, 9] introduce what they call "type-theoretic partial Galois connections", which are essentially partial type equivalences on an enriched $\alpha\ \mathsf{option}$ type. They allow for partiality on one side of the equivalence but not the other. Their framework is designed for effective program extraction and implemented using Coq's typeclass mechanism.

Ringer et al. [26] developed a Coq plugin to transport proof terms via type equivalences for inductive types. Their theory shares similarities with [28,29], but it directly transforms proof terms. This way, one can remove all references to the old datatype once the proof terms have been transported to the new target type. This is not readily achievable using other mentioned frameworks, including ours.

Type equivalences enjoy the property of having total and mutually inverse transport functions. This is not the case for partial Galois connections, which makes the transport of proofs harder. For example, the parametricity law for equality $(T \Rrightarrow T \Rrightarrow (\longleftrightarrow))\,(=)\,(=)$ holds only if T is left-unique and injective. This is the case if T is described by a type equivalence but not in general by a Galois connection. Kunčar [17] provides parametricity rules for all prominent logical connectives. These rules also apply to our setting and will be crucial when we polish the integration of white-box transports in our prototype.

The works mentioned above all transport terms via certain notions of equivalences. But there are also other approaches, particularly in the field of data refinement. An example is the CoqEAL framework [4], which automatically derives parametricity results using typeclass search. Another one is Isabelle's Autoref framework [18], which derives relational parametricity results using white-box transports. The core inspiration in both cases goes back to [21,25,34]. A comprehensive comparison of these frameworks can be found in [19].

Galois Connections in Computer Science. Galois connections are fundamental in the field of abstract interpretation. Cousot and Cousot's recent book [5] provides an overview of their applications. The closure of Galois connections under non-dependent function relators goes back to at least [6]. We generalised this result to partial Galois connections and dependent function relators in Sect. 4.1. Most work in abstract interpretation does not consider partially defined Galois connections and assumes partial orderings on relations. The work of Miné [20] is an exception, allowing for partiality on one side of the connection but not the other. Darais and Van Horn [10] formalise Galois connections constructively and apply it to tasks in abstract interpretation. An early application of Galois connections was by Hartmanis and Stearns [12]. Though they did not use Galois connections, they introduced an equivalent notion of *pair algebras* [11]. Our Galois relator indeed describes the pair algebra induced by a Galois connection.

7 Conclusion and Future Work

We explored existing notions of equivalences used for automatic transport. Based on this exploration, we identified a set of minimal expectations when transporting terms via equivalences. This essence led us to introduce a new class of equivalences, namely partial Galois connections. Partial Galois connections generalise (standard) Galois connections and apply to relations that are only defined on subsets of their types. We derived closure conditions for partial Galois connections and equivalences, and typical order properties under (dependent) function relators, relators for (co)datatypes, and composition. Our framework applies to simple type theory and – unlike prior solutions for simple type theory – can handle inter-argument dependencies. We implemented a prototype in Isabelle/HOL based on our results. The prototype needs to be further polished, but it can already handle relevant examples that are out of scope for existing tools.

Future Work. As our theory subsumes the one of Isabelle's Lifting package, one goal is to replace the package by a more general tool. To this end, we have to integrate our results into Isabelle's (co)datatypes package [2], extend our prototype to automate the construction of compositions, and polish the support of white-box transports (cf. Sect. 6).

Finally, based on our formalisation insights, we conjecture that one can adopt our theory to constructive logics, but only a formalisation in a constructive prover will give a definite answer.

Acknowledgements. The author thanks the anonymous reviewers of this and a previous submission for their valuable feedback and Mohammad Abdulaziz and Tobias Nipkow for their comments on a draft of this paper.

References

1. Angiuli, C., Cavallo, E., Mörtberg, A., Zeuner, M.: Internalizing representation independence with univalence. Proc. ACM Program. Lang. **5**(POPL), 1–30 (2021). https://doi.org/10.1145/3434293
2. Blanchette, J.C., Hölzl, J., Lochbihler, A., Panny, L., Popescu, A., Traytel, D.: Truly modular (co)datatypes for Isabelle/HOL. In: Klein, G., Gamboa, R. (eds.) ITP 2014. LNCS, vol. 8558, pp. 93–110. Springer, Cham (2014). https://doi.org/10.1007/978-3-319-08970-6_7
3. Church, A.: A formulation of the simple theory of types. J. Symb. Logic **5**(2), 56–68 (1940). https://doi.org/10.2307/2266170
4. Cohen, C., Dénès, M., Mörtberg, A.: Refinements for free! In: Gonthier, G., Norrish, M. (eds.) CPP 2013. LNCS, vol. 8307, pp. 147–162. Springer, Cham (2013). https://doi.org/10.1007/978-3-319-03545-1_10
5. Cousot, P.: Principles of Abstract Interpretation. MIT Press, Cambridge (2021)
6. Cousot, P., Cousot, R.: Static determination of dynamic properties of recursive procedures. In: Neuhold, E. (ed.) IFIP Conference on Formal Description of Programming Concepts, St-Andrews, N.B., CA, North-Holland, pp. 237–277 (1977)
7. Cousot, P., Cousot, R.: Abstract interpretation frameworks. J. Logic Comput. **2**(4), 511–547 (1992). https://doi.org/10.1093/logcom/2.4.511
8. Dagand, P.E., Tabareau, N., Tanter, E.: Partial type equivalences for verified dependent interoperability. SIGPLAN Not. **51**(9), 298–310 (2016). https://doi.org/10.1145/3022670.2951933
9. Dagand, P.E., Tabareau, N., Tanter, E.: Foundations of dependent interoperability. J. Funct. Program. **28** (2018). https://doi.org/10.1017/S0956796818000011
10. Darais, D., Van Horn, D.: Constructive galois connections. J. Funct. Program. **29** (2019). https://doi.org/10.1017/S0956796819000066
11. Derderian, J.C.: Galois connections and pair algebras. Can. J. Math. **21**, 498–501 (1969). https://doi.org/10.4153/CJM-1969-056-x

12. Hartmanis, J., Stearns, R.: Pair algebra and its application to automata theory. Inf. Control **7**(4), 485–507 (1964). https://doi.org/10.1016/S0019-9958(64)90181-0
13. Huffman, B., Kunčar, O.: Lifting and transfer: a modular design for quotients in Isabelle/HOL. In: Gonthier, G., Norrish, M. (eds.) CPP 2013. LNCS, vol. 8307, pp. 131–146. Springer, Cham (2013). https://doi.org/10.1007/978-3-319-03545-1_9
14. Kappelmann, K.: Transport via partial galois connections and equivalences (Extended Version) (2023). https://doi.org/10.48550/arXiv.2303.05244
15. Kappelmann, K., Josh, C., Krauss, A.: Isabelle/Set (2023). https://github.com/kappelmann/Isabelle-Set
16. Krishnaswami, N.R., Dreyer, D.: Internalizing relational parametricity in the extensional calculus of constructions. In: Rocca, S.R.D. (ed.) Computer Science Logic 2013 (CSL 2013). Leibniz International Proceedings in Informatics (LIPIcs), vol. 23, pp. 432–451. Schloss Dagstuhl-Leibniz-Zentrum fuer Informatik, Dagstuhl (2013). https://doi.org/10.4230/LIPIcs.CSL.2013.432
17. Kunčar, O.: Types, Abstraction and Parametric Polymorphism in Higher-Order Logic. Ph.D. thesis, Technische Universität München (2016)
18. Lammich, P.: Automatic data refinement. In: Blazy, S., Paulin-Mohring, C., Pichardie, D. (eds.) ITP 2013. LNCS, vol. 7998, pp. 84–99. Springer, Heidelberg (2013). https://doi.org/10.1007/978-3-642-39634-2_9
19. Lammich, P., Lochbihler, A.: Automatic refinement to efficient data structures: a comparison of two approaches. J. Autom. Reason. **63**(1), 53–94 (2019). https://doi.org/10.1007/s10817-018-9461-9
20. Miné, A.: Weakly Relational Numerical Abstract Domains. Theses, Ecole Polytechnique X (2004). https://pastel.archives-ouvertes.fr/tel-00136630
21. Mitchell, J.C.: Representation independence and data abstraction. In: Proceedings of the 13th ACM SIGACT-SIGPLAN Symposium on Principles of Programming Languages, POPL 1986, pp. 263–276. Association for Computing Machinery, New York (1986). https://doi.org/10.1145/512644.512669
22. de Moura, L., Kong, S., Avigad, J., van Doorn, F., von Raumer, J.: The lean theorem prover (system description). In: Felty, A.P., Middeldorp, A. (eds.) CADE 2015. LNCS (LNAI), vol. 9195, pp. 378–388. Springer, Cham (2015). https://doi.org/10.1007/978-3-319-21401-6_26
23. Moura, L., Ullrich, S.: The lean 4 theorem prover and programming language. In: Platzer, A., Sutcliffe, G. (eds.) CADE 2021. LNCS (LNAI), vol. 12699, pp. 625–635. Springer, Cham (2021). https://doi.org/10.1007/978-3-030-79876-5_37
24. Nipkow, T., Wenzel, M., Paulson, L.C. (eds.): Isabelle/HOL: A Proof Assistant for Higher-Order Logic. LNCS, vol. 2283. Springer, Heidelberg (2002). https://doi.org/10.1007/3-540-45949-9
25. Reynolds, J.C.: Types, abstraction and parametric polymorphism. In: Mason, R.E.A. (ed.) Information Processing 83, Proceedings of the IFIP 9th World Computer Congress, Paris, France, 19–23 September 1983, pp. 513–523. North-Holland/IFIP (1983)
26. Ringer, T., Porter, R., Yazdani, N., Leo, J., Grossman, D.: Proof repair across type equivalences. In: Proceedings of the 42nd ACM SIGPLAN International Conference on Programming Language Design and Implementation, PLDI 2021, pp. 112–127. Association for Computing Machinery, New York (2021). https://doi.org/10.1145/3453483.3454033
27. Sozeau, M., Oury, N.: First-class type classes. In: Mohamed, O.A., Muñoz, C., Tahar, S. (eds.) TPHOLs 2008. LNCS, vol. 5170, pp. 278–293. Springer, Heidelberg (2008). https://doi.org/10.1007/978-3-540-71067-7_23

28. Tabareau, N., Tanter, E., Sozeau, M.: Equivalences for free: univalent parametricity for effective transport. Proc. ACM Program. Lang. **2**(ICFP) (2018). https://doi.org/10.1145/3236787
29. Tabareau, N., Tanter, E., Sozeau, M.: The marriage of univalence and parametricity. J. ACM **68**(1), 1–44 (2021). https://doi.org/10.1145/3429979
30. Traytel, D., Popescu, A., Blanchette, J.C.: Foundational, compositional (co)datatypes for higher-order logic: category theory applied to theorem proving. In: 2012 27th Annual IEEE Symposium on Logic in Computer Science, pp. 596–605 (2012). https://doi.org/10.1109/LICS.2012.75
31. Univalent Foundations Program, T.: Homotopy Type Theory: Univalent Foundations of Mathematics. https://homotopytypetheory.org/book. Institute for Advanced Study (2013)
32. Vezzosi, A., Mörtberg, A., Abel, A.: Cubical Agda: a dependently typed programming language with univalence and higher inductive types. Proc. ACM Program. Lang. **3**(ICFP) (2019). https://doi.org/10.1145/3341691
33. Voevodsky, V.: The equivalence axiom and univalent models of type theory (2010). https://doi.org/10.48550/ARXIV.1402.5556
34. Wadler, P.: Theorems for free! In: Proceedings of the Fourth International Conference on Functional Programming Languages and Computer Architecture, FPCA 1989, pp. 347–359. Association for Computing Machinery, New York (1989). https://doi.org/10.1145/99370.99404

Argument Reduction of Constrained Horn Clauses Using Equality Constraints

Ryo Ikeda, Ryosuke Sato(✉), and Naoki Kobayashi

The University of Tokyo, Tokyo, Japan
rsato@is.s.u-tokyo.ac.jp

Abstract. Constrained Horn Clauses (CHCs) have recently been studied extensively as a common, uniform foundation for automated program verification. Various program verification problems have been shown to be reducible to CHC solving, and accordingly, CHC solvers have been developed by several research groups. We propose a new optimization method for CHC solving, which reduces the number of predicate arguments by finding (conditional) equality constraints among the predicate arguments. The optimization is especially effective for data-driven CHC solvers such as HoIce, as it significantly reduces the number of data required to infer a solution for CHCs. We have implemented our method and confirmed its effectiveness through experiments.

1 Introduction

Much progress has been made recently on Constrained Horn Clauses (CHCs, a.k.a., constraint logic programming) as a common, uniform foundation for automated program verification [1,5,9]. Indeed, various program verification methods [2,3,7,10,15,18,23] that utilize CHC solvers as backend solvers have been proposed, including verification methods for imperative/object-oriented programs [7,10,15,22], and functional programs (via refinement type inference) [3,23]. Accordingly, various CHC solvers [3,6,8,11,13] have been developed such as Z3/Spacer [13], Eldarica [8], HoIce [3], and FreqHorn [24].

As an example of verification problems, let us consider the following imperative program.

```
int x = 0, y = 0, z = 0;
while(x < 500) {
    y += x; z += x + 2; x += 1;
}
z += x;
assert(z >= y + 1000);
```

Suppose we wish to verify that the program above is safe, i.e., the assertion does not fail. This verification problem can be reduced to the satisfiability of the following CHCs, i.e., the problem of checking whether there exists an interpretation

C.-K. Hur (Ed.): APLAS 2023, LNCS 14405, pp. 246–265, 2023.
https://doi.org/10.1007/978-981-99-8311-7_12

for the predicate variable P that makes all the three clauses valid.

$$\begin{aligned} &P(0,0,0). \\ &\forall x,y,z.P(x,y,z) \land x < 500 \implies P(x+1, y+x, z+x+2). \\ &\forall x,y,z.P(x,y,z) \land x \geq 500 \implies z+x \geq y+1000. \end{aligned}$$

Here, each logical formula is a CHC, a Horn clause extended with constraints. The predicate P represents the invariant of the while loop of the original program, where the three arguments of P respectively correspond to the variables x, y, and z. The first clause means that the state $x = y = z = 0$ at the beginning of the loop should satisfy the invariant. The second clause means that the invariant is preserved by the loop, i.e., if $P(x, y, z)$ holds at the beginning of the loop and the loop condition $x < 500$ holds, then, after the execution of the loop body, the loop invariant $P(x+1, y+x, z+x+2)$ should still hold. The last clause means that the asserted condition $z \geq y + 1000$ holds just after the exit of the loop. As in this example, various verification problems can naturally be reduced to the satisfiability problem for CHCs. Although the CHC problem is undecidable in general, various CHC solvers have been developed [3,6,8,11,13], which can efficiently solve a number of instances that arise in practice.

Unfortunately, however, despite extensive efforts to develop efficient CHC solvers, the current CHC solvers are not fully satisfactory. In fact, the state-of-the-art CHC solvers (namely Z3, ELDARICA, HoIce, and FREQHORN) failed to solve the above CHCs (consisting of just three simple clauses!) within 10 min.

To improve the efficiency of CHC solvers, we propose an optimization for reducing the number of predicate arguments by finding linear equality constraints among the predicate arguments. For the example above, $z = 2x + y$ holds whenever $P(x, y, z)$ holds, if P is the least predicate that satisfies the first two clauses. Based on this equality, we can set

$$P(x,y,z) \equiv P'(x,y) \land z = 2x + y$$

for a new predicate $P'(x, y)$, and transform the CHCs above into the following constraints, by replacing $P(x, y, z)$ with $P'(x, y) \land z = 2x + y$.

$$\begin{aligned} &P'(0,0) \land 0 = 2 \cdot 0 + 0 \\ &P'(x,y) \land z = 2x + y \land x < 500 \implies \\ &\qquad P'(x+1, y+x) \land z+x+2 = 2(x+1) + (y+x) \\ &P'(x,y) \land z = 2x + y \land x \geq 500 \implies z+x \geq y+1000. \end{aligned}$$

They can be further simplified to the following CHCs:

$$\begin{aligned} &P'(0,0) \\ &P'(x,y) \land z = 2x + y \land x < 500 \implies P'(x+1, y+x) \\ &P'(x,y) \land z = 2x + y \land x \geq 500 \implies z+x \geq y+1000. \end{aligned}$$

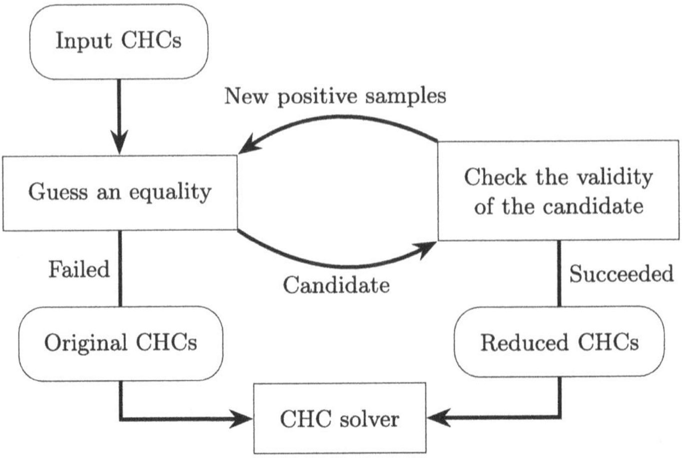

Fig. 1. Overall flow of CHC solving with discovering equality relations

The transformation preserves the satisfiability of CHCs, and given a solution of $P'(x, y) \equiv \varphi$ of the simplified CHCs, we can obtain $P(x, y, z) \equiv \varphi \wedge z = 2x + y$ as a solution of the original CHCs. In this manner, finding equality constraints on predicate arguments allows us to reduce the number of predicate arguments. The resulting CHCs are expected to be much easier to solve, especially for CHC solvers that work in a data-driven manner [3,24]. In fact, for the above example, the simplified CHCs have the trivial solution $P'(x, y) \equiv \textbf{true}$, from which we obtain the solution $P(x, y, z) \equiv z = 2x + y$ for the original CHCs.

To find equality constraints on predicate arguments, we introduce a counterexample-guided method. We collect a set of *positive samples* of a predicate that are combinations of values on which the predicate must evaluate to true, and find an equality relation among the arguments of predicates. For example, in the example above, $(0, 0, 0)$, $(1, 0, 2)$, and $(2, 1, 5)$ are positive samples of the predicate P. By using the positive samples, we can find the relation $z = 2x + y$ based on the Gaussian elimination.

Figure 1 shows the overall flow of our CHC solving method with a mechanism for finding equality relations among the arguments of a predicate. For each predicate in the constraints, we repeatedly (i) synthesize candidate equality constraints from a set of positive samples and (ii) check whether the candidate is an inductive invariant of the predicate (i.e., whether it satisfies the definite clauses); if that is the case, we return the equality constraints. Otherwise, (iii) we can find a new positive sample, which does not satisfy the candidate equality constraints. We then go back to step (i) with the new positive sample set. Once we have found the equality relation, we can reduce one of the arguments appearing in the equality relation as we have seen above. In the example, above, we actually start with the empty set of positive samples, and the initial candidate constraint is $\bot$. We then obtain $(0, 0, 0)$ as a new positive sample (since $P(x, y, z) \equiv \bot$

does not satisfy $P(0,0,0)$), and the candidate equality constraints are updated to $x = y = z = 0$. Then $(1,0,2)$ is found as a new positive sample that does not satisfy the constraints, and the candidate equality constraints are updated to $y = 0 \land z = 2x$. Since $P(x,y,z) \equiv y = 0 \land z = 2x$ does not satisfy the first two clauses either, a new positive sample $(2,1,5)$ is found. At this point, we find a valid equality constraint $z = 2x + y$.

Once an equality constraint is found, we generate a reduced CHC by removing some predicate arguments. The resulting CHC is then passed to an off-the-shelf CHC solver. If we are unable to find an equality constraint within a time limit (if we have set one) or there are no equality constraint that can be expressed in the target domain (such as linear expressions), we simply give the original CHCs to the solver.

We here remark that our method to find equality relations is useful not only for satisfiable instances but also for unsatisfiable instances. For example, suppose that we change the assertion in the first example to $z = y$. By using the equality relation $z = 2x + y$, the goal clause becomes $P'(x,y) \land z + x = 2x + y \land x \geq 500 \implies z = y$, which can be simplified to $P'(x,y) \implies \bot$. The resulting CHCs are trivially unsatisfiable because of the first clause $P'(0,0)$.

Our counterexample-guided method for finding equality constraints can be considered a generalization of Sharma et al. [20] for finding algebraic loop invariants to the setting of CHCs. In particular, the overall flow mentioned above corresponds to the guess-and-check loop of their method. Thanks to the formalization of the method for CHCs (rather than loop programs), our method is applicable to a wider range of program verification problems, including those for functional programs. Fedyukovich et al. [6] also proposed a data-driven method to find and utilize polynomial equalities for solving CHCs, but their method for finding equalities does not work in a counterexample-guided manner. There are other methods for reducing the number of arguments, such as RAF (Redundant Argument Filtering) [14], but they do not utilize arithmetic constraints and are not effective for the above example. Section 6 discusses related work in more detail.

Our contributions are summarized as follows:

- A method to discover (conditional) equality relations among the arguments of the predicates in CHCs by using Gaussian elimination.
- A method to reduce the number of predicate arguments by using discovered (conditional) equalities without changing the satisfiability of CHCs, which can be implemented as a preprocessor for any CHC solver.
- An implementation and experiments to confirm that our method indeed improves the efficiency of HoIce, a data-driven CHC solver.

The rest of this paper is structured as follows. Section 2 reviews the definition of CHCs. Section 3 describes the method to reduce arguments by using equality relations, and Sect. 4 describes an extension of the method introduced in the previous section to deal with conditional equalities. Section 5 reports an implementation and experimental results. Section 6 discusses related work, and Sect. 7 concludes the paper.

2 Preliminaries

In this section, we review the definition of constrained Horn clauses.

A *Constrained Horn Clause* (CHC) is a first-order logic formula of the following form:

$$\forall x_1, \ldots, x_n.\ \varphi \wedge L_1 \wedge \cdots \wedge L_m \implies H$$

where φ is an arithmetic formula, L and H are defined as follows.

$$L \text{ (literal)} ::= P(x_1, \ldots, x_n) \qquad H \text{ (head)} ::= L \mid \bot$$

We use the meta-variable P for predicate variables, e for arithmetic expressions, c for CHCs, and $\mathcal{C}$ for sets of CHCs. For clause $c = \forall x_1, \ldots, x_n.\ \varphi \wedge L_1 \wedge \cdots \wedge L_m \implies H$, we say $\varphi \wedge L_1 \wedge \cdots \wedge L_m$ is the body of c and H is the head of c. We call a clause a *definite clause* if the head of the clause is of the form L, and call a clause a *goal clause* if the head is $\bot$. We write $\mathit{Defs}(\mathcal{C})$ for the set of the definite clauses in $\mathcal{C}$, and write $PV(\mathcal{C})$ for the set of the predicate variables in $\mathcal{C}$. We write $\widetilde{\cdot}$ for a sequence or a tuple of variables/values and write $|\widetilde{\cdot}|$ for its length. For example, $\widetilde{x}$ represents a sequence $x_1, \ldots, x_n$ or a tuple $(x_1, \ldots, x_n)$ where $n = |\widetilde{x}|$. We often omit universal quantifiers of clauses.

In the definition of the CHC, we restrict the arguments of a predicate to only variables, restrict the head of a goal clause to $\bot$, and impose the order restriction on the formula and the literals in the body of a clause. Note that we do not lose the generality by these restrictions. For example, we can represent the CHCs mentioned in the introduction as follows.

Example 1.

$$\begin{array}{ll}
\forall x, y, z. & x = 0 \wedge y = 0 \wedge z = 0 \implies P(x, y, z) \\
\forall x, y, z, x', y', z'. & x < 500 \wedge x' = x + 1 \wedge y' = y + x \wedge z' = z + x + 2 \\
& \qquad \wedge P(x, y, z) \implies P(x', y', z') \\
\forall x, y, z. & x \geq 500 \wedge \neg(z + x \geq y + 1000) \wedge P(x, y, z) \implies \bot
\end{array}$$

In the rest of the paper, assuming such normalization is implicitly applied, we use arithmetic expressions as arguments and the heads of clauses.

We say a set $\mathcal{C}$ of CHCs is *satisfiable* if there exists an assignment of the predicate variables in $PV(\mathcal{C})$ that satisfies all the CHCs in $\mathcal{C}$, and call the assignment a solution of $\mathcal{C}$. Otherwise, we say $\mathcal{C}$ is *unsatisfiable*. For example, the set of CHCs in Example 1 is satisfiable by the solution $[P \mapsto \lambda(x, y, z).\ z = 2x + y]$.

We can check whether the given assignment is a solution of CHCs or not by using a Satisfiability Module Theories (SMT) solver if all the arithmetic formulae appearing in the CHCs and the assignment are decidable logic formulae, e.g., formulae in the quantifier-free linear integer arithmetic. We do not specify the underlying logic, but, for the effectiveness of the method, we assume that the underlying logic is decidable.

3 Argument Reduction by Equality Constraints

In this section, we describe our method for reducing arguments of predicates by finding equality relations among the arguments. As described in the introduction, our method repeatedly guesses equality relations and collects positive samples.

3.1 Guessing Equality Constraints

We first describe how to guess an equality relation from the given set of positive samples. Here, a *positive sample* of a n-arity predicate P is a n-tuple $\widetilde{v}$ of values that $P(\widetilde{v})$ must evaluate to true.

To reduce the arguments of predicate P whose arity is n, we wish to find an equation of the following form:

$$0 = c_0 + \sum_{1 \leq k \leq n} c_k x_k$$

where $x_1, \ldots, x_n$ are the arguments of P and $c_0, \ldots, c_n$ are integer coefficients. This means that, x_i can be represented by using other variables for each i such that $c_i \neq 0$.

Given a set of positive samples $\{(v_{11}, \ldots, v_{1n}), \ldots, (v_{m1}, \ldots, v_{mn})\}$ and we assume that there are at least one positive sample, i.e., $m \neq 0$. If a valid equation of the form above is given, the values v_{jk} in the positive samples also satisfy

$$0 = c_0 + \sum_{1 \leq k \leq n} c_k v_{jk}$$

for any $j \in \{1, \ldots, m\}$. By using vector notations, we can represent this as

$$\mathbf{0} = \left(\mathbf{1}\ \boldsymbol{v}_1 \cdots \boldsymbol{v}_{i-1}\ \boldsymbol{v}_{i+1} \cdots \boldsymbol{v}_n\right)\left(c_0\ c_1 \cdots c_n\right)^{\mathsf{T}}$$

where $\boldsymbol{v}_k = (v_{k1} \cdots v_{km})^{\mathsf{T}}$ for each $k \in \{1, \ldots, n\}$, and $\mathbf{0}$ (resp. $\mathbf{1}$) is the vector $(0 \ldots 0)^{\mathsf{T}}$ (resp. $(1 \ldots 1)^{\mathsf{T}}$). This means that $\boldsymbol{v}_i$ is a linearly dependent vector of the other vectors. Hence, by checking the linearly independencies of the vectors constructed from the positive samples, we can synthesize a candidate of a linear equality on the arguments. This can be performed by applying Gaussian elimination algorithm to the matrix $\left(\mathbf{1}\ \boldsymbol{v}_1 \cdots \boldsymbol{v}_n\right)^{\mathsf{T}}$.

Consider a predicate P whose arity is 5 and the following set of positive samples

$$\{(1,0,0,0,1), (1,0,1,2,2), (2,0,0,0,1), (2,2,2,5,2)\}\,.$$

The matrix we apply Gaussian elimination and the matrices obtained by the operations of Gaussian elimination are as follows:

$$\left(\begin{array}{c|c} 1\,1\,1\,1 & 1 \\ 1\,1\,2\,2 & x_1 \\ 0\,0\,0\,2 & x_2 \\ 0\,1\,0\,2 & x_3 \\ 0\,2\,0\,5 & x_4 \\ 1\,2\,1\,2 & x_5 \end{array}\right) \rightarrow \left(\begin{array}{c|c} 1\,1\,1\,1 & 1 \\ 0\,0\,1\,1 & -1+x_1 \\ 0\,0\,0\,2 & x_2 \\ 0\,1\,0\,2 & x_3 \\ 0\,2\,0\,5 & x_4 \\ 0\,1\,0\,1 & -1+x_5 \end{array}\right) \rightarrow \left(\begin{array}{c|c} 1\,1\,1\;\;1 & 1 \\ 0\,1\,0\;\;2 & x_3 \\ 0\,0\,0\;\;2 & x_2 \\ 0\,0\,1\;\;1 & -1+x_1 \\ 0\,0\,0\;\;1 & -2x_3+x_4 \\ 0\,0\,0\,-1 & -1-x_3+x_5 \end{array}\right)$$

$$\rightarrow \left(\begin{array}{c|c} 1\,1\,1\;\;1 & 1 \\ 0\,1\,0\;\;2 & x_3 \\ 0\,0\,1\;\;1 & -1+x_1 \\ 0\,0\,0\;\;2 & x_2 \\ 0\,0\,0\;\;1 & -2x_3+x_4 \\ 0\,0\,0\,-1 & -1-x_3+x_5 \end{array}\right) \rightarrow \left(\begin{array}{c|c} 1\,1\,1\,1 & 1 \\ 0\,1\,0\,2 & x_3 \\ 0\,0\,1\,1 & -1+x_1 \\ 0\,0\,0\,2 & x_2 \\ 0\,0\,0\,0 & -\frac{1}{2}x_2-2x_3+x_4 \\ 0\,0\,0\,0 & -1+\frac{1}{2}x_2-x_3+x_5 \end{array}\right).$$

Here, we also write the expression correspond to each row in the right-hand side of the coefficient matrix. For example, the bottom line of the first matrix represents that $1, 2, 1, 2$ are the values of the variable x_5 in the positive samples.

Therefore, when we get the row echelon form of the matrix, if all the values of a row are all zero, then the expression represents the equality relations on the variables. In the example above, since the last two lines of the last matrix consist of zeros, we obtain candidates of equality relations on the arguments as

$$0 = -\frac{1}{2}x_2 - 2x_3 + x_4, \qquad 0 = -1 + \frac{1}{2}x_2 - x_3 + x_5.$$

Furthermore, we can normalize the rational number coefficients to integers as

$$0 = -x_2 - 4x_3 + 2x_4, \qquad 0 = -2 + x_2 - 2x_3 + 2x_5.$$

Here, we can regarded x_4 and x_5 as dependent variables since the last two lines of the last matrix correspond to x_4 and x_5. Hence, if the candidate is a valid equality relation, we can remove x_4 and x_5 for the arguments of P.

We note here that, in the first iteration of the equality discovery procedure of Fig. 1, we have no positive samples. In this case, we just return $\lambda\widetilde{x}.\bot$ as the candidate, which can be viewed as the strongest equality.

3.2 Checking Equality Constraints

Once we obtain a candidate equality relation on the arguments of a predicate P, we next check that the candidate equality relation really holds for the values on which P evaluate to true.

Given a set $\mathcal{C}$ of CHCs and a set of equalities whose element is of the form $(P, \lambda\widetilde{x}.(\varphi, \{y_1, \ldots, y_k\}))$, in which φ represents a equality on the arguments $\widetilde{x}$ of P and $\{y_1, \ldots, y_k\}$ are the dependent variables that will be removed. For example, the equality candidate used in Sect. 3.1 can be represented as

$$\{(P, \lambda\widetilde{x}.(0 = -x_2 - 4x_3 + 2x_4 \wedge 0 = -2 + x_2 - 2x_3 + 2x_5, \{x_4, x_5\}))\}.$$

Below, we treat E as a function from predicate variables to equality relations, and assumes that E is total. Hence, if there is no equality relation on the argument of P in E, then $E(P) = \lambda\widetilde{x}.\,(\top, \emptyset)$. We also write $E^{eq}(P) = \lambda\widetilde{x}.\,\varphi$ and $E^{rm}(P) = X$ when $E(P) = \lambda\widetilde{x}.\,(\varphi, X)$.

We check that the candidate E is an inductive invariant of the predicate P by checking whether $[P_1 \mapsto E^{eq}(P_1), \ldots, P_m \mapsto E^{eq}(P_m)]$ is a solution of $\mathit{Defs}(\mathcal{C})$ where $\{P_1, \ldots, P_m\} = PV(\mathcal{C})$. If the candidate is really (inductive) invariant (and the least solution of P has this property), then we can use it to reduce the arguments as described in Sect. 3.3. Otherwise, there exists a counterexample of the constraint that is a tuple of values of the arguments on which P must evaluate to true but the current candidate evaluates to false. We use it as the new positive sample in the next iteration of the whole loop.

Consider the set $\mathcal{C}$ of the CHCs in Example 1 and candidate equality relation $(P, \lambda(x, y, z).\,(z = 2x + y, \{z\}))$. The definite clauses in $\mathcal{C}$ are $P(0, 0, 0)$ and $P(x, y, z) \land x < 500 \implies P(x + 1, y + x, z + x + 2)$. By replacing P with $\lambda(x, y, z).\, z = 2x + y$, we obtain the following constraint:

$$\begin{aligned}&\forall x, y, z.0 = 2 \cdot 0 + 0 \land \\ &\qquad (z = 2x + y \land x < 500 \implies z + x + 2 = 2(x + 1) + (y + x)).\end{aligned}$$

We then check the validity of the constraint by invoking a SMT solver. Since the constraint above is valid, we found the relation is really equality relation on x, y, and z. In contrast, if the candidate is $z = x + y$, which is not an inductive invariant of P, is given, then the constraint obtained by the substitution is:

$$\begin{aligned}&\forall x, y, z.0 = 0 + 0 \land \\ &\qquad (z = x + y \land x < 500 \implies z + x + 2 = (x + 1) + (y + x).\end{aligned}$$

Since this is not valid, there is a counterexample, for instance, $x = y = z = 0$. This counterexample comes from the clause $P(x, y, z) \land x < 500 \implies P(x + 1, y + x, z + x + 2)$. and indicates that $P(0 + 1, 0 + 0, 0 + 0 + 2)$ must be true, but $x = 1 \land y = 0 \land z = 2$ does not satisfy the candidate $z = x + y$. Hence, we use $(1, 0, 2)$ as the new positive sample in the next iteration.

We will see the correctness of the checking method later, but here we give the intuition of the correctness. The correctness can be derived from the property that, for any CHCs $\mathcal{C}$, $\mathcal{C}$ are satisfiable if and only if the least solution of $\mathit{Defs}(\mathcal{C})$ satisfies the goal clauses. If E satisfies $\mathit{Defs}(\mathcal{C})$, then the least solution of $\mathit{Defs}(\mathcal{C})$ satisfies E. Therefore, the whole $\mathcal{C}$ are satisfiable if and only if there is a solution that satisfies E.

3.3 Reducing Arguments by Equality Relation

By using equality relations on the argument of a predicate, we can reduce arguments of predicates.

Let $\mathcal{C}$ be a set of CHCs, E be a set of equality relations. We can reduce argument of predicates in $\mathcal{C}$ by transforming $\mathcal{C}$ into $\mathit{ArgRed}\,(\mathcal{C}, E)$ as defined in

$$ArgRed\,(\mathcal{C}, E) = \left\{ ArgRed^{E}\,(c) \;\middle|\; c \in \mathcal{C} \right\}$$

$$ArgRed^{E}\left(\forall \widetilde{y}.\, \varphi \wedge \bigwedge_{1 \le j \le m} P_j(\widetilde{z}_j) \implies H\right) = \forall \widetilde{y}.\, \varphi' \wedge \bigwedge_{1 \le j \le m} L_j \implies H'$$

where

$$\varphi' = \varphi \wedge \varphi'_1 \wedge \cdots \wedge \varphi'_n$$
$$(\varphi'_j, L_j) = (\varphi_j[\widetilde{x} \mapsto \widetilde{z}], P_j(\widetilde{z}_j|x)) \quad \text{if} \quad E(P_j) = \lambda\widetilde{x}.\,(\varphi_j, X_j)$$
$$\text{for each } j \in \{1, \dots, m\}$$
$$H' = \begin{cases} P(\widetilde{z}|x)) & \text{if } H = P(\widetilde{z}) \text{ and } E(P) = \lambda\widetilde{x}.\,(\varphi, X) \\ \bot & \text{if } H = \bot \end{cases}$$

Fig. 2. The definition of $ArgRed\,(\mathcal{C}, E)$

Fig. 2. In the definition, $\widetilde{z}|_X$ represents the sequence that can be obtained by removing the elements of X from the sequence $\widetilde{z}$, for example, $(x, y, z)|_{\{y\}} = (x, z)$. The substitution $[\widetilde{x} \mapsto \widetilde{z}]$ represents $[x_1 \mapsto z_1, \dots, x_n \mapsto z_n]$ where $n = |\widetilde{x}| = |\widetilde{z}|$. Function $ArgRed^{E}\,(c)$ just returns the new clause in which the argument $x_1, \dots, x_m$ of the predicate P are removed by replacing $P(\widetilde{z})$ with $E^{eq}(P)(\widetilde{z}) \wedge P\left(\widetilde{z}|_{E^{rm}(P)}\right)$ except for the heads of the clauses. When the head of a clause is $P(\widetilde{x})$, the head is replaced just with $P\left(\widetilde{z}|_{E^{rm}(P)}\right)$ instead of the conjunction with the equality $E^{eq}(P)(\widetilde{z})$. This removal of the conjunct does not change the satisfiability of the clause since the implication to the equality has already been checked by the validity checking step of the equality constraints.

The theorem below states the correctness of $ArgRed\,(\mathcal{C}, E)$.

Theorem 1. *Suppose $\mathcal{C}$ be a set of CHCs and E is a valid equality relation of $\mathcal{C}$. Then, $\mathcal{C}$ is satisfiable if and only if $ArgRed\,(\mathcal{C}, E)$ is satisfiable.*

Proof Sketch. In this proof sketch, we write $AR\,(P_j)$ for $\varphi'_j \wedge L_j$ where φ'_j and L_j are defined in Fig. 2 (The arguments of P_j is clear from the context below.)

"If" direction: Suppose $ArgRed\,(\mathcal{C}, E)$ has a solution

$$\sigma' = [P_1, \mapsto \lambda\widetilde{x_1}'.\,\varphi_1, \dots, P_n, \mapsto \lambda\widetilde{x_n}'.\,\varphi_n].$$

We can show that

$$\sigma = [P_1, \mapsto \lambda\widetilde{x_1}.\,\sigma'(AR\,(P_1)), \dots, P_n, \mapsto \lambda\widetilde{x_n}.\,\sigma'(AR\,(P_n))]$$

is a solution of $\mathcal{C}$ where $\widetilde{x_j}' = \widetilde{x_j}|_{E^{rm}(P_j)}$ for each $j \in \{1, \dots, n\}$. By the definition of σ, for each $j \in \{1, \dots, n\}$, the following holds:

$$\sigma P_j(\widetilde{x}_j) = \sigma'(AR\,(P_j)) = \varphi'_j \wedge \sigma' P_j(\widetilde{x}'_j).$$

The case of goal clauses is trivial from this equality. The case of definite clauses also follows from the equality above along with the validity of E.

"Only-if" direction: If $\mathcal{C}$ has a solution, then there exists a least solution

$$\sigma = [P_1, \mapsto \lambda\widetilde{x_1}.\varphi_1, \ldots, P_n, \mapsto \lambda\widetilde{x_n}.\varphi_n].$$

We can show that

$$\sigma' = [P_1, \mapsto \lambda\widetilde{x_1}'.\varphi_1'', \ldots, P_n, \mapsto \lambda\widetilde{x_n}'.\varphi_n'']$$

is a solution of *ArgRed* $(\mathcal{C})$. Here, for each $j \in \{1, \ldots, n\}$, $\widetilde{x_j}' = \widetilde{x_j}|_{E^{rm}(P_j)}$ and $\varphi_j'' = \varphi_j[\ldots, x_{ji} \mapsto e_{ji}, \ldots]$ where e_{ji} is the right-hand side of the equality obtained by rewriting the corresponding equality relation to the form of $x_{ji} = e_{ji}$ for each $x_{ji} \in E^{rm}(P_j)$. For each $j \in \{1, \ldots, n\}$, $\sigma'(AR(P_j))$ is logically equivalent to φ_j'' and, since σ is the least solution, $\sigma(P(\widetilde{x_j}))$ holds when φ_j'' holds. This implies that σ' is a solution of *ArgRed* $(\mathcal{C}, E)$.

4 Argument Reduction by Using Conditional Equalities

In this section, we introduce an extension to deal with more general equality relations than the equalities dealt by the method described in Sect. 3. In this extension, we find and use *conditional equality relations* that are equality relations of the form $\bigwedge_i(\varphi_i \implies \varphi_i')$.

For example, consider the following CHCs:

$$\begin{aligned}
&P(0,0)\\
&P(x,y) \land x \geq 0 \implies P(x+1, y+1)\\
&P(x,y) \land x \leq 0 \implies P(x-1, y+1)\\
&P(x,y) \implies y \geq x
\end{aligned}$$

The predicate $P(x,y)$ represents that y is the absolute value of integer x. If we have found the relation $(x \geq 0 \implies y = x) \land (x < 0 \implies y = -x)$, we can remove the argument y and obtain the following CHCs:

$$\begin{aligned}
&P'(0)\\
&(x \geq 0 \implies y = x) \land (x < 0 \implies y = -x) \land P'(x) \land x \geq 0 \implies P(x+1)\\
&(x \geq 0 \implies y = x) \land (x < 0 \implies y = -x) \land P'(x) \land x \leq 0 \implies P(x-1)\\
&(x \geq 0 \implies y = x) \land (x < 0 \implies y = -x) \land P'(x) \implies y \geq x
\end{aligned}$$

The satisfiability of them are trivial because the goal clause is valid for any assignment for P'.

To find such conditional equality relation, we first find the consequent parts of the conditional equality, e.g., $y = x$ and $y = -x$ in the example above. This is achieved by finding *disjunctive equalities* that are equalities of the form $\bigvee_j(x_i = e_j)$. Once we have found consequent parts, we synthesize the antecedent of each consequent.

For the example above, we first try to discover disjunctive equality, for instance, $y = x \vee y = -x$ as the consequent parts of the conditional equality above. If we have found the disjunctive equality, we next try to synthesize the conditional equality of the form $(\varphi_1 \implies x = y) \wedge (\varphi_2 \implies x = -y)$.

A conditional equality is typically needed for verification of a loop with conditional branch. For example, consider the following code snippet:

```
z = x; y = 0;
while(x != 0) {
    if(x > 0) then {
      y += 2; x -= 1;
    } else {
      y -= 1; x += 1;
    }
}
```

This loop has invariant $(z > 0 \implies 2z = 2x + y) \wedge (z \leq 0 \implies z = x + y)$, which can be useful for verification.

4.1 Guessing Disjunctive Equality

In this section, we describe how to guess *disjunctive equalities*. We will call an equality of the form used in Sect. 3 a *simple equality* in order to distinguish it from the equalities introduced in this section.

Given a set S of positive samples. For each predicate P and the i-th argument of P, we first calculate all possible candidate E of simple equalities by

$$E = \bigcup \{\mathit{SimpleEq}(S', i) \mid \emptyset \subsetneq S' \subsetneq S\}$$

where $\mathit{SimpleEq}(S, i)$ represents the set of all the candidate simple equalities of the form $\lambda\tilde{x}.\, x_i = e$ that can be synthesized by the method described in Sect. 3. For example, consider the set of positive samples $\{(0,0), (1,1), (-1,1), (2,2)\}$. Then, for each S', $\mathit{SimpleEq}(S', 2)$ is as follows:

$$\mathit{SimpleEq}(S', 2) = \begin{cases} \{\lambda(x,y).\, y = x\} \\ \qquad \text{if } S' \in \{\{s_0, s_1\}, \{s_0, s_2\}, \{s_1, s_2\}, \{s_0, s_1, s_2\}\} \\ \{\lambda(x,y).\, y = -x\} \\ \qquad \text{if } S' = \{s_0, s_{-1}\} \\ \emptyset \\ \qquad \text{otherwise} \end{cases}$$

where $s_0 = (0,0)$, $s_1 = (1,1)$, $s_{-1} = (-1,1)$, and $s_2 = (2,2)$.

We then try to find a subset of E such that each value of x_i in the positive samples can be representable by one of its element. More precisely, we try to find $E' \subseteq E$ such that

$$\forall \widetilde{v} \in S.\ \exists (x_i = e) \in E'.\ \models (x_i = e)[\widetilde{x} \mapsto \widetilde{v}].$$

This set E' represents a candidate disjunctive equalities. For example, since $E' = \{\lambda(x, y).\, y = x, \lambda(x, y).\, y = -x\}$ satisfy the property above, the corresponding disjunctive equality $\lambda(x, y).\, y = x \vee y = -x$ is the candidate for the example above.

We wish to calculate the smallest set with the property above. However, since this is a kind of the set cover problem, calculating such the smallest set is too expensive. Hence, we employ the greedy algorithm described below.

If we write $s \models \varphi$ when the sample s satisfy the equality relation φ, then the greedy algorithm $G(E, S)$ can be written as follows:

$$\begin{aligned}
&G(E, \emptyset) = \emptyset \\
&G(E, S) = \{e\} \cup G(E \setminus \{e\}, \{s \in S \mid s \not\models e\}) \\
&\qquad \text{where } e \text{ is the element of } E \text{ that maximizes } |\{s \in S \mid s \models e\}|
\end{aligned}$$

This algorithm repeatedly picks the greatest equality e in the sense that e covers the largest number of the positive samples, and quits if all the positive samples are covered.

4.2 Guessing Conditional Equality

Once we have found a candidate disjunctive equality $\lambda\widetilde{x}.\ \bigvee_j (x_i = e_j)$ on the i-th argument of the predicate P, we next try to discover the boundary (sufficient condition) of each disjunct.

For each disjunct $x_i = e_j$, we have the set S_j of positive samples that satisfy the equality, i.e., $S_j = \{\widetilde{v} \in S \mid \models (x_i = e_j)[\widetilde{x} \mapsto \widetilde{v}]\}$. By using S_j, we try to find the boundary φ of $x_i = e_j$ that satisfy $\varphi[\widetilde{x} \mapsto \widetilde{v}]$ for all $\widetilde{v} \in S_j$ and φ does not have x_i as a free variable.

We can find the boundaries by using a SMT solving if we restrict the form of a boundary to $0 \le c_0 + \sum_i c_i x_i$. If $\widetilde{v} \in S_j$ is given, then the coefficients $\widetilde{c}$ can be obtained by solving the following linear inequalities

$$\left(\forall \widetilde{v} \in S_j.\ 0 \le c_0 + \sum_i c_i v_i\right) \wedge \left(\forall \widetilde{v} \in S \setminus S_j.\ 0 > c_0 + \sum_i c_i v_i\right)$$

where S is the set of all the positive samples. Here, we must cover all the spaces of values by the union of the boundaries. Hence, for the last disjunct, we use the negation of the disjunction of the other boundaries, i.e., $\varphi_m = \neg(\varphi_1 \vee \cdots \vee \varphi_{m-1})$

where m is the number of disjuncts and, for each $k \in \{1, \ldots, m\}$, φ_k is the boundary of the k-th disjunct obtained above.

Consider the candidate $\lambda(x, y).\, y = x \vee y = -x$ and the set of positive samples $\{(0,0), (1,1), (-1,1), (2,2)\}$. The disjunct $y = x$ covers the samples $\{(0,0), (1,1), (2,2)\}$, and the disjunct $y = -x$ covers the samples $\{(0,0), (-1,1)\}$. By using a SMT solver, we could obtain $0 \leq x$ by the solution of

$$(0 \leq c_0 + 0 \cdot c_1 \ \wedge \ 0 \leq c_0 + 1 \cdot c_1 \ \wedge \ 0 \leq c_0 + 2 \cdot c_1) \ \wedge \ (0 > c_0 - 1 \cdot c_1)$$

as the boundary for $y = x$, and the boundary for $y = -x$ can be obtained by its negation, i.e., $0 > x$. Therefore, the candidate we obtained here is $(0 \leq x \implies y = x) \wedge (0 > x \implies y = -x)$.

The process after we have found the candidate conditional equality is the same as that for simple equalities. Sections 3.2 and 3.3 do not depend on the fact that E is a *simple* equality relation, only on the fact that E is an (inductive) invariant that expresses a total function to values of the target argument from ones of the other arguments. We can hence use the same procedure for checking the candidate and the same transformation $\mathit{ArgRed}\,(\mathcal{C})\,E$ to reduce arguments by using the equality.

5 Implementation and Experiments

We have implemented our method as a preprocess of the state-of-the-art CHC solvers, namely HoIce [3] and Z3/Spacer [12]. To evaluate the methods introduced in Sect. 3 and Sect. 4, we use two versions of the implementation: (i) HoIce-SEq and Z3-SEq that use the method for simple equalities introduced in Sect. 3, and (ii) HoIce-CEq and Z3-CEq that use the method for conditional equalities introduced in Sect. 4. Due to implementation reasons, we did not set a time limit for the equality inference in HoIce-SEq and HoIce-CEq, while we set the time limit to 2 s in Z3-SEq and Z3-CEq.

We evaluated our implementations against: Z3, ELDARICA [8], FREQHORN [24], and HoIce. The experiments were conducted on a machine with AMD Ryzen 9 5900X 3.7 GHz and 32 GB of memory, with a timeout of 1000 s.

We use the two benchmark sets `CHC-COMP` and `SyGuS-Comp`. The benchmark `CHC-COMP` is the benchmark set of the latest CHC competition (CHC-COMP 2023)[1], which consists of 850 CHC instances from various source, e.g., the benchmarks of FREQHORN, ELDARICA, LinearArbitrary, MoCHi, and so on. The benchmark `SyGuS-Comp` is the benchmark set of the invariant synthesis track (Inv) in the latest SyGuS competition (SyGuS-Comp 2019)[2]. Since the original benchmark instances are written in their original specification language, we translated these instances into general CHC instances written in the standard SMT-LIB format. The benchmark includes 858 instances. Therefore, the number of all the instances is 1708.

[1] https://chc-comp.github.io/.
[2] https://sygus.org/comp/2019/.

Figure 3 shows the comparison of all the solvers. The vertical axis shows an elapsed time (measured in seconds) in logarithmic scale, and the horizontal axis shows the number of instances solved in the time. While the numbers of solved instances by our tools are less than that of Z3, HoIce-SEq and Z3-SEq solved more instances than the original solvers with small additional costs (as discussed later). HoIce-CEq is inferior than HoIce and HoIce-SEq (located to the upper left of HoIce). This is because the current implementation of the method described in Sect. 4 in HoIce-CEq is naïve, where all the possible simple equalities are calculated for all the subsets of the positive samples. Thus, the cost to find candidates of conditional equalities is too high when the number of arguments and positive samples are large. The optimization to address this issue is left for future work.

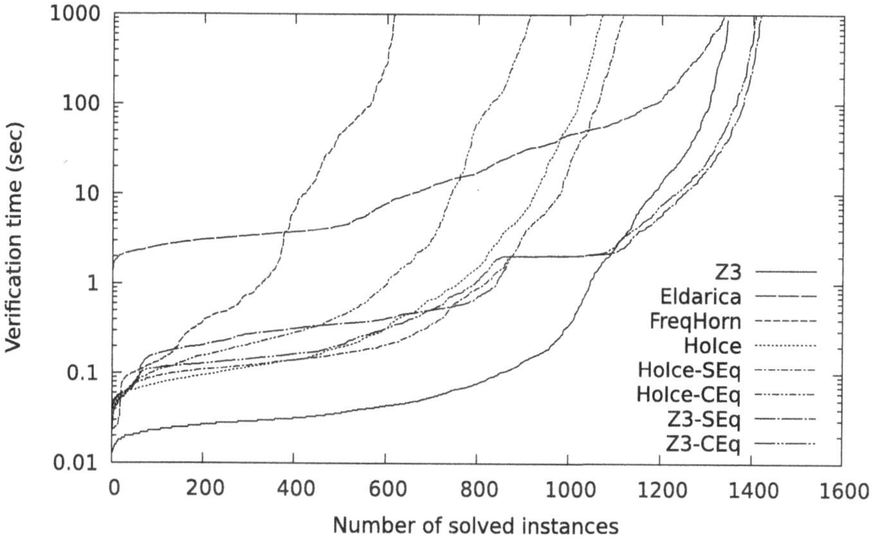

Fig. 3. Comparison with Z3, ELDARICA, FREQHORN, and HoIce

Table 1. Number of uniquely solved instances

Z3	ELDARICA	FREQHORN	HoIce	
3 (1,344)	30 (1,335)	7 (616)	0 (1,070)	
HoIce-SEq	HoIce-CEq	Z3-SEq	Z3-CEq	Ours
1 (1,115)	21 (913)	3 (1,416)	1 (1,405)	43

In spite of this naïve implementation, the method in Sect. 4 was effective for some instances. Table 1 shows the number of uniquely solved instances, i.e., the number of instances that can be solved by the solver but cannot be solved by the other solvers. In the table, the numbers in the parentheses represent the numbers of solved instances, and "Ours" represents the result of the parallel execution of HoIce-SEq, HoIce-CEq, Z3-SEq, and Z3-CEq. In other words, 43 instances were solved by at least one of HoIce-SEq, HoIce-CEq, Z3-SEq, and Z3-CEq, but could not be solved by the other solvers. As can be seen from the table, HoIce-CEq solves 21 instances that cannot be solved by the others. Interestingly, 20 out of 21 instances are unsat instances, which indicates that the invariant discovery is useful for finding not only a solution but also a counterexample as described in Sect. 1. Since our method is orthogonal to CHC solving methods, we can also improve the other CHC solvers by incorporating our method into them. We believe that optimizations on conditional equality findings may improve the overall performance further.

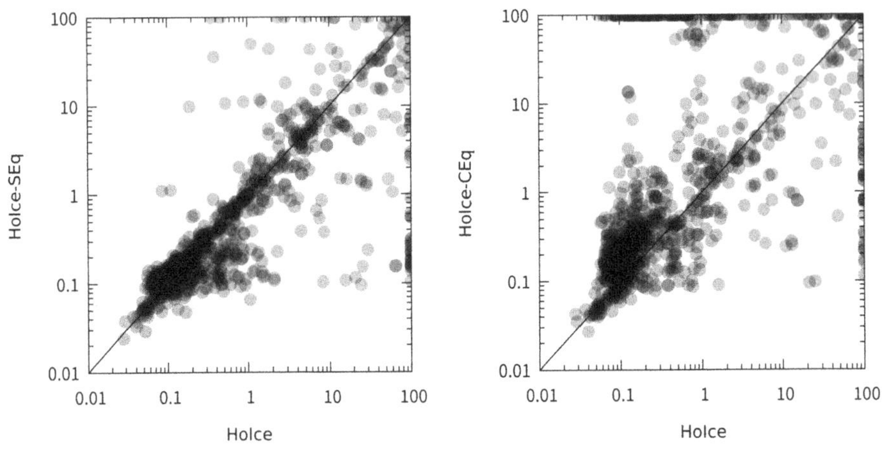

(a) HoIce-SEq vs HoIce (b) HoIce-CEq vs HoIce

Fig. 4. Comparison of ours with HoIce

Figure 4 shows the comparisons of ours and HoIce. The horizontal axis represents the solving time of HoIce and each vertical axis represents that of ours in logarithmic scale. As can be seen in Fig. 4(a), even for the instances that can be solved by HoIce, HoIce-SEq tends to solve the instances faster than HoIce except very easy instances (More points away from the center line.) In contrast, HoIce-CEq is slower than HoIce for such instances as can be seen in Fig. 4(b). This is because finding conditional equality has a high cost.

Figure 5 shows how much the argument reduction improves the overall performance. In the figure, the points on the upper line (resp. the lower line) represents that HoIce (resp. ours) was timeout for the instances. There is no explicit correlation between the number of reduced arguments and the speed-up ratio, which means that, at least for HoIce, the equality relation itself is more important than the number of reduced arguments. The important point here is that removals of one or more arguments enables HoIce to solve more instances, at least for HoIce-SEq, with small cost (i.e., not much points are below the center line).

Figure 6 shows the cost of finding equalities against the maximum number of integer arguments. The vertical axis represents the time spent in the procedure of finding equalities. For simple equalities (Fig. 6(a)), the procedure ends within a second for most of the instances (992 out of 1,115). Even for most instances that have predicates with several dozen integer arguments, the procedure ends within 10 s. For conditional equalities (Fig. 6(b)), if the number of integer arguments exceeds 4, the procedure takes much time for many instances.

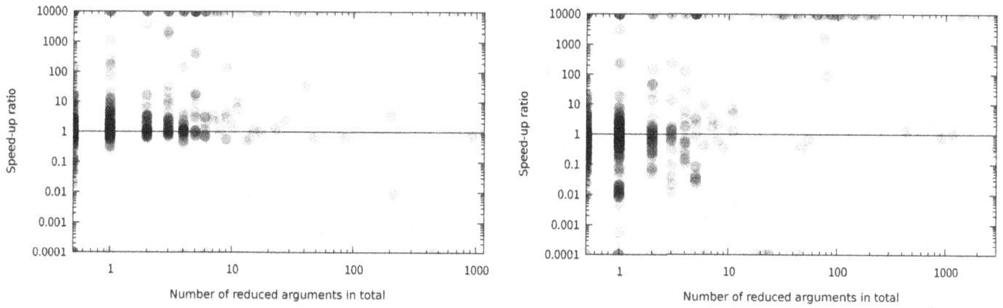

(a) HoIce-SEq (b) HoIce-CEq

Fig. 5. Speed-up ratio against the number of reduced arguments

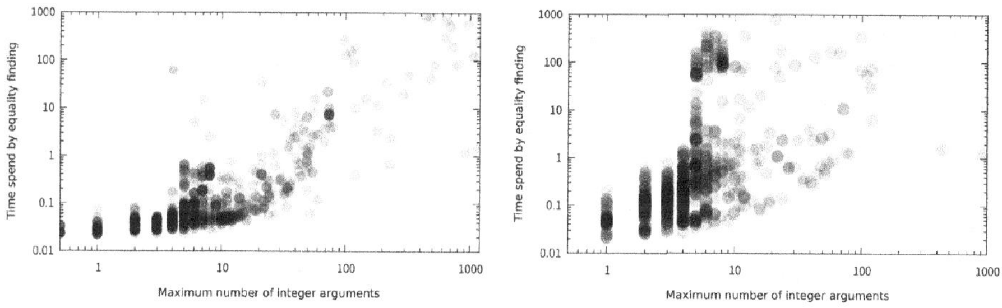

(a) Simple equalities (b) Conditional equalities

Fig. 6. Time spent by equality finding against the maximum number of integer arguments

6 Related Work

Several techniques have been developed [4,14,16] to reduce arguments of predicates for CHC and Constraint Logic Programming (CLP) with respect to its satisfiability/semantics. Leuschel and Sørensen [14] proposed methods, called RAF and FAR, for reducing predicate arguments, by detecting redundant arguments that do not affect the satisfiability of CHCs, based on certain syntactic conditions. Another method has been proposed by Proietti and Pettorossi [17], which utilizes the fold/unfold transformation technique to detect and eliminate unnecessary variables. Since those methods do not take into account arithmetic constraints, they are not effective for the examples presented in this paper.

Our technique of finding linear equalities described in Sects. 3.1 and 3.2 can be considered a transplant of the technique of Sharma et al. [20] for finding algebraic loop invariants to the setting of CHCs. More precisely, the method for guessing equalities from data in Sect. 3.1 is essentially the same as their method, and the method for checking equalities and finding new data in Sect. 3.2 is a generalization of their corresponding method to the setting of CHCs, which can deal with a wider class of control structures than loops, including mutually recursive functions. Moreover, Sharma et al.'s method first runs the program to collect the initial data set, but it is difficult to do so (at least efficiently) in the setting of CHCs. Thus, our procedure is made to work with an empty initial data set. The important point is that the impact of the generalization to the settings of CHCs is significant, as CHC solving can be used for verification of much larger classes of programs and properties. They [20] also proposed a method for finding disjunctive equalities from polynomial equalities, which may serve as a good alternative to our method in Sect. 4.1.

In the setting of CHCs, Fedyukovich et al. [6] also gave a data-driven method for discovering equality constraints. They used the discovered equalities as seeds for their syntax-guided approach to CHC solving. Instead, we have used equality constraints for a preprocessing to reduce predicate arguments. Our approach can be combined with any CHC solvers. Another difference is in the way data are collected: Fedyukovich et al. [6] collect data by unrolling CHCs, while we collect them in a counterexample-guided manner, following the approach of Sharma et al. [20].

Other data-driven approaches for finding invariants of loop programs or CHCs have been proposed [11,19,21,24]. For example, Zhu et al. [24] used support vector machines, and Ryan et al. [19] and Kobayashi et al. [11] used neural networks. While those methods can also deal with inequality constraints, those methods tend to be more costly than our approach to finding equality constraints.

7 Conclusion

We have proposed a method for reducing the number of arguments of predicates by finding equality relations among the arguments in a counterexample-guided manner. We have implemented the proposed method and confirmed its effectiveness through experiments.

Future work includes an extension of our method for finding polynomial equalities. To that end, we just need to fix the maximum degree d of polynomials, and add the rows corresponding to $x_1^{d_1} \cdots x_k^{d_k}$ for $d_1 + \cdots + d_k \leq d$ when applying the Gaussian elimination in Sect. 3.1.

It would also be interesting to extend our work to find invariants on data structures such as lists and trees, to improve the efficiency of solvers for CHCs with data structures. For example, if we can find relations on integer and data structure arguments such as "$x = y :: z$", "x is the first element of the integer list y", and "x is the depth of the tree y", (where x, y, z are the argument of some predicate), then we can remove the argument x from the predicate.

Acknowledgement. We would like to thank anonymous referees for useful comments. This work was supported by JSPS KAKENHI Grant Numbers JP20H05703.

References

1. Bjørner, N., Gurfinkel, A., McMillan, K., Rybalchenko, A.: Horn clause solvers for program verification. In: Beklemishev, L.D., Blass, A., Dershowitz, N., Finkbeiner, B., Schulte, W. (eds.) Fields of Logic and Computation II. LNCS, vol. 9300, pp. 24–51. Springer, Cham (2015). https://doi.org/10.1007/978-3-319-23534-9_2
2. Bjørner, N.S., McMillan, K.L., Rybalchenko, A.: Program verification as satisfiability modulo theories. In: Fontaine, P., Goel, A. (eds.) 10th International Workshop on Satisfiability Modulo Theories, SMT 2012, Manchester, UK, 30 June- 1 July 2012. EPiC Series in Computing, vol. 20, pp. 3–11. EasyChair (2012). https://doi.org/10.29007/117f
3. Champion, A., Chiba, T., Kobayashi, N., Sato, R.: ICE-based refinement type discovery for higher-order functional programs. J. Autom. Reason. **64**(7), 1393–1418 (2020). https://doi.org/10.1007/s10817-020-09571-y
4. De Angelis, E., Fioravanti, F., Pettorossi, A., Proietti, M.: Semantics-based generation of verification conditions via program specialization. Sci. Comput. Program. **147**, 78–108 (2017). https://doi.org/10.1016/j.scico.2016.11.002
5. Delzanno, G., Podelski, A.: Constraint-based deductive model checking. Int. J. Softw. Tools Technol. Transf. **3**(3), 250–270 (2001). https://doi.org/10.1007/s100090100049
6. Fedyukovich, G., Prabhu, S., Madhukar, K., Gupta, A.: Solving constrained Horn clauses using syntax and data. In: Bjørner, N.S., Gurfinkel, A. (eds.) 2018 Formal Methods in Computer Aided Design, FMCAD 2018, Austin, TX, USA, 30 October - 2 November 2018, pp. 1–9. IEEE (2018). https://doi.org/10.23919/FMCAD.2018.8603011
7. Gurfinkel, A., Kahsai, T., Komuravelli, A., Navas, J.A.: The SeaHorn verification framework. In: Kroening, D., Păsăreanu, C.S. (eds.) CAV 2015. LNCS, vol. 9206, pp. 343–361. Springer, Cham (2015). https://doi.org/10.1007/978-3-319-21690-4_20

8. Hojjat, H., Rümmer, P.: The ELDARICA horn solver. In: Bjørner, N.S., Gurfinkel, A. (eds.) 2018 Formal Methods in Computer Aided Design, FMCAD 2018, Austin, TX, USA, 30 October - 2 November 2018, pp. 1–7. IEEE (2018). https://doi.org/10.23919/FMCAD.2018.8603013
9. Jaffar, J., Santosa, A.E., Voicu, R.: A CLP method for compositional and intermittent predicate abstraction. In: Emerson, E.A., Namjoshi, K.S. (eds.) VMCAI 2006. LNCS, vol. 3855, pp. 17–32. Springer, Heidelberg (2005). https://doi.org/10.1007/11609773_2
10. Kahsai, T., Rümmer, P., Sanchez, H., Schäf, M.: JayHorn: a framework for verifying java programs. In: Chaudhuri, S., Farzan, A. (eds.) CAV 2016. LNCS, vol. 9779, pp. 352–358. Springer, Cham (2016). https://doi.org/10.1007/978-3-319-41528-4_19
11. Kobayashi, N., Sekiyama, T., Sato, I., Unno, H.: Toward neural-network-guided program synthesis and verification. In: Drăgoi, C., Mukherjee, S., Namjoshi, K. (eds.) SAS 2021. LNCS, vol. 12913, pp. 236–260. Springer, Cham (2021). https://doi.org/10.1007/978-3-030-88806-0_12
12. Komuravelli, A., Gurfinkel, A., Chaki, S.: SMT-based model checking for recursive programs. In: Biere, A., Bloem, R. (eds.) CAV 2014. LNCS, vol. 8559, pp. 17–34. Springer, Cham (2014). https://doi.org/10.1007/978-3-319-08867-9_2
13. Komuravelli, A., Gurfinkel, A., Chaki, S., Clarke, E.M.: Automatic abstraction in SMT-based unbounded software model checking. In: Sharygina, N., Veith, H. (eds.) CAV 2013. LNCS, vol. 8044, pp. 846–862. Springer, Heidelberg (2013). https://doi.org/10.1007/978-3-642-39799-8_59
14. Leuschel, M., Sørensen, M.H.: Redundant argument filtering of logic programs. In: Gallagher, J. (ed.) LOPSTR 1996. LNCS, vol. 1207, pp. 83–103. Springer, Heidelberg (1997). https://doi.org/10.1007/3-540-62718-9_6
15. Matsushita, Y., Tsukada, T., Kobayashi, N.: RustHorn: CHC-based verification for Rust programs. ACM Trans. Program. Lang. Syst. **43**(4), 15:1–15:54 (2021). https://doi.org/10.1145/3462205
16. Proietti, M., Pettorossi, A.: An automatic transfomation strategy for avoiding unnecessary variables in logic programs (extended abstract). In: Clement, T.P., Lau, K. (eds.) Logic Program Synthesis and Transformation, Proceedings of LOPSTR 91, International Workshop on Logic Program Synthesis and Transformation, University of Manchester, UK, 4–5 July 1991, pp. 126–128. Workshops in Computing. Springer (1991). https://doi.org/10.1007/978-1-4471-3494-7_10
17. Proietti, M., Pettorossi, A.: Unfolding - definition - folding, in this order, for avaoiding unnecessary variables in logic programs. Theor. Comput. Sci. **142**(1), 89–124 (1995). https://doi.org/10.1016/0304-3975(94)00227-A
18. Rondon, P.M., Kawaguchi, M., Jhala, R.: Liquid types. In: Gupta, R., Amarasinghe, S.P. (eds.) Proceedings of the ACM SIGPLAN 2008 Conference on Programming Language Design and Implementation, Tucson, AZ, USA, 7–13 June 2008, pp. 159–169. ACM (2008). https://doi.org/10.1145/1375581.1375602
19. Ryan, G., Wong, J., Yao, J., Gu, R., Jana, S.: CLN2INV: learning loop invariants with continuous logic networks. In: 8th International Conference on Learning Representations, ICLR 2020. OpenReview.net (2020)
20. Sharma, R., Gupta, S., Hariharan, B., Aiken, A., Liang, P., Nori, A.V.: A data driven approach for algebraic loop invariants. In: Felleisen, M., Gardner, P. (eds.) ESOP 2013. LNCS, vol. 7792, pp. 574–592. Springer, Heidelberg (2013). https://doi.org/10.1007/978-3-642-37036-6_31
21. Si, X., Naik, A., Dai, H., Naik, M., Song, L.: Code2Inv: a deep learning framework for program verification. In: Lahiri, S.K., Wang, C. (eds.) CAV 2020. LNCS, vol.

12225, pp. 151–164. Springer, Cham (2020). https://doi.org/10.1007/978-3-030-53291-8_9

22. Toman, J., Siqi, R., Suenaga, K., Igarashi, A., Kobayashi, N.: ConSORT: context- and flow-sensitive ownership refinement types for imperative programs. In: ESOP 2020. LNCS, vol. 12075, pp. 684–714. Springer, Cham (2020). https://doi.org/10.1007/978-3-030-44914-8_25
23. Unno, H., Kobayashi, N.: On-demand refinement of dependent types. In: Garrigue, J., Hermenegildo, M.V. (eds.) FLOPS 2008. LNCS, vol. 4989, pp. 81–96. Springer, Heidelberg (2008). https://doi.org/10.1007/978-3-540-78969-7_8
24. Zhu, H., Magill, S., Jagannathan, S.: A data-driven CHC solver. In: Foster, J.S., Grossman, D. (eds.) Proceedings of the 39th ACM SIGPLAN Conference on Programming Language Design and Implementation, PLDI 2018, Philadelphia, PA, USA, 18–22 June 2018, pp. 707–721. ACM (2018). https://doi.org/10.1145/3192366.3192416

Static Analysis and Testing

Incorrectness Proofs for Object-Oriented Programs via Subclass Reflection

Wenhua Li[1(✉)], Quang Loc Le[2], Yahui Song[1], and Wei-Ngan Chin[1]

[1] National University of Singapore, Singapore, Singapore
{liwenhua,yahuis,chinwn}@comp.nus.edu.sg
[2] University College London, London, UK
loc.le@ucl.ac.uk

Abstract. Inheritance and method overriding are crucial concepts in object-oriented programming (OOP) languages. These concepts support a hierarchy of classes that reuse common data and methods. Most existing works for OO verification focus on modular reasoning in which they could support dynamic dispatching and thus efficiently enforce the Liskov substitution principle on behavioural subtyping. They are based on *superclass abstraction* to reason about the correctness of OO programs. However, techniques to reason about the incorrectness of OOP are yet to be investigated.

In this paper, we present a mechanism that 1) specifies the normal and abnormal executions of OO programs by using ok specifications and er specifications respectively; 2) verifies these specifications by a novel under-approximation proof system based on incorrectness logic that can support dynamic modularity. We introduce *subclass reflection* with dynamic views and an adapted subtyping relation for under-approximation. Our proposal can deal with both OOP aspects (e.g., behavioural subtyping and casting) and under-approximation aspects (e.g., dropping paths). To demonstrate how the proposed proof system can soundly verify the specifications, we prove its soundness, prototype the proof system, and report on experimental results. The results show that our system can precisely reason about the incorrectness of programs with OOP aspects, such as proving the presence of casting errors and null-pointer-exceptions.

1 Introduction

Proving the correctness and incorrectness of programs are two sides of a coin. On one side is Hoare logic, the pioneering formal system for correctness reasoning. Its central feature is Hoare triple, denoted by $\{pre\}$ S $\{post\}$ where *pre* and *post* are assertion formulae in some logic, and S is a program written in some programming languages. This triple means if we execute S starting from any program state σ (σ are valuations of program variables) satisfying *pre* and if it terminates, we will obtain program states σ' satisfying *post*. We refer σ' as reachable states from *pre*. This interpretation implies:

- *post* may be an over-approximation of reachable states, i.e., some of its states may satisfy *post* but do not correspond to a terminating execution associated

C.-K. Hur (Ed.): APLAS 2023, LNCS 14405, pp. 269–289, 2023.
https://doi.org/10.1007/978-981-99-8311-7_13

with a starting state satisfying *pre*. As such, Hoare logic is primarily used for correctness proving. Given a program S, a precondition *pre*, and an assertion *bad* representing buggy states, to prove that S is safe, we can show $\{pre\}$ S $\{post\}$ is valid and the *post* does not contain any *bad* states.
- Hoare logic cannot be used to prove the incorrectness of programs (i.e., confirming that S has a *bad* property by establishing $post \wedge bad$ that is satisfiable is inaccurate). This is due to an over-approximating *post* state.

Recently, O'Hearn completed the other side of the puzzle with incorrectness logic (IL) [23]. Its centrepiece is IL triple, the under-approximation counterpart of Hoare triple. An IL triple, written as $[pre]$ S $[post]$, states that each state of σ', that satisfies *post*, is a reachable state from executing S from one or more inputs satisfying *pre*. Given an IL triple $[pre]$ S $[post]$ and a buggy assertion *bad*, S has a bug if $post \wedge bad$ is satisfiable. With this, we can always find a counterexample whose input value(s) satisfy *pre* from which S goes *bad*. Notably, Pulse-X, a recent IL analyser [11], found 15 new bugs in OpenSSL and showed the importance of incorrectness reasoning for the industrial codebase.

Though IL is a significant advance to under-approximating reasoning, it is currently limited to static modularity and does not support dynamic modularity for object-oriented programming (OOP). OOP is one of the vital components in many imperative programming languages (e.g., Java, Scala and C#). An OO program is a collection of classes, each of which contains a set of fields and methods. Classes could be subclasses of others to form a class hierarchy. Methods of the superclass can be inherited or overridden by the subclass. The design of OOP must adhere to the Liskov substitution principle (LSP) on behavioural subtyping [18]: An object of a subclass can always substitute an object of the superclass, and dynamic dispatching of a method is determined based on its actual type at the runtime. Most existing OO verification works focus on the support of dynamic modularity to enforce the substitutivity efficiently. While these works support correctness reasoning with *superclass abstraction* in Hoare logic (e.g., [8, 9, 13, 14]) or its extension, separation logic (e.g., [4, 20, 24, 25]), none focuses on the incorrectness of programs. Therefore, incorrectness reasoning in OO programs is worth investigating.

We introduce IL for OOP, with the following challenge: How to support dynamic modularity to enforce behavioural subtyping in under-approximation? A key observation is that the superclasses are unaware of the behaviours of extension fields in the subclasses. However, the subclasses can reflect the reachable states for fields inherited from the superclasses. Hence, the specifications of the subclass methods can be used to show the behaviours of the subclass itself and the superclasses. We call this *subclass reflection.*

In some prior works [4, 25] on correctness reasoning, they propose the coexistence of static and dynamic specifications. A static specification (spec) specifies the functional properties of each method, while a dynamic spec can be used to verify dynamic dispatching; and the specification subtyping relation between static/dynamic specs ensures behavioural subtyping. Similar to the prior works, we propose static specs and reflexive specs to specify OO programs in under-approximation: A static spec under-approximates a single method while a reflexive spec under-approximates methods of one class and its superclasses. Moreover, we propose dynamic views which can efficiently support *subclass reflection* and reason about casting operations. Our primary contributions are as follows.

- We present an under-approximate approach to OO verification. Our proposal extends incorrectness logic, with *subclass reflection* using dynamic views, to specify both normal and incorrect behaviours of OO programs.
- We introduce a proof system that supports dynamic modularity (including dynamic dispatching for class inheritance, casting operator and `instanceof` operator) and under-approximating reasoning via dropping paths and classes.
- We prototype the proposal in a verifier, called OURify (OO program Under-approximation Verifier), and demonstrate its capability of proving the incorrectness of OO programs, which is beyond the state-of-the-art.

Organization. Section 2 illustrates our proposal with examples. Section 3 presents the target language and the assertion language. The proof system and our approach to behaviour subtyping are shown in Sect. 4. Section 5 discusses our implementation OURify. Finally, Sect. 6 shows related work and concludes.

2 Motivation and Overview

We first explain the dynamic modularity problem and how existing proposals address it in correctness reasoning using Hoare logic and separation logic (Sect. 2.1). After that, in Sect. 2.2, we discuss the motivation of a novel foundation for incorrectness reasoning via incorrectness logic by highlighting the fundamental differences between Hoare logic and incorrectness logic. Afterwards, we informally describe our proposal for incorrectness reasoning.

2.1 Correctness Reasoning with Superclass Abstraction

When the type of an object is dynamically determined, is there a modular way to verify this object without explicitly considering all the method implementations? Liskov substitution principle answers this question: the subclass implementation must satisfy the specification of the superclass for each inherited or overridden method. This process requires re-verification as all subclasses need to be checked and could be polynomial in the numbers of inherited classes.

To avoid re-verification and enforce behavioural subtyping efficiently, prior works [4,25] suggest that each method has a pair of specs: a static spec for the verification of its implementation and a dynamic spec involving behaviour subtyping. Furthermore, a method's static spec is a subtype (written as $<:_O$) of its dynamic spec. A method's dynamic spec in the subclass is a subtype of the dynamic spec in its superclass. This mechanism enhances behavioural subtyping, such that the dynamic spec of a superclass's method abstracts (possibly over-approximating) behaviours of <u>all</u> its subclass methods. This is the so-called *superclass abstraction.* Suppose that superclass C has a method `mn` with spec $\{pre_C\}\_\{post_C\}$, and D is a subclass of C – denoted as $D \prec C$, and

D.mn overrides/inherits from C.mn. Then, for all D.mn's spec $\{pre_D\}$-$\{post_D\}$, $\{pre_D\}$-$\{post_D\}$<:$_O$$\{pre_C\}$-$\{post_C\}$, where the relation <:$_O$ is defined as:

$$\frac{pre_C \ \wedge type(this) \prec D \ \models \ pre_D \qquad\qquad post_D \ \models \ post_C}{\{pre_D\}\text{-}\{post_D\} \ <:_O \ \{pre_C\}\text{-}\{post_C\}}$$

(Note that the relations proposed in separation logic [4,24,25] consider frame inference in the premises, which is a generic form of entailment problem.) Regarding this relation, we have the following two observations.

- First, the entailment checks are not straightforward, as the specs are from two different classes. Various approaches [4,7,25] have been applied to address this issue. For example, the extension predicate [4] encodes fields from multiple objects (e.g., one superclass and its subclasses) in a single predicate. When the extension predicate is used with the subtype constraint $type(this) \prec D$, the entailments are checked for the subclass D.
- Second, the subtyping relation enforces subtyping behaviour without requiring re-verification. For any program S s.t. $\{pre_D\}\mathtt{S}\{post_D\}$ is valid, then the subtyping relation and the *consequence rule* of Hoare logic (rule HL-Conseq below) ensure so is $\{pre_C\}\mathtt{S}\{post_C\}$.

$$\frac{pre_C \models pre_D \qquad \{pre_D\}\ \mathtt{S}\ \{post_D\} \qquad post_D \models post_C}{\{pre_C\}\ \mathtt{S}\ \{post_C\}} \ (\mathtt{HL\text{-}Conseq})$$

We notice a phenomenon in which inheritance is not subtyping [6], i.e. subclass instances behave differently from instances of its superclass. One solution to address such odd instances is to provide over-approximation for *superclass abstraction* (shown in the following example). Alternatively, Dhara and Leavens [7] propose a *specification inheritance* technique in which the specification of the overriding method is strengthened by conjoining it with the specification of the overridden method. This technique was realized in separation logic via multiple specs [4] or specs with the *also* keyword [25].

We elaborate on subtyping behaviour through the code shown in Fig. 1. It defines two classes: the superclass `Cnt` and the subclass `DblCnt`. `Cnt` includes a field `val` and a method `tick`, which increases `val` by one. `DblCnt` inherits `val`, defines another field `bak` and overrides the method `tick`. Method `DblCnt.tick()` additionally backs up the value of `val` in `bak` and nondeterministically increases `val` by 1 (on line 10) or 2 (on line 12). While the `if` branch shows the subtyping behaviour of `DblCnt.tick()`, the `else` branch does not.

```
1  class Cnt {
2    int val;
3    void tick()
4    {this.val := this.val+1;}}
5
6  class DblCnt extends Cnt{
7    int bak;
8    override void tick()
9    {this.bak := this.val;
10   if (*) super.tick();
11   else
12    this.val := this.val+2;}}
```

Fig. 1. Illustrative example

To write method specifications, we need to define an abstraction that captures all fields of the two classes. For instance, we follow the approach introduced in [4] to define an extension predicate in separation logic. The abstraction is:

$$\mathit{this}::\mathtt{Cnt}\langle t, v, p\rangle * p::\mathtt{ExtAll}(\mathtt{Cnt}, t)$$

$\mathit{this}::\mathtt{Cnt}\langle t, v, p\rangle$ defines the superclass. t is the actual type of this object; value v is the field `val`. p is the reference to subclass extensions. $*$ is the separating conjunction, and predicate $p::\mathtt{ExtAll}(\mathtt{Cnt}, t)$ defines a chain of subclasses from `Cnt` to t. $\mathtt{ExtAll}(\mathtt{Cnt}, t)$ is defined as the following:

$$\begin{aligned} p :: \mathtt{ExtAll}(\mathtt{Cnt}, t) \equiv\ & t = \mathtt{Cnt} \wedge p = \mathit{null} \\ & \vee\ p::\mathtt{Ext}\langle t_1, \overline{v}, p_1\rangle * p_1::\mathtt{ExtAll}(t_1, t) \wedge (t_1 \prec_1 \mathtt{Cnt}) \wedge (t \prec t_1) \end{aligned}$$

where $t_1 \prec_1 \mathtt{Cnt}$ means t_1 is an immediate subclass of `Cnt` and $t \prec t_1$ means t is a subclass of t_1. With this abstraction, `Cnt` is realized as:

$$\mathit{this}::\mathtt{Cnt}\langle \mathtt{Cnt}, v, p\rangle * p::\mathtt{ExtAll}(\mathtt{Cnt}, \mathtt{Cnt}) = \mathit{this}::\mathtt{Cnt}\langle \mathtt{Cnt}, v, \mathit{null}\rangle$$

And `DblCnt` is $\mathit{this}::\mathtt{Cnt}\langle \mathtt{DblCnt}, v, p\rangle * p::\mathtt{ExtAll}(\mathtt{Cnt}, \mathtt{DblCnt})$ which is equivalent with $\mathit{this}::\mathtt{Cnt}\langle \mathtt{DblCnt}, v, p\rangle * p::\mathtt{Ext}\langle \mathtt{DblCnt}, b, \mathit{null}\rangle \wedge \mathtt{DblCnt} \prec_1 \mathtt{Cnt}$.

Using these predicates, we can write static and dynamic specs for two methods `tick`. First, methods `Cnt.tick` and `DblCnt.tick` are specified and statically verified by the following two static specs, respectively.

$$\begin{aligned} &\mathtt{static}\ \{\mathit{this}::\mathtt{Cnt}\langle \mathtt{Cnt}, v, \mathit{null}\rangle\}\ \mathtt{Cnt.tick()}\ \{\mathit{this}::\mathtt{Cnt}\langle \mathtt{Cnt}, v+1, \mathit{null}\rangle\} \\ &\mathtt{static}\ \{\mathit{this}::\mathtt{Cnt}\langle \mathtt{DblCnt}, v, p\rangle * p::\mathtt{Ext}\langle \mathtt{DblCnt}, \_, \mathit{null}\rangle \wedge \mathtt{DblCnt} \prec_1 \mathtt{Cnt}\} \\ &\qquad \mathtt{DblCnt.tick()} \\ &\quad \{\mathit{this}::\mathtt{Cnt}\langle \mathtt{DblCnt}, v', p\rangle * p::\mathtt{Ext}\langle \mathtt{DblCnt}, v, \mathit{null}\rangle \wedge \mathtt{DblCnt} \prec_1 \mathtt{Cnt} \\ &\qquad \wedge\ v+1 \le v' \le v+2\} \end{aligned}$$

Similarly, each method `tick` is annotated with another dynamic spec, which is used for dynamic dispatching verification.

$$\begin{aligned} \mathtt{dynamic}\quad & \{\mathit{this}::\mathtt{Cnt}\langle t, v, p\rangle * p::\mathtt{ExtAll}(\mathtt{Cnt}, t)\} \\ & \mathtt{Cnt.tick()} \\ & \{\mathit{this}::\mathtt{Cnt}\langle t, v', p\rangle * p::\mathtt{ExtAll}(\mathtt{Cnt}, t) \wedge v' > v\} \end{aligned}$$

$$\begin{aligned} \mathtt{dynamic}\quad & \{\mathit{this}::\mathtt{Cnt}\langle t, v, p\rangle * p::\mathtt{Ext}\langle \mathtt{DblCnt}, \_, p_1\rangle \\ & *p_1::\mathtt{ExtAll}(\mathtt{DblCnt}, t) \wedge \mathtt{DblCnt} \prec_1 \mathtt{Cnt}\} \\ & \mathtt{DblCnt.tick()} \\ & \{\mathit{this}::\mathtt{Cnt}\langle t, v', p\rangle * p::\mathtt{Ext}\langle \mathtt{DblCnt}, v, p_1\rangle \\ & *p_1::\mathtt{ExtAll}(\mathtt{DblCnt}, t) \wedge \mathtt{DblCnt} \prec_1 \mathtt{Cnt} \wedge\ v{+}1 \le v' \le v{+}2\} \end{aligned}$$

Next, to enforce behaviour subtyping, we first check whether the static spec of method `Cnt.tick()` is a subtype of its dynamic spec. Secondly, we check whether the dynamic spec of `DblCnt.tick()` is a subtype of the dynamic spec of `Cnt.tick()`. With these specs above, all these checks are valid. Hence, this validity guarantees behavioural subtyping without requiring re-verification. Moreover, any dynamic dispatching call with the receiver of static type `Cnt` can use the dynamic specification in class `Cnt`.

2.2 Incorrectness Reasoning with Subclass Reflection

Hoare logic and IL have different foundations. Technically, IL has another consequence rule with a reversed entailment in the premises.

$$\frac{pre_D \models pre_C \qquad [pre_D] \; \mathsf{S} \; [post_D] \qquad post_C \models post_D}{[pre_C] \; \mathsf{S} \; [post_C]} \; (\mathrm{IL - Conseq})$$

Second, an analyser using Hoare logic has to prove the safety of all program paths to show the absence of bugs in a program. In contrast, to show the presence of a bug, an analyser using IL could drop paths. A critical insight from the IL-Conseq rule is that the postcondition can be under-approximated, e.g., dropping paths/disjuncts for scalability. *Superclass abstraction* cannot be easily adapted to capture reachable states for subclasses in under-approximation. As the above example shows, the dynamic spec of `Cnt.tick` only records the change in the `val` field; we cannot conclude any information for the `bak` field. As a result, we cannot find precise reachable states for the subclass of `Cnt` when a dynamic dispatching call is performed.

We observe that while superclasses are unaware of reachable states of extended fields in the subclasses, the subclasses should satisfy the constraints (reachable states) over fields inherited from superclasses. To uphold the substitution principle in under-approximating reasoning, we require the inherited fields in the postcondition of a subclass method are not weaker than its counterpart in the superclass.

Based on this observation, we introduce *subclass reflection* to handle dynamic dispatching calls for under-approximating reasoning. *Superclass abstraction* is a top-down approach while *subclass reflection* is bottom-up. An abstraction for under-approximation could be behaviours of a subset of a class hierarchy. With this setting, we write reflexive specifications in subclasses to reflect their superclasses' behaviours. Hence, each subclass will take care of one class chain in a class hierarchy.

Given a subclass method D.mn, <u>for all D.mn's specs $[pre_D]$_$[post_D]$, there exists</u> some specs $[pre_C]$_$[post_C]$ of method mn in the superclass C such that $[pre_C]$_$[post_C] <:_U [pre_D]$_$[post_D]$ where the relation $<:_U$[1] is defined as:

$$\frac{pre_C \models pre_D \qquad post_D \wedge type(this) = C \models post_C}{[pre_C]\text{\_}[post_C] <:_U [pre_D]\text{\_}[post_D]}$$

If $[pre_C]$ _ $[post_C] <:_U [pre_D]$ _ $[post_D]$, then for all S, and $[pre_C] \; \mathsf{S} \; [post_C]$, we have $[pre_D] \; \mathsf{S} \; [post_D \wedge type(this) = C]$. Note that, the type constraint here

---

[1] This definition is slightly different from the version in Definition 2 for simplicity.

is $type(this) = C$ which is different from $type(this) \prec D$ in $<:_O$. This is because *subclass reflection* requires $post_D$ to reflect its superclass C. We now demonstrate our proposal through the example in Fig. 1. The reflexive spec of `Cnt.tick` is the same as its static spec since `Cnt` is the only type to be reflected by `Cnt`:

$$\texttt{static/reflex}\ [this{::}\texttt{Cnt}\langle v\rangle]\ \texttt{tick}()\ [\text{ok: } this{::}\texttt{Cnt}\langle v+1\rangle]$$

Note that, ok denotes postconditions in normal executions. Objects that need to be reflected by `DblCnt` are $this{::}\texttt{Cnt}\langle v\rangle \ \vee\ this{::}\texttt{DblCnt}\langle v, b\rangle$. We propose a dynamic view as: $this{::}\texttt{Cnt}\langle v\rangle\texttt{DblCnt}\langle b\rangle$ to represent this disjunction.

$$\texttt{static}\ [this{::}\texttt{DblCnt}\langle v, b\rangle]\ \texttt{tick}()\ [\text{ok: } this{::}\texttt{DblCnt}\langle v', v\rangle \wedge v{+}1{\le}v'{\le}v{+}2]$$
$$\texttt{reflex}\ \ [this{::}\texttt{Cnt}\langle v\rangle\texttt{DblCnt}\langle b\rangle]\ \texttt{tick}()\ [\text{ok: } this{::}\texttt{Cnt}\langle v{+}1\rangle\texttt{DblCnt}\langle v\rangle]$$

The `else` branch of `DblCnt.tick` has been dropped in the reflexive spec.

Let `reflex(mn)` (resp. `static(mn)`) be the reflexive (resp. static) spec of method `mn`. To show that `reflex(DblCnt.tick)` is valid for both `DblCnt.tick` and `Cnt.tick`, we prove both 1) `static(DblCnt.tick)` $<:_U$ `reflex(DblCnt.tick)` and 2) `reflex(Cnt.tick)` $<:_U$ `reflex(DblCnt.tick)`. We illustrate 1) here,

$$this{::}\texttt{DblCnt}\langle v, b\rangle \models this{::}\texttt{Cnt}\langle v\rangle\texttt{DblCnt}\langle b\rangle \qquad //\text{checking for } pre$$
$$this{::}\texttt{Cnt}\langle v{+}1\rangle\texttt{DblCnt}\langle v\rangle \wedge (type(this) = \texttt{DblCnt}) \qquad //\text{checking for } post$$
$$\Rightarrow (this{::}\texttt{Cnt}\langle v{+}1\rangle \vee this{::}\texttt{DblCnt}\langle v{+}1, v\rangle) \wedge (type(this) = \texttt{DblCnt})$$
$$\Rightarrow this{::}\texttt{DblCnt}\langle v{+}1, v\rangle \models this{::}\texttt{DblCnt}\langle v', v\rangle \wedge v{+}1{\le}v'{\le}v{+}2$$

By doing so, we validate `reflex(DblCnt.tick)` without verifying it against the method bodies. We show a simple example in Fig. 2. The precondition before the dispatching call (line 3) shows that object x has a dynamic view $x{::}\texttt{Cnt}\langle v\rangle\texttt{DblCnt}\langle b\rangle$. We will retrieve a reflexive spec according to the last type in this dynamic view. Hence, the reflexive spec in `DblCnt` is chosen as it also reflects the types before `DblCnt` in this dynamic view. Alternatively, if we want to capture the `else` branch of `DblCnt`, another reflexive spec in `DblCnt.tick()` could be: $[this{::}\texttt{Cnt}\langle v\rangle\texttt{DblCnt}\langle b\rangle]\_$ $[\text{ok: } this{::}\texttt{DblCnt}\langle v{+}2, v\rangle]$. This reflexive spec drops the path from `Cnt`. Hence, we do not have to check `reflex(Cnt.tick)` $<:_U$ `reflex(DblCnt.tick)` for this spec as the relation is trivially true.

Our dynamic view can reason about casting, which is extensively used in OOP. For instance, Fig. 2 shows a casting operation performed on object x. x's type is either `Cnt` or `DblCnt`. On line 5, as x is casting to `DblCnt`, based on x's possible types, our system splits into cases with ok spec on line 6 and er spec on line 7, respectively. By so doing, our system

```
1 void goo(Cnt x) {...
2     [x::Cnt⟨v⟩DblCnt⟨b⟩]
3     x.tick();
4     [ok: x::Cnt⟨v + 1⟩DblCnt⟨v⟩]
5     y := (DblCnt) x;
6     [ok: x::DblCnt⟨v + 1, v⟩ ∧ y = x]
7     [er: x::Cnt⟨v + 1⟩]
8   ...}
```

Fig. 2. Example on casting

can discover bugs relating to casting effectively. The efficiency is also confirmed by our experiments: Our system can prove casting bugs which are beyond Pulse, the bug checker used in products at Meta and other big-tech companies.

3 Language and Specifications

The section presents the core OO language and our assertion grammar.

3.1 Syntax of the Target Language

Figure 3 presents our core language. We assume the language uses single inheritance and pass-by-value mechanism. `Object` is an implicit superclass of all classes, x, y... for program variables, C, D... for class names, e and B for expressions and boolean expressions respectively, and $x.f$ for the field f of x. Boolean expression x `instanceof` C is true if x is in class C or a subclass of C.

$$
\begin{array}{rl}
\mathcal{P} ::= & \overline{\texttt{cdef};} \\
\texttt{cdef} ::= & \mathit{class}\ C_1\ \mathit{extends}\ C_2\ \{\overline{\texttt{t}}\ \overline{f};\ \overline{\texttt{meth}}\} \\
\tau ::= & \texttt{int} \mid \texttt{bool} \mid \texttt{void} \qquad\qquad \texttt{t} ::= C \mid \tau \\
\texttt{sp}, \texttt{rp} ::= & [P]\_[\epsilon{:}Q] \\
\texttt{meth} ::= & \texttt{mtype}\ \texttt{t}\ \texttt{mn}\ (\overline{\texttt{t}}\ \overline{x})\ [\mathit{static}\ \texttt{sp}]\ [\mathit{reflexive}\ \texttt{rp}]\ \{\texttt{S}; \texttt{return}\ y\} \\
\texttt{mtype} ::= & \mathit{virtual} \mid \mathit{inherit} \mid \mathit{override} \\
\texttt{S} ::= & \texttt{skip} \mid x{:=}e \mid x.f{:=}y \mid x{:=}y.f \mid \texttt{t}\ x; \texttt{S} \mid y{:=}(C)\ x \mid x{:=}\mathit{new}\ C(\overline{y}) \\
& \mid y{:=}x.\texttt{mn}(\overline{z}) \mid y{:=}x\ \texttt{instanceof}\ C \mid \texttt{S}; \texttt{S} \mid \mathit{assume}(B) \mid \texttt{S} + \texttt{S}
\end{array}
$$

Fig. 3. A core Object-Oriented language.

A program $\mathcal{P}$ is a collection of class definitions. A class declares its superclass via keyword *extends*. A class consists of fields, method declarations and definitions. Each method `meth` will be annotated as *virtual*, *inherit* or *override*. A *virtual* method only exists in the subclass but not its superclass. An *inherit* method uses the same method body as its superclass. Lastly, an *override* method re-defines the method body in the subclass. Each method is annotated with two specifications: one is static `sp` and another is reflexive `rp`. ϵ is program status: ok (for normal executions) and er (for abnormal ones).

3.2 Semantics

Val defines values of variables including integers, booleans, locations *Loc*, and *null*. A program state $\sigma \in \mathit{PState}$ is a tuple, including a stack $s \in \mathit{Stack}$, that maps variables to values, *Val*, and a heap $h \in \mathit{Heap}$, that partially maps addresses to the contents. A heap h includes two mappings: $h.1$ maps locations to class names (dynamic type of an object) and $h.2$ maps location-field tuples to *Val*. The semantics is the relation of statements S, exit conditions ϵ, and program states σ.

$$\sigma \in PState \stackrel{\text{def}}{=} Stack \times Heap \qquad s \in Stack \stackrel{\text{def}}{=} Var \rightarrow Val \qquad v \in Val$$
$$h \in Heap \stackrel{\text{def}}{=} (Loc \rightharpoonup Classes) \times (Loc \times Field \rightharpoonup Val) \qquad l \in Loc \subseteq Val$$
$$[\![\cdot]\!] \stackrel{\text{def}}{=} Statement \times Exit \times \mathcal{P}(PState \times PState) \qquad \epsilon \in Exit \stackrel{\text{def}}{=} \{ok, er\}$$

The relational denotational semantics is presented in our technical report [16]. We discuss the semantics of two commands: casting and `instanceof` in detail. The semantics of casting is as follows:

$$[\![y{:=}(C)\ x]\!]ok \stackrel{\text{def}}{=} \{((s,h),(s[y \mapsto s(x)],h))|\ (h.1(s(x)) = C_1 \wedge C_1{\prec}C) \vee s(x) = null\}$$
$$[\![y{:=}(C)\ x]\!]er \stackrel{\text{def}}{=} \{((s,h),(s,h))|\ h.1(s(x)) = C_1 \wedge C_1{\not\prec}C\}$$

Casting an object to its superclass is always successful, while it is erroneous another way around. For instance, downcasting a heap object with a type C to its subclass or any unrelated class causes an error. The statement `instanceof` is used to check object types before casting.

Class hierarchy is collected via *extends* keyword. When for each C_1 *extends* C_2, $\{C_1{\prec_1}C_2\}$ is added to the environment. The notation $C_2{\prec_1}C_1$ means C_2 is the immediate subclass of C_1 while $C_2{\prec}C_1$ means C_2 is a subclass of C_1 or C_2 equals C_1. We can query the class hierarchy environment for the subtyping relation between classes. x `instanceof` C is a side-effect-free Boolean expression. Its semantics is as follows:

$$B[\![x\ \texttt{instanceof}\ C]\!](s,h) \stackrel{\text{def}}{=} False\ \texttt{iff}\ s(x) = null \vee (h.1(s(x)) \not\prec C)$$
$$B[\![x\ \texttt{instanceof}\ C]\!](s,h) \stackrel{\text{def}}{=} True\ \texttt{iff}\ (h.1(s(x)) \prec C)$$

3.3 Assertion Language

We here present the assertion language, an extension of separation logic [4] with IL. Figure 4 presents the syntax of the specification language (while the semantics can be found in our technical report [16]). The separation conjunction $\kappa_1 * \kappa_2$ describes two non-overlapping heaps, κ_1 and κ_2. $x.f{\mapsto}e$ stands for an object x has a field f which points to e and $x : C$ stands for the type for x stored in a heap is C. To simplify the notation, we encode a heap object in the form of $x{\mapsto}C\langle\overline{e}\rangle$, meaning that the object x of exact type C has fields $x.f_1{\mapsto}e_1, x.f_2{\mapsto}e_2, \cdots x.f_n{\mapsto}e_n$. That said, $x{\mapsto}C\langle\overline{e}\rangle = x : C{*}x.f_1{\mapsto}e_1{*}x.f_2{\mapsto}e_2{*} \cdots x.f_n{\mapsto}e_n$.

$$P,Q ::= (\kappa{\wedge}\phi) \mid P \vee Q \mid \exists x.P \qquad \kappa ::= emp \mid x.f{\mapsto}e \mid x : C \mid x{\mapsto}C\langle\overline{e}\rangle \mid \kappa_1 * \kappa_2$$
$$\phi ::= False \mid C \prec C \mid x = e \mid x < e \mid \phi_1 \wedge \phi_2 \mid \phi_1{\vee}\phi_2 \mid \neg\phi \mid \phi_1{\Rightarrow}\phi_2$$

Fig. 4. Assertion language.

We also call $x \mapsto C\langle \overline{e} \rangle$ a static view, which describes a single object. In addition, we introduce the dynamic view to handle the dynamically dispatched method call. The dynamic view is in the form of $x{::}C_1\langle \overline{e_1} \rangle C_2 \langle \overline{e_2} \rangle \cdots C_n \langle \overline{e_n} \rangle$ which is a collection of static views of objects along a class chain from C_1 to C_n in a class hierarchy. Specifically, it is syntactic sugar for the disjunction of objects, i.e. $x \mapsto C_1 \langle \overline{e_1} \rangle \vee x \mapsto C_2 \langle \overline{e_1}, \overline{e_2} \rangle \cdots \vee x \mapsto C_n \langle \overline{e_1}, \cdots \overline{e_n} \rangle$. The subclass objects have to maintain the same state for the fields inherited from its superclass to form a valid dynamic view.

IL Triples. An IL triple is of the following form: $\vDash [P] \ \textsf{S} \ [\epsilon{:}Q]$. In contrast to Hoare logic, the postcondition Q is an under-approximation of all possible execution paths and any state in Q, is reachable from some states satisfying P. Formally,

$$\vDash [P] \ \textsf{S} \ [\epsilon{:}Q] \overset{\text{def}}{=} \forall \sigma \in \llbracket Q \rrbracket. \ \exists \sigma' \in \llbracket P \rrbracket.(\sigma', \sigma) \in \llbracket \textsf{S} \rrbracket \epsilon.$$

4 Proof System for Under-Approximating Reasoning

We propose specification subtyping in Sect. 4.1 and the mechanism of static and reflexive specifications in Sect. 4.2. Finally, proof rules are shown in Sect. 4.3.

4.1 Behavioural Subtyping

Liskov substitution principle (behaviour subtyping) [17,18] gives a general guideline for OOP design, which is crucial to the dynamic modularity problem. In under-approximation, we uphold this principle.

Definition 1 (Specification Subtyping).   *Given an IL specification* $[P_C]\_[\epsilon{:}Q_C]$ *and another IL specification* $[P_D]\_[\epsilon{:}Q_D]$. *We say* $[P_C]\_[\epsilon{:}Q_C]$ *is a subtype specification of* $[P_D]\_[\epsilon{:}Q_D]$ *if the following holds,*

$$\frac{Q_D \vDash Q_C * F \qquad F * P_C \vDash P_D}{[P_C]\_[\epsilon{:}Q_C] <: [P_D]\_[\epsilon{:}Q_D]}$$

This definition is a corollary of IL consequence rule and the frame rule. The frame F can be calculated via the postcondition entailment proving. Then, F will be carried forward for the precondition entailment proving. Any program satisfying $[P_C]\_[\epsilon{:}Q_C]$ will satisfy $[P_D]\_[\epsilon{:}Q_D]$.

Recap that the inherited fields in a behavioural subtype should not reach more states than the superclass. This is the key point to uphold Liskov substitution principle in under-approximation. For instance, we would not expect a buggy state to be reachable by a method in the subclass but unreachable in the superclass. Otherwise, the superclass is not replaceable as the program will introduce new errors with the subclass. Hence, according to the above definition, the under-approximation specification of a superclass should be a subtype of that in the subclass. In other words, the subclass specification needs to reflect its superclass's behaviours. We call it *subclass reflection*. With *subclass reflection*, the dynamic dispatching call can be handled efficiently.

However, as subclasses might extend superclasses with extra fields, checking Definition 1 is not straightforward. To address this issue, we incorporate static view and dynamic view. Recall that the dynamic view is a disjunction of multiple objects. We allow a constraint $type(x) \in T$ to assert if the type of object x is in a set T of types. Hence, we can check specifications for objects that only belong to T. For example,

$$\begin{aligned}
&this{::}C\langle\overline{e_1}\rangle D\langle\overline{e_2}\rangle \wedge type(this) \in \{C\}\\
\Rightarrow&(this{\mapsto}C\langle\overline{e_1}\rangle \vee this{\mapsto}D\langle\overline{e_1},\overline{e_2}\rangle) \wedge type(this) \in \{C\}\\
\Rightarrow&this{\mapsto}C\langle\overline{e_1}\rangle
\end{aligned}$$

We mainly need two kinds of implications between static view and dynamic view in our verification processes Sect. 4.2.

Lemma 1 (View Relationship).

$$this{::}C\langle\overline{e_1}\rangle D\langle\overline{e_2}\rangle E\langle\overline{e_3}\rangle \wedge type(this) \in \{E\} \Rightarrow this{\mapsto}E\langle\overline{e_1},\overline{e_2},\overline{e_3}\rangle$$

$$this{::}C\langle\overline{e_1}\rangle D\langle\overline{e_2}\rangle E\langle\overline{e_3}\rangle \wedge type(this) \in \{C, D\} \Rightarrow this{::}C\langle\overline{e_1}\rangle D\langle\overline{e_2}\rangle$$

Now, we introduce the specification subtyping for behavioural subtyping.

Definition 2 (Behavioural Subtyping). *We say that the under-approximation specification* $[P_C]$ _ $[\epsilon{:}Q_C]$ *for a method mn in superclass C and another* $[P_D]$ _ $[\epsilon{:}Q_D]$ *for mn in subclass D cater to behavioural subtyping if the following holds,*

$$\frac{Q_D \wedge type(this) \in T_C \models Q_C * F \qquad F * P_C \models P_D}{[P_C]\ \_\ [\epsilon{:}Q_C]\ <:_U\ [P_D]\ \_\ [\epsilon{:}Q_D]}$$

where T_C is the set of types pointed to by `this` *reference in C's specification. We use $<:_U$ to capture this relationship.*

4.2 Static and Reflexive Specifications

In some previous works [4,25], static and dynamic specification co-existence has been proposed to handle method verification and behavioural subtyping. We introduce a similar mechanism in an under-approximation flavour. We use the special variable *this* to denote the reference of the current object.

Static Specification. Static specification is a description of a single method. The static view must describe the object referred to by *this* in the static specification. Hence, the static specification should be precise (the precondition needs to be as strong as possible, and the postcondition needs to be as weak as possible).

Reflexive Specification. Reflexive specification is used for two purposes. Firstly, it ensures behavioural subtyping: i) The reflexive specification in the superclass is a subtype of the reflexive specification in the subclass; ii) the static specification of a method needs to be a subtype of the corresponding reflexive specification. Secondly, it is used for dynamically dispatching calls. To model dynamic dispatching, the dynamic views encode the state of multiple objects along a class chain. Any object in a dynamic view could be dispatched for a dynamic call. In contrast to the static specification, we use dynamic view for *this* reference in reflexive specifications.

Static/Reflexive Specification Verification. We now discuss the relationship between these two specifications in class inheritance. The first one is virtual method whose implementation only exists in subclasses. Note that, one specification can be both static and reflexive in the virtual method as there is no superclass to reflect.

$$\frac{\begin{array}{c}\texttt{sp}{=}[P]\_[\epsilon{:}Q] \\ [P]\ \texttt{S;return y}\ [\epsilon{:}Q] \qquad \textit{(Spec verification)}\end{array}}{\textit{virtual}\ \texttt{t}_1\ \texttt{mn}\ (\bar{\texttt{t}}_2\ \bar{x})\ [\textit{static}\ \texttt{sp}]\ [\textit{reflexive}\ \texttt{sp}]\ \{\texttt{S;return}\ y\}\ \texttt{in}\ C}$$

Spec verification is the verification of the static specification against the method body by using our proof rules in Sect. 4.3 and basic rules in [16].

Second, an inherited method in the subclass uses the same implementation from its superclass: Inherited methods are semantically equivalent in both classes. The prior work [4] defines a notion called "statically-inherited" methods. A method is statically inherited by the subclass if (1) it does not override the original implementation and (2) if the method calls any other method mn inside the body, mn must also be statically-inherited. For simplicity, we assume every inherited method is statically-inherited as a non-statically-inherited method can always be transferred into an overriding method. To verify the static specification for the inherited method in the subclass, we can check whether its specification is *compatible* with the corresponding static specification in the superclass. *Compatible*(sp', sp) means that sp is derivable from sp' using consequence rule or frame rule, i.e. $sp' <: sp$, which is defined in Definition 1.

$$\frac{\begin{array}{c}D{\prec_1}C \quad \texttt{sp}_\texttt{c}{=}\texttt{static}(C.\texttt{mn}) \quad \texttt{rp}_\texttt{c}{=}\texttt{reflex}(C.\texttt{mn}) \quad \texttt{sp}'_\texttt{c}{=}\texttt{sp}_\texttt{c}[\texttt{this} : D/\texttt{this} : C] \\ \textit{Compatible}(\texttt{sp}'_\texttt{c}, \texttt{sp}) \qquad \textit{(Spec verification)} \\ \texttt{sp} <:_U \texttt{rp} \qquad \textit{(Dynamic Dispatch)} \\ \texttt{rp}_\texttt{c} <:_U \texttt{rp} \qquad \textit{(Behavioural subtyping)}\end{array}}{\textit{inherit}\ \texttt{t}_1\ \texttt{mn}\ (\bar{\texttt{t}}_2\ \bar{x})\ [\textit{static}\ \texttt{sp}]\ [\textit{reflexive}\ \texttt{rp}]\ \{\}\ \textit{in}\ D}$$

Note that, $\texttt{sp}'_\texttt{c} = \texttt{sp}_\texttt{c}[\texttt{this} : \texttt{D}/\texttt{this} : \texttt{C}]$ is valid when the superclass implementation does not access the type information of *this*. If the implementation accesses the type information of *this*, we need to verify the implementation against the static specification of the subclass.

Lastly, an overriding method redefines the procedure performed in a subclass. Hence, the superclass and the subclass may behave differently. However, the subclass can still be behavioural subtyping if both classes obey the rule in Definition 2. Again, we require the same relation holds for those specifications.

$$\frac{\begin{array}{c} D{\prec_1}C \qquad \mathtt{rp_c}{=}\mathtt{reflex}(C.\mathtt{mn}) \qquad \mathtt{sp}{=}[P]\_[\epsilon{:}Q] \\ [P]\ \mathtt{S};\mathtt{return}\ y\ [\epsilon{:}Q] \quad (\textit{Spec verification}) \\ \mathtt{sp} <:_U \mathtt{rp} \quad (\textit{Dynamic Dispatch}) \\ \mathtt{rp_c} <:_U \mathtt{rp} \quad (\textit{Behavioural Subtyping}) \end{array}}{\textit{override}\ \mathtt{t_1}\ \mathtt{mn}\ (\bar{\mathtt{t}}_2\ \overline{x})\ [\textit{static}\ \mathtt{sp}]\ [\textit{reflexive}\ \mathtt{rp}]\ \{\mathtt{S};\mathtt{return}\ y\}\ \mathtt{in}\ D}$$

The constructor is a special type of method that initialises the fields of an object. We use C_{cs} to denote the constructor for class C. When the subclass's constructor is called, by default, the constructor of its superclass is called before the subclass constructor. As a constructor instantiates a concrete object, constructors only have a static specification. A concrete object should use static specifications for further method calls.

$$\frac{\begin{array}{c} D{\prec_1}C \qquad \mathtt{sp_c}{=}\textit{static}(C_{\mathtt{cs}}) \qquad \mathtt{sp_c}{=}[P_c]\_[\epsilon{:}Q_c] \\ \mathtt{sp}{=}[P]\_[\epsilon{:}Q] \qquad P_c * \mathtt{P_f} \vdash P \\ [P']{=}[\epsilon{:}Q_c[\mathtt{this}:D/\mathtt{this}:C] * \mathtt{P_f} * (\ast_{\mathtt{f_i}\in\mathtt{field(D)}}\ \mathtt{this.f_i}{\mapsto}\mathtt{null})] \\ [P']\ \mathtt{S}\ [\epsilon{:}Q] \quad (\textit{Spec verification}) \end{array}}{D_{\mathtt{cs}}\ (\bar{\mathtt{t}}_2\ \overline{x})\ [\textit{static}\ \mathtt{sp}]\ \{\mathtt{S}\}}$$

To ensure sp meets the precondition for calling the superclass's constructor, we do an entailment checking for $P_c * \mathtt{P_f} \vdash P$: the precondition of the superclass P_c should entail the precondition of the subclass P with a possible anti-frame $\mathtt{P_f}$ that captures the extra nodes (do not appear in P_c) in the separation formula P. This anti-frame $\mathtt{P_f}$ is carried forward as part of the pre-states for verification. In addition, all extension fields of class D will be set to `null` before executing the constructor body S.

4.3 Proof Rules

This section presents primary proof rules specific to our OO language in Fig. 5. We leave the remaining standard rules [23,26] in [16].

Rules Read, Write, NullRead and NullWrite are for object access (read/write). Programmers typically check object type using `instanceof` before applying casting. Rules for `instanceof`, including InsNull, Ins and DyIns, model the type checking. While the first two are for objects with static views, the last one is for objects with dynamic views. C_m represents some classes with fields before C_i while C_k is for those after C_i. If $C_i \prec C$, `intanceof` operator returns true and drops all classes before C_i, but keeps the field information (of the dropped classes) in C_i. Otherwise, it returns false and drops those classes after C_i.

The rules for casting operators are CastNull, CastOk, CastErr, DyCastOk and DyCastErr. A casting error happens when the type of an object is assigned to an incompatible type. Note that the casting operation does not change the type stored in a heap or which method to call. A casting operator applies on a `null` value without any exceptions. Upcasting is always successful, as an instance of the subclass is also an instance of the superclass. Downcasting fails if we cast an object of exact type C to its subclass D. Casting to an unrelated class will also lead to an error. Similar to DyIns, rules DyCastOk and DyCastErr are for objects with dynamic view. If $C_i \prec C$, all classes after C_i in a dynamic view can be cast to C. Otherwise, all classes before C_i in a dynamic view can lead to casting errors.

Rules for method invocation are Static MethodInv and Dynamic MethodInv. When an object has an exact type C, we apply its static specification. For the

$$\frac{}{[x.f\mapsto e \wedge y = y']\ y{:=}x.f\ [\text{ok: } x.f\mapsto e[y'/y] \wedge y = e[y'/y]]}\ \text{Read}$$

$$\frac{}{[x = \texttt{null}]\ y{:=}x.\_\ [\text{er: } x = \texttt{null}]}\ \text{NullRead}$$

$$\frac{}{[x.f\mapsto e]\ x.f{:=}\ y\ [\text{ok: } x.f\mapsto y]}\ \text{Write} \qquad \frac{}{[x{=}\texttt{null}]\ x.f{:=}y\ [\text{er: } x{=}\texttt{null}]}\ \text{NullWrite}$$

$$\frac{}{[x = \texttt{null} \wedge y = y']\ y{:=}x\ \texttt{instanceof}\ C\ [\text{ok: } x = \texttt{null} \wedge y = \mathit{False}]}\ \text{InsNull}$$

$$\frac{Q_1 \equiv x : C_1 \wedge y = \mathit{True} \wedge C_1 \prec C \qquad Q_2 \equiv x : C_1 \wedge y = \mathit{False} \wedge C_1 \not\prec C}{[x : C_1 \wedge y = y']\ \ y{:=}x\ \texttt{instanceof}\ C\ [\text{ok: } Q_i],\ i \in \{1;2\}}\ \text{Ins}$$

$$\frac{\begin{array}{c} Q_1 \equiv x :: C_i\langle\overline{e_m}, \overline{e_i}\rangle C_k \wedge y = \mathit{True} \wedge C_i \prec C \\ Q_2 \equiv x :: C_m C_i\langle\overline{e_i}\rangle \wedge y = \mathit{False} \wedge C_i \not\prec C \end{array}}{[x :: C_m C_i\langle\overline{e_i}\rangle C_k \wedge y = y']\ \ y{:=}x\ \texttt{instanceof}\ C\ [\text{ok: } Q_1 \vee Q_2]}\ \text{DyIns}$$

$$\frac{}{[x = \texttt{null} \wedge y = y']\ y{:=}(C)\ x\ [\text{ok: } x = \texttt{null} \wedge y = \texttt{null}]}\ \text{CastNull}$$

$$\frac{}{[x{\mapsto}C_1\langle\bar{e}\rangle \wedge y = y' \wedge C_1{\prec}C]\ y{:=}(C)\ x\ [\text{ok: } x{\mapsto}C_1\langle\bar{e}[y'/y]\rangle \wedge y = x \wedge C_1{\prec}C]}\ \text{CastOk}$$

$$\frac{}{[x : C_1 \wedge C_1 \not\prec C]\ y{:=}(C)\ x\ [\text{er: } x : C_1 \wedge C_1 \not\prec C]}\ \text{CastErr}$$

$$\frac{Q \equiv x :: (C_i\langle\overline{e_m}, \overline{e_i}\rangle C_k)[y'/y] \wedge y = x \wedge C_i \prec C}{[x :: C_m C_i\langle\overline{e_i}\rangle C_k \wedge y = y']\ y{:=}(C)\ x\ [\text{ok: } Q]}\ \text{DyCastOk}$$

$$\frac{Q \equiv x :: C_m C_i\langle\overline{e_i}\rangle \wedge y = y' \wedge C_i \not\prec C}{[x :: C_m C_i\langle\overline{e_i}\rangle C_k \wedge y = y']\ y{:=}(C)\ x\ [\text{er: } Q]}\ \text{DyCastErr}$$

$$\frac{x : C \qquad \texttt{static}(C.\texttt{mn}(\bar{w})) = [Pr]_{-}[\epsilon{:}Po] \qquad Pr[x, \bar{z}/\mathit{this}, \bar{w}] \Rightarrow P}{[P \wedge y = y']y = x.\texttt{mn}(\bar{z})[\epsilon{:}Po[x, \bar{z}, y/\mathit{this}, \bar{w}, \mathit{ret}]]}\ \text{Static MethodInv}$$

$$\frac{\begin{array}{c} \mathit{view}(x) = x :: ...D\langle...\rangle \\ \texttt{reflex}(D.\texttt{mn}(\bar{w})) = [Pr]_{-}[\epsilon{:}Po] \qquad Pr[x, \bar{z}/\mathit{this}, \bar{w}] \Rightarrow P \end{array}}{[P \wedge y = y']y = x.mn(\bar{z})[\epsilon{:}Po[x, \bar{z}, y/\mathit{this}, \bar{w}, \mathit{ret}]]}\ \text{Dynamic MethodInv}$$

$$\frac{\texttt{static}(C(\bar{w})) = [Pr]_{-}[\epsilon{:}Po] \quad Pr[\bar{y}/\bar{w}] \Rightarrow P}{[P \wedge x = x']x{:=}\mathit{new}\ C(\bar{y})[\epsilon{:}Po[\bar{y}, x/\bar{w}, \mathit{this}]]}\ \text{Constructor}$$

Fig. 5. Proof rules

dynamic method invocation ($view(x) = x :: ...D\langle...\rangle$ means the dynamic view of object x in the precondition ends with type D), our system extracts reflexive specs according to the last type of the object's dynamic view. Note that, a reflexive spec may describe more classes than necessary. For instance, the dynamic view of an object x before a dynamic method invocation is $x{::}D\langle\overline{e_2}\rangle E\langle\overline{e_3}\rangle$. However, the dynamic view of *this* object in the precondition of the corresponding reflexive spec (class E) might be $this{::}C\langle\overline{e_1}\rangle D\langle\overline{e_2}\rangle E\langle\overline{e_3}\rangle$. It seems we could not apply the Dynamic MethodInv rule. In this case, we can use the Constancy rule [23] and add a constrain $type(this) = \{D, E\}$ in the pre/post of the reflexive spec. Then, we can obtain a spec that can be used for this dynamic method invocation. Our case studies in [16] utilise this strategy to do the proving. Constructor is for object constructor and is similar to Static MethodInv. Note that, all method invocations may need extra efforts for anti-frame inference. As the precondition P could contain more heap components than Pr for method calls, we need to infer a formula F where $Pr * F \vdash P$ and then push F forward by using the frame rule.

Theorem 1 (Soundness). *If* $\vdash [P]\mathtt{S}[\epsilon{:}Q]$, *then* $\models [P]\mathtt{S}[\epsilon{:}Q]$.

5 Implementation and Evaluation

Implementation. We prototype our incorrectness verification system for OOP, OURify, which consists of 10,000 lines of OCaml codes. We discharge the entailment checking and the anti-frame inference using the off-the-shelf tool, SLEEK [5,12].

OURify is an automated verifier that performs under-approximation compositional reasoning in a bottom-up manner. Specifically, given a program written in our core language (shown in Fig. 3) with well-annotated static and reflexive specifications, OURify verifies (i) the implementation against the static specifications; and (ii) behaviour subtyping conformance via the proposed subtyping relation among reflexive specifications. Afterwards, OURify reports the verification results, SUCCESS or FAILED, to the user.

OURify implements the proof rules in Fig. 5, basic rules in [16,23,26], and a proof search algorithm. The algorithm takes a *specification table* T, that stores verified specifications of methods and uses a function $post(P, T, \mathtt{S})$, that computes the post-states ϵ': Q' of command $\mathtt{S}$ from its pre-condition P via applying the proof rules.

Given a method mn with the static specification $[P]\_[\epsilon{:}Q]$ and implementation m_c, OURify verifies the specification by first computing a set of post-states via $post(P, T, m_c)$. After that, for each post-state assertion $\epsilon' : Q'$, it invokes SLEEK to check whether ϵ' is the same with ϵ and $Q * emp \models Q'$. If there is no post-state that satisfies these checks, OURify returns FAILED. Otherwise, the static specification $[P]\_[\epsilon{:}Q]$ is verified. Theorem 1 ensures the correctness of the function *post*: $[P]\_[\epsilon{:}Q \mid \epsilon{:}\ Q \in post(P, T, m_c)]$. In addition, OURify checks the validity of the corresponding reflexive specification according to Definition 2 (specification subtyping between static and reflexive specifications of the method as well as reflexive specifications between methods of superclasses and subclasses), with the help of the back-end solver, SLEEK [5,12]. If all checks are successful, it returns SUCCESS. Otherwise, it produces FAILED.

Evaluation. The implementation is running on a Linux machine with an Intel i7 processor 3.40 GHz and 8 GB of memory. We have tested OURify on programs with null-pointer-exceptions (NPE) and class-casting-exceptions (CAST) and reported the results in Table 1 while the name with "OK" indicates an ok program.

We have chosen 15 programs as our benchmarks. Six of them are manually constructed (those with the prefix M). The manually constructed programs are used to validate our implementation. The rest of the programs are taken from some existing works and publicly available data set [2,19,21,28,29]. Those programs have been translated into our core language. We annotate specifications for each method to capture their functional properties. The benchmarks are collections of commonly occurring bugs from various projects. We keep the crucial parts for doing the experiments. For instance, we have selected some benchmarks from Pulse repository [2]. The current version of Pulse does not support the detection of some OO-related bugs in those benchmarks. We are interested in those bugs in our system.

Table 1. Experimental results.

Benchmark	LOC	TIME(s)	LoSpec	SUCCESS	FAILED
NPE_1	34	0.249	3	3	0
M_OK_2	61	0.815	8	6	2
M_NPE_3	60	0.811	9	9	0
M_CAST_4	79	0.695	13	11	2
M_OK_5	80	0.799	7	7	0
NPE_6	80	0.956	8	8	0
NPE_7	150	2.850	28	28	0
NPE_8	167	3.251	22	21	1
CAST_9	187	1.717	18	18	0
M_NPE&CAST_10	203	1.801	19	19	0
OK_11	321	5.418	49	43	6
NPE_12	331	4.907	42	38	4
NPE_13	335	5.962	53	53	0
M_NPE&CAST_14	524	9.498	84	84	0
NPE_15	709	13.282	99	99	0
Sum	3321	53.011	462	447	15

Table 1 summarises the experimental results. The table records: 1) LOC, the number of lines of code; 2) TIME, the running time (in seconds); 3) LoSpec, the number of lines of specifications – one pair of pre/post per line; 4) SUCCESS, the number of valid triples; and 5) FAILED, the number of invalid triples (all are false IL triples added to test OURify's soundness). The experimental results show that OURify verified all the triples correctly within a short running time and did not verify a false IL triple. Note that as our approach is compositional, the verification time increases linearly wrt. the number of specifications.

To demonstrate the practical impact of our proposal, we conduct the second experiment to reproduce the bugs reported by Pulse, an analyser developed within the Infer framework to find bugs in products at Meta [1]. Pulse applies under-approximate bi-abduction to infer static specifications automatically [11]. It reports a bug at a method only when it can derive a manifest er triple e.g., the triple is of the form $[emp \wedge true]$ *code* $[er : q]$, where q is satisfiable.

For this experiment, we take all real-world programs in the above experiment. For each program, if Pulse reports an NPE bug, we construct corresponding IL triples, some of them are manifest er triples. If OURify could verify these triples, we classify the bug as confirmed. Otherwise, if we could not verify manifest er triples, we write either ok triples or latent er triples (which are er triples but not in the form of manifest) where OURify can verify them and classify the bug as unconfirmed. Moreover, we also carefully validated that the ones in confirmed partition are real bugs and all in unconfirmed one are false positives.

Table 2 presents the experimental results from both tools: 1) OK_OR, the number of ok specifications proved by OURify; 2) Cast_OR, the number of error specifications for casting errors proved by OURify; 3) NPE_OR, the number of error specifications for NPE proved by OURify; 4) Manifest, the number of manifest bugs (the true bugs, in contrast to latent/possible bugs [11]); 5) NPE_PS, the number of NPE reported by Pulse; 6) Confirmed, the number of bugs reported by Pulse and confirmed by OURify; 7) FP_PS, the number of errors reported by Pulse but cannot be confirmed by OURify; and 8) FN_PS, the number of manifest bugs OURify could verify with er triples but Pulse did not discover.

Table 2. Incorrectness verification by OURify vs. bug finding by Pulse.

Benchmark	OK_OR	Cast_OR	NPE_OR	Manifest	NPE_PS	Confirmed	FP_PS	FN_PS
NPE_1	1	0	2	1	1	1	0	0
NPE_6	5	0	3	1	0	0	0	1
NPE_7	23	0	5	2	2	2	0	0
NPE_8	17	0	4	3	0	0	0	3
CAST_9	10	8	0	3	0	0	0	3
OK_11	43	0	0	0	0	0	0	0
NPE_12	37	0	1	1	1	0	1	1
NPE_13	40	0	13	12	8	5	3	7
NPE_15	75	0	24	11	9	8	1	3
Sum	251	8	52	34	21	16	5	18

To sum up, there are 34 manifest bugs, including 16 confirmed bugs and 18 false negatives (missed by Pulse), and Pulse also reported 5 false positives. Interestingly, NPE_OR (which is 52) is higher than NPE_PS (which is 21) as NPE_OR includes specifications for both latent (may) and manifest (must) bugs while NPE_PS reports manifest bugs only. Furthermore, OURify can prove several manifest bugs which Pulse could not discover. (We discuss two case studies in our technical report [16].) Most of these bugs relate to the hierarchical structure of OOP. For example, Pulse does not report bugs caused by the casting operator. In some situations, the superclass and the subclass behave differently (methods are overridden), as a result of which bugs are triggered when methods of the subclass are called but not the superclass. Pulse may miss such bugs. Requiring specification annotation is a drawback of OURify. It limits the applicability of OURify in large programs. However, writing specifications are always helpful to the program design. For instance, specifications can be used to support the regression analysis. Error specifications that are verified indicate the presence of bugs. They can kept to automatically remind programmers that certain errors should not re-appear (cannot be verified) when the code is modified in future. At the current stage, OURify works as a verification tool based on our proof system. We hope that our proof system could be the foundation for bug-finding tools, like Pulse, to hunt OO bugs more precisely in real codebases.

6 Related Work and Conclusion

Our work relates to the over-approximating verification for OOP [4,10,24,25]. To verify objects, Kassios [10] introduces a dynamic frame which describes data separation explicitly and could handle the aliasing problem. However, this work did not address behavioural subtyping which is essential for OOP. Parkinson and Bierman [24] propose the *abstract predicate family* to handle behavioural subtyping in separation logic, including a mechanism to capture specifications where subclasses own more fields than their superclasses. Predicates inside a family can change the arity freely. Hence, the implication between formulae with different heap sizes can be proved through existentially quantified arguments. Later, two independent papers [4,25] propose the co-existence of static and dynamic specifications for OOP to uphold the Liskov substitution principle.

Following the landscape of the proposals in separation logic [4,24,25], we introduce the first proof system for under-approximating reasoning over OOP. Similar to the abstract predicate family, our dynamic view specifies the behaviours of multiple objects in a class inheritance relationship. In contrast, while the abstract predicate is a conjunction set (for over-approximation), the dynamic view is based on disjuncts (i.e., describing a set of objects for under-approximation) such that it could support `instanceof` and *casting* effectively. Furthermore, we use reflexive specifications to support dynamic dispatching in a modular manner (e.g., avoid re-verification) while the static specification provides a precise verification for static method calls.

Another essential concept in OOP is class invariant, which describes classes' functions [8]. Using class invariants helps to achieve more precise analyses in over-approximately verifying OOP. There are several challenging problems and solutions for around this concept. For example, Barnett *et al.* [3] propose a methodology that can reason about class invariants which could be temporarily broken while class fields are being updated. They use a special field to explicitly record if an object's invariant is valid. Leino and Müller [15] generalise ownership-based reasoning to support interrelated object invariants. An analogy of class invariant in IL is beyond this proposal and would be investigated in future.

Under-approximating reasoning in IL helps to avoid false positives which some static analysis tools are suffering [27]. Like IL, De Vries and Koutavas [30] proposed the reverse Hoare logic for under-approximation. Incorrectness separation logic (ISL) [26] enhances the applicability of IL in heap-manipulating programs. It combines separation logic [22] and IL, which provides the fundamental framework for our work. Le *et al.* [11] bring the ISL theory into practice. They developed Pulse-X to capture manifest bugs (bugs that will be triggered regardless of the calling context) in real-world projects. Our work, an IL logic for OOP, is meant to help build a foundational framework for under-approximating reasoning that could systematically support bug finding in OOP codebase.

Conclusion. This paper presents a variant of incorrectness separation logic to show the presence of bugs in Java-like OO programs. In particular, we introduce the static view and static specification to verify the implementation of a static method and the dynamic view and reflexive specification to verify behavioural subtyping. When behavioural subtyping holds, we can avoid costly case analysis for class objects. The reflexive specification can be further re-used for the dynamically dispatched method calls. For future work, we plan to extend the system with the bi-abduction technology to infer specs and automatically find bugs in real-world OO programs.

Acknowledgements. The authors would like to thank anonymous reviewers for their comments. This work was partially supported by a Singapore Ministry of Education (MoE) Tier3 grant "Automated Program Repair", MOE-MOET32021-0001.

References

1. Infer Static Analyzer: Infer. https://fbinfer.com/. Accessed 02 June 2023
2. Pulse, an interprocedural memory safety analysis. https://github.com/facebook/infer/tree/main/infer/tests/codetoanalyze/java/pulse. Accessed 20 May 2023
3. Barnett, M., DeLine, R., Fähndrich, M., Leino, K.R.M., Schulte, W.: Verification of object-oriented programs with invariants. J. Object Technol. **3**(6), 27–56 (2004)
4. Chin, W.-N., David, C., Nguyen, H.H., Qin, S.: Enhancing modular OO verification with separation logic. ACM SIGPLAN Notices **43**(1), 87–99 (2008)
5. Chin, W.-N., David, C., Nguyen, H.H., Qin, S.: Automated verification of shape, size and bag properties via user-defined predicates in separation logic. Sci. Comput. Prog. **77**(9), 1006–1036 (2012)
6. Cook, W.R., Hill, W., Canning, P.S.: Inheritance is not subtyping. In: Proceedings of the 17th ACM SIGPLAN-SIGACT Symposium on Principles of Programming Languages (POPL 1990), New York, pp. 125–135. Association for Computing Machinery (1989)

7. Dhara, K.K., Leavens, G.T.: Forcing behavioral subtyping through specification inheritance. In: Proceedings of the 18th International Conference on Software Engineering (ICSE 1996), pp. 258–267. IEEE Computer Society (1996)
8. Hoare, C.A.R.: Proof of correctness of data representations. Acta Informatica **1**(4), 271–281 (1972)
9. Huisman, M., Jacobs, B.: Java program verification via a hoare logic with abrupt termination. In: Maibaum, T. (ed.) FASE 2000. LNCS, vol. 1783, pp. 284–303. Springer, Heidelberg (2000). https://doi.org/10.1007/3-540-46428-X_20
10. Kassios, I.T.: Dynamic frames: support for framing, dependencies and sharing without restrictions. In: Misra, J., Nipkow, T., Sekerinski, E. (eds.) FM 2006. LNCS, vol. 4085, pp. 268–283. Springer, Heidelberg (2006). https://doi.org/10.1007/11813040_19
11. Le, Q.L., Raad, A., Villard, J., Berdine, J., Dreyer, D., O'Hearn, P.W.: Finding real bugs in big programs with incorrectness logic. Proc. ACM Program. Lang. **6**(OOPSLA1) (2022)
12. Le, Q.L., Sun, J., Qin, S.: Frame inference for inductive entailment proofs in separation logic. In: Beyer, D., Huisman, M. (eds.) TACAS 2018. LNCS, vol. 10805, pp. 41–60. Springer, Cham (2018). https://doi.org/10.1007/978-3-319-89960-2_3
13. Leavens, G.T., Naumann, D.A.: Behavioral subtyping, specification inheritance, and modular reasoning. ACM Trans. Prog. Lang. Syst. **37**(4), 1–88 (2015)
14. Leavens, G.T., Weihl, W.E.: Specification and verification of object-oriented programs using supertype abstraction. Acta Informatica **32**(8), 705–778 (1995)
15. Leino, K.R.M., Müller, P.: Object invariants in dynamic contexts. In: Odersky, M. (ed.) ECOOP 2004. LNCS, vol. 3086, pp. 491–515. Springer, Heidelberg (2004). https://doi.org/10.1007/978-3-540-24851-4_22
16. Li, W., Le, Q.L., Song, Y., Chin, W.-N.: Incorrectness proofs for object-oriented programs via subclass reflection (technical report). https://www.comp.nus.edu.sg/~yahuis/APLAS2023.pdf (2023)
17. Liskov, B.: Keynote address-data abstraction and hierarchy. In: Addendum to the Proceedings on Object-Oriented Programming Systems, Languages and Applications (Addendum), pp. 17–34 (1987)
18. Liskov, B.H., Wing, J.M.: A behavioral notion of subtyping. ACM Trans. Program. Lang. Syst. **16**(6), 1811–1841 (1994)
19. Long, F., Amidon, P., Rinard, M.: Automatic inference of code transforms for patch generation. In: Proceedings of the 2017 11th Joint Meeting on Foundations of Software Engineering, pp. 727–739 (2017)
20. Luo, C., Qin, S.: Separation logic for multiple inheritance. Electron. Notes Theor. Comput. Sci. **212**, 27–40 (2008)
21. Madeiral, F., Urli, S., Maia, M., Monperrus, M.: Bears: an extensible java bug benchmark for automatic program repair studies. In: 2019 IEEE 26th International Conference on Software Analysis, Evolution and Reengineering (SANER), pp. 468–478. IEEE (2019)
22. O'Hearn, P., Reynolds, J., Yang, H.: Local reasoning about programs that alter data structures. In: Fribourg, L. (ed.) CSL 2001. LNCS, vol. 2142, pp. 1–19. Springer, Heidelberg (2001). https://doi.org/10.1007/3-540-44802-0_1
23. O'Hearn, P.W.: Incorrectness logic. Proc. ACM Prog. Lang. **4**(POPL), 10:1–10:32 (2020)
24. Parkinson, M., Bierman, G.: Separation logic and abstraction. In: Proceedings of the 32nd ACM SIGPLAN-SIGACT Symposium on Principles of Programming Languages, pp. 247–258 (2005)

25. Parkinson, M.J., Bierman, G.M.: Separation logic, abstraction and inheritance. ACM SIGPLAN Notices **43**(1), 75–86 (2008)
26. Raad, A., Berdine, J., Dang, H.-H., Dreyer, D., O'Hearn, P., Villard, J.: Local reasoning about the presence of bugs: incorrectness separation Logic. In: Lahiri, S.K., Wang, C. (eds.) CAV 2020. LNCS, vol. 12225, pp. 225–252. Springer, Cham (2020). https://doi.org/10.1007/978-3-030-53291-8_14
27. Sadowski, C., Aftandilian, E., Eagle, A., Miller-Cushon, L., Jaspan, C.: Lessons from building static analysis tools at google. Commun. ACM **61**(4), 58–66 (2018)
28. Tomassi, D.A., et al.: Bugswarm: mining and continuously growing a dataset of reproducible failures and fixes. In: 2019 IEEE/ACM 41st International Conference on Software Engineering (ICSE), pp. 339–349. IEEE (2019)
29. van Tonder, R., Le Goues, C.: Static automated program repair for heap properties. In: Proceedings of the 40th International Conference on Software Engineering, pp. 151–162 (2018)
30. de Vries, E., Koutavas, V.: Reverse hoare logic. In: Barthe, G., Pardo, A., Schneider, G. (eds.) SEFM 2011. LNCS, vol. 7041, pp. 155–171. Springer, Heidelberg (2011). https://doi.org/10.1007/978-3-642-24690-6_12

m-CFA Exhibits Perfect Stack Precision

Kimball Germane^(✉)

Brigham Young University, Provo, UT 84601, USA
kimball@cs.byu.edu

Abstract. m-CFA is a hierarchy of control-flow analyses (CFA) formulated as abstract machines and designed to exhibit polynomial time complexity while remaining usefully precise. The *Pushdown for Free* technique (P4F) prescribes a continuation allocator which induces *perfect stack precision* wherein each function invocation returns to only its call. Unfortunately, it is difficult to apply P4F to m-CFA as P4F is developed in an ANF setting but m-CFA is formulated in a CPS setting. In this paper, we recall that ANF corresponds to a CPS sublanguage without non-local control and show that m-CFA behaves identically on both. With an ANF-based m-CFA in hand, we turn to applying P4F only to discover that it already follows the prescription. In other words, m-CFA has always had perfect stack precision, a characteristic neither intended nor recognized, at its development or since. In addition to being surprising, we discuss how this result allows a spectrum of non-local control constructs to be supported more easily and with more precision than previous techniques.

Keywords: Static analysis · Control-flow analysis · Abstract interpretation

1 Introduction

A flow analysis of a functional program (i.e. control-flow analysis or CFA) computes, for each call $(f\,e)$, the set of (closures over) λs which flow to f (i.e. to which f may evaluate) and, for each function $\lambda x.e$, the set of enclosed λs which flow to x (i.e. to which x may be bound) [14]. Perhaps the most prevalent flow analysis is Shivers's k-CFA [16], a hierarchy of analyses in which the CFA at level k qualifies the analysis of each expression by the last-k call sites encountered during abstract evaluation. For instance, 0CFA does not qualify the analysis of expressions at all, and is thus context-insensitive; in contrast, 1CFA uses the most-recent call site to distinguish the analysis of otherwise-identical evaluation. To illustrate each, consider the program to the right, adapted from Gilray *et al.* [6], which we will use as a running example. The function `id` is called once at each of two sites with different arguments and, as a consequence, the analysis will bind `x`

```
(let* ([id (lambda (x) x)]
       [y (id 10)]
       [z (id 12)])
  (+ y z))
```


C.-K. Hur (Ed.): APLAS 2023, LNCS 14405, pp. 290–309, 2023.
https://doi.org/10.1007/978-981-99-8311-7_14

twice. A 0CFA analysis will conflate these two bindings so that each reference to `x` produces the values of *both* arguments. A 1CFA analysis, on the other hand, will qualify each binding by the most-recent call site, `(id 10)` and `(id 12)` respectively, so that references to it access only the values so qualified.

Since Shivers introduced k-CFA, techniques have been developed to improve its precision [12], its power [11,12,21], and its engineerability [19]. In this paper, we recall and reconcile two concurrent improvements, the development of m-CFA and the development of stack-precise CFA.

m-CFA [13] emerged from a kind of paradox: when k-CFA is applied to a functional language, its complexity is exponential (for $k > 0$); when k-CFA is applied to an object-oriented (OO) language, however, its complexity is polynomial. The discrepancy arises from the different ways in which environments are created in each setting. In a functional program, environments are created implicitly when a λ is encountered whereas, in an OO program, environments are created as part of explicit constructor invocation using `new`. Might *et al.* resolve this discrepancy to obtain a context-sensitive CFA hierarchy, m-CFA, with polynomial time complexity.

Stack-precise CFA emerged from the desire for a better model of control flow in functional languages. For two decades, CFAs modelled control flow as a finite state machine (FSM), a directed graph of control states connected by control transitions. While this model can be produced by relatively-simple workset algorithms, it cannot precisely capture the control behavior of higher-order programs whose execution is facilitated by a stack. Without precisely modeling the stack, it is impossible to capture the call–return behavior of programs with full precision, and FSM-producing CFAs routinely lose track of which particular caller to which a given call should return. The example program illustrates this well: although a 1CFA produces the expected value for each dynamic reference to `x`, a 1CFA without a precise stack model may associate both returns from `id` to each caller. In this case, `y` and `z` are each bound to both dynamic values of `x`, and the analysis calculates a result set $\{10+10, 10+12 = 12+10, 12+12\}$.

In the same year as m-CFA's presentation, Vardoulakis and Shivers [20] presented CFA2, a "context-free approach to control-flow analysis", which models control flow using a pushdown system. Using a pushdown system, rather than an FSM, allows CFA2 to precisely model the stack and perfectly associate each return to its corresponding call. Unfortunately, CFA2's summarization algorithm is substantially more complex than an FSM-producing workset algorithm and must be significantly modified to accommodate additional control features [22]. Moreover, its computational complexity is exponential, despite CFA2 not exhibiting call-site sensitivity à la k-CFA. Follow-on work produced stack-precise CFAs corresponding to FSM CFAs whose context-insensitive instances had polynomial complexity [7,10], but the techniques still imposed polynomial overhead and, in some cases, employed similarly-intricate summarization algorithms.

Somewhat surprisingly, Gilray *et al.* [6] discovered a technique to transform an FSM-based CFA into a stack-precise CFA "for free" in two senses: first, the technique prescribes a particular continuation allocator but requires no modification to the CFA, so it is free in terms of implementation effort; second, the allocator imposes only a constant factor overhead to running time above the CFA's, and so it is free in terms of computational complexity. Following the authors, we refer to this as the *pushdown for free* technique, abbreviated *P4F*.

Naturally, we would like to apply P4F to m-CFA to get the best of both worlds: a (1) polynomial-time, (2) stack-precise CFA hierarchy that (3) admits a straightforward workset-based implementation. Applying P4F requires care, however, because m-CFA is defined in terms of a CPS language but P4F is demonstrated in an ANF setting [4], and a naïve port will not necessarily result in the same analysis [15].

In this paper, we reformulate m-CFA so as to be able to directly apply P4F. After reviewing m-CFA (§2), we identify a subset of its CPS language free from non-local control (§3) and specialize a formulation of m-CFA to it (§4). We then translate this subset language to ANF (§5), formulate m-CFA for it (§6), and show that it is the same analysis as the CPS-based one (§7). Having arrived in ANF, we review P4F (§8). We observe that ANF-based CFA already uses it and show that it is indeed stack-precise (§9). We conclude by discussing ramifications of the corollary that, within the subset language, *m-CFA is and always has been stack-precise* (§10).

2 m-CFA

Might *et al.* [13] developed m-CFA in response to the paradox that, when formulated in an object-oriented (OO) setting, k-CFA [16] exhibits polynomial time complexity but, when formulated in a functional setting, exhibits exponential time complexity. After ensuring that k-CFA is implemented faithfully in both settings, Might *et al.* pinpoint environment construction to be the key distinction: in functional languages, environment bindings are captured implicitly within closures when lambda expressions are evaluated; in contrast, programmers explicitly pass data to constructors in OO languages when creating new objects. This difference leads to an exponential number of possible environments in the former case and a polynomial number in the latter, explaining the discrepancy.

Might *et al.* resolve this paradox by modifying k-CFA to produce only a polynomial number of environments by flattening the environment structure. To support this structure, their modified analysis explicitly copies bindings from old environments to new at each step, mimicking the manual construction that programmers carry out in OO programs. However, they observe that this rebinding policy leads to a precision decrease in typical programs, which is visible in the program to the right.

```
(define (f x)
  (log "f call")
  (g x))
```

In 1CFA, the bindings of `x` in `f` *before* the call to `log` are distinguished by the `f`'s caller, it being the most-recent call site. *After* the call to `log`, however, the most-recent call site is this call to `log`, or its last inner call, regardless of `f`'s caller. Consequently, rebinding `x` from the former environment to the latter combines bindings from distinct callers, jettisoning precision. Rather than revert the policy to avoid a precision decrease,

Might *et al.* manage the context abstraction differently. Instead of qualifying evaluation with the last-k call sites, they devise an approach which qualifies it with the top-m stack frames. The form of the context remains the same—a sequence of call sites—but its construction and consequent effect on the analysis differs. The resulting analysis, m-CFA, is characterized by both its rebinding policy and its context abstraction.

m-CFA is defined over a CPS language, in which all control is effected through function calls, in terms of a small-step abstract machine. We reproduce its formalism in Fig. 1, remaining vague about the details of the CPS language until §3. A machine state $\hat{\varsigma}$ is a tuple of a (CPS) call, environment, and store. A store $\hat{\sigma}$ maps addresses to denotable values. A denotable value $\hat{d}$ is a set of closures, each of which is a pair of a λ expression and an environment. An address $\hat{a}$ is a pair of a variable and an environment. An environment $\hat{\rho}$ is a sequence of call site labels up to length m, which is a parameter to the analysis. These labels are drawn from ULab which we define shortly.

$$\hat{\varsigma} \in \hat{\Sigma} = \mathsf{Call} \times \widehat{Env} \times \widehat{Store} \qquad \hat{\sigma} \in \widehat{Store} = \widehat{Addr} \to \hat{D}$$

$$\hat{d} \in \hat{D} = \mathcal{P}(\widehat{Clo} + \{\mathsf{halt}\}) \qquad \widehat{clo} \in \widehat{Clo} = \mathsf{Lam} \times \widehat{Env}$$

$$\hat{a} \in \widehat{Addr} = \mathsf{Var} \times \widehat{Env} \qquad \hat{\rho} \in \widehat{Env} = \mathsf{ULab}^{\leq m}$$

$$\Rightarrow_{\hat{\Sigma}} \subseteq \hat{\Sigma} \times \hat{\Sigma}$$

$$(call, \hat{\rho}, \hat{\sigma}) \Rightarrow_{\hat{\Sigma}} (call', \hat{\rho}'', \hat{\sigma}') \text{ where } call = [\![(f\, e_1 \ldots e_n)^\ell]\!] \text{ and}$$

$$\begin{aligned} (lam, \hat{\rho}') &\in \hat{\mathcal{E}}(f, \hat{\rho}, \hat{\sigma}) & \hat{d}_i &= \hat{\mathcal{E}}(f, \hat{\rho}, \hat{\sigma}) \\ lam &= [\![(\lambda\, (v_1 \ldots v_n)\; call')]\!] & \hat{a}_{x_j} &= (x_j, \hat{\rho}'') \\ \hat{\rho}'' &= \widehat{new}(\ell, \hat{\rho}, lam, \hat{\rho}') & \hat{a}_{v_i} &= (v_i, \hat{\rho}'') \\ \{x_1, \ldots, x_m\} &= free(lam) & \hat{d}'_j &= \hat{\sigma}(x_j, \hat{\rho}') \end{aligned}$$

$$\hat{\sigma}' = \hat{\sigma} \sqcup [\hat{a}_{v_i} \mapsto \hat{d}_i] \sqcup [\hat{a}_{x_j} \mapsto \hat{d}'_j]$$

Fig. 1. m-CFA state transition relation

Because of the uniformity of CPS, the machine state transition $\Rightarrow_{\hat{\Sigma}}$ can be characterized by a single rule: a machine step transitions control from a call to the body of its operator, which is also a call. In CPS, each argument to a call is trivial, and its value is provided by $\hat{\mathcal{E}} : \mathsf{Exp} \times \widehat{Env} \times \widehat{Store} \to \hat{D}$.

$$\hat{\mathcal{E}}(x, \hat{\rho}, \hat{\sigma}) = \hat{\sigma}(x, \hat{\rho}) \qquad \hat{\mathcal{E}}(lam, \hat{\rho}, \hat{\sigma}) = \{(lam, \hat{\rho})\}$$

The $\widehat{new}$ metafunction determines the destination environment as a function of the current call and its environment and the operator λ and its environment.

$$\widehat{new}(\ell, \hat{\rho}, lam, \hat{\rho}') = \begin{cases} \lfloor \ell{::}\hat{\rho} \rfloor_m & lam \text{ is a procedure} \\ \hat{\rho}' & lam \text{ is a continuation} \end{cases}$$

If the call is the application of a procedure, the destination environment is derived from the source environment by prepending the label of the call being performed and limiting the environment sequence to m calls overall. If the call is the application of a continuation, its environment is used as the destination environment. In the calculated environment m-CFA installs two distinct sets of bindings: first, the values of each parameter; second, the values of each free variable in the operator λ, resolved in the closure environment.

m-CFA's system space $\tilde{\Xi}$ factors the store from machine states so that an analysis consists of a single, global store and a set $\tilde{R}$ of store-less *configurations.*

$$\tilde{\xi} \in \tilde{\Xi} = \tilde{R} \times \widehat{Store} \qquad \tilde{r} \in \tilde{R} = \mathcal{P}(\tilde{C}) \qquad \tilde{c} \in \tilde{C} = \mathsf{Call} \times \widehat{Env}$$

An analysis is the least fixed point of the total monotonic function $\Rightarrow_{\tilde{\Xi}} : \tilde{\Xi} \to \tilde{\Xi}$.

$$(\tilde{C}, \hat{\sigma}) \Rightarrow_{\tilde{\Xi}} (\tilde{C}_0 \cup \tilde{C} \cup \tilde{C}', \hat{\sigma}_0 \sqcup \hat{\sigma}')$$

where $\tilde{C}_0 = \{(call, \langle\rangle)\}$ and $\hat{\sigma}_0 = [(k, \langle\rangle) \mapsto \{\mathsf{halt}\}]$ for program $(\lambda\,(k)\; call)$, and

$$\tilde{S}' = \{\tilde{\varsigma}' : \tilde{c} \in \tilde{C} \text{ and } (\tilde{c}, \hat{\sigma}) \Rightarrow_{\tilde{\Sigma}} \tilde{\varsigma}'\} \quad \tilde{C}' = \{\tilde{c} : (\tilde{c}, \hat{\sigma}) \in \tilde{S}'\} \quad \hat{\sigma}' = \bigsqcup_{(\tilde{c}, \hat{\sigma}) \in \tilde{S}'} \hat{\sigma}.$$

(Here $((call, \hat{\rho}), \hat{\sigma})$ is treated as $(call, \hat{\rho}, \hat{\sigma})$ for convenience.) The definition uses the standard semilattice definition for the store:

$$\bot_{\hat{\sigma}} = \lambda \hat{a}.\emptyset \quad \hat{\sigma}_0 \sqcup \hat{\sigma}_1 = \lambda \hat{a}.\hat{\sigma}_0(\hat{a}) \cup \hat{\sigma}_1(\hat{a}) \quad \hat{\sigma}_0 \sqsubseteq \hat{\sigma}_1 \iff \forall \hat{a} \in \widehat{Addr}.\hat{\sigma}_0(\hat{a}) \subseteq \hat{\sigma}_1(\hat{a})$$

3 CPS and Restricted CPS

Program processors, such as compilers and analyzers, often desugar a rich surface language into more uniform intermediate representation (IR). Modern languages a rich in control constructs, such as branching, function call, early return, and coroutines, and continuation-passing style (CPS) IRs, which express all control transfer via function call, capably regularize such features. m-CFA is defined over a quite general dialect of CPS in which λs can bind and calls can pass multiple continuations, and continuation references can be captured in closure environments just as value references can [11]. Despite this generality, the uniformity of CPS allows the m-CFA formalism to be given in terms of only a single rule.

Although CPS represents all control transfers as calls, CPS compilers do not typically interpret them naïvely; instead, they recognize the role of continuations in execution and keep them distinct from other values to apply particular compilation strategies, such as allocating continuation closures on the stack [4]. Compilers maintain this distinction by statically partitioning their CPS language into a user world and a continuation world. Terms in the user world correspond to terms in the source program whereas terms in the continuation world are those introduced by the CPS transformation. The distinction is carried into the dynamic semantics as a partition into user- and continuation-world values that respects the static partition: closures over λs are values from the λ's world, are bound exclusively to variables from that world, and are invoked exclusively at call sites from that world.

$$
\begin{array}{rclrcl}
pr \in \mathsf{Prgm} & ::= & (\lambda\,(k)\; call) & call \in \mathsf{Call} & = & \mathsf{UCall} + \mathsf{CCall} \\
ucall \in \mathsf{UCall} & ::= & (f\; e\; q)^{l} & ccall \in \mathsf{CCall} & ::= & (q\; e)^{\gamma} \\
f, e \in \mathsf{UExp} & = & \mathsf{UVar} + \mathsf{ULam} & q \in \mathsf{CExp} & = & \mathsf{CVar} + \mathsf{CLam} \\
u \in \mathsf{UVar} & = & \text{a set of identifiers} & k \in \mathsf{CVar} & = & \text{a set of identifiers} \\
ulam \in \mathsf{ULam} & ::= & (\lambda_l\,(u\,k)\; call) & clam \in \mathsf{CLam} & ::= & (\lambda_\gamma\,(u)\; call) \\
l \in \mathsf{ULab} & = & \text{a set of labels} & \gamma \in \mathsf{CLab} & = & \text{a set of labels}
\end{array}
$$

Fig. 2. A restricted CPS language

Figure 2 presents the grammar of a partitioned CPS language. A call comes from either the user or the continuation world. A call in the user world has operator, value, and continuation arguments; a call in the continuation world has only continuation and value arguments. Arguments are user or continuation expressions which consist of references and λs from the corresponding world. A user-world λ has parameters for its value and continuation, and its body consists of any kind of call. A continuation-world λ body is also any kind of call, but has a parameter only for its value. Each call and λ is annotated with a label specific to its world which distinguishes otherwise-identical terms. A program is a closed λ binding a single continuation which is α-converted, i.e., in which every binding instance of a variable is unique.

After converting the example program to this CPS language, we obtain the program to the right.

$$
\begin{array}{l}
(\lambda\ (\mathtt{k}_0) \\
\quad ((\lambda_a\ (\mathtt{id}) \\
\qquad (\mathtt{id}\ 10\ (\lambda_b\ (\mathtt{y}) \\
\qquad\qquad (\mathtt{id}\ 12\ (\lambda_c\ (\mathtt{z}) \\
\qquad\qquad\qquad (+\ \mathtt{y}\ \mathtt{z}\ \mathtt{k}_0)^B))^C))^D) \\
\quad\ (\lambda_A\ (\mathtt{x}\ \mathtt{k}_1)\ (\mathtt{k}_1\ \mathtt{x})^d))^e)
\end{array}
$$

The entire program becomes a λ awaiting a top-level continuation. The first `let*` binding becomes an immediate application of a `let`-continuation binding `id`. The two subsequent bindings become the corresponding calls to `id` whose continuations bind `y` and `z`, respectively. The body of the `let*` becomes a call to a continuation-aware definition of + which is passed the top-level continuation. User-world labels are drawn from $\{A, B, C, \ldots\}$ and continuation-world labels are drawn from $\{a, b, c, \ldots\}$.

This language is restricted relative to the expressive dialect of CPS that m-CFA supports in two ways: (1) calls pass exactly one continuation and (2) continuation references cannot appear free in the user-world λ which encloses them. These restrictions ensure that expressed programs exhibit only the simple push–pop stack behavior of function calls, in contrast to that of control constructs such as `call/cc` which goes far beyond. Vardoulakis and Shivers [21] present a variant of partitioned CPS they call *restricted CPS* or *RCPS* which imposes the latter restriction but not the former; we call our doubly-restricted variant *R2CPS*.

In R2CPS, the role of a CPS term in the source program can be determined merely from its shape. For example, a tail call in the source program is translated to a user-world call whose continuation argument is a reference whereas a proper call is translated to one whose continuation argument is a λ. We rely on this ability heavily in the sequel, beginning in the next section.

4 m-CFA^{cps}

R2CPS is a sublanguage of m-CFA's more-general CPS dialect, so a definition of m-CFA over it is no different than m-CFA itself. However, R2CPS allows us to distinguish terms according to the role they play in the source program and

$$\Rightarrow_{\tilde{\Sigma}_{cps}} \subseteq \tilde{\Sigma}_{cps} \times \tilde{\Sigma}_{cps}$$

$$((f\ e\ clam)^l, \hat{\rho}, \hat{\sigma}_{cps}) \Rightarrow_{\tilde{\Sigma}_{cps}} (call, \hat{\rho}', \hat{\sigma}'_{cps}), \text{ where}$$

$$\begin{array}{ll} ((\lambda_l\,(u\,k)\ call), \hat{\rho}') \in \hat{\mathcal{E}}_{cps}(f, \hat{\rho}, \hat{\sigma}_{cps}) & \hat{d} = \hat{\mathcal{E}}_{cps}(e, \hat{\rho}, \hat{\sigma}_{cps}) \\ \{x_1, \ldots, x_n\} = \mathit{free}((\lambda_l\,(u\,k)\ call)) & \hat{q} = \{(clam, \hat{\rho})\} \\ \hat{\rho}'' = \lfloor l :: \hat{\rho} \rfloor_m & \hat{d}_i = \hat{\sigma}_{cps}(x_i, \hat{\rho}') \end{array}$$

$$\hat{\sigma}'_{cps} = \hat{\sigma}_{cps} \sqcup [(u, \hat{\rho}'') \mapsto \hat{d}] \sqcup [(k, \hat{\rho}'') \mapsto \hat{q}] \sqcup [(x_i, \hat{\rho}'') \mapsto \hat{d}_i]$$

$$((k\ e)^\gamma, \hat{\rho}, \hat{\sigma}_{cps}) \Rightarrow_{\tilde{\Sigma}_{cps}} (call, \hat{\rho}', \hat{\sigma}'_{cps}), \text{ where}$$

$$((\lambda_\gamma\,(u)\ call), \hat{\rho}') \in \hat{\sigma}_{cps}(k, \hat{\rho}) \quad \hat{d} = \hat{\mathcal{E}}_{cps}(e, \hat{\rho}, \hat{\sigma}_{cps}) \quad \hat{\sigma}'_{cps} = \hat{\sigma}_{cps} \sqcup [(u, \hat{\rho}') \mapsto \hat{d}]$$

$$((f\ e\ k)^l, \hat{\rho}, \hat{\sigma}_{cps}) \Rightarrow_{\tilde{\Sigma}_{cps}} (call, \hat{\rho}', \hat{\sigma}'_{cps}), \text{ where}$$

$$\begin{array}{ll} ((\lambda_l\,(u\,k)\ call), \hat{\rho}') \in \hat{\mathcal{E}}_{cps}(f, \hat{\rho}, \hat{\sigma}_{cps}) & \hat{d} = \hat{\mathcal{E}}_{cps}(e, \hat{\rho}, \hat{\sigma}_{cps}) \\ \{x_1, \ldots, x_n\} = \mathit{free}((\lambda_l\,(u\,k)\ call)) & \hat{q} = \hat{\sigma}_{cps}(k, \hat{\rho}) \\ \hat{\rho}'' = \lfloor l :: \hat{\rho} \rfloor_m & \hat{d}_i = \hat{\sigma}_{cps}(x_i, \hat{\rho}') \end{array}$$

$$\hat{\sigma}'_{cps} = \hat{\sigma}_{cps} \sqcup [(u, \hat{\rho}'') \mapsto \hat{d}] \sqcup [(k, \hat{\rho}'') \mapsto \hat{q}] \sqcup [(x_i, \hat{\rho}'') \mapsto \hat{d}_i]$$

$$(((\lambda_\gamma\,(u)\ call)\ e)^\gamma, \hat{\rho}, \hat{\sigma}_{cps}) \Rightarrow_{\tilde{\Sigma}_{cps}} (call', \hat{\rho}', \hat{\sigma}'_{cps}), \text{ where}$$

$$((\lambda_\gamma\,(u')\ call'), \hat{\rho}') \in \{((\lambda_\gamma\,(u)\ call), \hat{\rho})\} \quad \hat{d} = \hat{\mathcal{E}}_{cps}(e, \hat{\rho}, \hat{\sigma}_{cps}) \quad \hat{\sigma}'_{cps} = \hat{\sigma}_{cps} \sqcup [(u', \hat{\rho}) \mapsto \hat{d}]$$

$$\hat{\mathcal{E}}_{cps} : \mathsf{UExp} \times \widehat{Env} \times \widehat{Store}_{cps}$$

$$\hat{\mathcal{E}}_{cps}(u, \hat{\rho}, \hat{\sigma}_{cps}) = \hat{\sigma}_{cps}(u, \hat{\rho}) \qquad \hat{\mathcal{E}}_{cps}(ulam, \hat{\rho}, \hat{\sigma}_{cps}) = \{(ulam, \hat{\rho})\}$$

Fig. 3. R2CPS-restricted m-CFA factored across user/continuation and tail/non-tail calls

specialize the state transition to each. Figure 3 presents m-CFA^{cps}, an R2CPS-restricted m-CFA whose state transition has been factored across (and specialized to) user/continuation and tail/non-tail calls. Because the shape of the continuation is known, we inline the use of $\hat{\mathcal{E}}_{cps}$ away in each rule. Similarly, because the source world of the operator is known, we inline the use of $\widehat{new}$—which computes the destination environment—away as well. A call $(f\ e\ clam)^l$ corresponds to a non-tail call to the pre-CPS version of f in the source program. A call $(k\ e)^\gamma$ corresponds to a return in the source program. A call $(f\ e\ k)^l$ corresponds to a tail call to the pre-CPS version of f in the source program. Finally, a call $((\lambda_\gamma\ (u)\ call)\ e)^\gamma$ corresponds to a let in the source program.

These rules are merely the sole m-CFA transition rule, limited to R2CPS terms, factored by and specialized to the shape of the call. We capture this fact in the following lemma.

Lemma 1. *For all $call, call' \in \mathsf{Call}$, $\hat{\rho}, \hat{\rho}' \in \widehat{Env}$, $\hat{\sigma}_{cps}, \hat{\sigma}'_{cps} \in \widehat{Store}$,*

$$(call, \hat{\rho}, \hat{\sigma}_{cps}) \Rightarrow_{\hat{\Sigma}} (call', \hat{\rho}', \hat{\sigma}'_{cps}) \text{ if and only if } (call, \hat{\rho}, \hat{\sigma}_{cps}) \Rightarrow_{\hat{\Sigma}_{cps}} (call', \hat{\rho}', \hat{\sigma}'_{cps}).$$

A 1CFA^{cps} analysis of the CPS'd example program yields $(\tilde{R}, \hat{\sigma})$ where

$$\tilde{R} = \{(e, \langle\rangle), (D, \langle\rangle), (d, \langle D\rangle), (C, \langle\rangle), (d, \langle C\rangle), (B, \langle\rangle), (+, \langle B\rangle)\}$$

and

$$\begin{array}{lllllllll}
\hat{\sigma} = [(\mathtt{k}_0, \langle\rangle) & \mapsto & \{\mathsf{halt}\}, & (\mathtt{id}, \langle\rangle) & \mapsto & \{(A, \langle\rangle)\}, & (\mathtt{x}, \langle D\rangle) & \mapsto & \{10\}, \\
(\mathtt{k}_1, \langle D\rangle) & \mapsto & \{(b, \langle\rangle)\}, & (\mathtt{y}, \langle\rangle) & \mapsto & \{10\}, & (\mathtt{x}, \langle C\rangle) & \mapsto & \{12\}, \\
(\mathtt{k}_1, \langle C\rangle) & \mapsto & \{(c, \langle\rangle)\}, & (\mathtt{z}, \langle\rangle) & \mapsto & \{12\}, & & & \\
(+_0, \langle B\rangle) & \mapsto & \{10\}, & (+_1, \langle B\rangle) & \mapsto & \{12\}] & & &
\end{array}$$

in which each call is represented by its label. Note that the variables $+_0$ and $+_1$, which correspond to the internal variables of the primitive $+$, are ultimately bound to single, precise values. This precision is an artifact of call-site sensitivity combined with precise call–return correspondence.

5 $\mathcal{A}$-Normal Form

Many compilers [1,8,9,16,17] convert source programs to CPS in the middle end to do analysis and transformation before generating code. This pipeline is depicted in the diagram to the right where a CPS translation carried out by Fischer's $\mathcal{F}$ [3] operates on a source (direct-style) program in λ_{ds}. However, the CPS translator $\mathcal{F}$ introduces many *administrative redexes* which abstract the continuation within a term. The $\bar{\beta}$ rule reduces these so that repeated application by $\bar{\beta}$ to a normal form results in a term in λ_{cps}. (For our purposes, we can consider λ_{cps} to be R2CPS.)

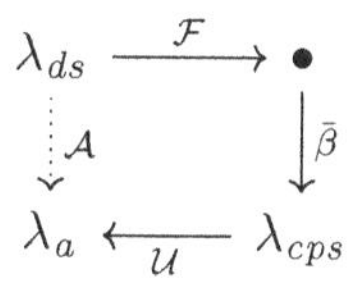

λ_{cps} terms can be evaluated with a CE machine [4], a machine which manipulates control and environment registers—m-CFA's abstract machine is a CE machine augmented with a store register. However, a CE machine models a naïve evaluator which directly interprets CPS terms, allowing the program itself to manage the continuation. In practice, compilers track the continuation by statically-partitioning the language (as in R2CPS) and manage it directly using a CE machine augmented with a **k**ontinuation register—a CEK machine [2]. This machine uses the shape of each call to determine its role in evaluation. In the call $(k\ e)^\gamma$, for example, the CEK does not look up k in the environment, as a CE machine would do, but instead recognizes this call as a function return and manipulates the continuation register accordingly.

By intercepting the program's continuation management, Flanagan *et al.* [4] observe:

1. Explicit continuation references are unnecessary; only the role of the call matters.
2. The CEK machine effectively inverts the CPS transformation (accurately modeling a code generator).

From these observations they respond in two ways.

First, Flanagan *et al.* devise a set of axioms $\mathcal{A}$ which carry out the corresponding reductions on a λ_{ds} term as $\bar{\beta}$ carries out on a CPS term, thus allowing a λ_a term to be obtained without a round trip through CPS. Reduction by the axioms $\mathcal{A}$ is normalizing, and a term in $\mathcal{A}$-normal form (or ANF) is in λ_a, defined below.

$$e \in \mathsf{Exp} \quad ::= \mathsf{let}_\gamma\, x := ce \;\mathsf{in}\; e \mid ce \qquad ce \in \mathsf{CExp} \quad ::= (ae_0\ ae_1)^l \mid ae^\gamma$$
$$ae \in \mathsf{AExp} \quad ::= \lambda_l x.e \mid x \qquad x \in \mathsf{Var} \quad = \text{a set of identifiers}$$

Programs in λ_a lack explicit continuations but, like CPS, name all intermediate values. A *proper expression* e is a let expression, which binds a call expression ce to a variable whose scope is another proper expression, or a call expression itself. A *call expression* ce is an atomic expression ae^γ or an application $(ae_0\ ae_1)^l$. An *atomic expression* ae is a variable reference x or a λ abstraction $\lambda_l x.e$. A program in λ_a is a closed expression that is α-converted. Call expressions are annotated with the user-world labels of λ_{cps}; let expressions and atomic expressions are annotated with continuation-world labels. The set of λs $\lambda_l x.e$ is Lam.

Second, Flanagan *et al.* define a function $\mathcal{U}$ that strips CPS terms of redundant continuation information, converting λ_{cps} terms to λ_a terms. We present $\mathcal{U}$ in Fig. 4 as well as its inverse $\mathcal{U}^{-1}$. Defining $\mathcal{U}^{-1}$ is less straightforward than defining $\mathcal{U}$ because $\mathcal{U}$ removes continuation references but $\mathcal{U}^{-1}$ must synthesize them. To make synthesis straightforward, we define the set λ_{cps}^{WN} of well-named R2CPS programs. A R2CPS program pr is *well-named* if, for each user-world function $(\lambda_l\,(u\,k)\ call)$, the name of k is derivable from $\mathcal{U}_e[\![call]\!]$ by $\mathcal{U}_k : \mathsf{Exp} \rightarrow \mathsf{CVar}$ and vice versa by $\mathcal{U}_k^{-1} : \mathsf{CVar} \rightarrow \mathsf{Exp}$. This correspondence between an ANF expression and a continuation-world variable helps us build a correspondence between different formulations of m-CFA (cf. §7). Any R2CPS program can be α-converted to one that is well-named, so λ_{cps}^{WN} is not materially smaller than λ_{cps}. The $\mathcal{U}$ and $\mathcal{U}^{-1}$ definitions are supported by variable conversion functions

$$\mathcal{U} : \lambda_{cps}^{WN} \rightarrow \lambda_a \qquad\qquad \mathcal{U}^{-1} : \lambda_a \rightarrow \lambda_{cps}^{WN}$$

$$\mathcal{U}[\![(\lambda\,(k)\ call)]\!] = \mathcal{U}_e[\![call]\!] \qquad \mathcal{U}^{-1}[\![pr]\!] = (\lambda\,(k)\,\mathcal{U}_e^{-1}[\![pr]\!](k)) \text{ where } k = \mathcal{U}_k[\![pr]\!]$$

$$\mathcal{U}_e : \mathsf{Call} \rightarrow \mathsf{Exp}$$

$$\mathcal{U}_e[\![((\lambda_{\gamma'}\,(u)\ call)\ e)^{\gamma}]\!] = \mathsf{let}_{\gamma'}\,\mathcal{U}_x[\![u]\!] := \mathcal{U}_{ae}[\![e]\!]^{\gamma}\ \mathsf{in}\,\mathcal{U}_e[\![call]\!]$$

$$\mathcal{U}_e[\![(f\ e\ (\lambda_{\gamma}\,(u)\ call))^{l}]\!] = \mathsf{let}_{\gamma}\,\mathcal{U}_x[\![u]\!] := (\mathcal{U}_{ae}[\![f]\!]\ \mathcal{U}_{ae}[\![e]\!])^{l}\ \mathsf{in}\,\mathcal{U}_e[\![call]\!]$$

$$\mathcal{U}_e[\![(k\ e)^{\gamma}]\!] = \mathcal{U}_{ae}[\![e]\!]^{\gamma}$$

$$\mathcal{U}_e[\![(f\ e\ k)^{l}]\!] = (\mathcal{U}_{ae}[\![f]\!]\ \mathcal{U}_{ae}[\![e]\!])^{l}$$

$$\mathcal{U}_e^{-1} : \mathsf{Exp} \rightarrow \mathsf{CVar} \rightarrow \mathsf{Call}$$

$$\mathcal{U}_e^{-1}[\![\mathsf{let}_{\gamma}\,x := (ae_0\ ae_1)^{l}\ \mathsf{in}\ e]\!](k) = (\mathcal{U}_{ae}^{-1}[\![ae_0]\!]\ \mathcal{U}_{ae}^{-1}[\![ae_1]\!]\ (\lambda_{\gamma}\,(\mathcal{U}_x^{-1}[\![x]\!])\,\mathcal{U}_e^{-1}[\![e]\!](k)))^{l}$$

$$\mathcal{U}_e^{-1}[\![\mathsf{let}_{\gamma}\,x := ae^{\gamma'}\ \mathsf{in}\ e]\!](k) = ((\lambda_{\gamma}\,(\mathcal{U}_x^{-1}[\![x]\!])\,\mathcal{U}_e^{-1}[\![e]\!](k))\ \mathcal{U}_{ae}^{-1}[\![ae]\!])^{\gamma'}$$

$$\mathcal{U}_e^{-1}[\![(ae_0\ ae_1)^{l}]\!](k) = (\mathcal{U}_{ae}^{-1}[\![ae_0]\!]\ \mathcal{U}_{ae}^{-1}[\![ae_1]\!]\ k)^{l}$$

$$\mathcal{U}_e^{-1}[\![ae^{\gamma}]\!](k) = (k\ \mathcal{U}_{ae}^{-1}[\![ae]\!])^{\gamma}$$

$$\mathcal{U}_{ae} : \mathsf{UExp} \rightarrow \mathsf{AExp}$$

$$\mathcal{U}[\![(\lambda_l\,(u\,k)\ call)]\!] = \lambda_l\mathcal{U}_x[\![u]\!].\mathcal{U}_e[\![call]\!]$$

$$\mathcal{U}[\![u]\!] = \mathcal{U}_x[\![u]\!]$$

$$\mathcal{U}^{-1} : \mathsf{AExp} \rightarrow \mathsf{UExp}$$

$$\mathcal{U}^{-1}[\![\lambda_l x.e]\!] = (\lambda_l\,(\mathcal{U}_x^{-1}[\![x]\!]\,k)\,\mathcal{U}_e^{-1}[\![e]\!](k)) \text{ where } k = \mathcal{U}_k[\![e]\!]$$

$$\mathcal{U}^{-1}[\![x]\!] = \mathcal{U}_x^{-1}[\![x]\!]$$

Fig. 4. The λ_{cps}^{WN}–λ_a bijection pair $\mathcal{U}/\mathcal{U}^{-1}$.

$\mathcal{U}_x : UVar \rightarrow Var$ and $\mathcal{U}_x^{-1}\, Var \rightarrow UVar$ which convert between user-world variables in λ_{cps} and variables in λ_a. These functions precisely preserve user- and continuation-world labels. The following lemma establishes that these functions are indeed mutual inverses.

Lemma 2. *$\mathcal{U}^{-1} \circ \mathcal{U} = I_{\lambda_{cps}^{WN}}$ and $\mathcal{U} \circ \mathcal{U}^{-1} = I_{\lambda_a}$*

Using $\mathcal{U}$ to convert the CPS version of the example program yields the program to the right. While user-world labels remain associated with their corresponding λ or call, continuation-world labels on λs annotate lets and on calls annotate atomic expressions.

$$\begin{array}{l} \mathsf{let}_a\ \mathtt{id} = (\lambda_A \mathtt{x}.\mathtt{x}^d)^e \\ \mathsf{in}\ \mathsf{let}_b\ \mathtt{y} = (\mathtt{id}\ 10)^D \\ \quad \mathsf{in}\ \mathsf{let}_c\ \mathtt{z} = (\mathtt{id}\ 12)^C \\ \qquad \mathsf{in}\ (+\ \mathtt{y}\ \mathtt{z})^B \end{array}$$

6 m-CFA^a

We now define m-CFA^a, m-CFA for λ_a. We then extend the term isomorphism of §5 to show that an m-CFA^a analysis is isomorphic to a m-CFA^{cps} analysis, thus demonstrating that the continuation references in λ_{cps} are redundant with respect to m-CFA just as they are for a CEK machine.

m-CFA^a is defined in terms of an abstract CEK machine using the *Abstracting Abstracting Machines* (AAM) methodology [19]. Whereas the continuation register contains a representation of continuation, such as a stack, in a concrete CEK machine, it contains the address of a store-allocated continuation in an abstract CEK machine. (Anticipating our application of P4F in §8, we separate values and continuations into dedicated stores.)

Continuation variables, used to form continuation addresses in m-CFA^{cps}, are not present in m-CFA^{a}. However, we can use $\mathcal{U}_k$ correspondence of each λ_{cps} continuation variable to the λ_a representation of its scope to obtain a m-CFA^{a} continuation address from each corresponding one in m-CFA^{cps}. Thus, a m-CFA^{a} continuation address consists of an expression entailing a continuation scope—a λ body or the program itself—paired with an environment. For a fixed program pr (with unique labels), the body of the innermost-enclosing λ of any expression is apparent; we assume a function $\zeta_{pr} : Exp \rightarrow Exp$ which produces the body of the innermost-enclosing λ of the given expression, or the entire program if it is not enclosed. This function allows us to derive the continuation address $(\zeta_{pr}(e), \hat{\rho})$ from the CE registers $(e, \hat{\rho})$ and in turn omit the K register from configurations altogether.

Figure 5 presents m-CFA^{a} system space and transfer function. Evaluation of the let-binding of a call creates an abstract frame $\mathsf{ar}(x, e, \hat{\rho})$ which consists of the bound variable, body expression, and environment. This frame contains a link to the previous frame, but only implicitly, as we will see momentarily. The transition constructs an environment for the call and extends the value store, copying bindings of free variables, in the standard way. For the continuation address, it uses the body expression of the called procedure paired with its environment, in correspondence to the continuation variable of its CPS representation. Evaluation of an atomic expression, which represents a function return, looks up the top frame to bind the return value and continue evaluation. The continuation address is derived from the atomic expression itself using ζ_{pr}. The atomic expression's value is bound in the store and the expression and environment within the stack frame are restored. Evaluation of a tail call is precisely the same as for a let-bound call, except that the current continuation is obtained by synthesizing the continuation address using ζ_{pr} and copied to the callee's continuation address. Similarly, evaluation of a let-bound atomic expression proceeds precisely the same as for an atomic expression, except that the continuation to which the value is "returned" is local.

An m-CFA^{a} analysis is defined as the least fixed point of the function $\Rightarrow_{\tilde{\Xi}_a}$, which is computed in the same way as $\Rightarrow_{\tilde{\Xi}_{cps}}$.

An $[m = 1]$-CFA^{a} analysis of the ANF'd example program yields $(\tilde{R}, \hat{\sigma}, \tilde{\sigma}_\kappa)$ where

$$\tilde{R} = \{(e, \langle\rangle), (D, \langle\rangle), (d, \langle D\rangle), (C, \langle\rangle), (d, \langle C\rangle), (B, \langle\rangle), (+, \langle B\rangle)\}$$

and

$$\begin{aligned} \hat{\sigma} = [(\mathtt{id}, \langle\rangle) &\mapsto \{(A, \langle\rangle)\}, & (\mathtt{x}, \langle D\rangle) &\mapsto \{10\}, & (\mathtt{y}, \langle\rangle) &\mapsto \{10\}, \\ (\mathtt{x}, \langle C\rangle) &\mapsto \{12\}, & (\mathtt{z}, \langle\rangle) &\mapsto \{12\}, & (+_0, \langle B\rangle) &\mapsto \{10\}, \\ (+_1, \langle B\rangle) &\mapsto \{12\}] \end{aligned}$$

and

$$\begin{aligned} \tilde{\sigma}_\kappa = [(\mathtt{k}_0, \langle\rangle) &\mapsto \{\mathsf{mt}\}, & (d, \langle D\rangle) &\mapsto \{(\mathtt{y}, b, \langle\rangle)\}, \\ (d, \langle C\rangle) &\mapsto \{(\mathtt{z}, c, \langle\rangle)\}]. \end{aligned}$$

$$\tilde{R} = \{(e, \langle\rangle), (D, \langle\rangle), (d, \langle D\rangle), (C, \langle\rangle), (d, \langle C\rangle), (B, \langle\rangle), (+, \langle B\rangle)\}$$

and

$$\begin{aligned}\hat{\sigma} = [(\mathtt{id}, \langle\rangle) &\mapsto \{(A, \langle\rangle)\}, & (\mathtt{x}, \langle D\rangle) &\mapsto \{10\}, & (\mathtt{y}, \langle\rangle) &\mapsto \{10\},\\ (\mathtt{x}, \langle C\rangle) &\mapsto \{12\}, & (\mathtt{z}, \langle\rangle) &\mapsto \{12\}, & (+_0, \langle B\rangle) &\mapsto \{10\},\\ (+_1, \langle B\rangle) &\mapsto \{12\}]\end{aligned}$$

and

$$\begin{aligned}\tilde{\sigma}_\kappa = [(\mathtt{k}_0, \langle\rangle) &\mapsto \{\mathsf{mt}\}, & (d, \langle D\rangle) &\mapsto \{(\mathtt{y}, b, \langle\rangle)\},\\ (d, \langle C\rangle) &\mapsto \{(\mathtt{z}, c, \langle\rangle)\}].\end{aligned}$$

$$\varsigma \in \tilde{\Sigma}_a = \mathsf{Exp} \times \widehat{Env} \times \widehat{Store}_a \times \widetilde{KStore}$$

$$\begin{aligned}\hat{\sigma}_a &\in \widehat{Store}_a &&= \widehat{Addr}_a \to \widehat{D}_a & \widehat{Addr}_a &= \mathsf{Var} \times \widehat{Env}\\ \tilde{\sigma}_\kappa &\in \widetilde{KStore} &&= \widetilde{KAddr} \to \mathcal{P}(\widetilde{Frame}) & \widetilde{KAddr} &= \mathsf{Exp} \times \widehat{Env}\\ \hat{d}^a &\in \widehat{D}_a &&= \mathcal{P}(\mathsf{Lam} \times \widehat{Env}) & \widetilde{Frame}_a &::= \mathsf{mt} \mid \mathsf{ar}(x, e, \hat{\rho})\end{aligned}$$

$$\Rightarrow_{\tilde{\Sigma}_a} \subseteq \tilde{\Sigma}_a \times \tilde{\Sigma}_a$$

$$(\mathsf{let}_\gamma\, x := (ae_0\ ae_1)^l\ \mathsf{in}\ e, \hat{\rho}, \hat{\sigma}_a, \tilde{\sigma}_\kappa) \Rightarrow_{\tilde{\Sigma}_a} (e', \hat{\rho}'', \hat{\sigma}'_a, \tilde{\sigma}'_\kappa), \text{ where}$$
$$\begin{aligned}(\lambda_l x'.e', \hat{\rho}') &\in \hat{\mathcal{E}}_a(ae_0, \hat{\rho}, \hat{\sigma}_a) & \hat{d}^a &= \hat{\mathcal{E}}_a(ae_1, \hat{\rho}, \hat{\sigma}_a)\\ \{x_1, \ldots, x_n\} &= \mathit{free}(\lambda_l x.e') & \tilde{\phi} &= \{\mathsf{ar}(x, e, \hat{\rho})\}\\ \hat{\rho}'' &= \lfloor l :: \hat{\rho} \rfloor_m & \hat{d}^a_i &= \hat{\sigma}_a(x_i, \hat{\rho}')\end{aligned}$$
$$\hat{\sigma}'_a = \hat{\sigma}_a \sqcup [(x, \hat{\rho}'') \mapsto \hat{d}^a] \sqcup [(x_i, \hat{\rho}'') \mapsto \hat{d}^a_i]$$
$$\tilde{\sigma}'_\kappa = \tilde{\sigma}_\kappa \sqcup [(e', \hat{\rho}'') \mapsto \tilde{\phi}]$$

$$(ae^\gamma, \hat{\rho}, \hat{\sigma}_a, \tilde{\sigma}_\kappa) \Rightarrow_{\tilde{\Sigma}_a} (e, \hat{\rho}', \hat{\sigma}'_a, \tilde{\sigma}_\kappa), \text{ where}$$
$$\mathsf{ar}(x, e, \hat{\rho}') \in \tilde{\sigma}_\kappa(\zeta_{pr}[\![ae^\gamma]\!], \hat{\rho}) \qquad \hat{d}^a = \hat{\mathcal{E}}_a(ae, \hat{\rho}, \hat{\sigma}_a) \qquad \hat{\sigma}'_a = \hat{\sigma}_a \sqcup [(x, \hat{\rho}') \mapsto \hat{d}^a]$$

$$((ae_0\ ae_1)^l, \hat{\rho}, \hat{\sigma}_a, \tilde{\sigma}_\kappa) \Rightarrow_{\tilde{\Sigma}_a} (e', \hat{\rho}'', \hat{\sigma}'_a, \tilde{\sigma}'_\kappa), \text{ where}$$
$$\begin{aligned}(\lambda_l x.e', \hat{\rho}') &\in \hat{\mathcal{E}}_a(ae_0, \hat{\rho}, \hat{\sigma}_a) & \hat{d}^a &= \hat{\mathcal{E}}_a(ae_1, \hat{\rho}, \hat{\sigma}_a)\\ \{x_1, \ldots, x_n\} &= \mathit{free}(\lambda_l x.e') & \tilde{\phi} &= \tilde{\sigma}_\kappa(\zeta_{pr}[\![(ae_0\ ae_1)^l]\!], \hat{\rho})\\ \hat{\rho}'' &= \lfloor l :: \hat{\rho} \rfloor_m & \hat{d}^a_i &= \hat{\sigma}_a(x_i, \hat{\rho}')\end{aligned}$$
$$\hat{\sigma}'_a = \hat{\sigma}_a \sqcup [(x, \hat{\rho}'') \mapsto \hat{d}^a] \sqcup [(x_i, \hat{\rho}'') \mapsto \hat{d}^a_i]$$
$$\tilde{\sigma}'_\kappa = \tilde{\sigma}_\kappa \sqcup [(e', \hat{\rho}'') \mapsto \tilde{\phi}]$$

Fig. 5. m-CFA^a

$$(\mathsf{let}_\gamma\, x := ae^\gamma \;\mathsf{in}\; e, \hat{\rho}, \hat{\sigma}_a, \tilde{\sigma}_\kappa) \Rightarrow_{\tilde{\Sigma}_a} (e', \hat{\rho}', \hat{\sigma}'_a, \tilde{\sigma}_\kappa), \text{ where}$$
$$\mathsf{ar}(x', e', \hat{\rho}') \in \{\mathsf{ar}(x, e, \hat{\rho})\} \qquad \hat{d}^a = \hat{\mathcal{E}}_a(ae, \hat{\rho}, \hat{\sigma}_a) \qquad \hat{\sigma}'_a = \hat{\sigma}_a \sqcup [(x', \hat{\rho}') \mapsto \hat{d}^a]$$

$$\hat{\mathcal{E}}_a : \mathsf{AExp} \times \widehat{Env} \times \widehat{Store}_a$$
$$\hat{\mathcal{E}}_a(x, \hat{\rho}, \hat{\sigma}_a) = \hat{\sigma}_a(x, \hat{\rho}) \qquad \hat{\mathcal{E}}_a(\lambda_l x.e, \hat{\rho}, \hat{\sigma}_a) = \{(\lambda_l x.e, \hat{\rho})\}$$

$$\tilde{\xi}_a \in \tilde{\Xi}_a = \tilde{R}_a \times \widehat{Store}_a \times \widetilde{KStore} \qquad \tilde{r}_a \in \tilde{R}_a = \mathcal{P}(\tilde{C}_a) \qquad \tilde{c}_a \in \tilde{C}_a = \mathsf{Exp} \times \widehat{Env}$$

$$\Rightarrow_{\tilde{\Xi}_a} : \tilde{\Xi}_a \to \tilde{\Xi}_a$$
$$(\tilde{C}_a, \hat{\sigma}_a, \tilde{\sigma}_\kappa) \Rightarrow_{\tilde{\Xi}_a} (\tilde{C}_a^{init} \cup \tilde{C} \cup \tilde{C}', \hat{\sigma}'_a, \tilde{\sigma}_\kappa^{init} \sqcup \tilde{\sigma}'_\kappa) \text{ where}$$
$$\tilde{C}_a^{init} = \{(pr, \langle\rangle)\} \qquad \tilde{\sigma}_\kappa^{init} = [(pr, \langle\rangle) \mapsto \{\mathsf{mt}\}]$$
$$\tilde{S}'_a = \{\tilde{\varsigma}'_a : \tilde{c}_a \in \tilde{C}_a \text{ and } (\tilde{c}_a, \hat{\sigma}_a, \tilde{\sigma}_\kappa) \Rightarrow_{\tilde{\Sigma}_a} \tilde{\varsigma}'_a\} \qquad \hat{\sigma}'_a = \bigsqcup_{(\tilde{c}_a, \hat{\sigma}_a, \tilde{\sigma}_\kappa) \in \tilde{S}'_a} \hat{\sigma}_a$$
$$\tilde{C}'_a = \{\tilde{c}_a : (\tilde{c}_a, \hat{\sigma}_a, \tilde{\sigma}_\kappa) \in \tilde{S}'_a\} \qquad \tilde{\sigma}'_\kappa = \bigsqcup_{(\tilde{c}_a, \hat{\sigma}_a, \tilde{\sigma}_\kappa) \in \tilde{S}'_a} \tilde{\sigma}_\kappa$$

Fig. 5. (*continued*)

Value store allocations are identical to user-world allocations in m-CFA^{cps}. Continuation frames (in which an expression is represented by its label) correspond directly to continuation-world allocations, as we show in the next section.

7 m-CFA^{cps}–m-CFA^a Correspondence

We extend the λ_{cps}^{WN}–λ_a isomorphism through $\mathcal{U}$ to m-CFA^{cps}–m-CFA^a, first to the state space, then to transition rules, and then finally to the entire analysis. The definitions

$$\mathcal{U}(call, \hat{\rho}, \hat{\sigma}_{cps}) = (\mathcal{U}_e[\![call]\!], \hat{\rho}, \hat{\sigma}_a, \tilde{\sigma}_\kappa) \text{ where } (\hat{\sigma}_a, \tilde{\sigma}_\kappa) = T(\hat{\sigma}_{cps})$$

and

$$\mathcal{U}^{-1}(e, \hat{\rho}, \hat{\sigma}_a, \tilde{\sigma}_\kappa) = (\mathcal{U}_e^{-1}[\![e]\!](\mathcal{U}_k^{-1}(\varsigma_{pr}[\![e]\!])), T^{-1}(\hat{\sigma}_a, \tilde{\sigma}_\kappa))$$

extend it to the state space. T_{pr}/T_{pr}^{-1}, seen in Fig. 6, is a lattice isomorphism (i.e. it is a bijection which commutes with the join operation and refinement relation) between the m-CFA^{cps} store lattice and the m-CFA^a value and continuation store product lattice. The T_{pr}/T_{pr}^{-1} isomorphism induces an isomorphism between the system spaces $\tilde{\Xi}_{cps}$ and $\tilde{\Xi}_a$ (elided for space). We also use T_{pr}/T_{pr}^{-1} to establish that $\Rightarrow_{\tilde{\Sigma}_{cps}}$ and $\Rightarrow_{\tilde{\Sigma}_a}$ are isomorphic, which is proved straightforwardly since each transition rule in m-CFA^a corresponds to a transition rule in m-CFA^{cps}.

$$T_{pr} : \widehat{Store}_{cps} \rightarrow \widehat{Store}_a \times \widetilde{KStore}$$

$$T_{pr}(\hat{\sigma}_{cps}) = (\hat{\sigma}_a, \tilde{\sigma}_\kappa) \text{ where}$$

$$\begin{aligned}
\hat{\sigma}_a &= \lambda(x, \hat{\rho}).\{(\lambda_l \mathcal{U}_x[\![u]\!].\mathcal{U}_e[\![call]\!], \hat{\rho}') : ((\lambda_l\,(u\,k)\;call), \hat{\rho}') \in \hat{\sigma}_{cps}(\mathcal{U}_x^{-1}[\![x]\!], \hat{\rho})\} \\
\tilde{\sigma}_\kappa &= \lambda(e, \hat{\rho}).\{\mathsf{ar}(\mathcal{U}_x[\![u]\!], \mathcal{U}_e[\![call]\!], \hat{\rho}') : ((\lambda_\gamma\,(u)\;call), \hat{\rho}') \in \hat{\sigma}_{cps}(\mathcal{U}_k^{-1}(\zeta_{pr}[\![e]\!]), \hat{\rho})\} \\
&\quad \cup \{\mathsf{mt} : \mathsf{halt} \in \hat{\sigma}_{cps}(\mathcal{U}_k^{-1}(\zeta_{pr}[\![e]\!]), \hat{\rho})\}
\end{aligned}$$

$$T_{pr}^{-1} : \widehat{Store}_a \times \widetilde{KStore} \rightarrow \widehat{Store}_{cps}$$

$$T_{pr}^{-1}(\hat{\sigma}_a, \tilde{\sigma}_\kappa) = \lambda(z, \hat{\rho}). \begin{cases} \{((\lambda_l\,(\mathcal{U}_x^{-1}[\![x]\!]\;k)\,\mathcal{U}_e^{-1}[\![e]\!](k)), \hat{\rho}') : (\lambda_l x.e, \hat{\rho}') \in \sigma(z, \hat{\rho})\}, \text{ if } z = (u, 0) \\ \{((\lambda_\gamma\,(\mathcal{U}_x^{-1}[\![x]\!])\,\mathcal{U}_e^{-1}[\![e]\!](k)), \hat{\rho}') : \mathsf{ar}(x, e, \hat{\rho}') \in \tilde{\sigma}_\kappa(\zeta_{pr}[\![\mathcal{U}_k^{-1}(k)]\!], \hat{\rho})\} \\ \cup\{\mathsf{halt} : \mathsf{mt} \in \tilde{\sigma}_\kappa(\zeta_{pr}[\![\mathcal{U}_k^{-1}(k)]\!], \hat{\rho})\}, \text{ if } z = (k, 1) \end{cases}$$

Fig. 6. T_{pr}/T_{pr}^{-1} lattice isomorphism between $\widetilde{Store}_{cps}$ and $\widetilde{Store}_a \times \widetilde{KStore}$

Lemma 3 (**$\Rightarrow_{\tilde{\Sigma}_{cps}}$–$\Rightarrow_{\tilde{\Sigma}_a}$ Isomorphism**)**.** *For all $\tilde{\varsigma}_{cps}, \tilde{\varsigma}'_{cps} \in \tilde{\Sigma}_{cps}$, $\tilde{\varsigma}_{cps} \Rightarrow_{\tilde{\Sigma}_{cps}} \tilde{\varsigma}'_{cps} \iff \mathcal{U}(\tilde{\varsigma}_{cps}) \Rightarrow_{\tilde{\Sigma}_a} \mathcal{U}(\tilde{\varsigma}'_{cps})$ and, for all $\tilde{\varsigma}, \tilde{\varsigma}' \in \tilde{\Sigma}_a$, $\tilde{\varsigma} \Rightarrow_{\tilde{\Sigma}_a} \tilde{\varsigma}' \iff \mathcal{U}^{-1}(\tilde{\varsigma}_a) \Rightarrow_{\tilde{\Sigma}_{cps}} \mathcal{U}^{-1}(\tilde{\varsigma}'_a)$.*

From the $\tilde{\Xi}_{cps}$–$\tilde{\Xi}_a$ isomorphism and the $\Rightarrow_{\tilde{\Sigma}_{cps}}$–$\Rightarrow_{\tilde{\Sigma}_a}$ isomorphism, we can show that $\Rightarrow_{\tilde{\Xi}_{cps}}$ and $\Rightarrow_{\tilde{\Xi}_a}$ commute with the isomorphism.

Theorem 1 (**m-CFA^{cps}–m-CFA^a Correspondence**)**.** *The following diagram commutes.*

$$\begin{array}{ccc}
\tilde{\Xi}_{cps} & \xrightarrow{cps} & \tilde{\Xi}_{cps} \\
\mathcal{U}/\mathcal{U}^{-1}\Big\updownarrow & & \Big\updownarrow\mathcal{U}/\mathcal{U}^{-1} \\
\tilde{\Xi}_a & \xrightarrow{a} & \tilde{\Xi}_a
\end{array}$$

An immediate corollary is that the least fixed points of $\Rightarrow_{\tilde{\Xi}_{cps}}$ and $\Rightarrow_{\tilde{\Xi}_a}$ correspond to one another so that m-CFA^{cps} and m-CFA^a compute the same analysis.

8 Perfect Stack Precision

k-CFA and m-CFA each model the execution of a program using a finite state machine (FSM) in which the nodes are execution states and the edges are control transitions. This model has the benefit that it is easy to construct using a straightforward workset algorithm. However, it is unable to capture the call–return behavior of programs whose execution is mediated by a stack. In particular, it cannot precisely associate returns to points of call, instead discovering spurious control paths within the program's execution.

In the same year that m-CFA was presented, Vardoulakis and Shivers [20] presented CFA2, a *stack-precise* CFA which models program execution with a pushdown system instead of an FSM. Unlike an FSM, a pushdown model allows to analysis to precisely associate each return to its corresponding call, thereby significantly increasing control precision. Unfortunately, CFA2 suffers from the shortcomings that (1) it is context-insensitive (i.e. *monovariant*); (2) its algorithm is in EXPTIME, and (3) its algorithm uses a relatively-complex summarization-based approach.

Follow-on work mitigated each of these shortcomings, achieving context sensitivity, low computational complexity, and algorithmic simplicity [7,10]. In one fell swoop, Gilray *et al.* [6] resolved them all with the *pushdown for free* (or *P4F*) technique to achieve perfect stack precision "for free" both in the sense that it requires essentially no implementation effort and also in the sense that it doesn't increase the computational complexity of the target CFA. The technique derives from two observations:

1. In an abstract-machine based CFA, the stack precision is determined by the continuation allocator, a (often implicit) function $\widehat{alloc}_\kappa : \hat{\Sigma} \times Exp \times \widehat{Env} \times \widehat{Store} \to \widehat{Addr}_\kappa$ of the source configuration $\hat{\varsigma} \in \hat{\Sigma}$ and the target expression $e \in Exp$, environment $\hat{\rho} \in \widehat{Env}$, and store $\sigma \in \widehat{Store}$.
2. Perfect stack precision is achieved when, within the same abstract invocation, the set of continuations for an exit configuration is no less precise than that of the corresponding entry configuration.

The technique entails only the following continuation allocator, by which an address consists solely of the target expression and environment.

$$\widehat{alloc}_\kappa(\hat{\varsigma}, e, \hat{\rho}, \hat{\sigma}) = (e, \hat{\rho})$$

In essence, the continuation address is the entry configuration itself (when the store is factored out into the system space), which ensures that it only ever refers to a single such configuration.

The P4F technique is formulated in an ANF setting; having formulated m-CFA in such a setting, we are now positioned to apply P4F to realize a stack-precise variant of m-CFA, which we set out to do in the next section.

9 m-CFA Is Stack-Precise

The application of P4F to achieve perfect stack precision is straightforward: on a call transition, allocate the continuation at an address consisting of the target configuration's expression and environment. By inspection, it is clear that m-CFA^a *already* uses this allocation strategy and consequently is already stack-precise. It follows from Theorem 1 that R2CPS-limited *m-CFA is and always has been stack-precise.* (We discuss this corollary in §10.)

While our primary result is largely in hand, we review the key pieces of the proof of precision and discuss the modifications needed to account for tail calls, which our setting has but P4F's doesn't.

9.1 Overview of Stack Precision

The property of *precision*—also called *completeness*—is dual to the property of *soundness*. Whereas soundness conveys that every behavior in the reference semantics is present in the abstract semantics, *completeness* conveys that no other behavior is present. With respect to stacks, completeness means that every stack implied by the abstract semantics is realizable by a reference semantics which represents stacks explicitly. We now present this reference semantics $\Rightarrow_{\hat{\Sigma}_a}$, show that the abstract semantics $\Rightarrow_{\tilde{\Sigma}_a}$ are sound with respect to $\Rightarrow_{\hat{\Sigma}_a}$, define what it means for a stack to be realizable by $\Rightarrow_{\hat{\Sigma}_a}$ and implied by $\Rightarrow_{\tilde{\Sigma}_a}$, and finally prove that every stack implied by $\Rightarrow_{\tilde{\Sigma}_a}$ is realizable by $\Rightarrow_{\hat{\Sigma}_a}$. (We elide the straightforward result that $\Rightarrow_{\tilde{\Sigma}_a}$ is sound with respect to a concrete reference semantics for space.)

Figure 7 presents a small-step semantics for λ_a in which each configuration includes a stack instead of a continuation store. Except for the handling of the continuation, this semantics is identical to the abstract semantics. When an atomic expression is let-bound or the call is a tail call, the continuation is undisturbed. When a call expression is let-bound, a frame is pushed on the continuation. Evaluation of an atomic expression pops the top frame and restores its expression and environment as it binds the result.

An analysis in the system space $\hat{\Xi}_a$ is defined as the least fixed point of $\Rightarrow_{\hat{\Sigma}_a}$, which is defined similarly to $\Rightarrow_{\tilde{\Sigma}_a}$. However, unlike the abstract system space $\tilde{\Xi}_a$, the system space $\hat{\Xi}_a$ is infinite due to unbounded stacks within configurations. Consequently, the least fixed point of $\Rightarrow_{\hat{\Sigma}_a}$ is well-defined but incomputable.

$$\tilde{\varsigma}_a \in \tilde{\Sigma}_a = \mathsf{Exp} \times \widehat{Env}_a \times \widehat{Store}_a \times \widehat{Stack}_a$$

$$\hat{\kappa}_a \in \widehat{Stack}_a ::= \mathsf{mt} \mid \mathsf{ar}(x, e, \hat{\rho}_a, \hat{\kappa}_a)$$

$$\Rightarrow_{\hat{\Sigma}_a} \subseteq \hat{\Sigma}_a \times \hat{\Sigma}_a$$

$$(\mathsf{let}_\gamma\, x := ae^\gamma\ \mathsf{in}\, e, \hat{\rho}, \hat{\sigma}_a, \hat{\kappa}) \Rightarrow_{\hat{\Sigma}_a} (e, \hat{\rho}, \hat{\sigma}'_a, \hat{\kappa})$$
$$\hat{d}^a = \hat{\mathcal{E}}_a(ae, \hat{\rho}, \hat{\sigma}_a) \quad \hat{\sigma}'_a = \hat{\sigma}_a \sqcup [(x, \hat{\rho}) \mapsto \hat{d}^a]$$

$$(ae^\gamma, \hat{\rho}, \hat{\sigma}_a, \hat{\kappa}) \Rightarrow_{\hat{\Sigma}_a} (e, \hat{\rho}', \hat{\sigma}'_a, \hat{\kappa}')$$
$$\hat{d}^a = \hat{\mathcal{E}}_a(ae, \hat{\rho}, \hat{\sigma}_a) \quad \hat{\kappa} = \mathsf{ar}(x, e, \hat{\rho}', \hat{\kappa}')$$
$$\hat{\sigma}'_a = \hat{\sigma}_a \sqcup [(x, \hat{\rho}') \mapsto \hat{d}^a]$$

$$(\mathsf{let}_\gamma\, x := (ae_0\ ae_1)^l\ \mathsf{in}\, e, \hat{\rho}, \hat{\sigma}_a, \hat{\kappa}) \Rightarrow_{\hat{\Sigma}_a} (e', \hat{\rho}'', \hat{\sigma}'_a, \hat{\kappa}')$$
$$(\lambda_l x'.e', \hat{\rho}') \in \hat{\mathcal{E}}_a(ae_0, \hat{\rho}, \hat{\sigma}_a) \quad \hat{d}^a = \hat{\mathcal{E}}_a(ae_1, \hat{\rho}, \hat{\sigma}_a)$$
$$\{x_1, \ldots, x_n\} = \mathit{free}(\lambda_l x.e') \quad \hat{\kappa}' = \mathsf{ar}(x, e, \hat{\rho}, \hat{\kappa})$$
$$\hat{\rho}'' = \lfloor l :: \hat{\rho} \rfloor_m \quad \hat{d}^a_i = \hat{\sigma}_a(x_i, \hat{\rho}')$$
$$\hat{\sigma}'_a = \hat{\sigma}_a \sqcup [(x, \hat{\rho}'') \mapsto \hat{d}^a] \sqcup [(x_i, \hat{\rho}'') \mapsto \hat{d}^a_i]$$

$$((ae_0\ ae_1)^l, \hat{\rho}, \hat{\sigma}_a, \hat{\kappa}) \Rightarrow_{\hat{\Sigma}_a} (e', \hat{\rho}'', \hat{\sigma}'_a, \hat{\kappa})$$
$$(\lambda_l x.e', \hat{\rho}') \in \hat{\mathcal{E}}_a(ae_0, \hat{\rho}, \hat{\sigma}_a) \quad \hat{d}^a = \hat{\mathcal{E}}_a(ae_1, \hat{\rho}, \hat{\sigma}_a)$$
$$\{x_1, \ldots, x_n\} = \mathit{free}(\lambda_l x.e') \quad \hat{d}^a_i = \hat{\sigma}_a(x_i, \hat{\rho}')$$
$$\hat{\rho}'' = \lfloor l :: \hat{\rho} \rfloor_m$$
$$\hat{\sigma}'_a = \hat{\sigma}_a \sqcup [(x, \hat{\rho}'') \mapsto \hat{d}^a] \sqcup [(x_i, \hat{\rho}'') \mapsto \hat{d}^a_i]$$

Fig. 7. State transition rules $\Rightarrow_{\hat{\Sigma}_a}$

We relate the abstract state space $\tilde{\Sigma}_a$ and stack state space $\hat{\Sigma}_a$ by way of an abstraction function $|\cdot| : \hat{\Sigma}_a \to \tilde{\Sigma}_a$ where

$$|(e, \hat{\rho}, \hat{\sigma}_a, \hat{\kappa})| = (e, \hat{\rho}, \hat{\sigma}_a, F(\zeta_{pr}[\![e]\!], \hat{\rho}, \hat{\kappa}))$$

The F metafunction allocates a stack frame-by-frame to produce a continuation store in which all frames are allocated. It relies on the ζ_{pr} metafunction which maps an expression to the body of its innermost-enclosing λ or the top-level program if it is not enclosed.

$$F(e,\hat{\rho},\mathsf{mt}) = \bot \quad F(e,\hat{\rho},\mathsf{ar}(x,e',\hat{\rho}',\hat{\kappa}')) = F(\zeta_{pr}[\![e']\!],\hat{\rho}',\hat{\kappa}') \sqcup [(e,\hat{\rho}) \mapsto \{\mathsf{ar}(x,e',\hat{\rho}')\}]$$

We now define a polymorphic refinement relation $\sqsubseteq$ over stack states and over abstract states. This relation descends componentwise: expressions, environments, and stacks each have a discrete refinement ordering (i.e. they are related only by equality); store and continuation store refinements are as follows.

$$\hat{\sigma}_a \sqsubseteq \hat{\sigma}'_a \iff \forall \hat{a} \in \widehat{Addr}_a . \hat{\sigma}_a(\hat{a}) \subseteq \hat{\sigma}'_a(\hat{a})$$
$$\tilde{\sigma}_\kappa \sqsubseteq \tilde{\sigma}'_\kappa \iff \forall \tilde{a}_\kappa \in \widetilde{KAddr} . \tilde{\sigma}_\kappa(\tilde{a}_\kappa) \subseteq \tilde{\sigma}'_\kappa(\tilde{a}_\kappa)$$

Using these definitions, stack state and abstract state refinements are as follows.

$$(e,\hat{\rho},\hat{\sigma}_a,\hat{\kappa}) \sqsubseteq (e,\hat{\rho},\hat{\sigma}'_a,\hat{\kappa}) \iff \hat{\sigma}_a \sqsubseteq \hat{\sigma}'_a$$
$$(e,\hat{\rho},\hat{\sigma}_a,\tilde{\sigma}_\kappa) \sqsubseteq (e,\hat{\rho},\hat{\sigma}'_a,\tilde{\sigma}'_\kappa) \iff \hat{\sigma}_a \sqsubseteq \hat{\sigma}'_a \text{ and } \tilde{\sigma}_\kappa \sqsubseteq \tilde{\sigma}'_\kappa$$

We now express the simulation property that constitutes soundness.

Theorem 2 (Simulation). *If $|\hat{\varsigma}| \sqsubseteq \tilde{\varsigma}$ and $\hat{\varsigma} \Rightarrow_{\hat{\Sigma}_a} \hat{\varsigma}'$, then there exists $\tilde{\varsigma}'$ such that $\tilde{\varsigma} \Rightarrow_{\tilde{\Sigma}_a} \tilde{\varsigma}'$ and $|\hat{\varsigma}'| \sqsubseteq \tilde{\varsigma}'$.*

The proof proceeds by cases on the expression, showing in each case that the abstract transition respects the relationship induced by F.

A *path* is a sequence of zero or more transitions from the initial state denoted $\hat{I}(pr) \Rightarrow^*_{\hat{\Sigma}_a} \hat{\varsigma}$. A stack $\hat{\kappa}$ is *realizable* with respect to a store $\hat{\sigma}_a$ if $(pr,\langle\rangle,\hat{\sigma}_a,\mathsf{mt}) \Rightarrow^*_{\hat{\Sigma}_a} (e,\hat{\rho},\hat{\sigma}'_a,\hat{\kappa})$ for some expression e, environment $\hat{\rho}$, and store $\hat{\sigma}'_a$. A stack $\hat{\kappa}$ is *implied* with respect to a continuation address $(e,\hat{\rho})$ and a continuation store $\tilde{\sigma}_\kappa$, which we denote $\hat{\kappa} \in_{\tilde{\sigma}_\kappa} (e,\hat{\rho})$, as follows.

$$\mathsf{mt} \in_{\tilde{\sigma}_\kappa} (e,\hat{\rho}) \iff \mathsf{mt} \in \tilde{\sigma}_\kappa(e,\hat{\rho})$$
$$\mathsf{ar}(x,e',\hat{\rho}',\hat{\kappa}') \in_{\tilde{\sigma}_\kappa} (e,\hat{\rho}) \iff \mathsf{ar}(x,e',\hat{\rho}') \in \tilde{\sigma}_\kappa(e,\hat{\rho}) \text{ and } \hat{\kappa}' \in_{\tilde{\sigma}_\kappa} (\zeta_{pr}[\![e']\!],\hat{\rho}')$$

An empty stack is implied at an address if mt resides there. A non-empty stack is implied at an address if its top frame resides there and the remaining stack is implied by the continuation address derived from that frame. A configuration uniquely determines a continuation address, so it is sensible to consider the stacks realizable at a configuration.

Now we are able to state the precision property which, essentially, is that every reachable configuration and continuation thereat is reachable by a stack-respecting path.

Theorem 3 (Stack Precision). *Suppose $\tilde{\xi} = (\tilde{r},\hat{\sigma}_a,\tilde{\sigma}_\kappa)$ is the least fixed point of $\Rightarrow_{\tilde{\Sigma}_a}$. For each $(e,\hat{\rho}) \in \tilde{r}$ and $\hat{\kappa}$ such that $\hat{\kappa} \in_{\tilde{\sigma}_\kappa} (\zeta_{pr}[\![e]\!],\hat{\rho})$, there exists a path $(pr,\langle\rangle,\hat{\sigma}_a,\mathsf{mt}) \Rightarrow_{\hat{\Sigma}_a} (e,\hat{\rho},\hat{\sigma}_a,\hat{\kappa})$.*

As with Gilray *et al.* [6], the theorem is proved with two inductions, first on the path length, and second on the continuation. We omit their well-formedness property, instead relying on the supposed analysis being a *least* fixed point, which serves the same purpose to ensure that each present configuration and continuation has a reason to be. It is this property that allows the proof to easily accommodate tail calls; namely, once proper callers are ruled out as predecessors to an invocation entry, there must be a tail call which has the continuation of the entry, by definition of the continuation store tail call transition.

10 Discussion

An immediate consequence of the result that m-CFA^a is stack-precise (Theorem 3) is that m-CFA^{cps} is too, since the two analyses are isomorphic (Theorem 1).

This consequence itself is a striking result since the development of m-CFA^{cps} (1) was concurrent to and independent of the development of CFA2, the first stack-precise CFA, (2) makes no mention of stack precision, and (3) preceded P4F by more than half a decade. It also places m-CFA in a sweet spot in the CFA space, being a (1) polynomial-time, (2) stack-precise, (3) context-sensitive CFA hierarchy (4) implementable using a straightforward workset-based algorithm.

However, m-CFA exhibits additional advantages when it comes to non-local control constructs, such as exceptions, escapes, coroutines, up to full continuations. To illustrate, consider stack-precise CFAs computed by summarization algorithms, such as CFA2. With such analyses, it is difficult to extend the analyzed language with non-local control constructs because the summarization algorithm is the sole manager of the stack. Thus, any stack-touching control feature requires the summarization algorithm to be modified in a nontrivial way. This complex algorithm lies at the heart of the analysis's soundness property, which means that such a modification requires the soundness of the analysis to be reestablished. To do this work once and for all, Vardoulakis and Shivers [22] extend the CFA2's summarization algorithm to support `call/cc`, in terms of which a host of non-local control constructs can be expressed. But, by expressing a control feature in terms of `call/cc` to obtain analysis support, one also obtains at best the precision at which `call/cc` is analyzed, and not the higher precision that weaker non-control constructs, such as exceptions and escapes, enjoy, using more-tailored modifications to the summarization algorithm [5].

In contrast, m-CFA appears to handle such constructs in its unrestricted CPS language seamlessly, with no modification to its workset algorithm, and with as much precision as current techniques. For example, when using the well-known "double-barrelled CPS" technique to encode exceptions [18], it appears that m-CFA is able to maintain perfect stack precision (also called "relative completeness" with reference to exceptions [5]) with no modification to the analysis whatsoever. We intend to formally characterize the precision m-CFA offers different continuation patterns to allow clients to engineer the CPS transformation instead of the analyzer.

The fact that m-CFA^{cps} implements P4F is due to the clever way in which Might *et al.* [13] are able to "pop" the stack of the top-m stack frames by treating the stack frame context with the discipline of a static environment—indeed, it *is* the static environment in the analysis. We can use this observation to completely isolate m-CFA's stack precision from its aggressive rebinding. That is, a variant of m-CFA which used the top-m-stack-frames context abstraction but a k-CFA-style environment would also be stack-precise (albeit exponential).

References

1. Appel, A.W.: Compiling with Continuations. Cambridge University Press, Cambridge (1992)
2. Felleisen, M., Friedman, D.P.: Control operators, the SECD-machine, and the λ-calculus. In: Wirsing, M. (ed.) Formal Description of Programming Concepts - III: Proceedings of the IFIP TC 2/WG 2.2 Working Conference on Formal Description of Programming Concepts - III, Ebberup, Denmark, 25–28 August 1986, pp. 193–222. North-Holland (1987)
3. Fischer, M.J.: Lambda calculus schemata. In: Proceedings of ACM Conference on Proving Assertions About Programs, 6–7 January 1972, Las Cruces, New Mexico, USA, pp. 104–109. ACM (1972)
4. Flanagan, C., Sabry, A., Duba, B.F., Felleisen, M.: The essence of compiling with continuations. SIGPLAN Not. **28**(6), 237–247 (1993)
5. Germane, K., Might, M.: Relatively complete pushdown analysis of escape continuations. In: Enea, C., Piskac, R. (eds.) VMCAI 2019. LNCS, vol. 11388, pp. 205–225. Springer, Cham (2019). https://doi.org/10.1007/978-3-030-11245-5_10
6. Gilray, T., Lyde, S., Adams, M.D., Might, M., Van Horn, D.: Pushdown control-flow analysis for free. In: Proceedings of the 43rd Annual ACM SIGPLAN-SIGACT Symposium on Principles of Programming Languages, POPL '16, pp. 691–704. ACM, New York (2016)
7. Johnson, J.I., Van Horn, D.: Abstracting abstract control. In: Proceedings of the 10th ACM Symposium on Dynamic Languages, DLS '14, pp. 11–22. ACM, New York (2014)
8. Kennedy, A.: Compiling with continuations, continued. In: Hinze, R., Ramsey, N. (eds.) Proceedings of the 12th ACM SIGPLAN International Conference on Functional Programming, ICFP 2007, 1–3 October 2007, Freiburg, Germany, pp. 177–190. ACM (2007)
9. Kranz, D.A., Kelsey, R., Rees, J., Hudak, P., Philbin, J.: ORBIT: an optimizing compiler for scheme. In: Wexelblat, R.L. (ed.) Proceedings of the 1986 SIGPLAN Symposium on Compiler Construction, 25–27 June 1986, Palo Alto, California, USA, pp. 219–233. ACM (1986)
10. Might, C.E.M., Horn, D.V.: Pushdown control-flow analysis of higher-order programs: precise, polyvariant and polynomial-time. In: Scheme Workshop (2010)
11. Might, M., Shivers, O.: Environment analysis via delta CFA. In: Morrisett, J.G., Jones, S.L.P. (eds.) Proceedings of the 33rd ACM SIGPLAN-SIGACT Symposium on Principles of Programming Languages, POPL 2006, 11–13 January 2006, Charleston, South Carolina, USA, pp. 127–140. ACM (2006)
12. Might, M., Shivers, O.: Improving flow analyses via gammaCFA: abstract garbage collection and counting. In: Proceedings of the Eleventh ACM SIGPLAN International Conference on Functional Programming, ICFP '06, pp. 13–25. ACM, New York (2006)

13. Might, M., Smaragdakis, Y., Van Horn, D.: Resolving and exploiting the k-CFA paradox: illuminating functional vs. object-oriented program analysis. In: Proceedings of the 31st ACM SIGPLAN Conference on Programming Language Design and Implementation, PLDI '10, pp. 305–315. ACM, New York (2010)
14. Palsberg, J.: Closure analysis in constraint form. ACM Trans. Program. Lang. Syst. **17**(1), 47–62 (1995)
15. Sabry, A., Felleisen, M.: Is continuation-passing useful for data flow analysis? In: Proceedings of the ACM SIGPLAN 1994 Conference on Programming Language Design and Implementation, PLDI '94, pp. 1–12. Association for Computing Machinery, New York (1994)
16. Shivers, O.: Control-Flow Analysis of Higher-Order Languages. Ph.D. thesis, Carnegie Mellon University, Pittsburgh, PA, USA (1991)
17. Steele, G.L., Jr.: RABBIT: A Compiler for Scheme. Massachusetts Institute of Technology, Cambridge (1978)
18. Thielecke, H.: Comparing control constructs by double-barrelled CPS. High. Order Symb. Comput. **15**(2–3), 141–160 (2002)
19. Van Horn, D., Might, M.: Abstracting abstract machines. In: Proceedings of the 15th ACM SIGPLAN International Conference on Functional Programming, ICFP '10, pp. 51–62. ACM, New York (2010)
20. Vardoulakis, D., Shivers, O.: CFA2: a context-free approach to control-flow analysis. In: Gordon, A.D. (ed.) ESOP 2010. LNCS, vol. 6012, pp. 570–589. Springer, Heidelberg (2010). https://doi.org/10.1007/978-3-642-11957-6_30
21. Vardoulakis, D., Shivers, O.: Ordering multiple continuations on the stack. In: Khoo, S., Siek, J.G. (eds.) Proceedings of the 2011 ACM SIGPLAN Workshop on Partial Evaluation and Program Manipulation, PEPM 2011, 24–25 January 2011, Austin, TX, USA, pp. 13–22. ACM (2011)
22. Vardoulakis, D., Shivers, O.: Pushdown flow analysis of first-class control. In: Chakravarty, M.M.T., Hu, Z., Danvy, O. (eds.) Proceeding of the 16th ACM SIGPLAN International Conference on Functional Programming, ICFP 2011, 19–21 September 2011, Tokyo, Japan, pp. 69–80. ACM (2011)

TorchProbe: Fuzzing Dynamic Deep Learning Compilers

Qidong Su[1,2], Chuqin Geng[1,3,4], Gennady Pekhimenko[1,2], and Xujie Si[1,2,4](✉)

[1] University of Toronto, Toronto, Canada
{qdsu,pekhimenko,six}@cs.toronto.edu, chuqin.geng@mail.mcgill.ca
[2] Vector Institute, Toronto, Canada
[3] McGill University, Montreal, Canada
[4] Mila - Quebec AI Institute, Montreal, Canada

Abstract. Static and dynamic computational graphs represent two distinct approaches to constructing deep learning frameworks. The former prioritizes compiler-based optimizations, while the latter focuses on programmability and user-friendliness. The recent release of PyTorch 2.0, which supports compiling arbitrary deep learning programs in Python, signifies a new direction in the evolution of deep learning infrastructure to incorporate compiler techniques in a more dynamic manner and support more dynamic language features like dynamic control flows and closures. Given PyTorch's seamless integration with Python, its compiler aims to support arbitrary deep learning code written in Python. However, the inherent dynamism of Python poses challenges to the completeness and robustness of the compiler. While recent research has introduced fuzzing to test deep learning compilers, there is still a lack of comprehensive analysis on how to test dynamic features. To address this issue, we propose several code transformations to generate test cases involving dynamic features. These transformations preserve the program's semantics, ensuring that any discrepancy between the transformed and original programs indicates the presence of a bug. Through our approach, we have successfully identified twenty previously unknown bugs in the PyTorch compiler and its underlying tensor compiler Triton.

Keywords: Debugging · Software engineering · Deep learning

1 Introduction

Deep Learning (DL) has recently achieved significant success in various critical fields such as vision [20,23], natural language processing [11,18,42], and autonomous driving [15]. This progress has led to the emergence of numerous algorithms, model architectures, and applications, necessitating highly flexible infrastructure. Python, with its highly dynamic features, has become the de facto standard programming language in the DL community. It is favored for its expressiveness, flexibility, and rich ecosystem. Popular DL frameworks like TensorFlow [7] and PyTorch [44] provide their programming interfaces as domain-specific languages (DSLs) embedded in Python.

C.-K. Hur (Ed.): APLAS 2023, LNCS 14405, pp. 310–331, 2023.
https://doi.org/10.1007/978-981-99-8311-7_15

However, executing high-level DL code efficiently in Python remains a challenging problem. Training and inference of deep learning models are known to be time and resource-consuming, particularly given the increasing number of parameters. Hardware vendors offer various accelerators such as GPUs [28,41], TPUs [26], and NPUs [1,2,6,25,31,36] to address this issue. These accelerators typically have distinct specifications, architectures, and programming models. Therefore, effectively mapping DL tasks onto the underlying hardware is crucial for maximizing the utilization of accelerators.

To bridge the gap between abstract deep neural network descriptions and the low-level hardware instructions of accelerators, the concept of "deep learning compilers" [32] has been introduced. The typical workflow of a deep learning compiler involves three steps: 1) writing high-level DL code in Python, 2) converting the DL model into an intermediate representation (IR) provided by the compiler, and 3) calling the DL compiler to generate optimized code. However, while Python itself is a highly flexible language, the IRs in DL compilers are usually more restricted as they rely on compile-time information to enable more optimization opportunities. For instance, static computational graphs allow for more advanced graph-level optimizations e.g., operator fusion [29,40]. Another example is fixing the shape of tensors involved in computations, which facilitates finding optimal configurations for the generated code, such as tiling size [13].

The misalignment in expressiveness between Python and deep learning compilers poses challenges and requires more manual intervention and engineering effort, hindering the widespread application of compiler techniques. TorchScript [17], the first-generation compiler of PyTorch, provides an intermediate representation (IR) that is incompatible with Python. As a result, users are faced with the options of either rewriting their code in a constrained subset of Python (scripting) or tracing the code's execution trajectory, which only captures partial information of the original code (tracing). On the other hand, Torch.fx [47], the second-generation compiler, offers an IR compatible with Python but requires the code to be purely functional.

In response to this issue, a recent trend in deep learning compiler development is to support more dynamic features, enabling the seamless application of compiler techniques within the original Python language. The newly released PyTorch 2.0 [60] includes a compiler component that facilitates the automatic optimization of *any* Python code through a simple API called `torch.compile`. This compiler component modifies the process of launching a Python function by analyzing the bytecode generated by the Python interpreter. It identifies code snippets that can be optimized, performs compiler optimizations on them, and caches the optimized code for future reuse. Given that deep learning tasks often involve high levels of repetition, this strategy can yield significant performance improvements in many scenarios.

However, the implementation of the new PyTorch compiler is complex and intertwined with the original Python interpreter, DL frameworks and libraries, and heterogeneous hardware. This complexity introduces the risk of potential bugs in the implementation, many of which may remain hidden and only manifest in specific corner cases. Manually creating test cases as a solution requires significant engineering effort and can only cover a limited range of possible inputs. Therefore, an automated testing framework that generates test cases for dynamic deep learning compilers would expedite the process of bug detection and enhance the robustness of the infrastructure. While previous works have utilized *fuzzing* techniques on DL infrastructures to identify bugs, they focus on static computational graphs [21,22,34,38,58], and the exploration of how to effectively fuzz dynamic deep learning compilers is still an area that lacks comprehensive analysis, to the best of our knowledge.

To address these challenges, we present a novel fuzzing framework called TorchProbe. This framework is designed to generate test cases that cover dynamic features such as control flows, in-place tensor mutation, list comprehension, and nested functions. For each generated test case, we perform three checks: 1) ensuring that the compiler can generate optimized code without encountering errors, 2) verifying that the optimized code can be executed successfully, and 3) validating that the output produced by the optimized code remains consistent with the original program.

To ensure the meaningfulness of the tests, it is crucial that they are both logically and numerically valid, capable of producing valid output even before being optimized by the compiler. For instance, the test cases should be free of numerical errors (e.g., division by zero) and undefined behaviors like `INFINITY` and `NaN` in floating-point numbers. Furthermore, the introduction of control flows can potentially lead to programs that never terminate, such as infinite loops.

To ensure the validity of the test cases, we employ two types of program mutation to generate new test cases based on a "seed" program: *Equivalent Mutation* and *Equivalence Modulo Inputs* (EMI) [51]. We ensure that the test cases generated through these mutations always produce the same output as the seed program if the compiler processes them correctly. In our approach, we convert the computational graphs generated by an existing fuzzer NNSmith [34] into straight-line code, which serves as the seed program. Since the methods for guaranteeing the validity of computational graphs have been extensively studied in prior works [34,38], we can ensure the validity of the mutated programs.

Moreover, these mutations are composable. Each mutation introduces more dynamic language features, and their composition enlarges the detected program space, which potentially exposes more bugs. A simple illustrative example is as follows in Fig. 1, where we derive a test case from one line of tensor declaration via several steps of program mutations. PyTorch compiler crashed on this program because it failed to handle hoisting, closures, and graph breaks correctly. One core developer of PyTorch refers to this bug as *'a lot of fun for a PL nerd'*.

The program mutations presented in this paper represent merely *one potential methodology* for generating valid test cases. It's important to note the validity of test cases does not necessarily rely on the equivalence. While equivalence-based program mutations can generate valid test cases, there exist huge numbers of valid test cases that are not covered by it. This work did not investigate how to synthesize valid test cases beyond equivalent program mutations, which is a vast space to explore for future works.

```
x = torch.zeros([1])
```

(a) Seed Program

```
x = torch.zeros([1])
def func():
    x[0] = backup
if x[0] >= -1e5:
    pass
backup = 1
func()
```

(b) Mutated Program

Fig. 1. An example of constructing more sophisticated test cases from a seed program. This test case triggers the PyTorch compiler to crash because it does not handle hoisting well.

We summarize the main contributions of this work as follows:

1. We observe the problem of how to automatically detect bugs in the emerging dynamic deep learning compilers, which aim to support more dynamic language features than previous ones.
2. We design novel program mutations to automatically generate test cases specifically for dynamic language features such as control flows, data mutation, and closure.
3. We find twenty previously undiscovered bugs in the latest compiler of PyTorch and its underlying backend compiler Triton. All of them are confirmed by the community, twelve of them have already been fixed, and five test cases have been integrated as unit tests.

2 Background

In this section, we introduce related background including the recent development of deep learning compilers and automatic testing techniques for deep learning systems.

2.1 Deep Learning Program and Systems

Deep learning applications differ from generic programs in several aspects, with the most significant one being their high computation intensity. DL code often involves heavy computations such as matrix multiplications and convolutions, which require a large number of floating-point operations. Running unoptimized DL tasks on regular hardware leads to unacceptable slowness.

To tackle this challenge, a domain-specific hardware-software stack has been established, encompassing accelerators, libraries, runtimes, frameworks, and languages. Hardware accelerators like GPUs, TPUs, and NPUs offer beneficial features for DL applications, such as highly parallel SIMT programming models and dedicated circuits for matrix multiplications [4]. However, new hardware also poses challenges for upper-level software. Developing high-performance code that is optimized for specialized hardware demands expertise in computer architecture and significant engineering effort. To address this, numerous solutions have been proposed.

High-performance Libraries. One solution is to use high-performance math libraries provided by hardware vendors. Hardware vendors often provide highly specialized and optimized libraries for their hardware products, such as cuBLAS [3] and cuDNN [14] for NVIDIA GPUs, and MKL-DNN [57] for Intel CPUs. These libraries contain many commonly used operators in the form of parallel functions called *kernels*. Most of them are written in C/C++ or assembly languages to provide high performance.

Deep Learning Frameworks. While high-performance libraries provide superior performance, their programming interface is not sufficiently friendly to DL researchers. Therefore, deep learning frameworks such as TensorFlow and PyTorch are invented for better user interface and programmability. A common abstraction of DL frameworks is *computational graphs*, which we elaborate on in Sect. 2.2.

2.2 Computational Graphs

Computational graphs are a widely used abstraction in deep learning programs, providing benefits in automatic differentiation and performance optimization. These graphs represent the data flow of DL programs, with nodes representing operators and edges representing data dependencies.

There are two types of computational graphs: static and dynamic. They are categorized based on when and how they are constructed.

Static Graph. Many frameworks such as Caffe [24], Theano [10], and early versions of Tensorflow [7] adopt static computation graphs. When writing DL programs, users explicitly describe the computational graph using the primitives provided by the framework. The computational graph is not executed until it is fully constructed (or *define-then-run*). The advantage of static graphs is that the framework can obtain complete information about the computational graph before the program is executed, which enables optimizations based on graph analysis [29], such as constant folding, common sub-expression elimination, and operator fusion.

Dynamic Graph. While static graphs provide opportunities for various optimizations, the define-then-run programming interface is not aligned with the imperative programming paradigm and other well-known matrix libraries such as `numpy` [55], which imposes additional demands on users. PyTorch [44] and TensorFlow Eager [8] adopt another strategy called dynamic graphs. In PyTorch, the code of forward propagation is similar to imperative numpy code. When an operator is called, its computation will be triggered immediately, and it will also be book-kept by a *tape*, which constructs the computational graph on the fly (or *define-by-run*). The computational graph is later used in the backward propagation. While dynamic graphs provide a better programming interface, it makes performance optimizations more challenging [47] (Fig. 2).

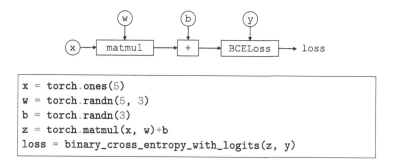

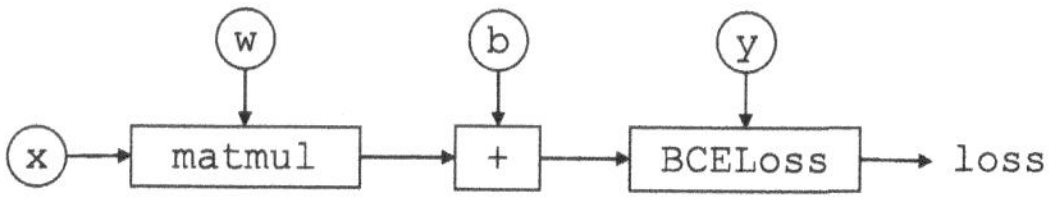


```
x = torch.ones(5)
w = torch.randn(5, 3)
b = torch.randn(3)
z = torch.matmul(x, w)+b
loss = binary_cross_entropy_with_logits(z, y)
```

Fig. 2. An example of computational graph and its corresponding PyTorch code.

2.3 Deep Learning Compilers

Compilers play an important role in many layers of the DL software stack. The CUDA compiler `nvcc` compiles CUDA code into lower-level binary code. Tensor compilers such as Halide [46], TVM [12], and Hidet [19] translate high-level mathematical tensor expressions into efficient kernels for different target hardware. This process is called *scheduling*, which is finished either manually or automatically. Triton is an intermediate language between CUDA and other loop-based tensor compilers, providing a programming model at the tile level.

Generally speaking, most DL compilers work on two distinct levels, namely the graph level and operator (or kernel) level. They take computational graphs as inputs, divide them into smaller subgraphs, and generate efficient kernels for each subgraph.

However, there is a misalignment between the language which DL researchers use and the frontend language used by the DL compilers. While a lot of DL researchers write programs in Python, most DL compilers take static graphs as their input. So it is necessary to convert the DL models to formats that can be accepted by DL compilers. Some examples of these formats are ONNX [5] and TorchScript [17]. The conversion is far from seamless due to different operator sets and implementation details.

The PyTorch community provides several solutions to ease the process of translating PyTorch code into compilable formats. TorchScript [17] is a language designed for DL model deployment. There are two methods to convert PyTorch code into TorchScript namely scripting and tracing. Scripting requires users to write in a subset of Python, which will be later parsed and translated into TorchScipt directly. Tracing is to actually run the code and record which operators are launched, and the recorded trace is later translated into TorchScript. Both scripting and tracing have weaknesses. Scripting does not support all language features of Python so users often need to rewrite the code, while tracing loses many key information such as control flows.

`Torch.fx` [47] is purely functional language designed for compiling PyTorch code, which is equivalent to computational graphs. Users can translate PyTorch code into torch.fx via symbolic tracing. However, many language features are still not supported. Figure 3 shows two examples that torch.fx cannot handle.

```
x[0] = 1
```

(a) Tensor mutation

```
if x[0] > 1:
    ...
else:
    ...
```

(b) Dynamic control flows

Fig. 3. Two examples of PyTorch code that torch.fx fails to trace, as it is a purely functional language design.

2.4 Dynamic Deep Learning Compilers

The recently released PyTorch 2.0 [60] adopts a new strategy of compilation, which is called *TorchDynamo*. The workflow of the PyTorch compiler is shown in Fig. 4. While computational graphs cannot represent all PyTorch programs, TorchDynamo analyzes the bytecode generated by the Python interpreter and capture *partial* computational graphs and translate them into torch.fx graphs. Therefore, a Python function might be broken down into multiple partial graphs, and the parts which cannot be compiled will be executed as normal Python code by the interpreter. In this manner, TorchDynamo has the ability to support *arbitrary* Python code.

Captured computational graphs will be compiled by one of the *backend* compilers in a Just-in-time way and cached for future reuse. Since DL tasks are repetitive, the compiled code has a high chance to be reused. Every time one function is called, TorchDynamo will check whether it has already been compiled and the conditions of reuse are satisfied (called *guards*, e.g. the shape of the input tensors is not changed), and will execute the compiled version if all requirements are met, which leads to substantial speedup.

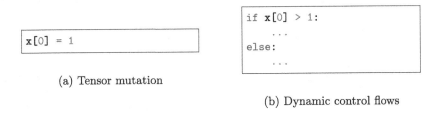

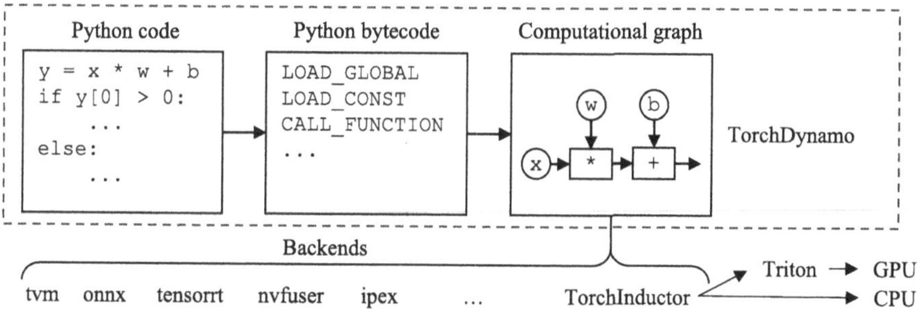

Fig. 4. Overview of the compiler of PyTorch 2.0 – TorchDynamo. TorchDynamo analyzes bytecode and captures partial computational graphs. It translates these graphs into torch.fx graphs, which can be compiled by backend compilers like TensorRT in a Just-in-Time manner.

TorchDynamo now supports many backend compilers including TorchInductor, TVM [12], TensorRT [56], and ONNX [5]. The official backend compiler is TorchInductor, which can generate high-performance CPU kernels, or relies on the Triton [53] intermediate language to generate GPU kernels.

2.5 Fuzzing Deep Learning Systems

As deep learning is applied to many critical scenarios, how to guarantee the robustness of deep learning systems has become an important topic. Fuzzing as an automatic testing technique has been introduced to detect bugs in DL systems. NNSmith [34] generates random valid computational graphs and input data to check if the tested DL system can produce expected outputs. A more detailed discussion about related work is included in Sect. 5.

3 Approach

This section presents our proposed deep learning fuzzer for testing dynamic deep learning compilers.

3.1 Overview

Figure 5 illustrates the overall workflow of our fuzzer. Let $\mathcal{L}$ be the language space of all possible programs, which specifically refers to code written in Python and PyTorch in our case. Let $\mathcal{I}$ be the input space which includes all possible input data, e.g. tuples of tensors.

A correctly implemented compiler should guarantee that the optimized code should generate the same output as the original code. More formally, let $[\![\mathcal{P}]\!](x)$ be the output of the program $\mathcal{P} \in \mathcal{L}$ given the input $x \in \mathcal{I}$, executed on the original Python interpreter and eager-mode PyTorch, and $[\![\mathcal{P}]\!]_{\mathcal{C}}(x)$ be the output of the compiled version of $\mathcal{P}$ produced by the compiler $\mathcal{C}$, which is executed on

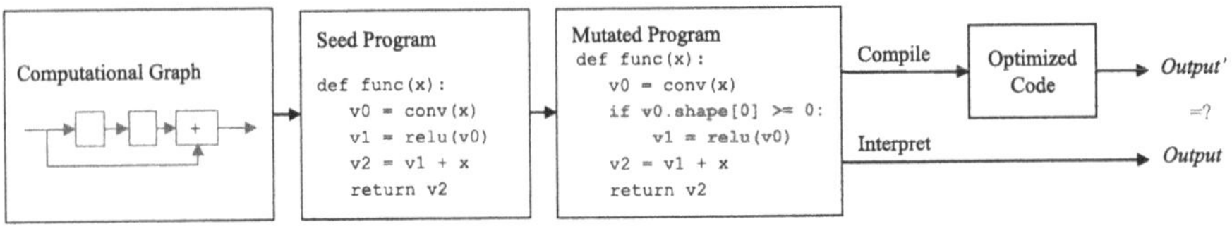

Fig. 5. The TorchProbe workflow involves translating input computational graphs into Python code, which serves as seed programs. These seed programs undergo numerical-equivalence mutations to create corresponding mutated programs. Finally, we verify if the compiler can produce the same results from the original Python interpreter and eager-mode PyTorch.

the modified runtime system for compiled code. The correctness of a compiler could be represented as

$$\forall \mathcal{P} \in \mathcal{L}, x \in \mathcal{I}, [\![P]\!](x) \text{ is valid} \Rightarrow [\![\mathcal{P}]\!](x) = [\![\mathcal{P}]\!]_{\mathcal{C}}(x) \tag{1}$$

where '$[\![\mathcal{P}]\!](x)$ is valid' means the program $\mathcal{P}$ is executed correctly and produces meaningful results without any syntax or semantic errors, runtime errors, numerical errors, or undefined behaviors including `INFINITY` and `NaN` in tensors. The compiler can pass the test case if 1) It can finish the compilation without errors, 2) the compiled code is runnable, 3) the compiled code can produce consistent outputs as the original program.

A fuzzer can sample valid test cases $(\mathcal{P}, x)$ containing a program $\mathcal{P} \in \mathcal{L}$ and input data $x \in \mathcal{I}$, and check whether the compiled code can produce consistent results as the original code. In order to ensure the validity of samples, we start from a valid 'seed' test case and perform a series of numerical-equivalence *mutations*, which preserves its validity in each step. We introduce two categories of mutations, namely *equivalent mutations* and *equivalence module inputs*. Therefore, as long as the seed test case is valid, the validity of derived test cases can also be guaranteed. We also design these mutations to be composable so that the composition of mutations form more sophisticated test cases, which might expose more bugs.

In order to obtain a valid test case, we use NNSmith [34], a fuzzer for DL systems based on computational graphs. It can automatically generate valid test cases, including the computational graph and input data. We then translate the computational graphs into straight-line Python code in static single-assignment form (SSA), which we use as the seed program. A seed program consists of a list of statements in the form of

$$out = op(in_1, in_2, \ldots, in_n)$$

where *op* is a DL operator, such as matrix multiplication or convolution, in_i-s are input tensors, and *out* is the output tensor. Each variable will appear as the output in at most one statement, that is, be defined once and remain constant.

3.2 Equivalent Mutations

Given a target deep learning program, the most direct approach to diversify the program is through equivalent mutations. Equivalent mutations ensure that both the seed program $\mathcal{P}$ and the mutated program $\mathcal{P}'$ yield the same output results for any random input x within the valid domain $\mathcal{I}$:

$$\forall x \in \mathcal{I}, \quad [\![P]\!](x) \text{ is valid} \Rightarrow [\![\mathcal{P}]\!](x) = [\![\mathcal{P}']\!](x) \tag{2}$$

The validity of the mutated test case $(\mathcal{P}', x)$ comes from the fact that $[\![\mathcal{P}]\!](x)$ is valid. Compiler bugs can be detected if the compiler crashes or the mutated program $\mathcal{P}'$ produces results that differ from the original program and the reference (oracle) program. In other words, the compiler passes the test if $[\![\mathcal{P}']\!](x) = [\![\mathcal{P}']\!]_{\mathcal{C}}(x)$.

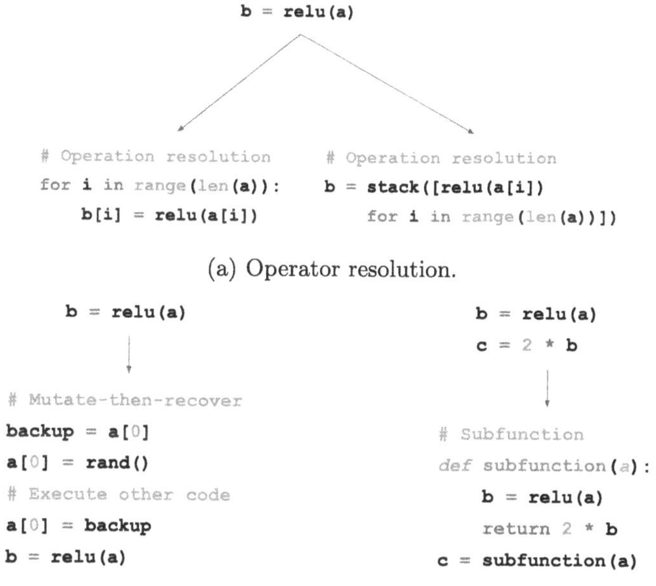

(a) Operator resolution.

(b) Mutate-then-recover.

(c) Functionalize

Fig. 6. The three types of equivalent mutations.

Our equivalent mutation method iteratively introduces more dynamic components to the target program. Specifically, we consider three types of mutations (also illustrated in Fig. 6):

1. **Operator resolution**. Deep learning operators are primarily vectorized operators. These operators can be fully or partially serialized with basic Python code blocks, such as for loops and list comprehensions. Specifically in this paper, we implemented operator resolution for element-wise operators,

such as ReLU and element-wise addition. The computation of each entry of the input tensor is independent, so we can unroll the operator along one axis. For example, suppose the tensor **a** and **b** both have a shape of $d_1 \times d_2 \times d_3$ in the assignment statement $\mathbf{b} = ReLU(\mathbf{a})$. We first randomly choose a dimension as the axis of the resolution, and unroll the operator in an equivalent form using loops or list comprehensions. Taking the second dimension as an example, the expression can be expanded as:

```
b = torch.empty_like(a)
for i in range(a.shape[1]):
    b[:, i, :] = torch.relu(a[:, i, :])
```

2. **Mutate-then-recover**. The straight-line code converted from computational graphs is in the static single-assignment form where each variable will be assigned only once and remain constant, while real-world code often involves the mutation of values of variables. To introduce tensor value mutation while preserving the numerical equivalence, we adopt the mutate-then-recover strategy, as shown in Fig. 6b. We randomly choose a tensor and an entry of it, back up its value in a temporary variable, and modify its value with a random value. Then we scan the following code to find the next statement which depends on the chosen tensor, and we insert a statement to recover its value. Therefore, the final output of the mutated program would not be changed.
3. **Functionalization**. Python supports nested functions and closures. To test this feature, we randomly choose a sequence of operations in the program and wrap them into a function, as shown in 6c. All variables defined or mutated in the function will be returned as reflected in the upper-level scope. Since Python supports hoisting (using a variable defined after the definition of a function), we can move the constructed function anywhere before it is called.

3.3 Equivalence Modulo Inputs (EMI)

The second mutation method guarantees conditional program equivalence that depends directly on the specific given program input x_0, which is called *Equivalance Modulo Inputs* (EMI). We want the mutated program gives the same result as the seed program on the given inputs, that is

$$[\![\mathcal{P}]\!](x_0) = [\![\mathcal{P}']\!](x_0)$$

Leveraging the fixed inputs enlarge the range of possible mutations. A class of EMI program mutations is *Always True Conditional Block* (TCB). As shown in Figure 7, we can randomly select a subset of consecutive statements and wrap them up with an `if` statement. As long as the condition expression (highlighted as red in Fig. 7) is true, the wrapped statements will be executed as the original program, which is supposed to lead to identical outputs. Synthesizing a true condition expression takes two steps, 1) program profiling, where we collect the runtime information which depends on x_0, and 2) condition synthesis.

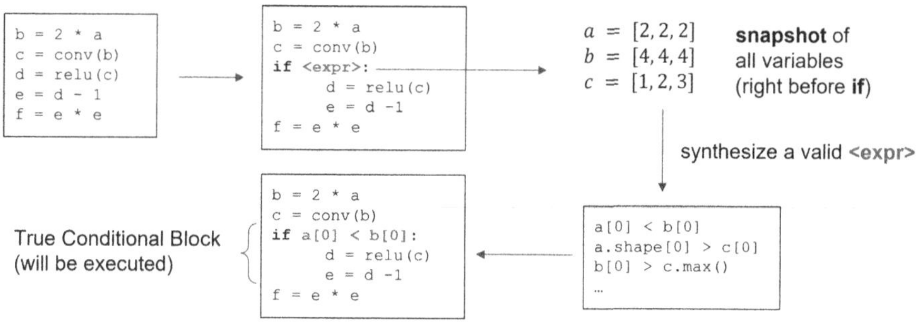

Fig. 7. By leveraging program profiling (runtime information that depends on x_0) and condition synthesis, Equivalence Modulo Inputs (EMI) ensures that mutated programs execute in the same order as the original programs.

Program Profiling. We execute the original program step by step until the position to insert the `if` statement while maintaining a symbol table to book-keep the value of each tensor variable. Note that it is possible that the program is not in SSA form after other mutations, that is the value of a variable might be changed. In order to support the composition of mutations, we need to stop the profiling exactly before the `if` statement.

Condition Synthesis. Following the grammar defined by Fig. 8, we synthesize an arithmetic comparison expression based on the execution profile we collect in the previous step. The comparison expression takes two scalars as operands, which are either an element of a tensor, the length of a certain dimension of a tensor, the number of dimensions of a tensor, or the maximum or minimum of a tensor. Since the input x_0 is fixed, all of these values are determined, and so is the order between two operands. Therefore the operator can also be determined.

$$
\begin{aligned}
\langle cond \rangle \quad &::= \langle scalar \rangle \ \langle op \rangle \ \langle scalar \rangle \\
\langle scalar \rangle \quad &::= \langle v \rangle \ \text{`}\texttt{[}\text{'} \ \langle pos \rangle \ \text{`}\texttt{]}\text{'} \\
&\ \ \mid \ \langle v \rangle \ \text{`}\texttt{.shape[}\text{'} \ \langle pos \rangle \ \text{`}\texttt{]}\text{'} \mid \text{`}\texttt{len(}\text{'} \ \langle v \rangle \ \text{`}\texttt{.shape)}\text{'} \\
&\ \ \mid \ \langle v \rangle \ \text{`}\texttt{.max()}\text{'} \mid \langle v \rangle \ \text{`}\texttt{.min()}\text{'} \mid \langle c \rangle \\
\langle v \rangle \quad &::= \text{variables} \\
\langle c \rangle \quad &::= \mathbb{Z} \\
\langle pos \rangle \quad &::= \langle c \rangle \mid \langle pos \rangle \ \text{`,'} \ \langle c \rangle \\
\langle op \rangle \quad &::= \text{`>'} \mid \text{`<'} \mid \text{`>='} \mid \text{`<='}
\end{aligned}
$$

Fig. 8. BNF Grammar of Synthesized Expressions

3.4 Mutations Beyond Equivalence

It's noteworthy that the equivalence-based program mutations mentioned are only one possible approach for generating valid test cases. Their primary purpose is to ensure the meaningfulness of test cases, aligning them with real-world programs developed by machine learning engineers.

However, it is important to clarify that equivalence is not a strict requirement for machine learning compiler fuzzing. Since we assume the interpreter always produces the correct results, the correctness of the compiled program can be verified by comparing it with the ground truth generated by the interpreter, as long as the test case is valid. Valid test cases are not necessarily derived from a seed program using equivalent mutations, and there can be other mutations that are not based on equivalence, which have the potential to enhance testing coverage. Nevertheless, how to design such mutations is beyond the scope of this work and remains a subject for future research.

4 Evaluation

4.1 Testing Settings

We implemented TorchProbe in approximately 1000 lines of Python code on the top of NNSmith, including 4 types of program mutations mentioned in Sect. 3.

We ran TorchProbe on a workstation equipped with an NVIDIA RTX 2070 GPU. The operating system is Ubuntu 20.04. We build PyTorch from source in the latest main branch of PyTorch project on GitHub. Both CPU and GPU backends of the PyTorch compiler are tested.

We use NNSmith [34] as the seed program generator. Note that TorchProbe is orthogonal to the seed program generator. Any fuzzing tools for DL systems based on computational graphs can be used as the seed program generator for TorchProbe, and any improvements (e.g. supporting more operators) could benefit TorchProbe.

We set the number of operators in one computational graph as 20. Computational graphs that are too large will slow down the testing process and tend to trigger commonly seen bugs more frequently, impeding the discovery of new bugs in corner cases. Graphs with too few operators cannot cover a wide range of combinations of operators.

4.2 Quantitative Results

All bugs have been minimized and de-duplicated. We only list bugs that have distinct root causes in this section. The related GitHub issues can be found in https://github.com/pytorch/pytorch/issues/created_by/soodoshll and https://github.com/openai/triton/issues/created_by/soodoshll.

Bug Counts. Within one month, we found 17 bugs in PyTorch's main branch and three PyTorch's underlying GPU backend compiler Triton. All bugs have been minimized and reported to the community, and we list them in Table 1. These bugs have been confirmed by the community and 12 of them have already been fixed. Five test cases have been integrated as unit tests of the main branch.

Bug Types. We discovered different types of bugs in multiple layers of the software stack. According to which part of the software the bugs happen in, they can be classified into:

- TorchDynamo: The graph capturer fails to capture computational graphs. We find 4 such bugs and all of them are discovered by composite program mutations involving dynamic language features.

Table 1. We find 17 bugs in PyTorch's main branch and 3 bugs in PyTorch's underlying GPU backend compiler.

GitHub Issue ID	Crashed Component	Category	Fixed
96432	CPU Backend	Inconsistent Results	Yes
96446	CPU Backend	Compiler Crash	Yes
96484	CPU Backend	Compiler Crash	Yes
96487	CPU & GPU Backend	Compiler Crash	No
96604	GPU Backend	Inconsistent Results	Yes
96609	GPU Backend	Compiler Crash	No
96625	CPU & GPU Backend	Compiler Crash	Yes
96728	CPU Backend	Inconsistent Results	Yes
97081	Dynamo	Compiler Crash	No
97082	Dynamo	Compiler Crash	No
97083	CPU & GPU Backend	Inconsistent Results	No
97115	Dynamo	Compiler Crash	No
97117	GPU Backend	Inconsistent Results	Yes
97124	CPU Backend	Compiler Crash	Yes
97127	CPU Backend	Compiler Crash	Yes
97130	Dynamo	Inconsistent Results	No
97807	GPU Backend	Compiler Crash	No
1328	Triton	Compiler Hang	Yes
1337	Triton	Inconsistent Results	Yes
1342	Triton	Inconsistent Results	Yes

- CPU backend: The CPU backend of TorchInductor fails to generate the correct code. We found 9 such bugs (3 of which also cause errors in the GPU backend), which are the most among all categories. Type casting and operator fusion are two fragile parts.

- GPU backend: The GPU backend of TorchInductor fails to generate the correct code. We found 7 such bugs.
- Triton: Bugs related to the underlying Triton compiler, which is maintained by another community. We found three bugs in Triton, and a fundamental one of them is that Triton evaluates the expression `True < False` as true.

According to the error type the bugs, they can be categorized into:

- Compiler Crash: The compiler crashes without producing runnable code.
- Compiler Hang: We found one bug in the Triton compiler where the compilation never terminates.
- Inconsistent Results: The results given by the original and compiled programs are different.

4.3 Sample Bugs

We select some typical bugs to demonstrate the efficacy of different program mutations.

Example 1: Mutate-then-recover + EMI. Here `b` is a scalar parameter of the upper-level function. In the first step, as shown in Fig. 9b, we insert a mutate-then-recover snippet before the `max` statement (the mutation statement is omitted since it will not affect the bug). In the second step, we insert a TCB statement between the two statements we inserted in the last step. This example causes TorchDynamo to crash, and the root cause is still under investigation by the developers. This example demonstrates how the interaction between two different types of program mutation exposes undiscovered bugs.

```
a.max()
```

(a) seed program

```
backup = a[0]
a[0] = backup
a.max()
```

(b) mutate-then-recover

```
backup = a[0]
if b < 1e5:
    a[0] = backup
    a.max()
```

(c) EMI

Fig. 9. Mutate-then-recover + EMI. The three snippets show how to derive new test cases step by step via mutations. This test case will cause TorchDynamo to crash due to an error in AOT Autograd (ahead-of-time auto-differentiation). The root cause is still under investigation.

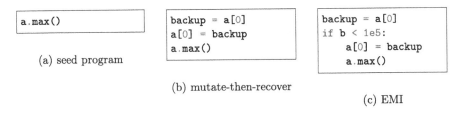

Example 2: Mutate-then-recover + EMI + functionalize. Figure 10 shows an example where three different types of mutation collaboratively triggered an error. It first creates three variables sharing the same underlying storage, i.e. they point to the same address. Therefore, any mutation of any one of the three tensors will also manifest in the other two. More specifically, this example

modifies one element of the tensor `b` from 1 to 2. So the value of tensor `b` and `c` is supposed to change accordingly, which is the behavior of the original code before compilation. The compiled code, however, incorrectly returns the `c` with the unchanged value.

Example 3: A bug caused by hoisting. Figure 11 shows an *Pythonic* example, which one of the core developers of PyTorch compiler refers to as an '*interesting puzzle*' and '*a lot of fun for a PL nerd*'. This example is generated by three transformations collaboratively and has been minimized manually. It involves dynamic language features including nested functions, closure and variable hoisting.

```
a = torch.ones((2,))
b = a.reshape(2)
c = a[0:2]
# So a, b, c share the same storage

def subfunc():
    b[0] = 2
    if b.sum() >= -1e5:
        pass

subfunc()
```

Fig. 10. Mutate-then-recover + EMI + Functionalize. The variables `a`, `b`, and `c` are pointed to the same underlying memory address, so any mutation to one tensor should manifest on the other two. However, the compiled code does not behave as expected. The root cause of this bug is that TorchInductor does not handle in-place copy (`copy_`) well.

5 Related Work

5.1 Compiler Testing

Testing has been the dominating technique to validate the robustness of compilers. As an alternative to manually write test cases, automatic testing has been introduced to improve the testing coverage more efficiently. CSmith [61] gains great success in automatically finding bugs in C compilers including GCC and LLVM. It synthesizes programs from scratch and is used to generate seed programs by other mutation-based fuzzers. Hermes [51] introduces several novel EMI mutations for live code regions and TCB is one of them. We borrow the idea from Hermes and extend it to Python and tensor operations.

5.2 Fuzzing DL Systems

Fuzzing has been applied to deep learning systems to automatically detect bugs and improve their robustness. CRADLE [45] leverages existing DL models to run differential testing on deep learning systems. AUDEE [22] and LEMON [58] extend CRADLE with mutation-based search strategies to improve the testing coverage. GraphFuzzer [38] and Muffin [38] enlarge the search space using the `reshape` operators. NNSmith [34], which TorchProbe is built upon, adopts SMT-solving to generate valid computational graphs and gradient-based search to find valid inputs, which further enlarge the search space. These works all focus on the computational graph level, while our work can generate test cases that cannot be represented by computational graphs. Furthermore, any graph-level fuzzers can be used as the seed program generator of TorchProbe.

Besides graph-level fuzzers, there are also fuzzers like TVMFuzz [43] and Tzer [35] designed for lower-level tensor program compilers such as TVM. These tensor compilers correspond to the backends of PyTorch compilers and therefore the fuzzers targeting on them are not aware of the high-level dynamic language features. Other techniques like Predoo [62], FreeFuzz [59], and DeepREL [16] are helpful for testing DL operators, they are insufficient for identifying bugs in graph-level optimizations.

```
x = torch.zeros([1], device='cuda')
def subfunc():
    x[0] = backup

if x[0] >= -1e5:
    pass

backup = 1
subfunc()
```

Fig. 11. A bug caused by hoisting. The function `subfunc` uses a variable `backup` in the upper-level scope, which appears after the definition of `subfunc`. PyTorch compiler crashes on this code snippet.

5.3 Verified Compilers

Verified compilers ensure their correctness by formal proofs. Liu *et al.* [33] implemented a verified Coq framework for optimizing tensor programs written in a purely functional language with a set of verified program rewrites. For traditional compilers, CompCert [30] is a verified compiler for the C language. While formal verification can guarantee the correctness of compilers, it requires expertise in theorem proving and heavy manual intervention. What makes it worse is that programming languages and compilers for DL are still rapidly evolving, demanding extra efforts to update the corresponding proofs.

5.4 Translation Validation

Translation validation is another method to validate compiler optimizations, which verifies the compiled code is equivalent to the source code. Unlike verified compilers, translation validation checks the equivalence between the target and source code of a specific input program. Bang *et al.* [9] uses SMT solver to verify the behavior of code compiled by the tensor program compiler MLIR is identical to the source code. It leverages to lower the complexity of high dimensional tensor data. There are also studies of applying translation validation on traditional languages like assembly [48], C [39,49], Java [52], and LLVM [27,37,50,54].

6 Conclusions

The introduction of PyTorch 2.0 signifies a remarkable milestone in the evolution of deep learning infrastructure by aiming to incorporate compiler techniques in a more dynamic manner. Nevertheless, the dynamic nature of Python poses challenges to the compiler's completeness and robustness.

While recent research has introduced fuzzing as a method to test deep learning compilers, there is still a lack of investigation concerning the testing of dynamic features. To bridge this gap, our proposed approach suggests multiple code transformations to generate test cases involving dynamic features. These transformations ensure the preservation of the program's semantics, thereby indicating the presence of a bug if any discrepancies arise between the transformed and original programs. Through this approach, we have identified a total of twenty bugs in the PyTorch compiler and its underlying tensor compiler Triton.

Acknowledgment. We thank the anonymous reviewers for their insightful comments. This work was supported, in part, by Individual Discovery Grants from the Natural Sciences and Engineering Research Council of Canada and the Canada CIFAR AI Chair Program.

References

1. AWS Inferentia. https://aws.amazon.com/machine-learning/inferentia/
2. AWS Trainium. https://aws.amazon.com/machine-learning/trainium/
3. cuBLAS. https://docs.nvidia.com/cuda/cublas/
4. NVIDIA Tensor Core. https://developer.nvidia.com/tensor-cores
5. ONNX: Open neural network exchange. https://github.com/onnx/onnx
6. SambaNova DataScale. https://sambanova.ai/products/datascale/
7. Abadi, M., et al.: TensorFlow: a system for large-scale machine learning. In: Keeton, K., Roscoe, T., (eds.) 12th USENIX Symposium on Operating Systems Design and Implementation, OSDI 2016, Savannah, GA, USA, November 2–4, 2016, pp. 265–283. USENIX Association (2016). https://www.usenix.org/conference/osdi16/technical-sessions/presentation/abadi
8. Agrawal, A., et al.: TensorFlow Eager: a multi-stage, Python-embedded DSL for machine learning. Proc. Mach. Learn. Syst. **1**, 178–189 (2019)

9. Bang, S., Nam, S., Chun, I., Jhoo, H.Y., Lee, J.: SMT-based translation validation for machine learning compiler. In: Computer Aided Verification: 34th International Conference, CAV 2022, Haifa, Israel, August 7–10, 2022, Proceedings, Part II, pp. 386–407. Springer, Cham (2022). https://doi.org/10.1007/978-3-031-13188-2_19
10. Bergstra, J., et al.: Theano: deep learning on GPUs with Python. In: NIPS 2011, BigLearning Workshop, Granada, Spain, vol. 3. Citeseer (2011)
11. Brown, T., et al.: Language models are few-shot learners. Adv. Neural. Inf. Process. Syst. **33**, 1877–1901 (2020)
12. Chen, T., et al.: TVM: an automated end-to-end optimizing compiler for deep learning. In: Arpaci-Dusseau, A.C., Voelker, G. (eds.) 13th USENIX Symposium on Operating Systems Design and Implementation, OSDI 2018, Carlsbad, CA, USA, October 8–10, 2018, pp. 578–594. USENIX Association (2018). https://www.usenix.org/conference/osdi18/presentation/chen
13. Chen, T., et al.: Learning to optimize tensor programs. In: Advances in Neural Information Processing Systems 31 (2018)
14. Chetlur, S., et al.: cuDNN: efficient primitives for deep learning. arXiv preprint arXiv:1410.0759 (2014)
15. Cordts, M., et al.: The cityscapes dataset for semantic urban scene understanding. In: Proceedings of the IEEE Conference on Computer Vision and Pattern Recognition, pp. 3213–3223 (2016)
16. Deng, Y., Yan, C., Wei, A., Zhang, L.: Fuzzing deep-learning libraries via automated relational API inference. In: Roychoudhury, A., Cadar, C., Kim, M. (eds.) Proceedings of the 30th ACM Joint European Software Engineering Conference and Symposium on the Foundations of Software Engineering, ESEC/FSE 2022, Singapore, Singapore, November 14–18, 2022, pp. 44–56. ACM (2022). https://doi.org/10.1145/3540250.3549085
17. DeVito, Z.: Torchscript: Optimized execution of PyTorch programs. Retrieved January (2022)
18. Devlin, J., Chang, M.W., Lee, K., Toutanova, K.: BERT: pre-training of deep bidirectional transformers for language understanding. arXiv preprint arXiv:1810.04805 (2018)
19. Ding, Y., Yu, C.H., Zheng, B., Liu, Y., Wang, Y., Pekhimenko, G.: Hidet: task-mapping programming paradigm for deep learning tensor programs. In: Proceedings of the 28th ACM International Conference on Architectural Support for Programming Languages and Operating Systems, vol. 2, pp. 370–384 (2023)
20. Dosovitskiy, A., et al.: An image is worth 16×16 words: transformers for image recognition at scale. arXiv preprint arXiv:2010.11929 (2020)
21. Gu, J., Luo, X., Zhou, Y., Wang, X.: Muffin: testing deep learning libraries via neural architecture fuzzing. In: Proceedings of the 44th International Conference on Software Engineering, pp. 1418–1430 (2022)
22. Guo, Q., et al.: Audee: automated testing for deep learning frameworks. In: Proceedings of the 35th IEEE/ACM International Conference on Automated Software Engineering, pp. 486–498 (2020)
23. He, K., Zhang, X., Ren, S., Sun, J.: Deep residual learning for image recognition. In: Proceedings of the IEEE Conference on Computer Vision and Pattern Recognition, pp. 770–778 (2016)
24. Jia, Y., et al.: Caffe: convolutional architecture for fast feature embedding. In: Proceedings of the 22nd ACM international conference on Multimedia, pp. 675–678 (2014)
25. Jia, Z., Tillman, B., Maggioni, M., Scarpazza, D.P.: Dissecting the graphcore IPU architecture via microbenchmarking. arXiv preprint arXiv:1912.03413 (2019)

26. Jouppi, N., Young, C., Patil, N., Patterson, D.: Motivation for and evaluation of the first tensor processing unit. IEEE Micro **38**(3), 10–19 (2018)
27. Kasampalis, T., Park, D., Lin, Z., Adve, V.S., Roşu, G.: Language-parametric compiler validation with application to LLVM. In: Proceedings of the 26th ACM International Conference on Architectural Support for Programming Languages and Operating Systems, pp. 1004–1019 (2021)
28. Keckler, S.W., Dally, W.J., Khailany, B., Garland, M., Glasco, D.: GPUs and the future of parallel computing. IEEE Micro **31**(5), 7–17 (2011)
29. Larsen, R.M., Shpeisman, T.: Tensorflow graph optimizations (2019)
30. Leroy, X.: Formal certification of a compiler back-end or: programming a compiler with a proof assistant. In: Conference record of the 33rd ACM SIGPLAN-SIGACT Symposium on Principles of Programming Languages, pp. 42–54 (2006)
31. Lewington, R.: An AI chip with unprecedented performance to do the unimaginable (2021)
32. Li, M., et al.: The deep learning compiler: a comprehensive survey. IEEE Trans. Parallel Distrib. Syst. **32**(3), 708–727 (2020)
33. Liu, A., Bernstein, G.L., Chlipala, A., Ragan-Kelley, J.: Verified tensor-program optimization via high-level scheduling rewrites. In: Proceedings of the ACM on Programming Languages 6(POPL) (2022)
34. Liu, J., et al.: NNSmith: generating diverse and valid test cases for deep learning compilers. In: Proceedings of the 28th ACM International Conference on Architectural Support for Programming Languages and Operating Systems, vol. 2, pp. 530–543 (2023)
35. Liu, J., Wei, Y., Yang, S., Deng, Y., Zhang, L.: Coverage-guided tensor compiler fuzzing with joint IR-pass mutation. Proc. ACM on Program. Lang. **6**(OOPSLA1), 1–26 (2022)
36. Liu, S., et al.: Cambricon: an instruction set architecture for neural networks. In: 2016 ACM/IEEE 43rd Annual International Symposium on Computer Architecture (ISCA), pp. 393–405. IEEE (2016)
37. Lopes, N.P., Lee, J., Hur, C.K., Liu, Z., Regehr, J.: Alive2: bounded translation validation for LLVM. In: Proceedings of the 42nd ACM SIGPLAN International Conference on Programming Language Design and Implementation, pp. 65–79 (2021)
38. Luo, W., Chai, D., Ruan, X., Wang, J., Fang, C., Chen, Z.: Graph-based fuzz testing for deep learning inference engines. In: 2021 IEEE/ACM 43rd International Conference on Software Engineering (ICSE), pp. 288–299. IEEE (2021)
39. Necula, G.C.: Translation validation for an optimizing compiler. In: Proceedings of the ACM SIGPLAN 2000 Conference on Programming Language Design and Implementation, pp. 83–94 (2000)
40. Niu, W., Guan, J., Wang, Y., Agrawal, G., Ren, B.: DNNFusion: accelerating deep neural networks execution with advanced operator fusion. In: Proceedings of the 42nd ACM SIGPLAN International Conference on Programming Language Design and Implementation, pp. 883–898 (2021)
41. Otterness, N., Anderson, J.H.: AMD GPUs as an alternative to NVIDIA for supporting real-time workloads. In: 32nd Euromicro Conference on Real-Time Systems (ECRTS 2020). Schloss Dagstuhl-Leibniz-Zentrum für Informatik (2020)
42. Ouyang, L., et al.: Training language models to follow instructions with human feedback. Adv. Neural. Inf. Process. Syst. **35**, 27730–27744 (2022)
43. Pankratz, D.: TVMFuzz: fuzzing tensor-level intermediate representation in TVM (2020)
44. Paszke, A., et al.: PyTorch: an imperative style, high-performance deep learning library. In: Advances in Neural Information Processing Systems 32 (2019)

45. Pham, H.V., Lutellier, T., Qi, W., Tan, L.: CRADLE: cross-backend validation to detect and localize bugs in deep learning libraries. In: 2019 IEEE/ACM 41st International Conference on Software Engineering (ICSE), pp. 1027–1038. IEEE (2019)
46. Ragan-Kelley, J., Barnes, C., Adams, A., Paris, S., Durand, F., Amarasinghe, S.: Halide: a language and compiler for optimizing parallelism, locality, and recomputation in image processing pipelines. ACM Sigplan Not. **48**(6), 519–530 (2013)
47. Reed, J., Devito, Z., He, H., Ussery, A., Ansel, J.: Torch.fx: practical program capture and transformation for deep learning in Python. Proc. Mach. Learn. Syst. **4**, 638–651 (2022)
48. Samet, H.: Automatically proving the correctness of translations involving optimized code, vol. 259. Citeseer (1975)
49. Siegel, M., Pnueli, A., Singerman, E.: Translation validation. In: TACAS, pp. 151–166 (1998)
50. Stepp, M., Tate, R., Lerner, S.: Equality-based translation validator for LLVM. In: Gopalakrishnan, G., Qadeer, S. (eds.) CAV 2011. LNCS, vol. 6806, pp. 737–742. Springer, Heidelberg (2011). https://doi.org/10.1007/978-3-642-22110-1_59
51. Sun, C., Le, V., Su, Z.: Finding compiler bugs via live code mutation. In: Proceedings of the 2016 ACM SIGPLAN International Conference on Object-Oriented Programming, Systems, Languages, and Applications, pp. 849–863 (2016)
52. Tate, R., Stepp, M., Tatlock, Z., Lerner, S.: Equality saturation: a new approach to optimization. In: Proceedings of the 36th Annual ACM SIGPLAN-SIGACT Symposium on Principles of Programming Languages, pp. 264–276 (2009)
53. Tillet, P., Kung, H.T., Cox, D.: Triton: an intermediate language and compiler for tiled neural network computations. In: Proceedings of the 3rd ACM SIGPLAN International Workshop on Machine Learning and Programming Languages, pp. 10–19 (2019)
54. Tristan, J.B., Govereau, P., Morrisett, G.: Evaluating value-graph translation validation for LLVM. In: Proceedings of the 32nd ACM SIGPLAN Conference on Programming Language Design and Implementation, pp. 295–305 (2011)
55. Van Der Walt, S., Colbert, S.C., Varoquaux, G.: The NumPy Array: a structure for efficient numerical computation. Comput. Sci. Eng. **13**(2), 22–30 (2011)
56. Vanholder, H.: Efficient inference with TensorRT. In: GPU Technology Conference, vol. 1, p. 2 (2016)
57. Wang, E., et al.: Intel math kernel library. High-Performance Computing on the Intel® Xeon Phi™: How to Fully Exploit MIC Architectures, pp. 167–188 (2014)
58. Wang, Z., Yan, M., Chen, J., Liu, S., Zhang, D.: Deep learning library testing via effective model generation. In: Proceedings of the 28th ACM Joint Meeting on European Software Engineering Conference and Symposium on the Foundations of Software Engineering, pp. 788–799 (2020)
59. Wei, A., Deng, Y., Yang, C., Zhang, L.: Free lunch for testing: fuzzing deep-learning libraries from open source. In: Proceedings of the 44th International Conference on Software Engineering, pp. 995–1007 (2022)
60. Wu, P.: PyTorch 2.0: the journey to bringing compiler technologies to the core of PyTorch (keynote). In: Proceedings of the 21st ACM/IEEE International Symposium on Code Generation and Optimization, pp. 1–1 (2023)

61. Yang, X., Chen, Y., Eide, E., Regehr, J.: Finding and understanding bugs in C compilers. In: Proceedings of the 32nd ACM SIGPLAN Conference on Programming Language Design and Implementation, pp. 283–294 (2011)
62. Zhang, X., et al.: Predoo: precision testing of deep learning operators. In: Proceedings of the 30th ACM SIGSOFT International Symposium on Software Testing and Analysis, pp. 400–412 (2021)

Author Index

A
Accattoli, Beniamino 69
Affeldt, Reynald 182
Aotani, Tomoyuki 3

B
Barenbaum, Pablo 69

C
Chen, Sheng 24
Chin, Wei-Ngan 269

F
Forsberg, Fredrik Nordvall 135
Forster, Yannick 155

G
Geng, Chuqin 310
Germane, Kimball 290

H
Hao, Dan 24

I
Ikeda, Ryo 246

K
Kappelmann, Kevin 225
Kirst, Dominik 155
Kobayashi, Naoki 246
Kupke, Clemens 135

L
Le, Quang Loc 269
Li, Wenhua 269
Lubis, Luthfan Anshar 3

M
Masuhara, Hidehiko 3
Mück, Niklas 155

N
Nantes-Sobrinho, Daniele 112

P
Paulus, Joseph W. N. 112
Pekhimenko, Gennady 310
Pérez, Jorge A. 112
Poulsen, Casper Bach 46

S
Saito, Ayumu 182
Sato, Ryosuke 246
Si, Xujie 310
Song, Yahui 269
Song, Yichen 205
Su, Qidong 310
Sun, Ke 24
Sun, Meng 205

T
Tanabe, Yudai 3

V
van den Heuvel, Bas 112
van der Rest, Cas 46

W
Wang, Meng 24
Wang, Yuting 205
Watters, Sean 135
Wu, Jinhua 205
Wu, Jui-Hsuan 91

X
Xu, Xiangzhe 205

C.-K. Hur (Ed.): APLAS 2023, LNCS 14405, p. 333, 2023.
https://doi.org/10.1007/978-981-99-8311-7

Printed in the United States
by Baker & Taylor Publisher Services